Microsoft®

Office 4.2

for Windows™

VISUAL 3D SERIES

by: maranGraphics' Development Group

Corporate Sales
Contact maranGraphics
Phone: (905) 890-3300, ext.206
(800) 469-6616, ext.206
Fax: (905) 890-9434

Canadian Trade Sales
Contact Prentice Hall Canada
Phone: (416) 293-3621
(800) 567-3800
Fax: (416) 299-2529

Microsoft® Office 4.2 for Windows™

Canadian Cataloguing in Publication Data

Maran, Ruth, 1970 –
Microsoft Office 4.2 for Windows

(Visual 3-D series)
Written by Ruth Maran.
Includes index.
ISBN 1-896283-04-7

1. Microsoft Office for Windows (Computer file).
2. Microsoft Word for Windows (Computer file).
3. Microsoft Excel for Windows (Computer file).
4. Microsoft PowerPoint for Windows (Computer file).
5. Microsoft Mail for Windows (Computer file).
6. Business - Computer programs. I. maranGraphics' Development Group. II. Title. III. Series.

HF5548.4.M525M37 1995 650'.0285'5369 C95-930977-2

Printed in the United States of America

10 9 8 7 6 5 4 3 2

Trademark Acknowledgments

maranGraphics Inc. has attempted to include trademark information for products, services and companies referred to in this guide. Although maranGraphics Inc. has made reasonable efforts in gathering this information, it cannot guarantee its accuracy.

Microsoft, the Microsoft Logo, MS, MS-DOS, Microsoft Mouse, Microsoft PowerPoint, Microsoft Mail, Microsoft Access and XL design (the Microsoft Excel logo) are registered trademarks and AutoSum, Windows, and Windows NT are trademarks of Microsoft Corporation in the United States of America and other countries.

Dell® is a registered trademark of Dell Computer Corporation.

The animated characters are the copyright of maranGraphics, Inc.

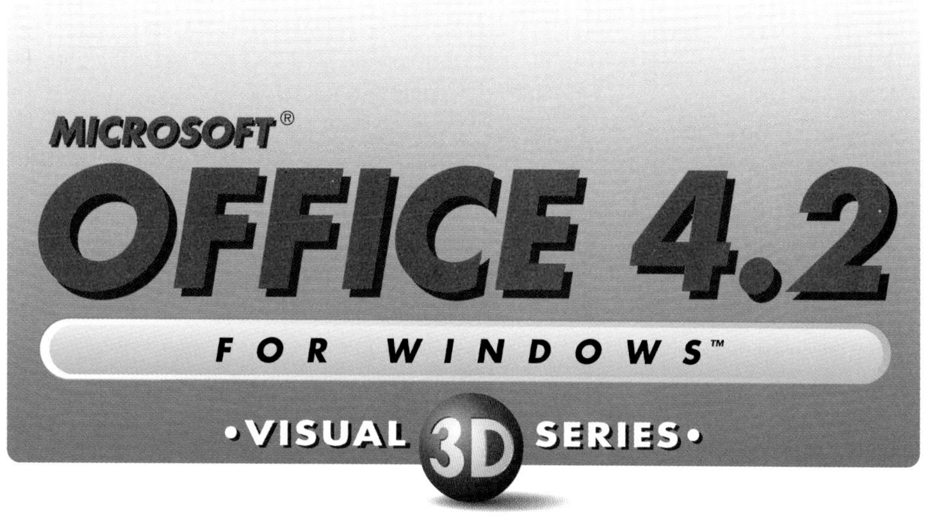

maranGraphics™

Credits

Author & Architect:
Ruth Maran

Technical Consultant:
Wendi Blouin Ewbank

Illustrations:
Dave Ross
David de Haas
Suzanna Pereira

Layout:
Christie Van Duin
Carol Walthers

Screens:
Tamara Poliquin

Editors:
Judy Maran
Kelleigh Wing

Proofreaders:
Paul Lofthouse
Brad Hilderley

Indexer:
Mark Kmetzko

Post Production:
Robert Maran

Acknowledgments

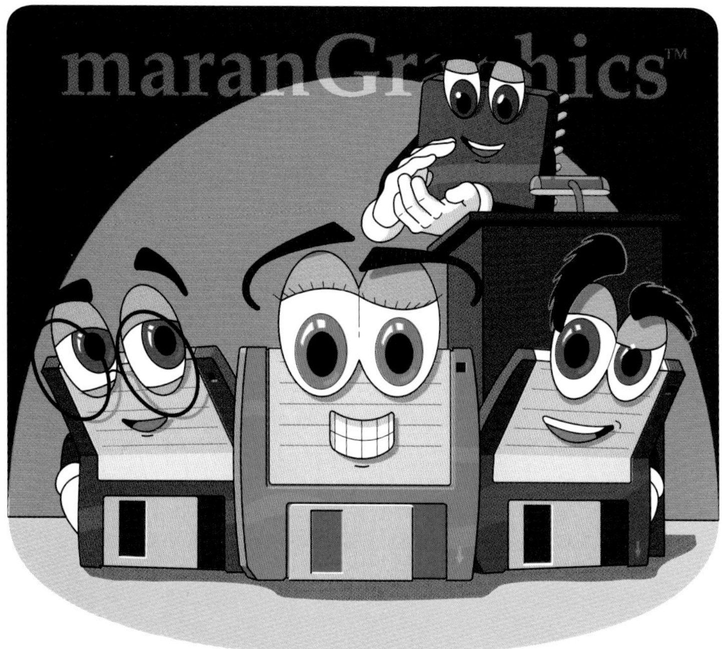

Special thanks to Wendi B. Ewbank for her insight and dedication in ensuring the technical accuracy of this book.

Thanks to Saverio C. Tropiano for his assistance and expert advice.

Thanks to the dedicated staff of maranGraphics, including Robin Clark, David de Haas, Brad Hilderley, Paul Lofthouse, Judy Maran, Maxine Maran, Robert Maran, Sherry Maran, Suzanna Pereira, Tamara Poliquin, Dave Ross, Christie Van Duin, Carol Walthers and Kelleigh Wing.

Finally, to Richard Maran who originated the easy-to-use graphic format of this guide. Thank you for your inspiration and guidance.

TABLE OF CONTENTS

INTRODUCTION TO MICROSOFT OFFICE

WORD

Getting Started

Edit Your Documents

Smart Editing

Save And Open Your Documents

H. Smith, Aeronautical Refrigeration Repair (California: Quest Publishing, 1989) 10.
R. Anderson, Volatile Cold Gases (Alaska: Inert Publishing, 1992) 31.

EXCEL

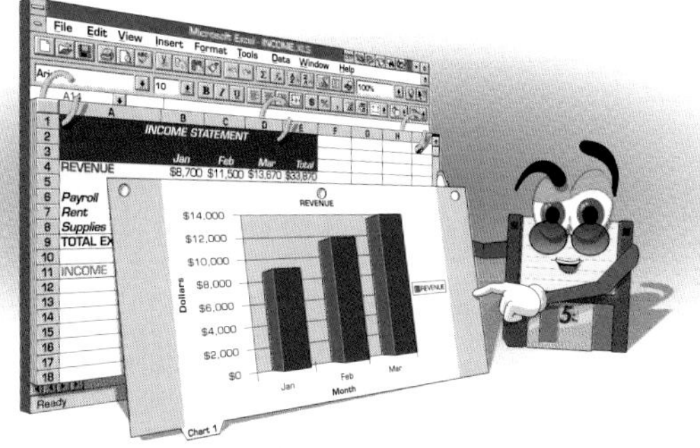

INCOME STATEMENT
REVENUE

INDEX

Print Your Worksheets

Using Multiple Worksheets

Charting Data

POWERPOINT

Getting Started

Create Presentations

Save And Open Presentations

Edit Presentations

Add Objects

Enhance Presentations

Fine-Tune Presentations

MAIL

EXCHANGE OBJECTS BETWEEN PROGRAMS

INDEX

Microsoft Office
KRYO
MO
DELL
DIMENSION XPS P90

INTRODUCTION TO MICROSOFT OFFICE

Microsoft® Office includes Word, Excel, PowerPoint and a license to use Mail. These programs will help you accomplish everyday tasks.

The Professional version of Microsoft Office also includes the Microsoft Access program. This program is useful for managing a large collection of information called a database.

This book does not cover the Microsoft Access program.

WORD

Word is a word processing program that lets you create letters, reports, memos and newsletters quickly and efficiently.

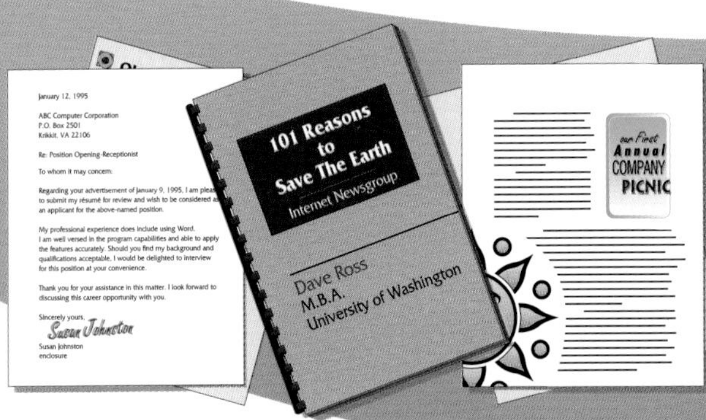

- **Microsoft Office**
- Using the Mouse
- Start a Program
- Switch Between Programs
- Exit a Program
- Select Commands

EXCEL

Excel is a spreadsheet program that helps you manage, present and analyze financial information.

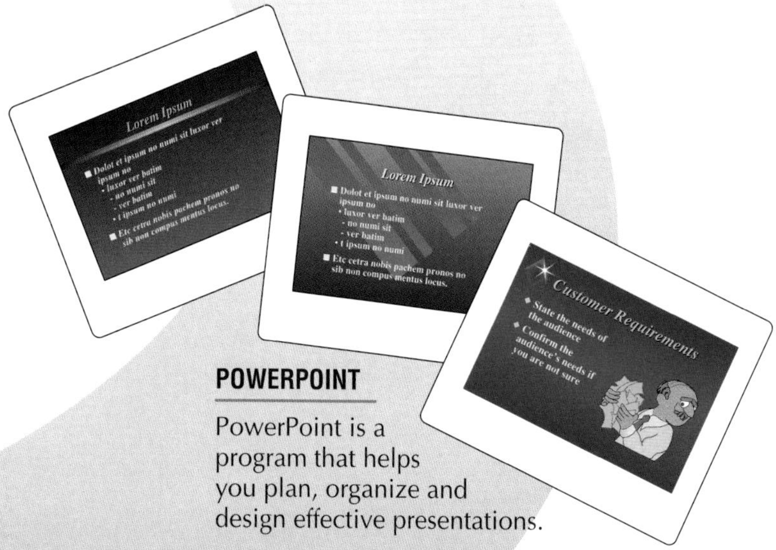

POWERPOINT

PowerPoint is a program that helps you plan, organize and design effective presentations.

MAIL

Mail is an electronic mail program that lets you exchange messages with other people connected to a network.

Note: Microsoft Office provides a license to use Mail; it does not supply the program. To use Mail, you must buy the program separately.

USING THE MOUSE

The mouse is a hand-held device that lets you quickly select commands and perform tasks.

USING THE MOUSE

◆ Hold the mouse as shown in the diagram. Use your thumb and two rightmost fingers to guide the mouse while your two remaining fingers press the mouse buttons.

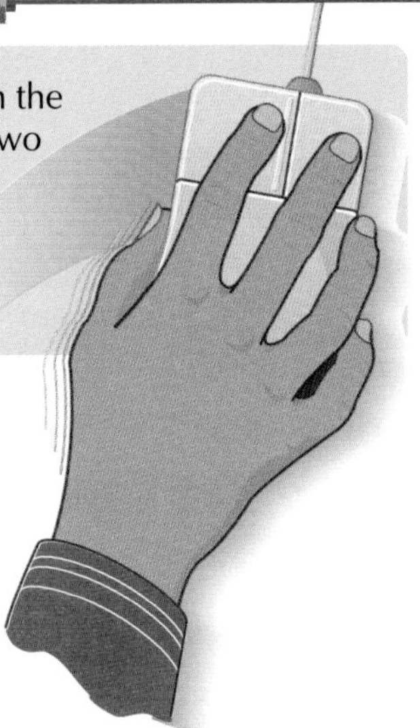

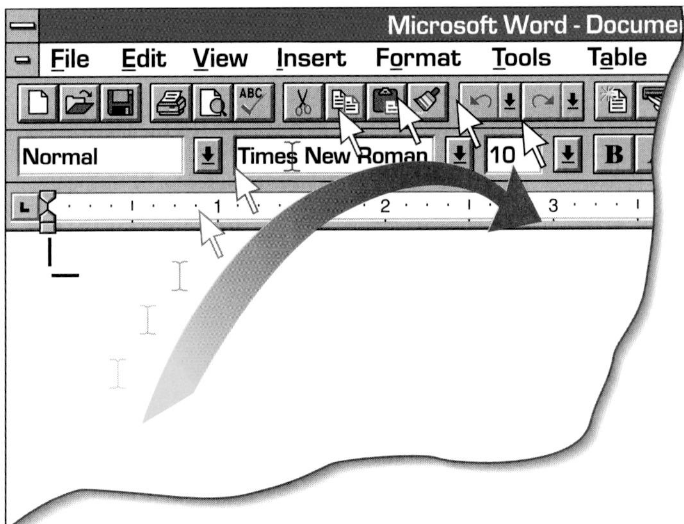

◆ When you move the mouse on your desk, the mouse pointer (I or ↖) on your screen moves in the same direction. The mouse pointer changes shape, depending on its location on your screen and the action you are performing.

PARTS OF THE MOUSE

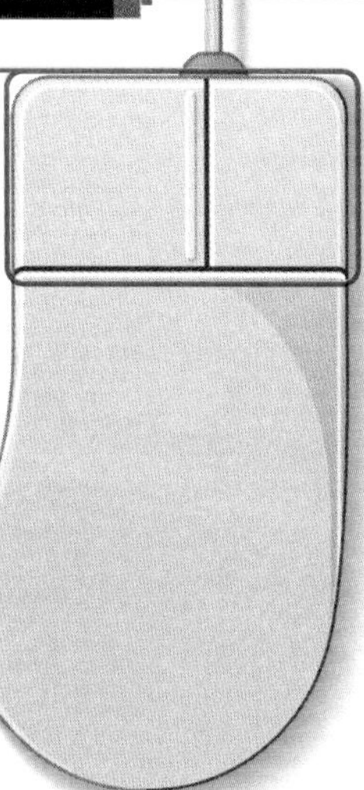

◆ The mouse has a left and right button. You can use these buttons to select commands and choose options.

Note: You will use the left button most of the time.

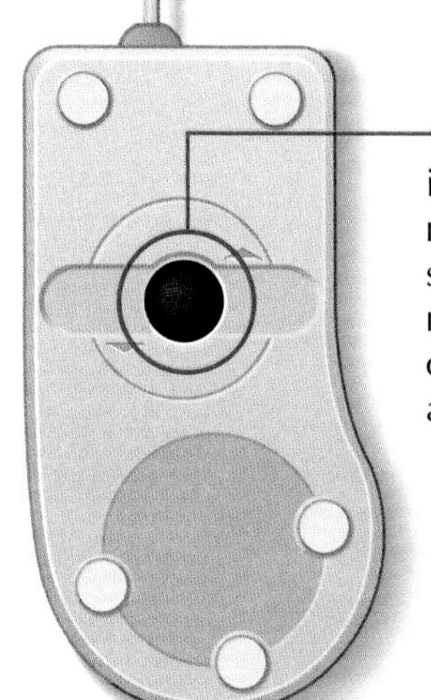

◆ Under the mouse is a ball that senses movement. To ensure smooth motion of the mouse, you should occasionally remove and clean this ball.

MOUSE TERMS

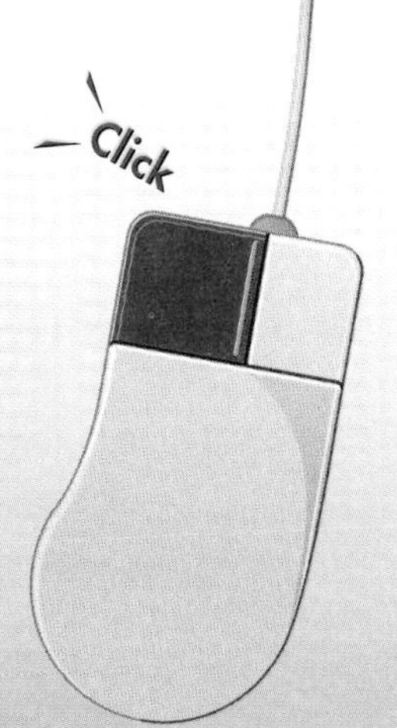

CLICK

Press and release the left mouse button once.

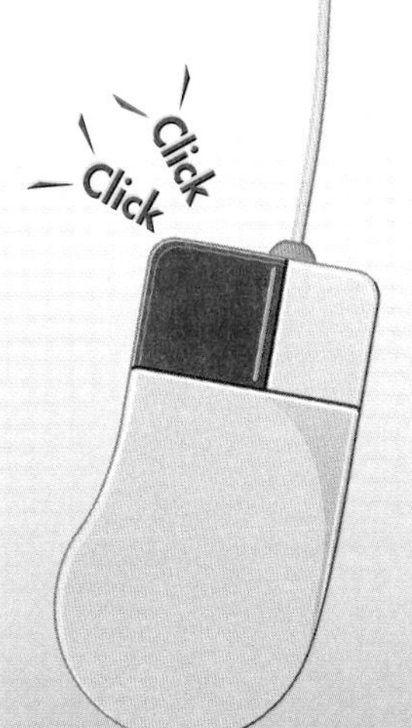

DOUBLE-CLICK

Quickly press and release the left mouse button twice.

DRAG

When the mouse pointer (I or ↖) is over an object on your screen, press and hold down the left mouse button and then move the mouse.

START A PROGRAM

You can use the Microsoft Office Manager to quickly start a program.

START A PROGRAM

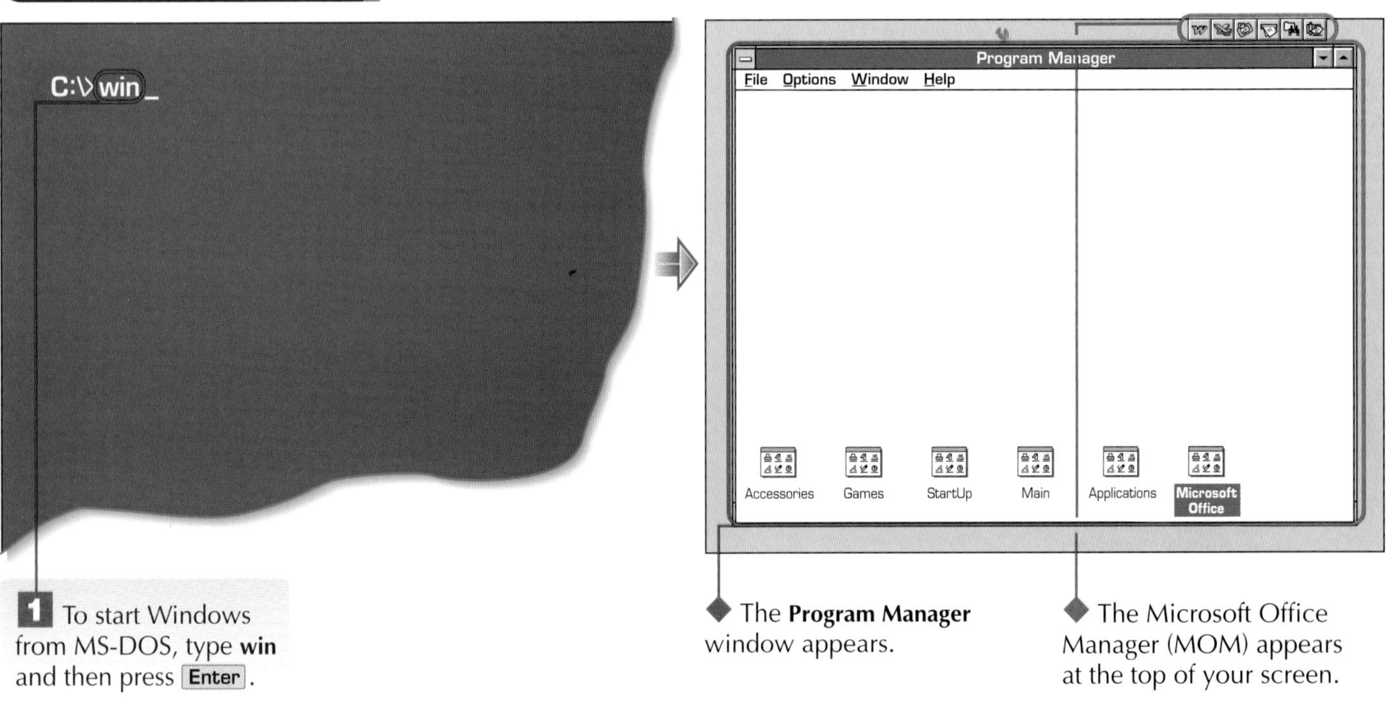

1 To start Windows from MS-DOS, type **win** and then press **Enter**.

◆ The **Program Manager** window appears.

◆ The Microsoft Office Manager (MOM) appears at the top of your screen.

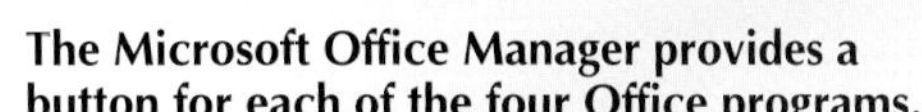

The Microsoft Office Manager provides a button for each of the four Office programs.

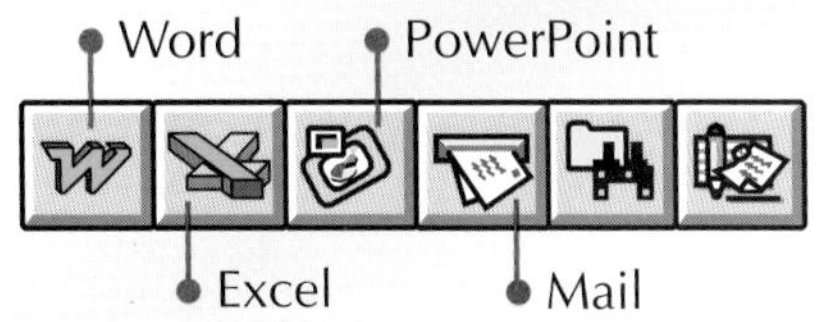

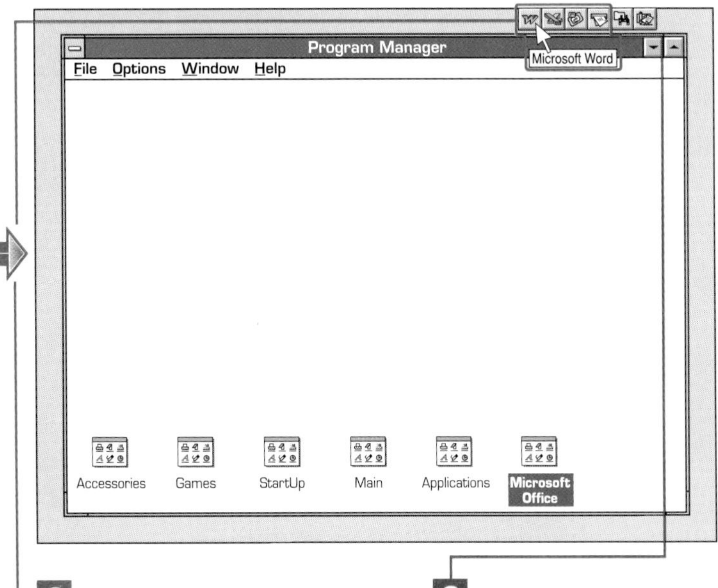

2 To display the name of a button, move the mouse over the button (example:).

◆ After a few seconds, the name of the button appears.

3 To start a program, move the mouse over the button (example: for Word) and then press the left button.

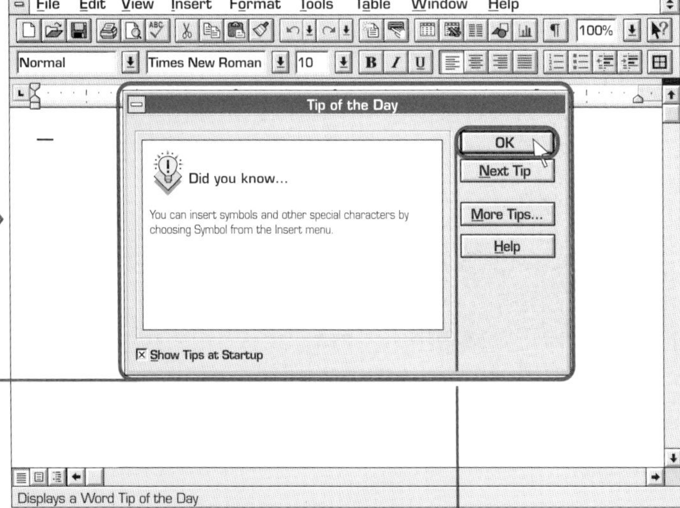

◆ The program appears on your screen.

◆ When you start the Word program, the **Tip of the Day** dialog box appears.

4 To close the dialog box, move the mouse over **OK** and then press the left button.

SWITCH BETWEEN PROGRAMS

EXIT A PROGRAM

You can work with several programs at the same time. For example, you can create a presentation while preparing an income statement.

SWITCH BETWEEN PROGRAMS

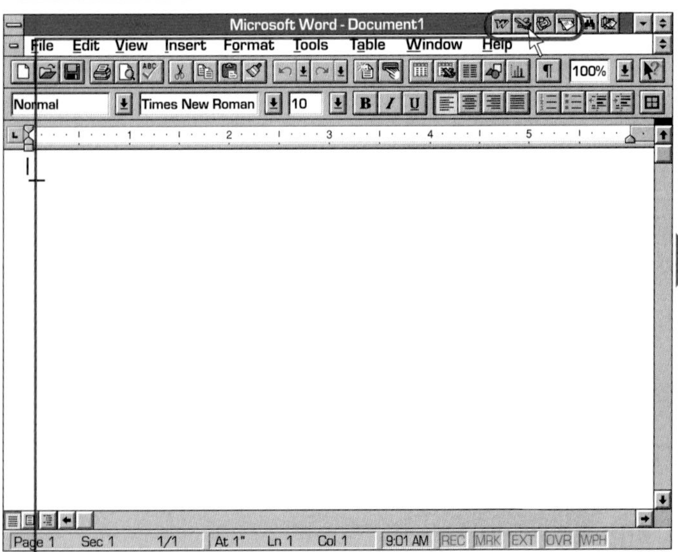

1 To open a second program, move the mouse over the button (example: for Excel) and then press the left button.

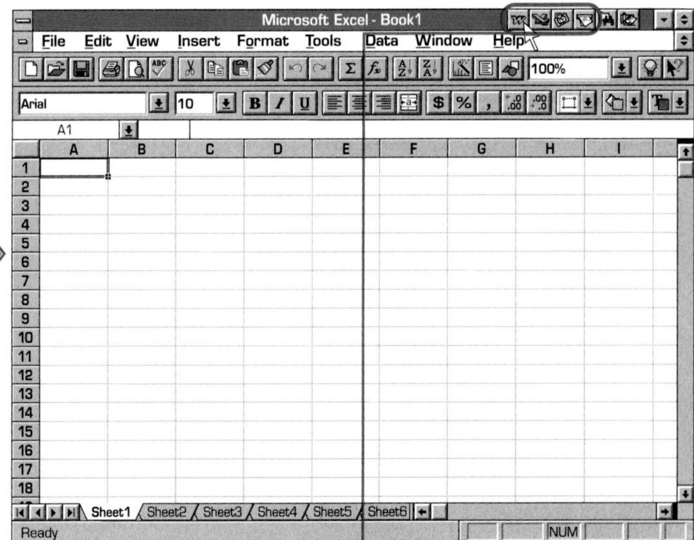

◆ The program appears on your screen.

Note: In this example, the Excel program covers the Word program.

2 To return to the original program, move the mouse over the button (example: for Word) and then press the left button.

When you finish using a program, you can exit the program.
EXIT

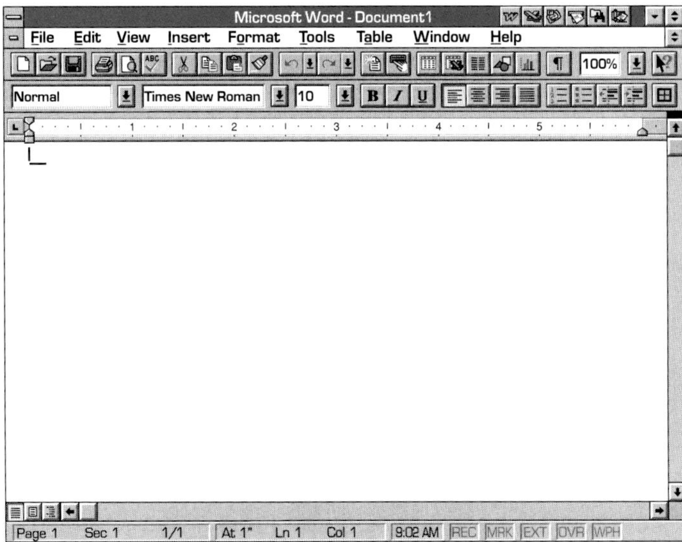

◆ The original program reappears.

Note: In this example, the Word program covers the Excel program.

EXIT A PROGRAM

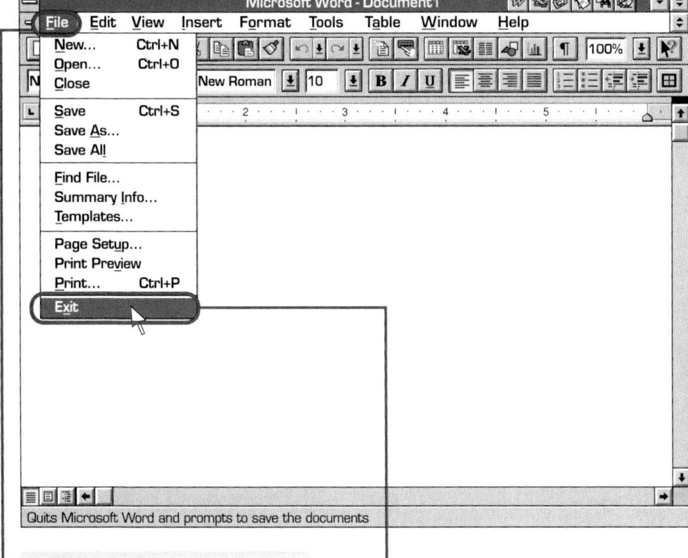

1 Move the mouse over **File** and then press the left button.

2 Move the mouse over **Exit** and then press the left button.

SELECT COMMANDS

You can open a menu to display a list of related commands. You can then select the command you want to use.
Save As...

USING THE MENUS WITH THE MOUSE

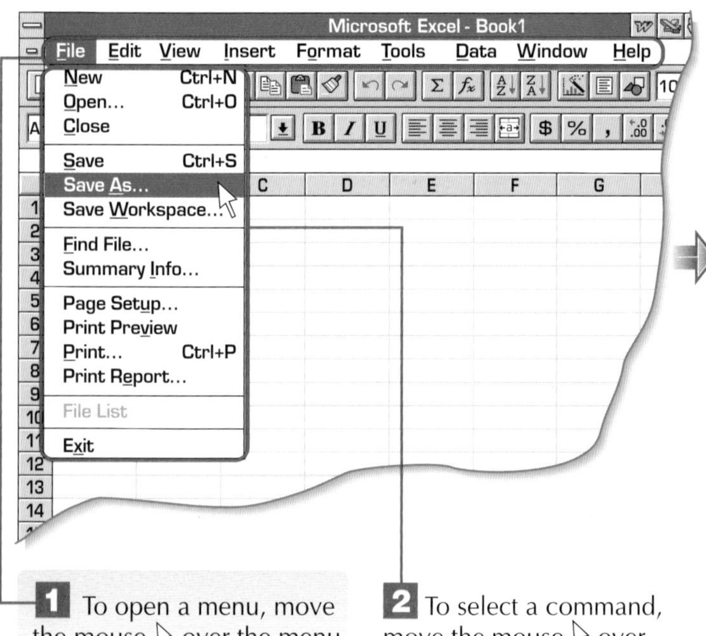

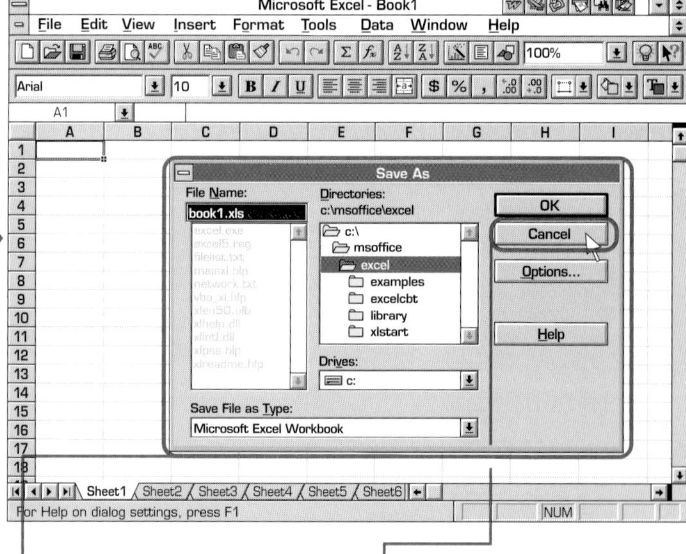

1 To open a menu, move the mouse over the menu name (example: **File**) and then press the left button.

Note: To close a menu, move the mouse outside the menu area and then press the left button.

2 To select a command, move the mouse over the command name (example: **Save As**) and then press the left button.

◆ A dialog box appears if the program requires more information to carry out the command.

3 To close a dialog box, move the mouse over **Cancel** or **Close** and then press the left button.

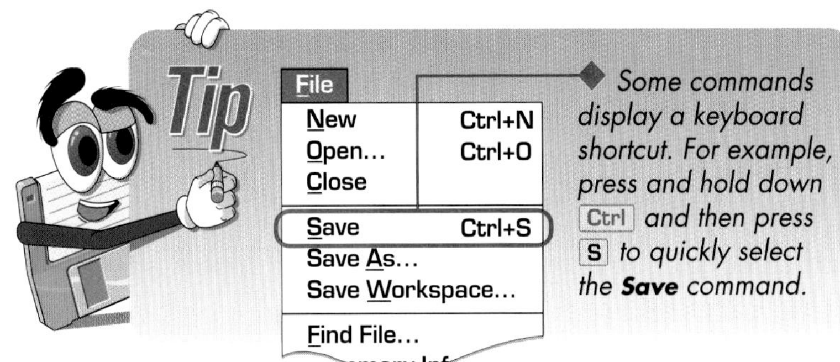

◆ *Some commands display a keyboard shortcut. For example, press and hold down* Ctrl *and then press* S *to quickly select the* ***Save*** *command.*

USING THE MENUS WITH THE KEYBOARD

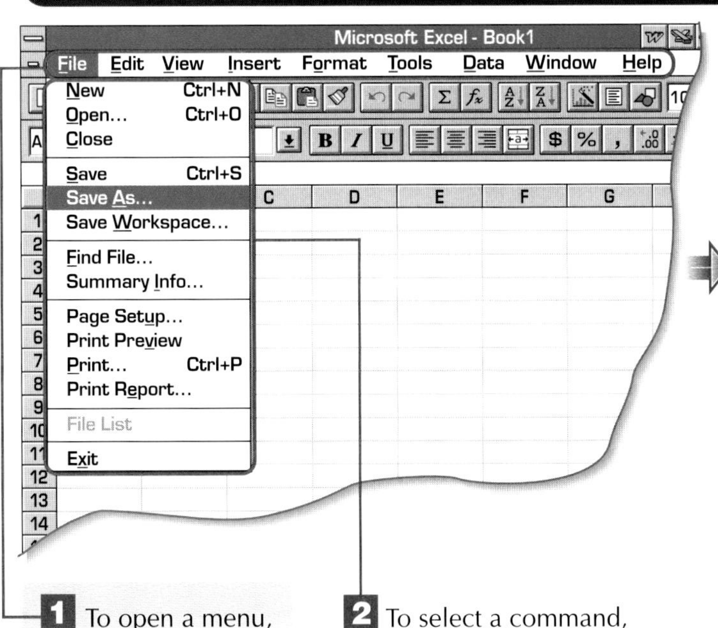

1 To open a menu, press Alt followed by the underlined letter in the menu name (example: F for **File**).

Note: To close a menu, press Alt.

2 To select a command, press the underlined letter in the command name (example: A for **Save As**).

◆ A dialog box appears if the program requires more information to carry out the command.

3 To close a dialog box, press Esc.

SELECT COMMANDS

You can use the buttons on your screen to quickly select the most commonly used commands.

USING THE BUTTONS

Each button displayed on your screen provides a fast method of selecting a menu command.

For example, you can use [Save button] to quickly select the **Save** command.

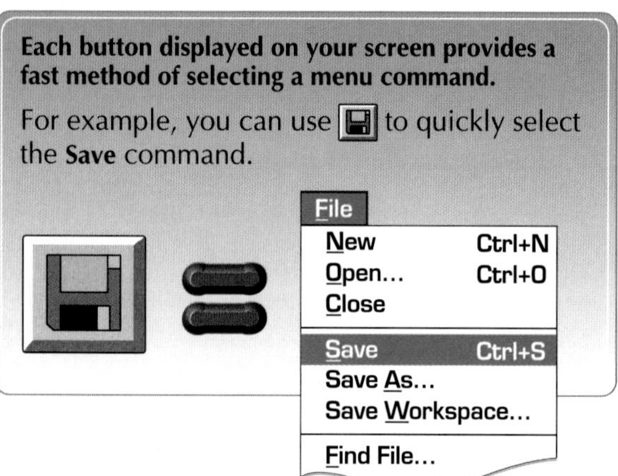

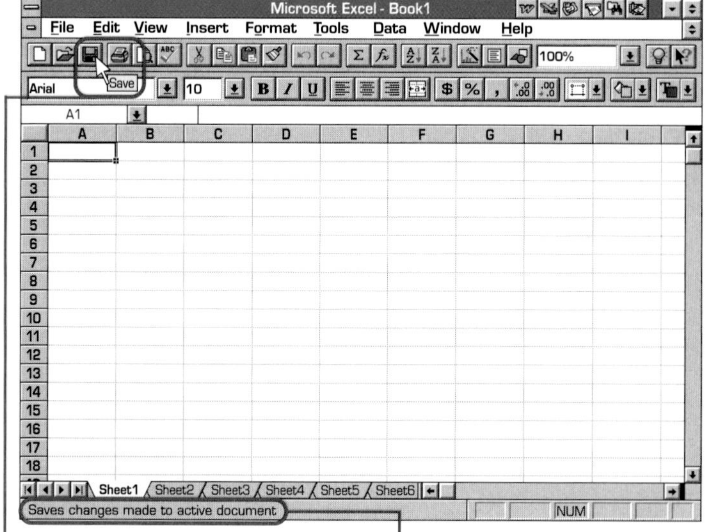

1 Move the mouse over a button of interest (example: [Save button]).

◆ After a few seconds, the name of the button appears.

◆ A short description of the button also appears at the bottom of your screen.

2 To select the button, press the left mouse button.

USING THE SHORTCUT MENUS

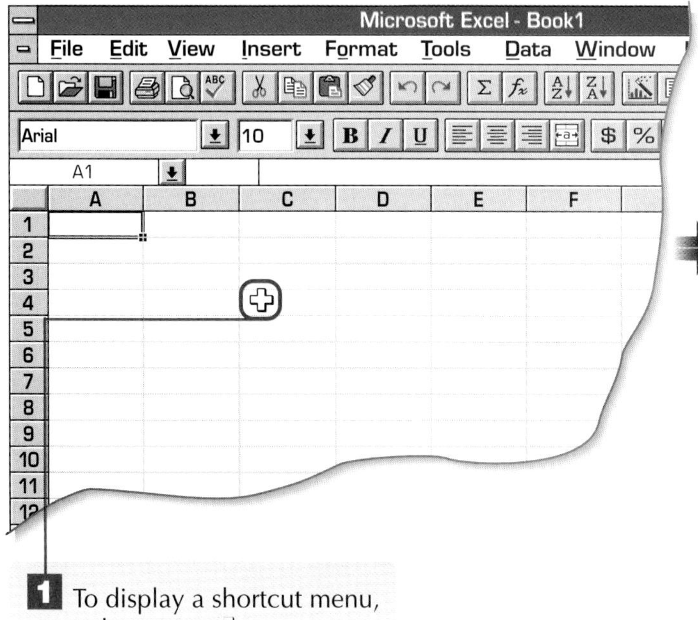

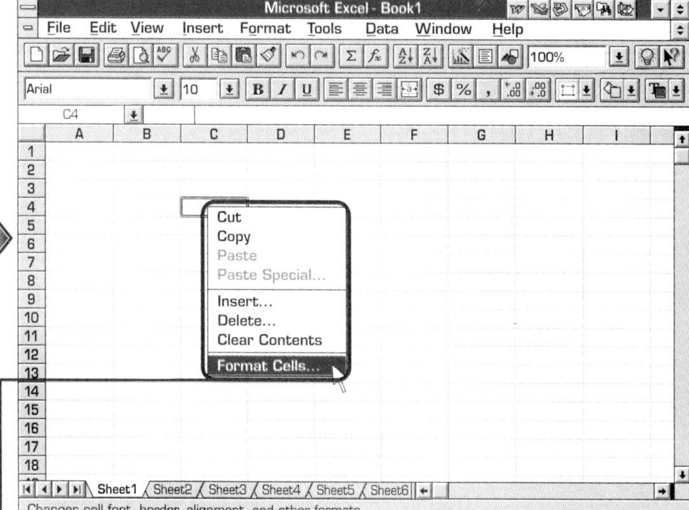

1 To display a shortcut menu, move the mouse over an area on your screen and then press the **right** button.

◆ A shortcut menu appears.

2 Move the mouse over the command you want to use and then press the left button.

Note: To close a shortcut menu, move the mouse outside the menu area and then press the left button.

In this section you will learn how to use Word to create professional-looking documents quickly and efficiently.
Dear Mr. Dent,

WORD

Word lets you produce impressive-looking documents quickly and efficiently.

WHAT YOU CAN CREATE WITH WORD

January 12, 1995

ABC Computer Corporation
P.O. Box 2501
Krikkit, VA 22106

Re: Position Opening-Receptionist

To whom it may concern:

Regarding your advertisement of January 9, 1995, I am pleased to submit my résumé for review and wish to be considered as an applicant for the above-named position.

My professional experience does include using Word. I am well versed in the program capabilities and able to apply the features accurately. Should you find my background and qualifications acceptable, I would be delighted to interview for this position at your convenience.

Thank you for your assistance in this matter. I look forward to discussing this career opportunity with you.

Sincerely yours,
Susan Johnston
Susan Johnston
enclosure

PERSONAL AND BUSINESS LETTERS

Word helps you efficiently produce personal and business letters.

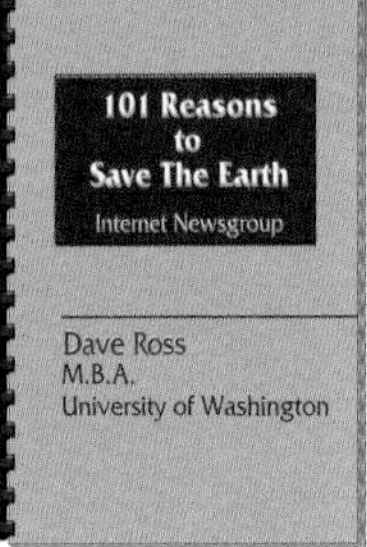

101 Reasons
to
Save The Earth
Internet Newsgroup
Dave Ross
M.B.A.
University of Washington

REPORTS AND MANUALS

Word provides editing and formatting features that make it ideal for producing longer documents, such as reports and manuals.

NEWSLETTERS AND BROCHURES

You can use the formatting features and graphics that Word provides to produce attractive newsletters and brochures.

When you start Word, a blank document appears. You can type text into this document.

START WORD

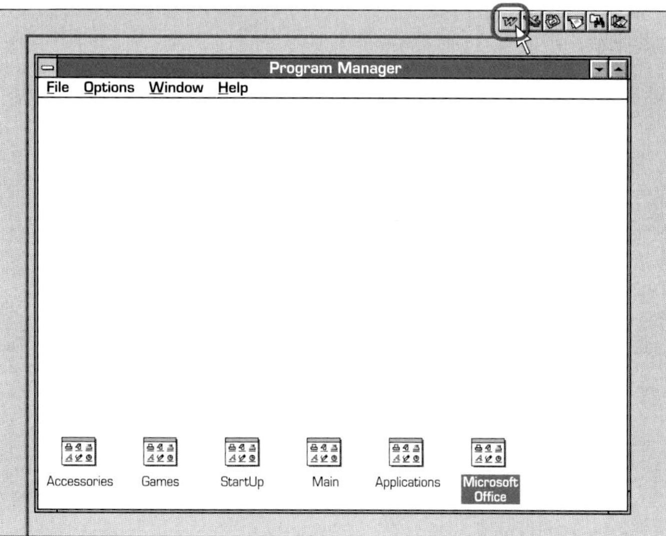

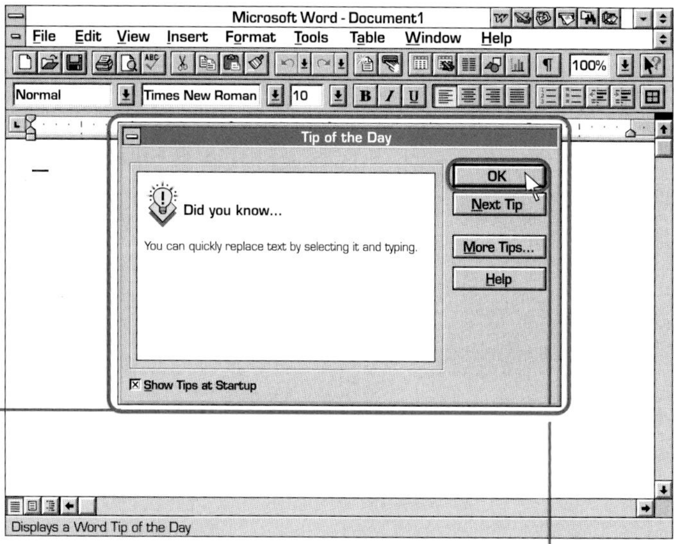

1 To start Word, move the mouse over and then press the left button.

◆ The **Microsoft Word** window appears, displaying a blank document.

◆ Each time you start Word, a tip about using the program appears.

2 To close the **Tip of the Day** dialog box, move the mouse over **OK** and then press the left button.

ENTER TEXT

When typing text in your document, you do not need to press Enter at the end of a line. Word automatically moves the text to the next line. This is called word wrapping.

When you use a word processor to type a letter, the text au...

When you use a word processor to type a letter, the text automatically wraps to the next line as you type.

ENTER TEXT

◆ In this book, the design and size of text were changed to make the document easier to read.

Initial or default font		New font
Times New Roman 10 point	→	Arial 12 point

Note: To change the design and size of text, refer to page 88.

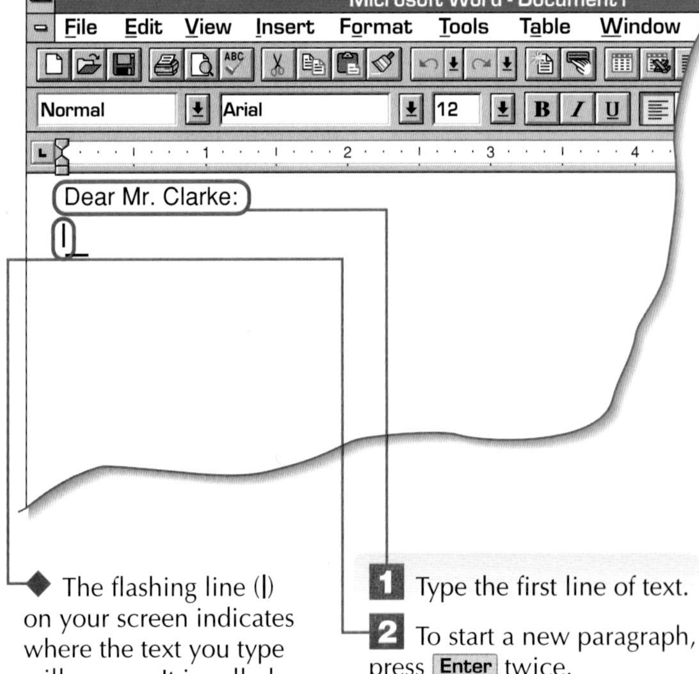

◆ The flashing line (|) on your screen indicates where the text you type will appear. It is called the **insertion point**.

1 Type the first line of text.

2 To start a new paragraph, press Enter twice.

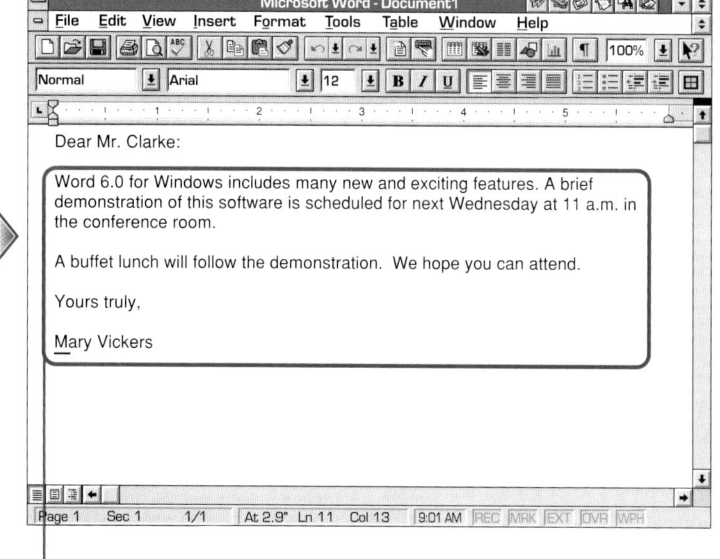
Microsoft Word - Document1
File Edit View Insert Format Tools Table Window Help
Normal
Arial
12
100%
Dear Mr. Clarke:
Word 6.0 for Windows includes many new and exciting features. A brief demonstration of this software is scheduled for next Wednesday at 11 a.m. in the conference room.
A buffet lunch will follow the demonstration. We hope you can attend.
Yours truly,
Mary Vickers
Page 1 Sec 1 1/1 At 2.9" Ln 11 Col 13 9:01 AM REC MRK EXT OVR WPH

3 Type the remaining text.

◆ Press Enter only when you want to start a new line or paragraph.

STATUS BAR

The status bar provides information about the position of the insertion point and the text displayed on your screen.

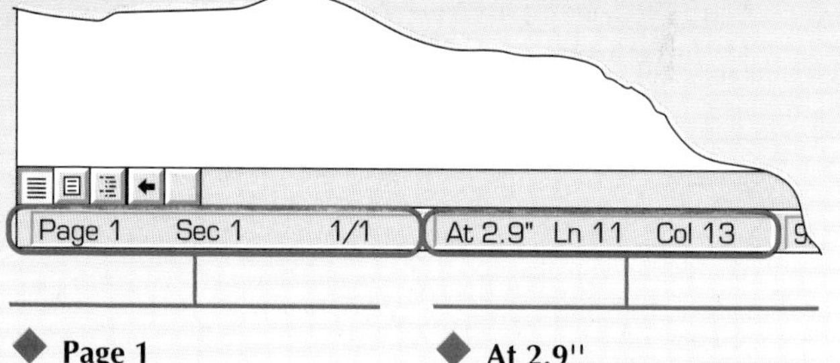
Page 1 Sec 1 1/1
At 2.9" Ln 11 Col 13

◆ **Page 1**
The page displayed on your screen.

◆ **Sec 1**
The section of the document displayed on your screen.

◆ **1/1**
The page displayed on your screen. / The total number of pages in your document.

◆ **At 2.9"**
The distance (in inches) from the top of the page to the insertion point.

◆ **Ln 11**
The number of lines from the top of the page to the insertion point.

◆ **Col 13**
The number of characters from the left margin to the insertion point, including spaces.

MOVE THROUGH A DOCUMENT

If you create a long document, your computer screen cannot display all the text at the same time. You must move through the document to view other areas of text.

IMPORTANT!

You cannot move the insertion point below the horizontal line (_) displayed on your screen. To move this line, position the insertion point after the last character in your document and then press Enter.

MOVE TO ANY POSITION

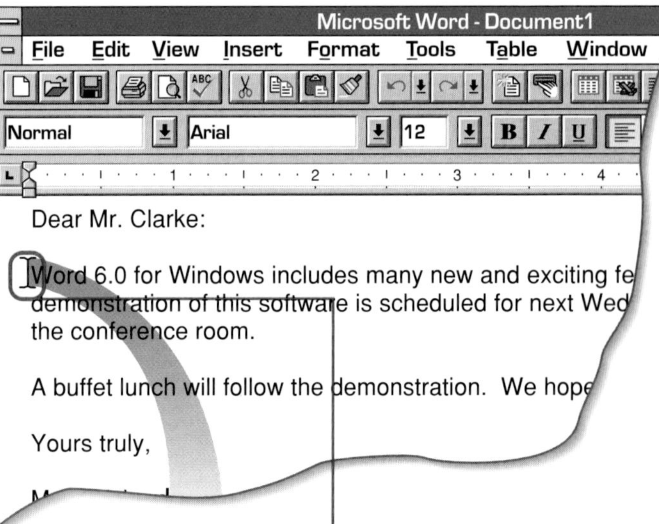
Microsoft Word - Document1
File Edit View Insert Format Tools Table Window
Normal
Arial
12
Dear Mr. Clarke:
Word 6.0 for Windows includes many new and exciting fe
demonstration of this software is scheduled for next Wed
the conference room.
A buffet lunch will follow the demonstration. We hope
Yours truly,

The insertion point indicates where the text you type will appear in your document.

1 To position the insertion point at another location on your screen, move the mouse I over the new location and then press the left button.

SCROLL UP OR DOWN

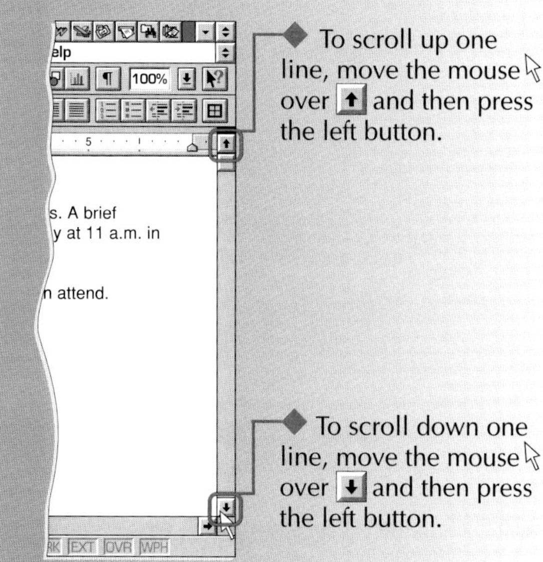

◆ To scroll up one line, move the mouse over ⬆ and then press the left button.

◆ To scroll down one line, move the mouse over ⬇ and then press the left button.

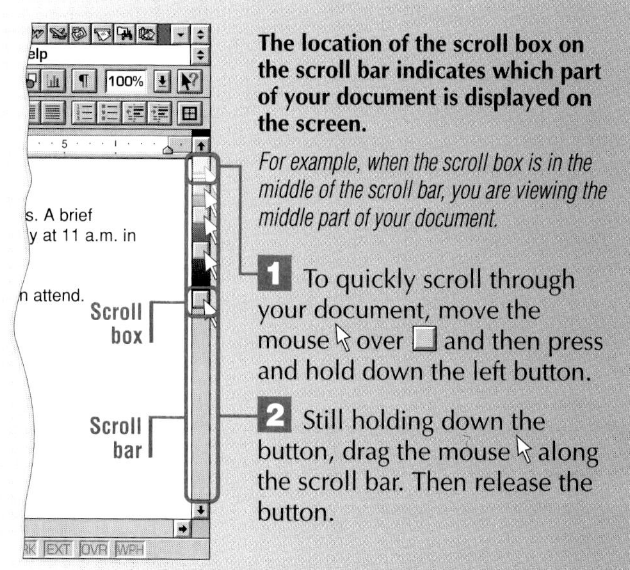

The location of the scroll box on the scroll bar indicates which part of your document is displayed on the screen.

For example, when the scroll box is in the middle of the scroll bar, you are viewing the middle part of your document.

1 To quickly scroll through your document, move the mouse over ☐ and then press and hold down the left button.

2 Still holding down the button, drag the mouse along the scroll bar. Then release the button.

KEYBOARD SHORTCUTS

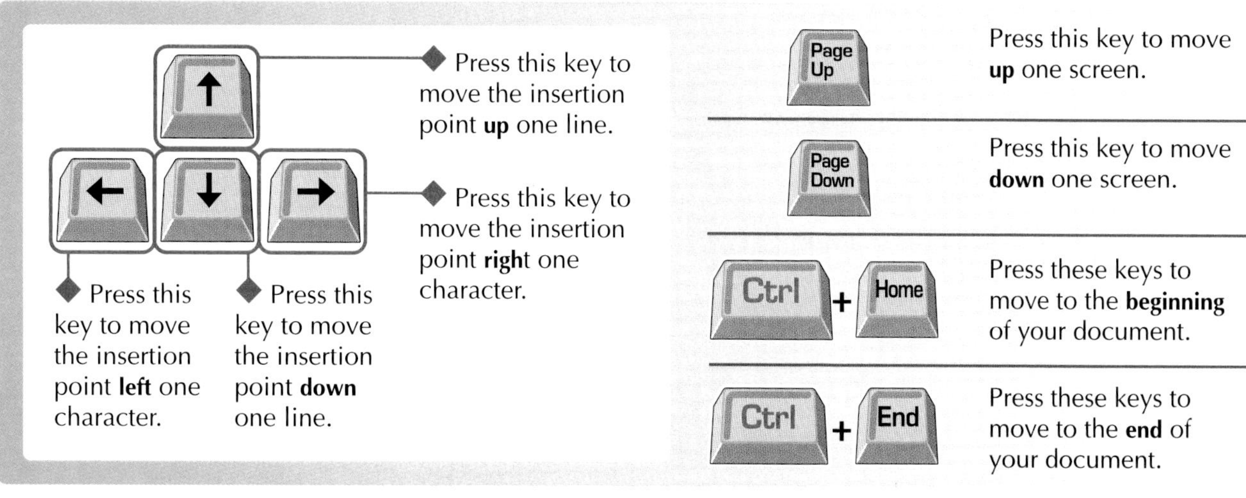

◆ Press this key to move the insertion point **up** one line.

◆ Press this key to move the insertion point **right** one character.

◆ Press this key to move the insertion point **left** one character.

◆ Press this key to move the insertion point **down** one line.

Press this key to move **up** one screen.

Press this key to move **down** one screen.

Press these keys to move to the **beginning** of your document.

Press these keys to move to the **end** of your document.

SELECT TEXT

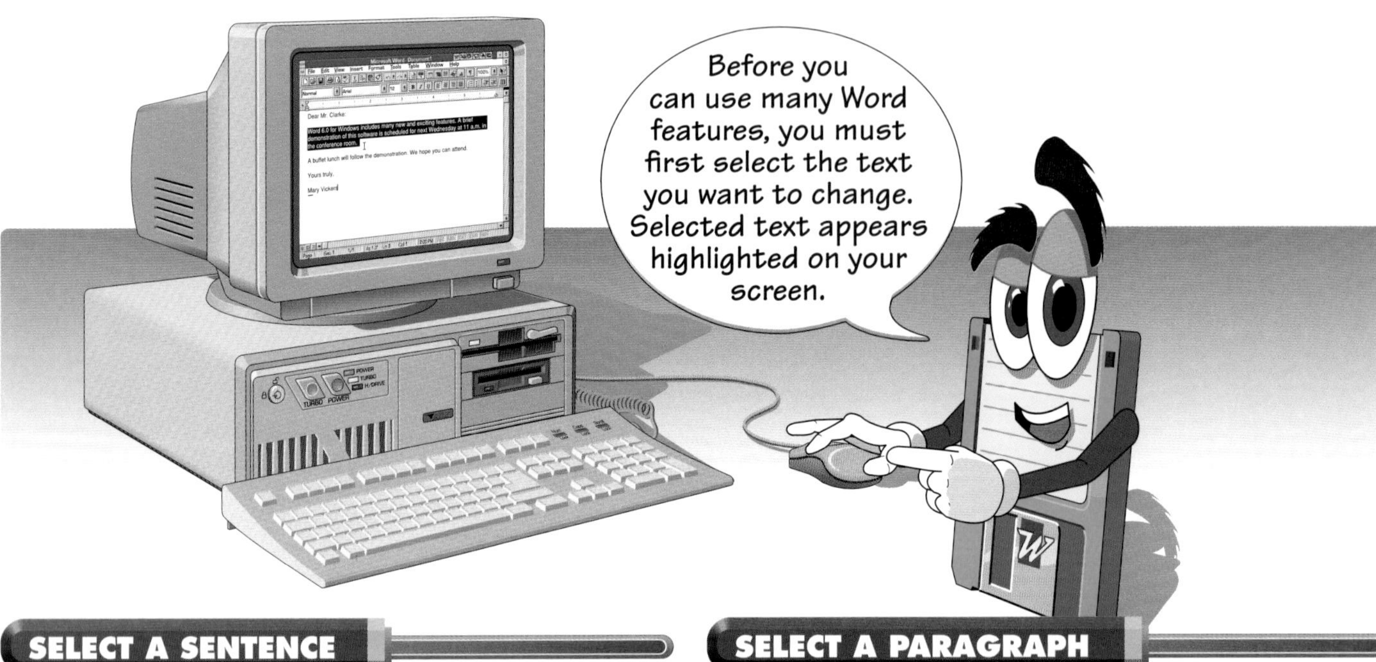

Before you can use many Word features, you must first select the text you want to change. Selected text appears highlighted on your screen.

SELECT A SENTENCE

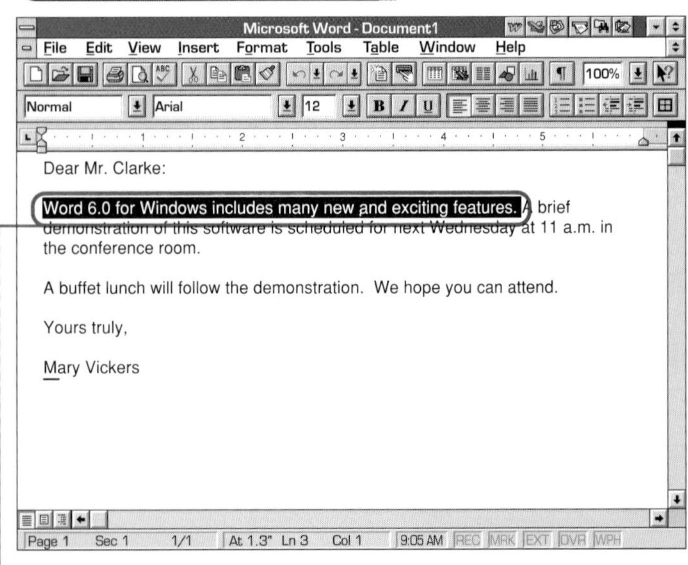

1. Press and hold down Ctrl.
2. Still holding down Ctrl, move the mouse I anywhere over the sentence you want to select and then press the left button. Then release Ctrl.

TO CANCEL A TEXT SELECTION

Move the mouse I outside the selected area and then press the left button.

SELECT A PARAGRAPH

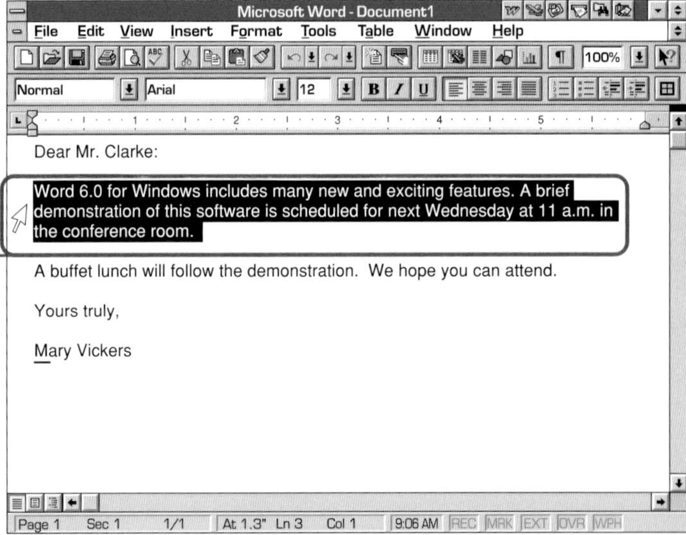

1. Move the mouse I to the left of the paragraph you want to select (I changes to ↖) and then quickly press the left button twice.

SELECT A WORD

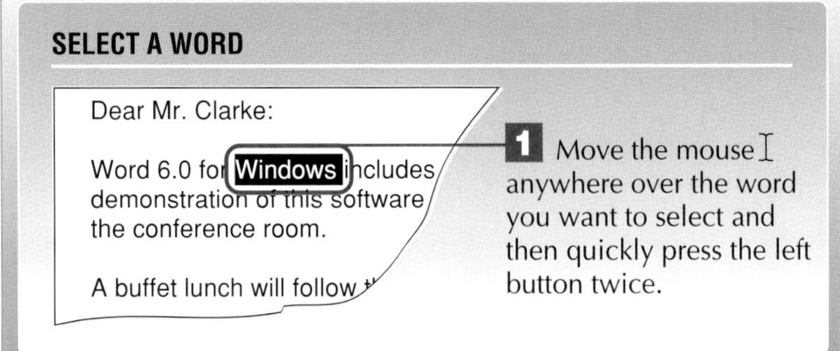

1 Move the mouse I anywhere over the word you want to select and then quickly press the left button twice.

SELECT YOUR ENTIRE DOCUMENT

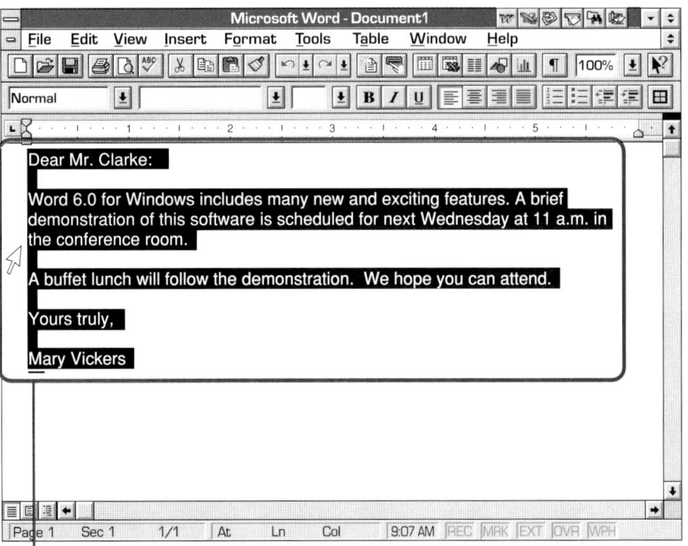

1 Move the mouse I anywhere to the left of the text in your document (I changes to ↗) and then quickly press the left button three times.

SELECT ANY AMOUNT OF TEXT

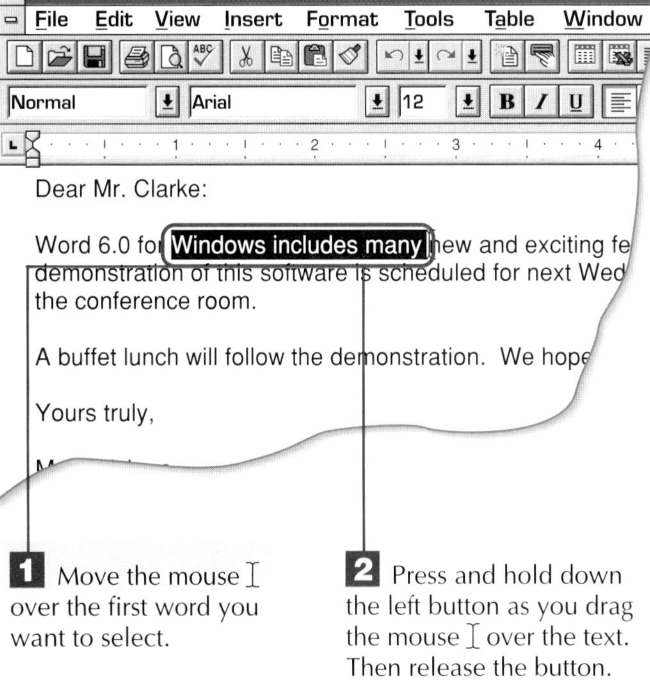

1 Move the mouse I over the first word you want to select.

2 Press and hold down the left button as you drag the mouse I over the text. Then release the button.

GETTING HELP

If you forget how to perform a task, you can use the Word Help feature to obtain information. This can save you time by eliminating the need to refer to other sources.

GETTING HELP

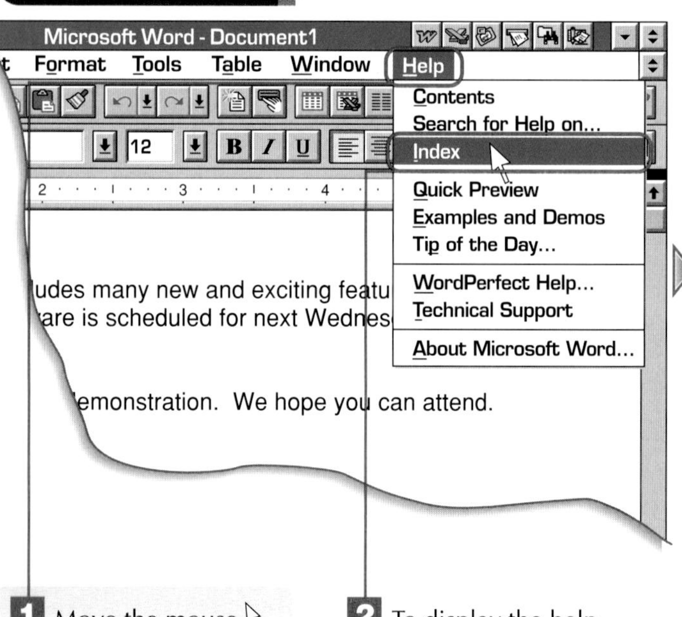

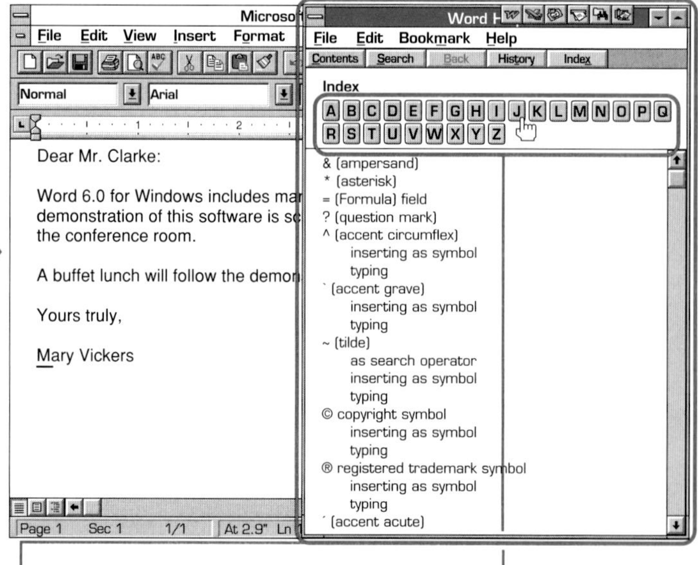

1 Move the mouse over **Help** and then press the left button.

2 To display the help index, move the mouse over **Index** and then press the left button.

◆ The **Word Help** window appears.

3 Move the mouse over the first letter of the topic you want information on (example: J for **Justification**) and then press the left button.

Tip

You can easily print the help topic displayed on your screen.

◆ *Move the mouse over* Print *in the* ***How To*** *window and then press the left button.*

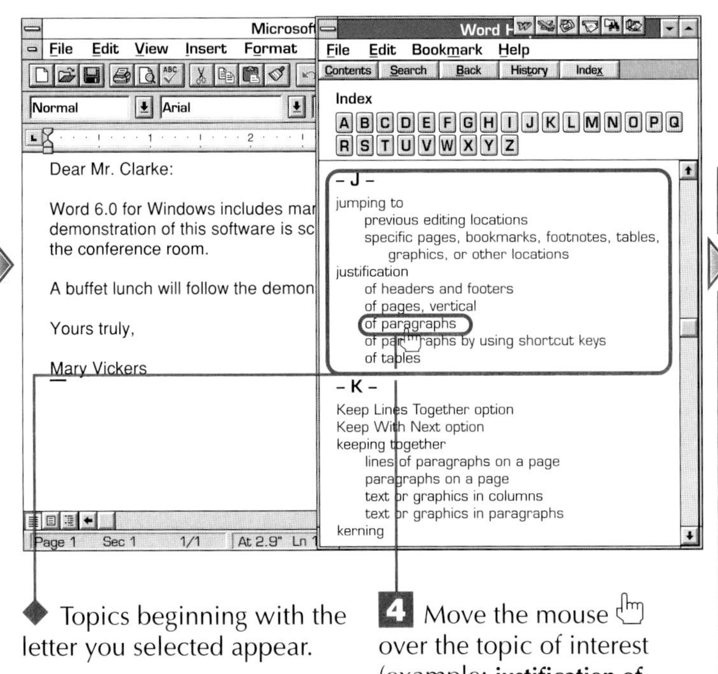

◆ Topics beginning with the letter you selected appear.

Note: You can use the scroll bar to view other topics in the index. For more information, refer to page 23.

4 Move the mouse over the topic of interest (example: **justification of paragraphs**) and then press the left button.

◆ Information on the topic you selected appears.

5 To close the **How To** window, move the mouse over **Close** and then press the left button.

6 To close the **Word Help** window, move the mouse over ▭ and then quickly press the left button twice.

INSERT TEXT

Word makes it easy to edit your document. To make changes, you no longer have to use correction fluid or retype a page.

INSERT A BLANK LINE

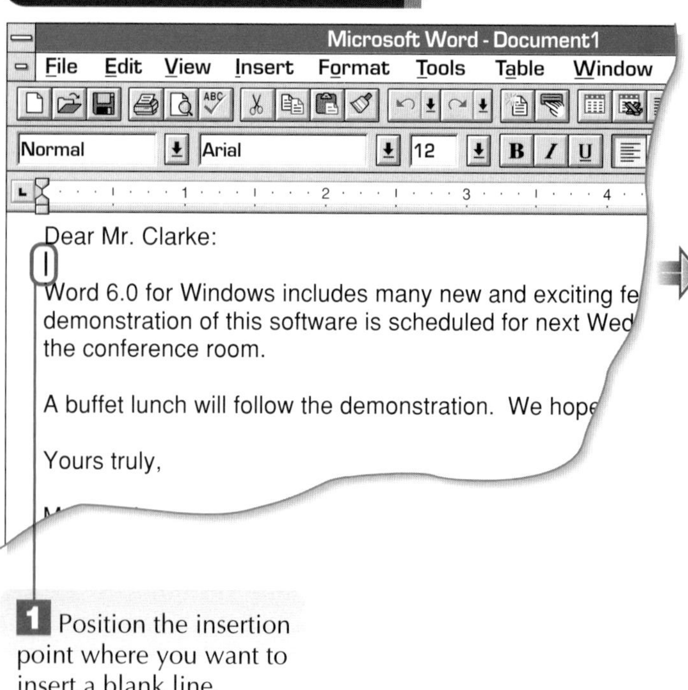

1 Position the insertion point where you want to insert a blank line.

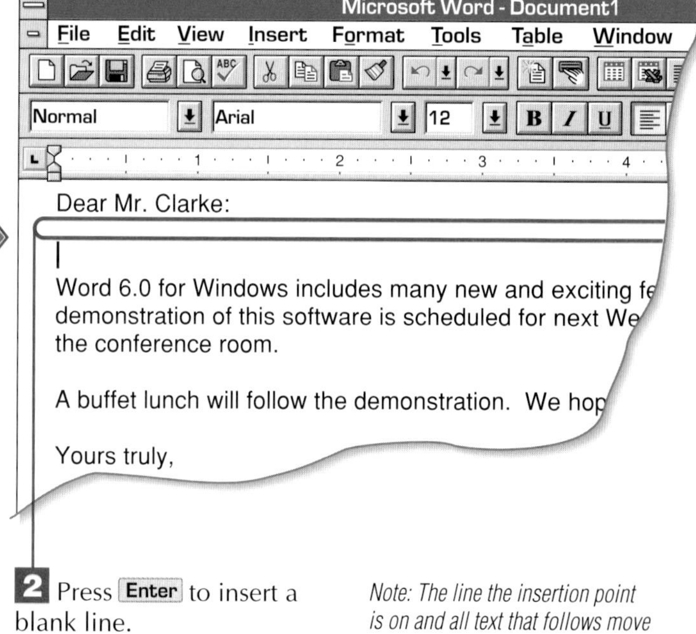

2 Press Enter to insert a blank line.

Note: The line the insertion point is on and all text that follows move down one line.

IMPORTANT!

Make sure you save your document to store it for future use. If you do not save your document, it will disappear when you turn off your computer.

Note: To save a document, refer to page 64.

SPLIT AND JOIN PARAGRAPHS

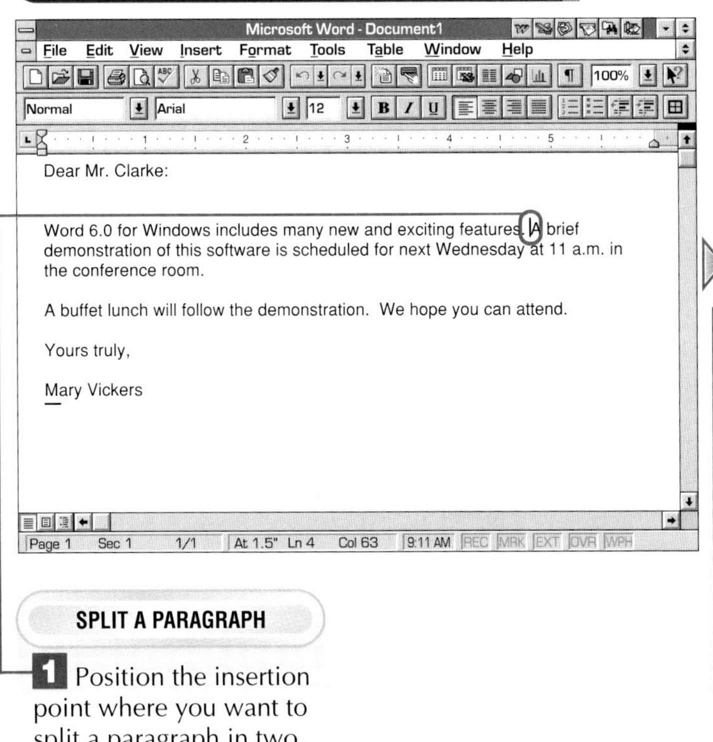

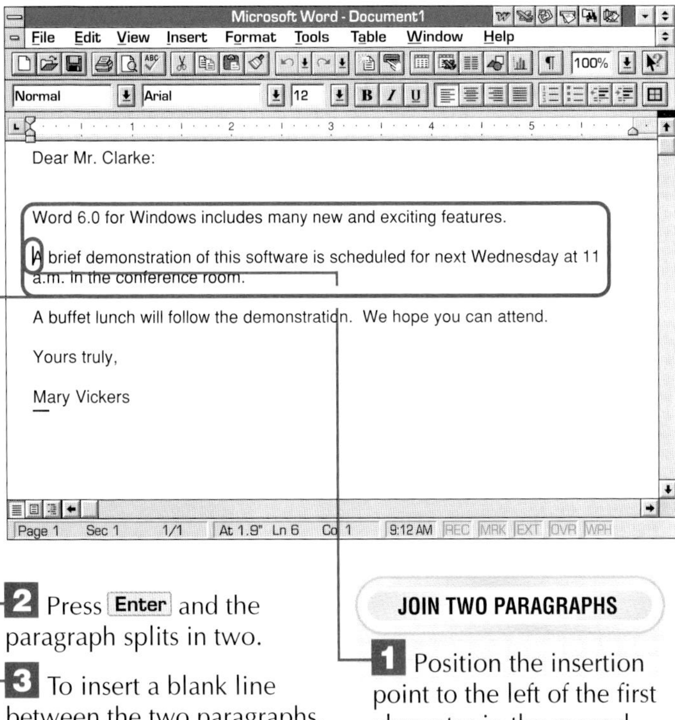

SPLIT A PARAGRAPH

1 Position the insertion point where you want to split a paragraph in two.

2 Press Enter and the paragraph splits in two.

3 To insert a blank line between the two paragraphs, press Enter again.

JOIN TWO PARAGRAPHS

1 Position the insertion point to the left of the first character in the second paragraph.

2 Press ←Backspace until the paragraphs are joined.

INSERT TEXT

In the Insert mode, the text you type appears at the insertion point location. Any existing text moves forward to make room for the new text.

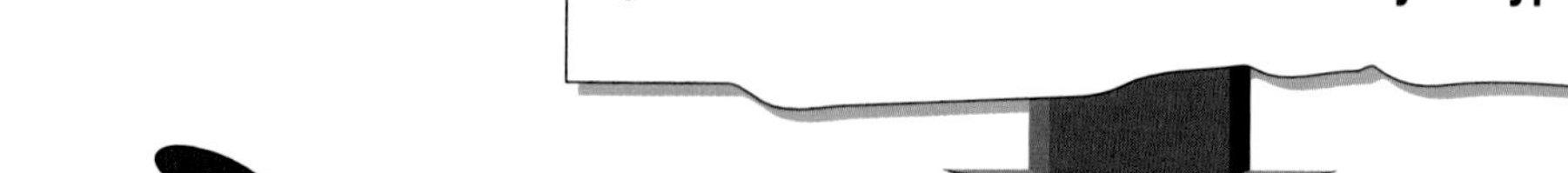
This sentence moves forward as you type.
This sentence moves forward as you type.

INSERT TEXT

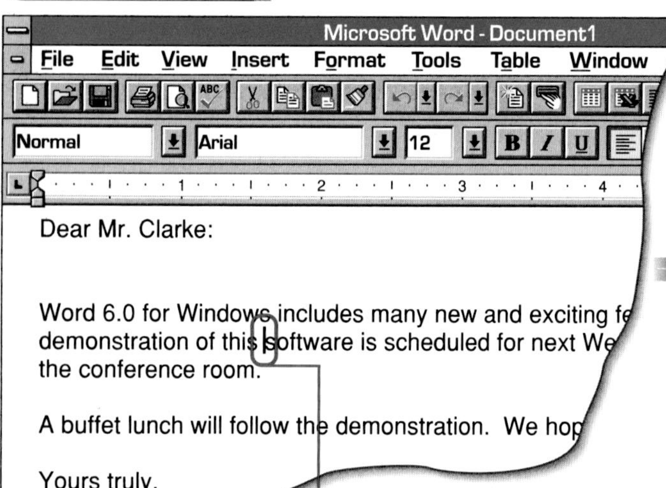
Microsoft Word - Document1
File Edit View Insert Format Tools Table Window
Normal
Arial
12
Dear Mr. Clarke:
Word 6.0 for Windows includes many new and exciting fe
demonstration of this software is scheduled for next We
the conference room.
A buffet lunch will follow the demonstration. We hop
Yours truly,

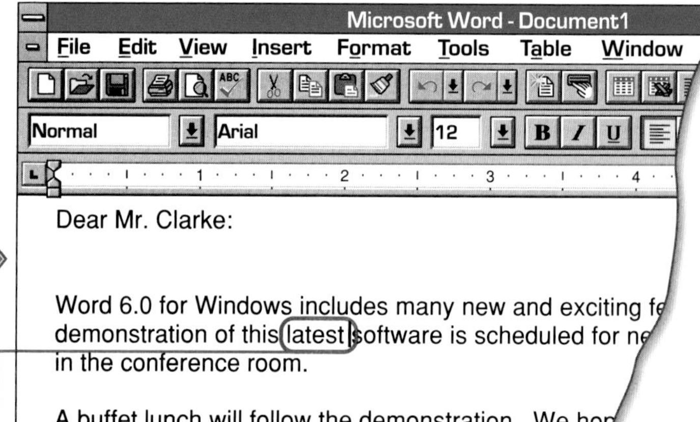
Microsoft Word - Document1
File Edit View Insert Format Tools Table Window
Normal
Arial
12
Dear Mr. Clarke:
Word 6.0 for Windows includes many new and exciting fe
demonstration of this latest software is scheduled for ne
in the conference room.
A buffet lunch will follow the demonstration. We hop
Yours truly,

When you start Word, the program is in the Insert mode.

1 Position the insertion point where you want to insert the new text.

*Note: If the letters **OVR** appear in black (OVR) at the bottom of your screen, press Insert on your keyboard to switch to the **Insert** mode.*

2 Type the text you want to insert (example: **latest**).

3 To insert a blank space, press the **Spacebar**.

Note: The words to the right of the inserted text move forward.

This sentence disappears as you type.
xxxxxxxxxxxxxxxxxxpears as you type.

OVERTYPE TEXT

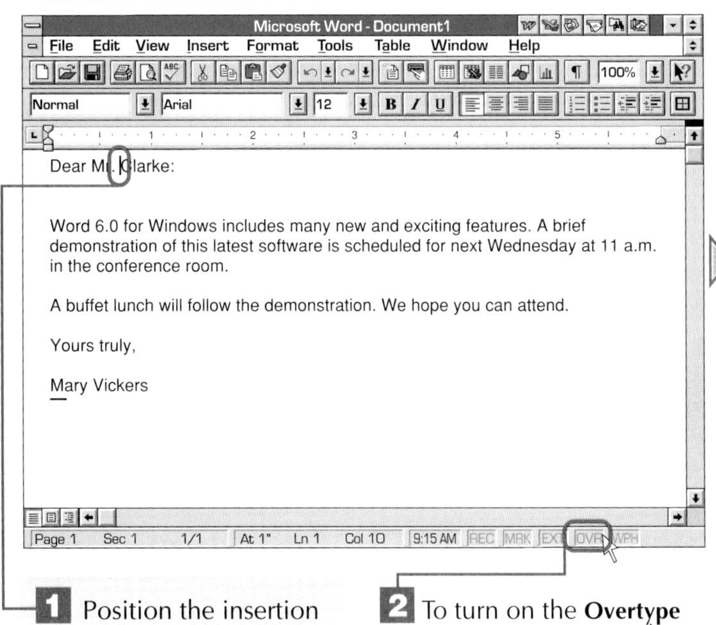

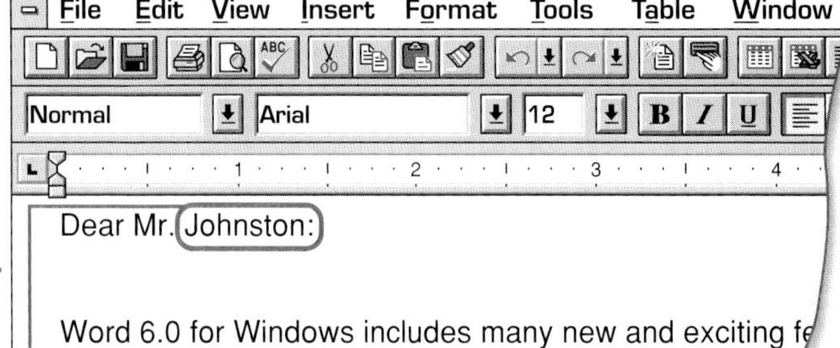

1 Position the insertion point to the left of the first character you want to replace.

2 To turn on the **Overtype** mode, move the mouse over OVR and then quickly press the left button twice (OVR changes to OVR).

3 Type the text you want to replace the existing text (example: **Johnston:**).

Note: The new text types over the existing text.

4 To turn off the **Overtype** mode, repeat step **2** (OVR changes to OVR).

Note: You can also press Insert *on your keyboard to turn on or off the* ***Overtype*** *mode.*

DELETE TEXT

DELETE A BLANK LINE

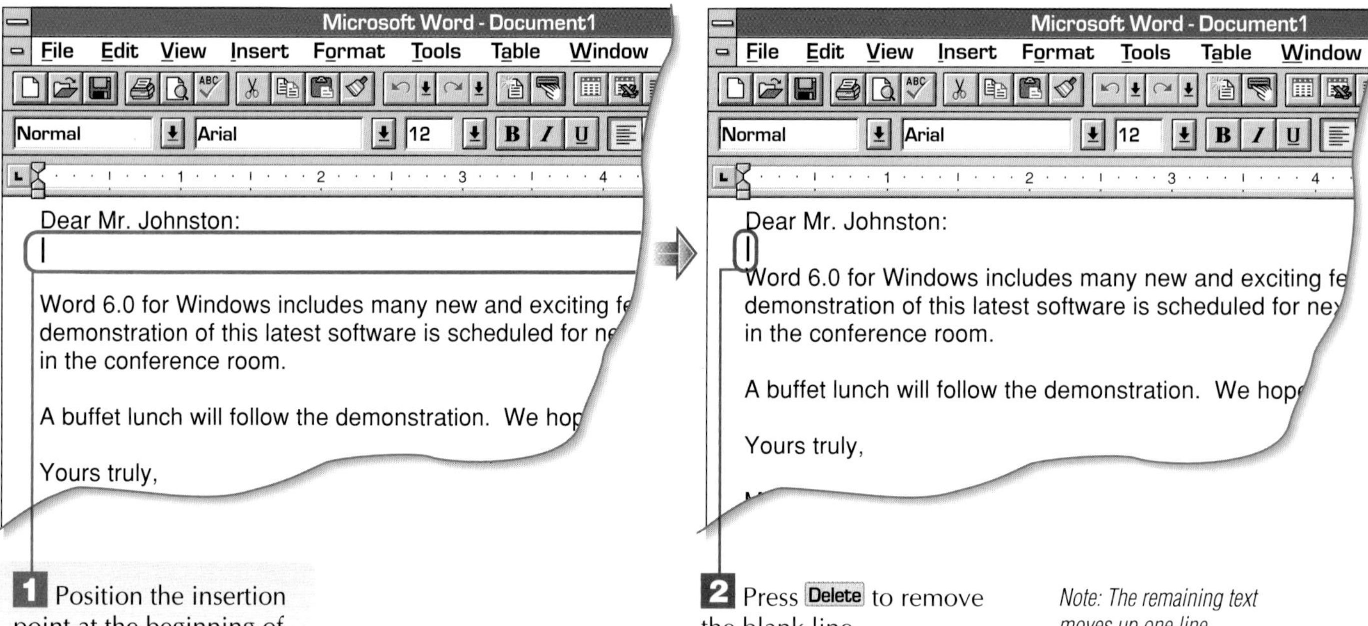

1 Position the insertion point at the beginning of the blank line you want to delete.

2 Press Delete to remove the blank line.

Note: The remaining text moves up one line.

You can use Delete to remove the character to the right of the insertion point. The remaining text moves to the left.

DELETE A CHARACTER

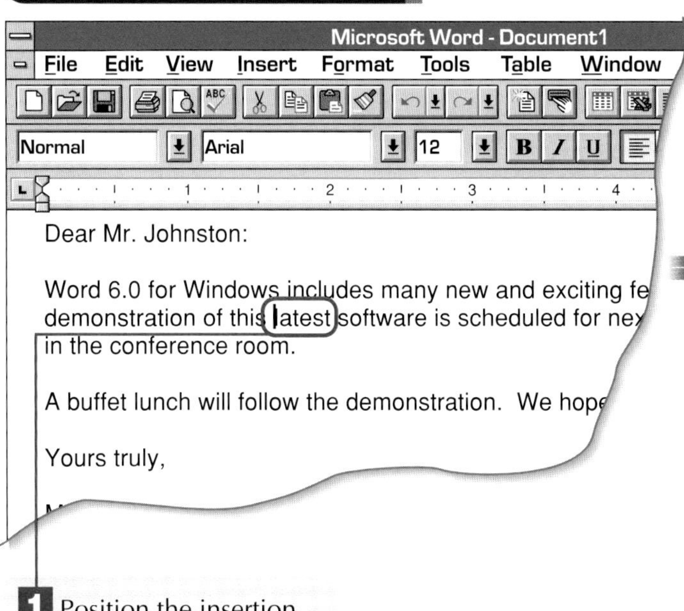
Microsoft Word - Document1
File Edit View Insert Format Tools Table Window
Normal
Arial
12
Dear Mr. Johnston:
Word 6.0 for Windows includes many new and exciting fe
demonstration of this latest software is scheduled for nex
in the conference room.
A buffet lunch will follow the demonstration. We hope
Yours truly,

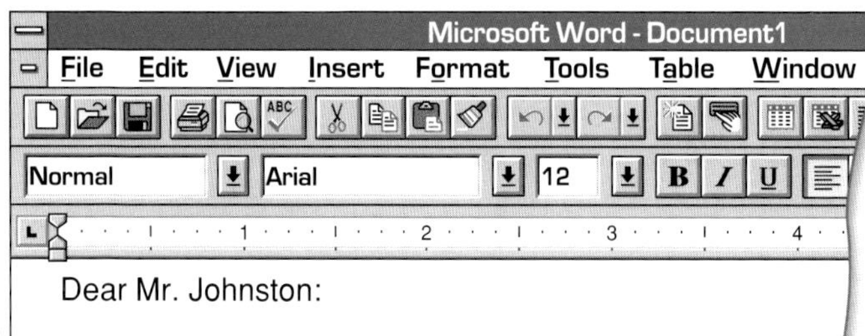
Microsoft Word - Document1
File Edit View Insert Format Tools Table Window
Normal
Arial
12
Dear Mr. Johnston:
Word 6.0 for Windows includes many new and exciting fe
demonstration of this software is scheduled for next Wed
the conference room.
A buffet lunch will follow the demonstration. We hope
Yours truly,

1 Position the insertion point to the left of the first character you want to delete (example: **l** in **l**atest).

2 Press Delete once for each character or space you want to delete (example: press Delete seven times).

You can also use this key to delete characters. Position the insertion point to the right of the character(s) you want to delete and then press ←Backspace.

←Backspace

DELETE TEXT

REPLACE SELECTED TEXT

DELETE SELECTED TEXT

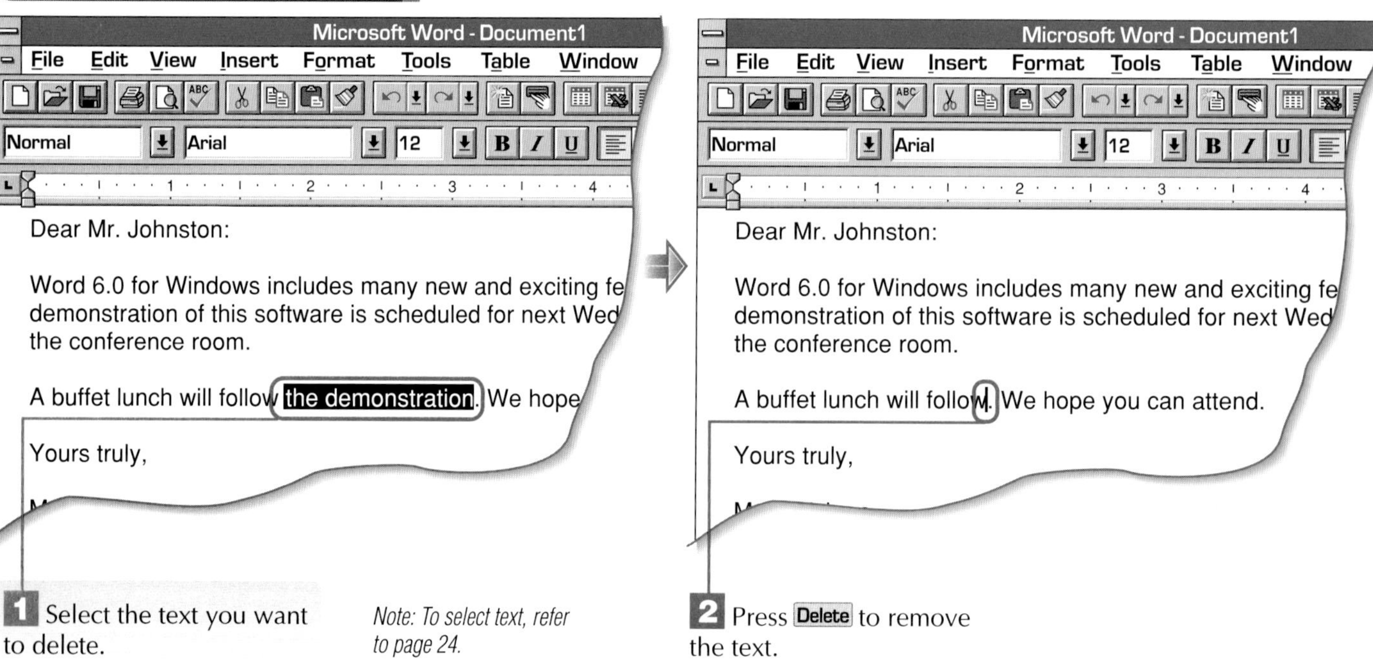

1 Select the text you want to delete.

Note: To select text, refer to page 24.

2 Press Delete to remove the text.

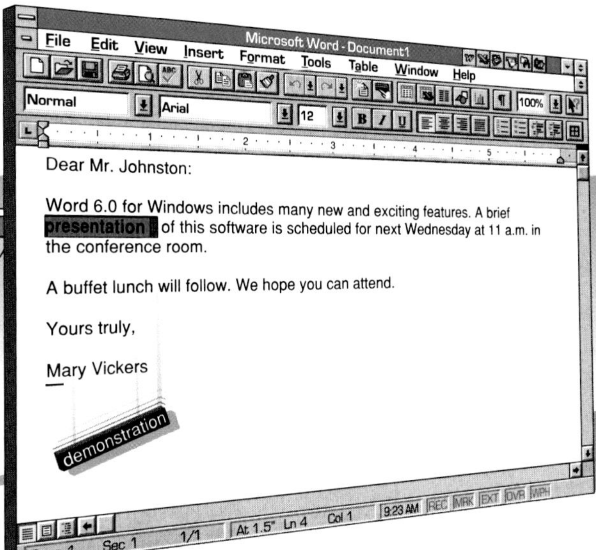

REPLACE SELECTED TEXT

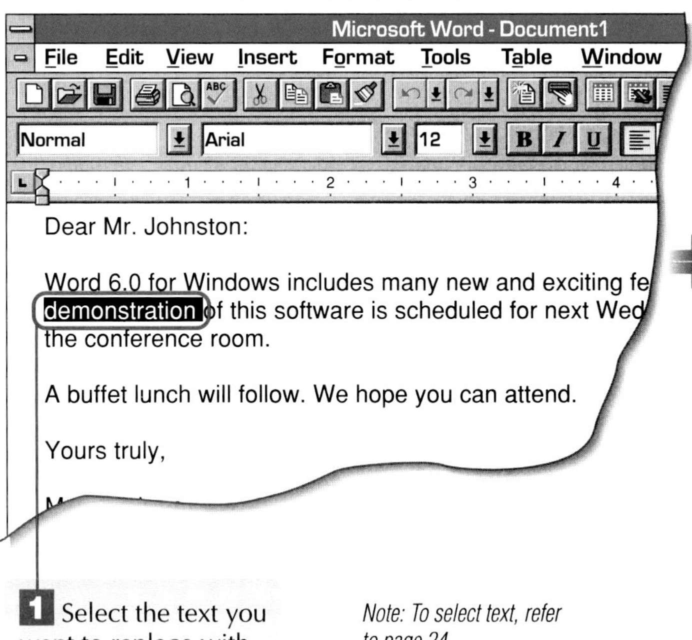

1 Select the text you want to replace with new text.

Note: To select text, refer to page 24.

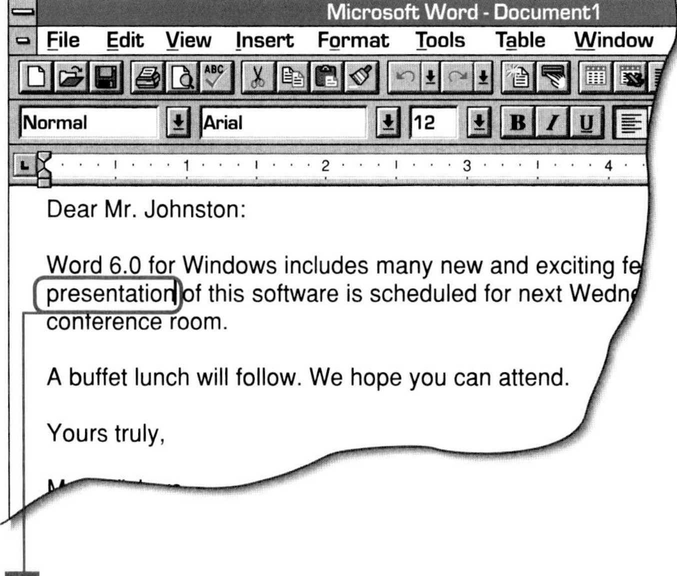

2 Type the new text (example: **presentation**). This text replaces the text you selected.

UNDO CHANGES

REDO CHANGES

Microsoft Word - Document1
POK
Dear Mr. Johnston:
Yours truly,
Mary Vickers

Word remembers the last 100 changes you made to your document. If you regret these changes, you can cancel them by using the Undo feature.

UNDO CHANGES

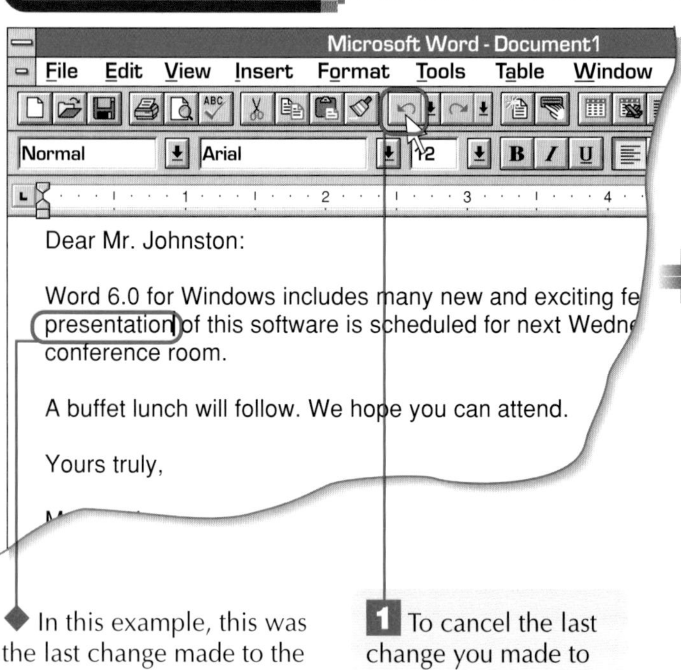

Microsoft Word - Document1
Dear Mr. Johnston:
Word 6.0 for Windows includes many new and exciting fe
presentation of this software is scheduled for next Wedn
conference room.
A buffet lunch will follow. We hope you can attend.
Yours truly,

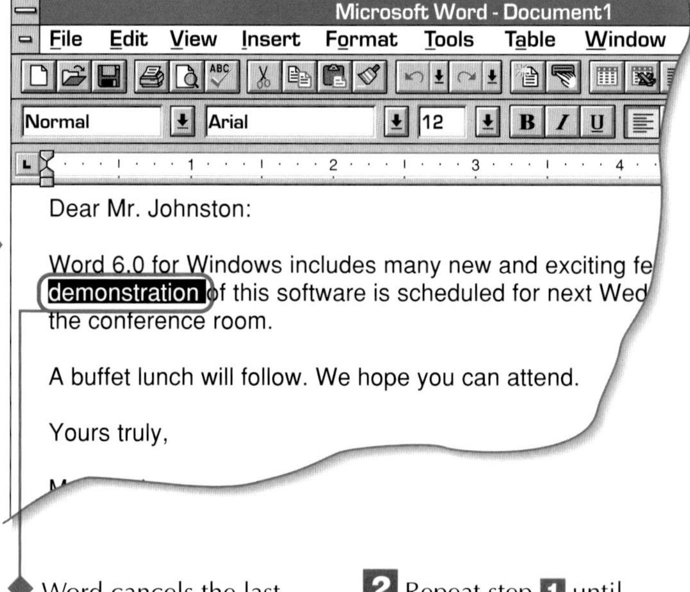

Microsoft Word - Document1
Dear Mr. Johnston:
Word 6.0 for Windows includes many new and exciting fe
demonstration of this software is scheduled for next Wed
the conference room.
A buffet lunch will follow. We hope you can attend.
Yours truly,

◆ In this example, this was the last change made to the document. The word **demonstration** was changed to **presentation**.

1 To cancel the last change you made to your document, move the mouse over the Undo button and then press the left button.

◆ Word cancels the last change you made to your document.

2 Repeat step **1** until you restore all the changes you regret.

The Undo and Redo features are very helpful, but there are some commands that Word cannot undo.

For example, you cannot use the Undo feature to cancel the save and print commands.

REDO CHANGES

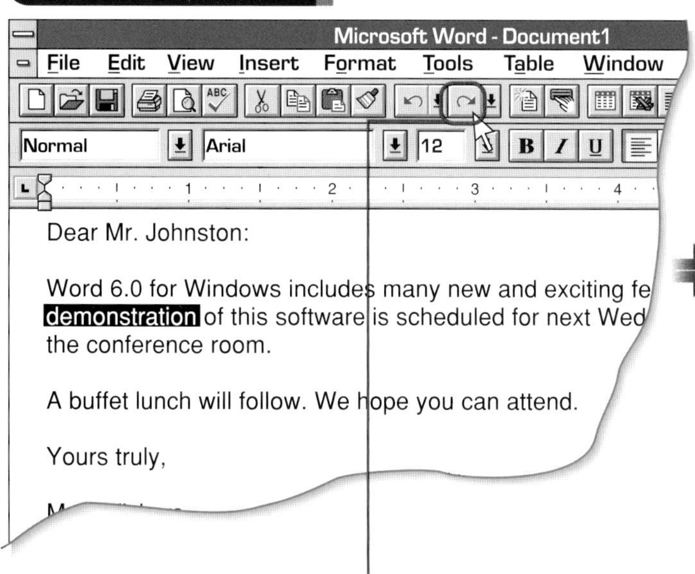
Microsoft Word - Document1
File Edit View Insert Format Tools Table Window
Normal
Arial
12
Dear Mr. Johnston:
Word 6.0 for Windows includes many new and exciting fe
demonstration of this software is scheduled for next Wed
the conference room.
A buffet lunch will follow. We hope you can attend.
Yours truly,

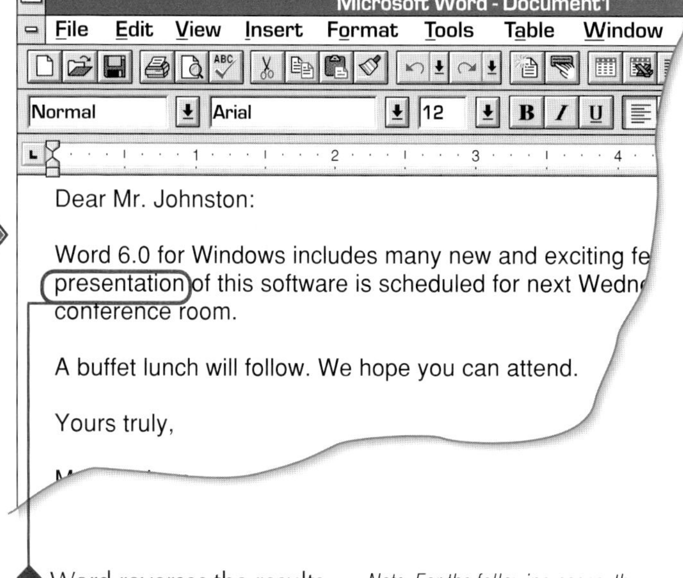
Microsoft Word - Document1
File Edit View Insert Format Tools Table Window
Normal
Arial
12
Dear Mr. Johnston:
Word 6.0 for Windows includes many new and exciting fe
presentation of this software is scheduled for next Wedn
conference room.
A buffet lunch will follow. We hope you can attend.
Yours truly,

If you are not satisfied with the results of the Undo feature, you can use the Redo feature to return the document to the way it was.

1. To reverse the results of using the Undo feature, move the mouse over and then press the left button.

◆ Word reverses the results of the last undo command.

2. Repeat step 1 until you reverse the results of all the undo commands you regret.

*Note: For the following pages, the word **presentation** was returned to **demonstration**.*

CHANGE THE CASE OF TEXT

CHANGE THE CASE OF TEXT

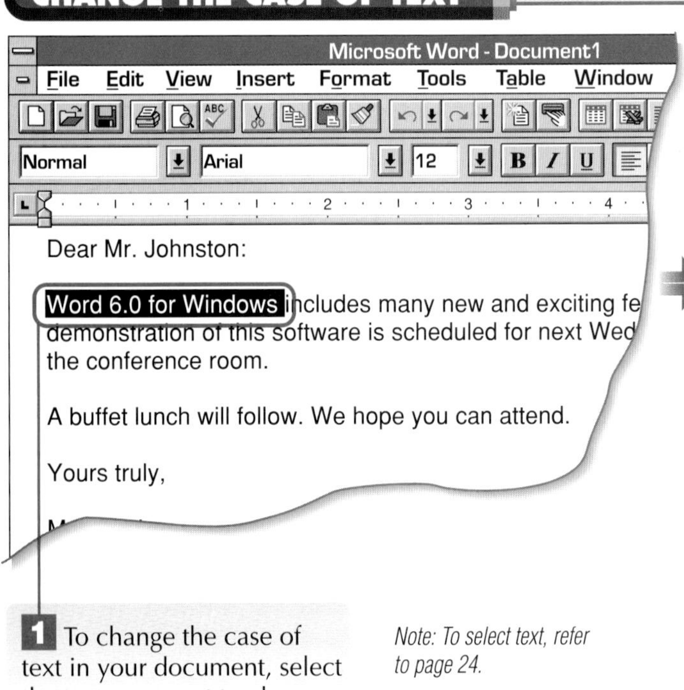

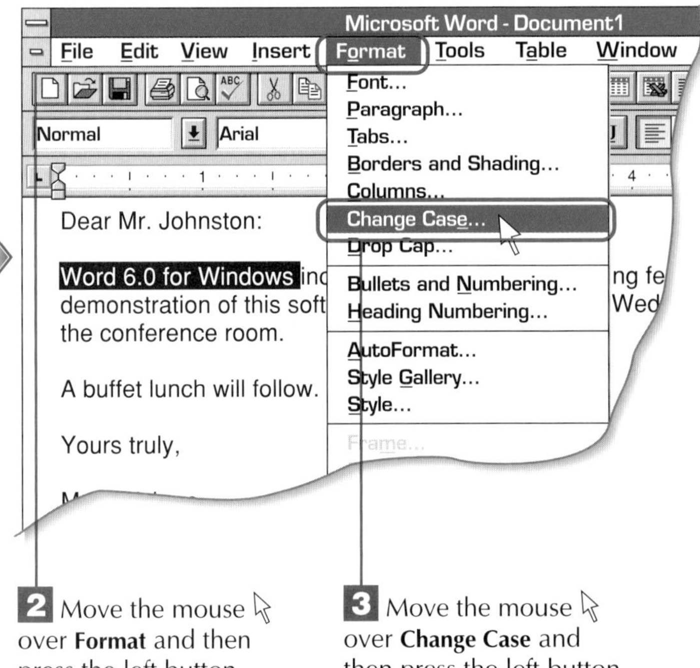

1 To change the case of text in your document, select the text you want to change.

Note: To select text, refer to page 24.

2 Move the mouse over **Format** and then press the left button.

3 Move the mouse over **Change Case** and then press the left button.

1 To quickly change the case of text in your document, select the text you want to change.

2 Press Shift + F3 to change the case of the text. Continue pressing Shift + F3 until the text appears in the case you want.

◆ Each time you press Shift + F3, your text appears in one of three cases:

UPPERCASE

lowercase

Title Case

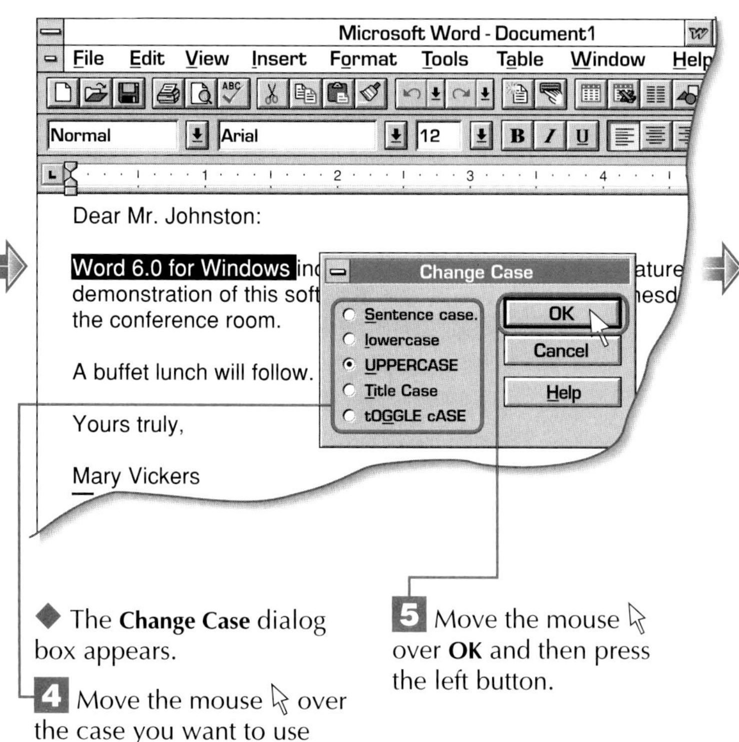

◆ The **Change Case** dialog box appears.

4 Move the mouse over the case you want to use (example: **UPPERCASE**) and then press the left button (O changes to ◉).

5 Move the mouse over **OK** and then press the left button.

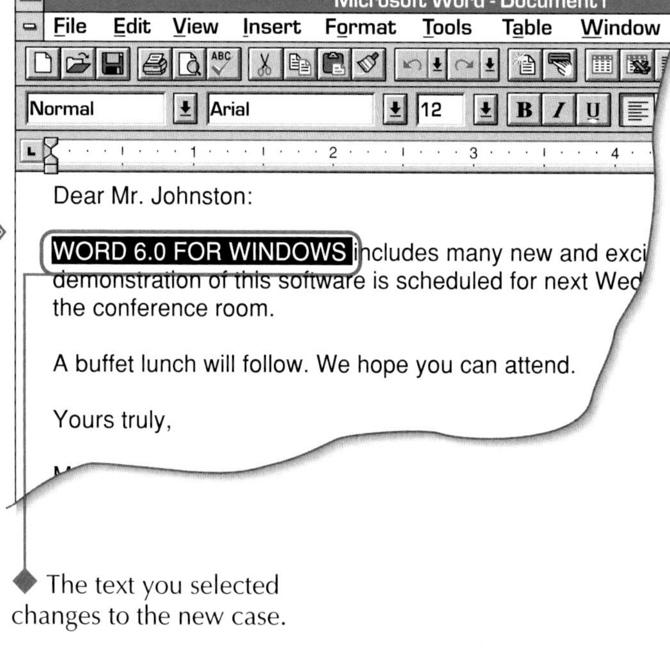

◆ The text you selected changes to the new case.

MOVE TEXT

You can move text from one location in your document to another.

MOVE TEXT

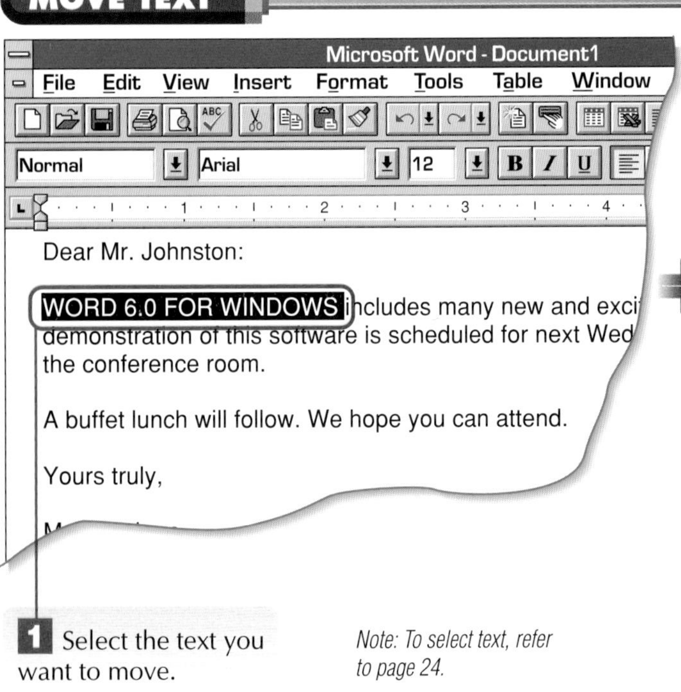

Microsoft Word - Document1
File Edit View Insert Format Tools Table Window
Normal
Arial
12
Dear Mr. Johnston:
WORD 6.0 FOR WINDOWS includes many new and exci
demonstration of this software is scheduled for next Wed
the conference room.
A buffet lunch will follow. We hope you can attend.
Yours truly,

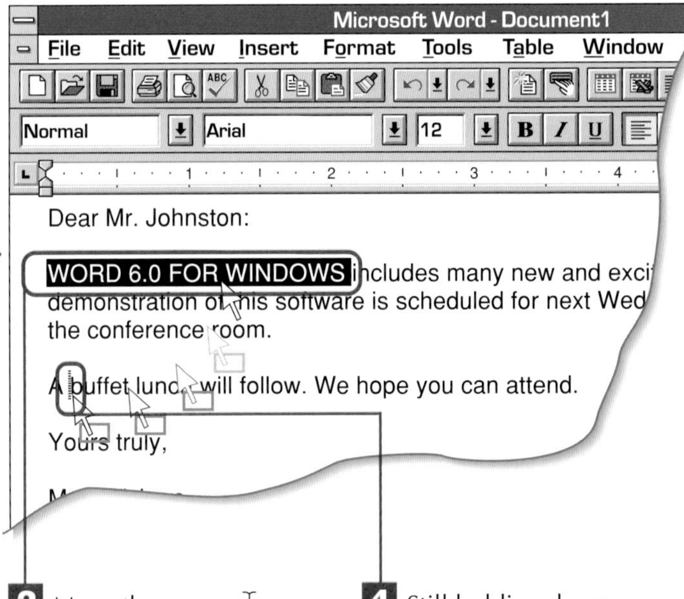

Microsoft Word - Document1
File Edit View Insert Format Tools Table Window
Normal
Arial
12
Dear Mr. Johnston:
WORD 6.0 FOR WINDOWS includes many new and exci
demonstration of this software is scheduled for next Wed
the conference room.
A buffet lunch will follow. We hope you can attend.
Yours truly,

1 Select the text you want to move.

Note: To select text, refer to page 24.

2 Move the mouse I anywhere over the selected text (I changes to ↖).

3 Press and hold down the left button (↖ changes to ↖).

4 Still holding down the left button, drag the mouse ↖ to where you want to place the text.

Note: The text will appear where you position the dotted insertion point on your screen.

You can also use these buttons to move text.

1 *Select the text you want to move.*

2 *Move the mouse over* ✂ *and then press the left button. The text you selected disappears from your screen.*

3 *Position the insertion point where you want to move the text.*

4 *Move the mouse over* 📋 *and then press the left button. The text appears in the new location.*

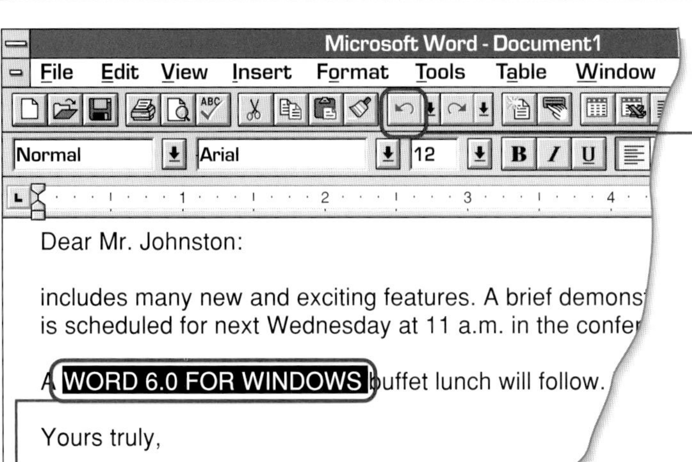

Microsoft Word - Document1
File Edit View Insert Format Tools Table Window
Normal
Arial
12
B I U
Dear Mr. Johnston:
includes many new and exciting features. A brief demons
is scheduled for next Wednesday at 11 a.m. in the confer
A WORD 6.0 FOR WINDOWS buffet lunch will follow.
Yours truly,
Mary Vickers

5 Release the button and the text moves to the new location.

You can cancel the last change you made to your document.

◆ To move the text back to its original location, position the mouse over ↶ and then press the left button.

Note: For more information on canceling changes made to your document, refer to page 36.

COPY TEXT

You can place a copy of text in a different location in your document. This will save you time since you do not have to retype the text.

COPY TEXT

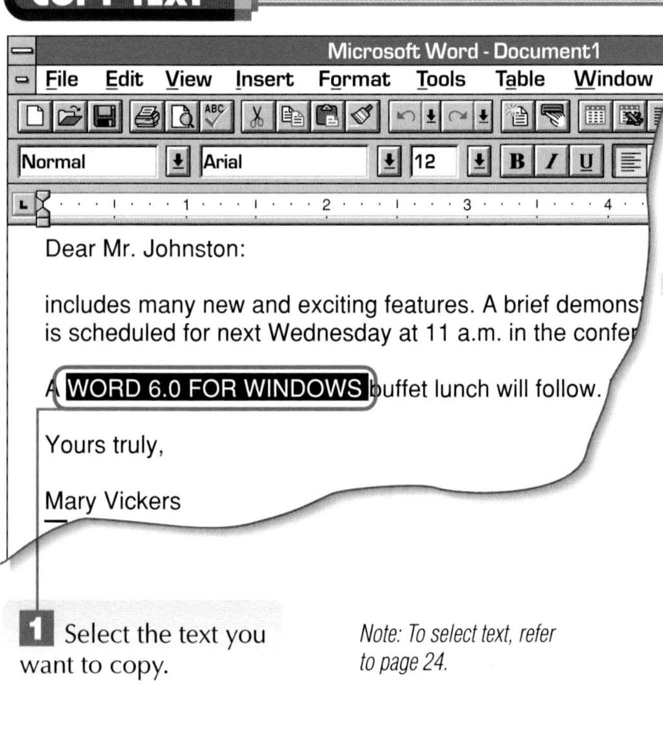

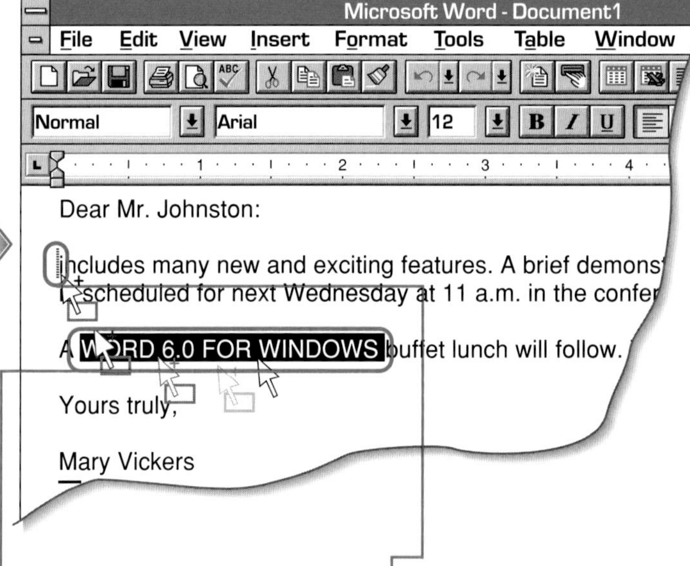

1 Select the text you want to copy.

Note: To select text, refer to page 24.

2 Move the mouse I anywhere over the selected text (I changes to ↖).

3 Press and hold down Ctrl and press and hold down the left button (↖ changes to ↖).

4 Still holding down Ctrl and the left button, drag the mouse ↖ to where you want to place the copy.

Note: The text will appear where you position the dotted insertion point on your screen.

Tip

You can also use these buttons to copy text.

1 *Select the text you want to copy.*

2 *Move the mouse over and then press the left button. The text you selected remains on your screen.*

3 *Position the insertion point where you want to place the copy.*

4 *Move the mouse over and then press the left button. A copy of the text appears in the new location.*

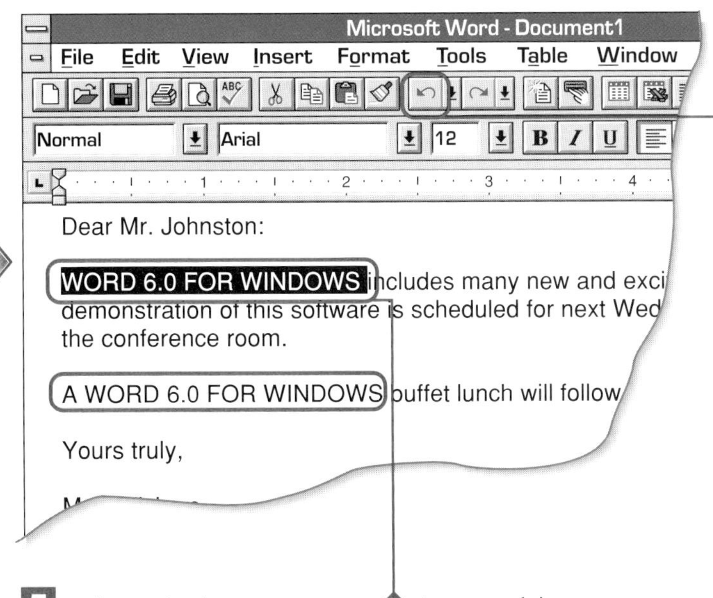
Microsoft Word - Document1
File Edit View Insert Format Tools Table Window
Normal
Arial
12
Dear Mr. Johnston:
WORD 6.0 FOR WINDOWS includes many new and exci
demonstration of this software is scheduled for next Wed
the conference room.
A WORD 6.0 FOR WINDOWS buffet lunch will follow
Yours truly,

5 Release the button and then release Ctrl.

◆ A copy of the text appears in the new location.

You can cancel the last change you made to your document.

◆ To remove the copy, move the mouse over and then press the left button.

Note: For more information on canceling changes made to your document, refer to page 36.

CHANGE VIEWS

Word offers three ways to display your document. You can choose the view that best suits your needs.

CHANGE VIEWS

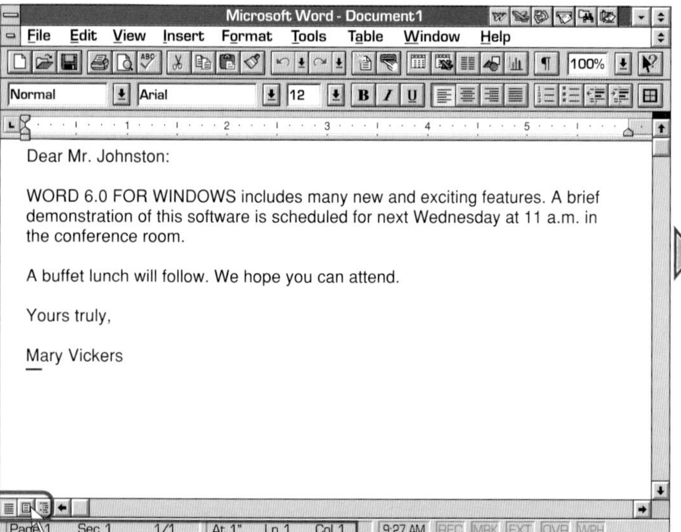

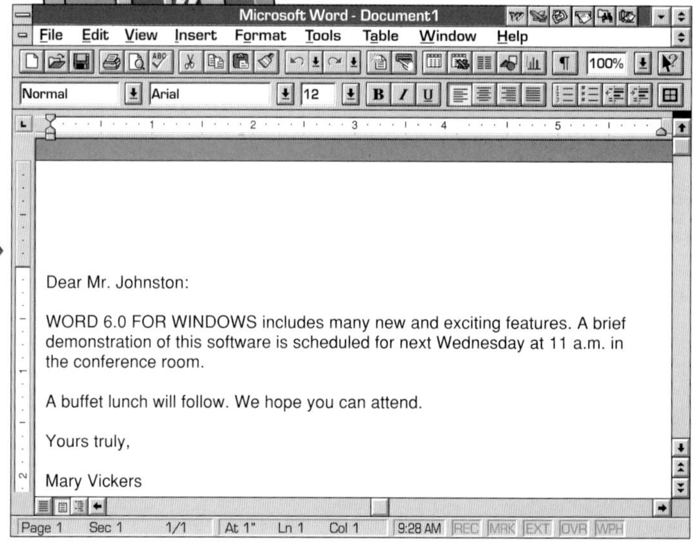

When you first start Word, your document appears in the Normal view.

1 To change to another view, move the mouse over one of the options listed below (example: ▤) and then press the left button.

- ▤ Normal view
- ▤ Page Layout view
- ▤ Outline view

◆ Your document appears in the new view (example: **Page Layout**).

THREE WAYS TO VIEW YOUR DOCUMENT

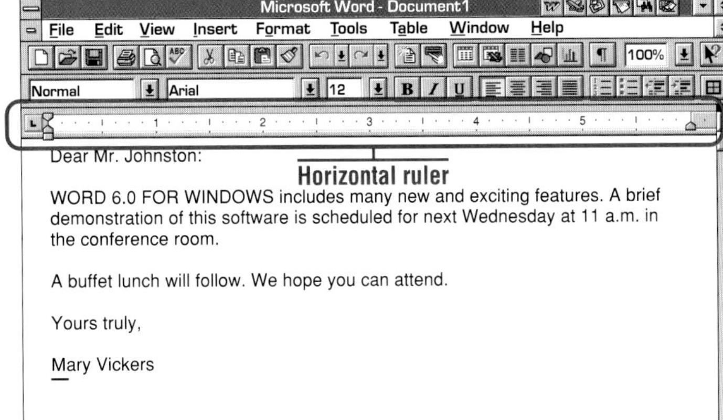

1 NORMAL VIEW

◆ The Normal view simplifies the page layout so you can type and edit the document quickly.

◆ This view does not display top or bottom margins, headers, footers or page numbers.

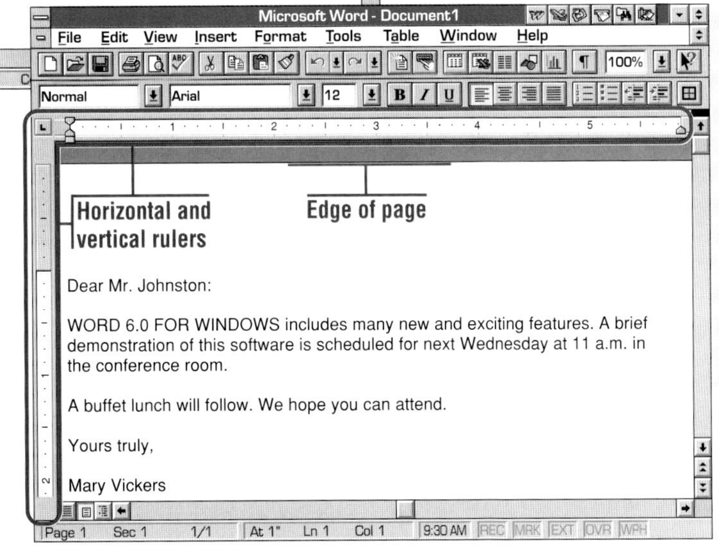

2 PAGE LAYOUT VIEW

◆ The Page Layout view displays your document exactly the way it will appear on a printed page.

◆ This view displays all features in your document, including top and bottom margins, headers, footers and page numbers.

3 OUTLINE VIEW

◆ The Outline view lets you create an outline of your document, similar to a Table of Contents. You can display the headings and subheadings and hide the body text. This view helps you work more efficiently with longer documents.

FIND TEXT

FIND TEXT

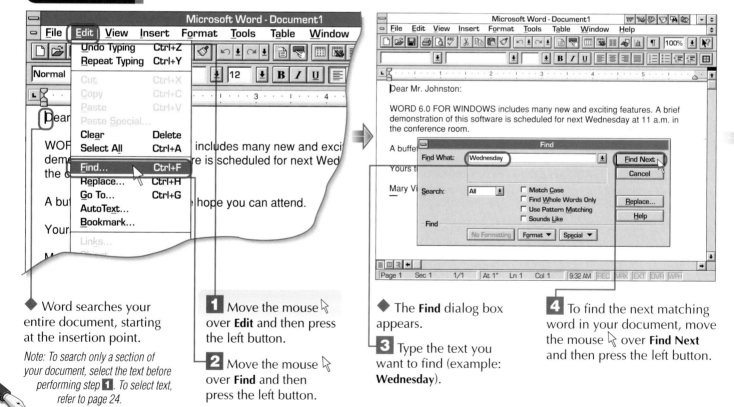

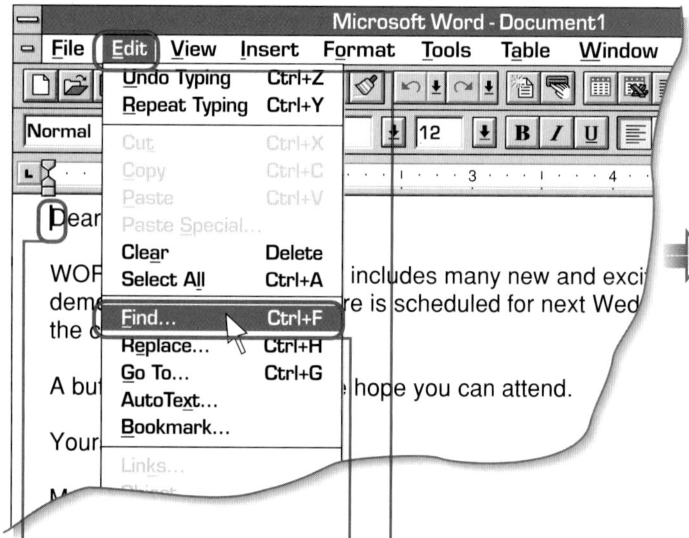

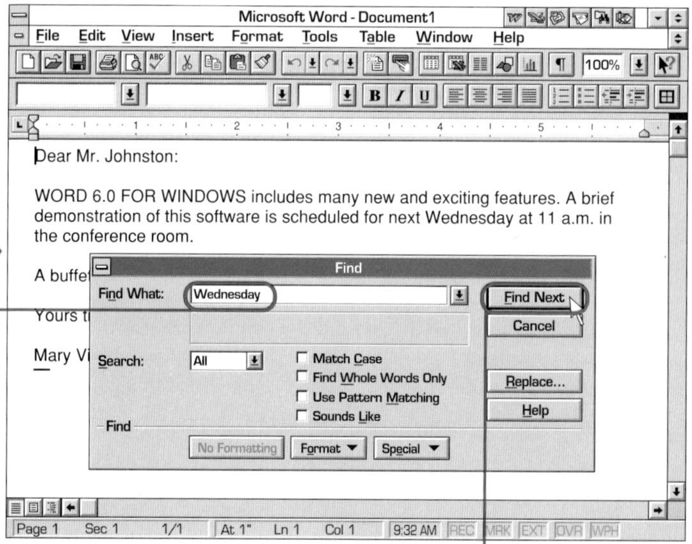

◆ Word searches your entire document, starting at the insertion point.

Note: To search only a section of your document, select the text before performing step 1. To select text, refer to page 24.

1 Move the mouse over **Edit** and then press the left button.

2 Move the mouse over **Find** and then press the left button.

◆ The **Find** dialog box appears.

3 Type the text you want to find (example: **Wednesday**).

4 To find the next matching word in your document, move the mouse over **Find Next** and then press the left button.

Tip

*The **Sounds Like** option finds words that sound the same but are spelled differently. For example, if you search for **there**, Word will also find **their** and **they're**.*

☐ Match Case
☐ Find Whole Words Only
☐ Use Pattern Matching
☒ Sounds Like

◆ *To select the **Sounds Like** option, move the mouse over the option and then press the left button (☐ changes to ☒).*

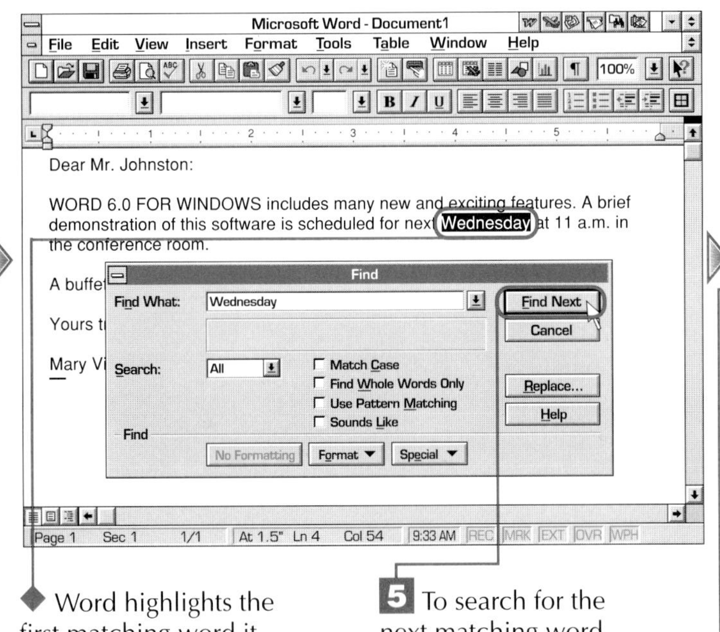

◆ Word highlights the first matching word it finds.

5 To search for the next matching word, repeat step **4**.

Note: To cancel the search at any time, press **Esc**.

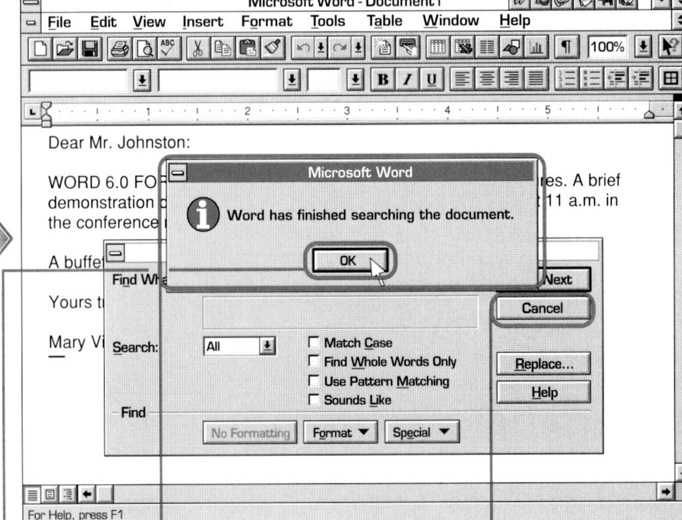

◆ This dialog box appears when there are no more matching words in your document.

6 To close the dialog box, move the mouse over **OK** and then press the left button.

7 To close the **Find** dialog box, move the mouse over **Cancel** and then press the left button.

REPLACE TEXT

REPLACE TEXT

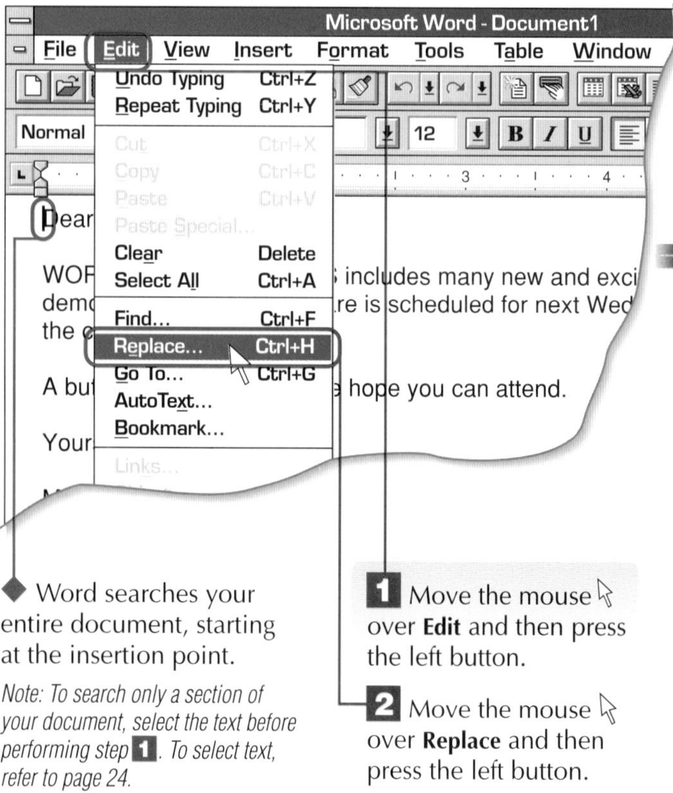

◆ Word searches your entire document, starting at the insertion point.

Note: To search only a section of your document, select the text before performing step 1. To select text, refer to page 24.

1 Move the mouse over **Edit** and then press the left button.

2 Move the mouse over **Replace** and then press the left button.

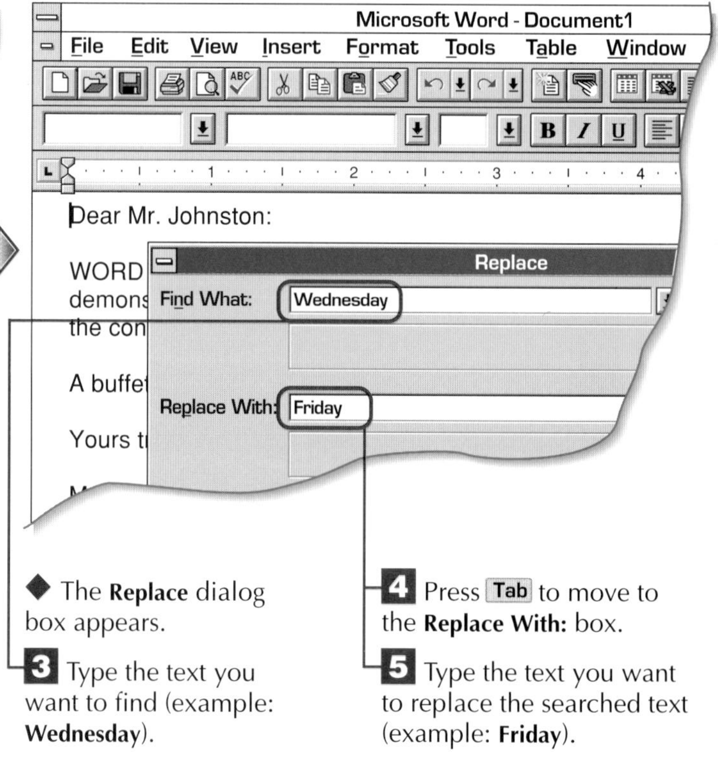

◆ The **Replace** dialog box appears.

3 Type the text you want to find (example: **Wednesday**).

4 Press Tab to move to the **Replace With:** box.

5 Type the text you want to replace the searched text (example: **Friday**).

- Find Text
- **Replace Text**
- Check Spelling
- Using AutoCorrect
- Using AutoText
- Using the Thesaurus
- Check Grammar

You can replace all matching words or phrases in your document at the same time.

Replace steps 6 to 8 below with the following:

Replace All

◆ *Move the mouse over* ***Replace All*** *and then press the left button.*

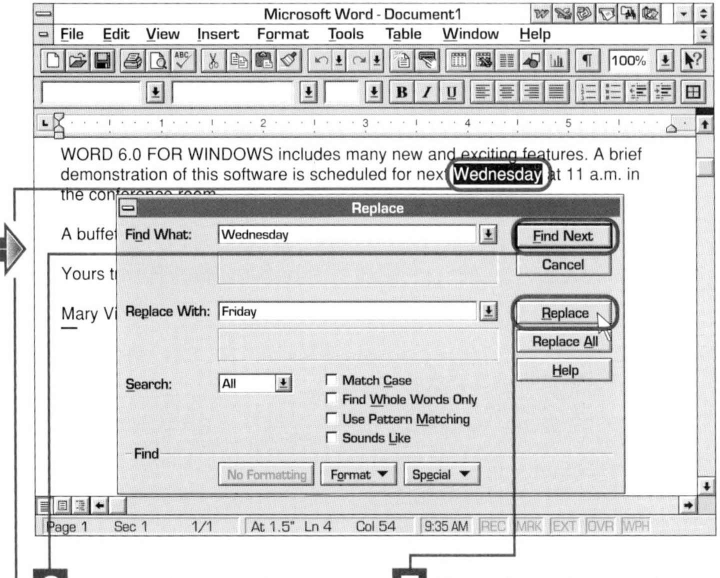

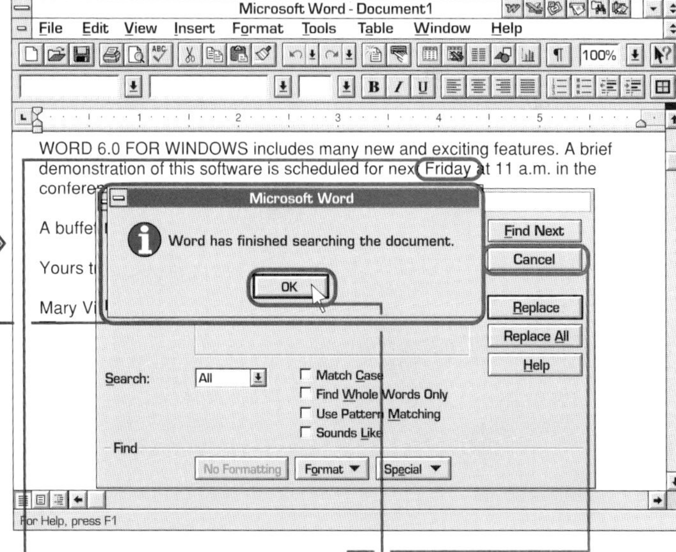

6 To start the search, move the mouse over **Find Next** and then press the left button.

◆ Word highlights the first matching word it finds.

7 To replace the word, move the mouse over **Replace** and then press the left button.

Note: If you do not want to replace the word, repeat step 6 to find the next matching word in your document.

◆ Word replaces the word and searches for the next matching word.

8 Repeat step 7 for each word you want to replace.

◆ This dialog box appears when there are no more matching words in your document.

9 To close this dialog box, move the mouse over **OK** and then press the left button.

10 To close the **Replace** dialog box, move the mouse over **Cancel** or **Close** and then press the left button.

CHECK SPELLING

You can use the Spelling feature to find and correct spelling errors in your document.
Sciense
Science
Word Dictionary
Expanded 6.0 Version

CHECK SPELLING

The spell check will find:	Example:
Misspelled words	The girl is six **yeers** old.
Duplicate words	The girl is **six six** years old.

The spell check will not find:	Example:
A correctly spelled word used in the wrong context.	The girl is **sit** years old.

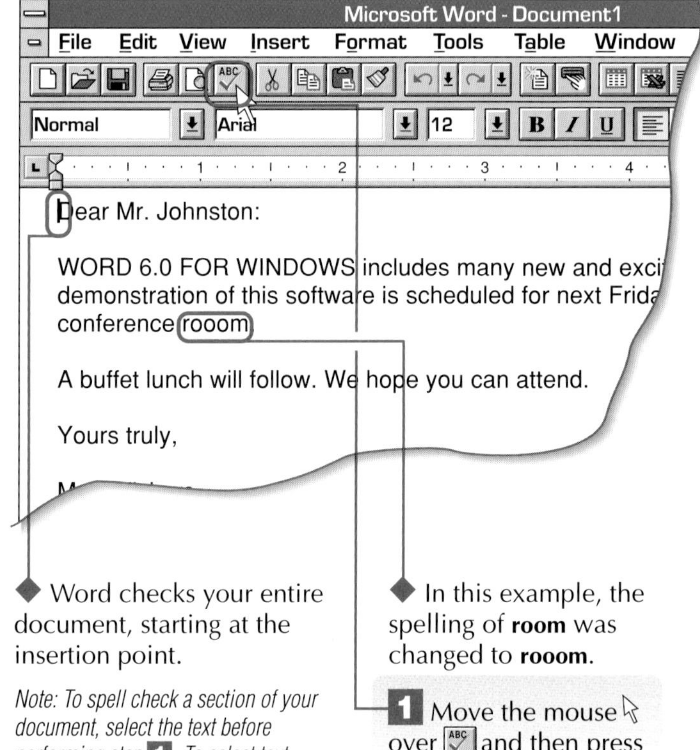
Microsoft Word - Document1
File Edit View Insert Format Tools Table Window
Normal
Arial
12
Dear Mr. Johnston:
WORD 6.0 FOR WINDOWS includes many new and exci
demonstration of this software is scheduled for next Frida
conference rooom
A buffet lunch will follow. We hope you can attend.
Yours truly,

◆ Word checks your entire document, starting at the insertion point.

Note: To spell check a section of your document, select the text before performing step 1. To select text, refer to page 24.

◆ In this example, the spelling of **room** was changed to **rooom**.

1 Move the mouse over the spelling button and then press the left button.

IMPORTANT!

You should save your document to store it for future use. If you do not save your document, it will disappear when you turn off your computer.

Note: To save your document, refer to page 64.

Once you have stored your document, save it every 5 to 10 minutes to reduce the possibility of work loss due to system or power failure.

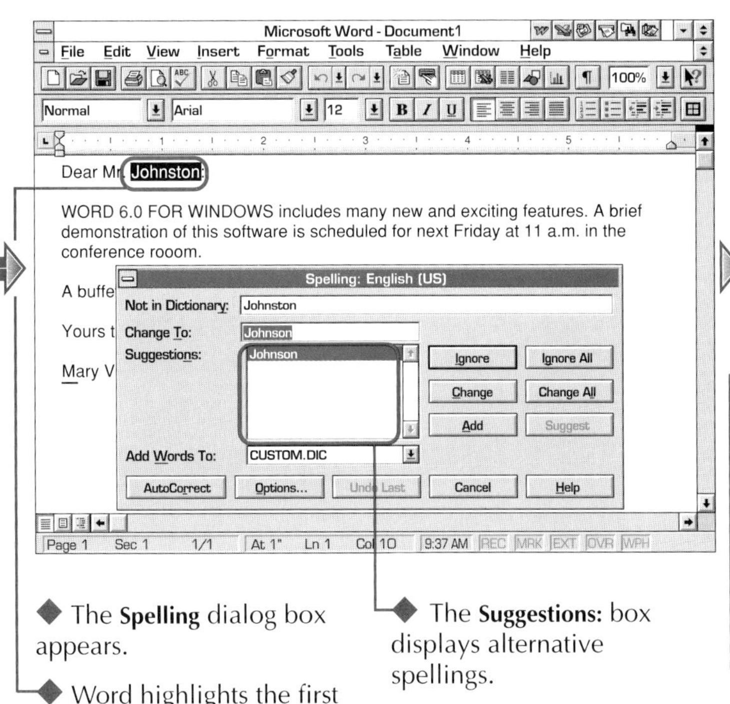

- The **Spelling** dialog box appears.
- Word highlights the first word it does not recognize (example: **Johnston**).
- The **Suggestions:** box displays alternative spellings.

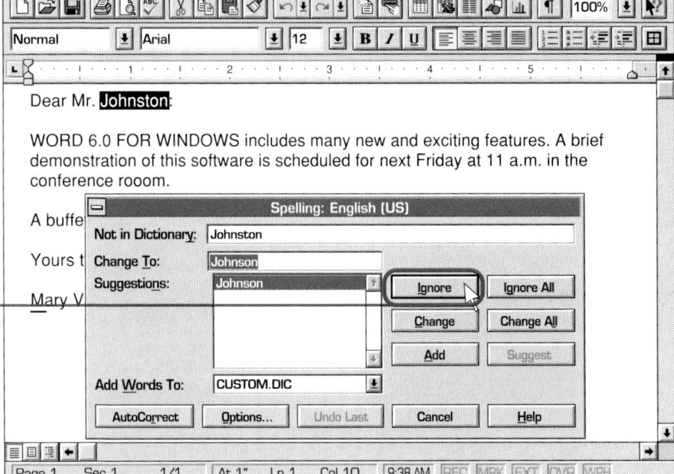

IGNORE MISSPELLED WORD

2 If you do not want to change the spelling of the highlighted word, move the mouse over **Ignore** and then press the left button.

CHECK SPELLING

Word compares every word in your document to words in its dictionary. If a word does not exist in the dictionary, Word considers it misspelled.

CHECK SPELLING (CONTINUED)

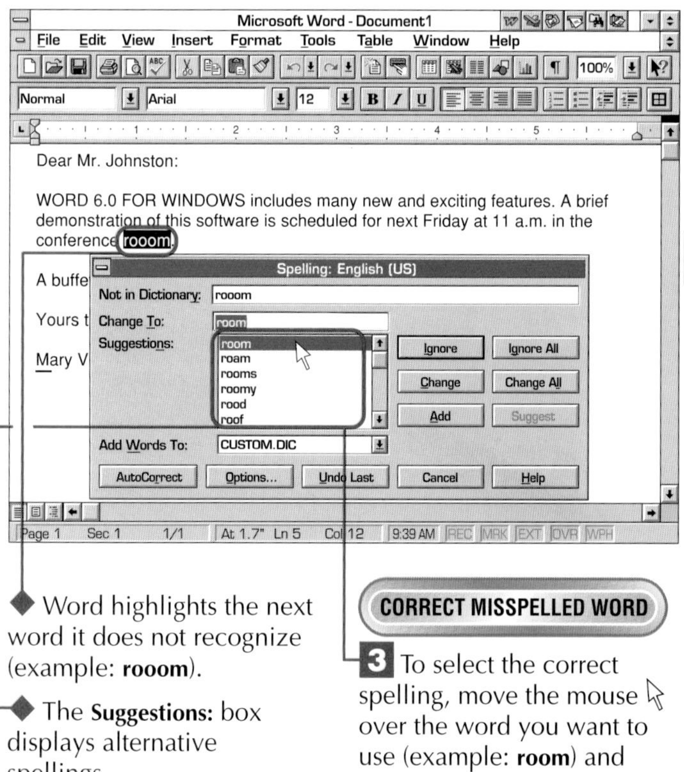

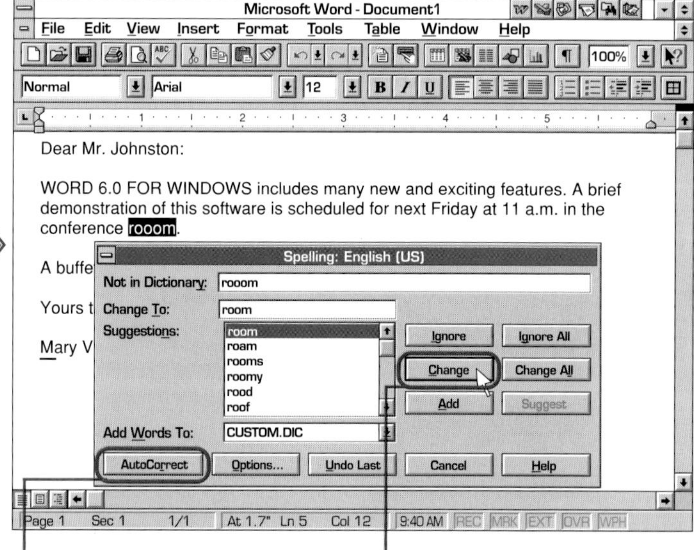

◆ Word highlights the next word it does not recognize (example: **rooom**).

◆ The **Suggestions:** box displays alternative spellings.

CORRECT MISSPELLED WORD

3 To select the correct spelling, move the mouse over the word you want to use (example: **room**) and then press the left button.

◆ If you want to have Word automatically correct the misspelled word every time you type it in your document, move the mouse over **AutoCorrect** and then press the left button.

Note: For more information on the AutoCorrect feature, refer to page 54.

4 To replace the misspelled word in your document with the correct spelling, move the mouse over **Change** and then press the left button.

You can cancel the spell check at any time.

◆ *To cancel the spell check, move the mouse over **Cancel** or **Close** and then press the left button.*

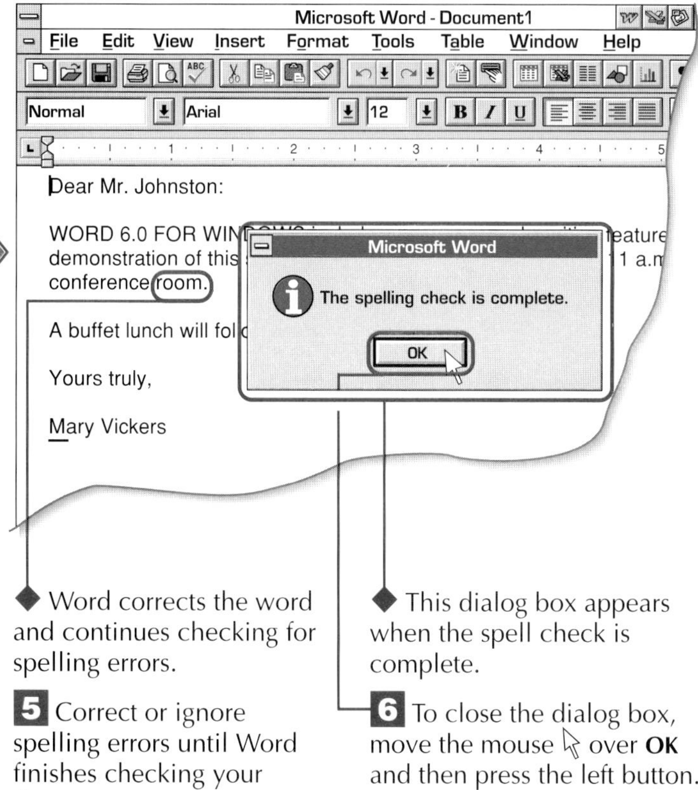

◆ Word corrects the word and continues checking for spelling errors.

5 Correct or ignore spelling errors until Word finishes checking your document.

◆ This dialog box appears when the spell check is complete.

6 To close the dialog box, move the mouse over **OK** and then press the left button.

DUPLICATE WORDS

If you accidentally typed a word twice in your document, Word will find this error during the spell check.

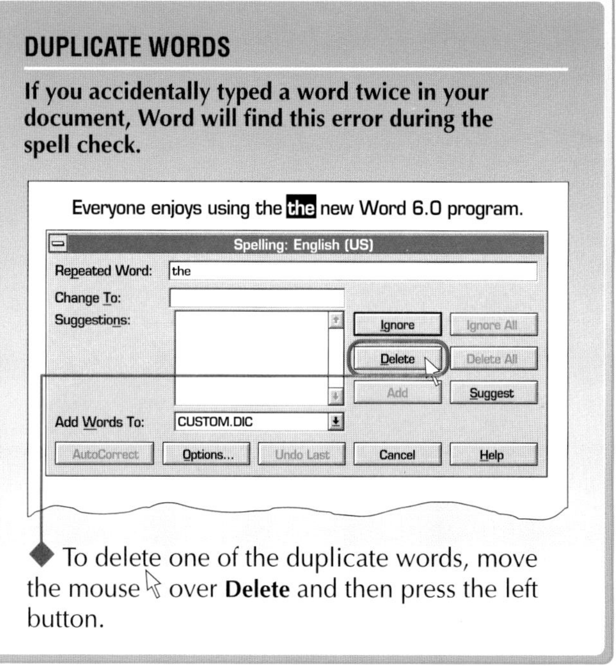

◆ To delete one of the duplicate words, move the mouse over **Delete** and then press the left button.

USING AUTOCORRECT

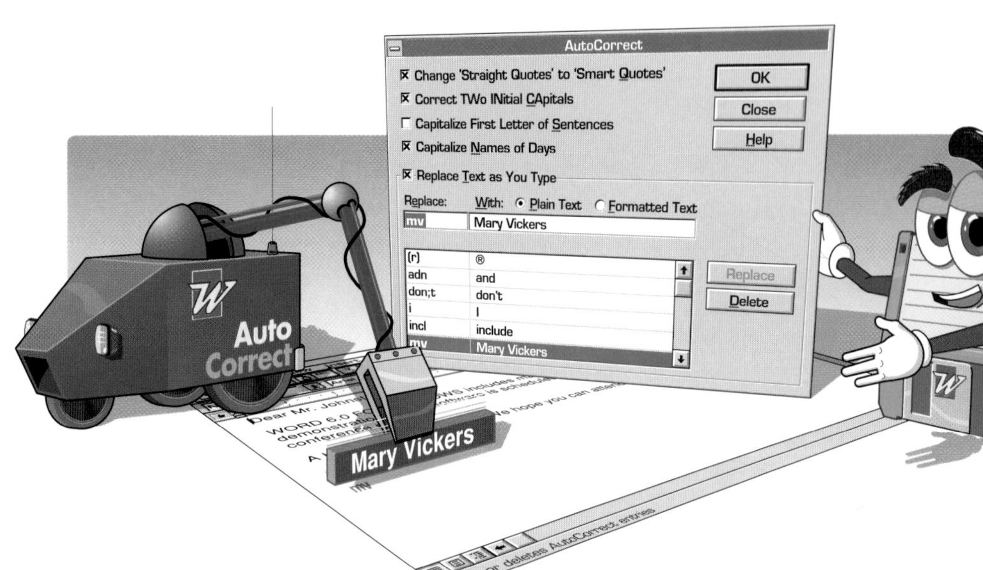

Word automatically corrects common spelling errors as you type. You can customize the AutoCorrect list to include words you often misspell or words you frequently use.

ADD TEXT TO AUTOCORRECT

If you type one of the following words and then press the Spacebar, Word will automatically change the word for you.

Text You Type	Replace With
(r)	®
adn	and
don;t	don't
i	I
incl	include
occurence	occurrence
recieve	receive
seperate	separate
teh	the

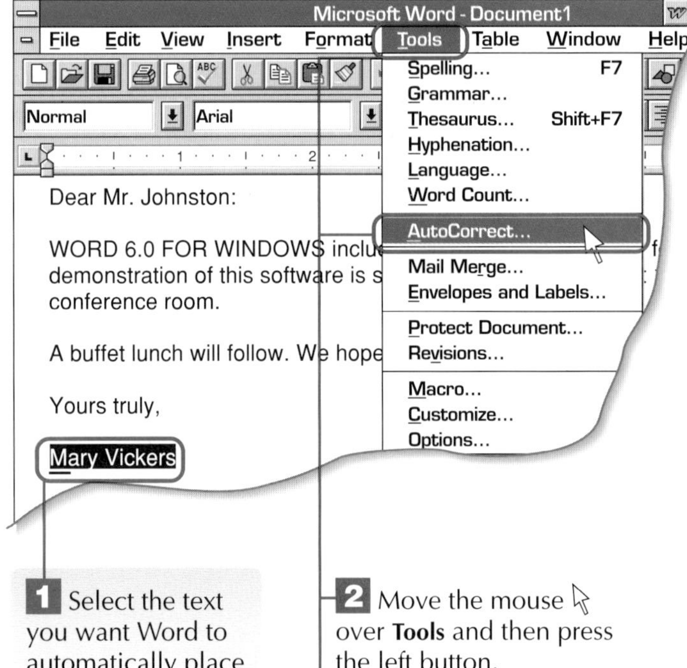

1 Select the text you want Word to automatically place in your documents.

Note: To select text, refer to page 24.

2 Move the mouse over **Tools** and then press the left button.

3 Move the mouse over **AutoCorrect** and then press the left button.

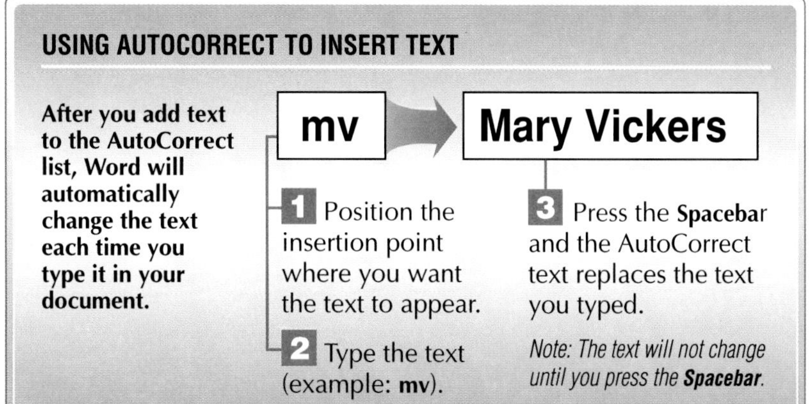

USING AUTOCORRECT TO INSERT TEXT
After you add text to the AutoCorrect list, Word will automatically change the text each time you type it in your document.
mv
Mary Vickers
1 Position the insertion point where you want the text to appear.
2 Type the text (example: mv).
3 Press the Spacebar and the AutoCorrect text replaces the text you typed.
Note: The text will not change until you press the Spacebar.

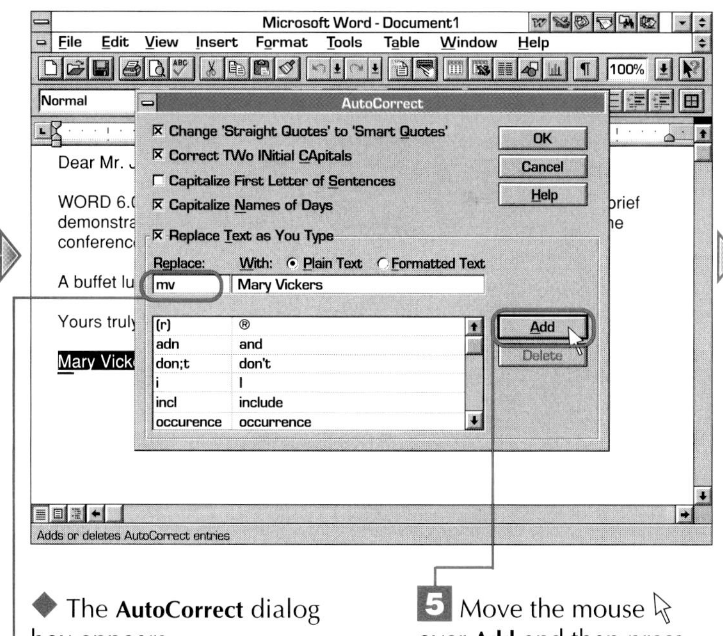

◆ The **AutoCorrect** dialog box appears.

4 Type the text you want Word to automatically replace every time you type it in a document (example: **mv**).

Note: This text cannot contain any spaces. Also, do not use a real word.

5 Move the mouse over **Add** and then press the left button.

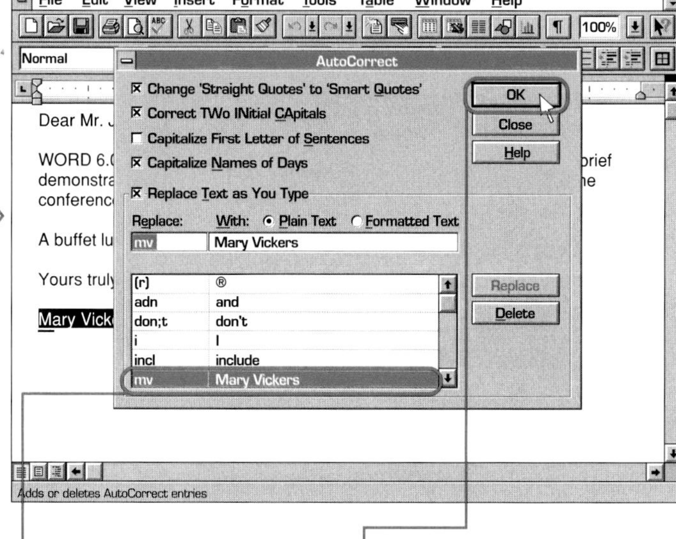

◆ The entry appears in the AutoCorrect list.

6 To close the **AutoCorrect** dialog box and return to your document, move the mouse over **OK** and then press the left button.

USING AUTOTEXT

The AutoText feature lets you store frequently used words, phrases and sentences. You can then insert them into your document by typing an abbreviated version of the text.
Microsoft Word - Document1
File Edit View Insert Format Tools Table Window Help
Dear Mr. Johnston:
WORD 6.0 FOR WINDOWS includes many new and exciting features. A brief demonstration of this software is scheduled for next Friday at 11 a.m. in the conference room.
Yours truly,
Mary Vickers
Auto Text

ADD TEXT TO AUTOTEXT

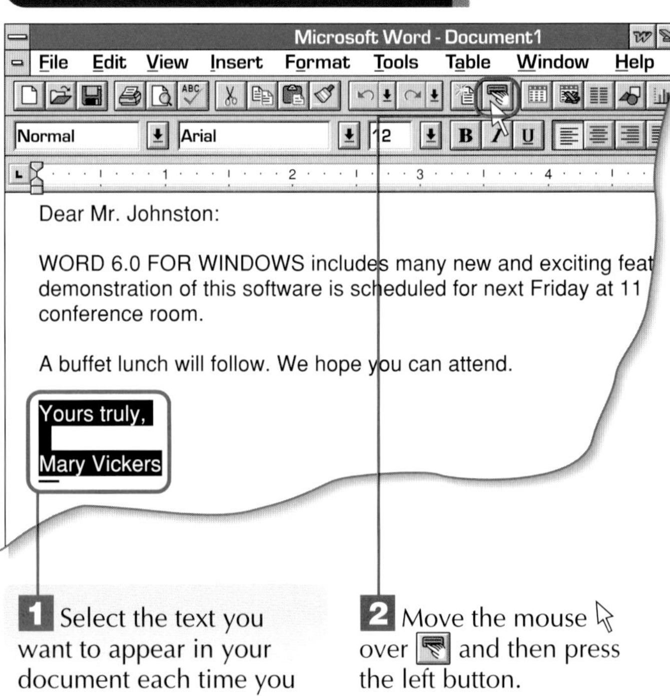
Microsoft Word - Document1
File Edit View Insert Format Tools Table Window Help
Normal
Arial
Dear Mr. Johnston:
A buffet lunch will follow. We hope you can attend.
Yours truly,
Mary Vickers

1 Select the text you want to appear in your document each time you type the abbreviated name.

Note: To select text, refer to page 24.

2 Move the mouse over the AutoText button and then press the left button.

Tip

The AutoText and AutoCorrect features both insert text into your document. However, there are two distinct differences:

Note: For information on the AutoCorrect feature, refer to page 54.

AUTOTEXT

◆ *Use AutoText to insert groups of text or to insert text you use occasionally.*

◆ *Word inserts the text only when you instruct it to do so.*

AUTOCORRECT

◆ *Use AutoCorrect to correct your most common spelling errors or to insert text you use frequently (i.e., every day).*

◆ *Word automatically inserts the text as you type.*

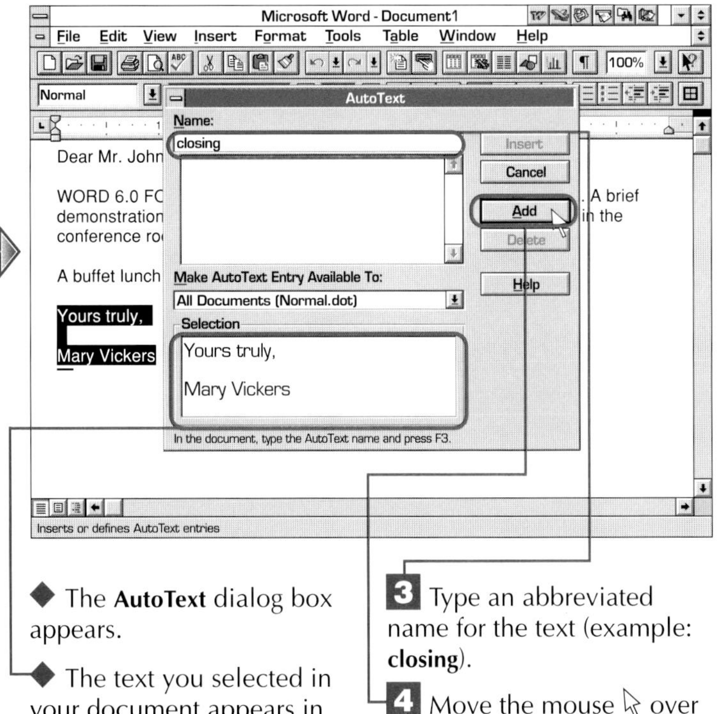

◆ The **AutoText** dialog box appears.

◆ The text you selected in your document appears in the **Selection** box.

3 Type an abbreviated name for the text (example: **closing**).

4 Move the mouse over **Add** and then press the left button.

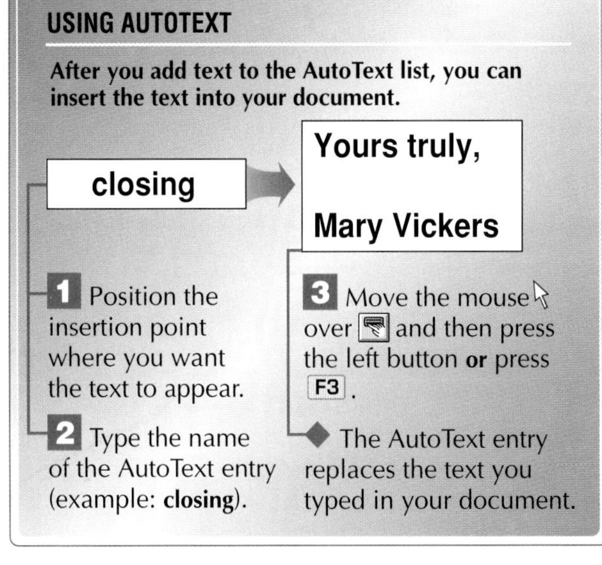

USING AUTOTEXT

After you add text to the AutoText list, you can insert the text into your document.

1 Position the insertion point where you want the text to appear.

2 Type the name of the AutoText entry (example: **closing**).

3 Move the mouse over the toolbar button and then press the left button **or** press F3.

◆ The AutoText entry replaces the text you typed in your document.

USING THE THESAURUS

You can use the Thesaurus to add variety to your writing. This feature lets you replace a word in your document with one that is more suitable.

USING THE THESAURUS

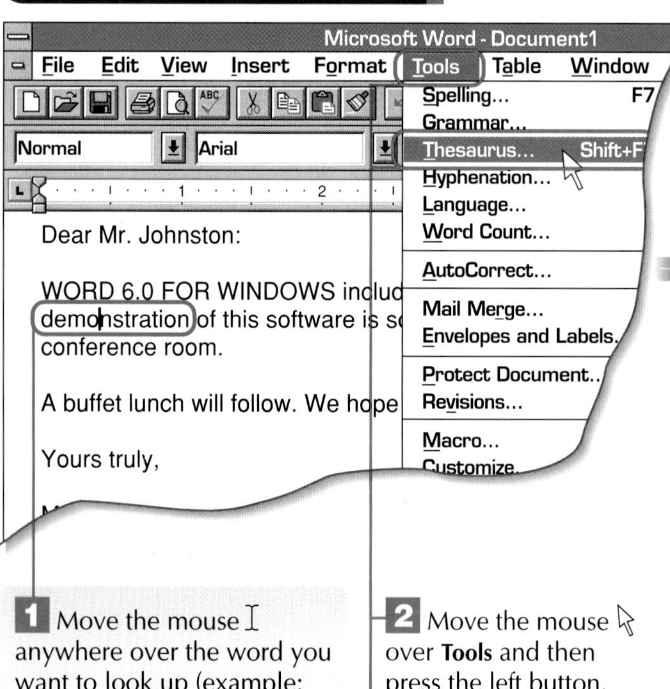

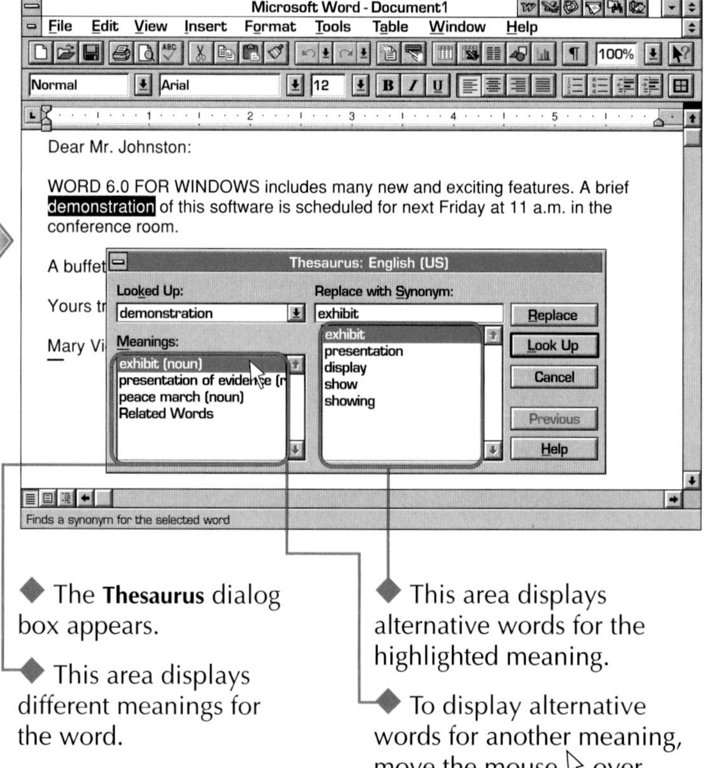

1 Move the mouse I anywhere over the word you want to look up (example: **demonstration**) and then press the left button.

2 Move the mouse over **Tools** and then press the left button.

3 Move the mouse over **Thesaurus** and then press the left button.

◆ The **Thesaurus** dialog box appears.

◆ This area displays different meanings for the word.

◆ This area displays alternative words for the highlighted meaning.

◆ To display alternative words for another meaning, move the mouse over the meaning and then press the left button.

- Find Text
- Replace Text
- Check Spelling
- Using AutoCorrect
- Using AutoText
- **Using the Thesaurus**
- Check Grammar

LOOK UP A WORD

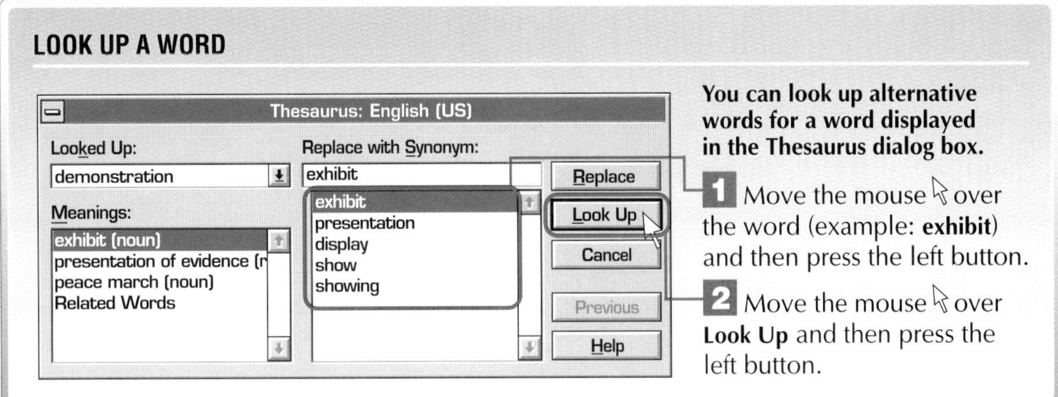

You can look up alternative words for a word displayed in the Thesaurus dialog box.

1 Move the mouse over the word (example: **exhibit**) and then press the left button.

2 Move the mouse over **Look Up** and then press the left button.

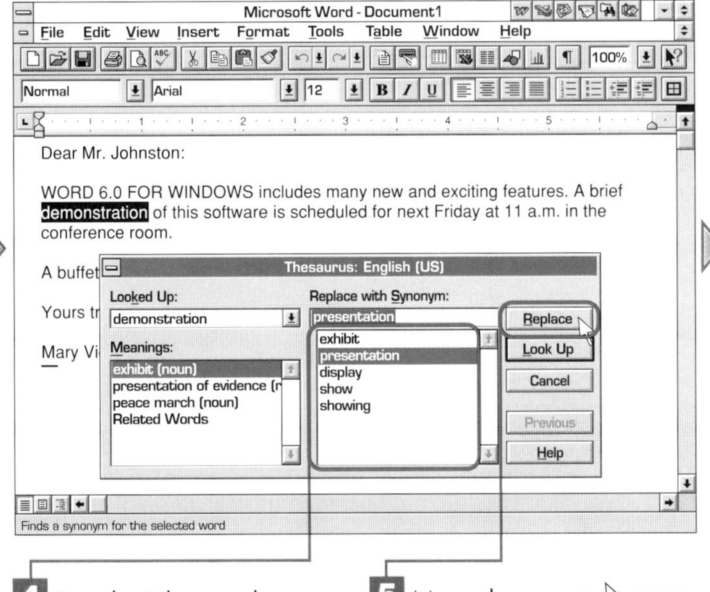

4 To select the word you want to use, move the mouse over the word (example: **presentation**) and then press the left button.

5 Move the mouse over **Replace** and then press the left button.

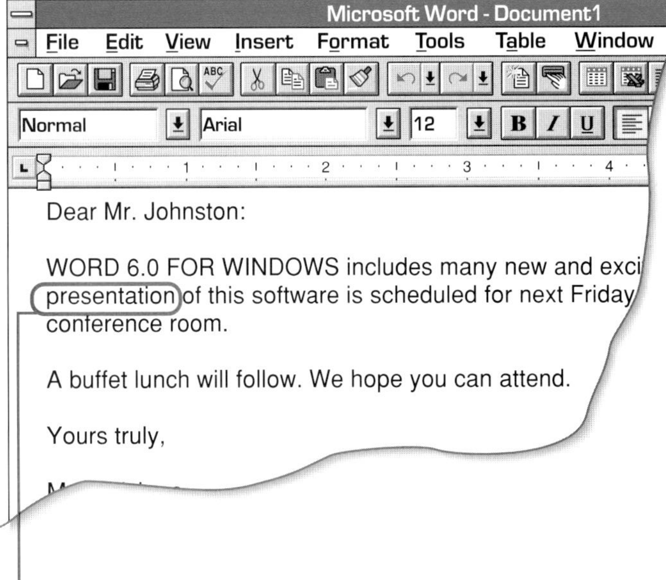

◆ The word from the Thesaurus replaces the word in your document.

CHECK GRAMMAR

You can use the Grammar feature to find and correct grammar and spelling errors in your document.

CHECK GRAMMAR

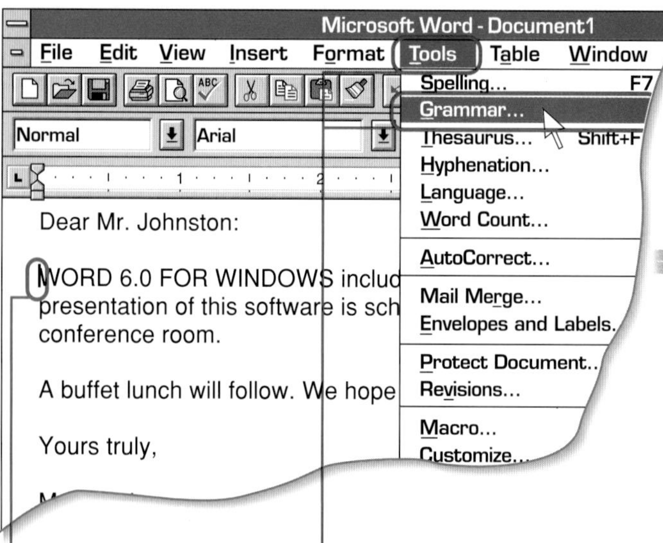

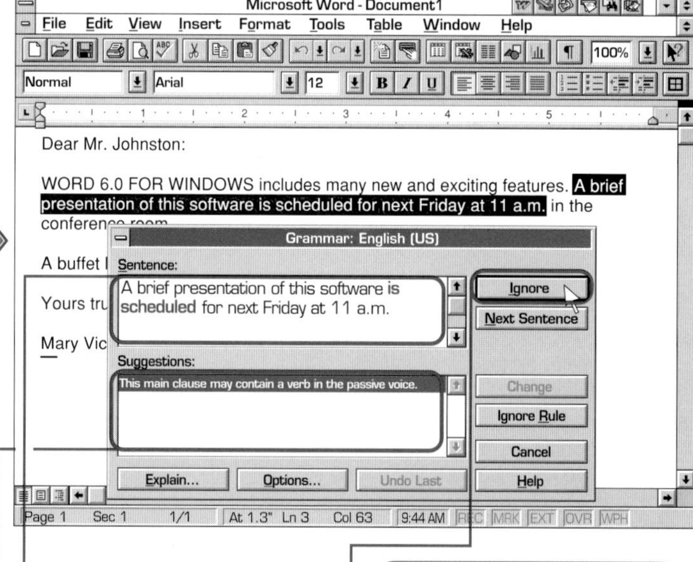

◆ Word checks your entire document, starting at the insertion point.

*Note: To check only a section of your document, select the text before performing step **1**. To select text, refer to page 24.*

1 Move the mouse over **Tools** and then press the left button.

2 Move the mouse over **Grammar** and then press the left button.

◆ If Word finds a grammatical error, the **Grammar** dialog box appears. This area displays the sentence containing the error.

◆ This area tells you what is wrong with the sentence and may offer a suggestion to correct the error.

IGNORE GRAMMATICAL ERROR

3 If you want to ignore the error and continue checking your document, move the mouse over **Ignore** and then press the left button.

*If Word finds a spelling error during a grammar check, the **Spelling** dialog box appears.*

*For more information on using the **Spelling** dialog box to correct a misspelled word, refer to page 52.*

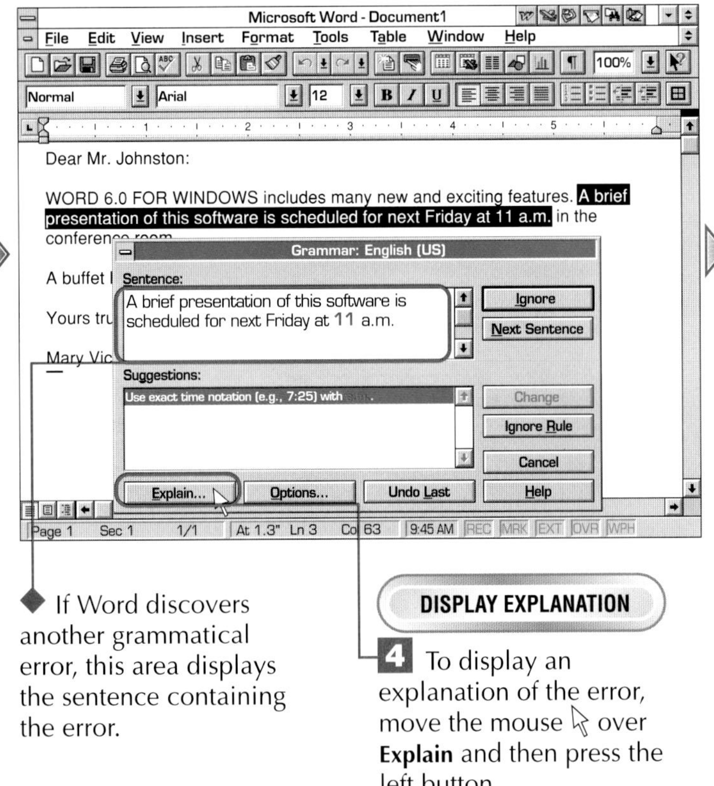

◆ If Word discovers another grammatical error, this area displays the sentence containing the error.

DISPLAY EXPLANATION

4 To display an explanation of the error, move the mouse over **Explain** and then press the left button.

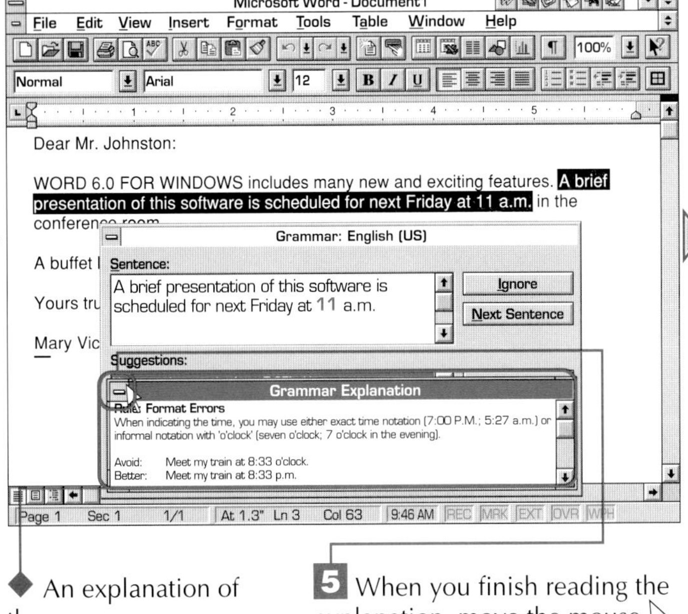

◆ An explanation of the error appears.

5 When you finish reading the explanation, move the mouse over ▭ and then quickly press the left button twice.

CONTINUED

CHECK GRAMMAR

The Grammar feature will improve the accuracy of your document.
I did not buy no books.
I did not buy any books.

CHECK GRAMMAR (CONTINUED)

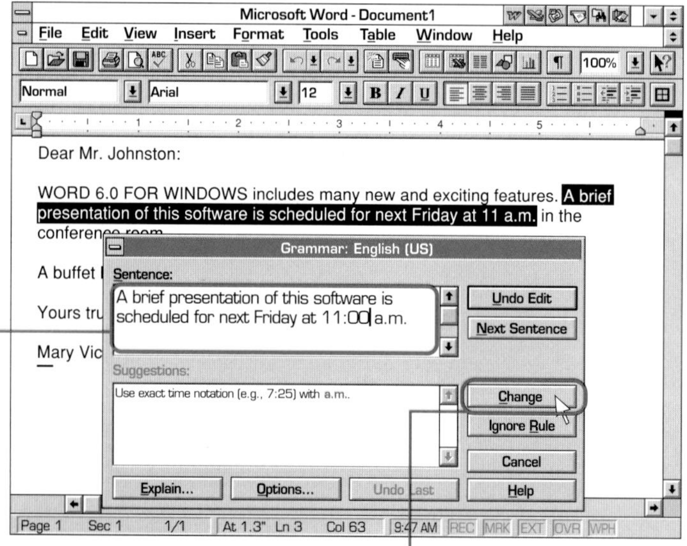

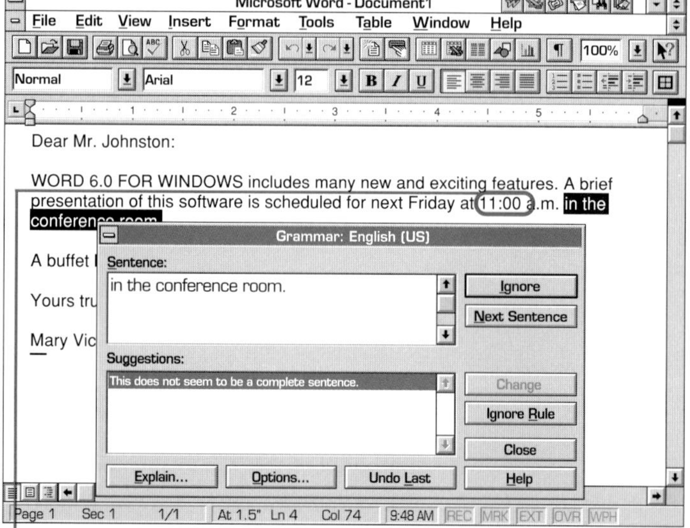

CORRECT GRAMMATICAL ERROR

6 Edit the text in the dialog box as you would any text in your document (example: change **11** to **11:00**).

Note: To insert and delete text, refer to pages 28 to 35.

7 Move the mouse over **Change** and then press the left button.

◆ The change appears in your document and Word continues checking for grammatical and spelling errors.

8 Correct or ignore grammatical errors until Word finishes checking your document.

You can cancel the grammar check at any time.

*To cancel the grammar check, move the mouse over **Cancel** or **Close** and then press the left button.*

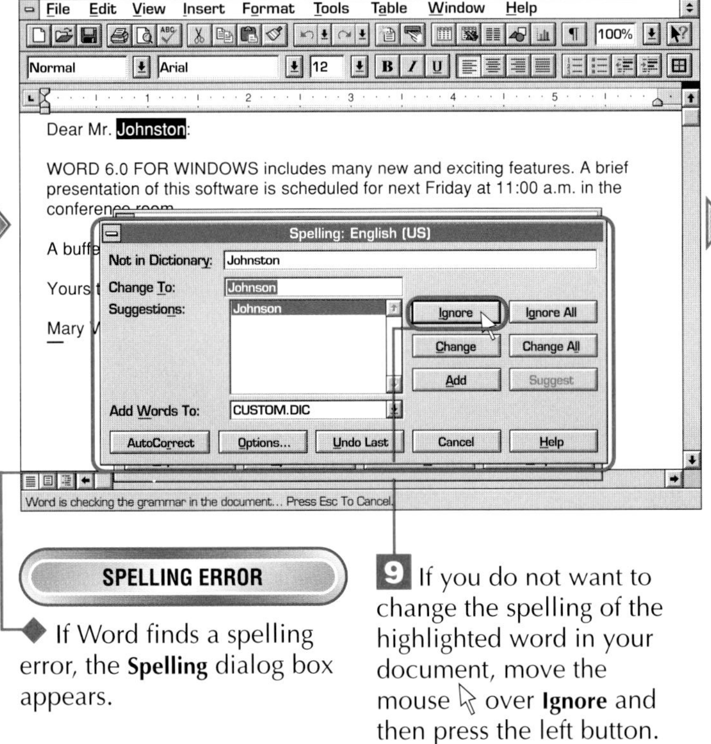

SPELLING ERROR

If Word finds a spelling error, the **Spelling** dialog box appears.

9 If you do not want to change the spelling of the highlighted word in your document, move the mouse over **Ignore** and then press the left button.

Note: For more information on checking your document for spelling errors, refer to pages 50 to 53.

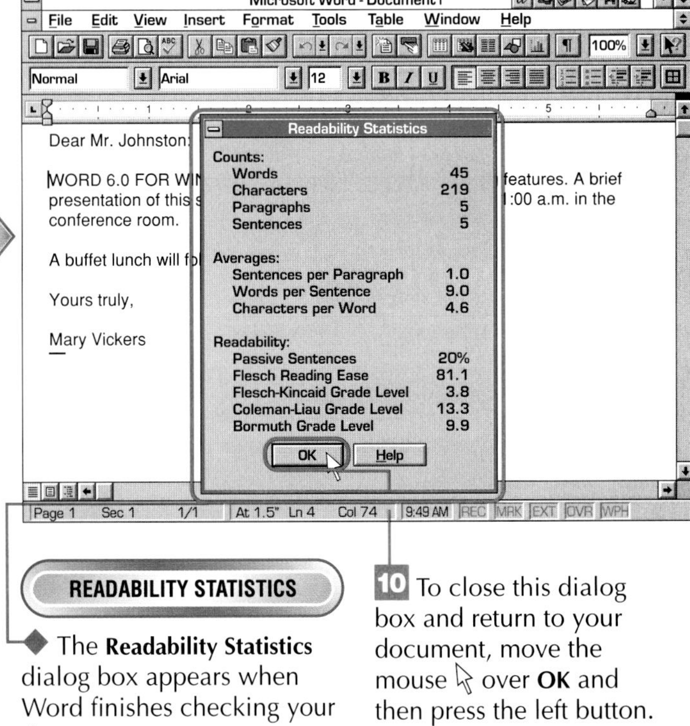

READABILITY STATISTICS

The **Readability Statistics** dialog box appears when Word finishes checking your document.

10 To close this dialog box and return to your document, move the mouse over **OK** and then press the left button.

SAVE A NEW DOCUMENT

You should save your document to store it for future use. This enables you to later retrieve the document for reviewing or editing purposes.

SAVE A NEW DOCUMENT

When you save a document for the first time, you must give it a name. The name of a document consists of two parts: a name and an extension. You must separate these parts with a period.

notice . doc

◆ **Name**
The name describes the contents of a document. It can have up to eight characters.

◆ **Period**
A period separates the name and the extension.

◆ **Extension**
The extension describes the type of information a document contains. It can have up to three characters.

*Note: **doc** stands for **document**.*

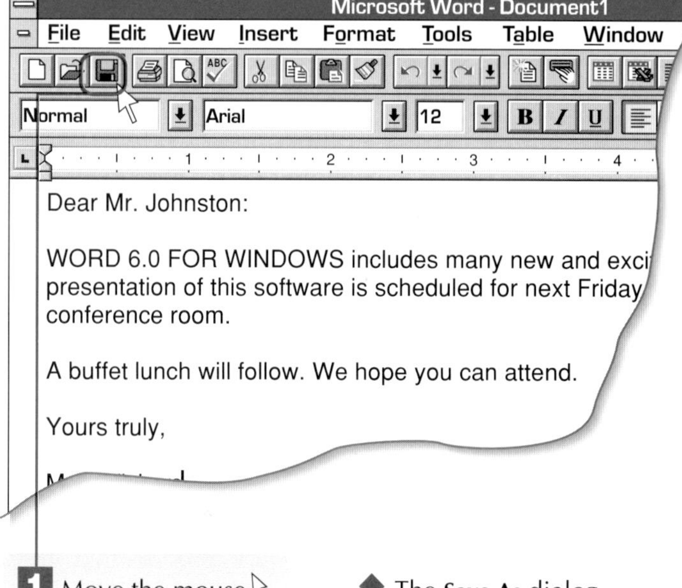

Microsoft Word - Document1
File Edit View Insert Format Tools Table Window
Normal
Arial
12
Dear Mr. Johnston:
WORD 6.0 FOR WINDOWS includes many new and exci
presentation of this software is scheduled for next Friday
conference room.
A buffet lunch will follow. We hope you can attend.
Yours truly,

1 Move the mouse over the save button and then press the left button.

◆ The **Save As** dialog box appears.

*Note: If you previously saved your document, the **Save As** dialog box will not appear since you have already named the document.*

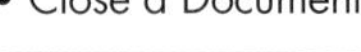

Rules for Naming a Document

The name of a document *can* contain the following characters:

- The letters A to Z
- The numbers 0 to 9
- The symbols _ ^ $ ~ ! # % & { } @ ( )

The name of a document *cannot* contain the following characters:

- A comma (,)
- A blank space
- The symbols * ? ; [ ] + = \ / : < >

Each document in a directory must have a unique name.

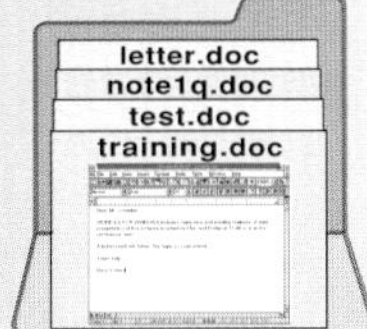

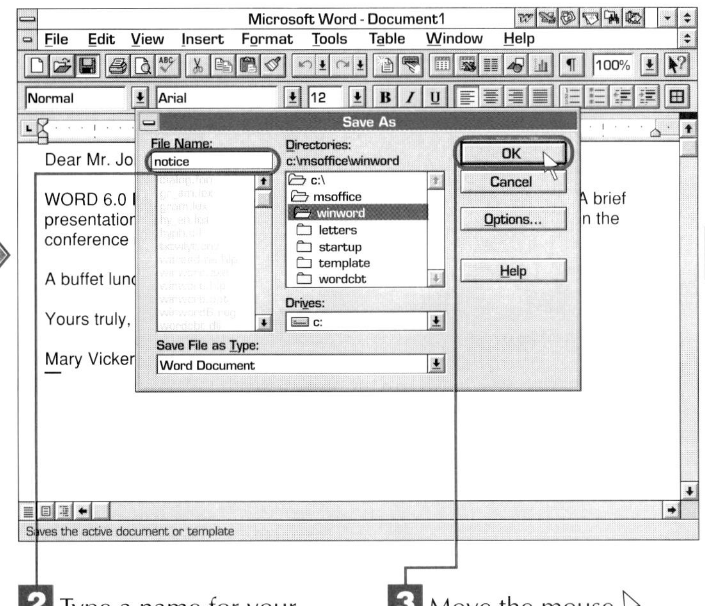

2 Type a name for your document (example: **notice**).

*Note: To make it easier to find your document later on, do not type an extension. Word will then automatically add the **doc** extension to the name.*

3 Move the mouse over **OK** and then press the left button.

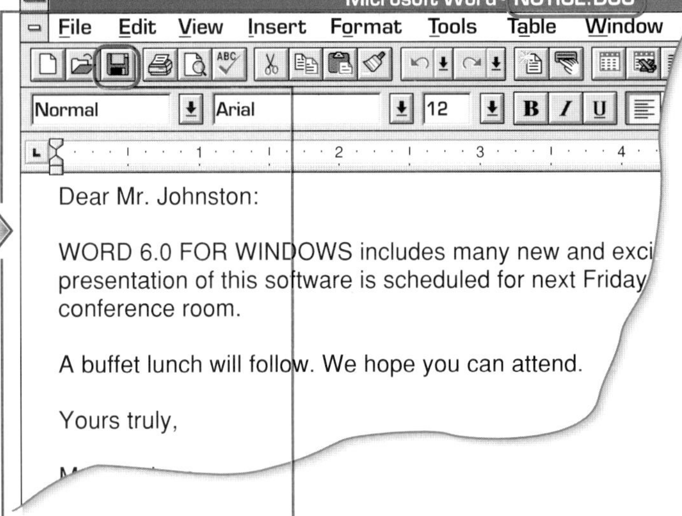

◆ Word saves your document and displays the name at the top of your screen.

◆ You should save your document every 5 to 10 minutes to store any changes made since the last time you saved the document. To save changes, move the mouse over the save button and then press the left button.

SAVE A DOCUMENT TO A DISKETTE

If you want to give your colleagues a copy of a document, you can save the document to a diskette. They can then review the document on their own computers.

SAVE A DOCUMENT TO A DISKETTE

1 Insert a diskette into a floppy drive (example: **a:**).

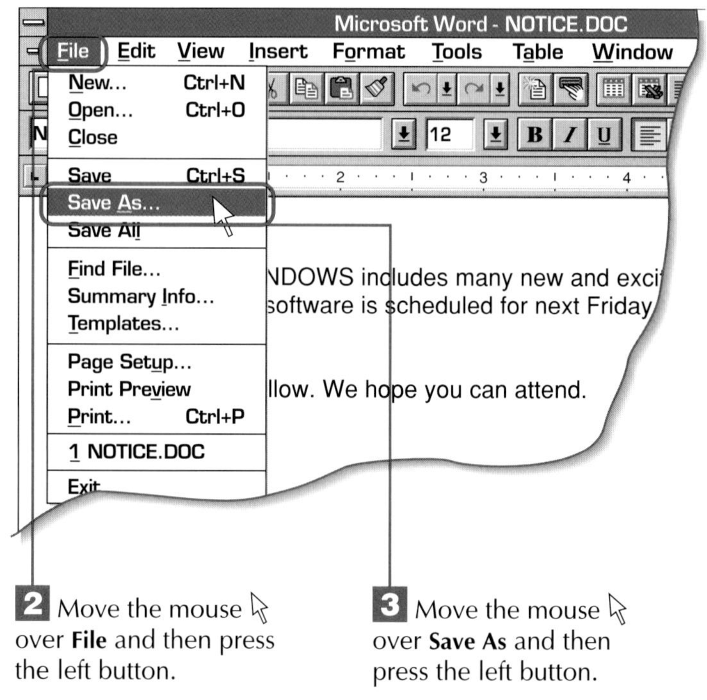

2 Move the mouse over **File** and then press the left button.

3 Move the mouse over **Save As** and then press the left button.

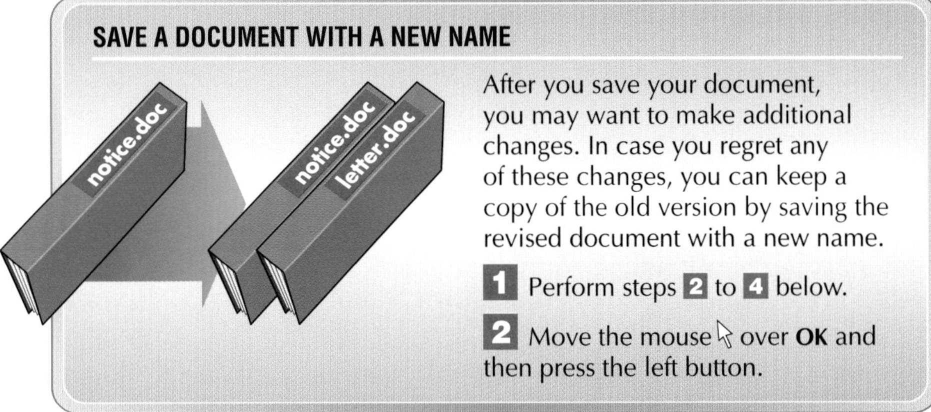

SAVE A DOCUMENT WITH A NEW NAME

After you save your document, you may want to make additional changes. In case you regret any of these changes, you can keep a copy of the old version by saving the revised document with a new name.

1 Perform steps **2** to **4** below.

2 Move the mouse over **OK** and then press the left button.

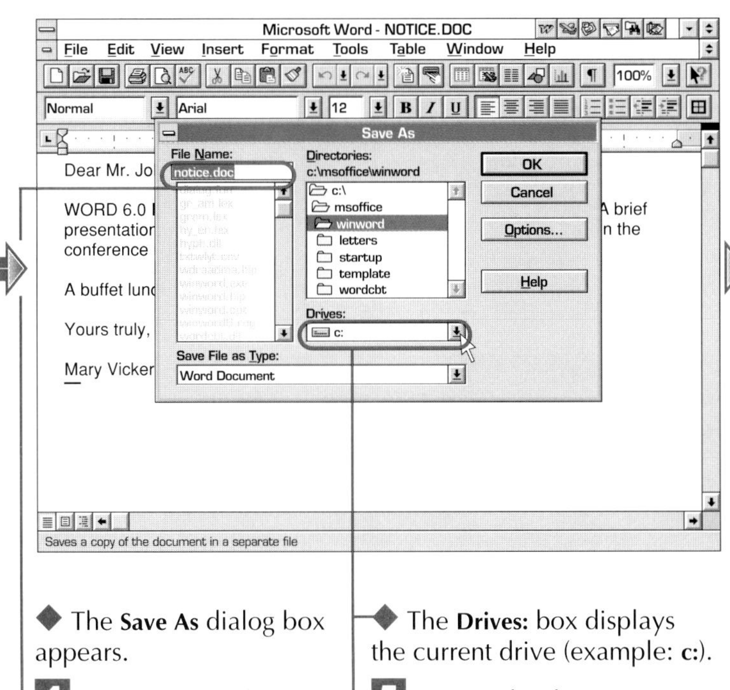

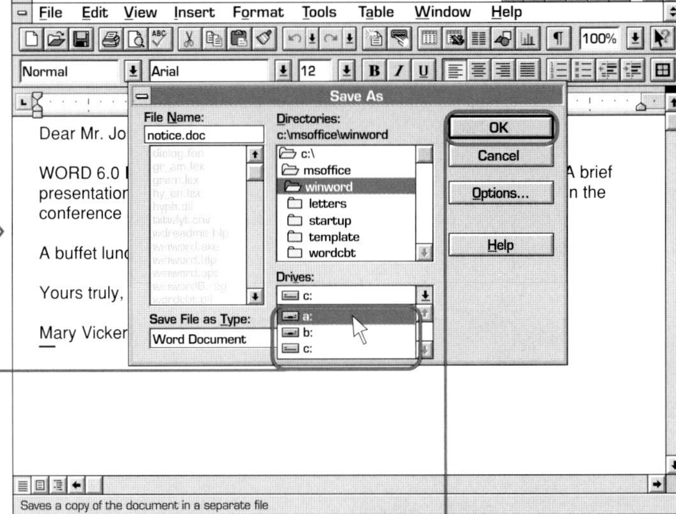

◆ The **Save As** dialog box appears.

4 The **File Name:** box displays the current file name. To save your document with a different name, type a new name.

◆ The **Drives:** box displays the current drive (example: **c:**).

5 To save the document to a diskette, move the mouse over ⬇ in the **Drives:** box and then press the left button.

◆ A list of the available drives for your computer appears.

6 Move the mouse over the drive that contains the diskette (example: **a:**) and then press the left button.

7 To save your document, move the mouse over **OK** and then press the left button.

CLOSE A DOCUMENT

EXIT WORD

When you finish working with a document, you can close the document to remove it from your screen.

CLOSE A DOCUMENT

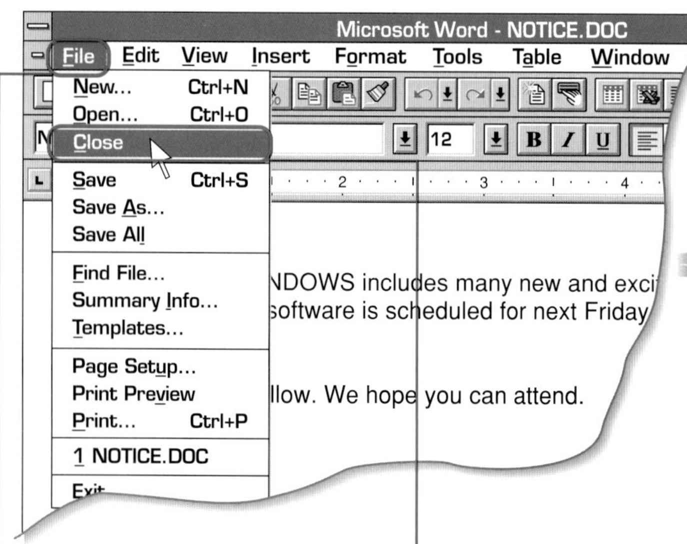

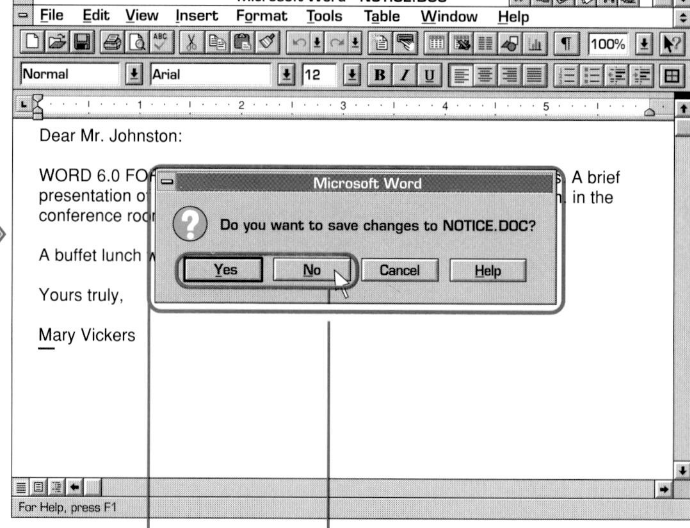

1 To close the document displayed on your screen, move the mouse over **File** and then press the left button.

2 Move the mouse over **Close** and then press the left button.

◆ This dialog box appears if you have not saved changes made to your document.

Note: For information on saving a document, refer to page 64.

3 To close the document without saving the changes, move the mouse over **No** and then press the left button.

◆ To save the changes, move the mouse over **Yes** and then press the left button.

When you finish using Word, you can easily exit the program.
EXIT

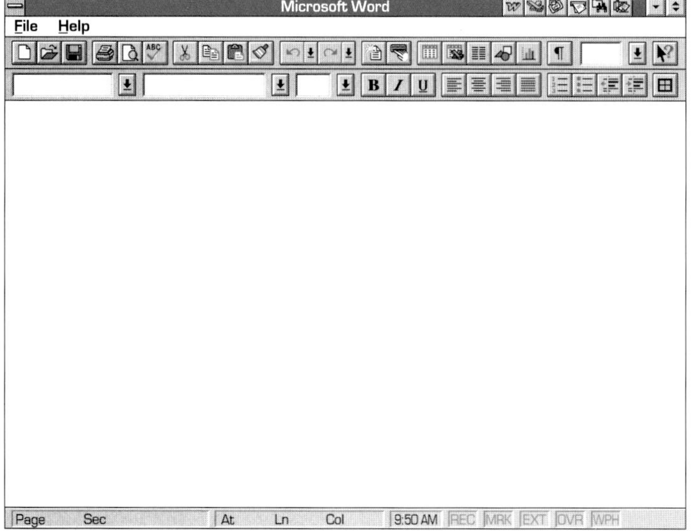

◆ Word removes the document from your screen.

EXIT WORD

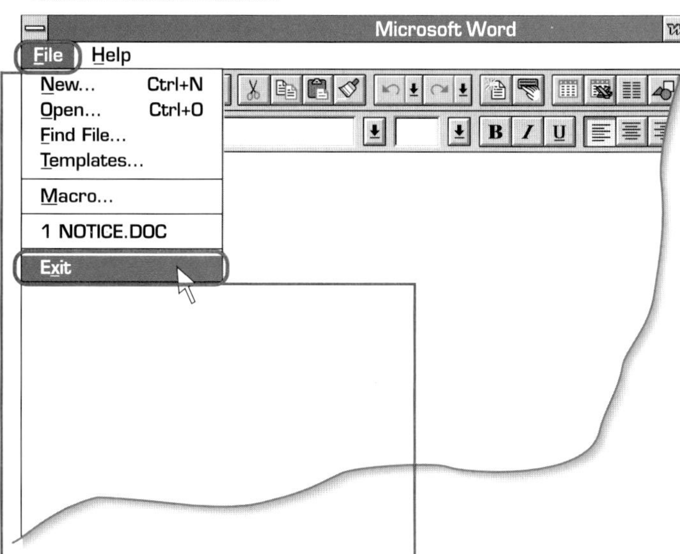

1 To exit Word, move the mouse over **File** and then press the left button.

2 Move the mouse over **Exit** and then press the left button.

Note: To restart Word, refer to page 19.

OPEN A DOCUMENT

You can open a saved document and display it on your screen. This lets you review and edit the document.

OPEN A DOCUMENT

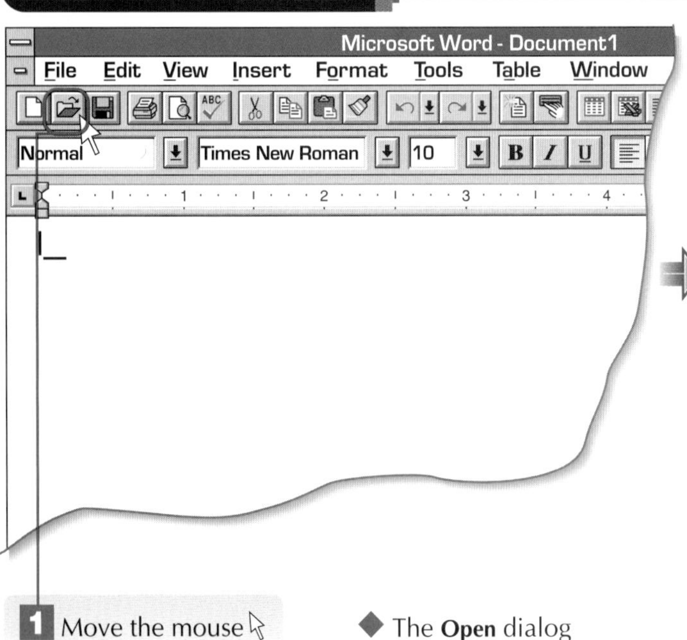

1 Move the mouse over the Open button and then press the left button.

◆ The **Open** dialog box appears.

◆ The **Drives:** box displays the current drive (example: **c:**).

2 To open a document on a different drive, move the mouse over the arrow button in the **Drives:** box and then press the left button.

◆ A list of the available drives for your computer appears.

3 Move the mouse over the drive containing the document you want to open and then press the left button.

SHORTCUT

The File menu displays the names of the last four documents you opened.

Note: In this example, only one document has been opened.

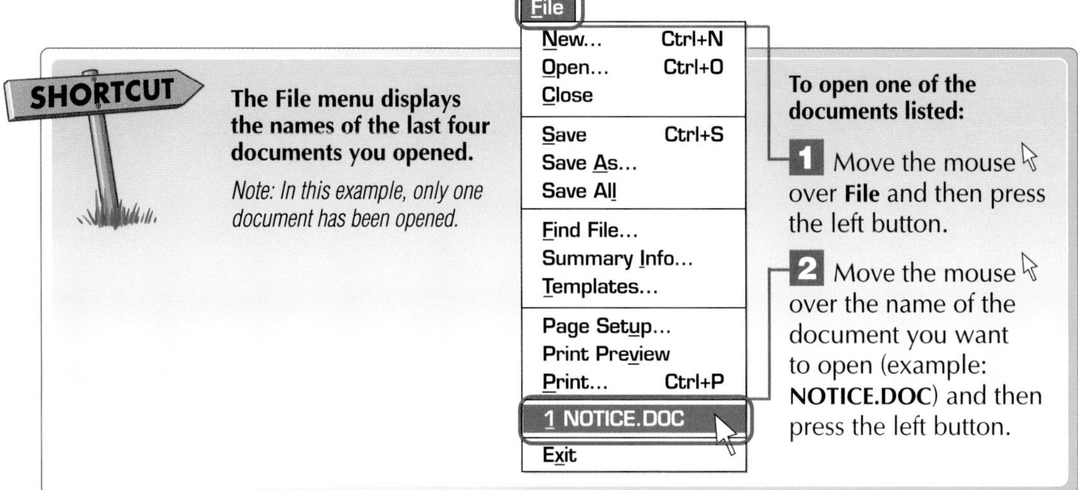

To open one of the documents listed:

1 Move the mouse over **File** and then press the left button.

2 Move the mouse over the name of the document you want to open (example: **NOTICE.DOC**) and then press the left button.

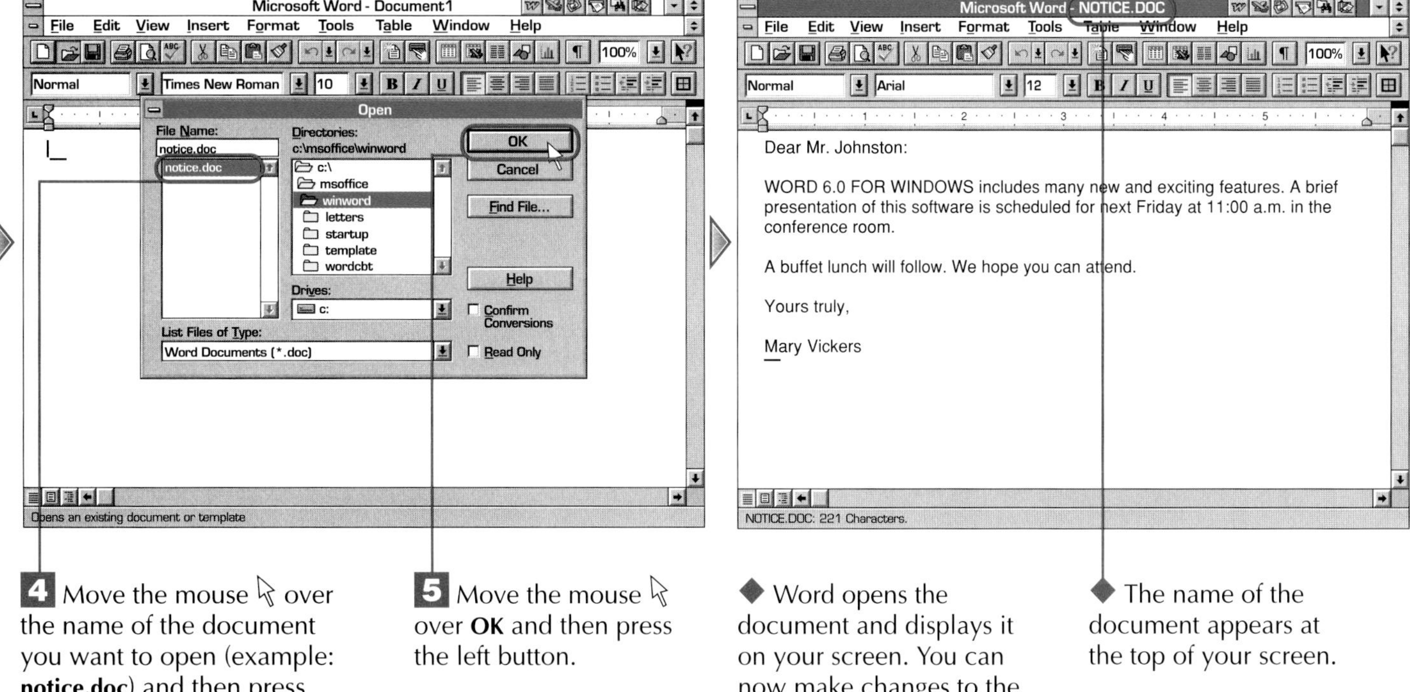

4 Move the mouse over the name of the document you want to open (example: **notice.doc**) and then press the left button.

5 Move the mouse over **OK** and then press the left button.

◆ Word opens the document and displays it on your screen. You can now make changes to the document.

◆ The name of the document appears at the top of your screen.

CREATE A NEW DOCUMENT

ARRANGE OPEN DOCUMENTS

CREATE A NEW DOCUMENT

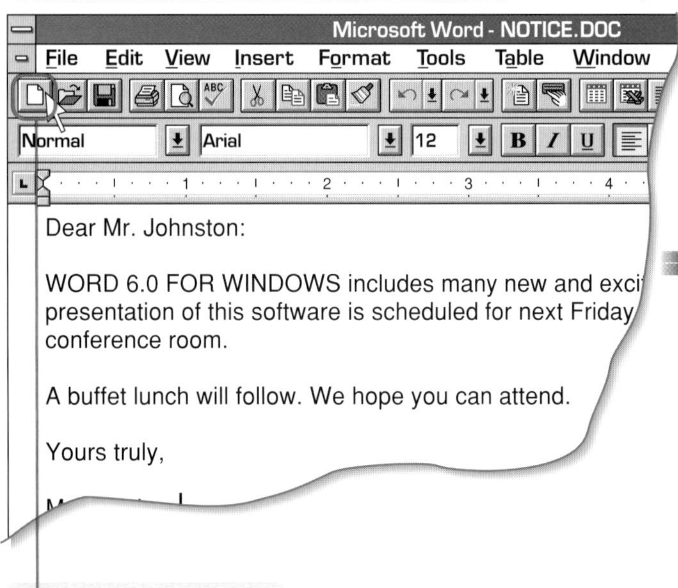

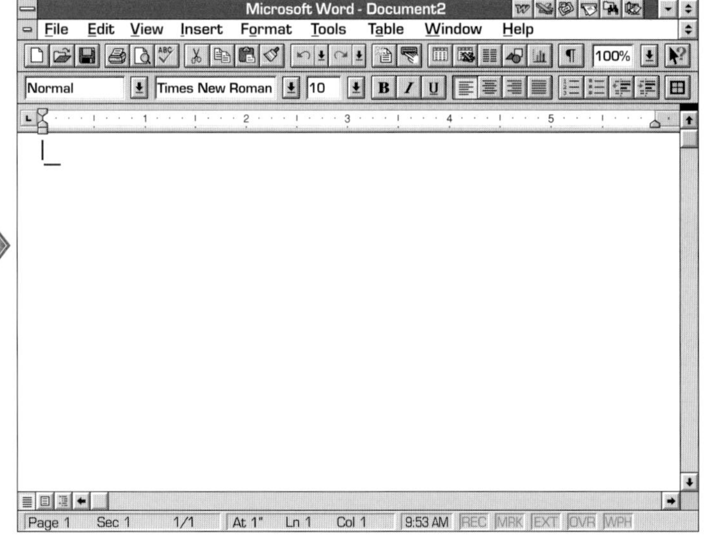

1 Move the mouse over and then press the left button.

◆ A new document appears.

Note: The previous document is now hidden behind the new document.

◆ Think of each document as a separate piece of paper. When you create a document, you are placing a new piece of paper on your screen.

- **Create a New Document**
- **Arrange Open Documents**
- Copy or Move Text Between Documents
- Maximize a Document
- Switch Between Documents

If you have several documents open, some of them may be hidden from view. To view the contents of each document, you can use the Arrange All command.
NOTICE.DOC
Dear Mr. Johnston:
WORD 6.0 FOR WINDOWS includes many new and exciting features. A brief presentation of this software is scheduled for next Friday at 11:00 a.m. in the conference room.

ARRANGE OPEN DOCUMENTS

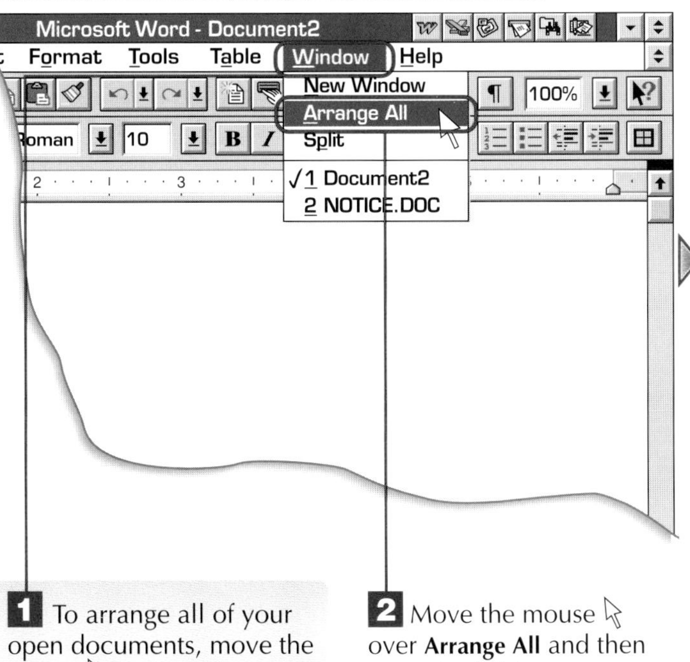

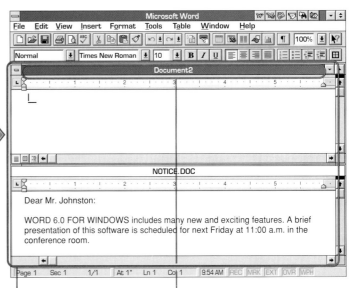

1 To arrange all of your open documents, move the mouse over **Window** and then press the left button.

2 Move the mouse over **Arrange All** and then press the left button.

◆ You can now view the contents of all your open documents at the same time.

◆ You can only work in the current document, which displays a highlighted title bar.

Note: To make another document current, move the mouse anywhere over the document and then press the left button.

COPY OR MOVE TEXT BETWEEN DOCUMENTS

Copying or moving text between documents saves you time when you are working in one document and want to use text from another.
text

COPY OR MOVE TEXT BETWEEN DOCUMENTS

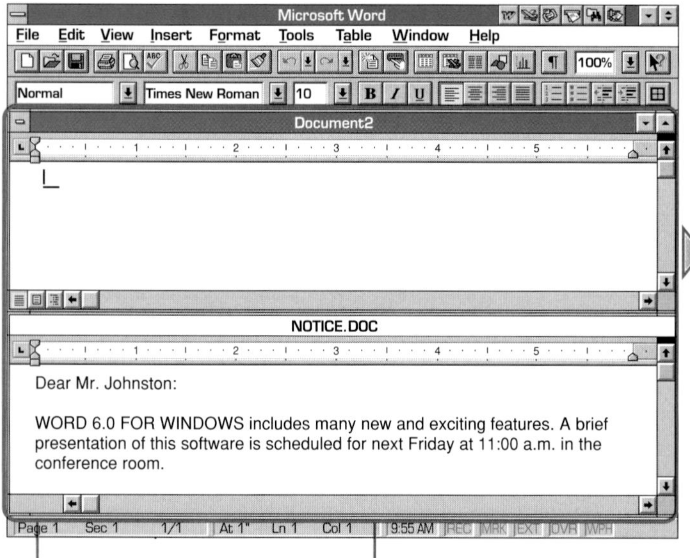

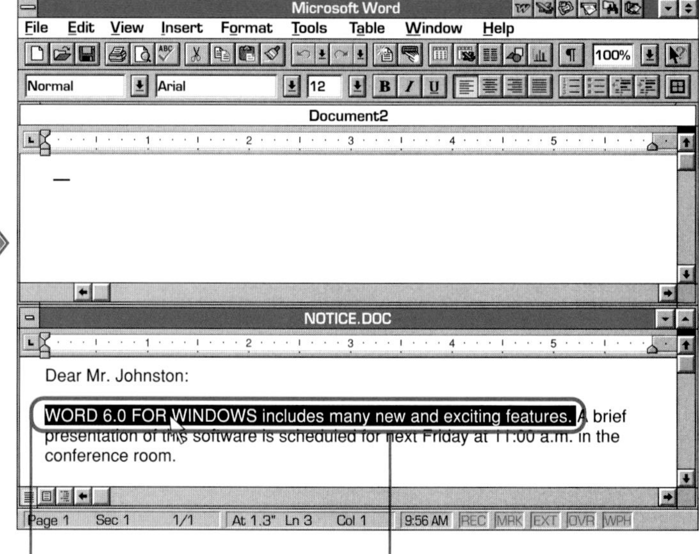

1 Open the documents you want to copy or move text between.

Note: To open a saved document, refer to page 70. To create a new document, refer to page 72.

2 Display the contents of both documents by using the **Arrange All** command.

*Note: For information on the **Arrange All** command, refer to page 73.*

3 Select the text you want to copy or move to another document.

Note: To select text, refer to page 24.

4 Move the mouse I anywhere over the selected text and I changes to ↖.

- Create a New Document
- Arrange Open Documents
- **Copy or Move Text Between Documents**
- Maximize a Document
- Switch Between Documents

The Copy and Move features both place text in a new location, but they have one distinct difference.

COPY TEXT

When you copy text, the original text remains in its place.

MOVE TEXT

When you move text, the original text disappears.

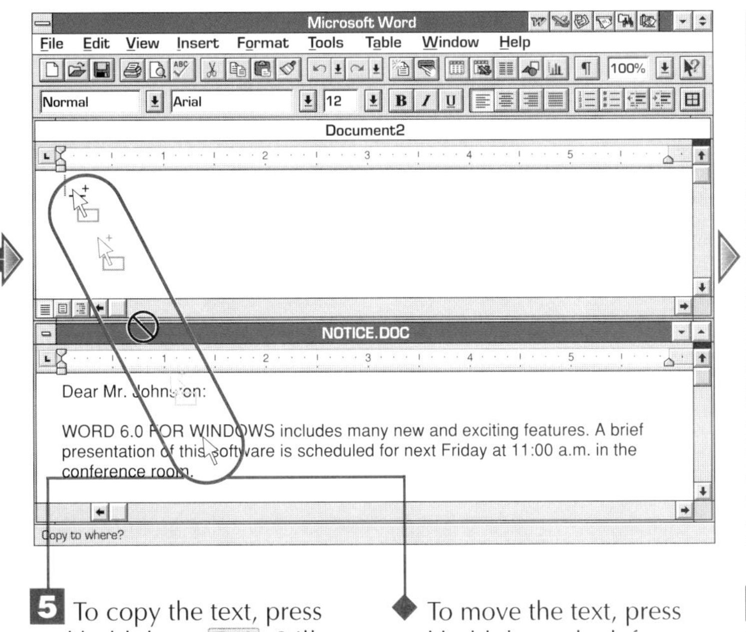

Microsoft Word
File Edit View Insert Format Tools Table Window Help
Normal
Arial
12
100%
Document2
NOTICE.DOC
Dear Mr. Johnston:
WORD 6.0 FOR WINDOWS includes many new and exciting features. A brief presentation of this software is scheduled for next Friday at 11:00 a.m. in the conference room.
Copy to where?

5 To copy the text, press and hold down Ctrl. Still holding down Ctrl, press and hold down the left button as you drag the mouse to where you want to place the copy.

◆ To move the text, press and hold down the left button as you drag the mouse to where you want to move the text.

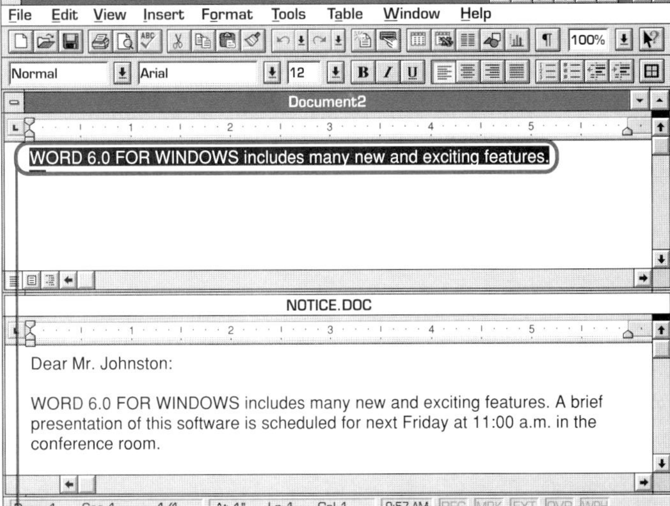

Microsoft Word
File Edit View Insert Format Tools Table Window Help
Normal
Arial
12
100%
Document2
WORD 6.0 FOR WINDOWS includes many new and exciting features.
NOTICE.DOC
Dear Mr. Johnston:
WORD 6.0 FOR WINDOWS includes many new and exciting features. A brief presentation of this software is scheduled for next Friday at 11:00 a.m. in the conference room.
Page 1 Sec 1 1/1 At 1" Ln 1 Col 1 9:57 AM REC MRK EXT OVR WPH

6 Release the button (and Ctrl) and the text appears in the new location.

Note: To deselect text, move the mouse I outside the selected area and then press the left button.

MAXIMIZE A DOCUMENT

SWITCH BETWEEN DOCUMENTS

You can enlarge a document to fill your screen. This lets you view more of its contents.

MAXIMIZE A DOCUMENT

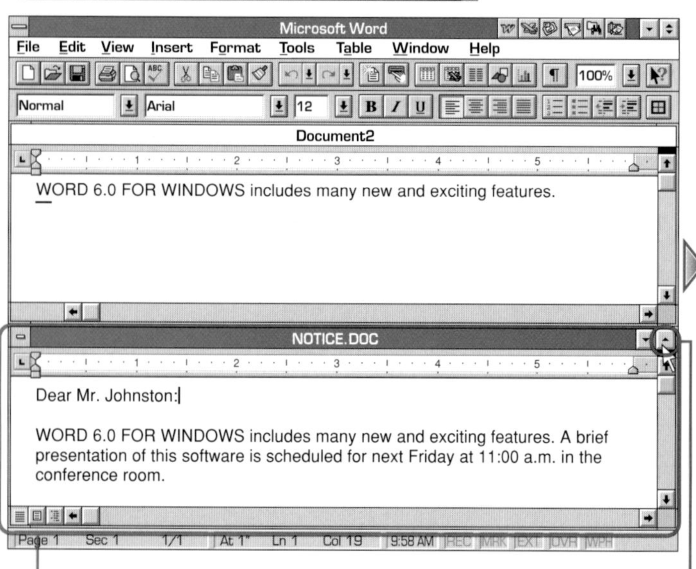

1 To select the document you want to maximize, move the mouse anywhere over the document and then press the left button.

2 Move the mouse over ▲ in the document you want to maximize and then press the left button.

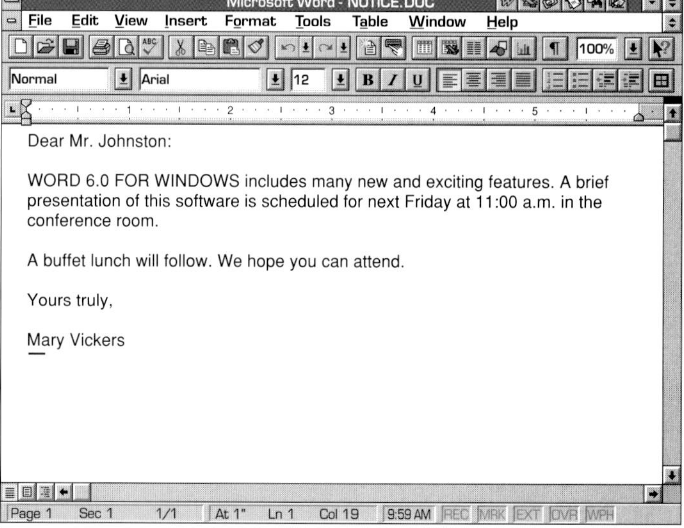

◆ The document enlarges to fill your screen.

Note: The document you maximized covers all of your open documents.

- Create a New Document
- Arrange Open Documents
- Copy or Move Text Between Documents
- **Maximize a Document**
- **Switch Between Documents**

You can easily switch between all of your open documents.
Microsoft Word - NOTICE.DOC
Format Tools Table Window Help
New Window
Arrange All
Split
1 Document2
√2 NOTICE.DOC
VS includes many new and exciting features. A brief
re is scheduled for next Friday at 11:00 a.m. in the
hope you can attend.
Microsoft Word Document2
File Edit View Insert Format Tools Table Window Help
WORD 6.0 FOR WINDOWS includes many new and exciting features.

SWITCH BETWEEN DOCUMENTS

1 To display a list of all your open documents, move the mouse over **Window** and then press the left button.

2 Move the mouse over the document you want to switch to and then press the left button.

◆ The document appears. Word displays its name at the top of your screen.

Note: When you finish working with a document, you can close the document to remove it from your screen. For more information, refer to page 68.

PREVIEW A DOCUMENT

PREVIEW A DOCUMENT

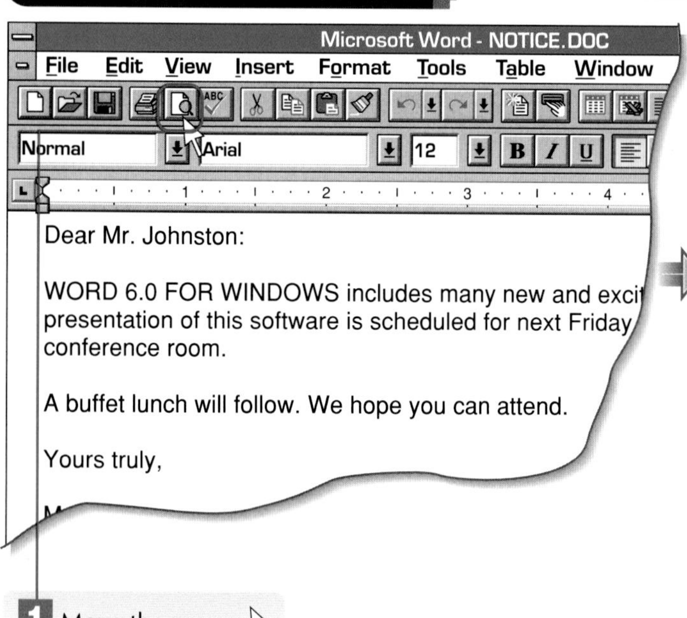

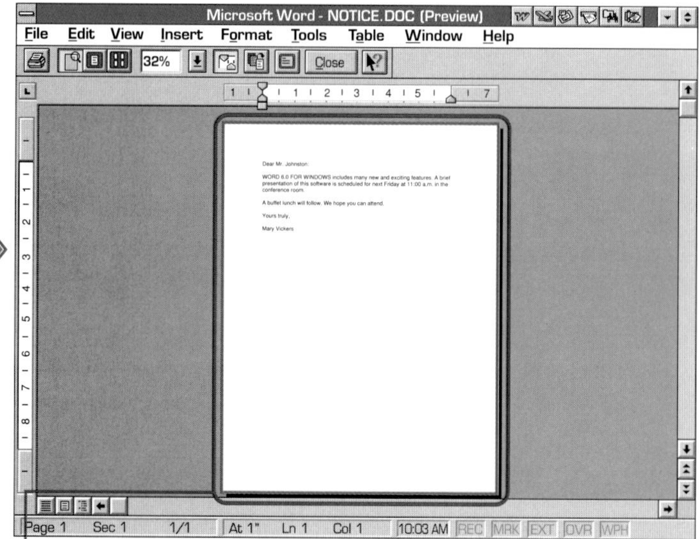

1 Move the mouse over and then press the left button.

◆ The page you are currently working on appears in the Print Preview window.

◆ If your document contains more than one page, press **PageDown** on your keyboard to display the next page. Press **PageUp** to display the previous page.

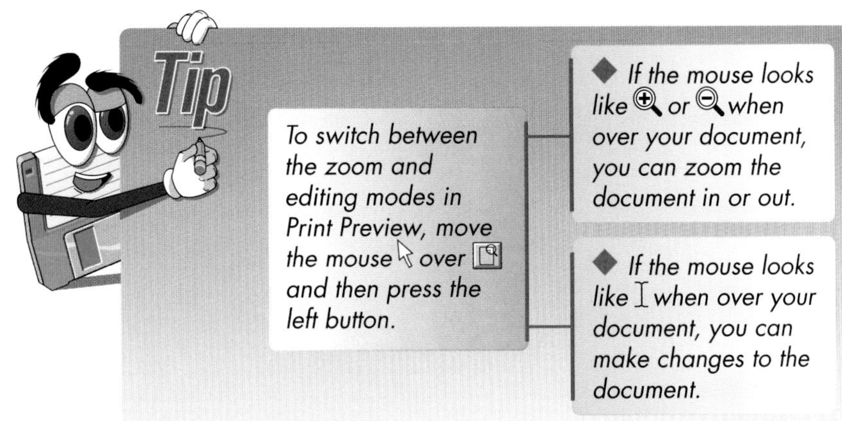

To switch between the zoom and editing modes in Print Preview, move the mouse over and then press the left button.

◆ If the mouse looks like or when over your document, you can zoom the document in or out.

◆ If the mouse looks like I when over your document, you can make changes to the document.

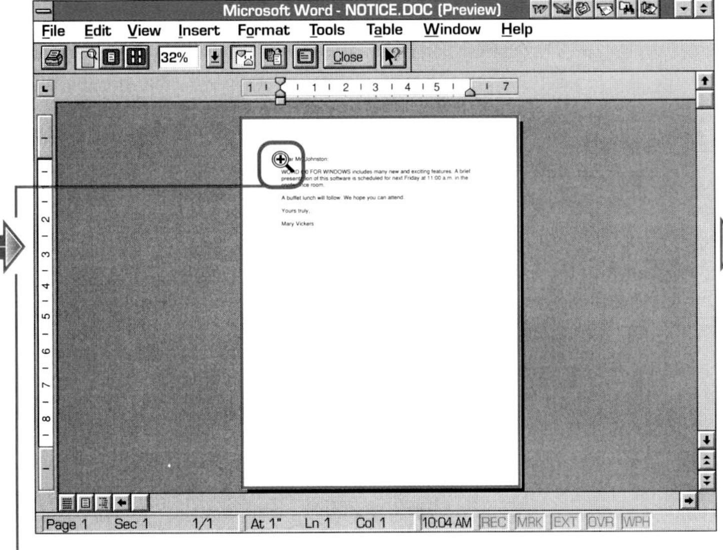

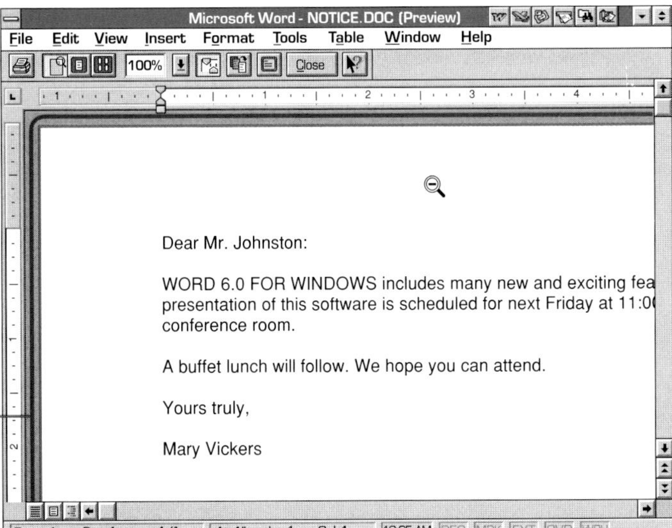

ZOOM IN OR OUT

1 To magnify a section of the page, move the mouse over the section (changes to) and then press the left button.

*Note: If the mouse looks like I when over your document, refer to the **Tip** above to change to the zoom mode.*

◆ A magnified view of the page appears and the mouse changes to .

2 To again display the entire page, move the mouse anywhere over the page and then press the left button.

PREVIEW A DOCUMENT

In Print Preview, Word can display more than one page at a time. This lets you view the overall style of multiple pages at once.

PREVIEW A DOCUMENT

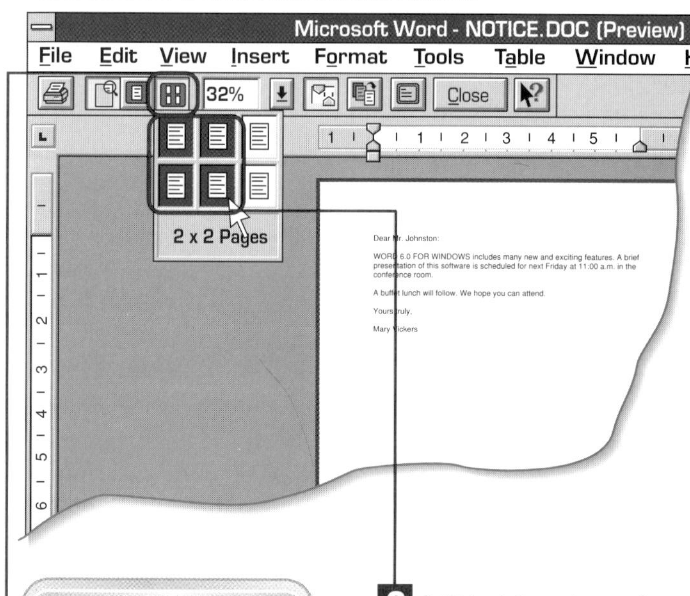

DISPLAY MULTIPLE PAGES

1 Move the mouse over ▦ and then press and hold down the left button.

2 Still holding down the button, move the mouse over the number of pages you want to display at once.

Note: If you drag the mouse down or to the right, more choices appear.

SHRINK TO FIT

The Shrink to Fit feature is useful if the last page in your document contains only a few lines of text and you want it to fit on one less page.

1 Move the mouse over on the Print Preview toolbar and then press the left button.

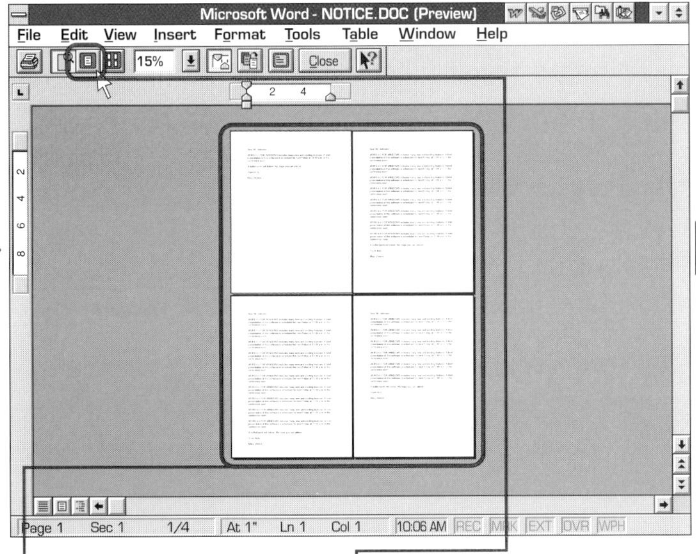

3 Release the button and the number of pages you specified appears on your screen.

Note: In this example, the document contains four pages.

DISPLAY ONE PAGE

1 To display a single page, move the mouse over and then press the left button.

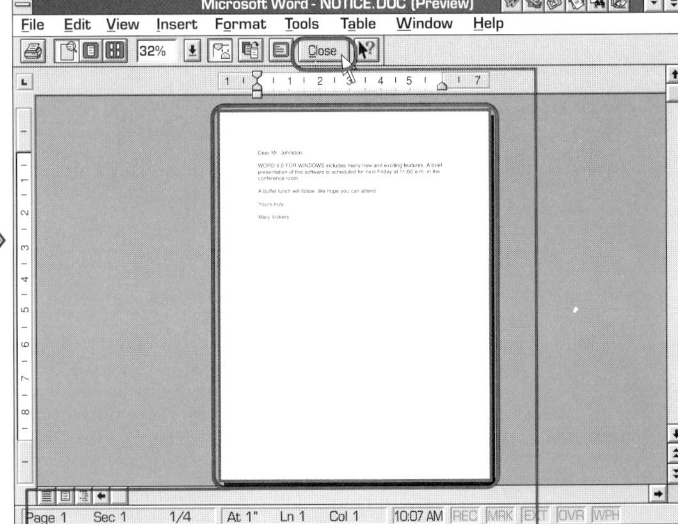

◆ A single page appears on your screen.

◆ Press PageDown on your keyboard to display the next page. Press PageUp to display the previous page.

CLOSE PRINT PREVIEW

1 To close Print Preview and return to your document, move the mouse over **Close** and then press the left button.

PRINT A DOCUMENT

You can print a single page, specific pages or your entire document. Before printing, make sure your printer is on and contains paper.

PRINT A DOCUMENT

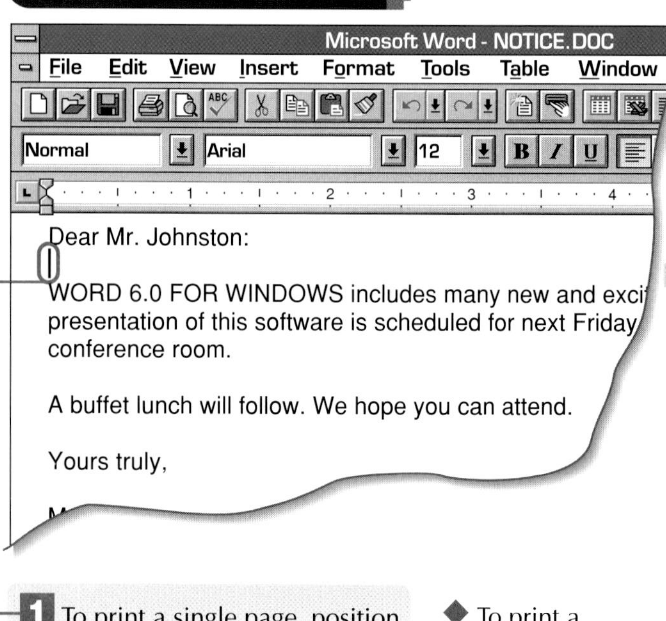

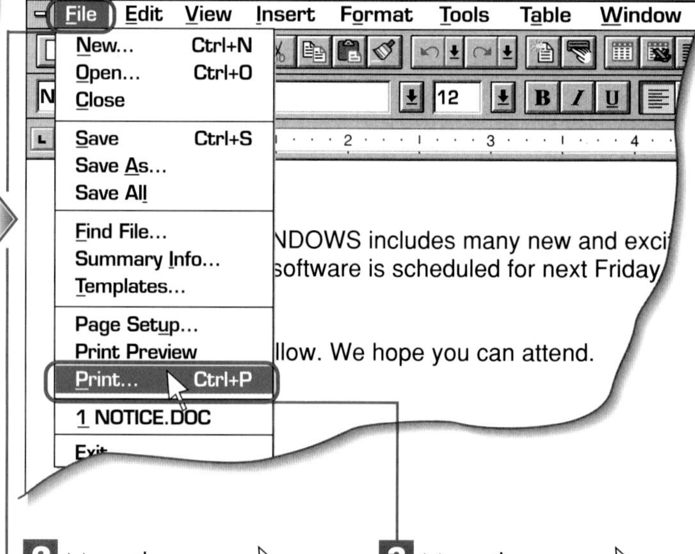

1 To print a single page, position the insertion point anywhere on the page you want to print.

◆ To print your entire document or specific pages, position the insertion point anywhere in the document.

◆ To print a section of text, select the text.

Note: To select text, refer to page 24.

2 Move the mouse over **File** and then press the left button.

3 Move the mouse over **Print** and then press the left button.

PRINT YOUR ENTIRE DOCUMENT

◆ To quickly print your entire document, move the mouse over [print button] and then press the left button.

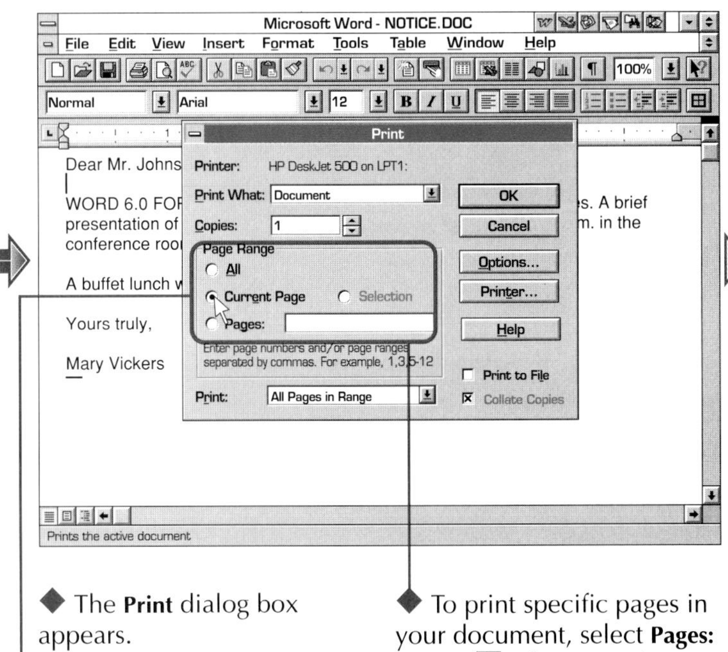

◆ The **Print** dialog box appears.

4 Move the mouse over the range you want to print (example: **Current Page**) and then press the left button.

◆ To print specific pages in your document, select **Pages:** in step **4**. Then type the page numbers separated by commas (example: **1,3,5**) or type the first and last page numbers separated by a dash (example: **3-5**).

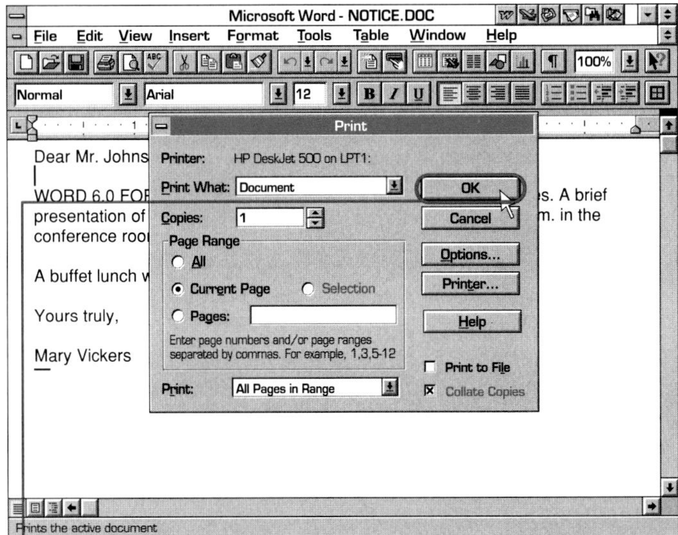

5 Move the mouse over **OK** and then press the left button.

PRINT AN ENVELOPE

PRINT AN ENVELOPE

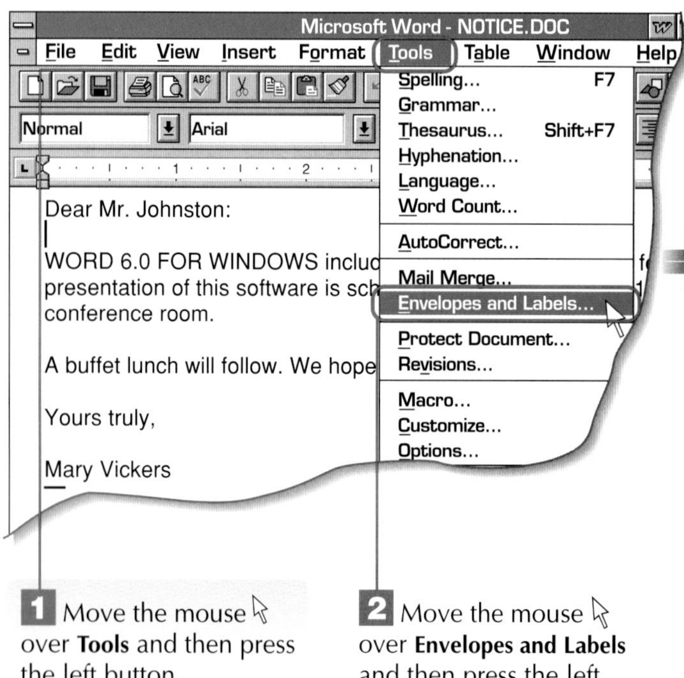

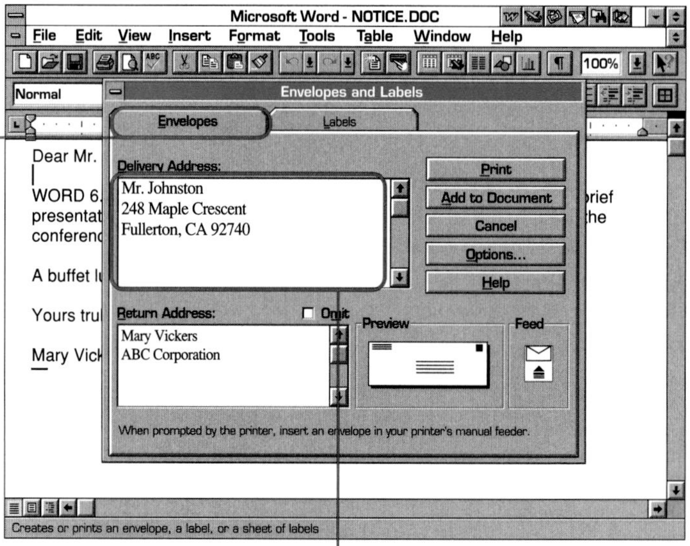

1 Move the mouse over **Tools** and then press the left button.

2 Move the mouse over **Envelopes and Labels** and then press the left button.

◆ The **Envelopes and Labels** dialog box appears.

3 Move the mouse over the **Envelopes** tab and then press the left button.

◆ A delivery address appears in this area if Word found one in your document.

4 If a delivery address did not appear, move the mouse over this area and then press the left button. Then type the address.

This dialog box appears if you made changes to the return address.

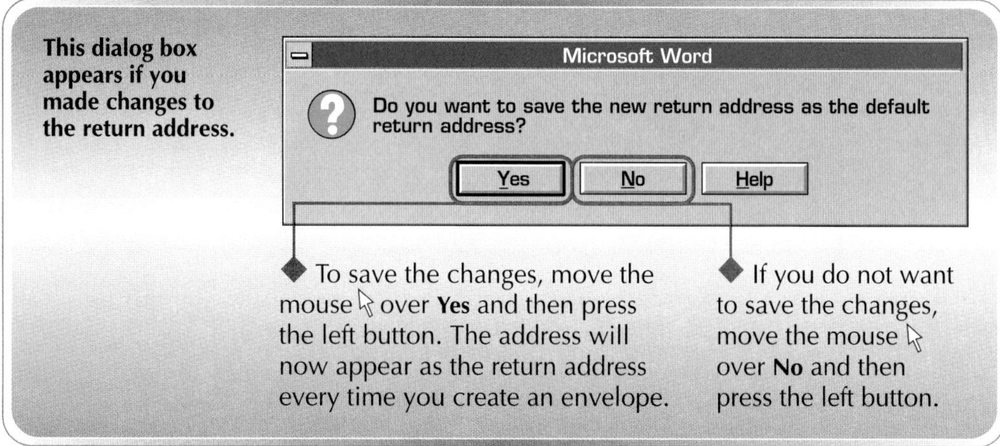

◆ To save the changes, move the mouse over **Yes** and then press the left button. The address will now appear as the return address every time you create an envelope.

◆ If you do not want to save the changes, move the mouse over **No** and then press the left button.

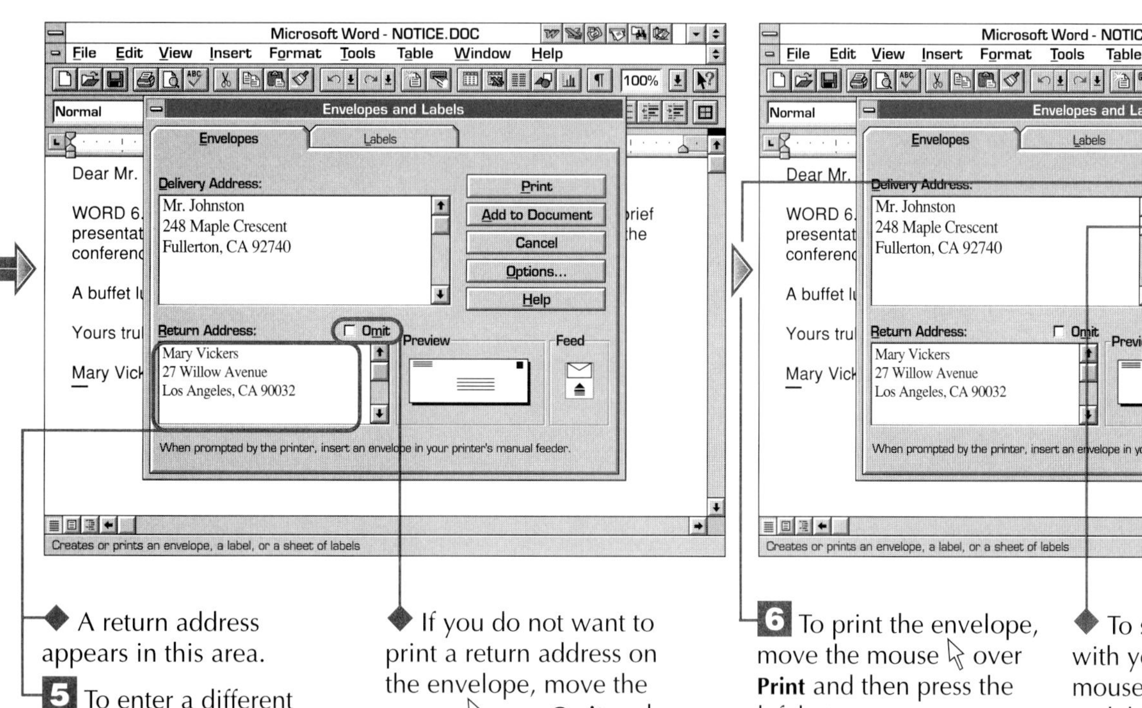

◆ A return address appears in this area.

5 To enter a different return address, press **Tab** twice to highlight the text. Then type a return address.

◆ If you do not want to print a return address on the envelope, move the mouse over **Omit** and then press the left button (☐ changes to ☒).

6 To print the envelope, move the mouse over **Print** and then press the left button.

◆ To save and print the envelope with your document, move the mouse over **Add to Document** and then press the left button. Word will attach the envelope to the top of your document.

BOLD, UNDERLINE AND ITALICS

You can use the Bold, Underline and Italic features to emphasize important information. This will improve the overall appearance of your document.

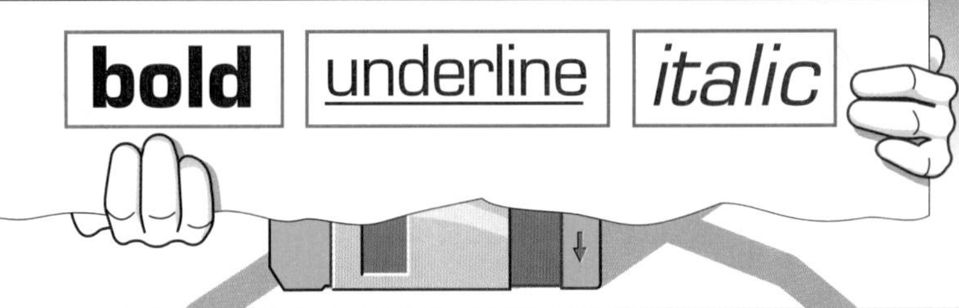

bold
underline
italic

BOLD TEXT

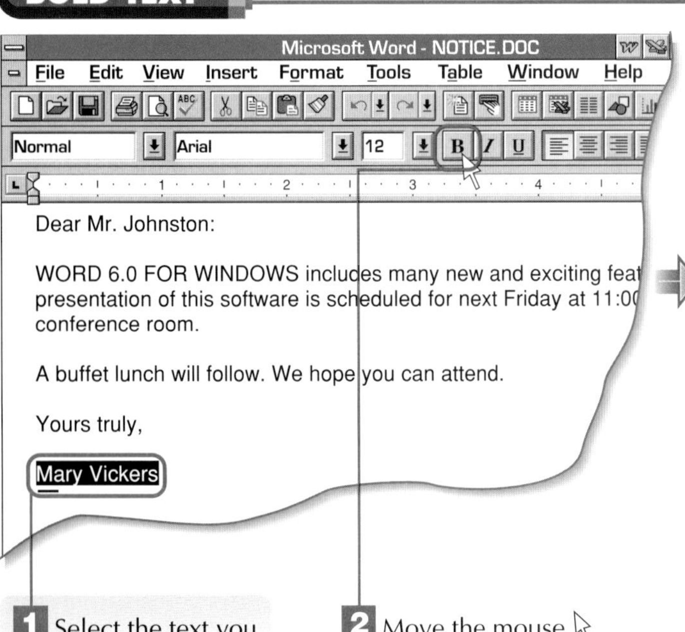

Microsoft Word - NOTICE.DOC
File Edit View Insert Format Tools Table Window Help
Normal Arial 12
Dear Mr. Johnston:
WORD 6.0 FOR WINDOWS includes many new and exciting feat
presentation of this software is scheduled for next Friday at 11:0
conference room.
A buffet lunch will follow. We hope you can attend.
Yours truly,
Mary Vickers

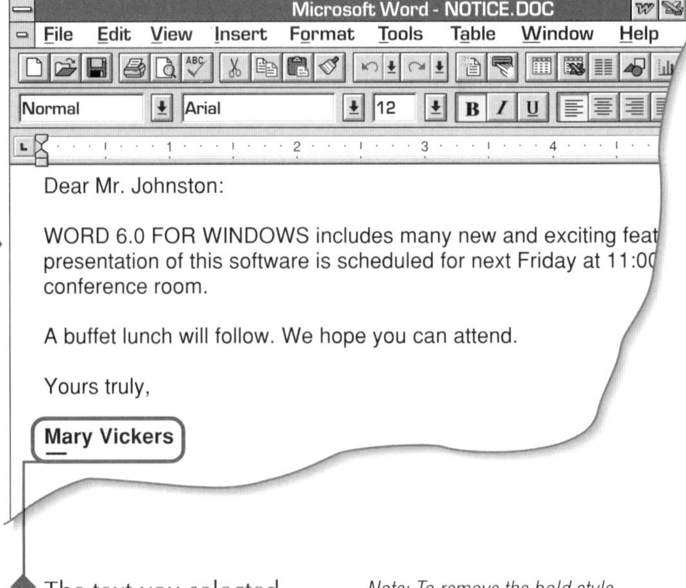

Microsoft Word - NOTICE.DOC
File Edit View Insert Format Tools Table Window Help
Normal Arial 12
Dear Mr. Johnston:
WORD 6.0 FOR WINDOWS includes many new and exciting feat
presentation of this software is scheduled for next Friday at 11:0
conference room.
A buffet lunch will follow. We hope you can attend.
Yours truly,
Mary Vickers

1 Select the text you want to bold.

Note: To select text, refer to page 24.

2 Move the mouse over **B** and then press the left button.

◆ The text you selected appears in the bold style.

Note: To deselect text, move the mouse outside the selected area and then press the left button.

Note: To remove the bold style, repeat steps **1** *and* **2**.

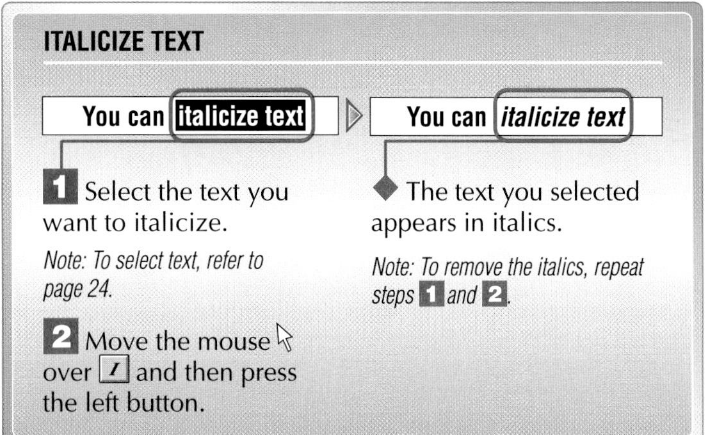

ITALICIZE TEXT
You can italicize text
You can italicize text

1 Select the text you want to italicize.

Note: To select text, refer to page 24.

2 Move the mouse over I and then press the left button.

◆ The text you selected appears in italics.

Note: To remove the italics, repeat steps 1 and 2.

UNDERLINE TEXT

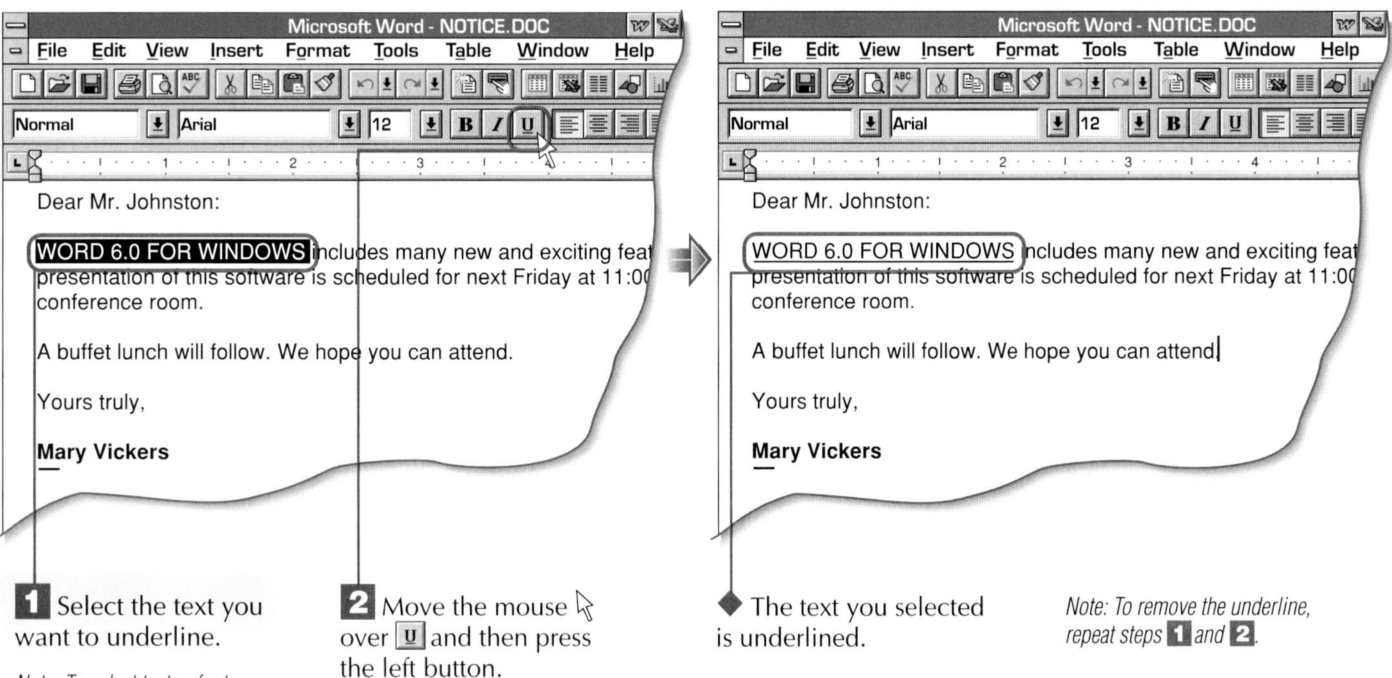

1 Select the text you want to underline.

Note: To select text, refer to page 24.

2 Move the mouse over U and then press the left button.

◆ The text you selected is underlined.

Note: To remove the underline, repeat steps 1 and 2.

CHANGE FONTS

You can change the design and size of characters in your document to emphasize headings and make text easier to read.

CHANGE FONTS

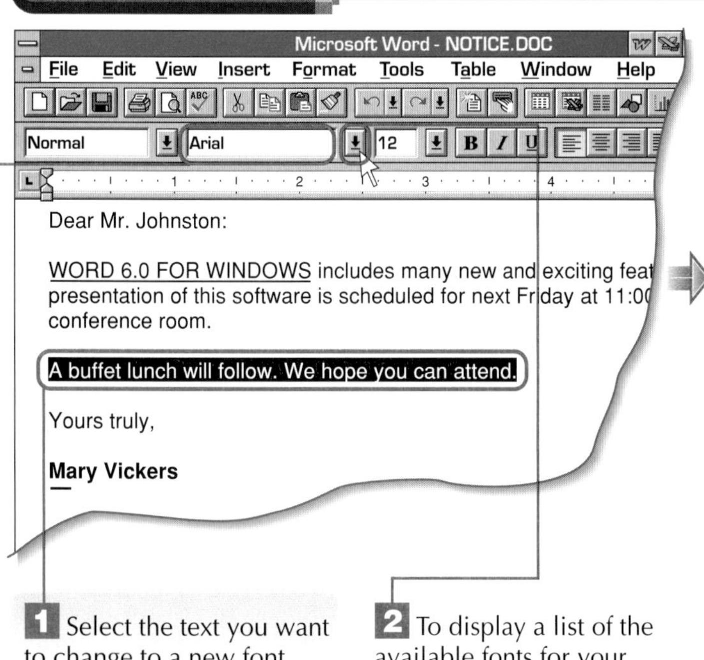

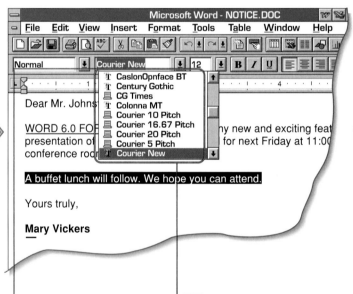

1 Select the text you want to change to a new font.

Note: To select text, refer to page 24.

◆ The **Font** box displays the font of the text you selected (example: **Arial**).

2 To display a list of the available fonts for your computer, move the mouse over ⬇ to the right of the **Font** box and then press the left button.

◆ A list of the available fonts appears.

3 Press ⬇ or ⬆ on your keyboard until you highlight the font you want to use (example: **Courier New**).

4 To select the highlighted font, press **Enter**.

REMOVE ALL CHARACTER FORMATTING

You can instantly remove all character formatting from text in your document.

1 Select the text that displays the character formatting you want to remove.

2 Press Ctrl + **Spacebar** on your keyboard.

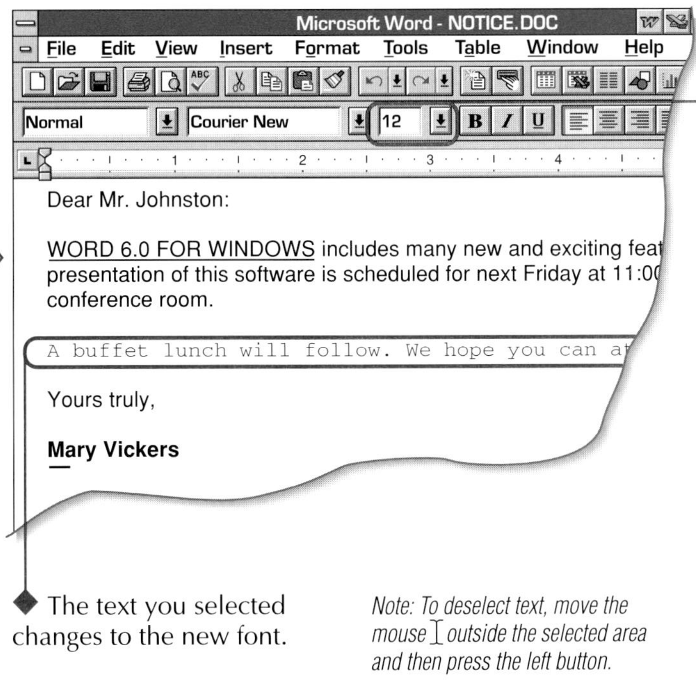
Microsoft Word - NOTICE.DOC
File Edit View Insert Format Tools Table Window Help
Normal
Courier New
12
Dear Mr. Johnston:
WORD 6.0 FOR WINDOWS includes many new and exciting feat
presentation of this software is scheduled for next Friday at 11:0
conference room.
A buffet lunch will follow. We hope you can at
Yours truly,
Mary Vickers

◆ The text you selected changes to the new font.

Note: To deselect text, move the mouse outside the selected area and then press the left button.

CHANGE FONT SIZE

You can increase or decrease the size of text in your document.

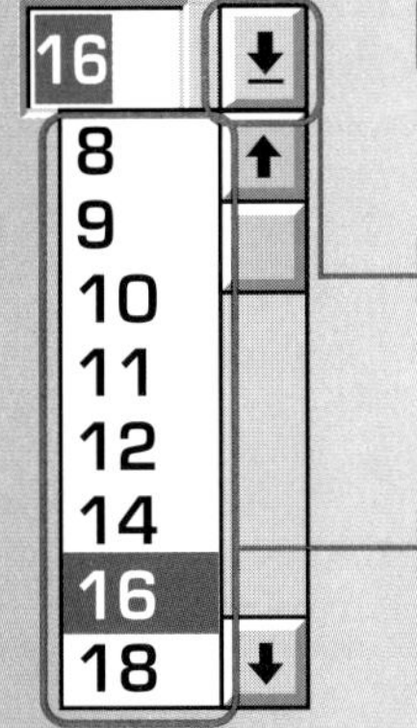
16
8
9
10
11
12
14
16
18

1 Select the text you want to change to a new font size.

Note: To select text, refer to page 24.

2 Move the mouse over ⬇ to the right of the **Font Size** box and then press the left button. A list of the available font sizes appears.

3 Press ⬇ or ⬆ on your keyboard until you highlight the font size you want to use (example: **16**).

4 To select the highlighted font size, press Enter.

Note: Word measures the size of text in points. There are approximately 72 points per inch.

CHANGE FONTS

You can use the Font dialog box to change the design and size of characters at the same time.

CHANGE FONTS

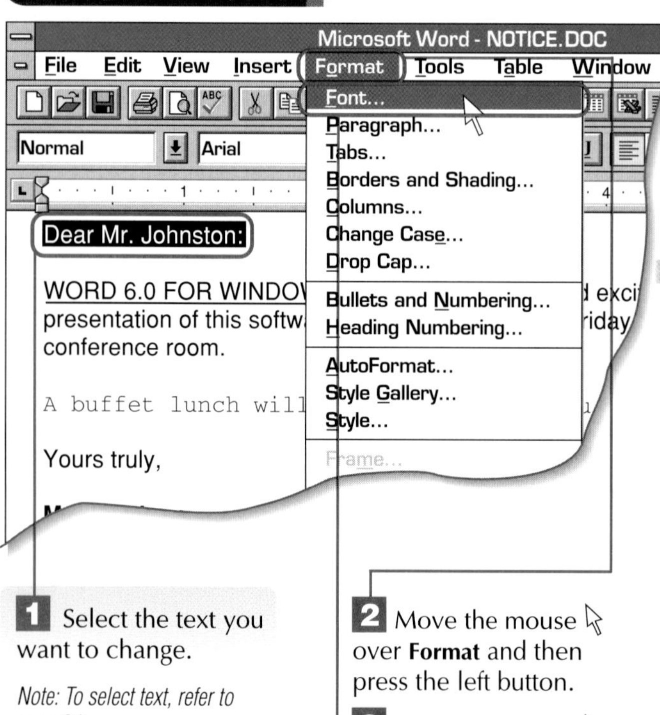

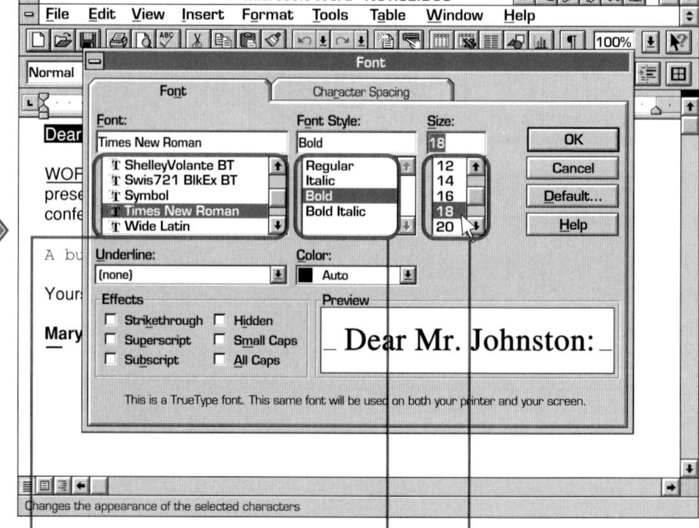

1 Select the text you want to change.

Note: To select text, refer to page 24.

2 Move the mouse over **Format** and then press the left button.

3 Move the mouse over **Font** and then press the left button.

4 Move the mouse over the font you want to use (example: **Times New Roman**) and then press the left button.

Note: To view all of the available font options, use the scroll bar. To use the scroll bar, refer to page 23.

5 Move the mouse over the font style you want to use (example: **Bold**) and then press the left button.

6 Move the mouse over the font size you want to use (example: **18**) and then press the left button.

- Bold, Underline and Italics
- **Change Fonts**
- Insert a Symbol

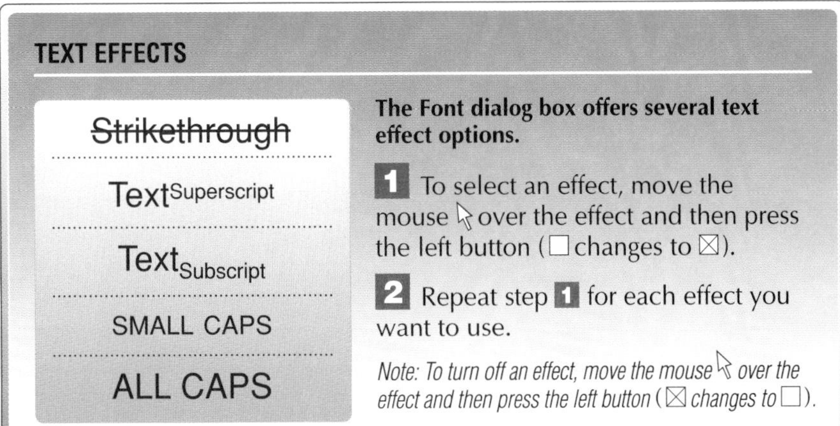

TEXT EFFECTS
Strikethrough
Text Superscript
Text Subscript
SMALL CAPS
ALL CAPS
The Font dialog box offers several text effect options.
1 To select an effect, move the mouse over the effect and then press the left button (☐ changes to ☒).
2 Repeat step 1 for each effect you want to use.
Note: To turn off an effect, move the mouse over the effect and then press the left button (☒ changes to ☐).

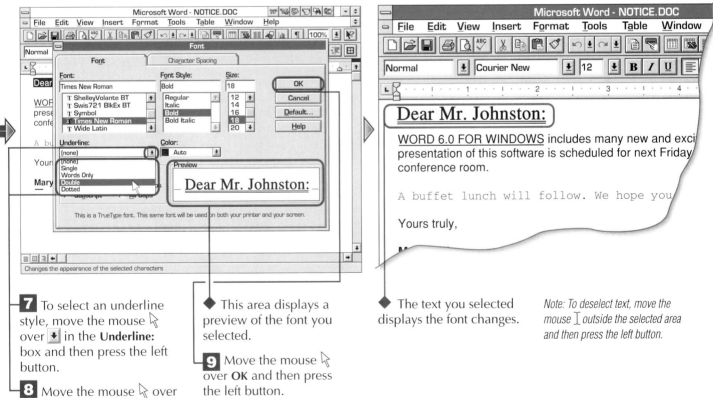

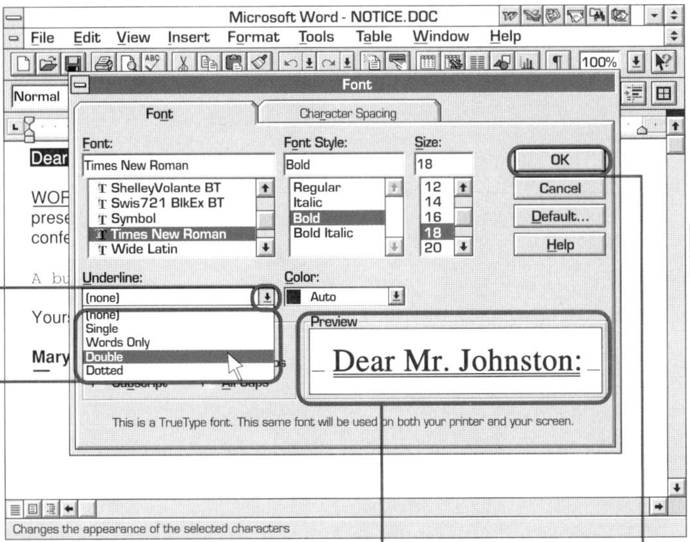

7 To select an underline style, move the mouse over ⬇ in the **Underline:** box and then press the left button.

8 Move the mouse over the underline style you want to use (example: **Double**) and then press the left button.

◆ This area displays a preview of the font you selected.

9 Move the mouse over **OK** and then press the left button.

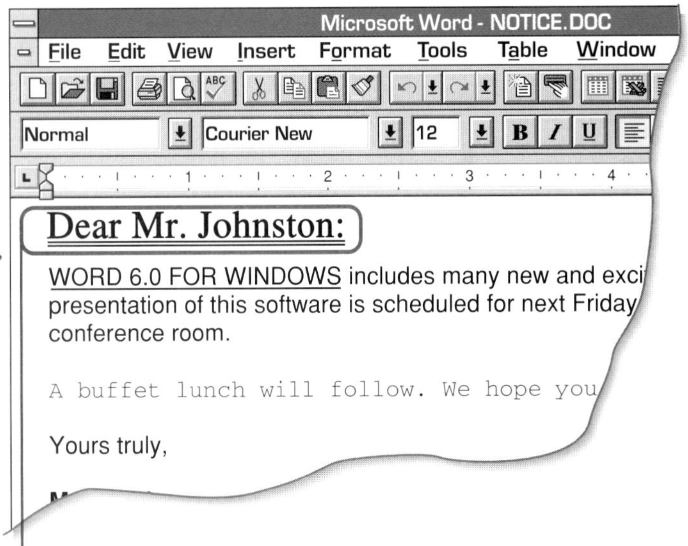

◆ The text you selected displays the font changes.

Note: To deselect text, move the mouse outside the selected area and then press the left button.

INSERT A SYMBOL

TM
Word lets you insert symbols into your document that do not appear on your keyboard.

INSERT A SYMBOL

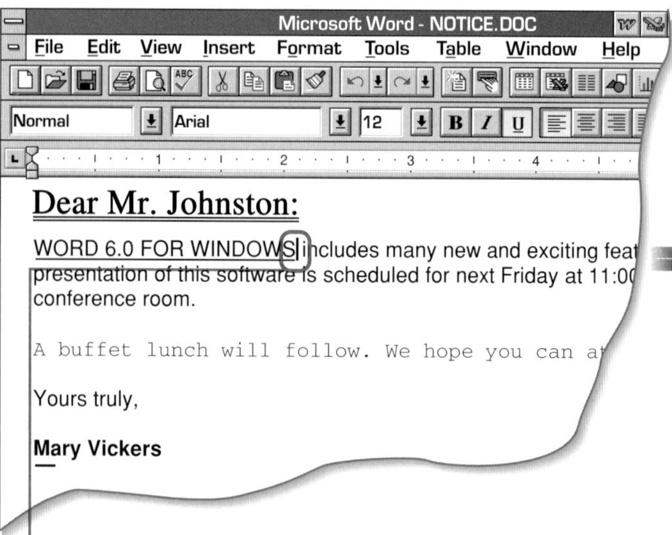

1 Position the insertion point where you want a symbol to appear in your document.

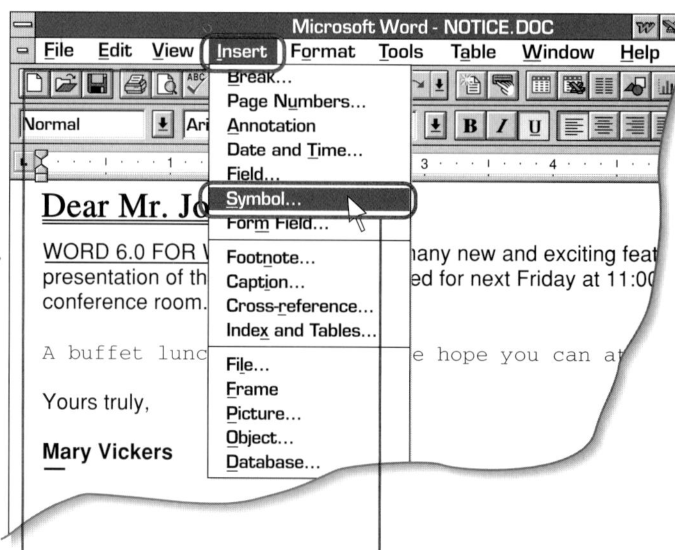

2 Move the mouse over **Insert** and then press the left button.

3 Move the mouse over **Symbol** and then press the left button.

DISPLAY MORE SYMBOLS

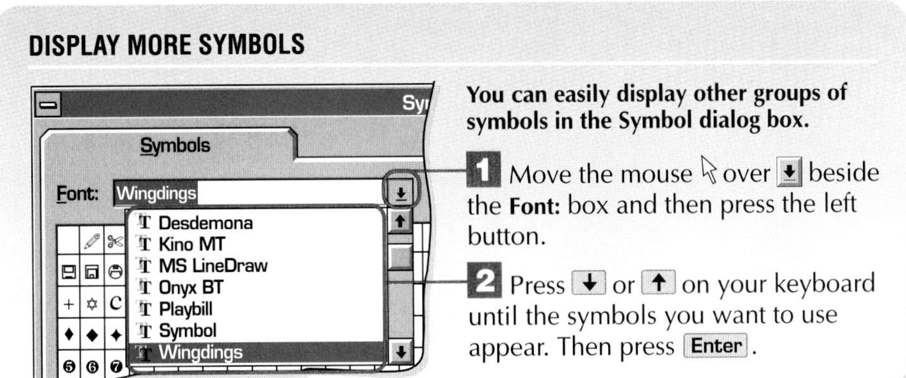

You can easily display other groups of symbols in the Symbol dialog box.

1 Move the mouse over ⬇ beside the **Font:** box and then press the left button.

2 Press ⬇ or ⬆ on your keyboard until the symbols you want to use appear. Then press Enter.

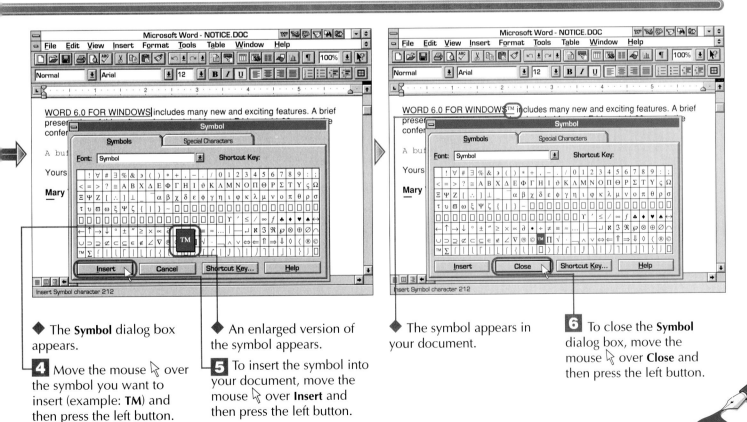

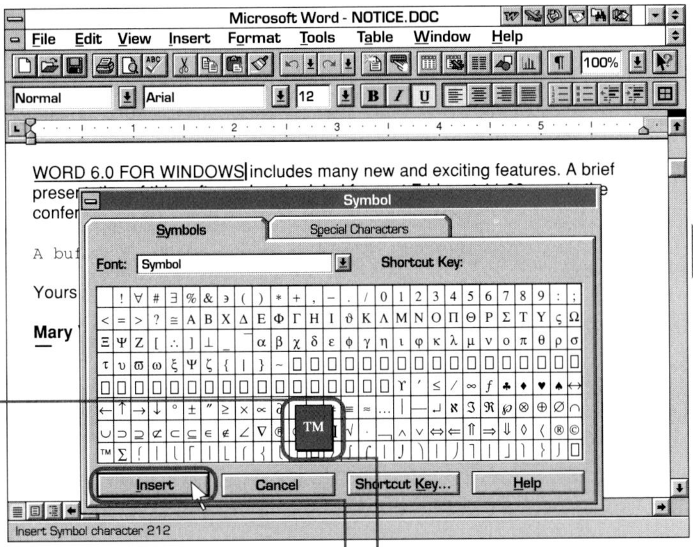

◆ The **Symbol** dialog box appears.

4 Move the mouse over the symbol you want to insert (example: **TM**) and then press the left button.

◆ An enlarged version of the symbol appears.

5 To insert the symbol into your document, move the mouse over **Insert** and then press the left button.

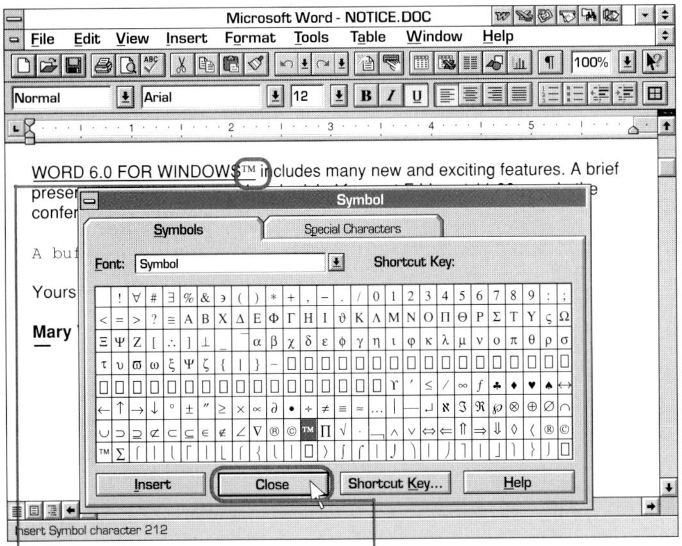

◆ The symbol appears in your document.

6 To close the **Symbol** dialog box, move the mouse over **Close** and then press the left button.

CHANGE LINE SPACING

Single line spacing
This is the initial (or default) setting.
1.5 line spacing
Double line spacing
1
FORMAT
You can make your document easier to read by changing the amount of space between the lines of text.

CHANGE LINE SPACING

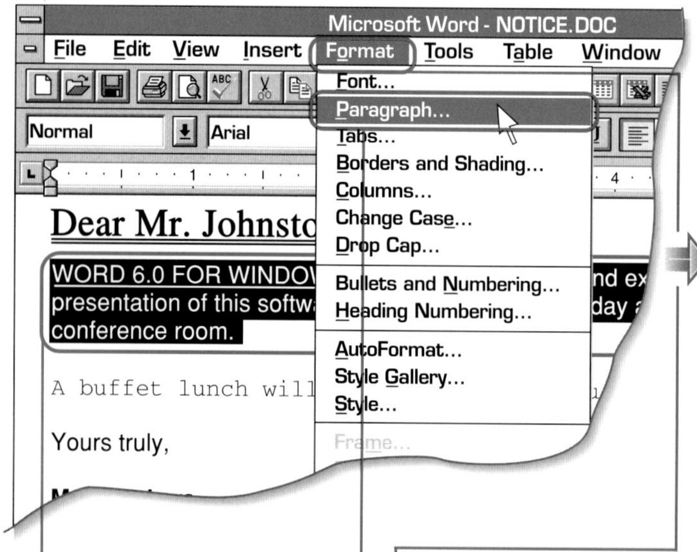

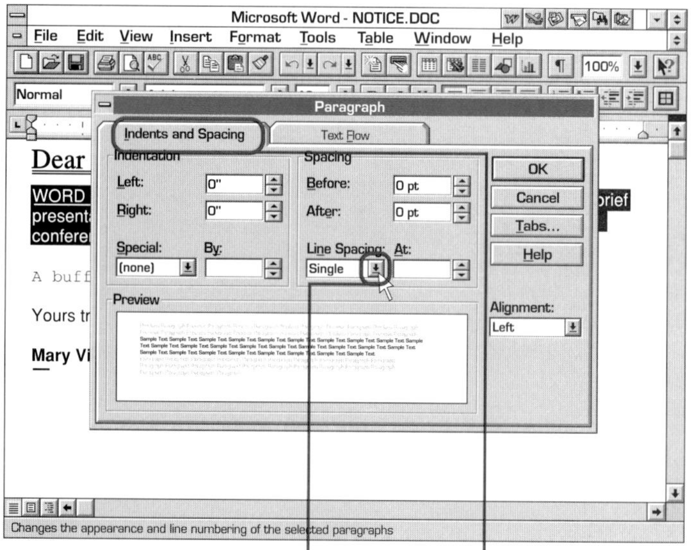

1 Select the paragraph(s) you want to change to a new line spacing.

Note: To select text, refer to page 24.

2 Move the mouse over **Format** and then press the left button.

3 Move the mouse over **Paragraph** and then press the left button.

◆ The **Paragraph** dialog box appears.

4 Move the mouse over the **Indents and Spacing** tab and then press the left button.

5 Move the mouse over ⬇ in the **Line Spacing:** box and then press the left button.

- **Change Line Spacing**
- Change Paragraph Alignment
- Display or Hide the Ruler
- Change Tab Settings
- Indent Paragraphs
- Create Numbered and Bulleted Lists

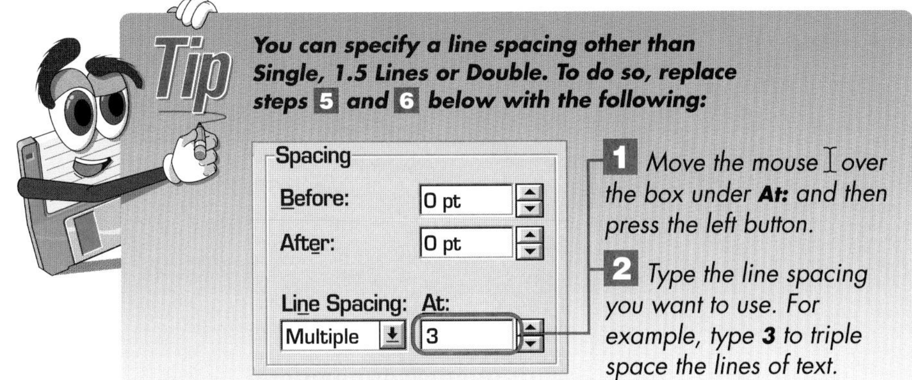

Tip ***You can specify a line spacing other than Single, 1.5 Lines or Double. To do so, replace steps 5 and 6 below with the following:***

*1 Move the mouse over the box under **At:** and then press the left button.*

*2 Type the line spacing you want to use. For example, type **3** to triple space the lines of text.*

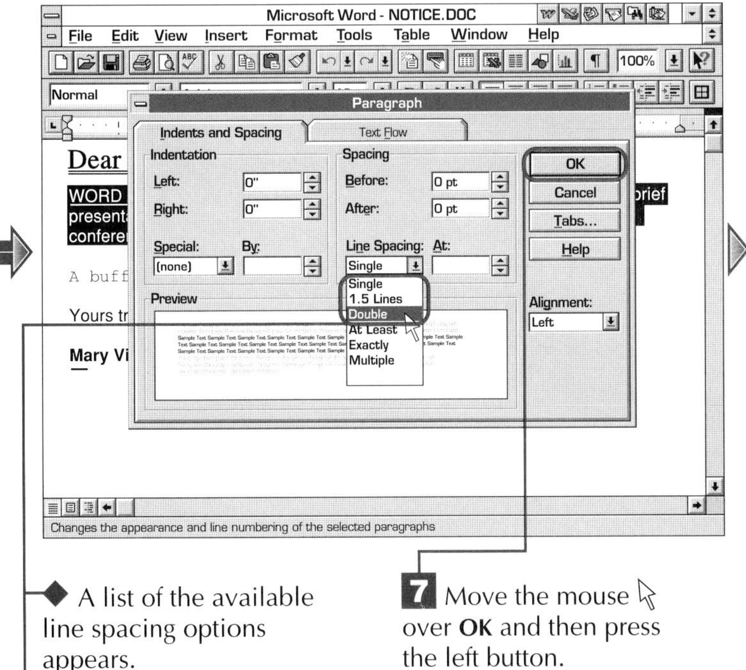

◆ A list of the available line spacing options appears.

6 Move the mouse over the line spacing you want to use (example: **Double**) and then press the left button.

7 Move the mouse over **OK** and then press the left button.

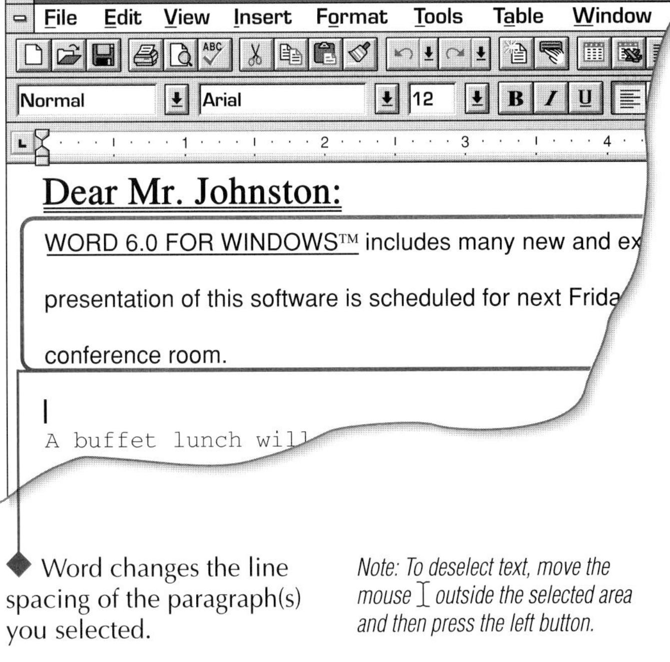

◆ Word changes the line spacing of the paragraph(s) you selected.

Note: To deselect text, move the mouse outside the selected area and then press the left button.

CHANGE PARAGRAPH ALIGNMENT

DISPLAY OR HIDE THE RULER

You can enhance the appearance of your document by aligning text in different ways. Word offers four alignment options.

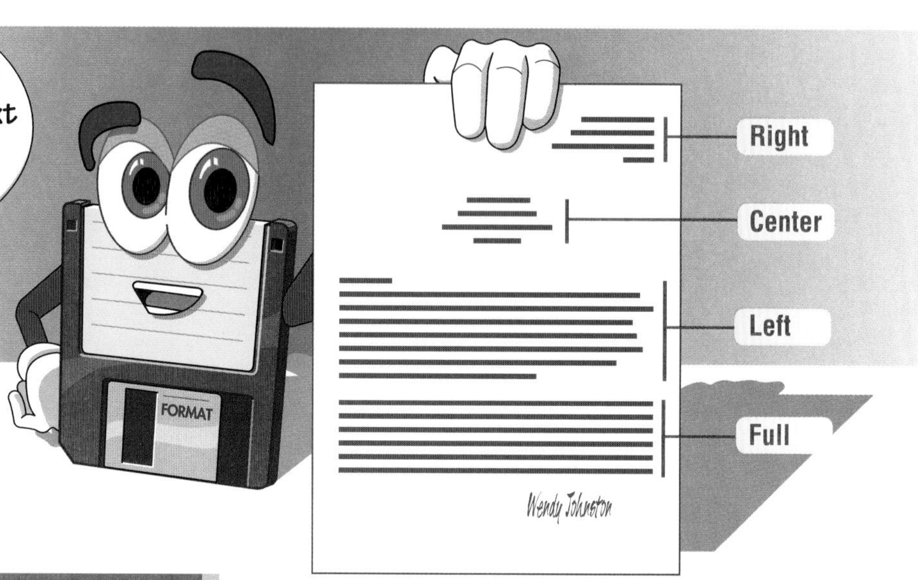
Right
Center
Left
Full
FORMAT

CHANGE PARAGRAPH ALIGNMENT

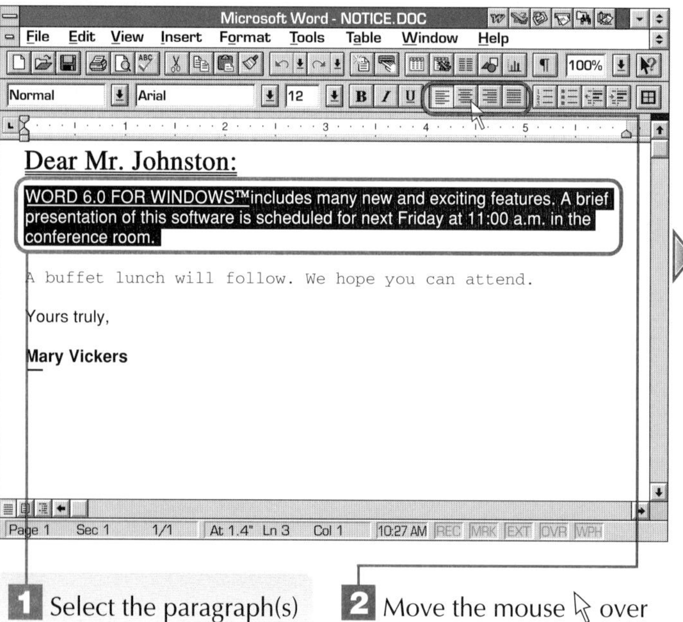
Microsoft Word - NOTICE.DOC
File Edit View Insert Format Tools Table Window Help
Dear Mr. Johnston:
WORD 6.0 FOR WINDOWS™ includes many new and exciting features. A brief presentation of this software is scheduled for next Friday at 11:00 a.m. in the conference room.
A buffet lunch will follow. We hope you can attend.
Yours truly,
Mary Vickers

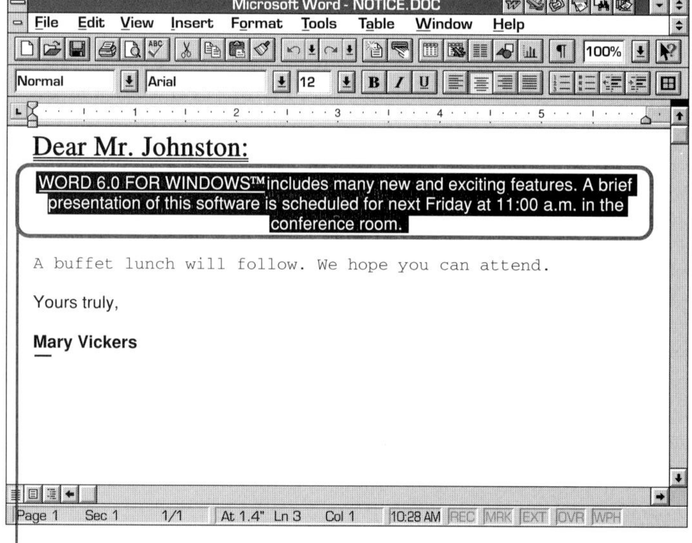
Microsoft Word - NOTICE.DOC
File Edit View Insert Format Tools Table Window Help
Dear Mr. Johnston:
WORD 6.0 FOR WINDOWS™ includes many new and exciting features. A brief presentation of this software is scheduled for next Friday at 11:00 a.m. in the conference room.
A buffet lunch will follow. We hope you can attend.
Yours truly,
Mary Vickers

1 Select the paragraph(s) you want to change.

Note: To select text, refer to page 24.

2 Move the mouse over the alignment option you want to use (example: **Center**) and then press the left button.

- Left
- Center
- Right
- Full

◆ The paragraph displays the new alignment.

*Note: To return to the original alignment, repeat steps **1** and **2**, selecting **Left** in step **2**.*

- Change Line Spacing
- **Change Paragraph Alignment**
- **Display or Hide the Ruler**
- Change Tab Settings
- Indent Paragraphs
- Create Numbered and Bulleted Lists

The ruler lets you indent paragraphs and change margin and tab settings. If you are not using the ruler, you can hide it to provide a larger and less cluttered working area.

DISPLAY OR HIDE THE RULER

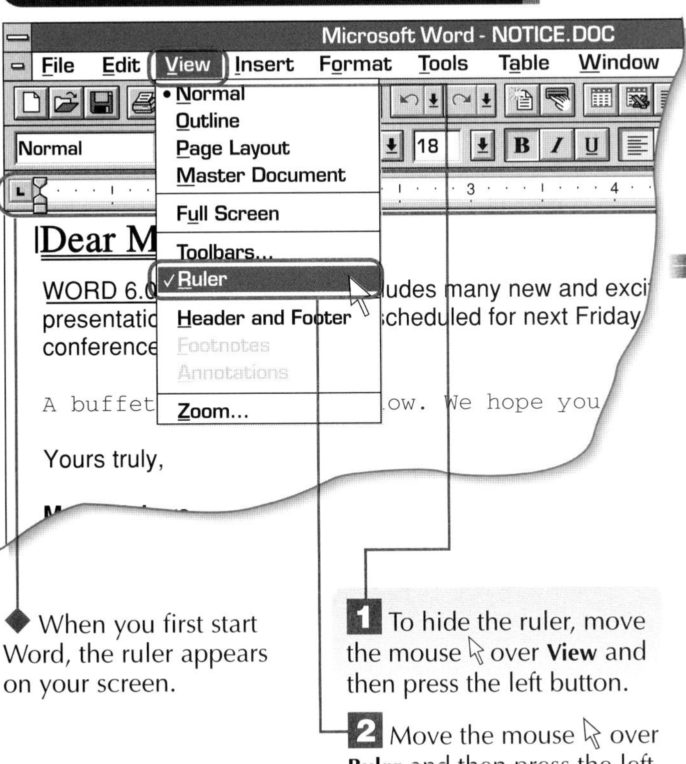

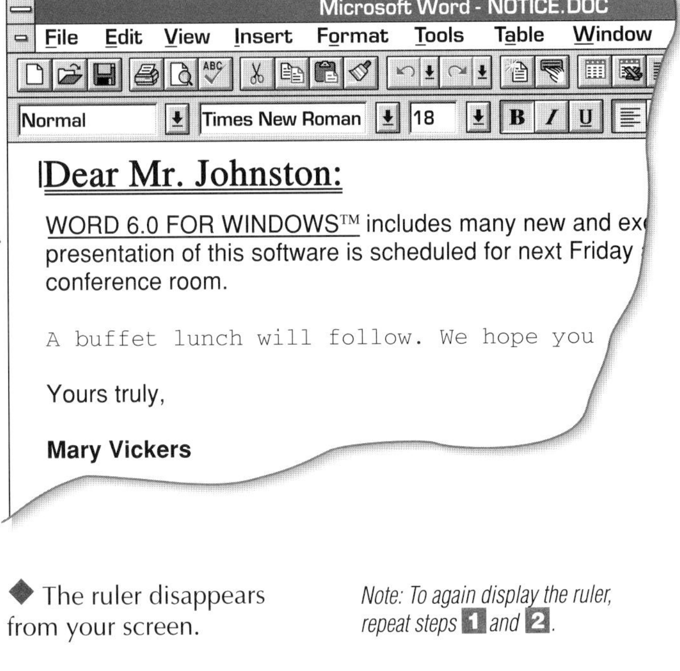

◆ When you first start Word, the ruler appears on your screen.

1 To hide the ruler, move the mouse over **View** and then press the left button.

2 Move the mouse over **Ruler** and then press the left button.

◆ The ruler disappears from your screen.

Note: To again display the ruler, repeat steps **1** *and* **2**.

CHANGE TAB SETTINGS

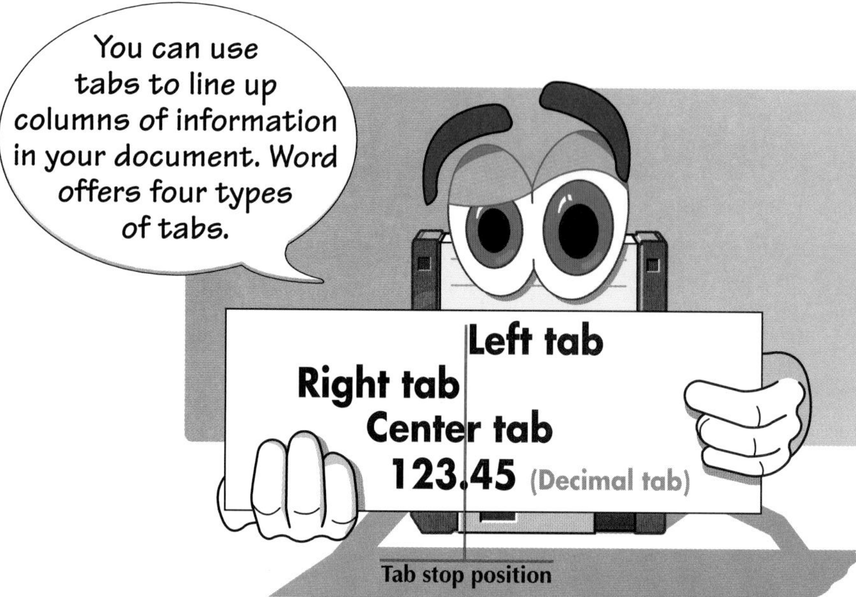

You can use tabs to line up columns of information in your document. Word offers four types of tabs.
Left tab
Right tab
Center tab
123.45 (Decimal tab)
Tab stop position

ADD A TAB STOP

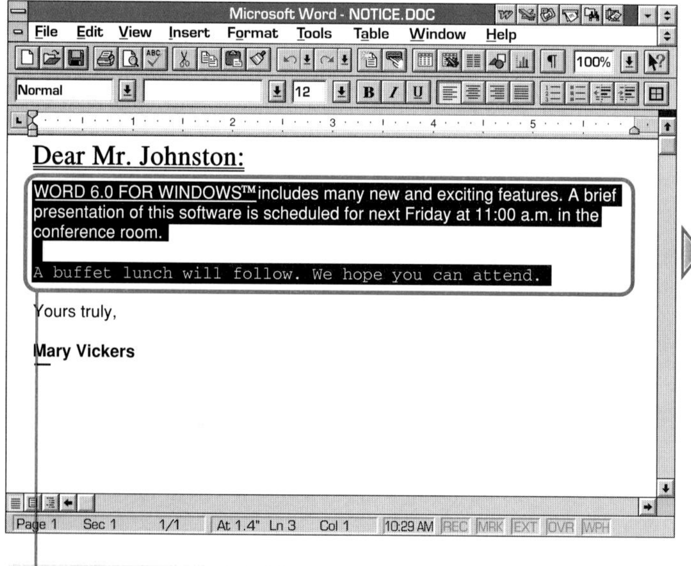

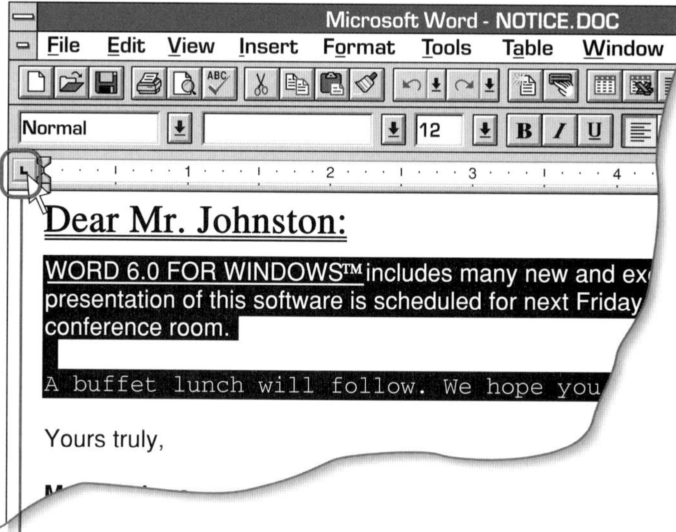

1 Select the paragraph(s) you want to contain the new tab stops.

Note: To select text, refer to page 24.

◆ To add tab stops to text you are about to type, position the insertion point where you want to begin typing the text.

2 Move the mouse over this box and then press the left button. Repeat this step until the type of tab you want to add appears (example:).

Note: If the ruler is not displayed on your screen, refer to page 97.

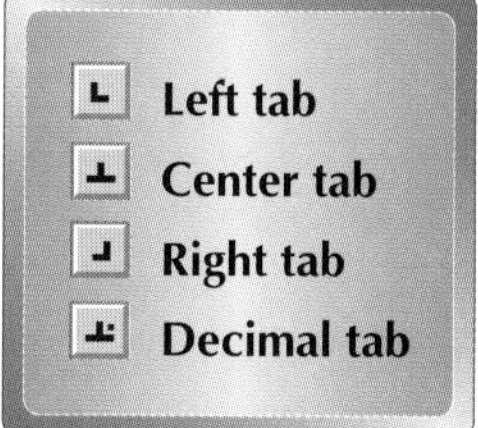

Left tab
Center tab
Right tab
Decimal tab

- Change Line Spacing
- Change Paragraph Alignment
- Display or Hide the Ruler
- **Change Tab Settings**
- Indent Paragraphs
- Create Numbered and Bulleted Lists

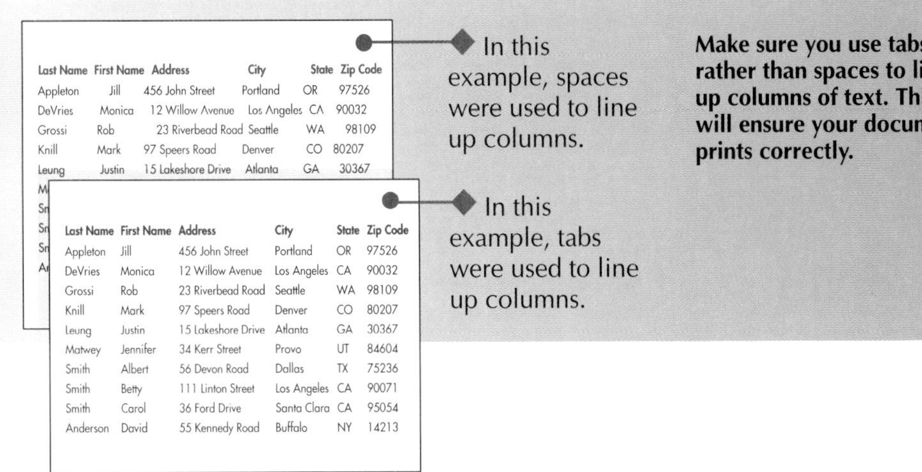

Last Name	First Name	Address	City	State	Zip Code
Appleton	Jill	456 John Street	Portland	OR	97526
DeVries	Monica	12 Willow Avenue	Los Angeles	CA	90032
Grossi	Rob	23 Riverbead Road	Seattle	WA	98109
Knill	Mark	97 Speers Road	Denver	CO	80207
Leung	Justin	15 Lakeshore Drive	Atlanta	GA	30367
Matwey	Jennifer	34 Kerr Street	Provo	UT	84604
Smith	Albert	56 Devon Road	Dallas	TX	75236
Smith	Betty	111 Linton Street	Los Angeles	CA	90071
Smith	Carol	36 Ford Drive	Santa Clara	CA	95054
Anderson	David	55 Kennedy Road	Buffalo	NY	14213

◆ In this example, spaces were used to line up columns.

◆ In this example, tabs were used to line up columns.

Make sure you use tabs rather than spaces to line up columns of text. This will ensure your document prints correctly.

USING TABS

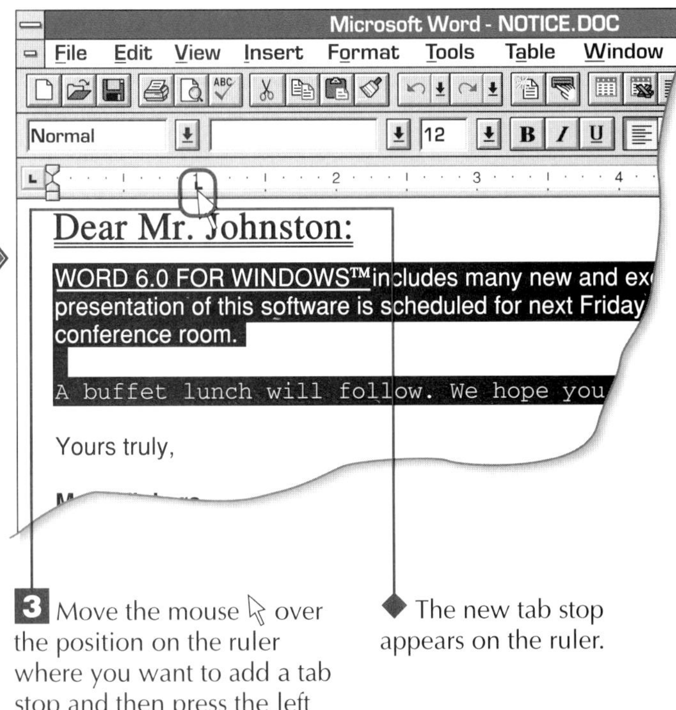
Microsoft Word - NOTICE.DOC
File Edit View Insert Format Tools Table Window
Normal
12
Dear Mr. Johnston:
WORD 6.0 FOR WINDOWS™includes many new and ex
presentation of this software is scheduled for next Friday
conference room.
A buffet lunch will follow. We hope you
Yours truly,

3 Move the mouse over the position on the ruler where you want to add a tab stop and then press the left button.

Note: Make sure you position the mouse over the lower half of the ruler.

◆ The new tab stop appears on the ruler.

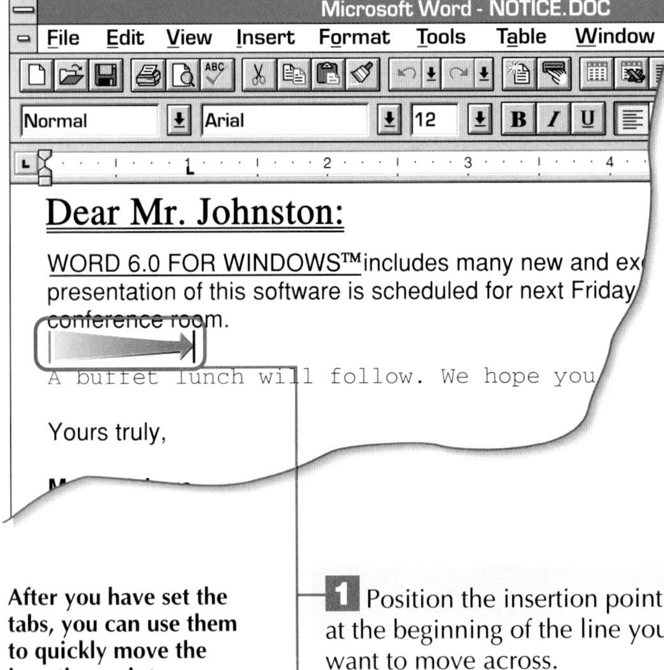
Microsoft Word - NOTICE.DOC
File Edit View Insert Format Tools Table Window
Normal
Arial
12
Dear Mr. Johnston:
WORD 6.0 FOR WINDOWS™includes many new and ex
presentation of this software is scheduled for next Friday
conference room.
A buffet lunch will follow. We hope you
Yours truly,

After you have set the tabs, you can use them to quickly move the insertion point across your screen.

1 Position the insertion point at the beginning of the line you want to move across.

2 Press Tab. The insertion point and any text that follows move to the first tab stop.

CHANGE TAB SETTINGS

You can easily move a tab stop to a different location on the ruler.
Dear Mr. Johnston:
WORD 6.0 FOR WINDOWS™ includes many new and exciting features. A brief presentation of this software is scheduled for next Friday at 11:00 a.m. in the conference room.

MOVE A TAB STOP

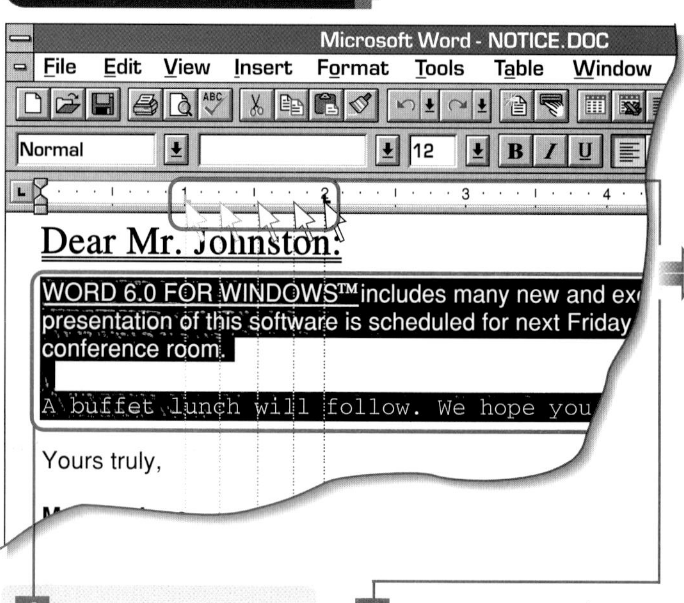

Microsoft Word - NOTICE.DOC
File Edit View Insert Format Tools Table Window
Normal
12
Dear Mr. Johnston:
WORD 6.0 FOR WINDOWS™ includes many new and ex
presentation of this software is scheduled for next Friday
conference room.
A buffet lunch will follow. We hope you
Yours truly,

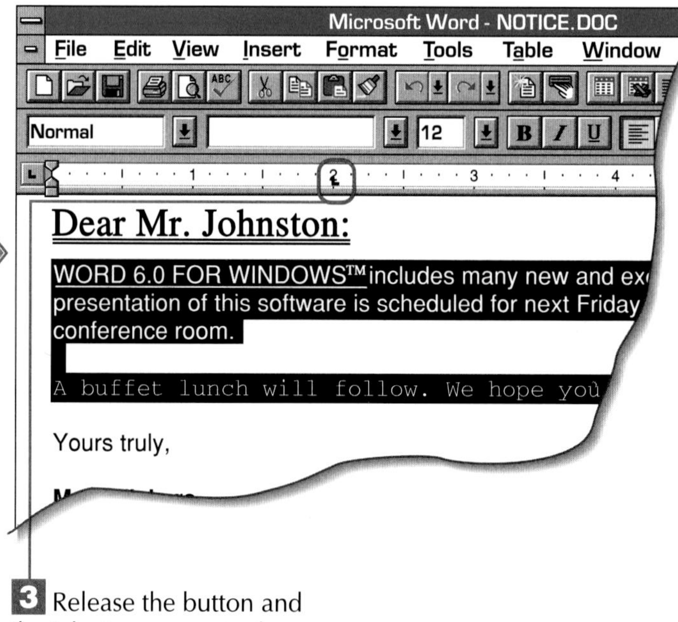

Microsoft Word - NOTICE.DOC
File Edit View Insert Format Tools Table Window
Normal
12
Dear Mr. Johnston:
WORD 6.0 FOR WINDOWS™ includes many new and ex
presentation of this software is scheduled for next Friday
conference room.
A buffet lunch will follow. We hope you
Yours truly,

1 Select the paragraph(s) containing the tab stop you want to move.

Note: To select text, refer to page 24.

2 Move the mouse over the tab stop and then press and hold down the left button as you drag the tab stop to a new position.

◆ A dotted line indicates the new tab stop position.

3 Release the button and the tab stop moves to the new position.

REMOVE A TAB STOP

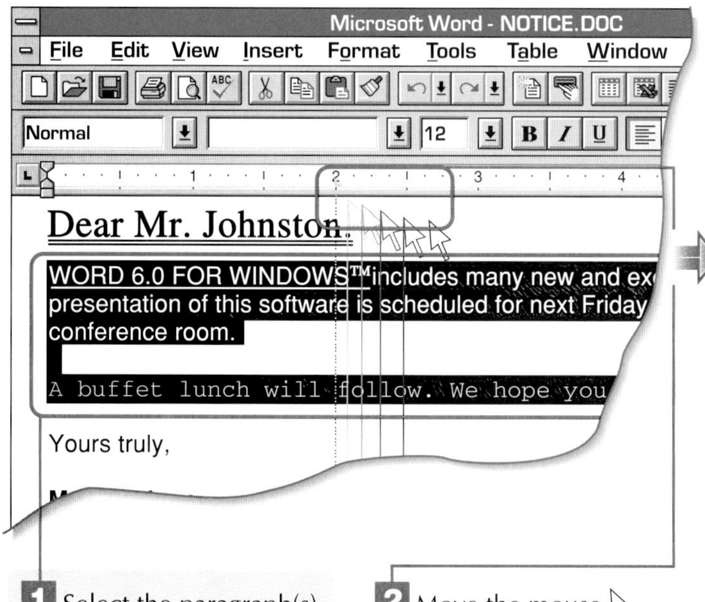

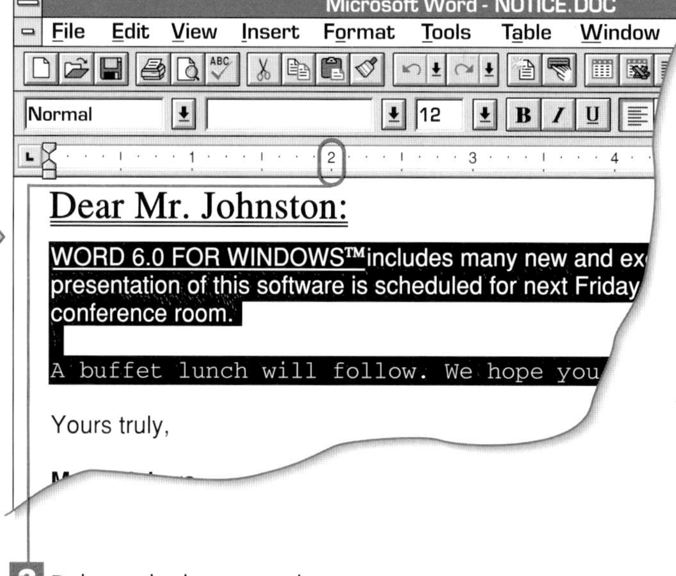

1 Select the paragraph(s) containing the tab stop you want to remove.

Note: To select text, refer to page 24.

2 Move the mouse over the tab stop and then press and hold down the left button as you drag the tab stop downward off the ruler.

3 Release the button and the tab stop disappears.

INDENT PARAGRAPHS

INDENT PARAGRAPHS

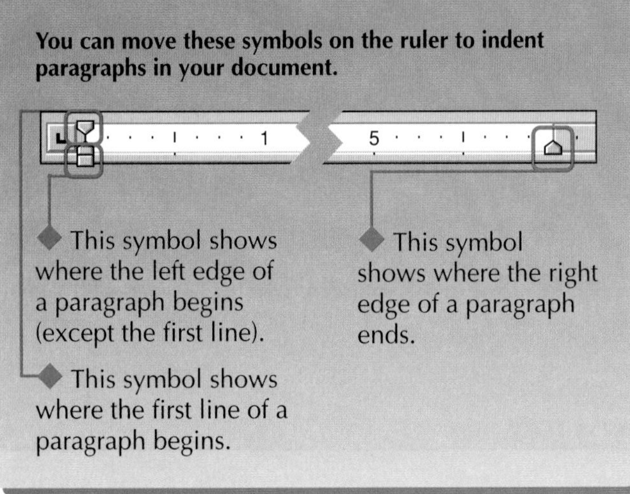

You can move these symbols on the ruler to indent paragraphs in your document.
1
5

◆ This symbol shows where the left edge of a paragraph begins (except the first line).

◆ This symbol shows where the first line of a paragraph begins.

◆ This symbol shows where the right edge of a paragraph ends.

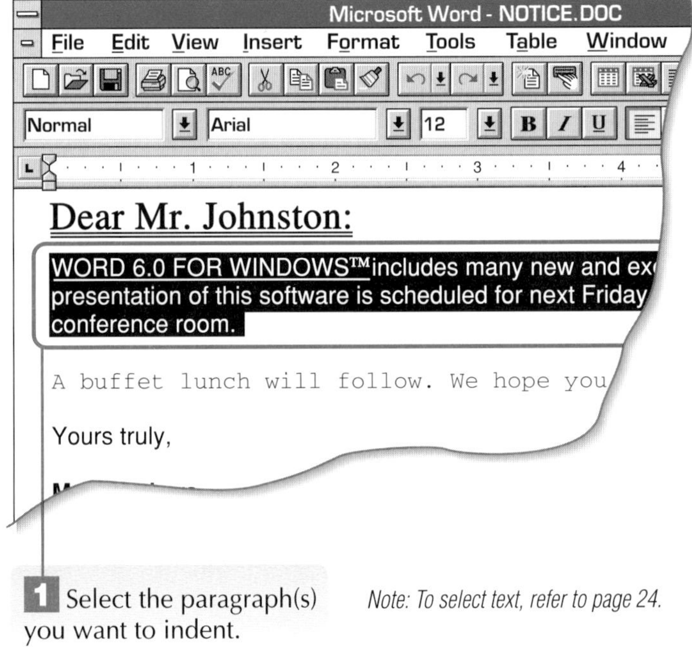

1 Select the paragraph(s) you want to indent.

Note: To select text, refer to page 24.

- Change Line Spacing
- Change Paragraph Alignment
- Display or Hide the Ruler
- Change Tab Settings
- **Indent Paragraphs**
- Create Numbered and Bulleted Lists

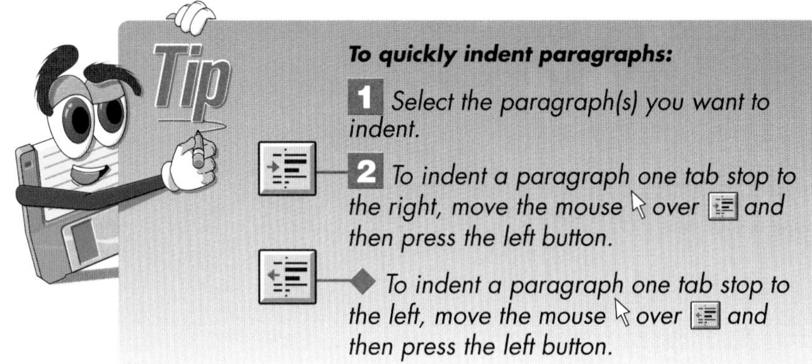
Tip

To quickly indent paragraphs:

1 Select the paragraph(s) you want to indent.

2 To indent a paragraph one tab stop to the right, move the mouse over and then press the left button.

◆ To indent a paragraph one tab stop to the left, move the mouse over and then press the left button.

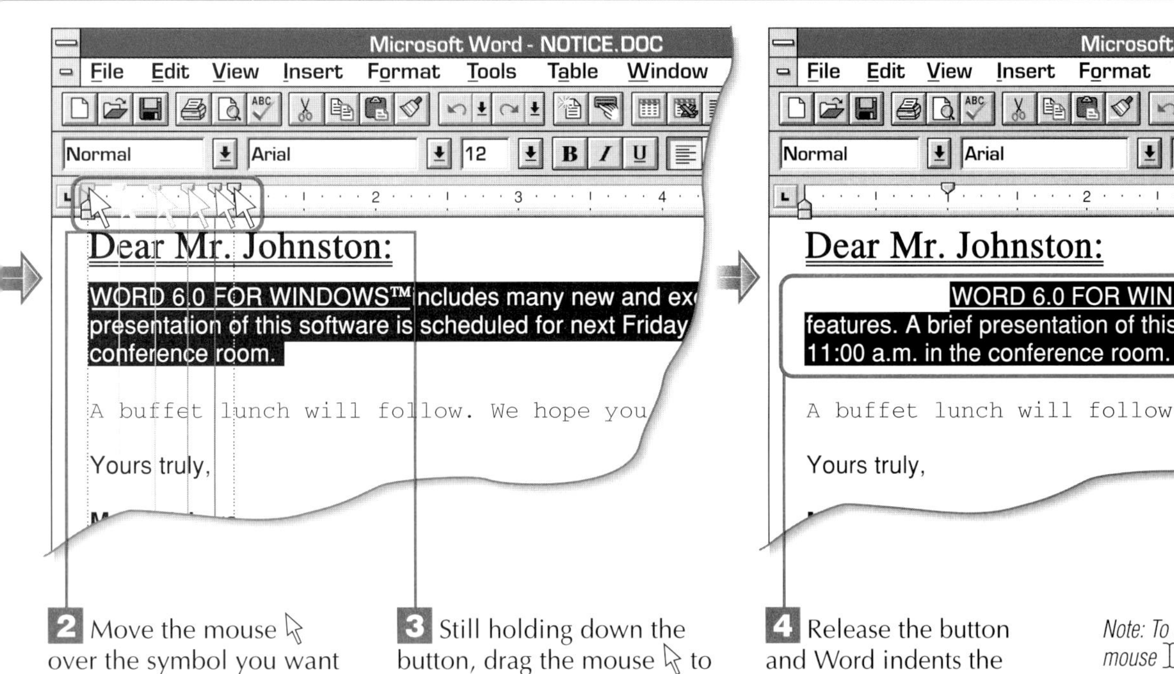
Microsoft Word - NOTICE.DOC
File Edit View Insert Format Tools Table Window
Normal
Arial
12
Dear Mr. Johnston:
WORD 6.0 FOR WINDOWS™ includes many new and ex
presentation of this software is scheduled for next Friday
conference room.
A buffet lunch will follow. We hope you
Yours truly,

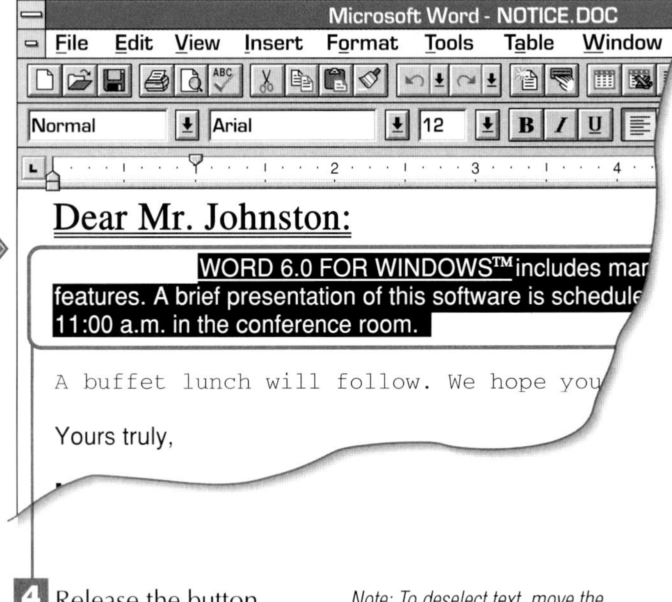
Microsoft Word - NOTICE.DOC
File Edit View Insert Format Tools Table Window
Normal
Arial
12
Dear Mr. Johnston:
WORD 6.0 FOR WINDOWS™ includes mar
features. A brief presentation of this software is schedule
11:00 a.m. in the conference room.
A buffet lunch will follow. We hope you
Yours truly,

2 Move the mouse over the symbol you want to move (example: ▽) and then press and hold down the left button.

3 Still holding down the button, drag the mouse to where you want to position the symbol.

4 Release the button and Word indents the paragraph(s) you selected.

Note: To deselect text, move the mouse outside the selected area and then press the left button.

CREATE NUMBERED AND BULLETED LISTS

You can separate items in a list by beginning each item with a bullet or number.

◆ **Numbers** are useful for items in a specific order, such as a recipe.

◆ **Bullets** are useful for items in no particular order, such as a list of goals.

CREATE NUMBERED AND BULLETED LISTS

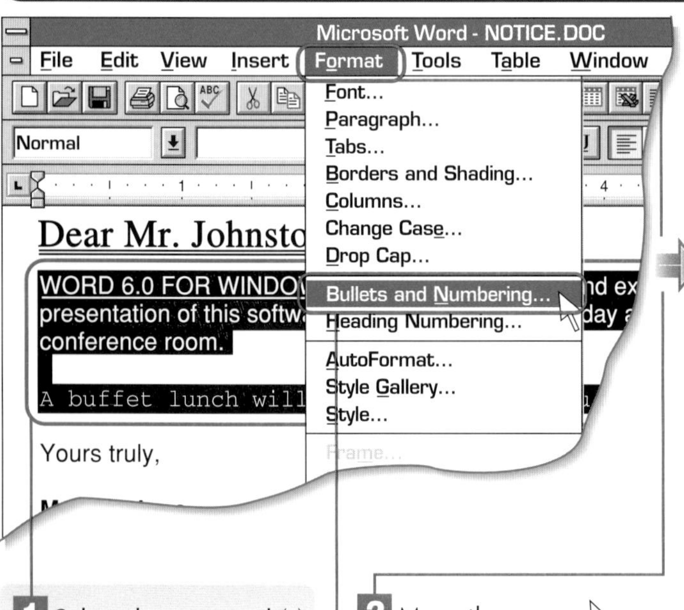

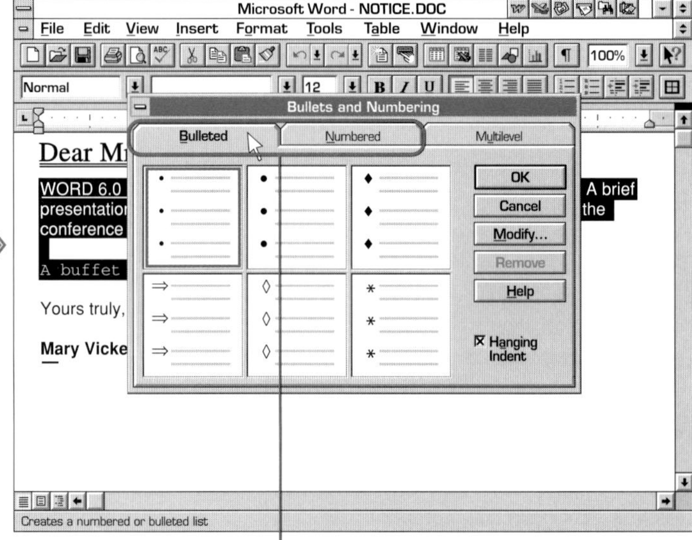

1 Select the paragraph(s) you want to display bullets or numbers.

Note: To select text, refer to page 24.

2 Move the mouse over **Format** and then press the left button.

3 Move the mouse over **Bullets and Numbering** and then press the left button.

◆ The **Bullets and Numbering** dialog box appears.

4 To create a bulleted list, move the mouse over the **Bulleted** tab and then press the left button.

◆ To create a numbered list, move the mouse over the **Numbered** tab and then press the left button.

- Change Line Spacing
- Change Paragraph Alignment
- Display or Hide the Ruler
- Change Tab Settings
- Indent Paragraphs
- **Create Numbered and Bulleted Lists**

To quickly create a bulleted or numbered list:

1 Select the paragraph(s) you want to display bullets or numbers.

2 To create a bulleted list, move the mouse over ☰ and then press the left button.

◆ To create a numbered list, move the mouse over ☰ and then press the left button.

To remove bullets or numbers:

1 Select the paragraph(s) displaying the bullets or numbers you want to remove.

2 To remove bullets, move the mouse over ☰ and then press the left button.

◆ To remove numbers, move the mouse over ☰ and then press the left button.

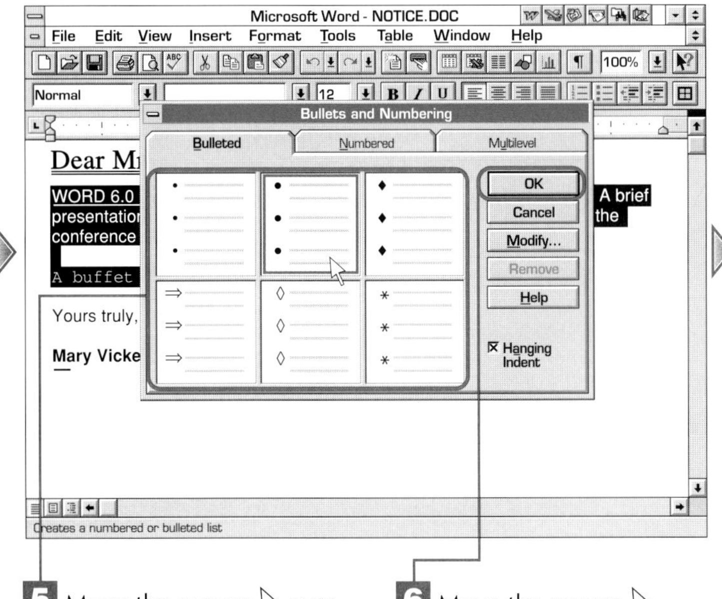

5 Move the mouse over the style you want to use and then press the left button.

6 Move the mouse over **OK** and then press the left button.

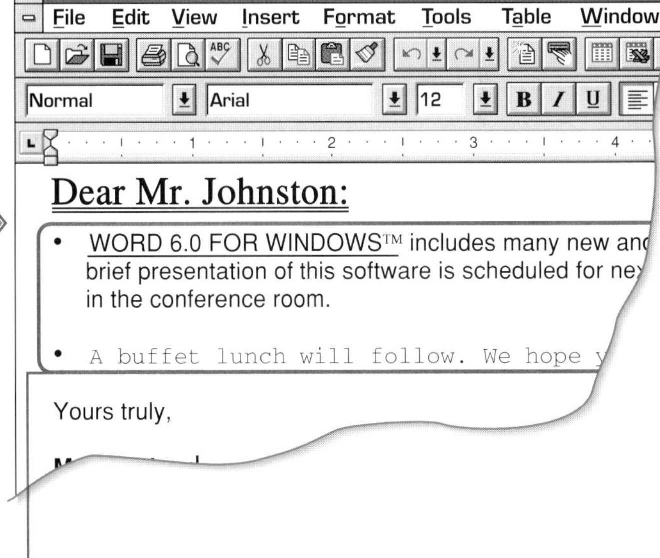

◆ The bullets or numbers appear in your document.

Note: To deselect text, move the mouse outside the selected area and then press the left button.

INSERT A PAGE BREAK

If you want to start a new page at a specific place in your document, you can insert a page break. A page break defines where one page ends and another begins.
A page break you inserted.
When you fill an entire page with text, Word automatically starts a new one by inserting a page break.
A page break Word inserted.

INSERT A PAGE BREAK

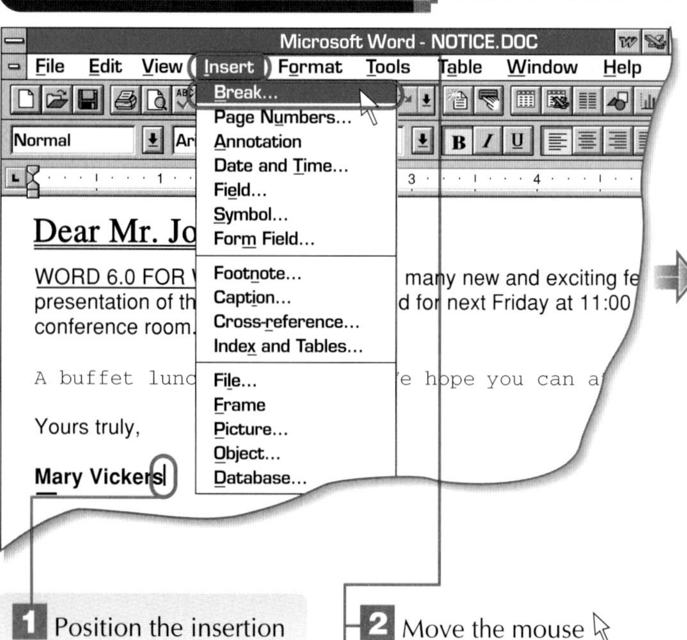

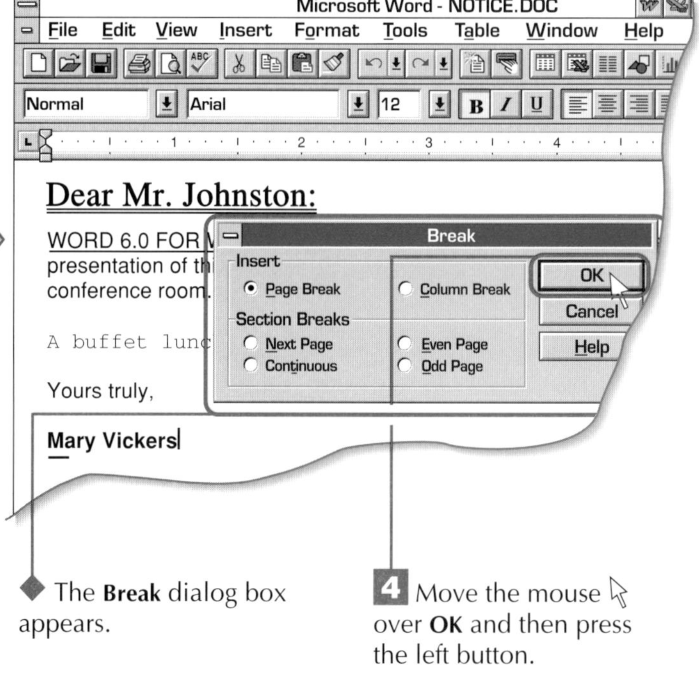

1 Position the insertion point where you want to start a new page.

2 Move the mouse over **Insert** and then press the left button.

3 Move the mouse over **Break** and then press the left button.

◆ The **Break** dialog box appears.

4 Move the mouse over **OK** and then press the left button.

- **Insert a Page Break**
- Create a New Section
- Change Margins
- Add Headers or Footers
- Add Footnotes
- Add Page Numbers
- Center a Page

To quickly insert a page break:

1 _Position the insertion point where you want to start a new page._

2 _Press Ctrl + Enter._

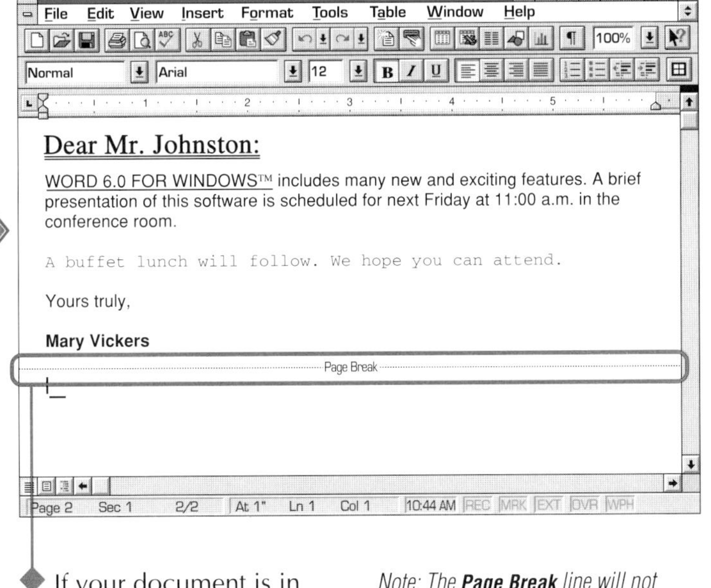

◆ If your document is in the Normal view, a dotted line with the words **Page Break** appears across your screen. This line defines where one page ends and another begins.

Note: The **Page Break** line will not appear when you print your document.

DELETE A PAGE BREAK

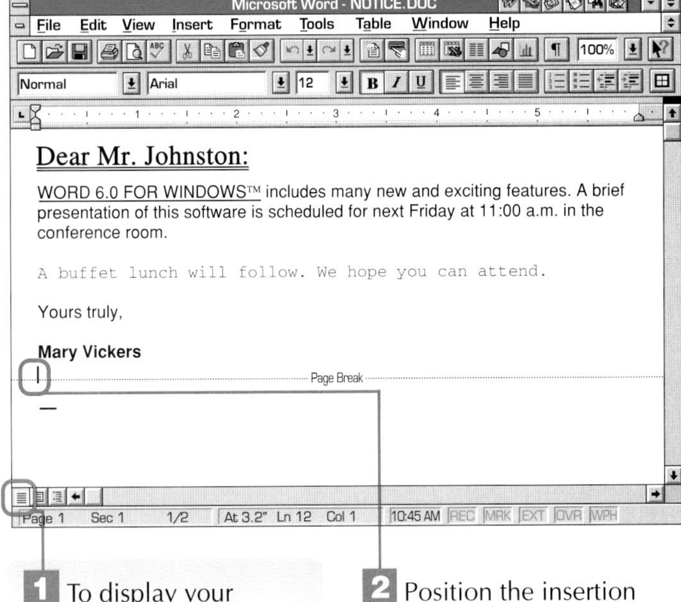

1 To display your document in the Normal view, move the mouse over ▤ and then press the left button.

2 Position the insertion point on the **Page Break** line and then press Delete.

CREATE A NEW SECTION

If you want to change the page formatting of a part of your document, you must divide the document into separate sections. Otherwise, the changes will affect your entire document.

CREATE A NEW SECTION

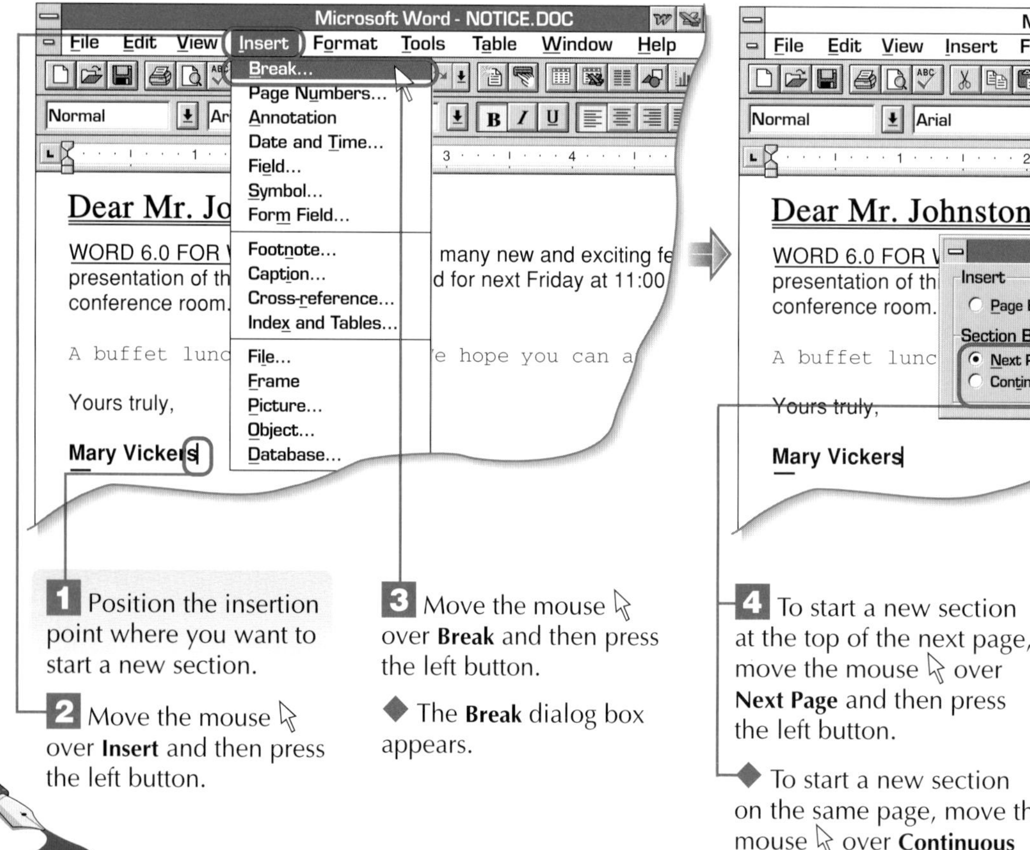

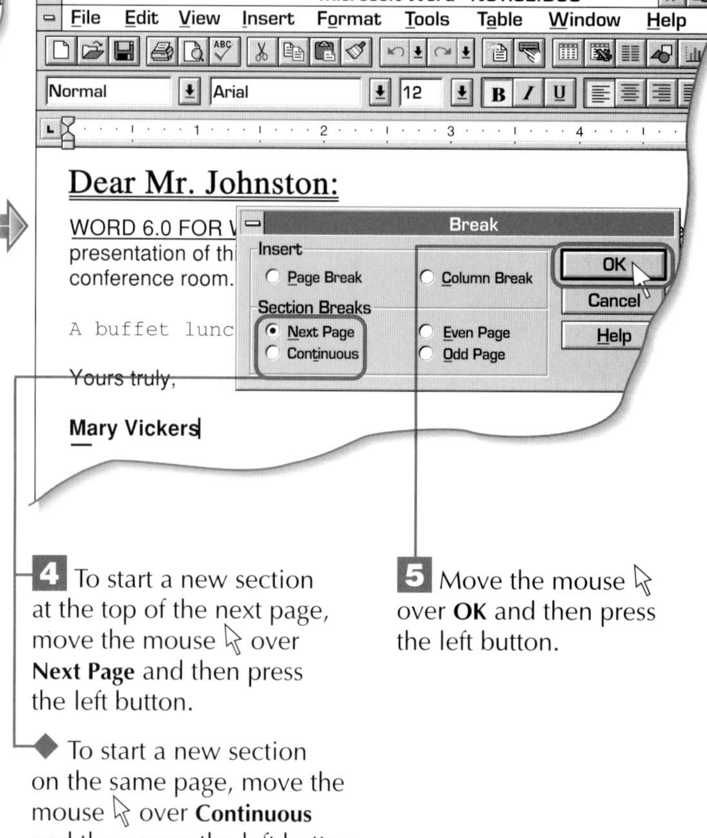

1 Position the insertion point where you want to start a new section.

2 Move the mouse over **Insert** and then press the left button.

3 Move the mouse over **Break** and then press the left button.

◆ The **Break** dialog box appears.

4 To start a new section at the top of the next page, move the mouse over **Next Page** and then press the left button.

◆ To start a new section on the same page, move the mouse over **Continuous** and then press the left button.

5 Move the mouse over **OK** and then press the left button.

- Insert a Page Break
- **Create a New Section**
- Change Margins
- Add Headers or Footers
- Add Footnotes
- Add Page Numbers
- Center a Page

When you delete a section break, the text above the break assumes the formatting of the following section.

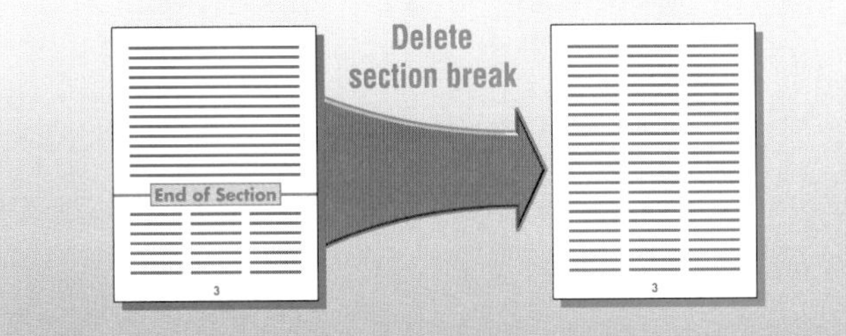

DELETE A SECTION BREAK

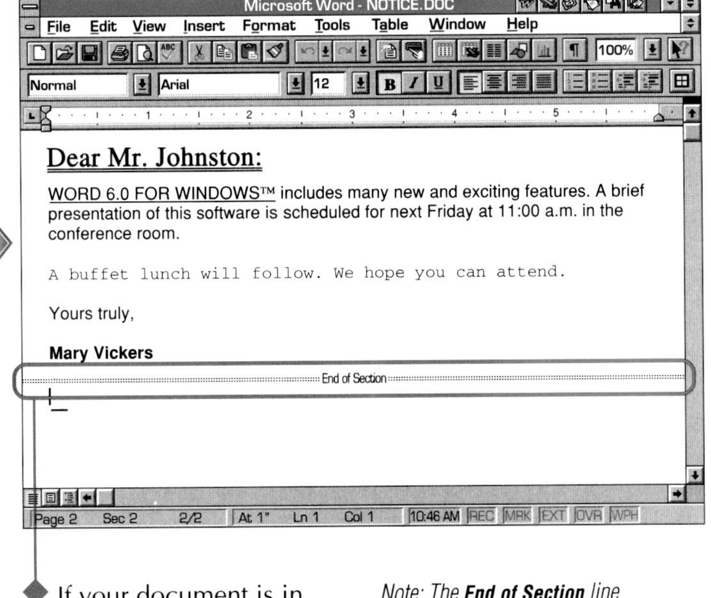

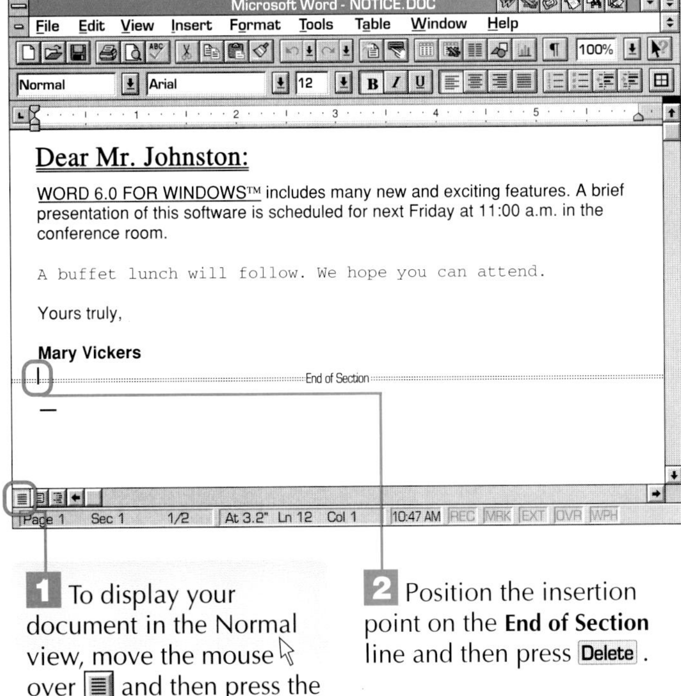

◆ If your document is in the Normal view, a dotted line with the words **End of Section** appears across your screen. This line defines where one section ends and another begins.

*Note: The **End of Section** line will not appear when you print your document.*

1 To display your document in the Normal view, move the mouse over ▤ and then press the left button.

2 Position the insertion point on the **End of Section** line and then press **Delete**.

CHANGE MARGINS

A margin is the amount of space between text and an edge of your paper.
Top
Left
Right
Bottom

◆ When you create a document, the top and bottom margins are set at 1 inch. You can change these settings to accommodate letterhead or other specialty paper.

◆ The left and right margins are set at 1.25 inches. You can change these settings to increase or decrease the amount of text on a page.

CHANGE MARGINS

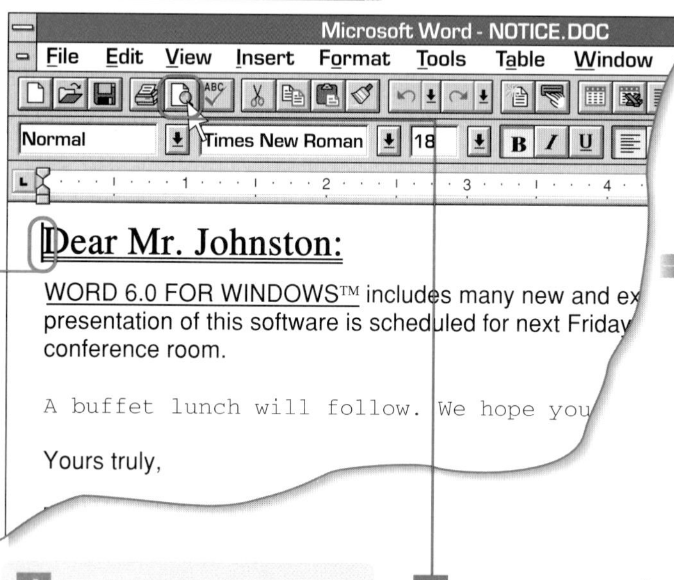

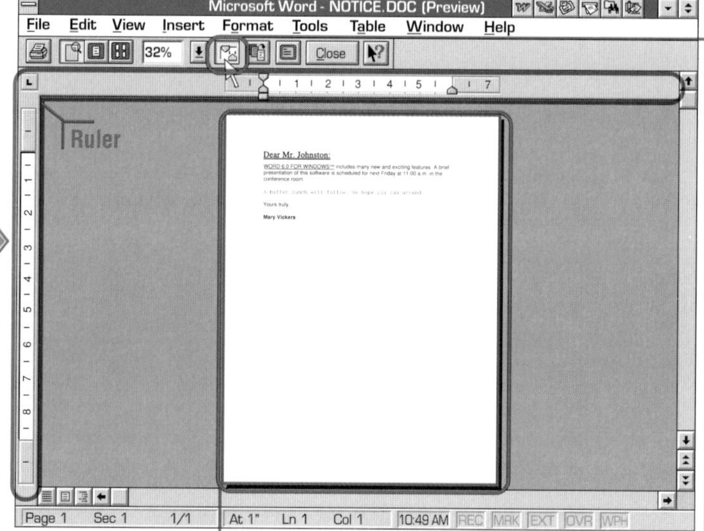

1 To change the margins for your entire document, position the insertion point anywhere in the document.

◆ To change the margins for a part of your document, position the insertion point in the section you want to change.

Note: For information on sections, refer to page 108.

2 Move the mouse over and then press the left button.

◆ The page you were working on appears in the Print Preview window.

Note: For more information on using Print Preview, refer to pages 78 to 81.

3 If the ruler is not displayed, move the mouse over and then press the left button.

If you want to change the left and right margins for a part of your document, it is much easier to change the indentation.

Note: To indent paragraphs, refer to page 102.

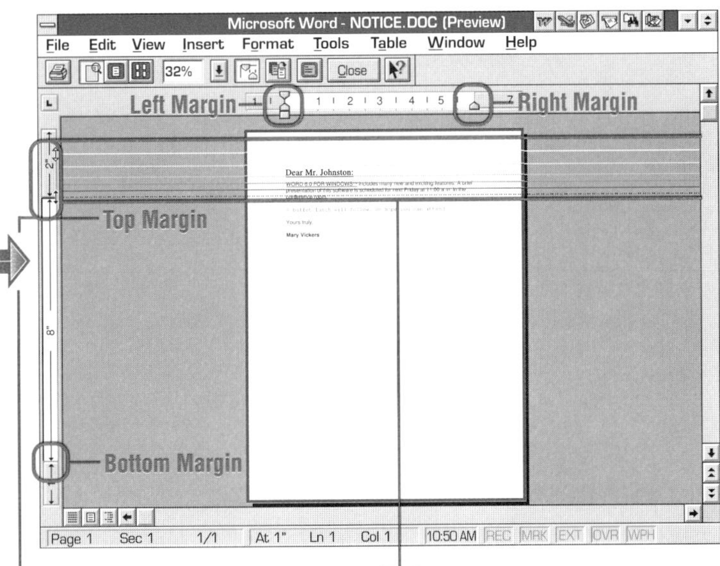

4 Move the mouse ↖ over the margin boundary you want to move and ↖ changes to ↕ or ↔.

5 To display the page measurements as you drag the margin boundary, press and hold down Alt.

6 Still holding down Alt, press and hold down the left button as you drag the margin boundary to a new location. A dotted line shows the location of the new margin.

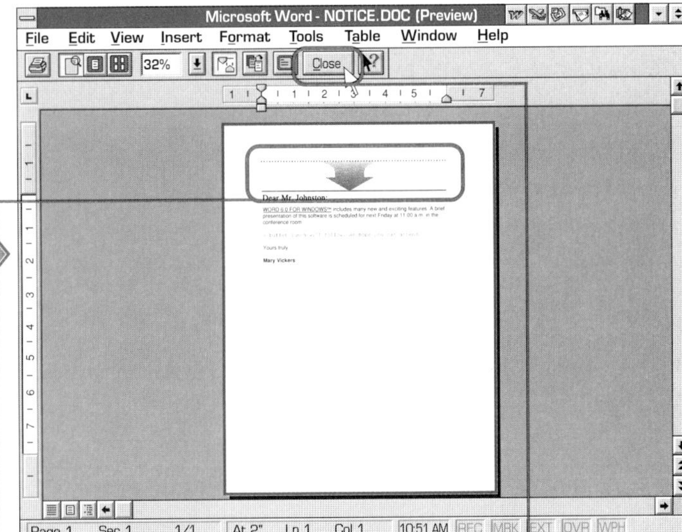

7 Release the button and then Alt to display the margin changes.

8 Repeat steps **4** to **7** for each margin you want to change.

9 To close Print Preview and return to your document, move the mouse ↖ over **Close** and then press the left button.

Note: The top and bottom margins are not visible on your screen when in the Normal view.

ADD HEADERS OR FOOTERS

You can add a header or footer to your document to display such information as the date or your company name.

ABC Corporation

◆ **Header**
A header appears at the top of a page.

October 10

◆ **Footer**
A footer appears at the bottom of a page.

ADD HEADERS OR FOOTERS

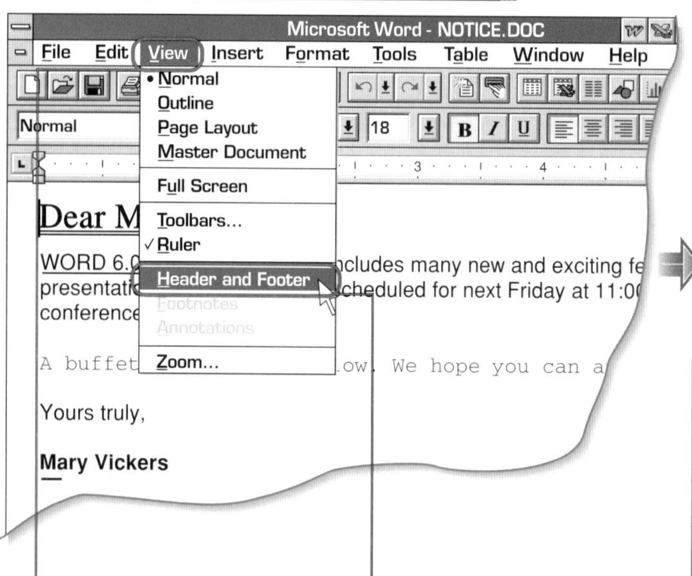

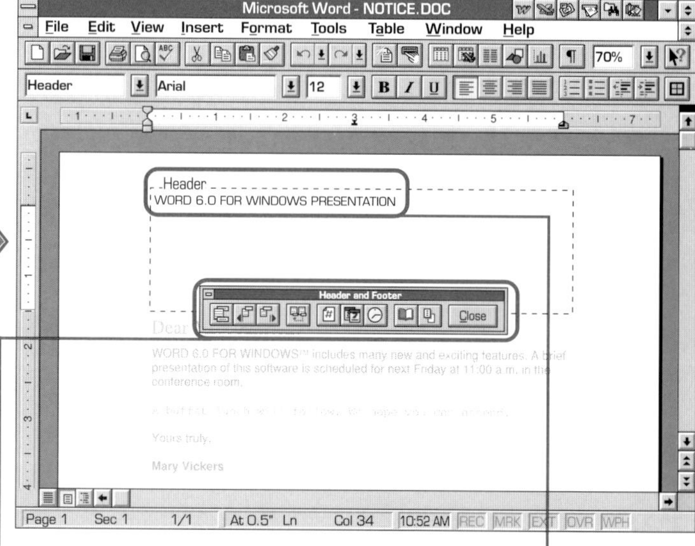

1 To add a header or footer to every page in your document, move the mouse ↖ over **View** and then press the left button.

2 Move the mouse ↖ over **Header and Footer** and then press the left button.

◆ The text in your document appears dimmed.

◆ The **Header and Footer** toolbar appears.

3 To create a header, type the header text. You can format the header text as you would any text in your document.

Headers and footers will not appear on your screen if you are in the Normal view.

1 To view headers or footers, move the mouse over and then press the left button.

Note: For more information on Print Preview, refer to pages 78 to 81.

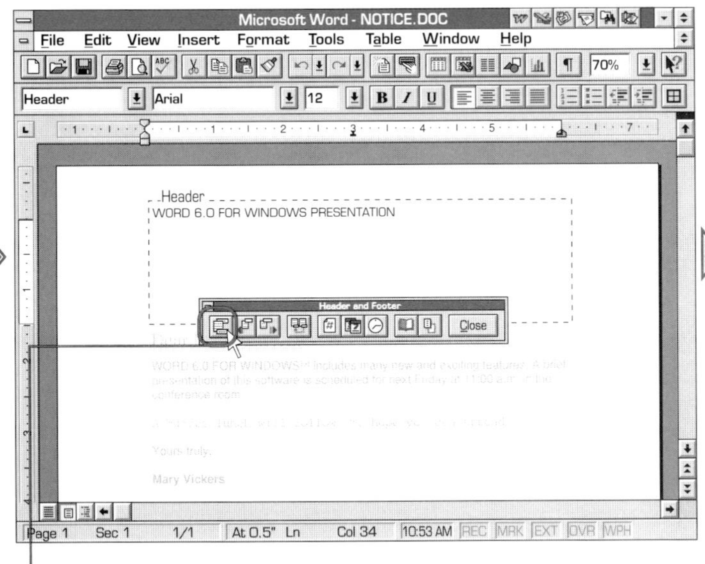

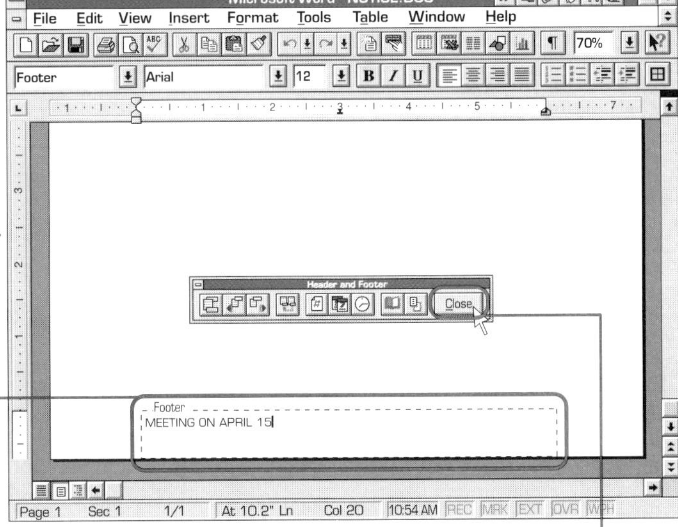

4 To create a footer, move the mouse over and then press the left button.

Note: You can return to the header area at any time by repeating step 4.

◆ The **Footer** area appears.

5 Type the footer text. You can format the footer text as you would any text in your document.

6 To return to your document, move the mouse over **Close** and then press the left button.

ADD FOOTNOTES

A footnote appears at the bottom of a page to provide additional information about text in your document.

H. Smith, Aeronautical Refrigeration Repair (California: Quest Publishing, 1989) 10.
R. Anderson, Volatile Cold Gases (Alaska: Inert Publishing, 1992) 31.

Word automatically numbers a footnote and places the footnote on the same page as the text it refers to.

ADD FOOTNOTES

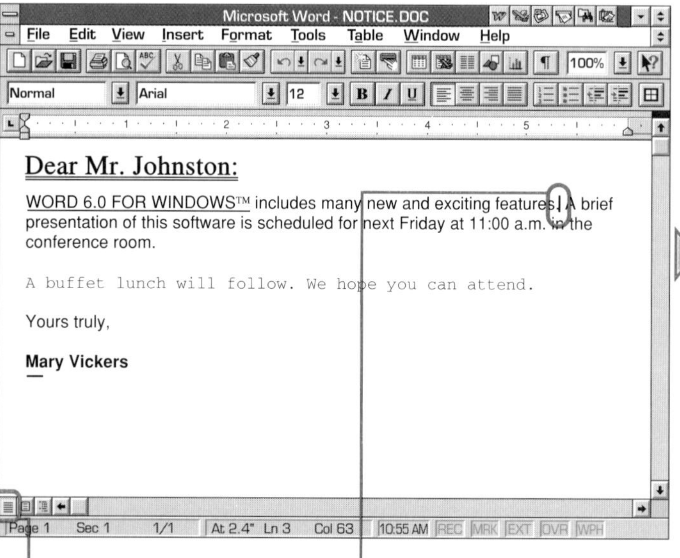

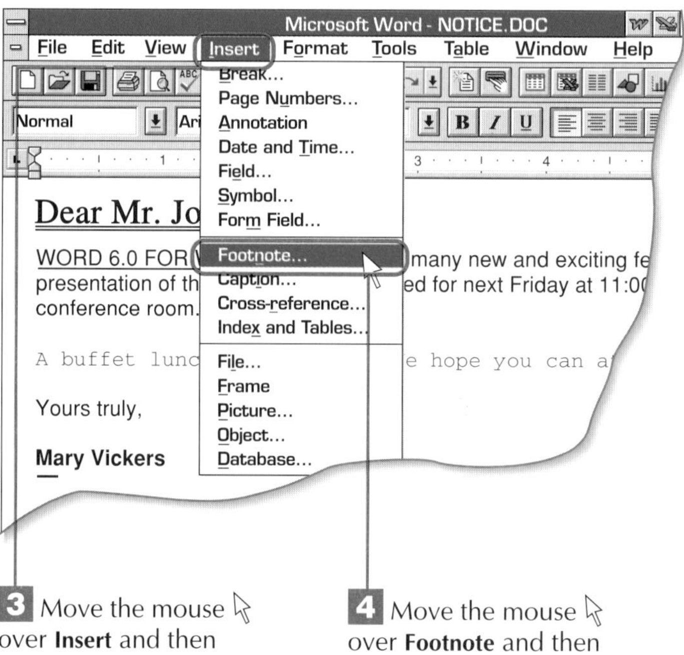

1 To display your document in the Normal view, move the mouse over ▤ and then press the left button.

2 Position the insertion point where you want the number for the footnote to appear in your document.

3 Move the mouse over **Insert** and then press the left button.

4 Move the mouse over **Footnote** and then press the left button.

EDIT A FOOTNOTE

1 To edit a footnote, move the mouse I over the footnote number in your document and then quickly press the left button twice. The footnote appears.

2 Edit the footnote as you would any text in your document.

3 When you finish editing the footnote, move the mouse over **Close** and then press the left button.

DELETE A FOOTNOTE

1 To delete a footnote, select the footnote number in your document and then press Delete.

Note: To select text, refer to page 24.

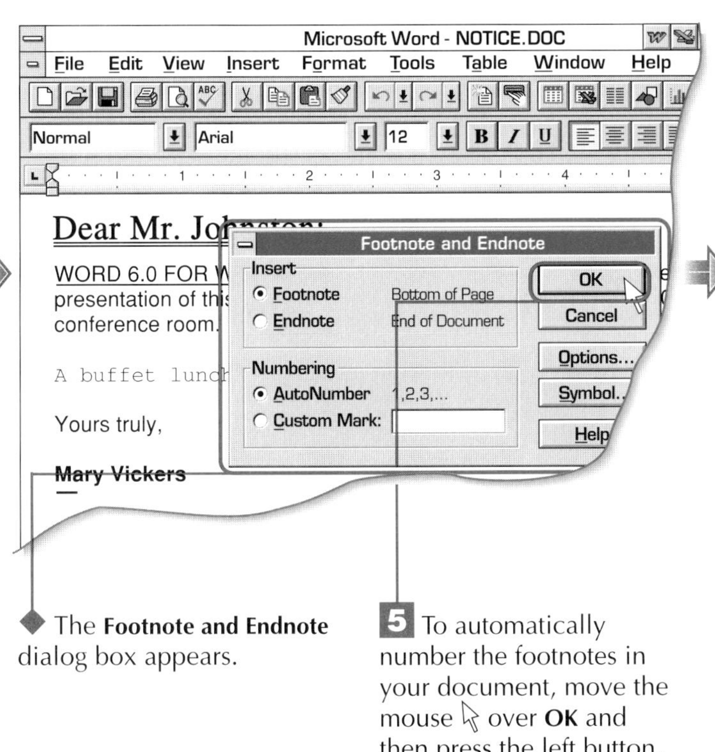

◆ The **Footnote and Endnote** dialog box appears.

5 To automatically number the footnotes in your document, move the mouse over **OK** and then press the left button.

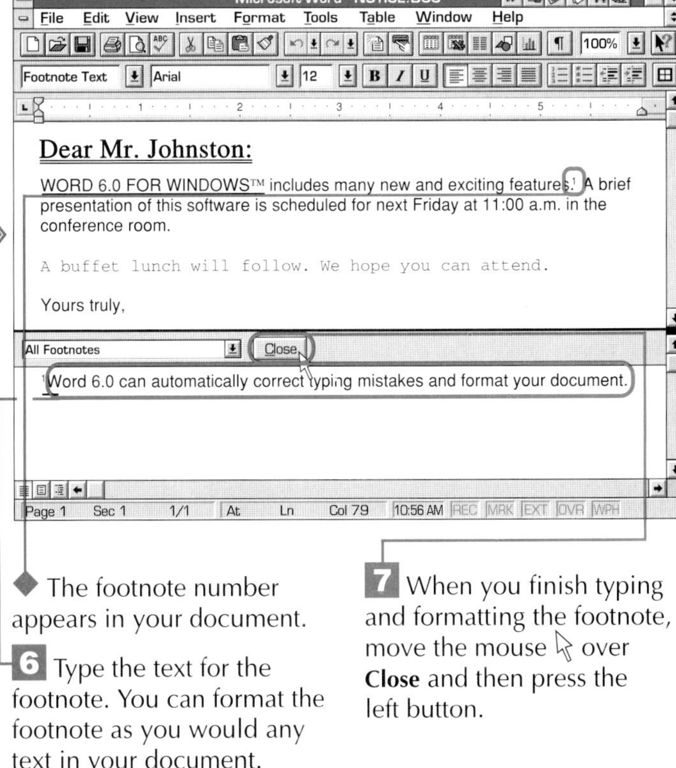

◆ The footnote number appears in your document.

6 Type the text for the footnote. You can format the footnote as you would any text in your document.

7 When you finish typing and formatting the footnote, move the mouse over **Close** and then press the left button.

ADD PAGE NUMBERS

You can have Word number the pages in your document.
FORMAT
42

ADD PAGE NUMBERS

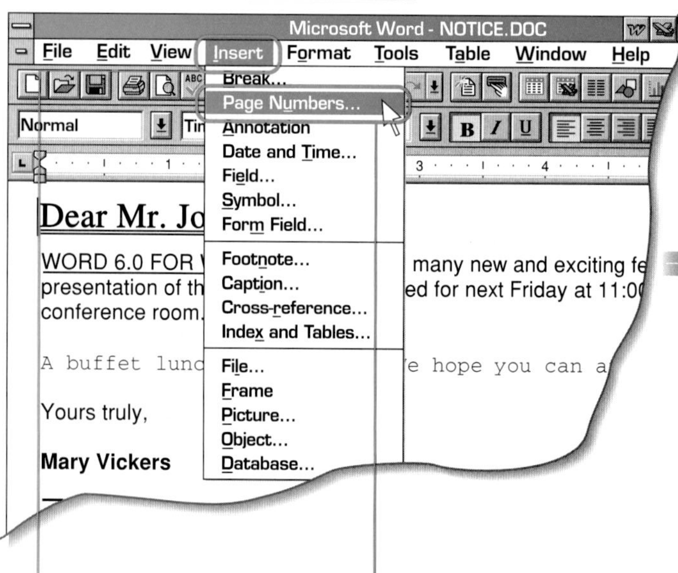

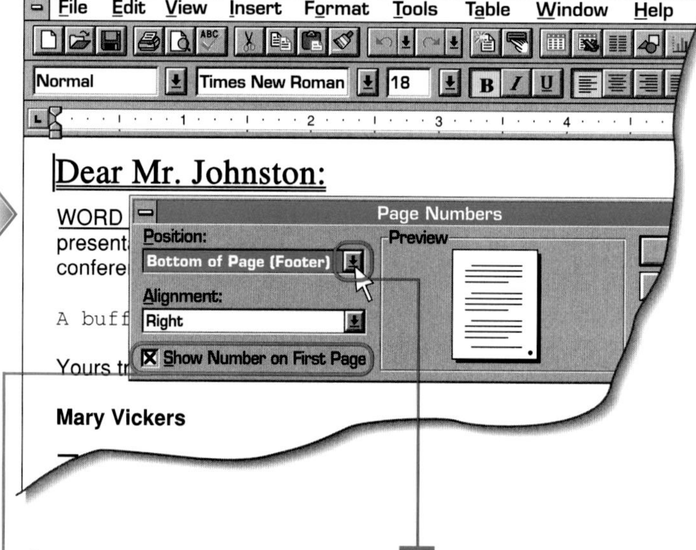

1 Move the mouse over **Insert** and then press the left button.

2 Move the mouse over **Page Numbers** and then press the left button.

◆ The **Page Numbers** dialog box appears.

◆ To hide the page number on the first page of your document, move the mouse over **Show Number on First Page** and then press the left button (☒ changes to ☐).

3 To select a position for the page numbers, move the mouse over ⬇ in the **Position:** box and then press the left button.

- Insert a Page Break
- Create a New Section
- Change Margins
- Add Headers or Footers
- Add Footnotes
- **Add Page Numbers**
- Center a Page

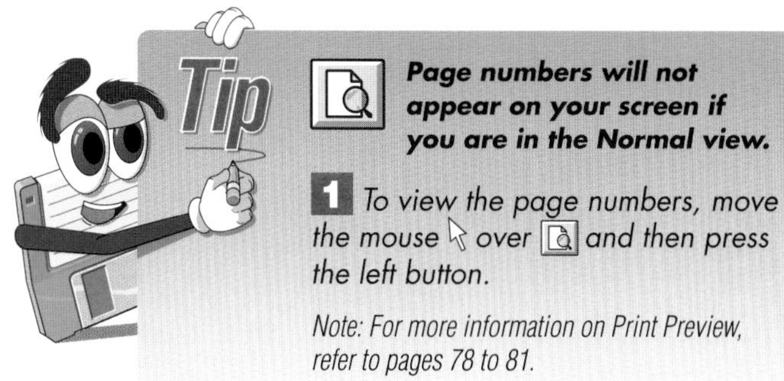

Page numbers will not appear on your screen if you are in the Normal view.

1 *To view the page numbers, move the mouse over and then press the left button.*

Note: For more information on Print Preview, refer to pages 78 to 81.

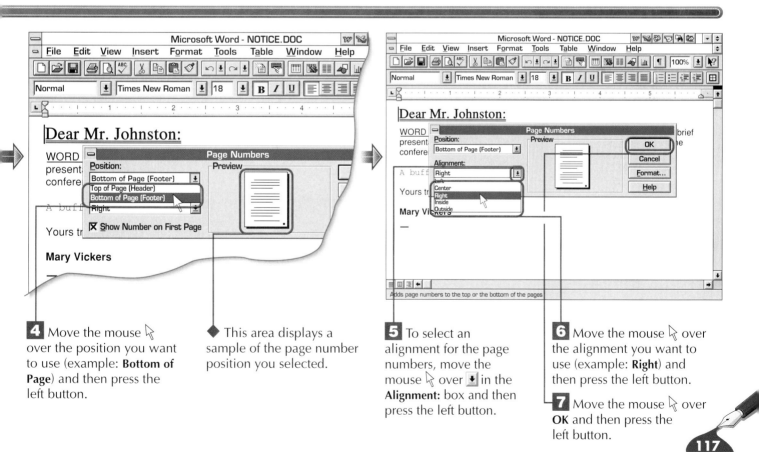

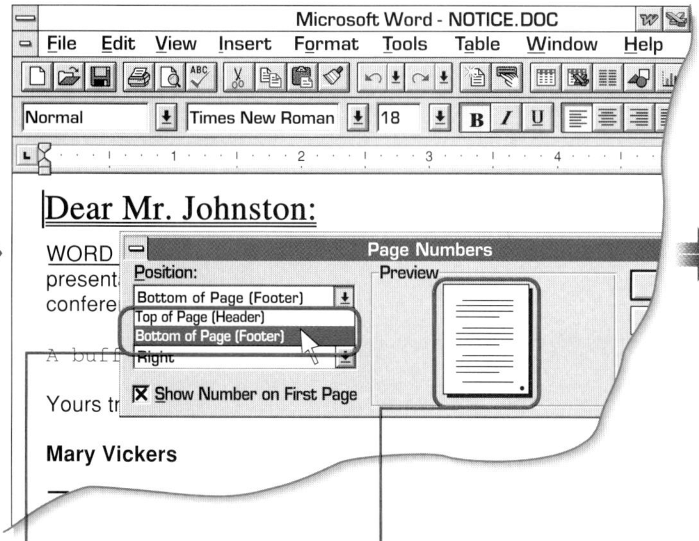

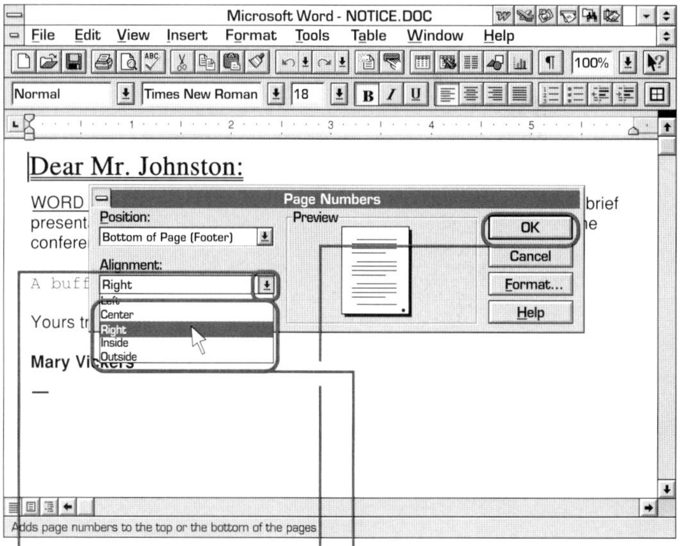

4 Move the mouse over the position you want to use (example: **Bottom of Page**) and then press the left button.

◆ This area displays a sample of the page number position you selected.

5 To select an alignment for the page numbers, move the mouse over in the **Alignment:** box and then press the left button.

6 Move the mouse over the alignment you want to use (example: **Right**) and then press the left button.

7 Move the mouse over **OK** and then press the left button.

CENTER A PAGE

You can vertically center text on a page. This is useful when creating title pages or short memos.
FORMAT
Dear Mr. Johnston:
Yours truly,
Mary Vickers

CENTER A PAGE

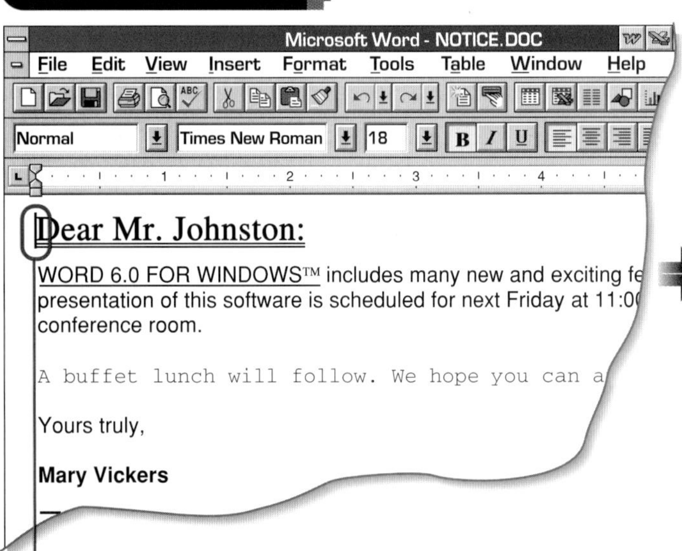

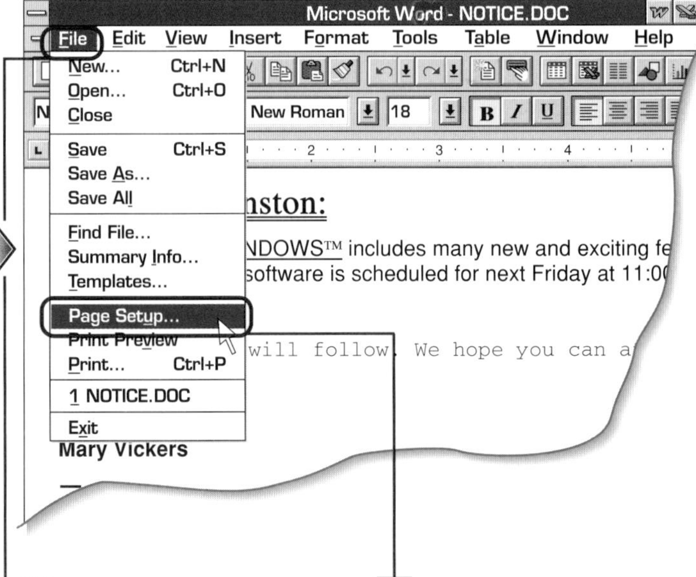

1 To center the text on all pages in your document, position the insertion point anywhere in the document.

◆ To center the text for a part of your document, position the insertion point in the section you want to change.

Note: For information on sections, refer to page 108.

2 Move the mouse over **File** and then press the left button.

3 Move the mouse over **Page Setup** and then press the left button.

- Insert a Page Break
- Create a New Section
- Change Margins
- Add Headers or Footers
- Add Footnotes
- Add Page Numbers
- **Center a Page**

Text will not appear centered on your screen if you are in the Normal view.

1 *To view the text centered on a page, move the mouse over and then press the left button.*

Note: For more information on Print Preview, refer to pages 78 to 81.

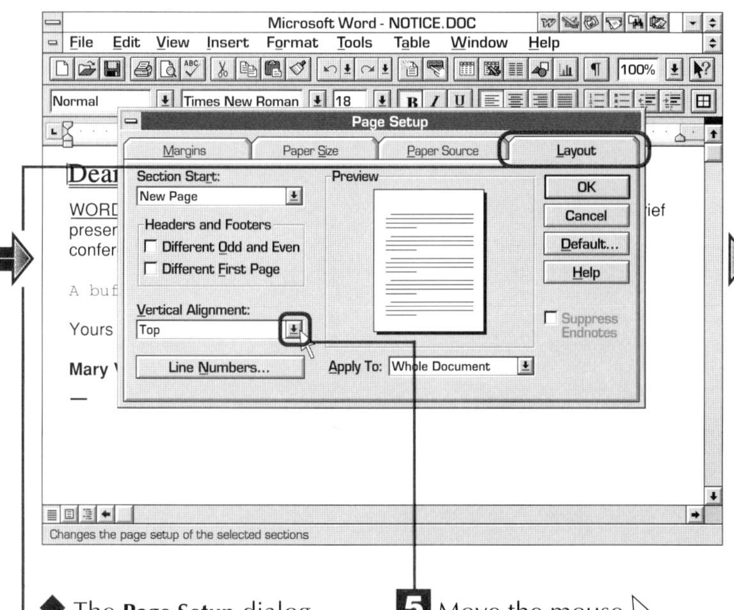

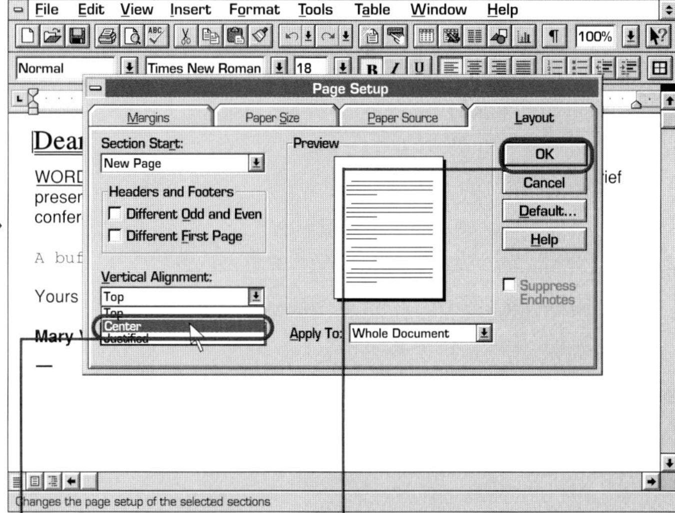

◆ The **Page Setup** dialog box appears.

4 Move the mouse over the **Layout** tab and then press the left button.

5 Move the mouse over in the **Vertical Alignment:** box and then press the left button.

6 Move the mouse over **Center** and then press the left button.

7 Move the mouse over **OK** and then press the left button.

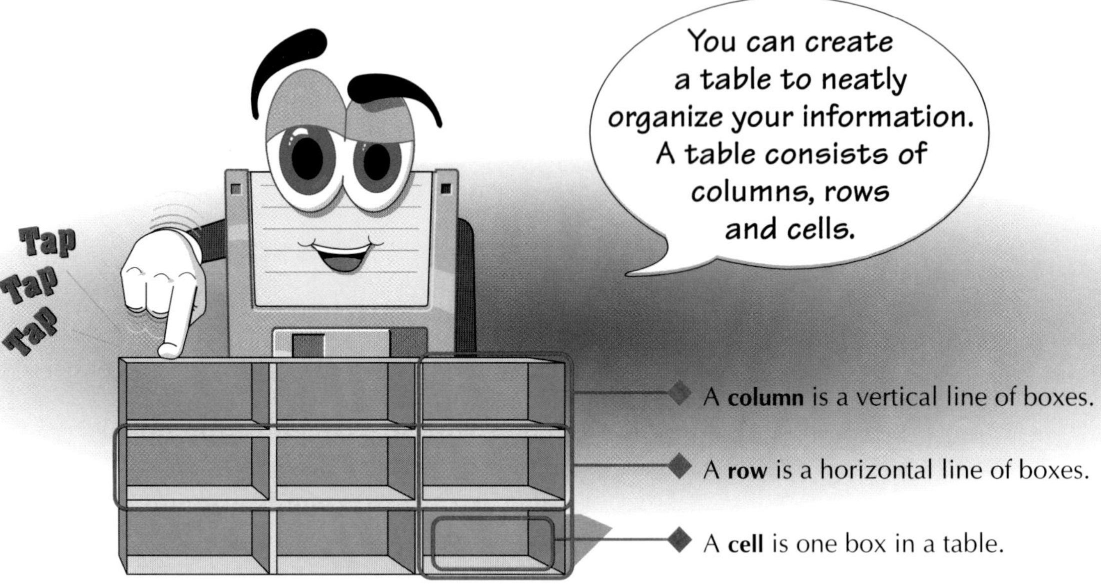

You can create a table to neatly organize your information. A table consists of columns, rows and cells.
Tap
Tap
Tap
A **column** is a vertical line of boxes.
A **row** is a horizontal line of boxes.
A **cell** is one box in a table.

CREATE A TABLE

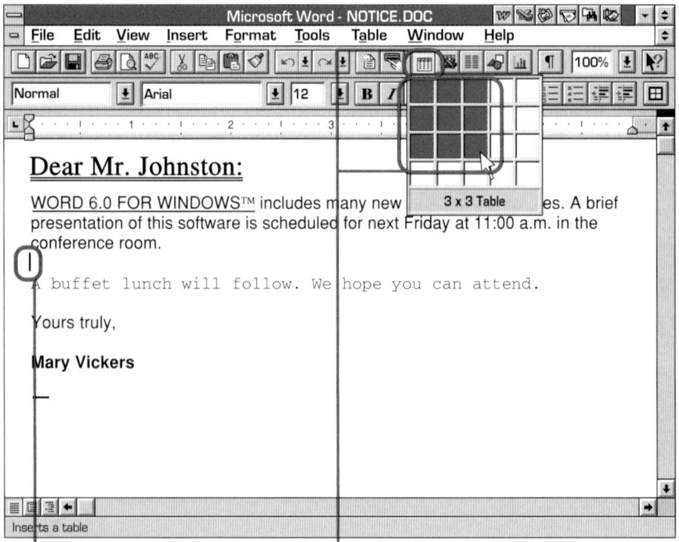

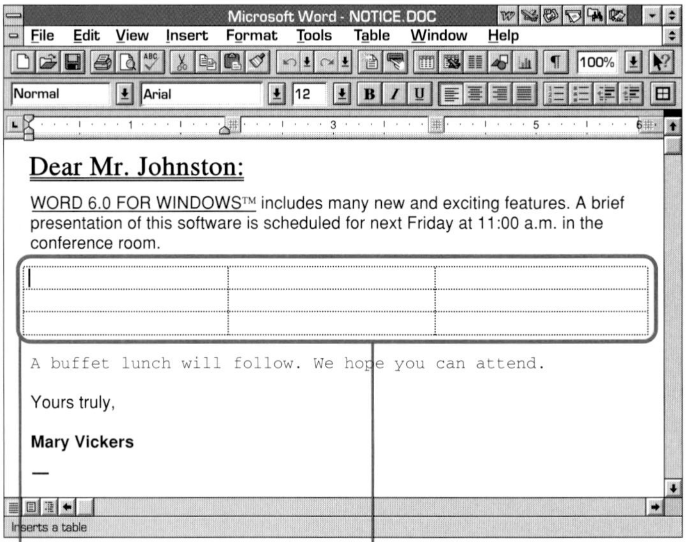

1 Position the insertion point where you want the table to appear in your document.

2 Move the mouse over the table button.

3 Press and hold down the left button as you move the mouse over the number of rows and columns you want in your table (example: **3 x 3**).

4 Release the button and the table appears.

◆ The dotted lines around the cells in the table will not appear when you print your document. To print table lines, you can add borders using the **Table AutoFormat** feature. For more information, refer to page 128.

- **Create a Table**
- **Type Text**
- Add a Row or Column
- Delete a Row or Column
- Change Column Width
- Format a Table
- Merge Cells

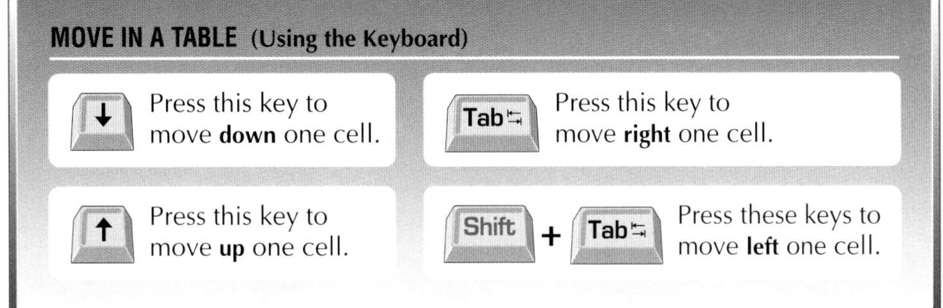

MOVE IN A TABLE (Using the Keyboard)
Press this key to move **down** one cell.
Tab
Press this key to move **right** one cell.
Press this key to move **up** one cell.
Shift + Tab
Press these keys to move **left** one cell.

TYPE TEXT IN A TABLE

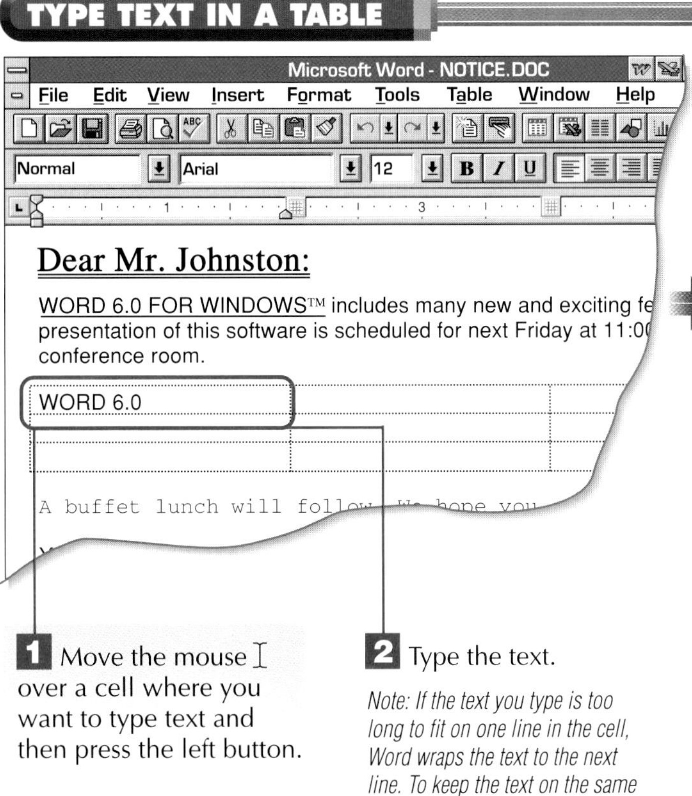

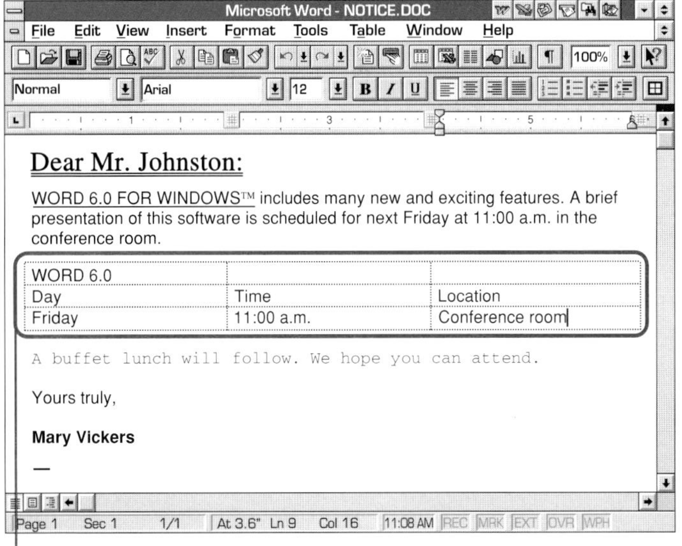

1 Move the mouse I over a cell where you want to type text and then press the left button.

2 Type the text.

Note: If the text you type is too long to fit on one line in the cell, Word wraps the text to the next line. To keep the text on the same line, refer to page 126 to change the column width.

3 Repeat steps **1** and **2** until you have typed all the text.

◆ Pressing **Enter** after typing text in a cell will begin a new line and increase the row height. If you accidentally press **Enter**, immediately press **←Backspace** to cancel the action.

ADD A ROW OR COLUMN

You can add a row or column to your table if you want to insert new information.

Tables

ADD A ROW

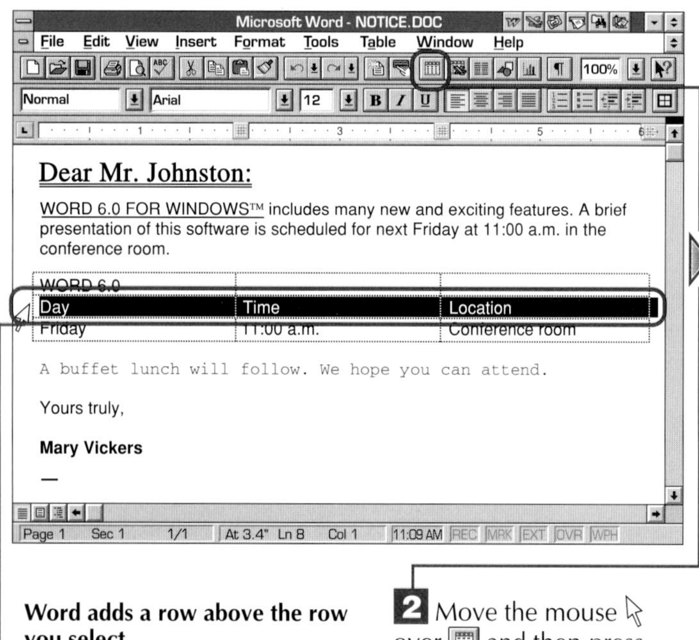

Microsoft Word - NOTICE.DOC
File Edit View Insert Format Tools Table Window Help
Dear Mr. Johnston:
WORD 6.0 FOR WINDOWS™ includes many new and exciting features. A brief presentation of this software is scheduled for next Friday at 11:00 a.m. in the conference room.
WORD 6.0
Day
Time
Location
Friday
11:00 a.m.
Conference room
A buffet lunch will follow. We hope you can attend.
Yours truly,
Mary Vickers

Word adds a row above the row you select.

1 To select a row, move the mouse I to the left edge of the row (I changes to ↖) and then press the left button.

2 Move the mouse ↖ over ▦ and then press the left button.

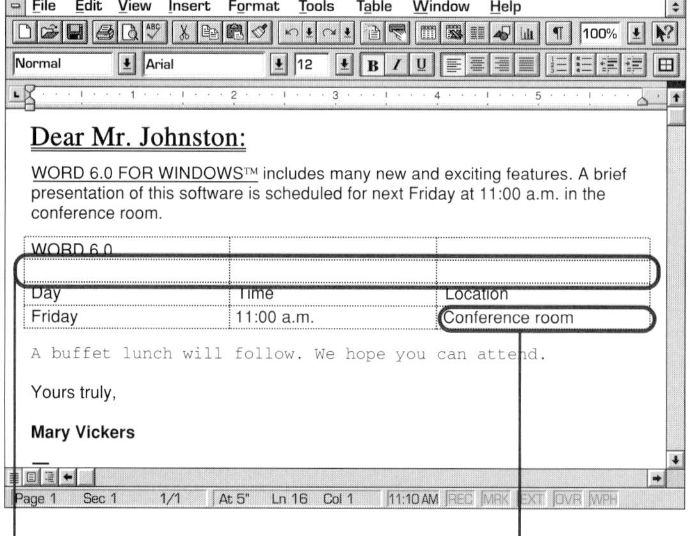

Microsoft Word - NOTICE.DOC
File Edit View Insert Format Tools Table Window Help
Dear Mr. Johnston:
WORD 6.0 FOR WINDOWS™ includes many new and exciting features. A brief presentation of this software is scheduled for next Friday at 11:00 a.m. in the conference room.
WORD 6.0
Day
Time
Location
Friday
11:00 a.m.
Conference room
A buffet lunch will follow. We hope you can attend.
Yours truly,
Mary Vickers

◆ The new row appears.

Note: To deselect a row, move the mouse I outside the table and then press the left button.

To add a row to the bottom of your table:

1 Position the insertion point in the bottom right cell of your table.

2 Press Tab and the new row appears.

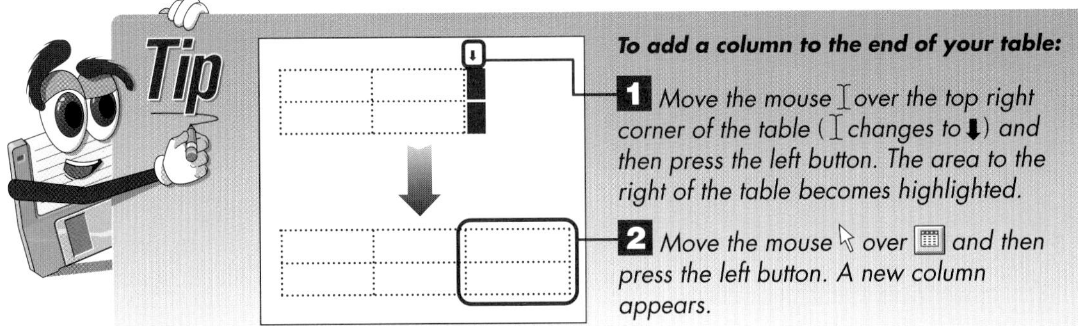

To add a column to the end of your table:

1 *Move the mouse over the top right corner of the table (changes to ⬇) and then press the left button. The area to the right of the table becomes highlighted.*

2 *Move the mouse over and then press the left button. A new column appears.*

ADD A COLUMN

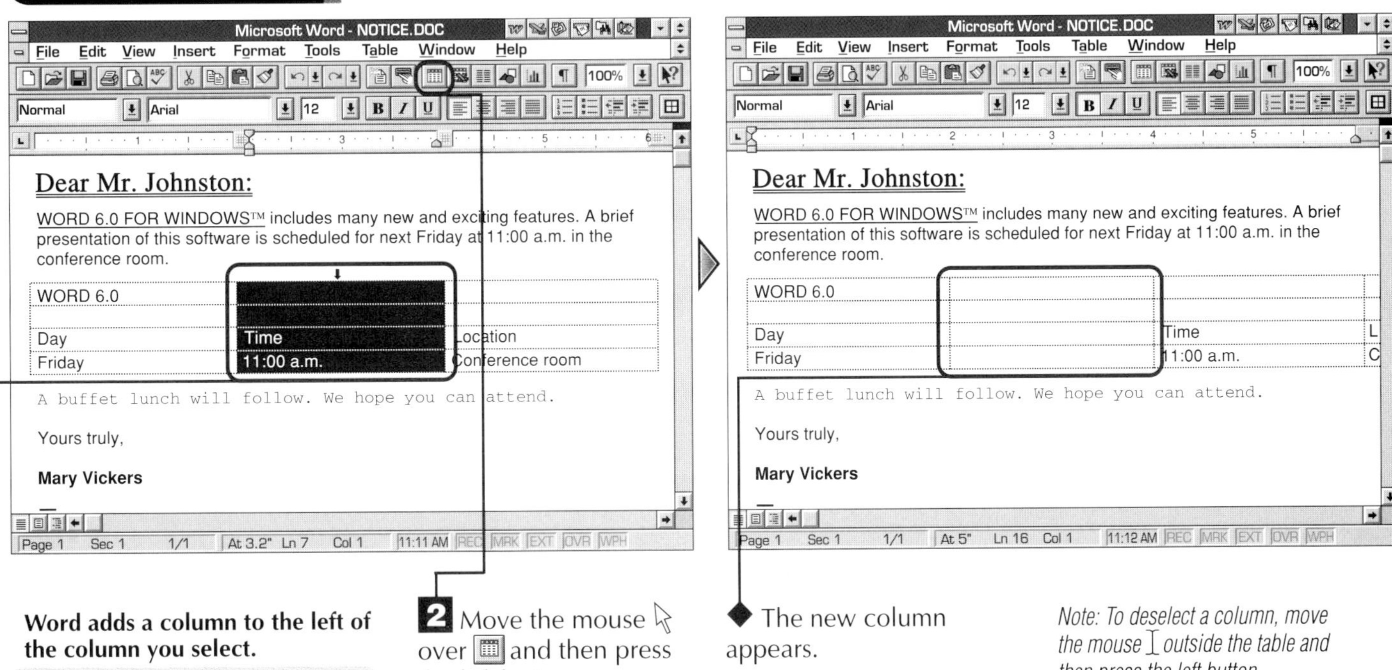

Word adds a column to the left of the column you select.

1 To select a column, move the mouse to the top edge of the column (changes to ⬇) and then press the left button.

2 Move the mouse over and then press the left button.

◆ The new column appears.

Note: To deselect a column, move the mouse outside the table and then press the left button.

DELETE A ROW OR COLUMN

DELETE A ROW

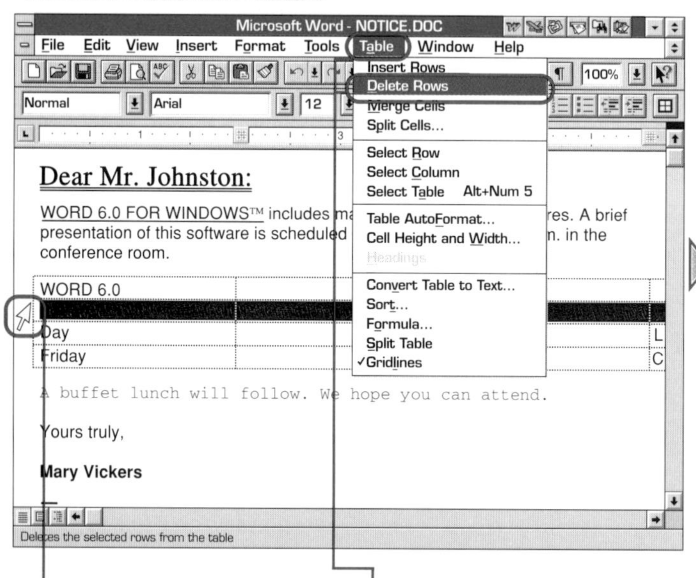

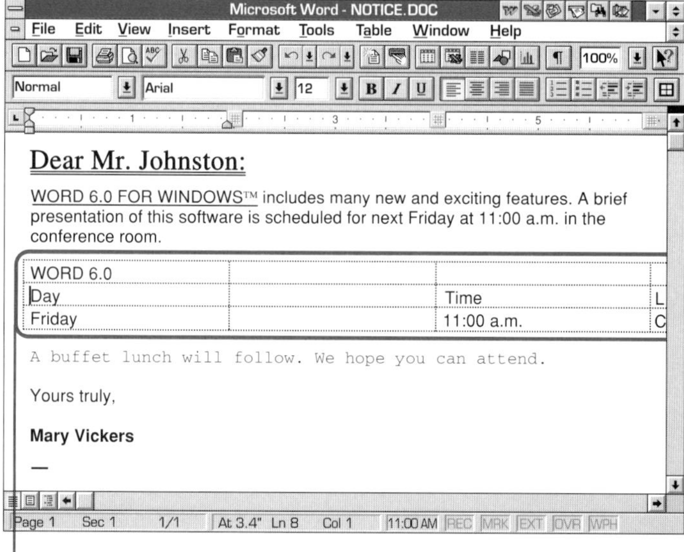

1 To select the row you want to delete, move the mouse I to the left edge of the row (I changes to ↗) and then press the left button.

2 Move the mouse ↖ over **Table** and then press the left button.

3 Move the mouse ↖ over **Delete Rows** and then press the left button.

◆ The row disappears from your screen.

- Create a Table
- Type Text
- Add a Row or Column
- **Delete a Row or Column**
- Change Column Width
- Format a Table
- Merge Cells

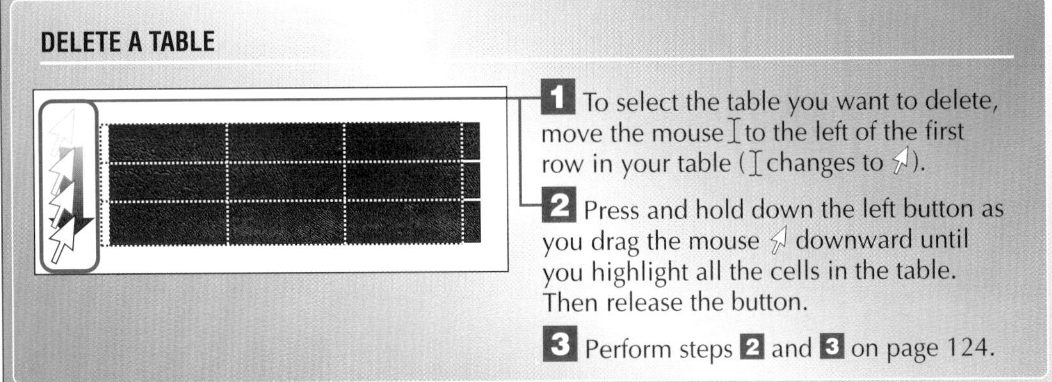

DELETE A TABLE

1 To select the table you want to delete, move the mouse I to the left of the first row in your table (I changes to ↗).

2 Press and hold down the left button as you drag the mouse ↗ downward until you highlight all the cells in the table. Then release the button.

3 Perform steps 2 and 3 on page 124.

DELETE A COLUMN

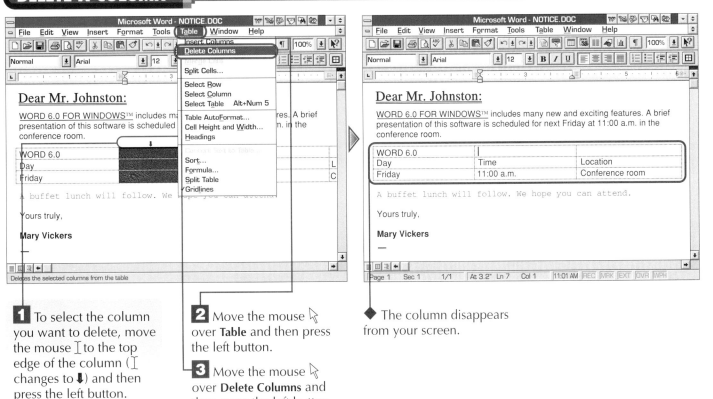

1 To select the column you want to delete, move the mouse I to the top edge of the column (I changes to ⬇) and then press the left button.

2 Move the mouse ↖ over **Table** and then press the left button.

3 Move the mouse ↖ over **Delete Columns** and then press the left button.

◆ The column disappears from your screen.

CHANGE COLUMN WIDTH

CHANGE COLUMN WIDTH

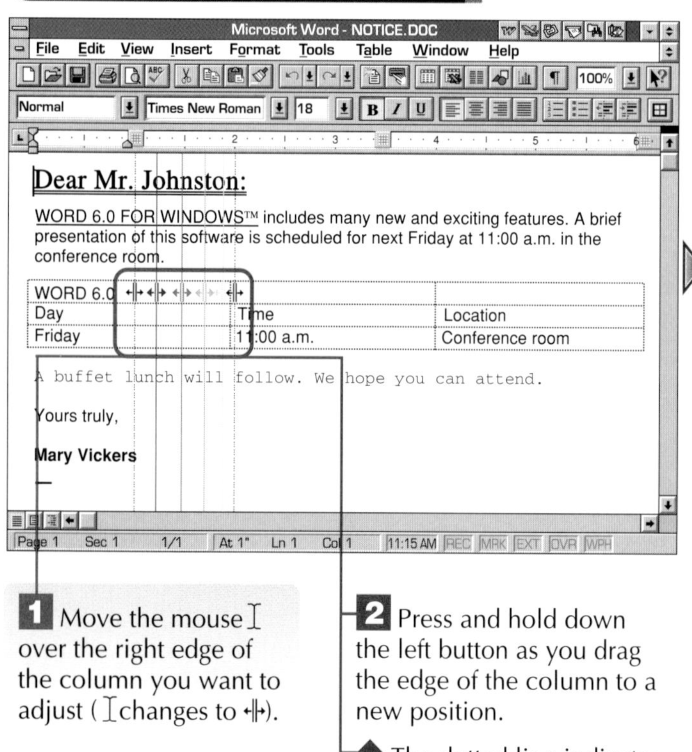

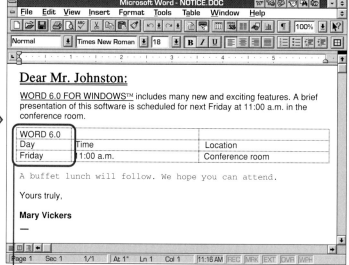

1 Move the mouse I over the right edge of the column you want to adjust (I changes to ⇹).

2 Press and hold down the left button as you drag the edge of the column to a new position.

◆ The dotted line indicates the new position.

3 Release the button and the new column width appears.

Note: The width of the entire table remains the same.

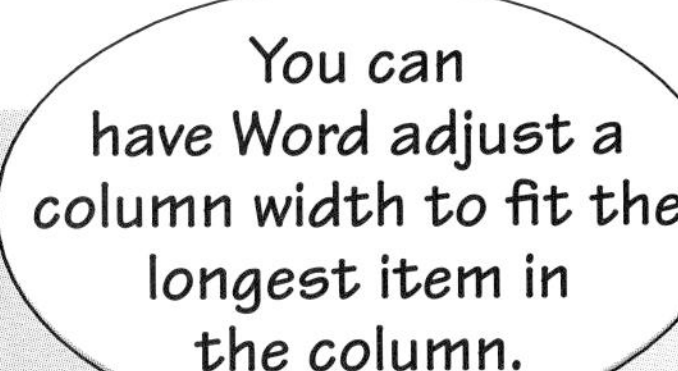

CHANGE COLUMN WIDTH AUTOMATICALLY

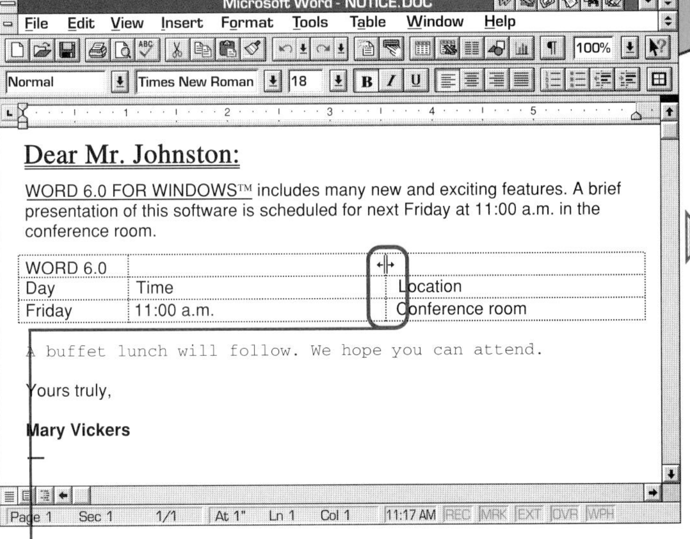

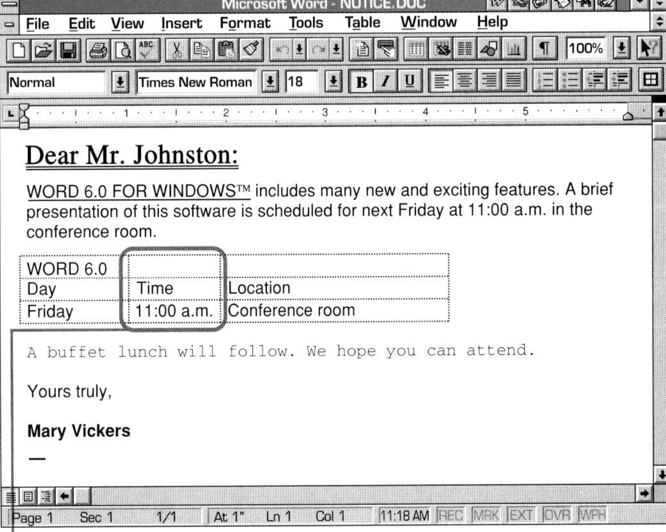

1 Move the mouse I over the right edge of the column you want to adjust (I changes to ⇹).

2 Quickly press the left button twice.

◆ The column width changes to fit the longest item in the column.

Note: The width of the entire table changes.

FORMAT A TABLE

You can use the Table AutoFormat feature to emphasize information and enhance the appearance of your table.

FORMAT A TABLE

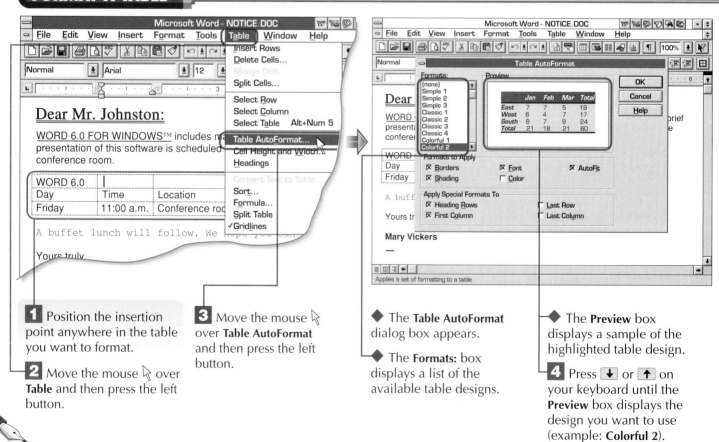

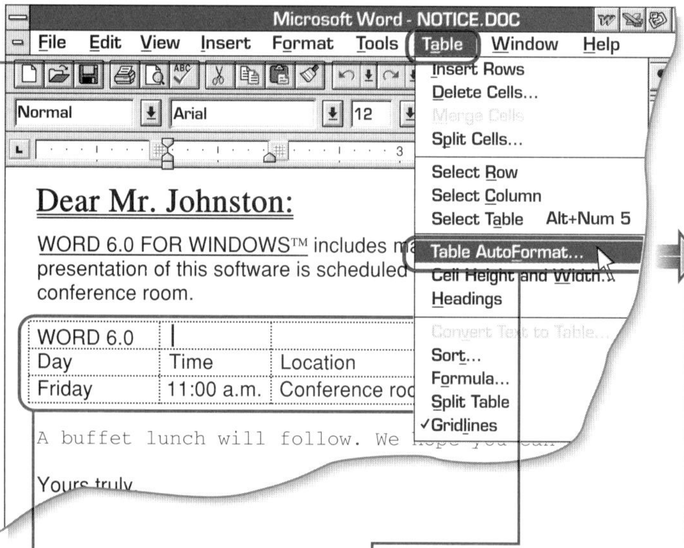

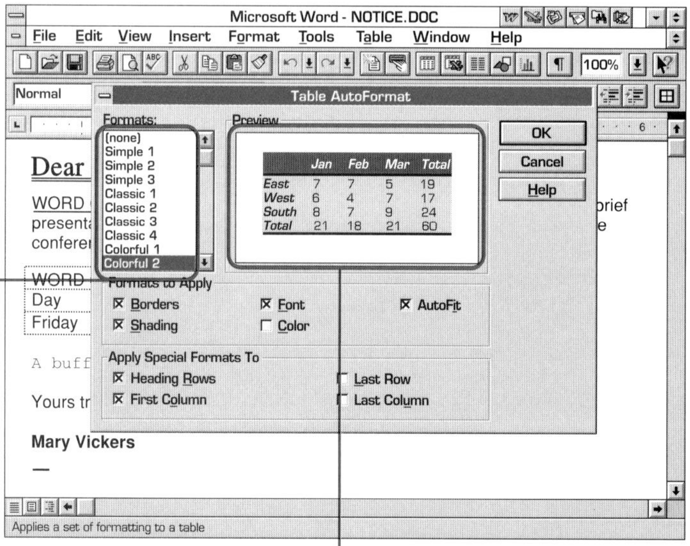

1 Position the insertion point anywhere in the table you want to format.

2 Move the mouse over **Table** and then press the left button.

3 Move the mouse over **Table AutoFormat** and then press the left button.

◆ The **Table AutoFormat** dialog box appears.

◆ The **Formats:** box displays a list of the available table designs.

◆ The **Preview** box displays a sample of the highlighted table design.

4 Press ↓ or ↑ on your keyboard until the **Preview** box displays the design you want to use (example: **Colorful 2**).

- Create a Table
- Type Text
- Add a Row or Column
- Delete a Row or Column
- Change Column Width
- **Format a Table**
- Merge Cells

When you create a table, Word places dotted lines around the cells. These lines will not appear when you print your document. To print table lines, you must use the Table AutoFormat feature to add borders to the table.

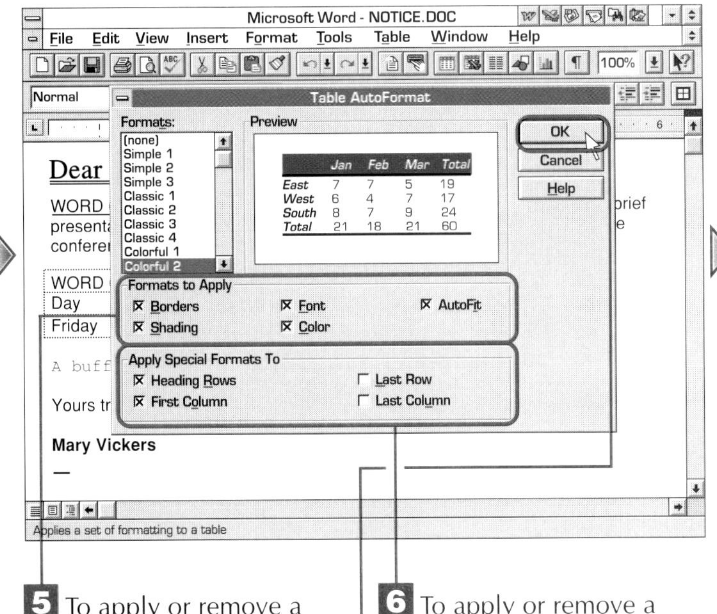

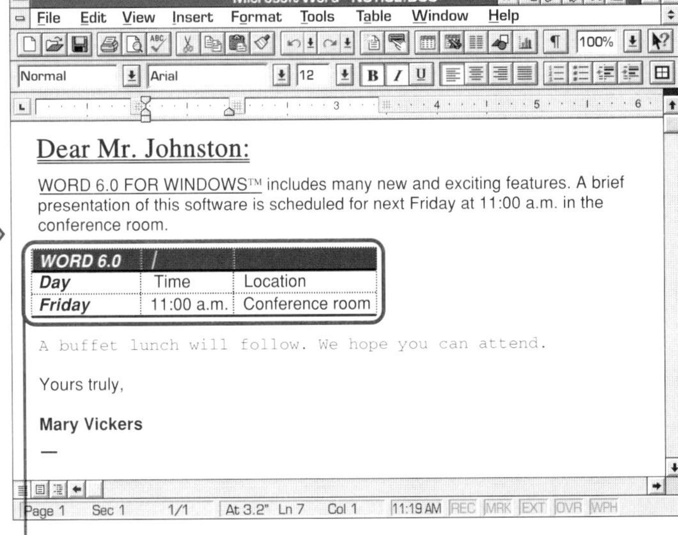

5 To apply or remove a format such as shading or color, move the mouse over an option (example: **Color**) and then press the left button.

Note: ☒ indicates an option is on. ☐ indicates an option is off.

6 To apply or remove a format from specific rows or columns, move the mouse over an option and then press the left button.

7 When the **Preview** box displays the table appearance you want, move the mouse over **OK** and then press the left button.

◆ Word applies the formats you selected to the table.

REMOVE FORMATS

To remove the formats from the table, perform steps **1** to **3**, select (**none**) in step **4** and then perform step **7**.

MERGE CELLS

You can combine two or more cells in your table to create one large cell. This is useful if you want to display a title at the top of your table.
Tables

MERGE CELLS

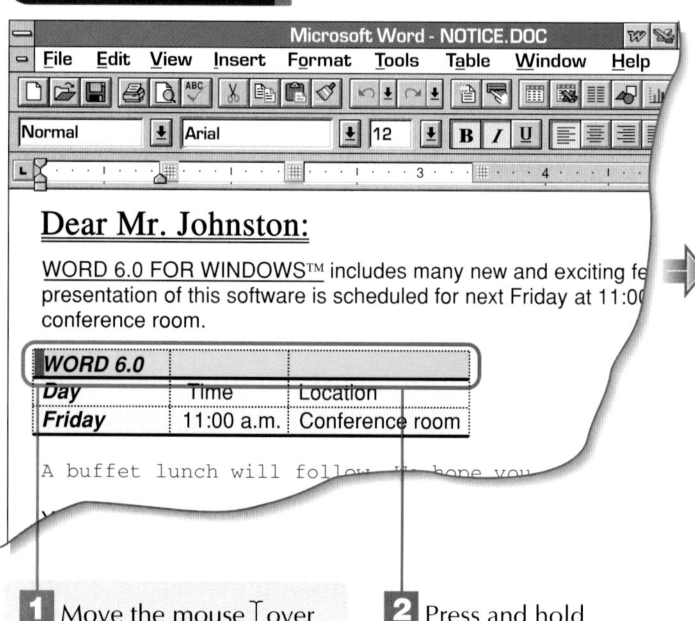

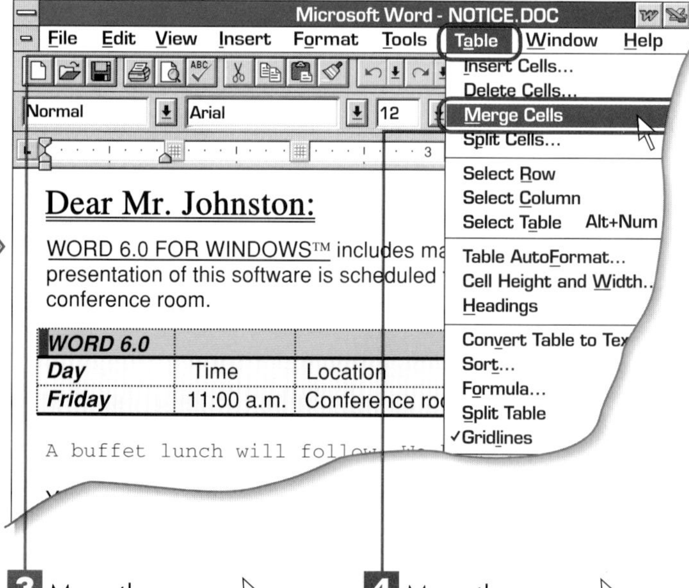

1 Move the mouse I over the first cell you want to join with other cells.

Note: You can only join cells in the same row. You cannot join cells in the same column.

2 Press and hold down the left button as you move the mouse I to highlight the cells you want to join. Then release the button.

3 Move the mouse ↖ over **Table** and then press the left button.

4 Move the mouse ↖ over **Merge Cells** and then press the left button.

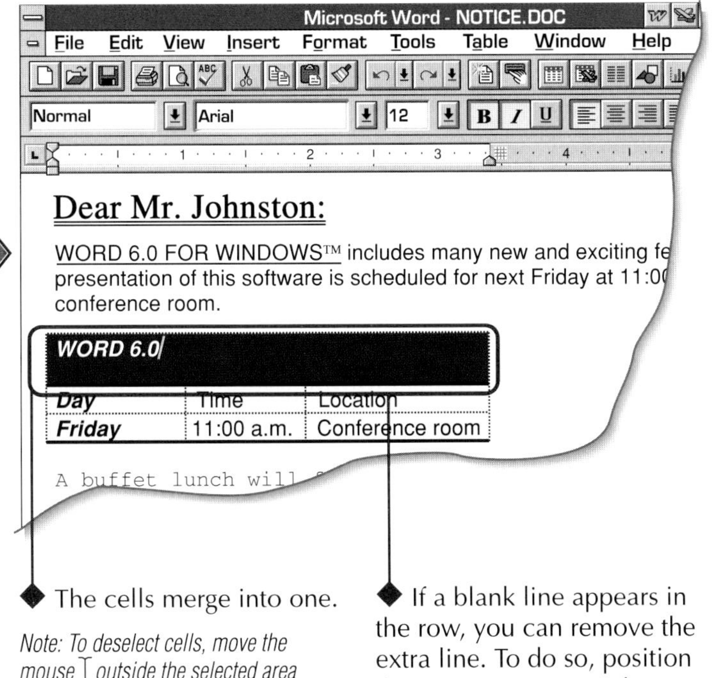

◆ The cells merge into one.

Note: To deselect cells, move the mouse outside the selected area and then press the left button.

◆ If a blank line appears in the row, you can remove the extra line. To do so, position the insertion point to the right of the text in the cell and then press Delete.

SPLIT CELLS

You can split one cell into two or more cells.

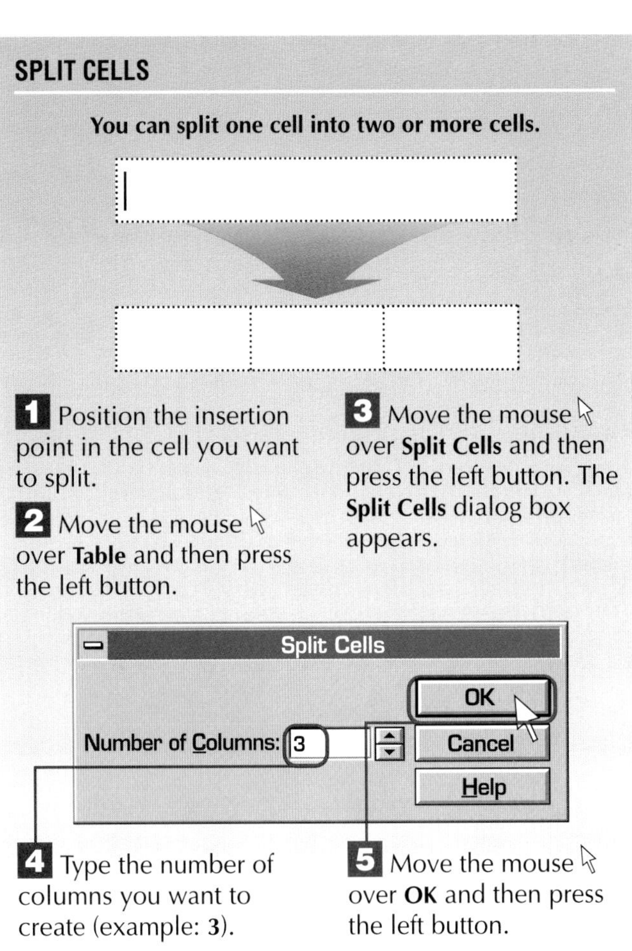

1 Position the insertion point in the cell you want to split.

2 Move the mouse over **Table** and then press the left button.

3 Move the mouse over **Split Cells** and then press the left button. The **Split Cells** dialog box appears.

4 Type the number of columns you want to create (example: **3**).

5 Move the mouse over **OK** and then press the left button.

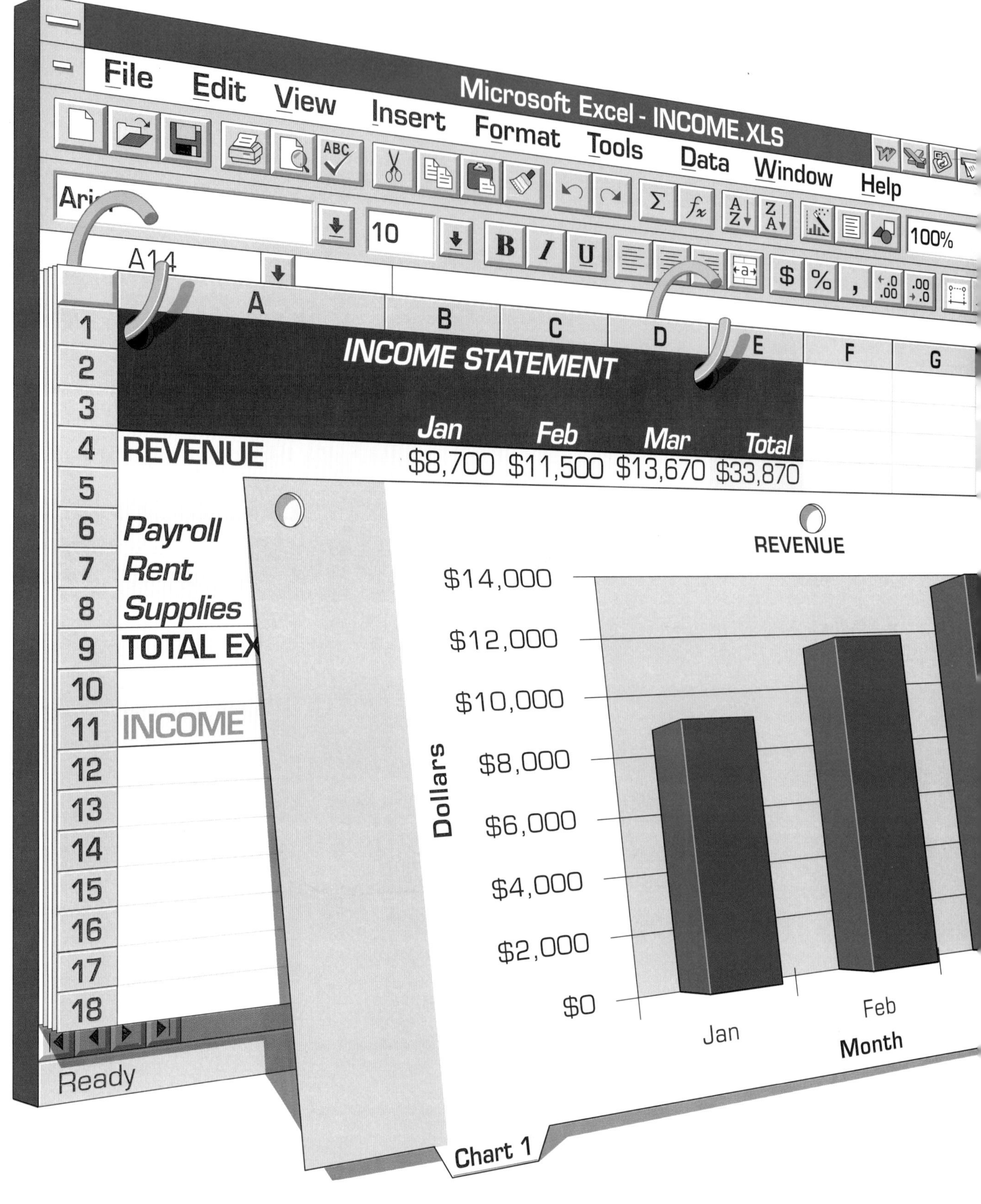

File
Edit
View
Insert
Format
Tools
Data
Window
Help
Microsoft Excel - INCOME.XLS
Ari
10
100%
A14
INCOME STATEMENT
Jan
Feb
Mar
Total
REVENUE
$8,700
$11,500
$13,670
$33,870
Payroll
Rent
Supplies
TOTAL EX
INCOME
Ready
REVENUE
$14,000
$12,000
$10,000
$8,000
$6,000
$4,000
$2,000
$0
Dollars
Jan
Feb
Month
Chart 1

EXCEL

In this section you will learn how to use Excel to manage, analyze and present financial information.
REVENUE

HOW YOU CAN USE EXCEL

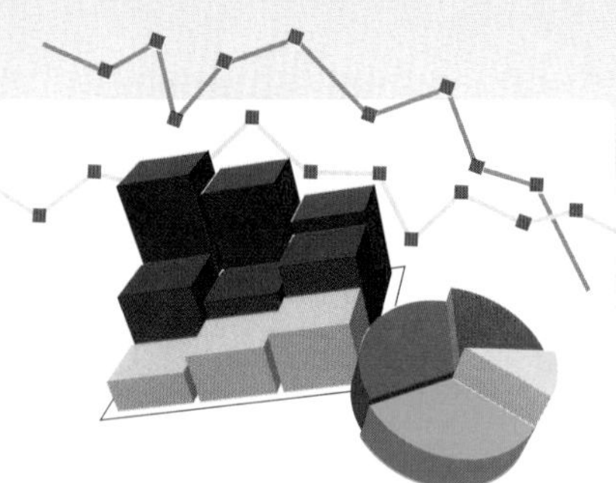

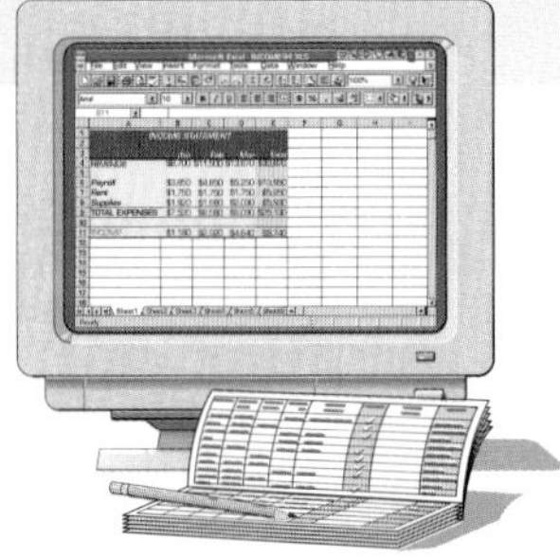

CHARTS

You can create charts from your worksheet data. A chart illustrates the relationship between different items.

PERSONAL FINANCES

Excel can help you keep track of your personal finances. You can use Excel to:

- balance your checkbook
- create a budget
- keep track of your mortgage
- compare investments
- prepare your taxes

FINANCIAL REPORTS

Businesses of all sizes use Excel to analyze and present financial information. Formatting and charting features help you present your results in professional-looking documents.

START EXCEL

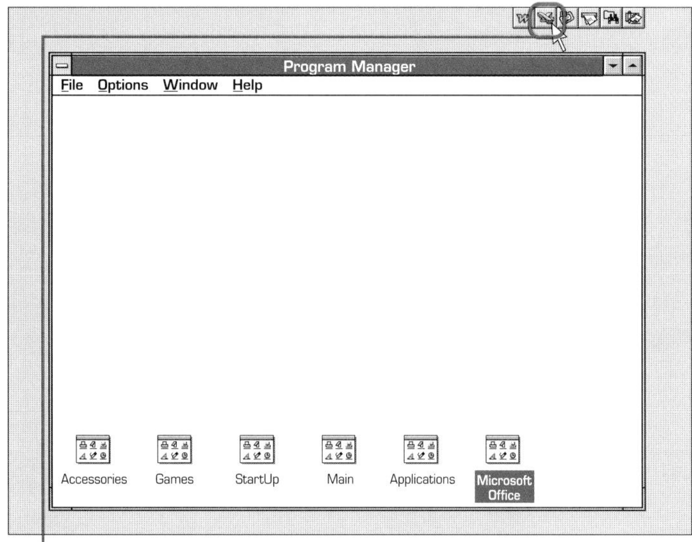

1 To start Excel, move the mouse over and then press the left button.

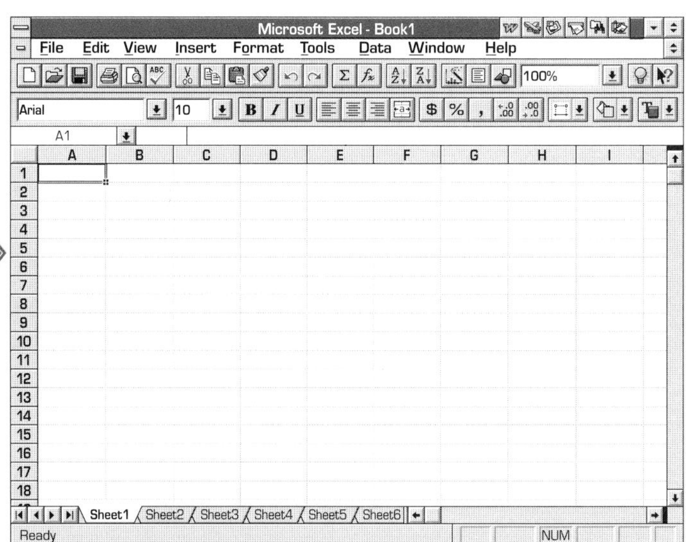

◆ The **Microsoft Excel** window appears, displaying a blank worksheet.

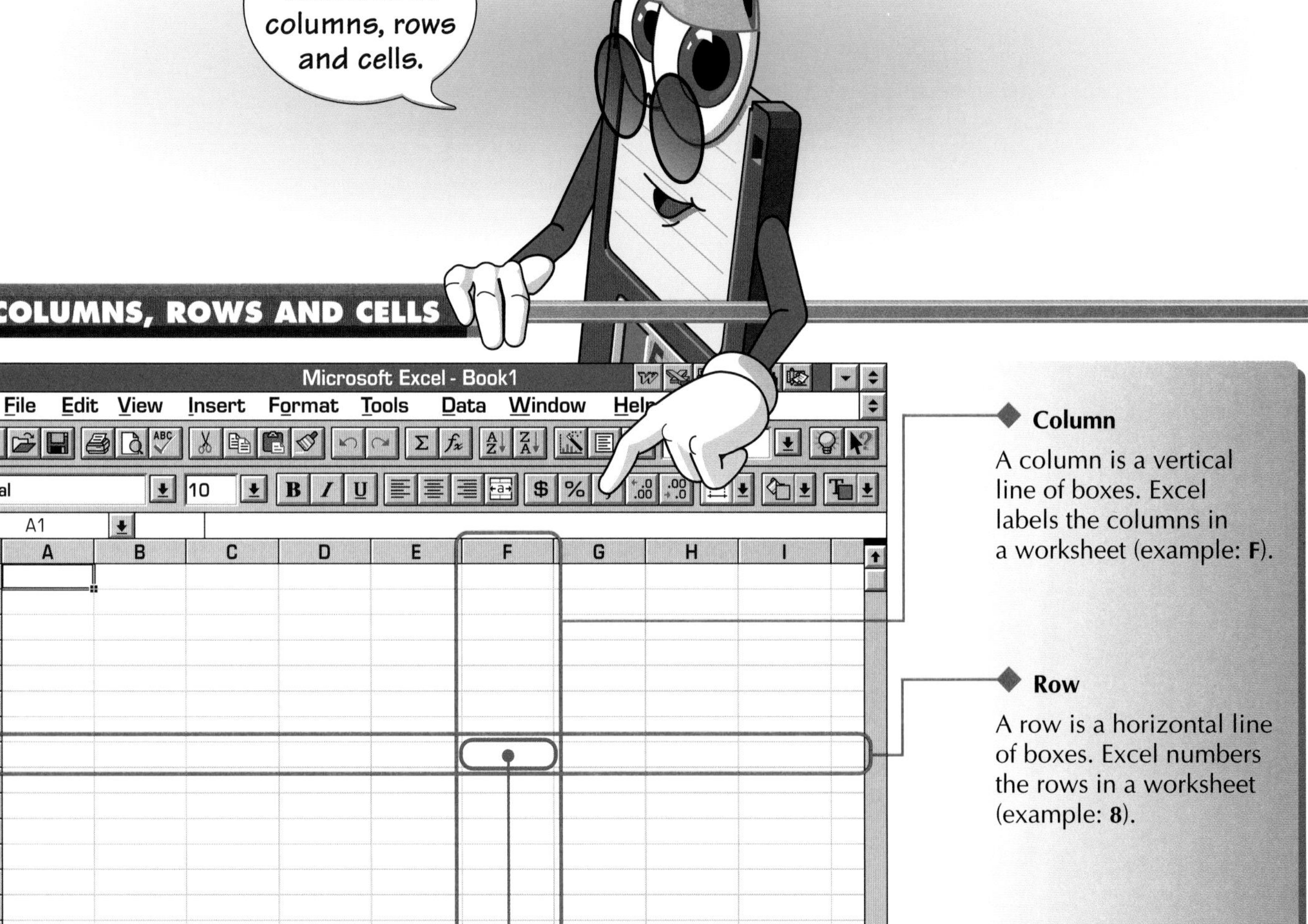

Column

A column is a vertical line of boxes. Excel labels the columns in a worksheet (example: **F**).

Row

A row is a horizontal line of boxes. Excel numbers the rows in a worksheet (example: **8**).

Cell

A cell is one box in a worksheet (example: **F8**).

THE ACTIVE CELL

ACTIVE CELL

◆ The active cell displays a thick border. You can only enter data into the active cell.

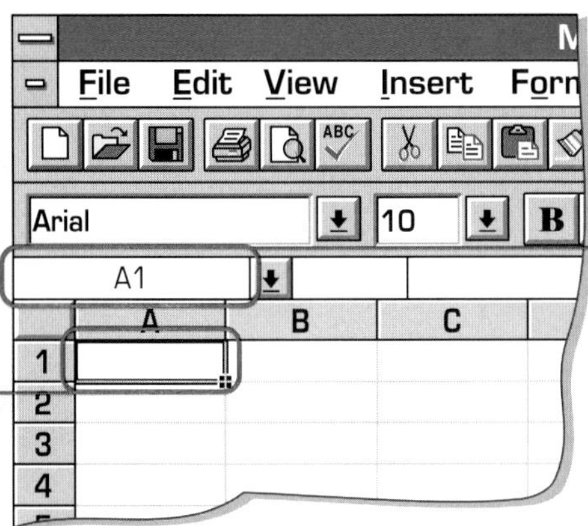

CELL REFERENCE

◆ A cell reference defines the location of each cell. It consists of a column letter followed by a row number (example: **A1**).

The cell reference of the active cell appears at the top of your worksheet.

CHANGE THE ACTIVE CELL

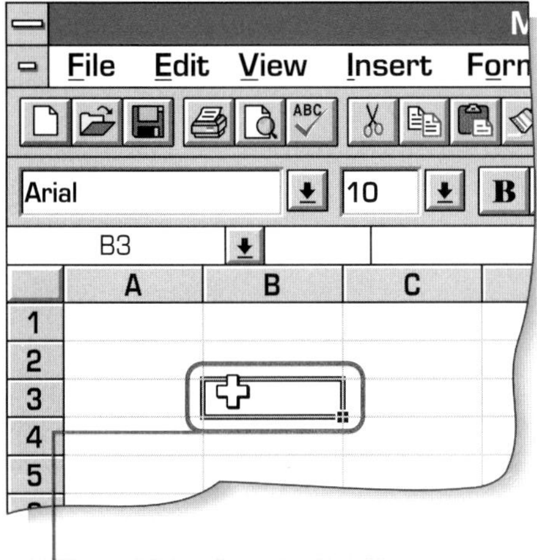

1 To make another cell on your screen the active cell, move the mouse ✚ over the cell and then press the left button.

◆ The cell now displays a thick border.

USING THE KEYBOARD

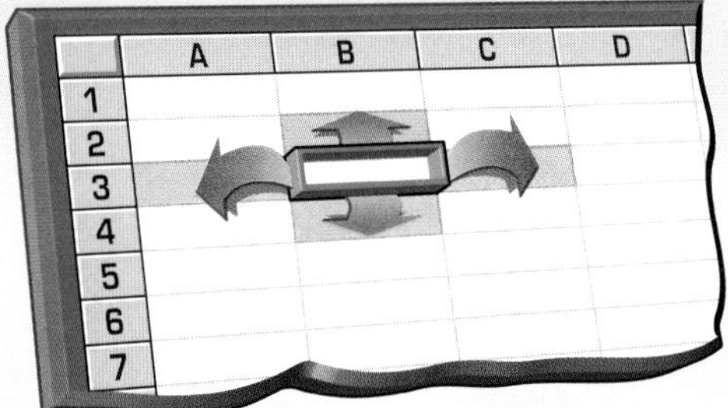

← Press this key to move **left** one cell.

→ Press this key to move **right** one cell.

↓ Press this key to move **down** one cell.

↑ Press this key to move **up** one cell.

ENTER DATA

You enter data into the cells of your worksheet using your keyboard.

ENTER DATA

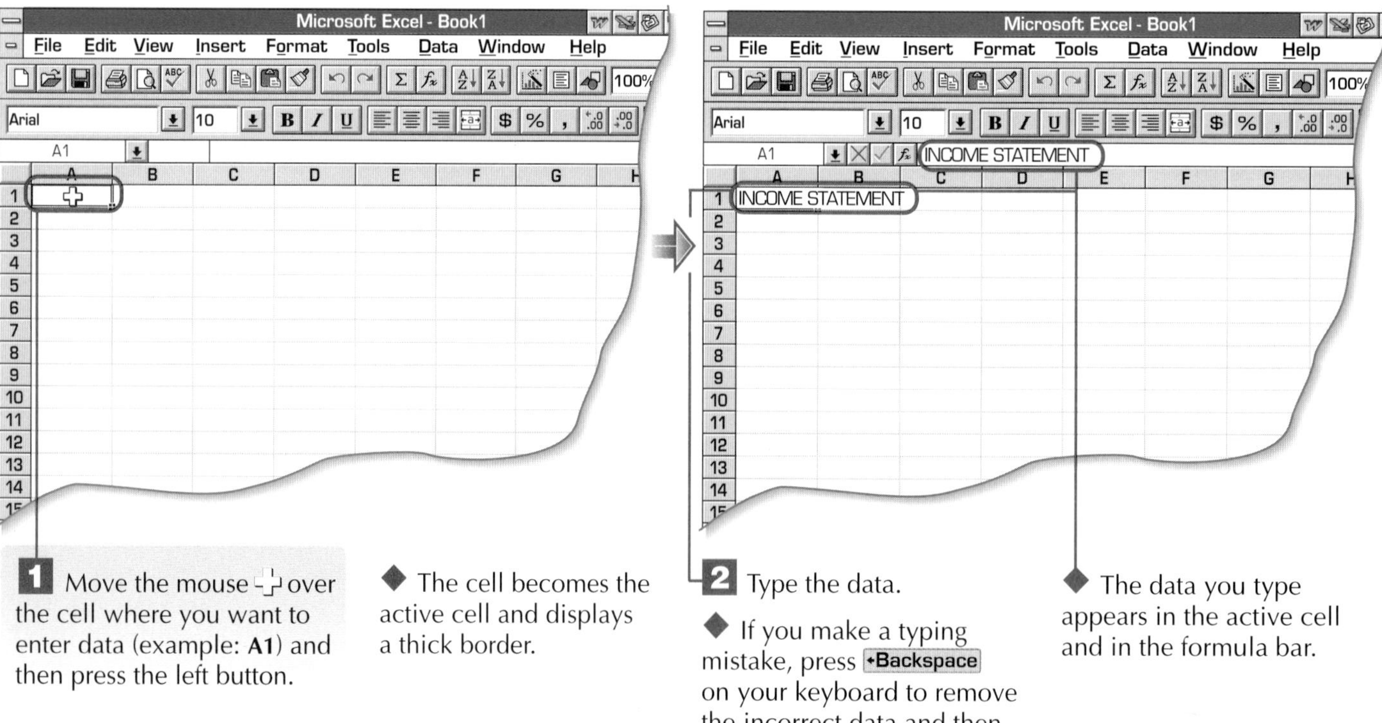

1 Move the mouse over the cell where you want to enter data (example: **A1**) and then press the left button.

◆ The cell becomes the active cell and displays a thick border.

2 Type the data.

◆ If you make a typing mistake, press **Backspace** on your keyboard to remove the incorrect data and then retype.

◆ The data you type appears in the active cell and in the formula bar.

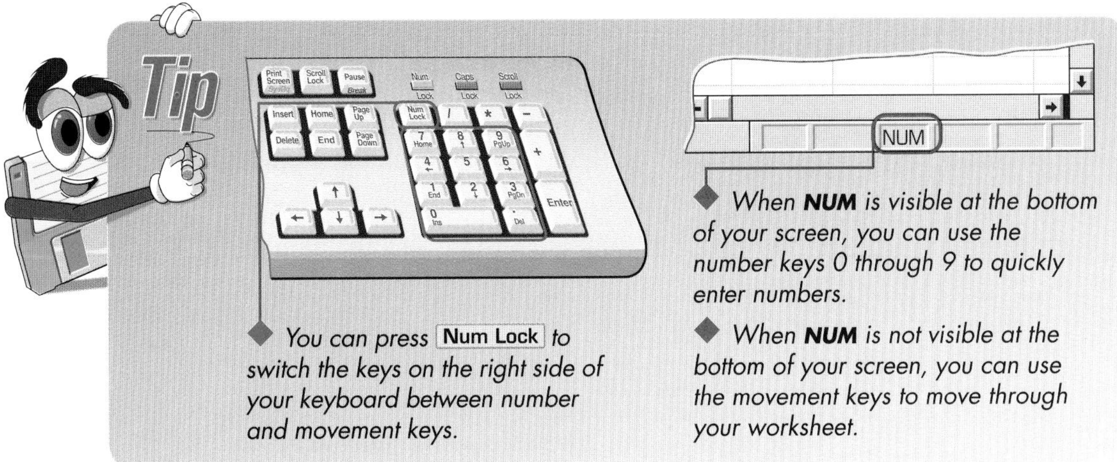

◆ You can press Num Lock to switch the keys on the right side of your keyboard between number and movement keys.

◆ When **NUM** is visible at the bottom of your screen, you can use the number keys 0 through 9 to quickly enter numbers.

◆ When **NUM** is not visible at the bottom of your screen, you can use the movement keys to move through your worksheet.

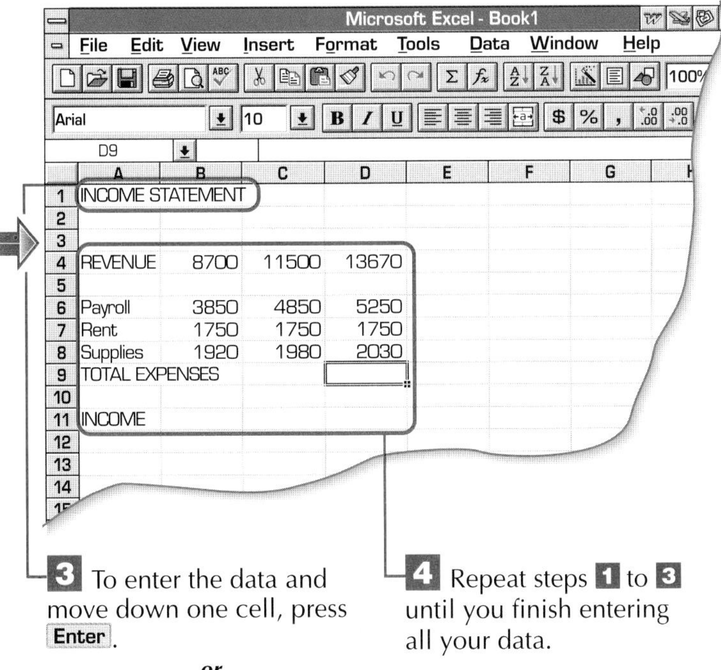

3 To enter the data and move down one cell, press Enter.

or

To enter the data and move one cell in any direction, press →, ←, ↓ or ↑.

4 Repeat steps **1** to **3** until you finish entering all your data.

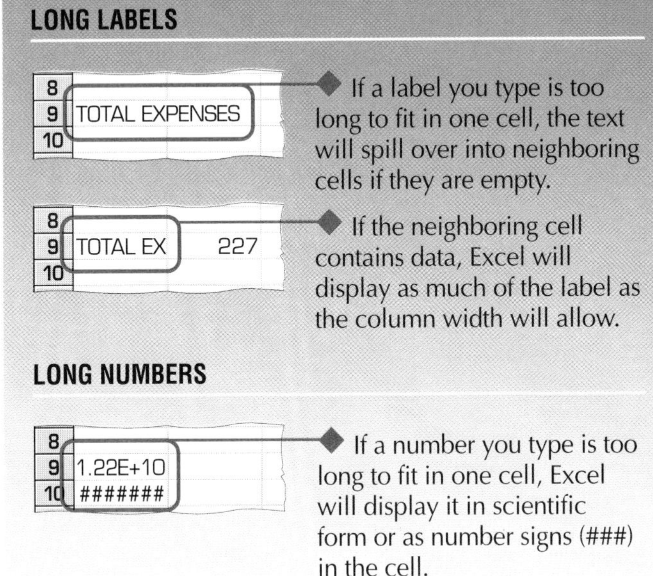

LONG LABELS

◆ If a label you type is too long to fit in one cell, the text will spill over into neighboring cells if they are empty.

◆ If the neighboring cell contains data, Excel will display as much of the label as the column width will allow.

LONG NUMBERS

◆ If a number you type is too long to fit in one cell, Excel will display it in scientific form or as number signs (###) in the cell.

Note: To display an entire label or number, you must increase the column width. For more information, refer to page 190.

SELECT CELLS

Before you can use many Excel features, you must first select the cells you want to work with. Selected cells appear highlighted on your screen.

SELECT A ROW

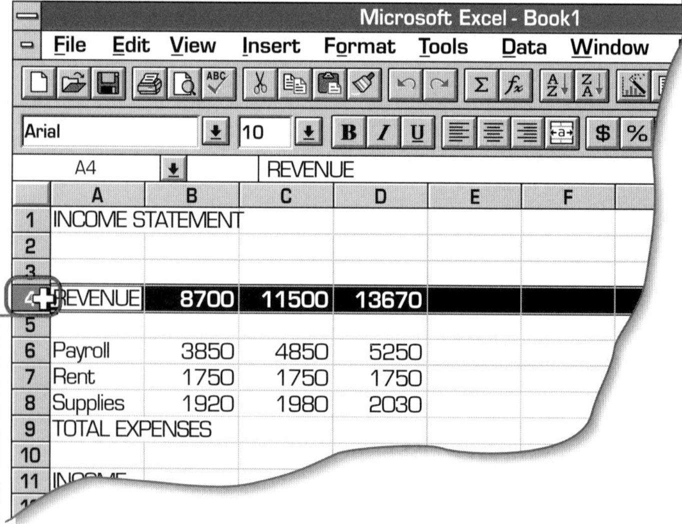

1 Move the mouse over the row number you want to select (example: **4**) and then press the left button.

◆ Make sure the mouse looks like ✣ (not ‡) before pressing the button.

TO CANCEL A SELECTION

Move the mouse over any cell in your worksheet and then press the left button.

SELECT A COLUMN

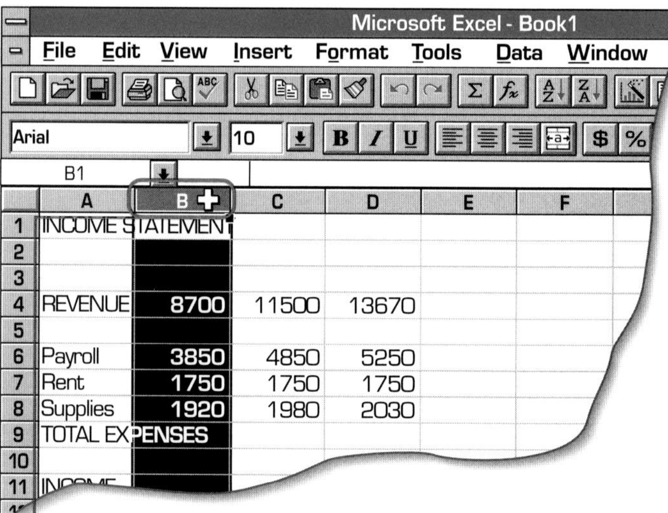

1 Move the mouse over the column letter you want to select (example: **B**) and then press the left button.

◆ Make sure the mouse looks like ✣ (not ↔) before pressing the button.

SELECT THE ENTIRE WORKSHEET

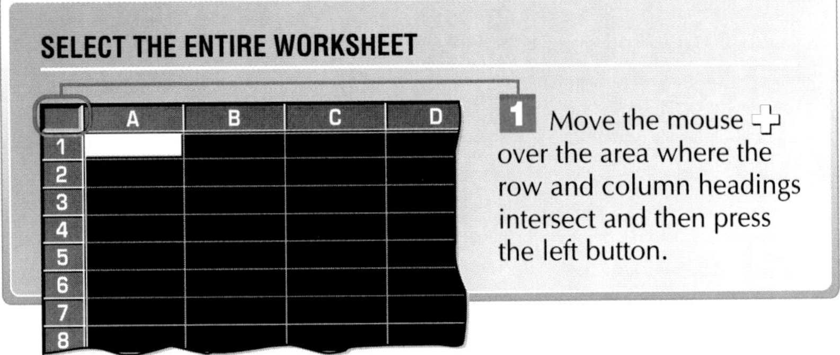

1 Move the mouse over the area where the row and column headings intersect and then press the left button.

SELECT A GROUP OF CELLS

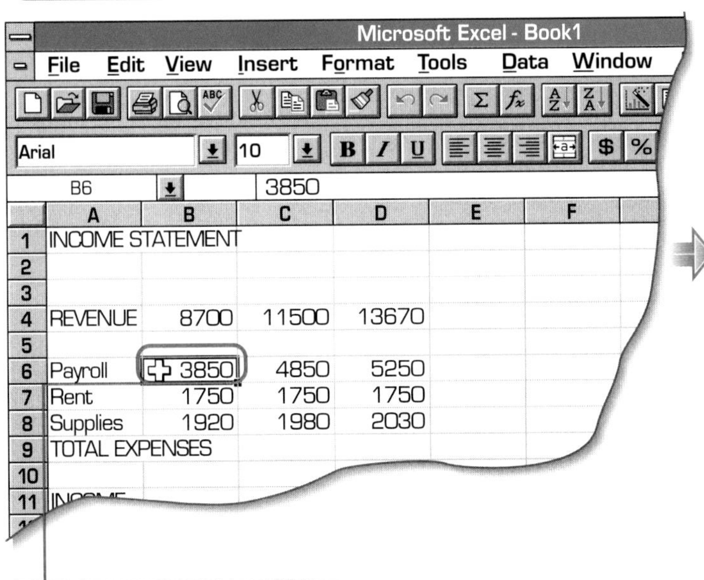

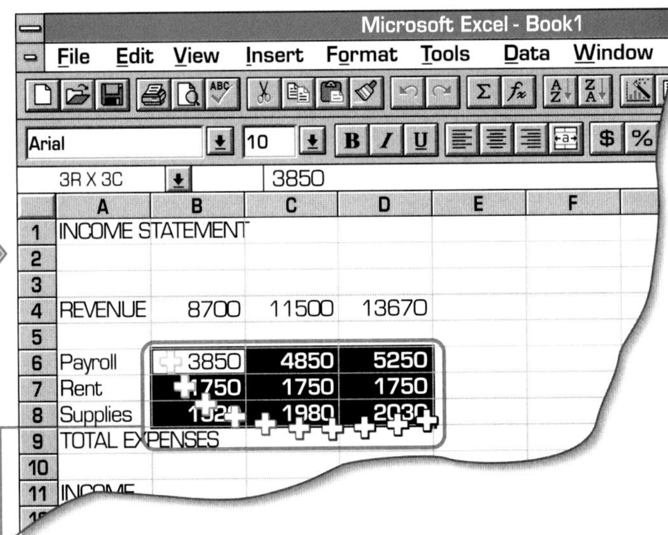

1 Move the mouse over the first cell you want to select (example: **B6**) and then press and hold down the left button.

2 Still holding down the button, drag the mouse until you highlight all the cells you want to select.

3 Release the button.

SELECT TWO GROUPS OF CELLS

To select another group of cells, press and hold down Ctrl while repeating steps 1 to 3.

USING AUTOFILL

USING AUTOFILL TO COMPLETE A SERIES

Complete a Series of Labels

Monday	Tuesday	Wednesday	Thursday
Product 1	Product 2	Product 3	Product 4
Q1	Q2	Q3	Q4

◆ Excel completes a series of labels based on the label in the first cell.

Complete a Series of Numbers

1993	1994	1995	1996
1	2	3	4
5	10	15	20

◆ Excel completes a series of numbers based on the numbers in the first two cells. These numbers tell Excel how much to add to each number to complete the series.

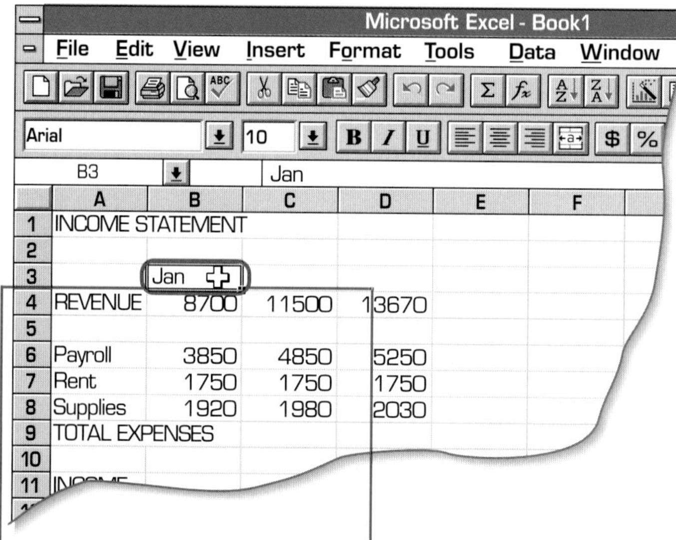

1 To create a series of labels, type and enter the first label in the series (example: **Jan**).

◆ To create a series of numbers, type and enter the first two numbers in the series.

2 Select the cell(s) containing the label or numbers you entered.

Note: To select cells, refer to page 140.

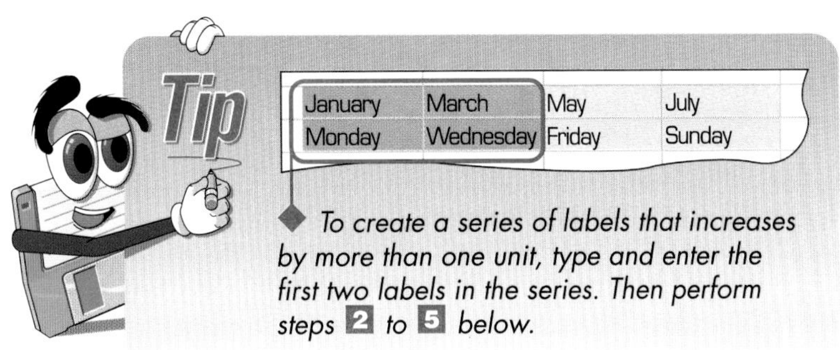

Tip
January
March
May
July
Monday
Wednesday
Friday
Sunday

To create a series of labels that increases by more than one unit, type and enter the first two labels in the series. Then perform steps 2 to 5 below.

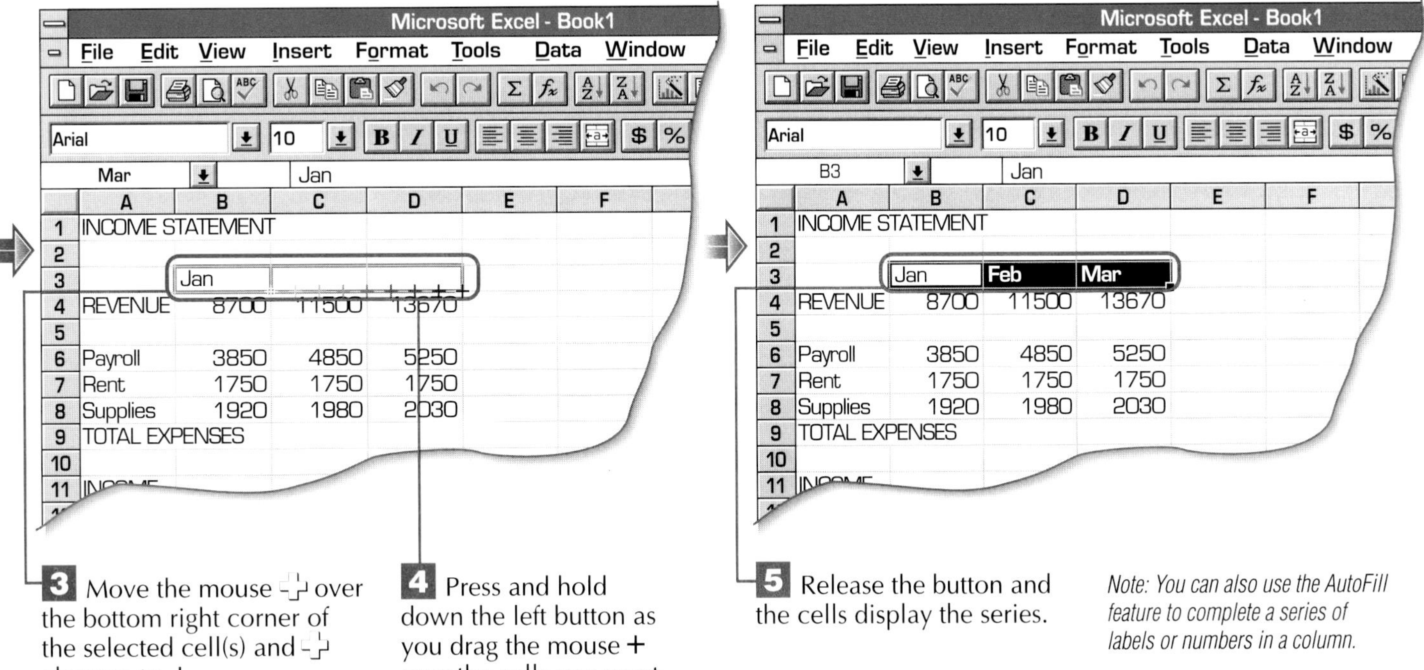

3 Move the mouse ⊹ over the bottom right corner of the selected cell(s) and ⊹ changes to +.

4 Press and hold down the left button as you drag the mouse + over the cells you want to include in the series.

5 Release the button and the cells display the series.

Note: You can also use the AutoFill feature to complete a series of labels or numbers in a column.

MOVE THROUGH A WORKSHEET

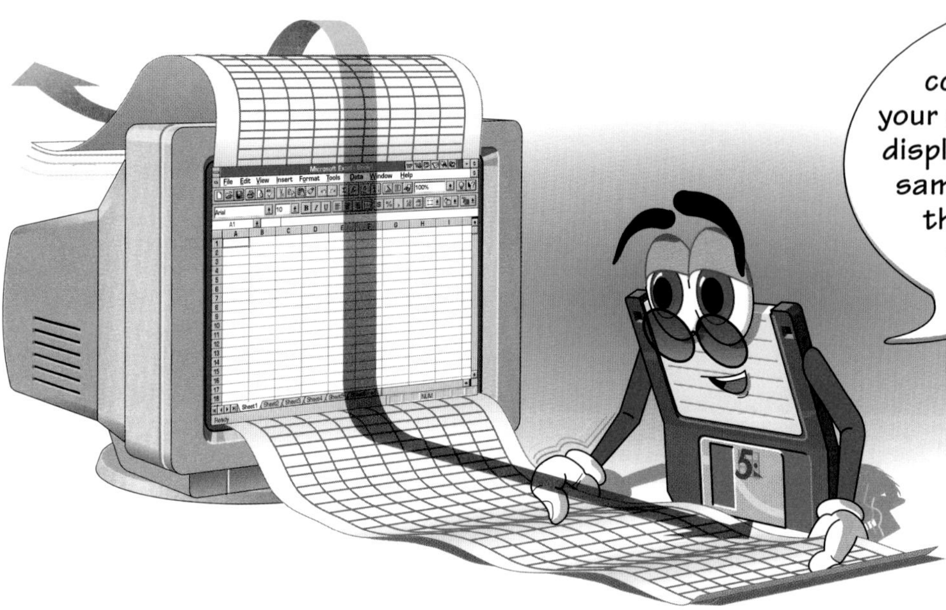

If your worksheet contains a lot of data, your computer screen cannot display all of the data at the same time. You must move through the worksheet to view other areas of data.

MOVE TO CELL A1

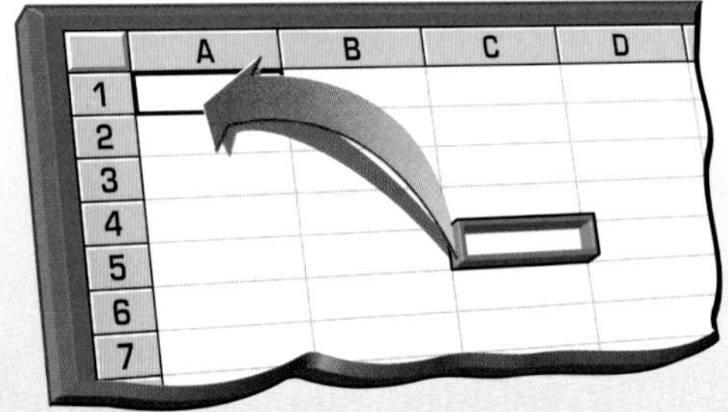

◆ Press Ctrl + Home to move to cell **A1** from any cell in your worksheet.

MOVE ONE SCREEN IN ANY DIRECTION

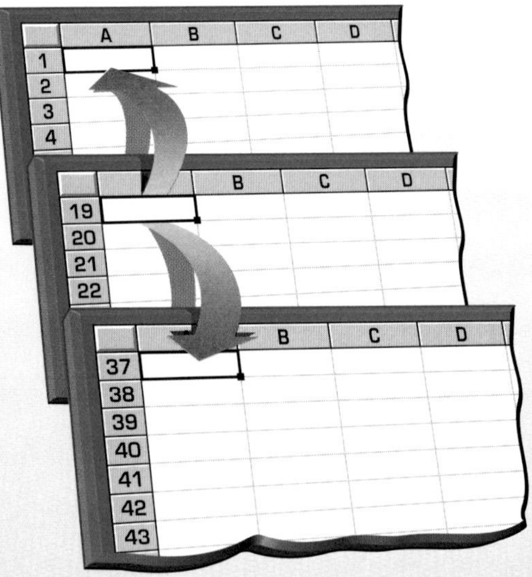

◆ Press PageDown to move **down** one screen.

◆ Press PageUp to move **up** one screen.

◆ Press Alt + PageDown to move **right** one screen.

◆ Press Alt + PageUp to move **left** one screen.

SCROLL UP OR DOWN

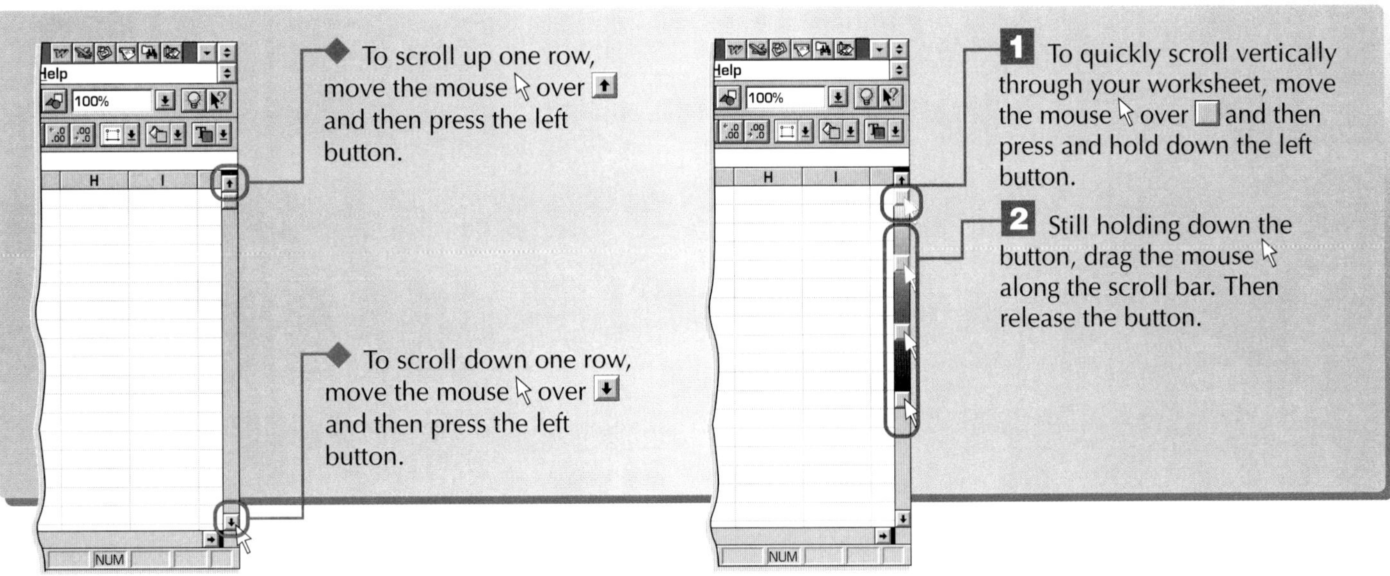

◆ To scroll up one row, move the mouse over and then press the left button.

◆ To scroll down one row, move the mouse over and then press the left button.

1 To quickly scroll vertically through your worksheet, move the mouse over and then press and hold down the left button.

2 Still holding down the button, drag the mouse along the scroll bar. Then release the button.

SCROLL LEFT OR RIGHT

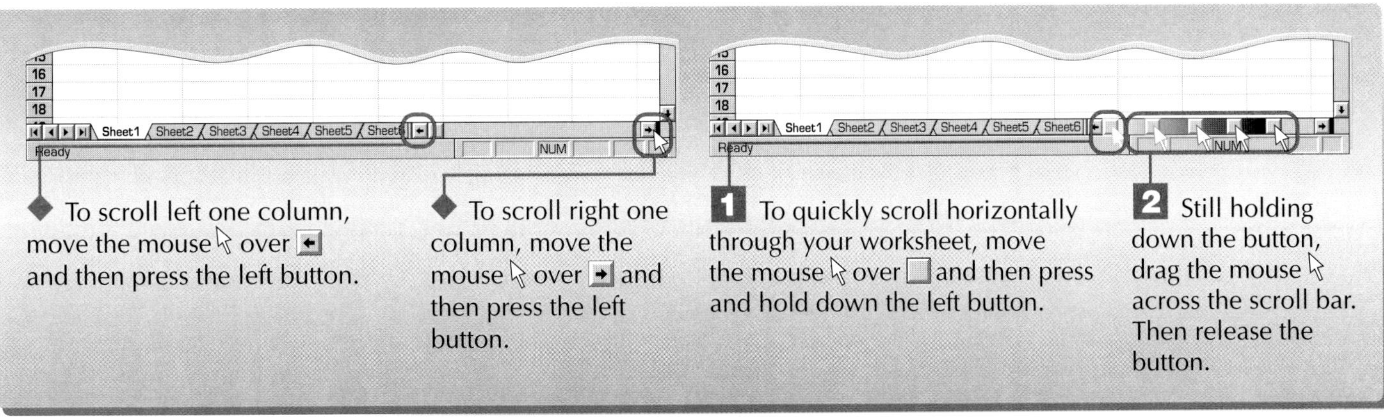

◆ To scroll left one column, move the mouse over and then press the left button.

◆ To scroll right one column, move the mouse over and then press the left button.

1 To quickly scroll horizontally through your worksheet, move the mouse over and then press and hold down the left button.

2 Still holding down the button, drag the mouse across the scroll bar. Then release the button.

GETTING HELP

If you forget how to perform a task, you can use the Help feature to obtain information. This can save you time by eliminating the need to refer to other sources.

GETTING HELP

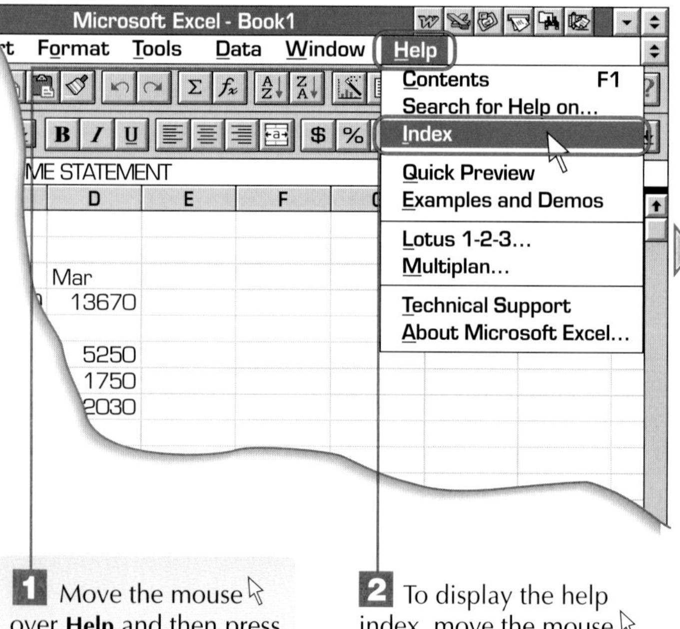

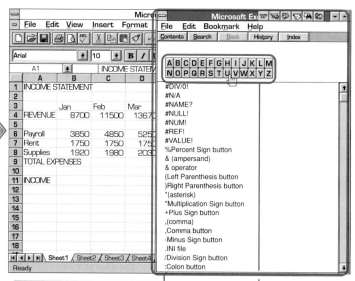

1 Move the mouse over **Help** and then press the left button.

2 To display the help index, move the mouse over **Index** and then press the left button.

◆ The **Microsoft Excel Help** window appears.

3 Move the mouse over the first letter of the topic you want information on (example: **U** for **Underlining**) and then press the left button.

THE TIPWIZARD

If Excel knows a better way to accomplish a task you are performing, the TipWizard button will turn from white to yellow.

1 To display the tip, move the mouse over and then press the left button. The tip appears.

Note: To hide the tip, repeat step **1**.

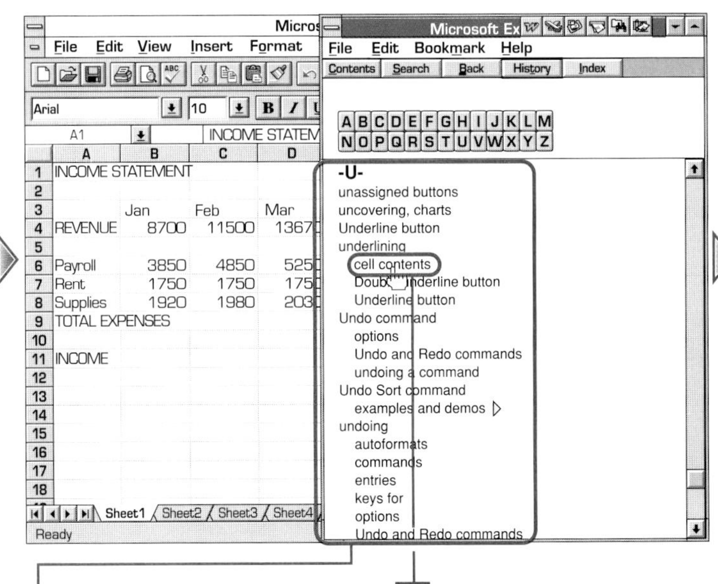

◆ Topics beginning with the letter you selected appear.

◆ To view more topics beginning with that letter, press PageDown on your keyboard.

4 Move the mouse over the topic of interest and then press the left button.

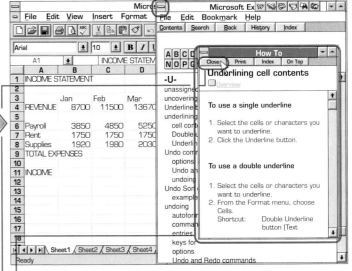

◆ Information on the topic you selected appears.

5 To close the **How To** window, move the mouse over **Close** and then press the left button.

6 To close the **Microsoft Excel Help** window, move the mouse over and then quickly press the left button twice.

SAVE A WORKBOOK

You should save your workbook to store it for future use. This lets you later retrieve the workbook for reviewing or editing purposes.

SAVE A WORKBOOK

When you save a workbook for the first time, you must give it a name. The name of a workbook consists of two parts: a name and an extension. You must separate these parts with a period.

INCOME.XLS

◆ **Name**

The name describes the contents of a workbook. It can have up to eight characters.

◆ **Period**

A period separates the name and the extension.

◆ **Extension**

The extension identifies the program you used to create the workbook. It can have up to three characters.

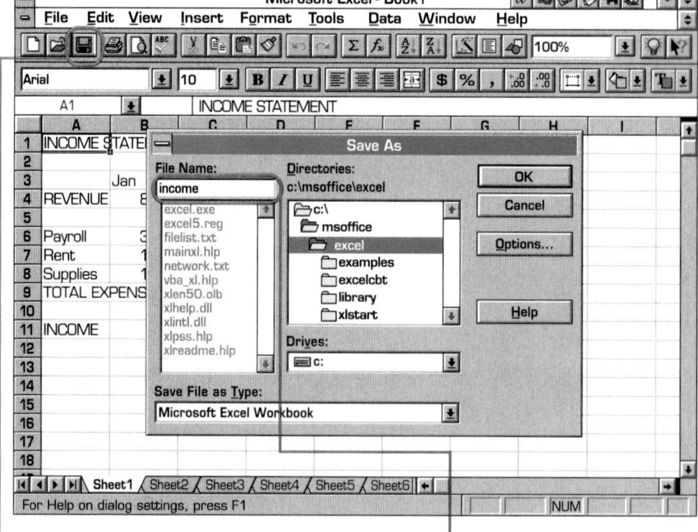

1 Move the mouse over the Save button and then press the left button.

◆ The **Save As** dialog box appears.

*Note: If you previously saved your workbook, the **Save As** dialog box will **not** appear since you have already named the workbook.*

2 Type a name for your workbook (example: **income**) and then press **Enter**.

*Note: To make it easier to find your workbook later on, do not type an extension. Excel will automatically add the **xls** extension to the name.*

Rules for Naming a Workbook

The name of a workbook *can* contain the following characters:

- The letters A to Z
- The numbers 0 to 9
- The symbols _ ^ $ ~ ! # % & { } @ ( )

The name of a workbook *cannot* contain the following characters:

- A comma (,)
- A blank space
- The symbols * ? ; [ ] + = \ / : < >

Each workbook in a directory must have a unique name.

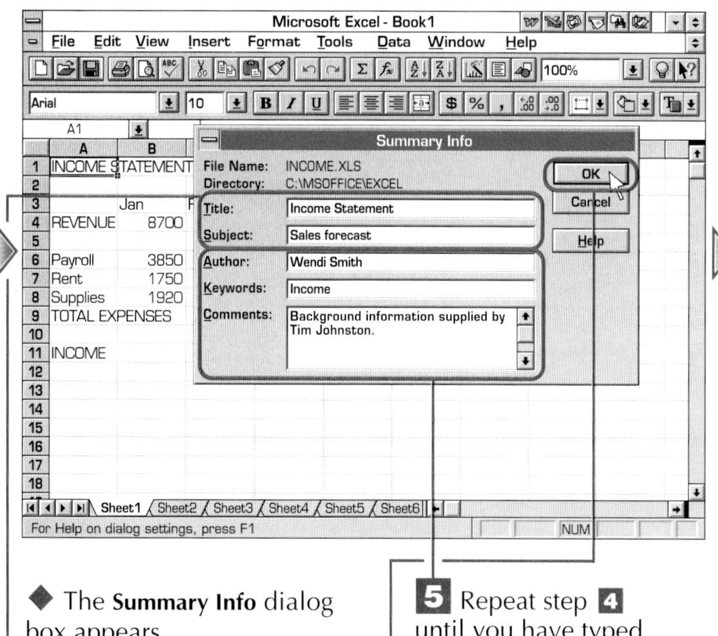

- The **Summary Info** dialog box appears.

3 Type a title for your workbook.

4 Press Tab to move to the next category. Type the corresponding information.

5 Repeat step **4** until you have typed all the information.

6 Move the mouse over **OK** and then press the left button.

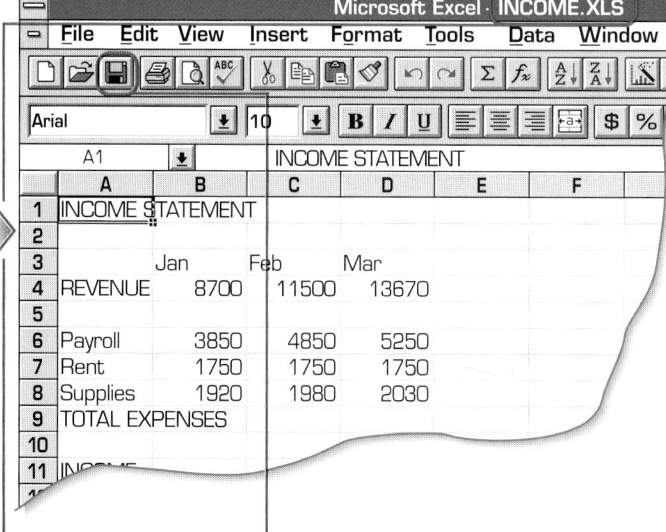

- Excel saves your workbook and displays the name at the top of your screen.

- You should save your workbook every 5 to 10 minutes to store any changes made since the last time you saved the workbook. To save changes, move the mouse over the save button and then press the left button.

SAVE A WORKBOOK TO A DISKETTE

If you want to give your colleagues a copy of a workbook, you can save the workbook to a diskette. They can then review the workbook on their own computers.

SAVE A WORKBOOK TO A DISKETTE

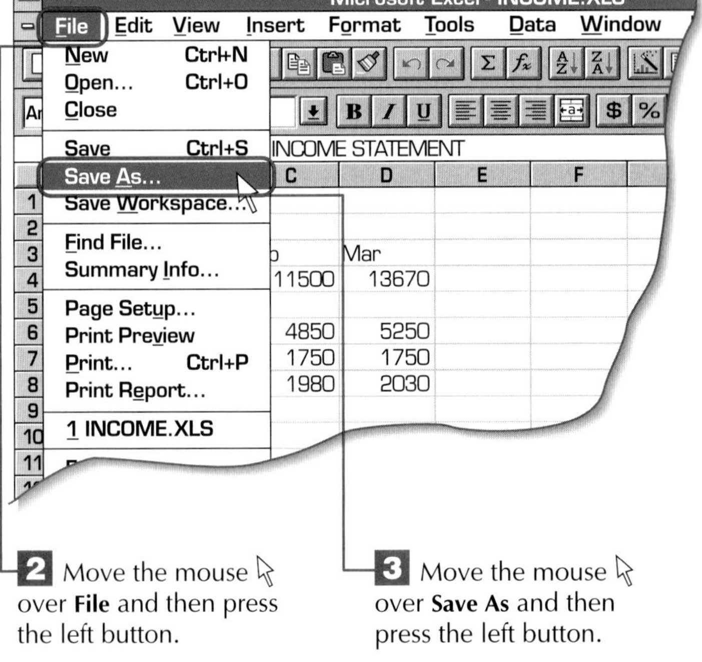

1 Insert a diskette into a floppy drive (example: **a:**).

2 Move the mouse over **File** and then press the left button.

3 Move the mouse over **Save As** and then press the left button.

- Save a Workbook
- **Save a Workbook to a Diskette**
- Close a Workbook
- Exit Excel
- Open a Workbook
- Create a New Workbook
- Switch Between Workbooks

SAVE A WORKBOOK WITH A NEW NAME

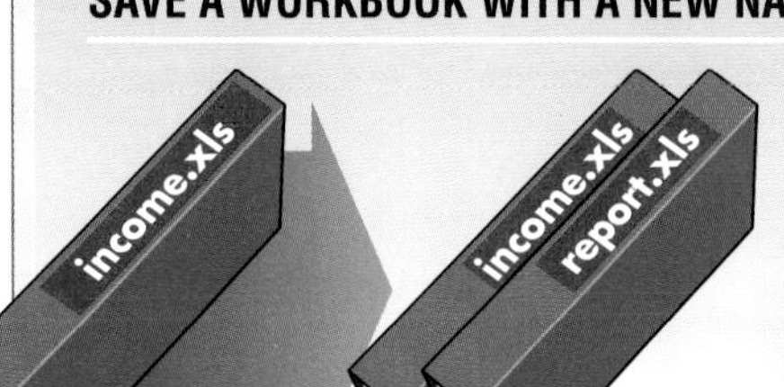

After you save your workbook, you may want to make additional changes. In case you regret any of these changes, you can keep a copy of the old version by saving the workbook with a new name.

1 Perform steps 2 to 4 below.

2 Move the mouse over **OK** and then press the left button.

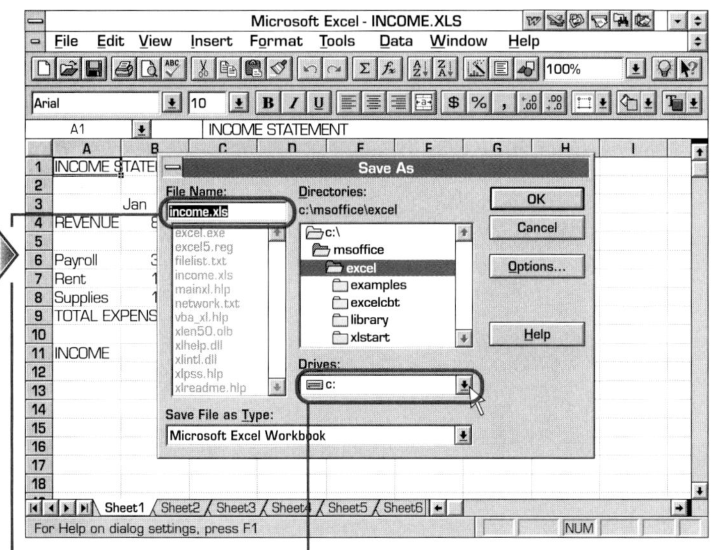

◆ The **Save As** dialog box appears.

4 The **File Name:** box displays the current file name. To save your workbook with a different name, type a new name.

◆ The **Drives:** box displays the current drive (example: **c:**).

5 To save the file to a diskette, move the mouse over ⬇ in the **Drives:** box and then press the left button.

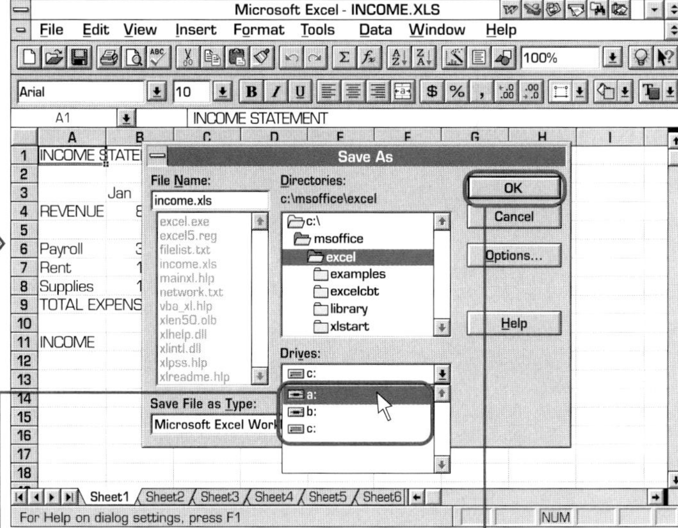

◆ A list of the available drives for your computer appears.

6 Move the mouse over the drive that contains the diskette (example: **a:**) and then press the left button.

7 To save your workbook, move the mouse over **OK** and then press the left button.

CLOSE A WORKBOOK

EXIT EXCEL

When you finish using a workbook, you can close the workbook to remove it from your screen.

CLOSE A WORKBOOK

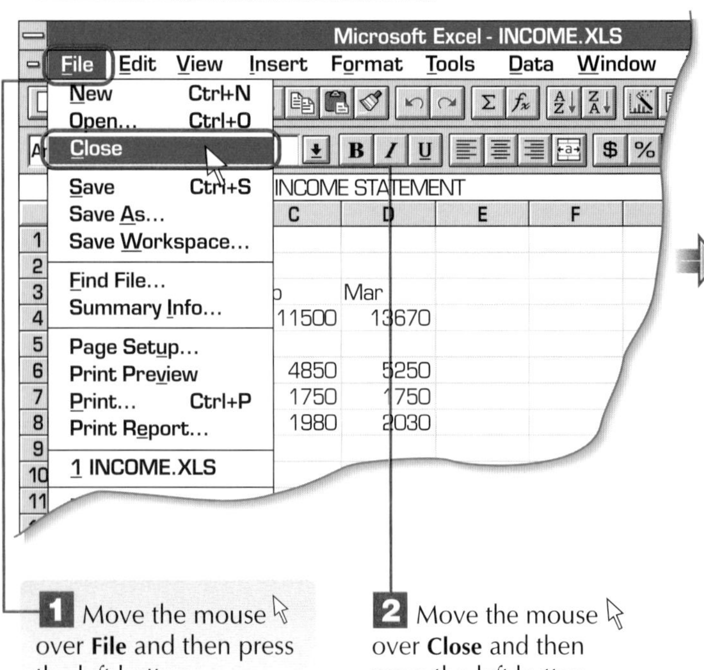

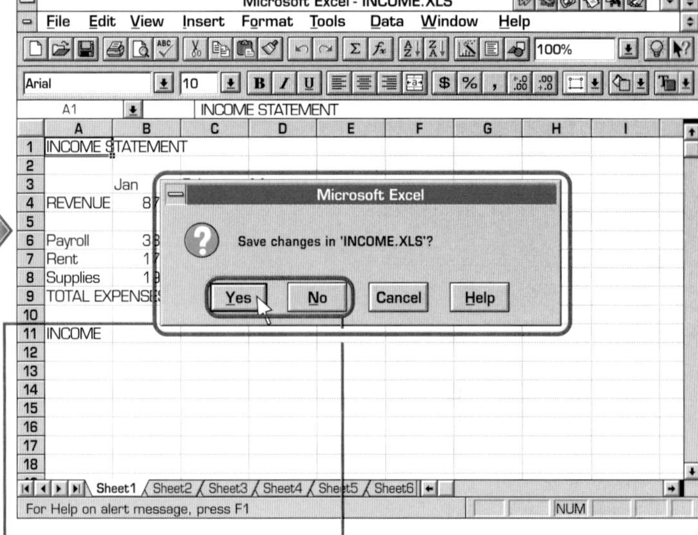

1 Move the mouse over **File** and then press the left button.

2 Move the mouse over **Close** and then press the left button.

◆ This dialog box appears if you have not saved changes made to your workbook.

3 To save the changes, move the mouse over **Yes** and then press the left button.

◆ To close the workbook without saving the changes, move the mouse over **No** and then press the left button.

When you finish using Excel, you can easily exit the program.
EXIT

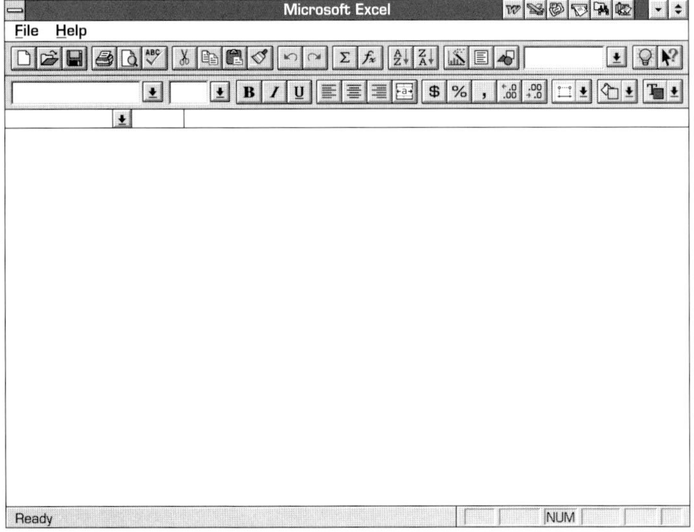

◆ The workbook disappears from your screen.

EXIT EXCEL

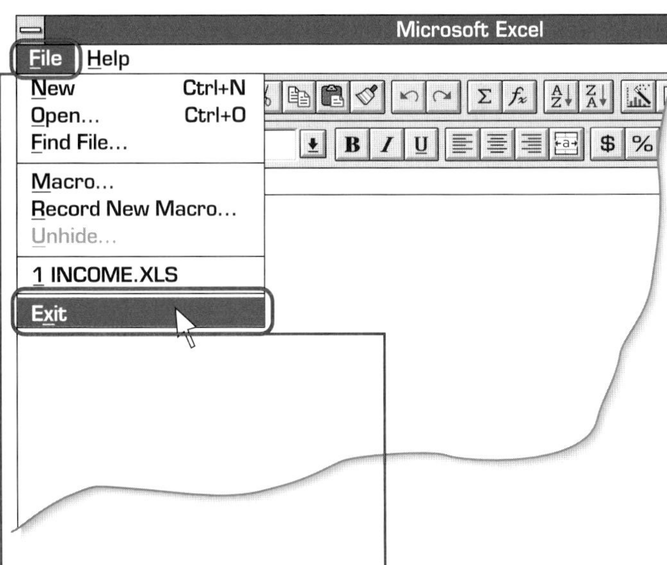

1 Move the mouse over **File** and then press the left button.

2 Move the mouse over **Exit** and then press the left button.

Note: To restart Excel, refer to page 135.

OPEN A WORKBOOK

You can open a saved workbook and display it on your screen. This lets you review and edit the workbook.
income.xls

OPEN A WORKBOOK

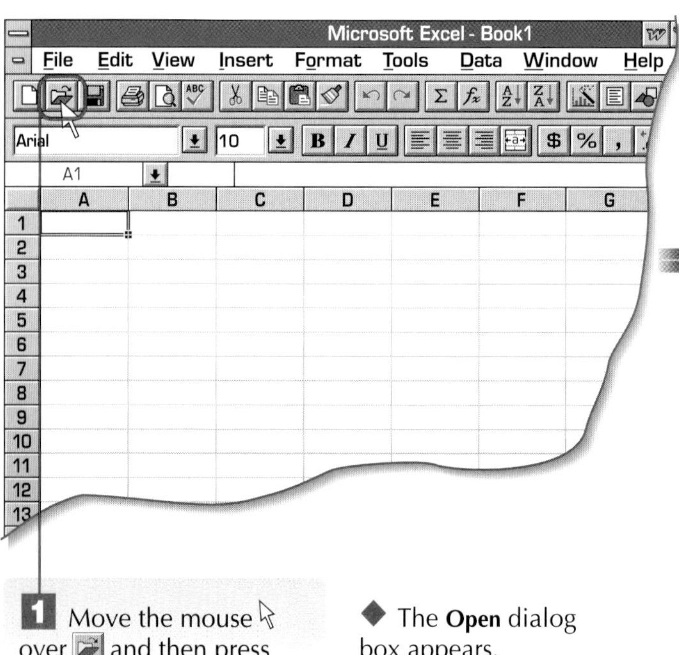

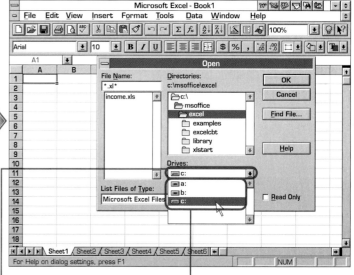

1 Move the mouse over and then press the left button.

◆ The **Open** dialog box appears.

◆ The **Drives:** box displays the current drive (example: **c:**).

2 To open a workbook on a different drive, move the mouse over in the **Drives:** box and then press the left button.

◆ A list of the available drives for your computer appears.

3 Move the mouse over the drive containing the workbook you want to open and then press the left button.

- Save a Workbook
- Save a Workbook to a Diskette
- Close a Workbook
- Exit Excel
- **Open a Workbook**
- Create a New Workbook
- Switch Between Workbooks

SHORTCUT

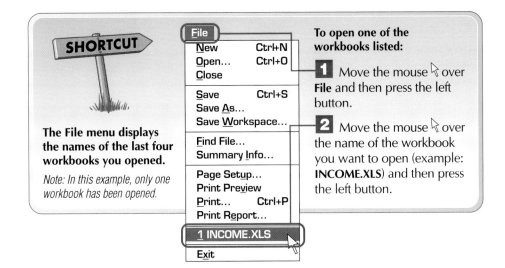

The File menu displays the names of the last four workbooks you opened.

Note: In this example, only one workbook has been opened.

File
New Ctrl+N
Open... Ctrl+O
Close
Save Ctrl+S
Save As...
Save Workspace...
Find File...
Summary Info...
Page Setup...
Print Preview
Print... Ctrl+P
Print Report...
1 INCOME.XLS
Exit

To open one of the workbooks listed:

1 Move the mouse over **File** and then press the left button.

2 Move the mouse over the name of the workbook you want to open (example: **INCOME.XLS**) and then press the left button.

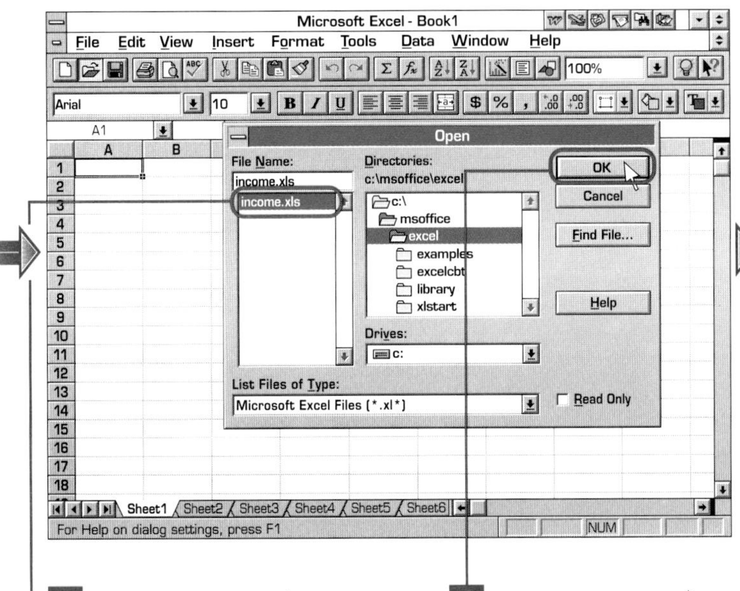

Microsoft Excel - INCOME.XLS

	A	B	C	D
1	INCOME STATEMENT			
2				
3		Jan	Feb	Mar
4	REVENUE	8700	11500	13670
5				
6	Payroll	3850	4850	5250
7	Rent	1750	1750	1750
8	Supplies	1920	1980	2030
9	TOTAL EXPENSES			
10				
11	INCOME			

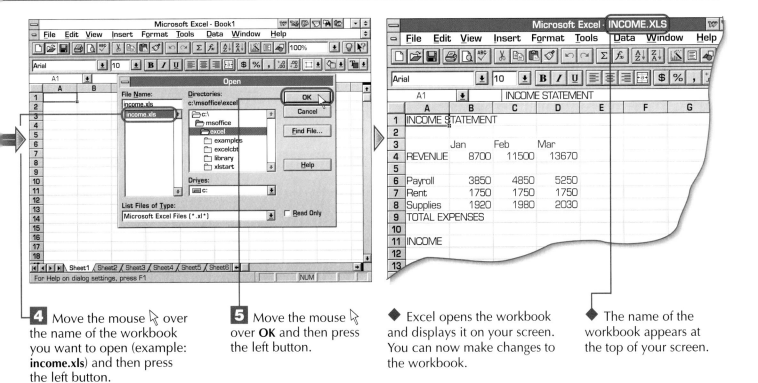

4 Move the mouse over the name of the workbook you want to open (example: **income.xls**) and then press the left button.

5 Move the mouse over **OK** and then press the left button.

◆ Excel opens the workbook and displays it on your screen. You can now make changes to the workbook.

◆ The name of the workbook appears at the top of your screen.

CREATE A NEW WORKBOOK

SWITCH BETWEEN WORKBOOKS

You can create a new workbook to store data on a different topic. Excel lets you easily switch between all of your open workbooks.
File
Edit
View
Insert
10
Arial
A
B
C

CREATE A NEW WORKBOOK

Microsoft Excel - INCOME.XLS

File Edit View Insert Format Tools Data Window

	A	B	C	D	E	F
1	INCOME STATEMENT					
2						
3		Jan	Feb	Mar		
4	REVENUE	8700	11500	13670		
5						
6	Payroll	3850	4850	5250		
7	Rent	1750	1750	1750		
8	Supplies	1920	1980	2030		
9	TOTAL EXPENSES					
10						

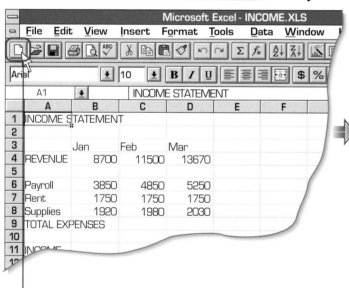

1 To create a new workbook, move the mouse over and then press the left button.

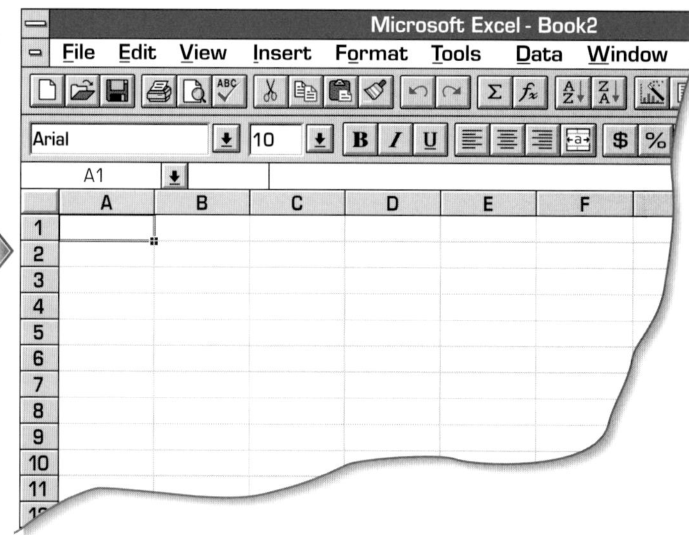

◆ A new workbook appears.

Note: The previous workbook is now hidden behind the new workbook.

Think of each new workbook as a new 3-ring binder. Each workbook contains worksheets that you can use to organize your data.

Note: For information on using multiple worksheets in a workbook, refer to pages 216 to 221.

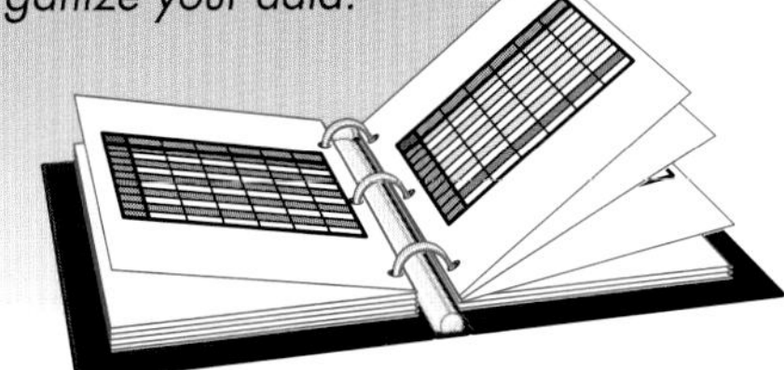

SWITCH BETWEEN WORKBOOKS

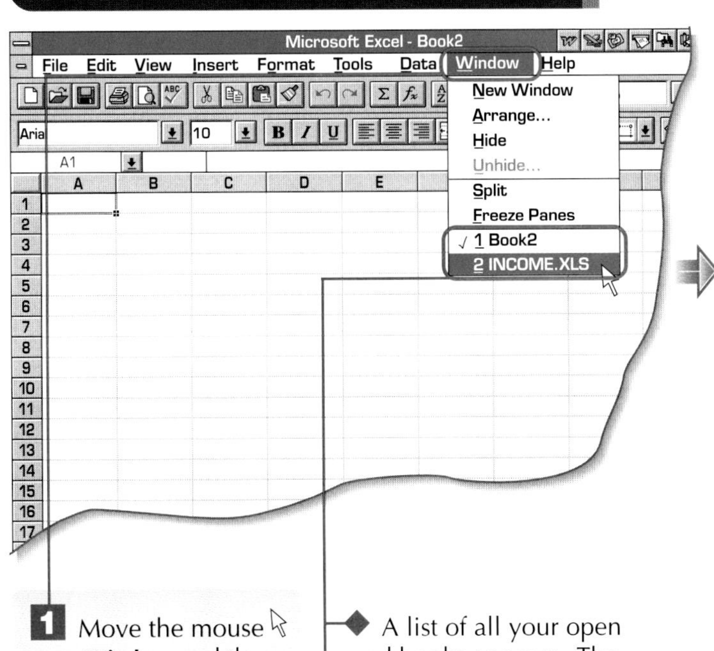

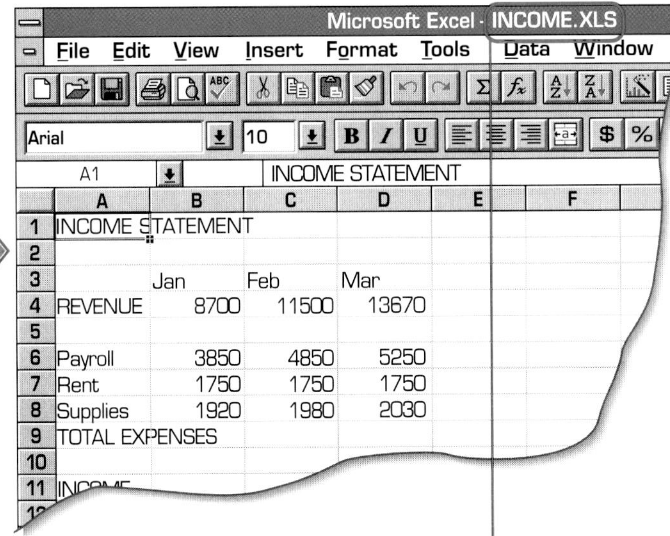

1 Move the mouse over **Window** and then press the left button.

◆ A list of all your open workbooks appears. The current workbook displays a check mark (√) beside its name.

2 Move the mouse over the workbook you want to switch to (example: **INCOME.XLS**) and then press the left button.

◆ The workbook appears.

◆ Excel displays the name of the workbook at the top of your screen.

EDIT DATA

After you enter data into your worksheet, you can correct a typing error or revise the data.

EDIT DATA IN A CELL

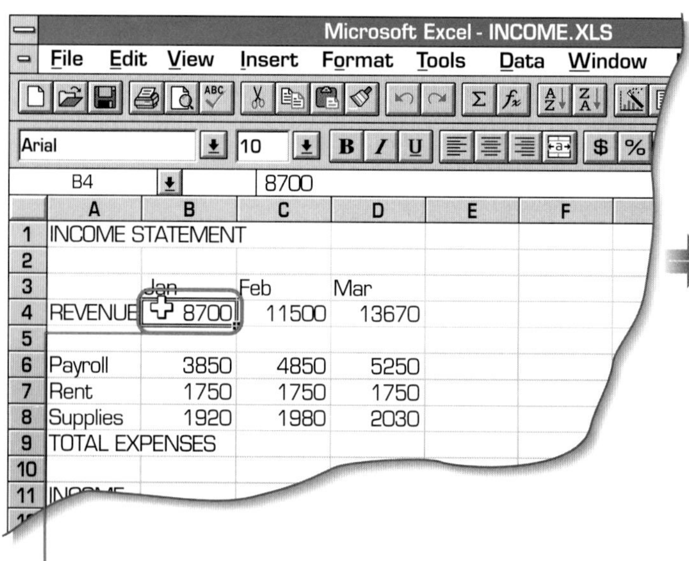

1 Move the mouse ✚ over the cell containing the data you want to change (example: **B4**) and then quickly press the left button twice.

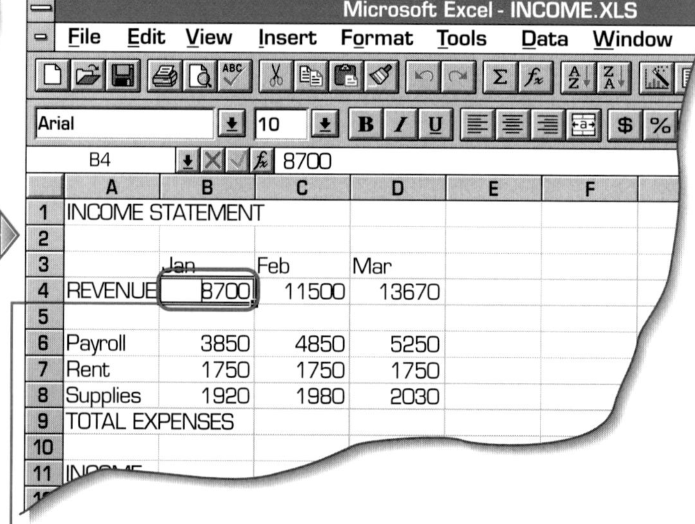

◆ A flashing insertion point appears in the cell.

2 Move the mouse I over the position where you want to add or delete characters and then press the left button.

Note: You can also press → or ← on your keyboard to move the insertion point.

REPLACE ENTIRE CELL CONTENTS

You can completely replace the contents of a cell with new data.

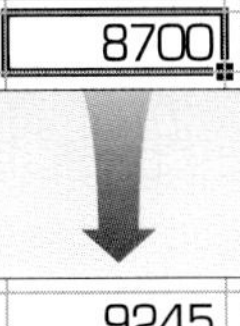

1 Move the mouse over the cell containing the data you want to replace with new data and then press the left button.

2 Type the new data and then press Enter.

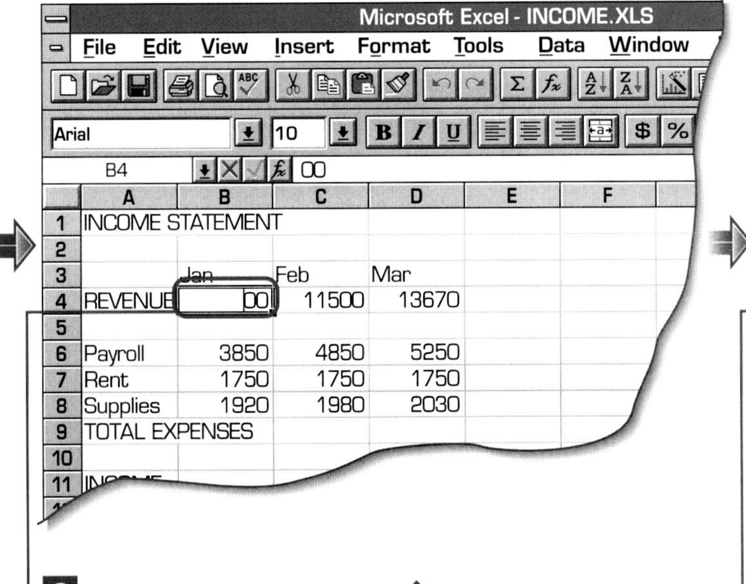

3 To remove the character to the right of the insertion point, press Delete.

◆ To remove the character to the left of the insertion point, press ←Backspace.

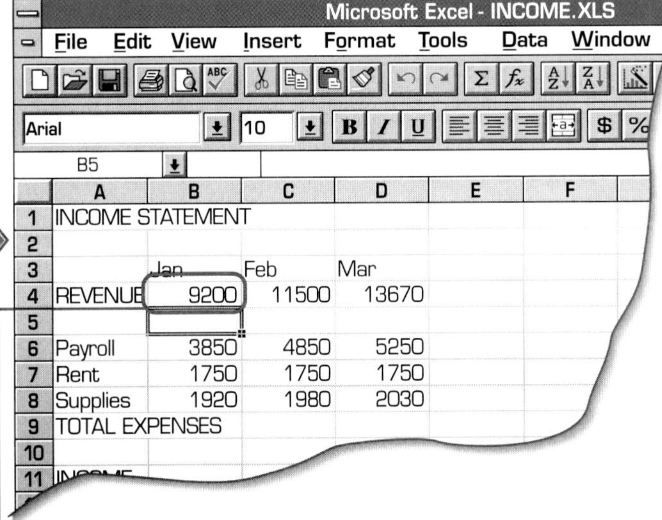

4 To insert data where the insertion point flashes on your screen, type the data.

5 When you finish making the changes, press Enter.

CLEAR DATA

UNDO LAST CHANGE

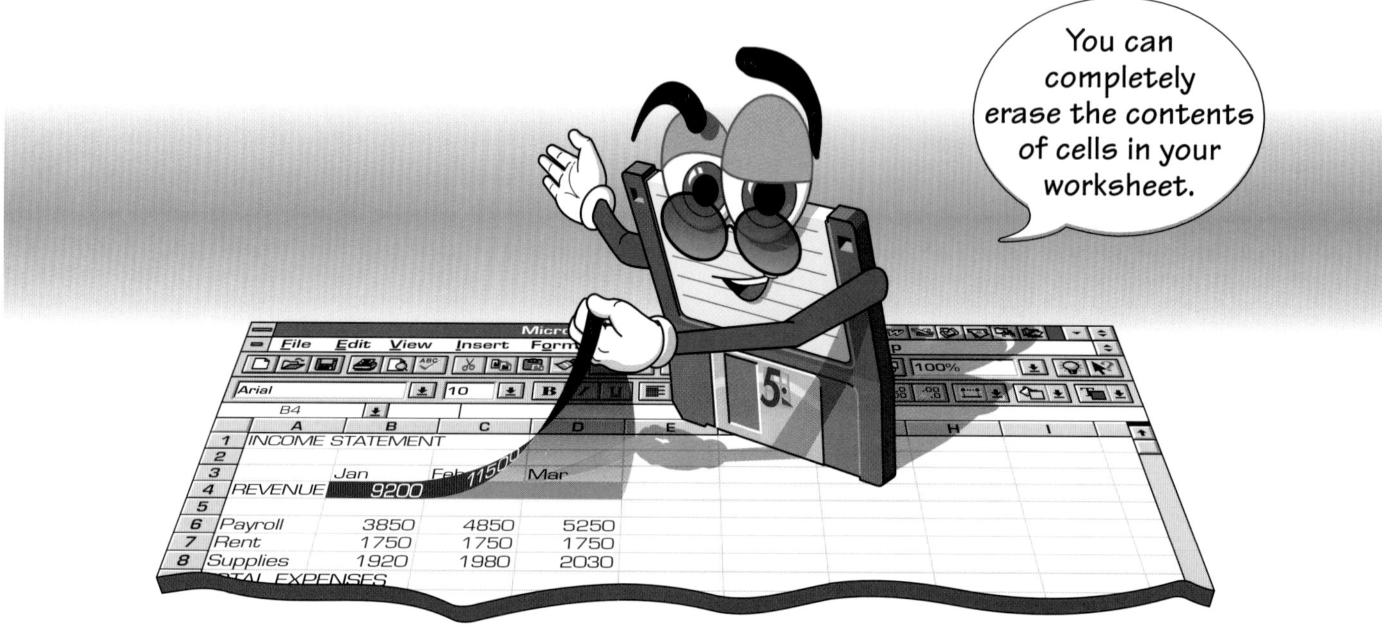

You can completely erase the contents of cells in your worksheet.

CLEAR DATA

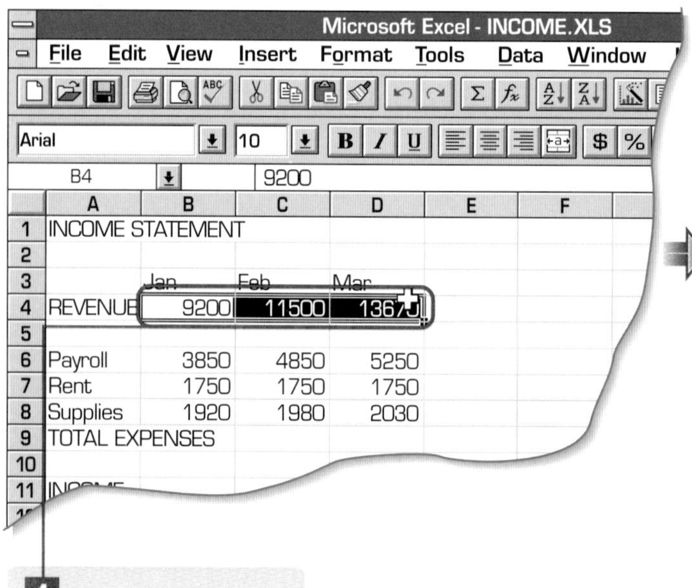

1 Select the cells containing the data you want to remove.

Note: To select cells, refer to page 140.

2 Press **Delete** and the contents of the cells you selected disappear.

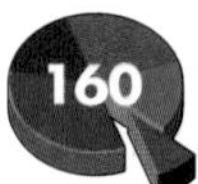

Excel remembers the last change you made to your worksheet. If you regret this change, you can cancel it by using the Undo feature.

UNDO YOUR LAST CHANGE

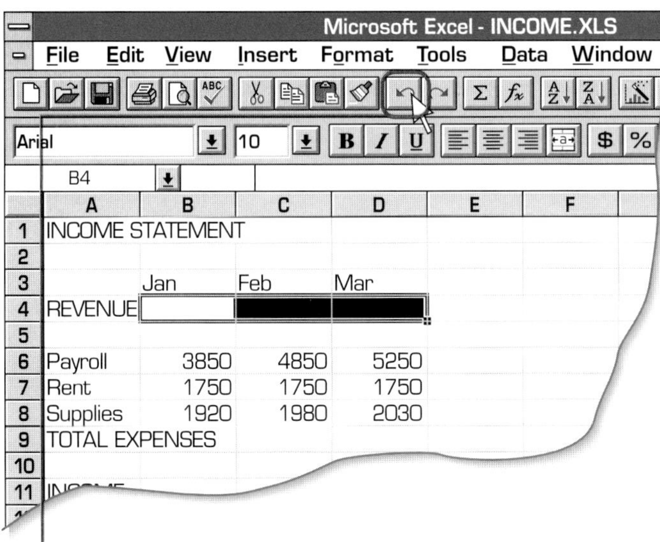

1 To cancel the last change made to your worksheet, move the mouse over the Undo button and then press the left button.

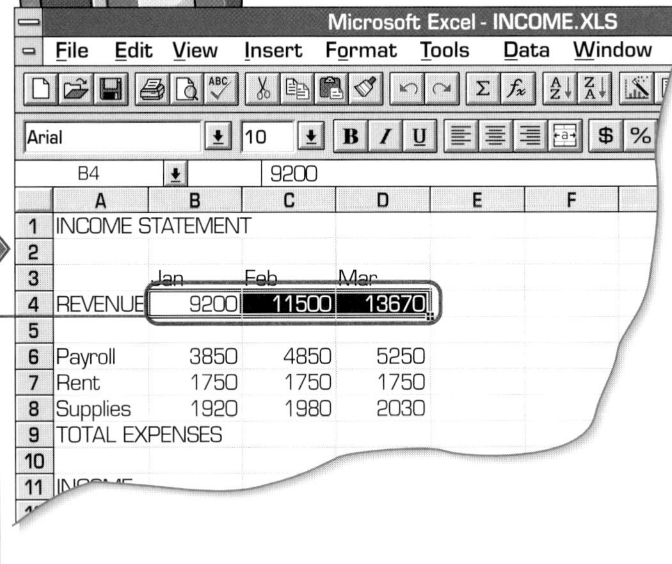

◆ Excel cancels your last change.

You can move data from one location in your worksheet to another. Excel cuts the data and pastes it in a new location. The original data disappears.

MOVE DATA

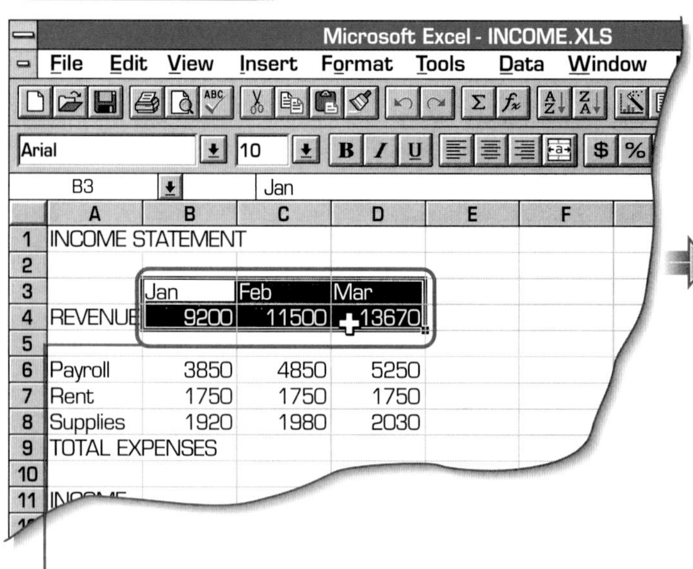

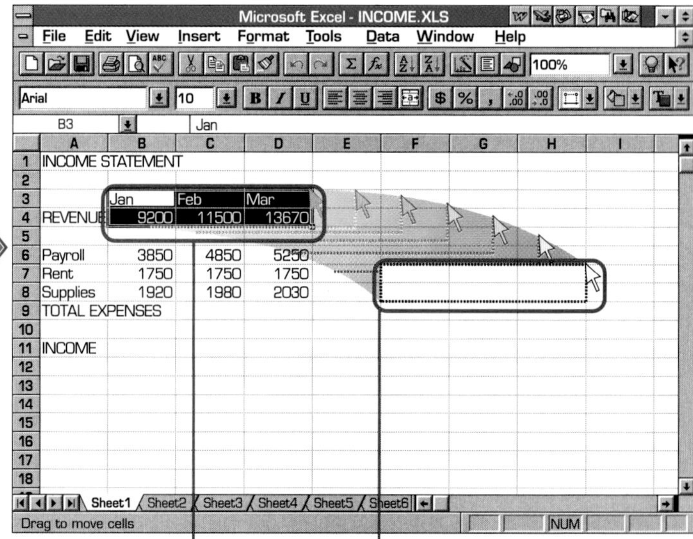

1 Select the cells containing the data you want to move to a new location.

Note: To select cells, refer to page 140.

2 Move the mouse ✚ over any border of the selected cells and ✚ changes to ↖.

3 Press and hold down the left button and then drag the mouse ↖ to where you want to place the data.

◆ A rectangular box indicates where the data will appear.

You can also move data to another worksheet.

Note: For more information, refer to page 218.

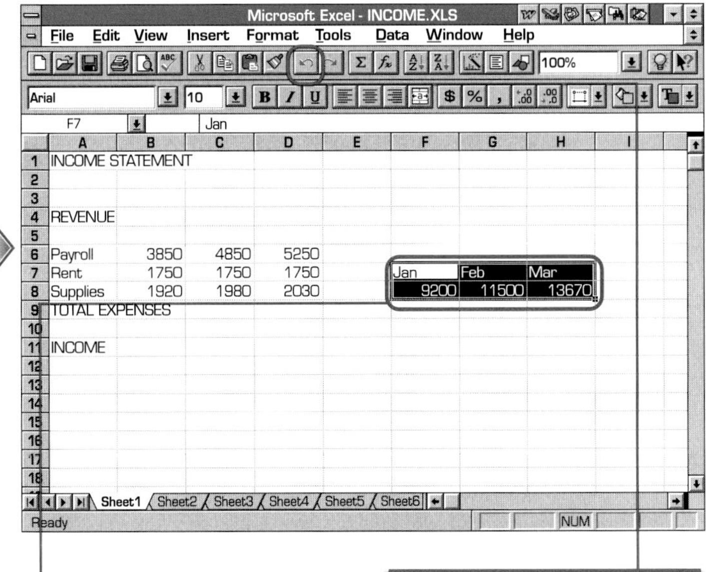

4 Release the left button and the data moves to the new location.

CANCEL THE MOVE

◆ To immediately cancel the move, position the mouse over the Undo button and then press the left button.

You can also use these buttons to move data.

1 Select the cells containing the data you want to move to a new location.

2 Move the mouse over the Cut button and then press the left button.

3 Select the cell where you want to place the data. This cell will become the top left cell of the new location.

4 Move the mouse over the Paste button and then press the left button. The data appears in the new location.

COPY DATA

Like a photocopy machine, you can make an exact copy of data and then place the copy in a new location.

COPY DATA

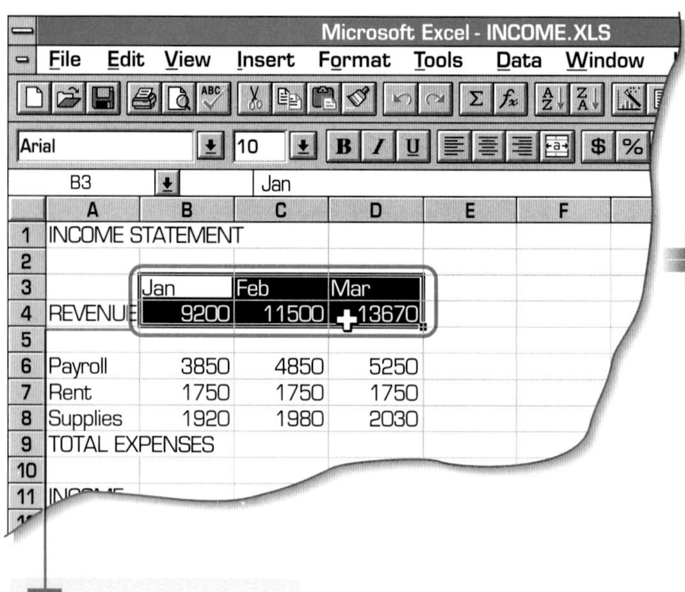

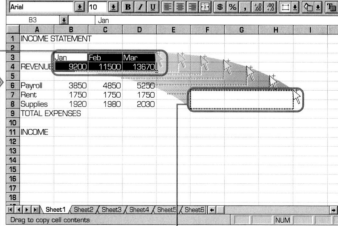

1 Select the cells containing the data you want to copy to a new location.

Note: To select cells, refer to page 140.

2 Move the mouse over any border of the selected cells (changes to).

3 Press and hold down **Ctrl** and the left button (changes to).

4 Still holding down **Ctrl** and the left button, drag the mouse to where you want to place the data.

◆ A rectangular box indicates where the data will appear.

You can also copy data to another worksheet.

Note: For more information, refer to page 218.

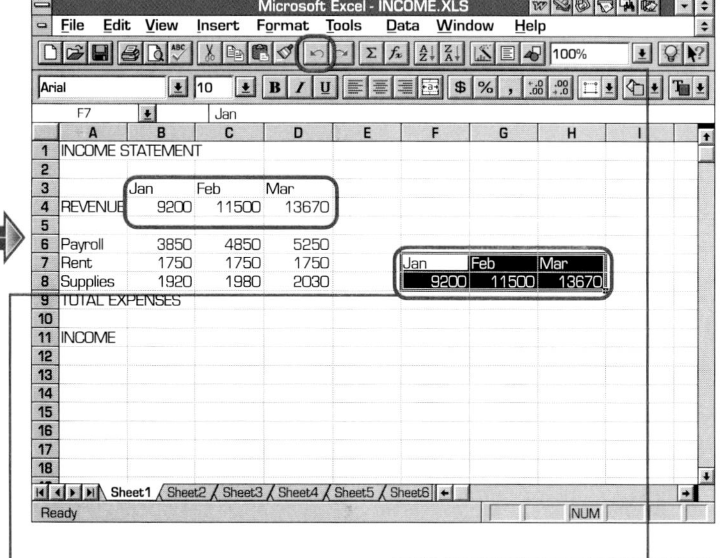

5 Release the left button and then release Ctrl .

◆ A copy of the data appears in the new location.

CANCEL THE COPY

◆ To immediately cancel the copy, position the mouse over and then press the left button.

You can also use these buttons to copy data.

1 Select the cells containing the data you want to copy to a new location.

2 Move the mouse over and then press the left button.

3 Select the cell where you want to place the data. This cell will become the top left cell of the new location.

4 Move the mouse over and then press the left button. A copy of the data appears in the new location.

*Note: You can repeat steps **3** and **4** to place the data in multiple locations in your worksheet.*

CHECK SPELLING

CHECK SPELLING

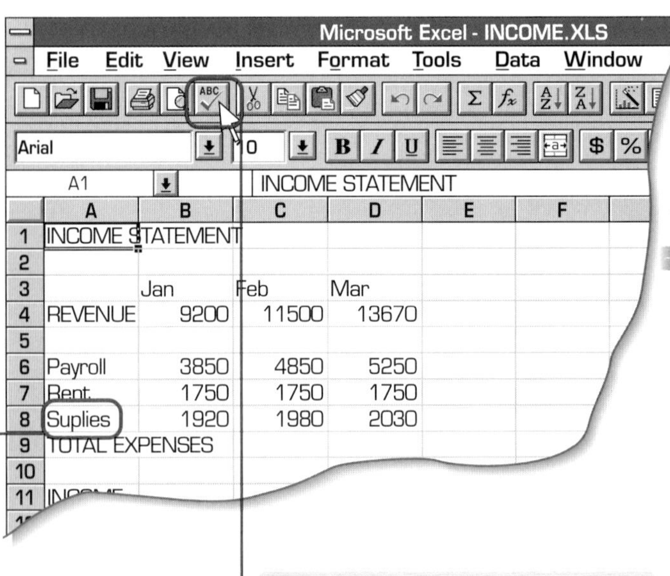

◆ In this example, the letter **p** was removed from **Supplies**.

1 To start the spell check at the beginning of your worksheet, press Ctrl + Home to move to cell **A1**.

Note: To spell check a section of your worksheet, select the cells before performing step **2**. *To select cells, refer to page 140.*

2 Move the mouse over the spelling button and then press the left button.

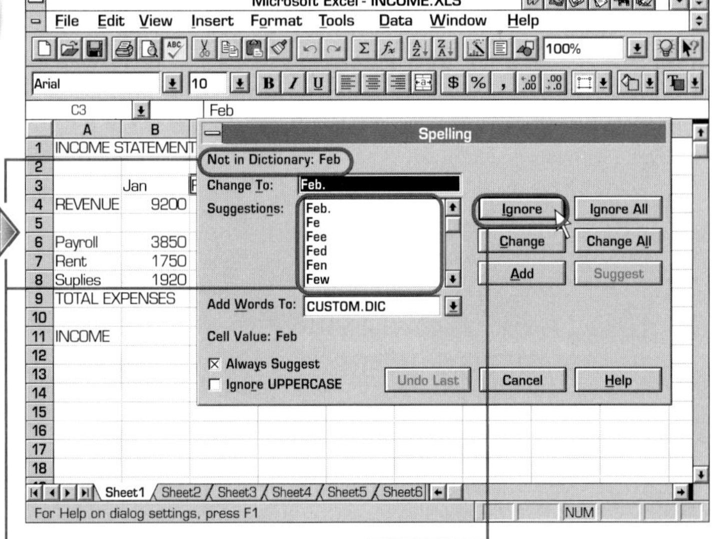

◆ If Excel finds a spelling error, the **Spelling** dialog box appears.

◆ Excel displays the word it does not recognize and suggestions to correct the error.

Ignore misspelled word

3 If you do not want to change the spelling of the word, move the mouse over **Ignore** and then press the left button.

Excel compares every word in your worksheet to words in its own dictionary. If a word does not exist in the dictionary, Excel considers it misspelled.

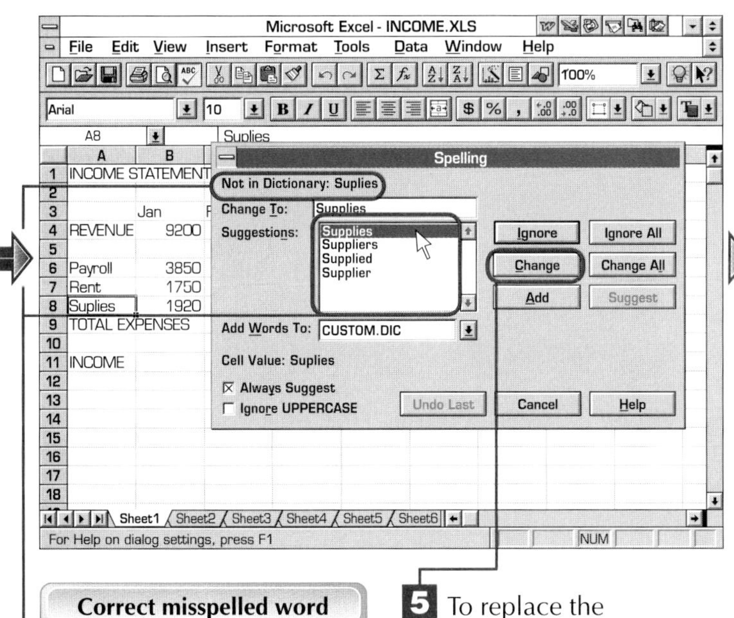

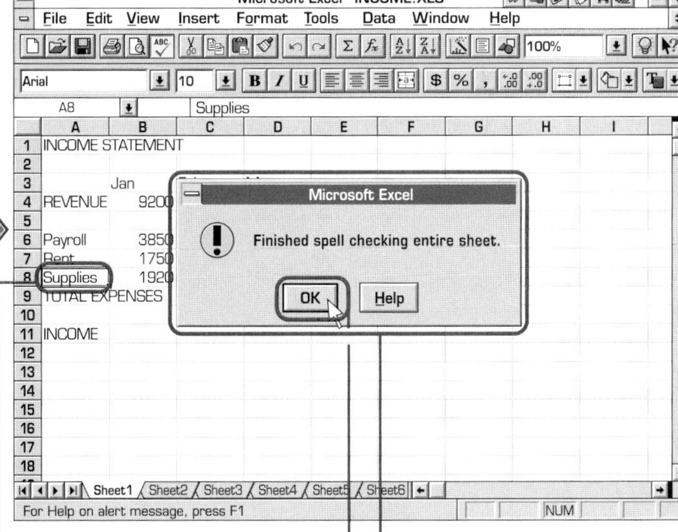

Correct misspelled word

◆ Excel displays the next word it does not recognize.

4 To correct the spelling, move the mouse over the word you want to use and then press the left button.

5 To replace the misspelled word in your worksheet with the correct spelling, move the mouse over **Change** and then press the left button.

◆ Excel corrects the word and continues checking for spelling errors.

6 Ignore or correct spelling errors until Excel finishes checking your worksheet.

◆ This dialog box appears when the spell check is complete.

7 To close the dialog box, move the mouse over **OK** and then press the left button.

You can use formulas to perform calculations on your worksheet data.
5.0

INTRODUCTION TO FORMULAS

◆ You must begin a formula with an equal sign (=).

◆ You should use cell references (example: **A1**) instead of actual numbers whenever possible. This way, if your data changes, Excel will automatically redo the calculations.

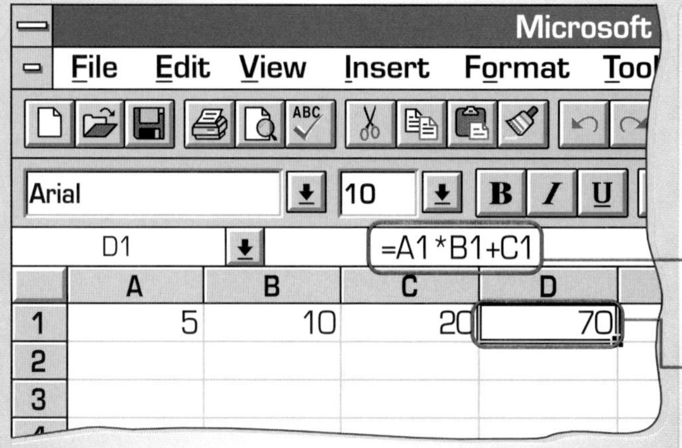

In this example, cell D1 contains the formula:

=A1*B1+C1

=5*10+20

=70

◆ The formula for the active cell appears in the formula bar.

◆ The result of the calculation appears in the cell containing the formula (example: **D1**).

You can use these operators in your formulas:

+	Addition
-	Subtraction
*	Multiplication
/	Division
^	Exponentiation

Excel will perform calculations in the following order:

1. Exponentiation
2. Multiplication and Division
3. Addition and Subtraction

You can change the order that Excel calculates your formulas by using parentheses ( ).

◆ Excel will calculate the numbers in parentheses first.

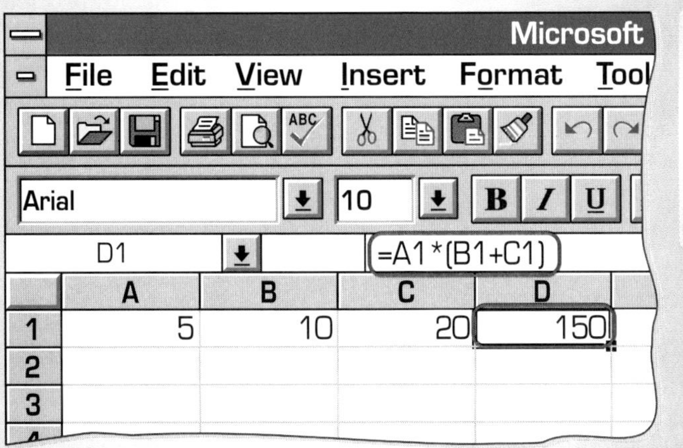

In this example, cell D1 contains the formula:

=A1*(B1+C1)

=5*(10+20)

=150

ENTER A FORMULA

You can enter a formula into any cell in your worksheet.

ENTER A FORMULA

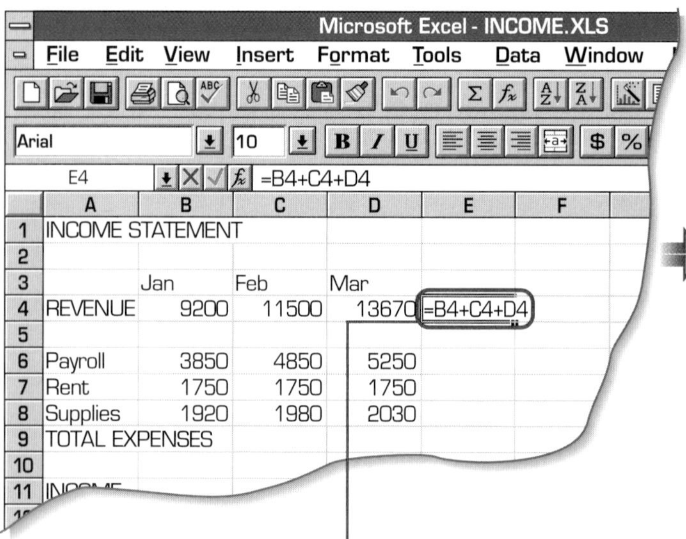

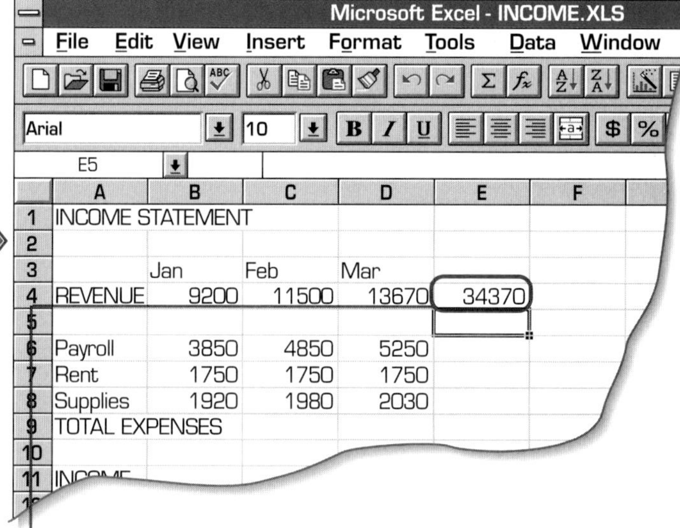

1 Move the mouse over the cell where you want to enter a formula (example: **E4**) and then press the left button.

2 Type an equal sign (=) to begin the formula.

3 Type the calculation you want to perform (example: **B4+C4+D4**).

Note: This formula will calculate the total Revenue.

4 Press Enter and the result of the calculation appears in the cell (example: **34370**).

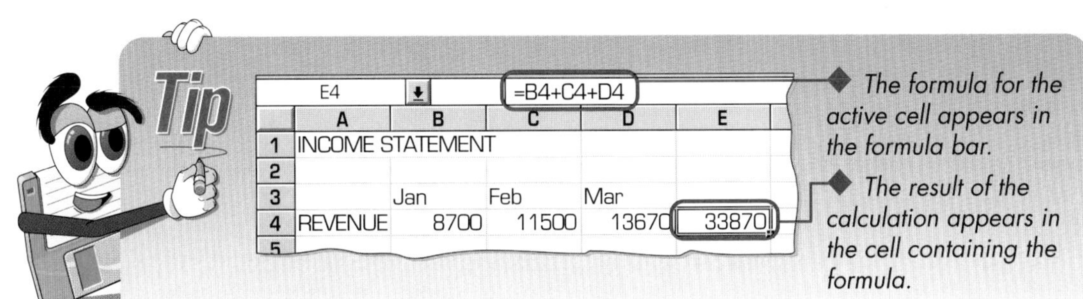

◆ *The formula for the active cell appears in the formula bar.*

◆ *The result of the calculation appears in the cell containing the formula.*

AUTOMATIC RECALCULATION

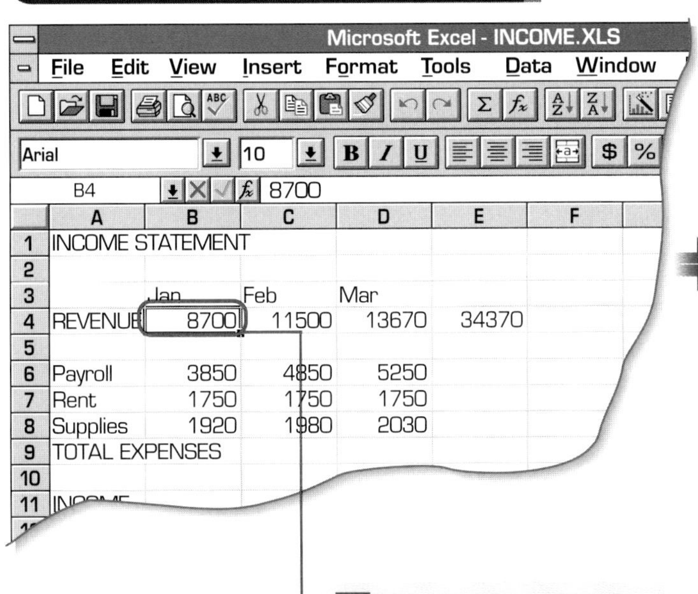

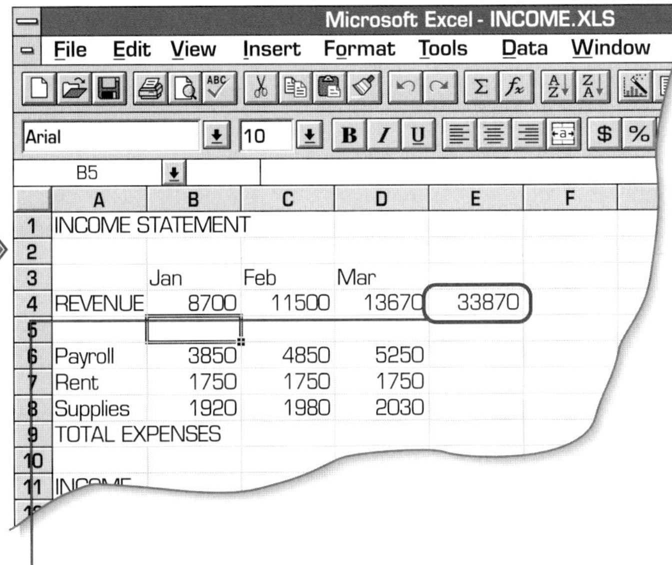

If you change a number used in a formula, Excel will automatically calculate a new result.

1 Move the mouse over the cell you want to change (example: **B4**) and then press the left button.

2 Type a new number (example: **8700**).

3 Press Enter and Excel automatically recalculates the formula using the new number.

FUNCTIONS

A function is a ready-to-use formula. Excel offers over 300 functions to perform specialized calculations on your worksheet data.
Functions
Instant!
Ready to Use!!
MAX AVERAGE
ROUND

INTRODUCTION TO FUNCTIONS

You must tell Excel what data to use to calculate a function. This data is enclosed in parentheses ( ).

=SUM(A1,A3,A5)

◆ When there is a comma (,) between cell references in a function, Excel uses each cell to perform the calculation.

Example: =SUM(A1,A3,A5) is the same as the formula =A1+A3+A5.

=SUM(A1:A4)

◆ When there is a colon (:) between cell references in a function, Excel uses the displayed cells and all cells between them to perform the calculation.

Example: =SUM(A1:A4) is the same as the formula =A1+A2+A3+A4.

Common Functions

Function	Description
AVERAGE	Calculates the average value of a list of numbers. *Example: =AVERAGE(B1:B6)*
COUNT	Counts the number of values in a list of numbers. *Example: =COUNT(B1:B6)*
MAX	Finds the largest value in a list of numbers. *Example: =MAX(B1:B6)*
MIN	Finds the smallest value in a list of numbers. *Example: =MIN(B1:B6)*
ROUND	Rounds a number to a specific number of digits. *Example: =ROUND(B6,2)*
SUM	Adds a list of numbers. *Example: =SUM(B1:B6)*

◆ A function starts with an equal sign (=).

◆ You should use cell references (example: **A1**) instead of actual numbers whenever possible. This way, if your data changes, Excel will automatically redo the calculations.

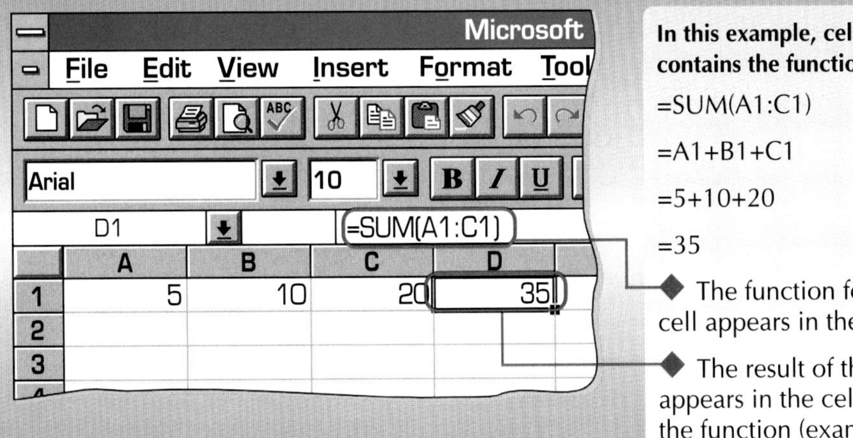

In this example, cell D1 contains the function:

=SUM(A1:C1)

=A1+B1+C1

=5+10+20

=35

◆ The function for the active cell appears in the formula bar.

◆ The result of the calculation appears in the cell containing the function (example: **D1**).

ENTER A FUNCTION

ENTER A FUNCTION

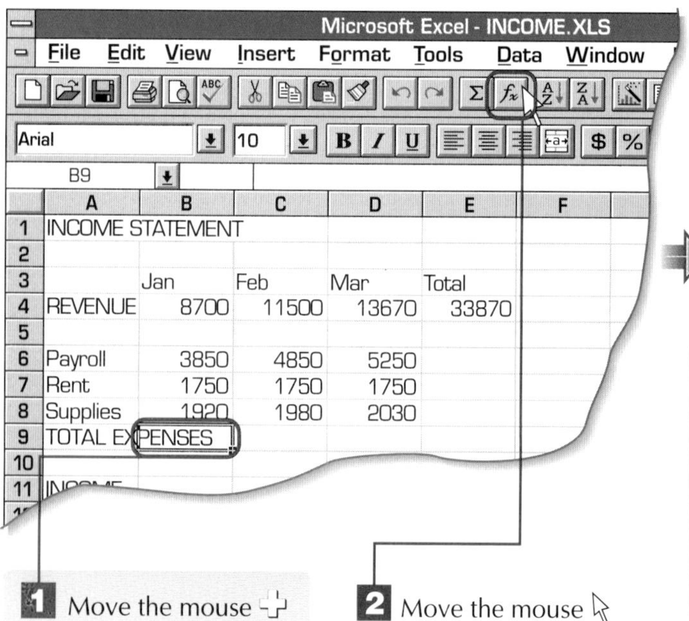

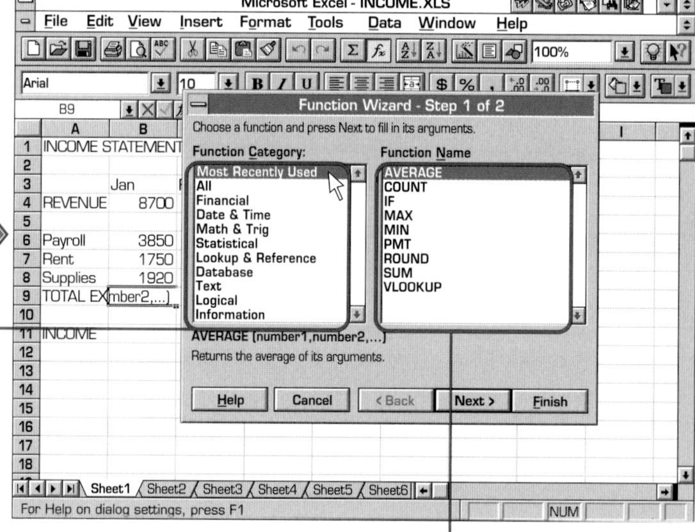

1 Move the mouse over the cell where you want to enter a function (example: **B9**) and then press the left button.

2 Move the mouse over and then press the left button.

◆ The **Function Wizard** dialog box appears.

3 Move the mouse over the category containing the function you want to use and then press the left button.

*Note: If you do not know which category contains the function you want to use, select **All**. This will display a list of all the functions.*

◆ This area displays the functions in the category you selected.

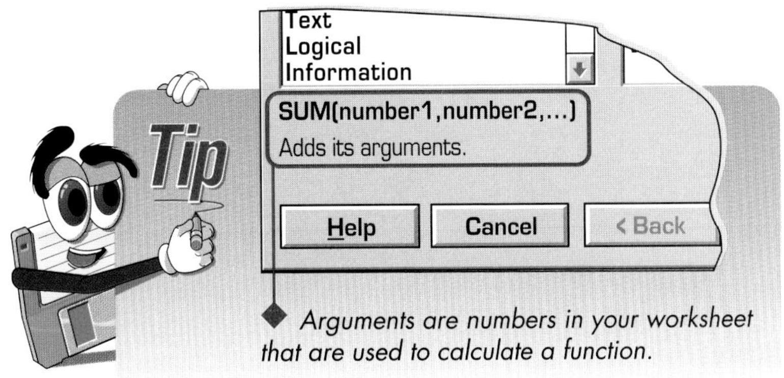

Arguments are numbers in your worksheet that are used to calculate a function.

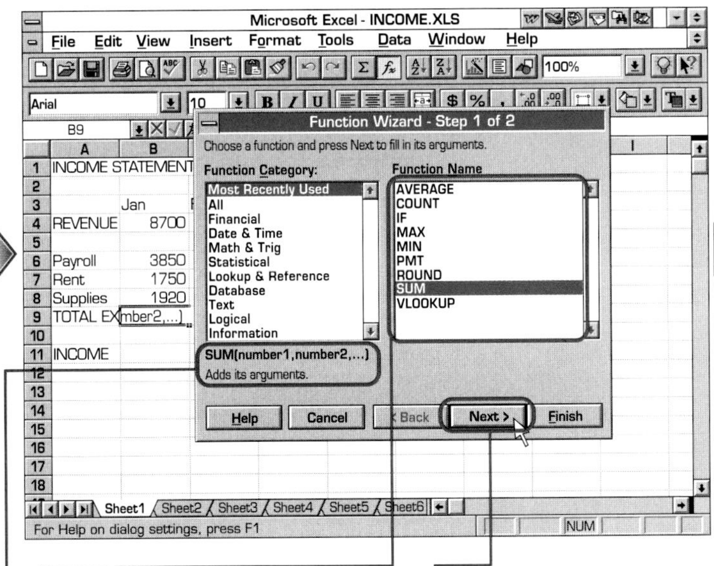

4 Move the mouse over the function you want to use (example: **SUM**) and then press the left button.

◆ A description of the function you selected appears.

5 To select the function, move the mouse over **Next** and then press the left button.

◆ This dialog box appears. The text in the dialog box depends on the function you selected in step **4**.

ENTER A FUNCTION

If the Function Wizard dialog box covers the data you want to use in the function, you can move the dialog box to another location on your screen.

ENTER A FUNCTION (CONTINUED)

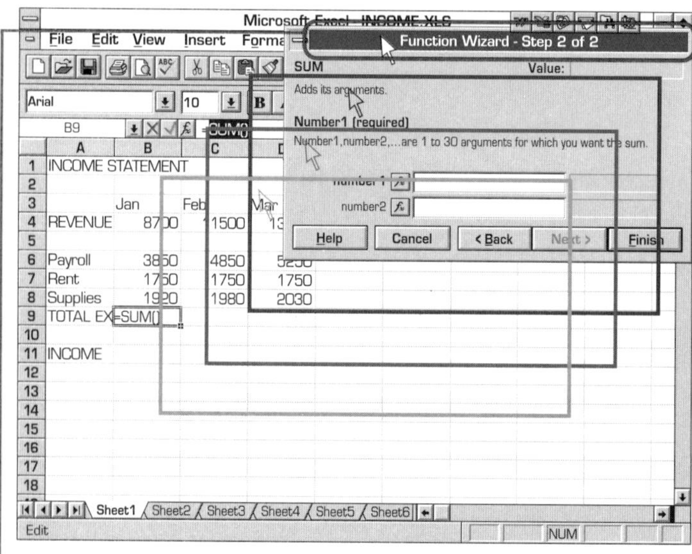

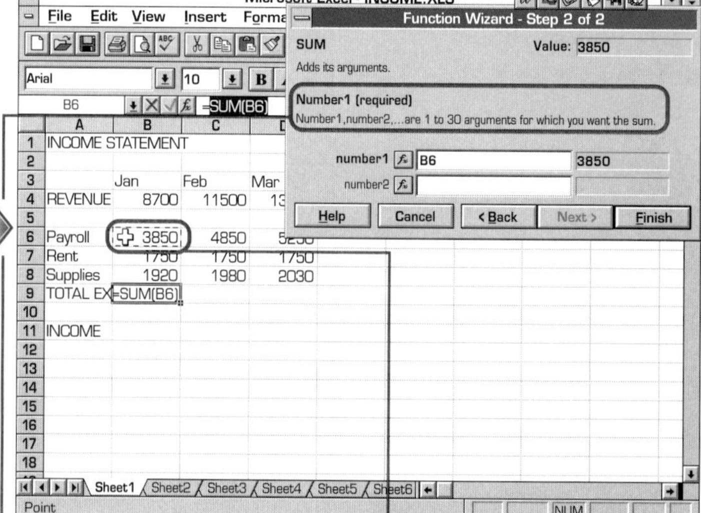

6 To move the **Function Wizard** dialog box, position the mouse over the title bar and then press and hold down the left button.

7 Still holding down the button, drag the box to a new location.

8 Release the button and the dialog box moves to the new location.

◆ This area describes the first number Excel needs to perform the function.

9 To select a number, move the mouse over the cell containing the data you want to use and then press the left button.

Note: If the number you want to enter does not appear in your worksheet, type the number.

◆ *In the example below, you can quickly enter numbers in the* ***Function Wizard*** *dialog box. Replace steps* **9** *to* **11** *by selecting cells* ***B6*** *to* ***B8****.*

Note: To select cells, refer to page 140.

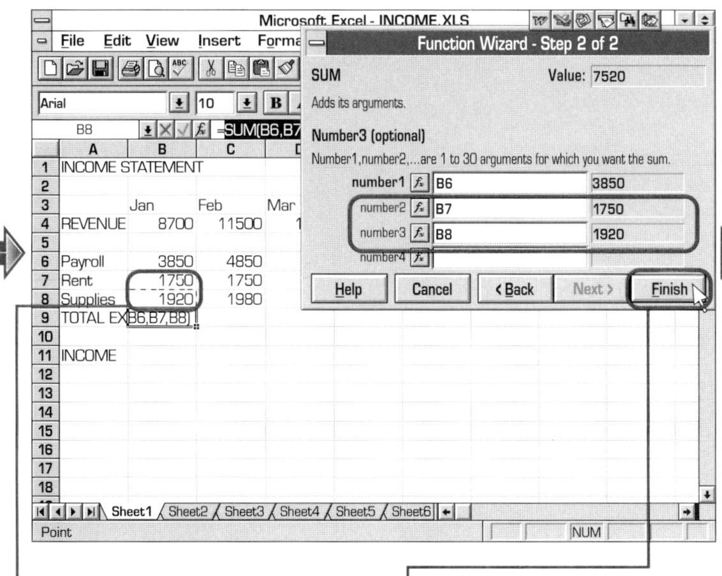

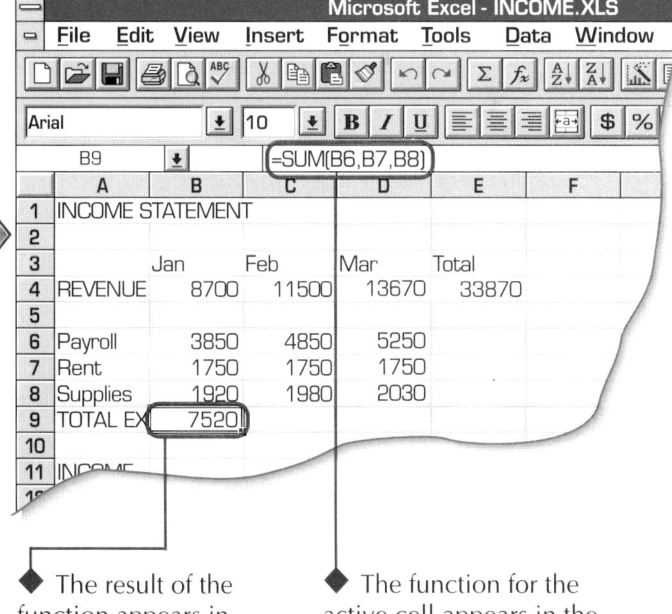

10 To display a description of the next number Excel needs to perform the function, press **Tab**.

11 Repeat steps **9** and **10** until you have selected all the cells you want to use in the function.

12 Move the mouse over **Finish** and then press the left button.

◆ The result of the function appears in the cell.

◆ The function for the active cell appears in the formula bar.

ADD NUMBERS

You can use the AutoSum feature to quickly add a list of numbers in your worksheet.

ADD A LIST OF NUMBERS

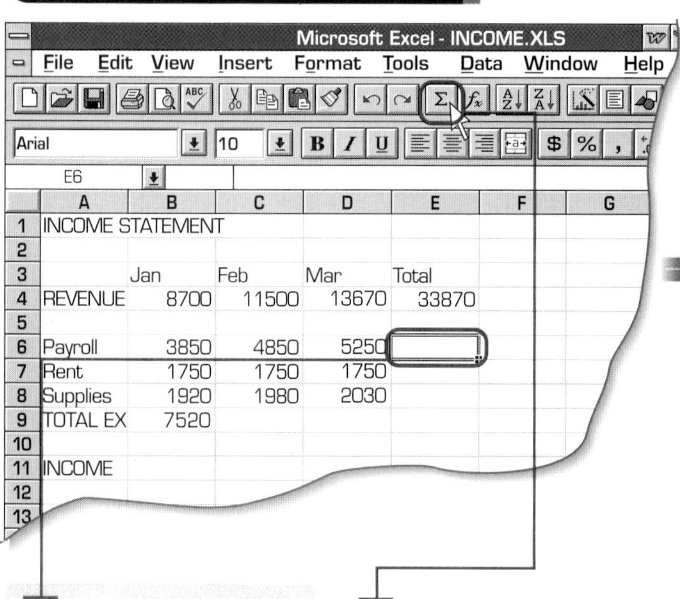

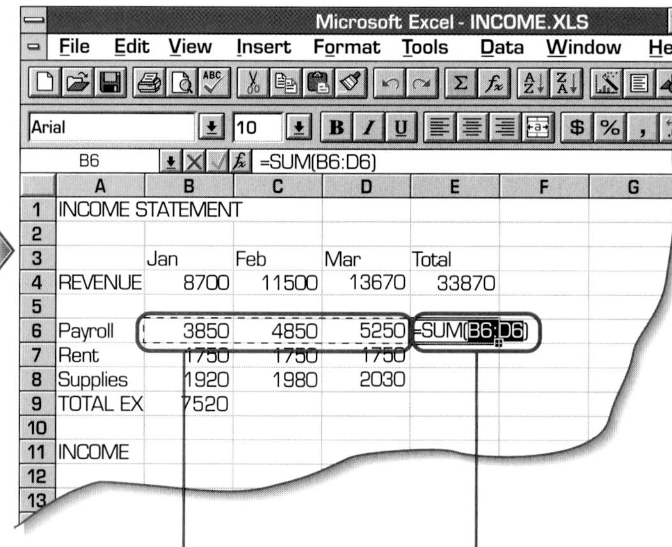

1 Move the mouse over the cell you want to display the sum (example: **E6**) and then press the left button.

2 Move the mouse over Σ and then press the left button.

Note: Σ is the Greek symbol for sum.

◆ A moving border appears around the cells Excel will add together.

◆ The SUM function appears. It displays the first and last cells Excel will add together, separated by a colon (:).

◆ To add a different list of cells, select the cells.

Note: To select cells, refer to page 140.

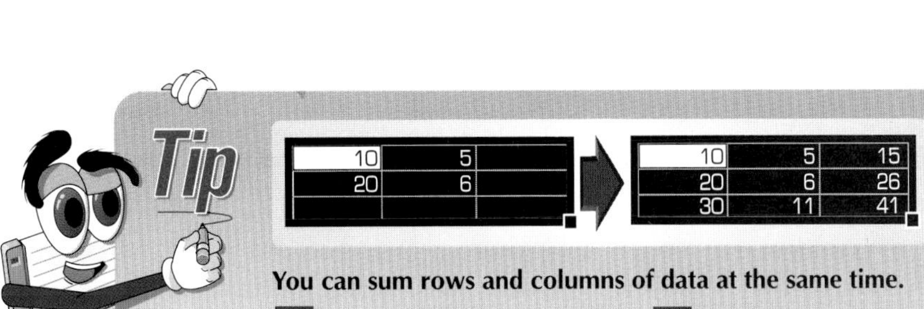

Tip

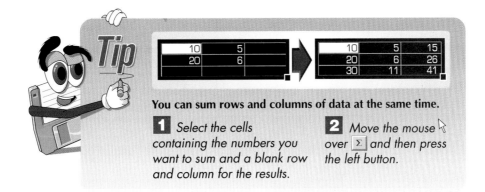

You can sum rows and columns of data at the same time.

1 *Select the cells containing the numbers you want to sum and a blank row and column for the results.*

2 *Move the mouse over Σ and then press the left button.*

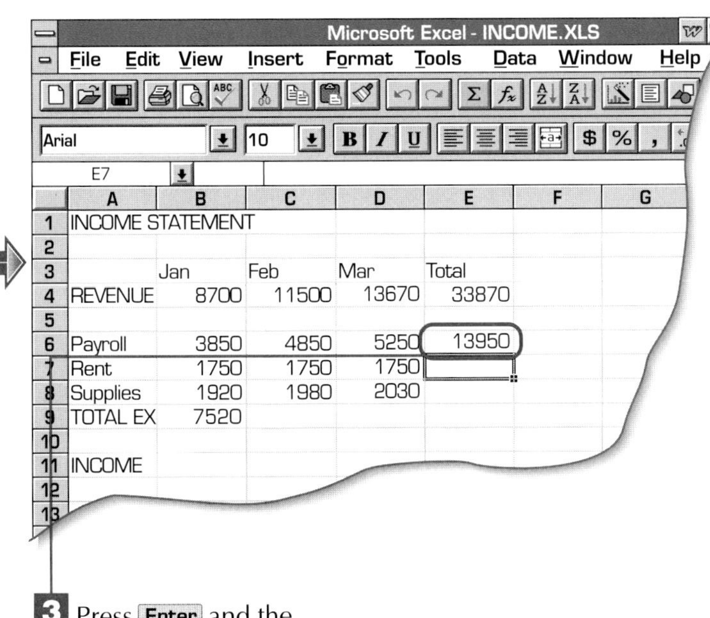

3 Press Enter and the result appears in the cell.

ADD SEVERAL LISTS OF NUMBERS

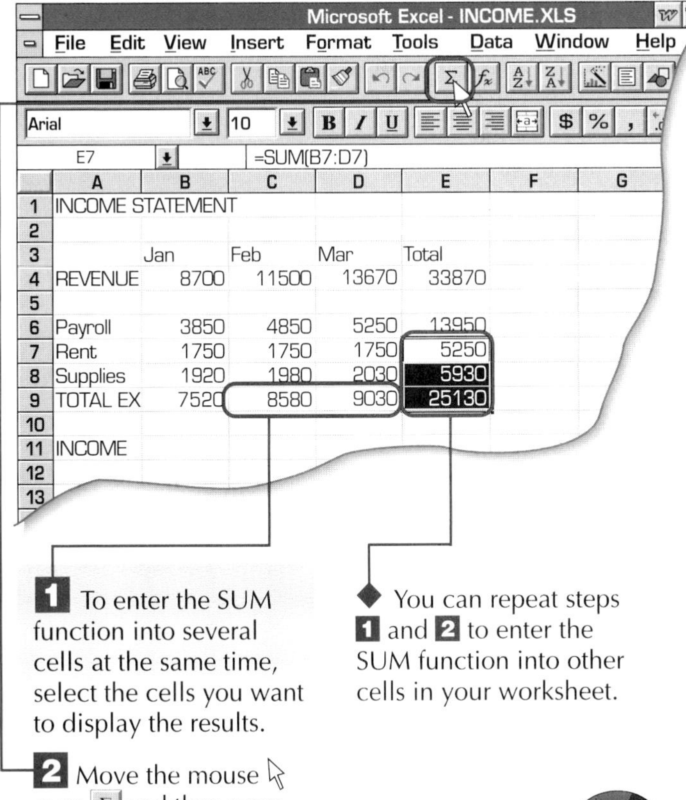

1 To enter the SUM function into several cells at the same time, select the cells you want to display the results.

2 Move the mouse over Σ and then press the left button.

◆ You can repeat steps **1** and **2** to enter the SUM function into other cells in your worksheet.

ERRORS IN FORMULAS

An error message appears when Excel cannot properly calculate a formula. You can correct an error by editing the cell displaying the error message.

COMMON ERRORS IN FORMULAS

#DIV/0!

This error message appears in a cell if the formula you entered divides a number by zero.

	A	B	C	D
1	50		35	
2	0			
3	#DIV/0!		#DIV/0!	
4				
5				

This cell contains the formula **=A1/A2 = 50/0**

The formula divides a number by 0.

This cell contains the formula **=C1/C2 = 35/0**

The formula divides a number by 0.

Note: Excel considers a blank cell to contain the zero value.

#NAME?

This error message appears in a cell if the formula you entered contains a name Excel does not recognize.

	A	B	C	D
1	5		30	
2	10		5	
3	20		10	
4	#NAME?		#NAME?	
5				

This cell contains the formula **=A1+A2A3**

The formula is missing a plus sign (+).

This cell contains the function **=SUMM(C1:C3)**

The name of the function is misspelled.

CORRECT AN ERROR

1 To correct an error, move the mouse over the cell displaying the error message and then quickly press the left button twice.

2 Edit the formula as you would any data in your worksheet.

Note: To edit data, refer to page 158.

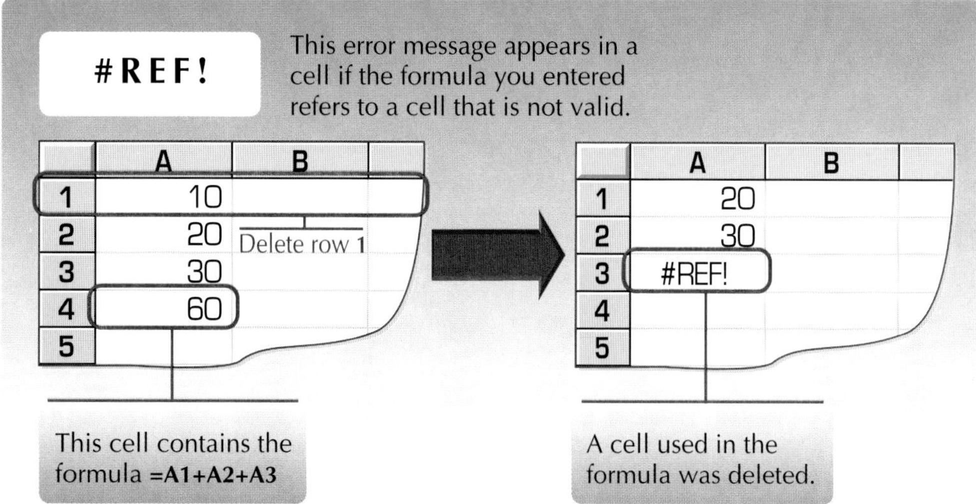

#REF!
This error message appears in a cell if the formula you entered refers to a cell that is not valid.
A
B
1
10
2
20
Delete row 1
3
30
4
60
5
This cell contains the formula **=A1+A2+A3**
A
B
1
20
2
30
3
#REF!
4
5
A cell used in the formula was deleted.

COPY FORMULAS

After entering a formula in your worksheet, you can copy the formula to other cells. This saves you time when entering the same formula into several cells.

COPY FORMULAS (USING RELATIVE REFERENCES)

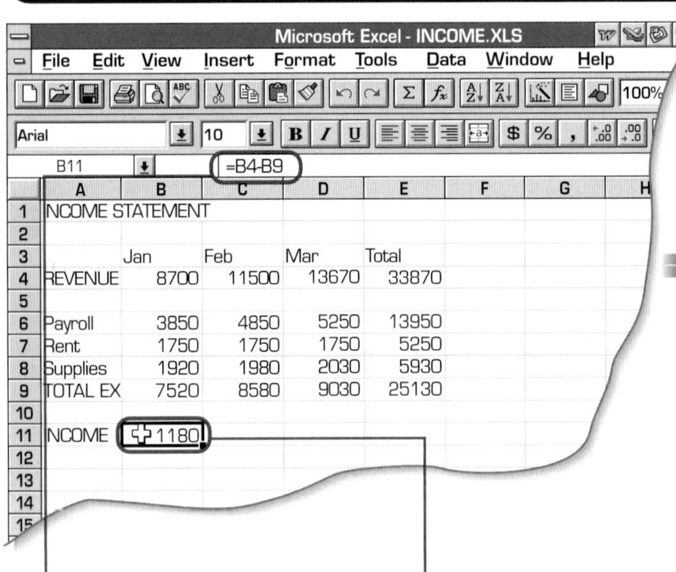

1 Enter the formula you want to copy to other cells (example: to calculate INCOME, enter **=B4-B9** in cell **B11**).

2 Move the mouse ✥ over the cell containing the formula and then press the left button.

3 Move the mouse ✥ over the bottom right corner of the cell and ✥ changes to +.

4 Press and hold down the left button as you drag the mouse + over the cells you want to receive a copy of the formula.

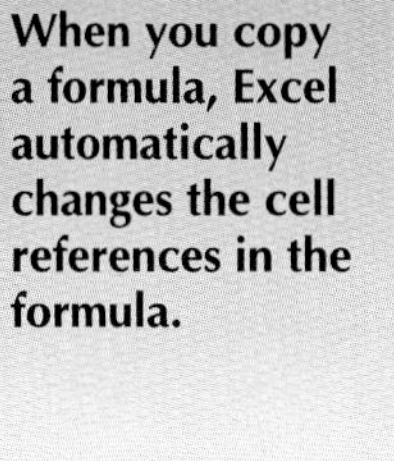

When you copy a formula, Excel automatically changes the cell references in the formula.

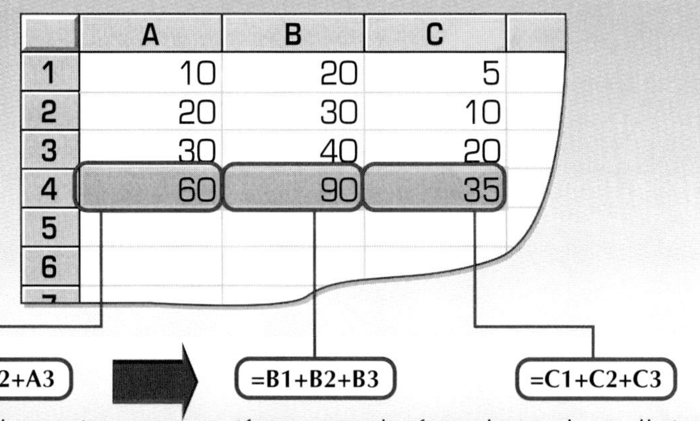

A
B
C
1 10 20 5
2 20 30 10
3 30 40 20
4 60 90 35
5
6
=A1+A2+A3
=B1+B2+B3
=C1+C2+C3

This cell contains the formula =A1+A2+A3

If you copy the formula to other cells in the worksheet, the cell references in the new formulas automatically change.

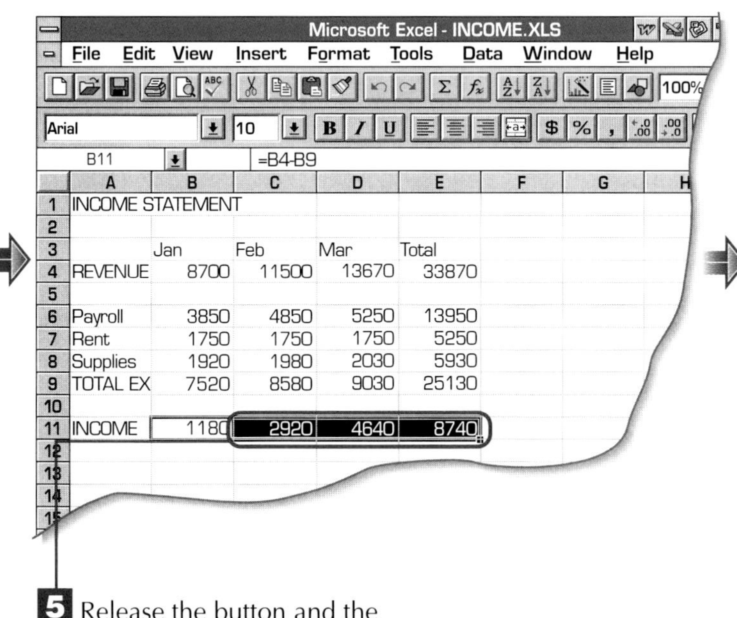

5 Release the button and the results of the formulas appear.

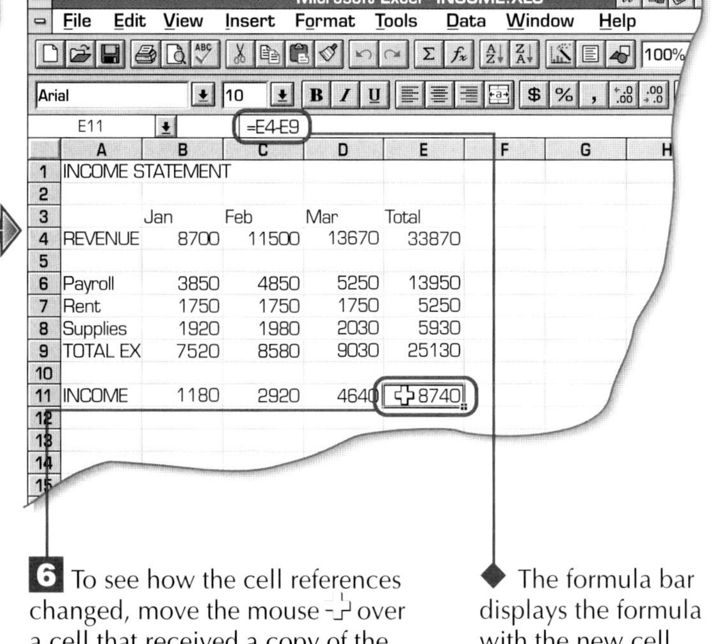

6 To see how the cell references changed, move the mouse over a cell that received a copy of the formula (example: **E11**) and then press the left button.

◆ The formula bar displays the formula with the new cell references.

COPY FORMULAS

To save time, you can copy a formula to other cells in your worksheet. If you do not want Excel to change a cell reference when copying the formula, you must lock the cell. A locked cell reference is called an absolute reference.

COPY FORMULAS (USING ABSOLUTE REFERENCES)

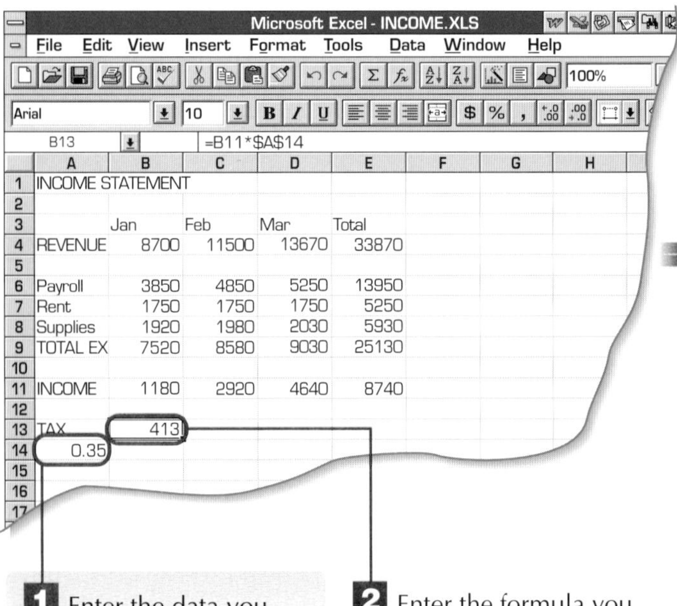

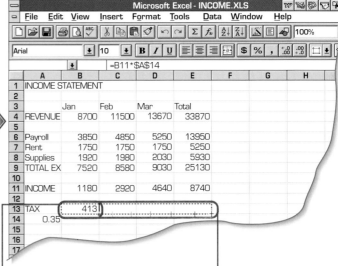

1 Enter the data you want to use as an absolute cell reference (example: **0.35** in cell **A14**).

2 Enter the formula you want to copy to other cells (example: to calculate TAX, enter **=B11*A14** in cell **B13**).

*Note: To lock a cell reference during the copy process, type a dollar sign (**$**) before both the column letter and row number (example: **A14**).*

3 Move the mouse over the cell containing the formula you want to copy (example: **B13**) and then press the left button.

4 Move the mouse over the bottom right corner of the cell and changes to +.

5 Press and hold down the left button as you drag the mouse + over the cells you want to receive a copy of the formula.

To make a cell reference absolute, type a dollar sign ($) before both the column letter and row number (example: B1).

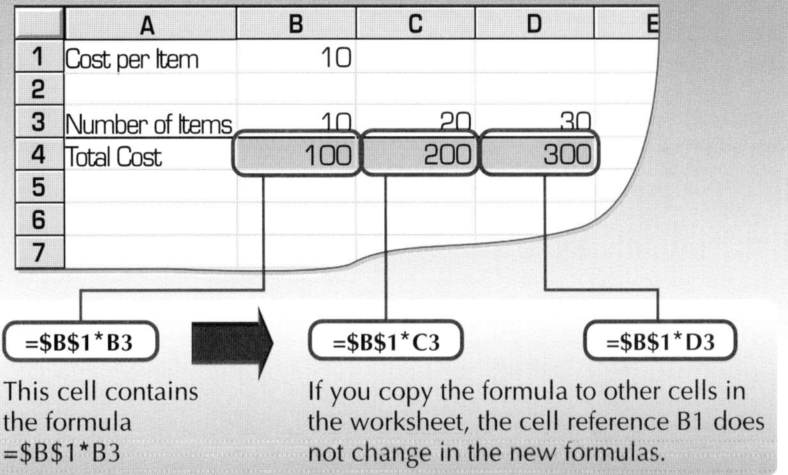

This cell contains the formula =B1*B3

If you copy the formula to other cells in the worksheet, the cell reference B1 does not change in the new formulas.

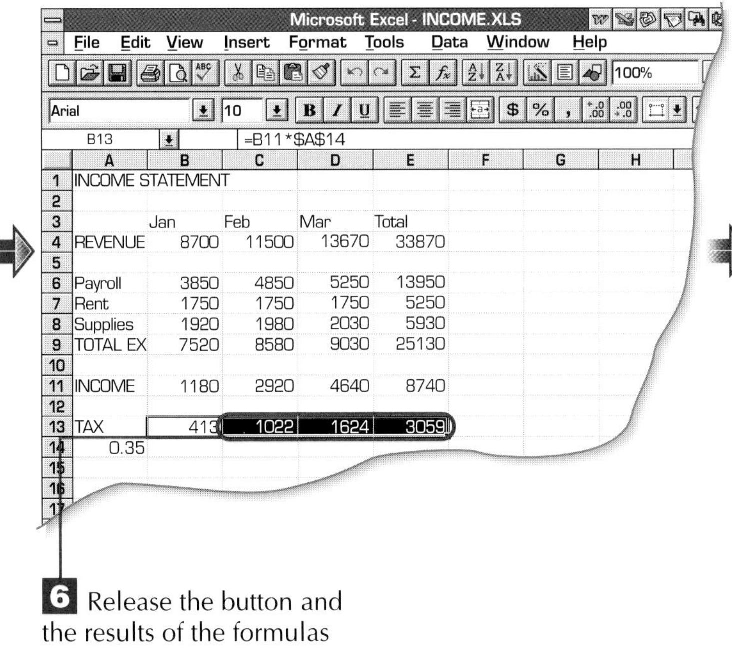

6 Release the button and the results of the formulas appear.

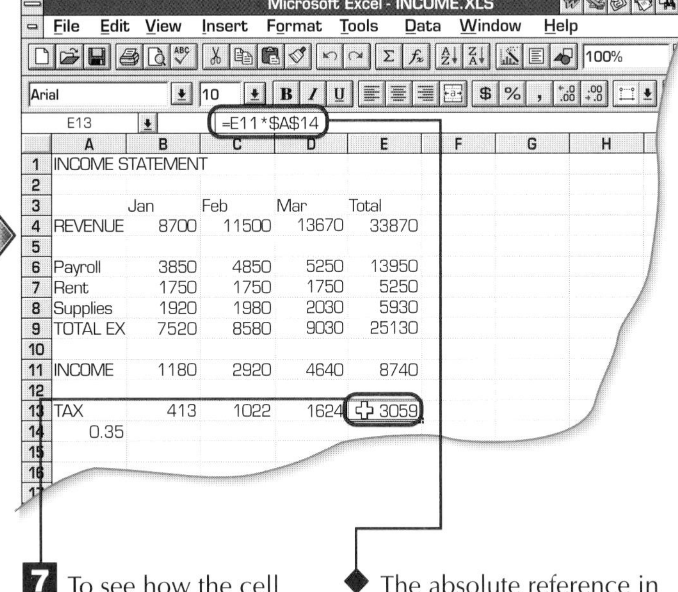

7 To see how the cell references changed, move the mouse over a cell that received a copy of the formula (example: **E13**) and then press the left button.

◆ The absolute reference in the formula did not change (example: **A14**). The relative reference in the formula did change (example: **E11**).

INSERT A ROW OR COLUMN

You can add a row or column to your worksheet if you want to insert new data.

INSERT A ROW

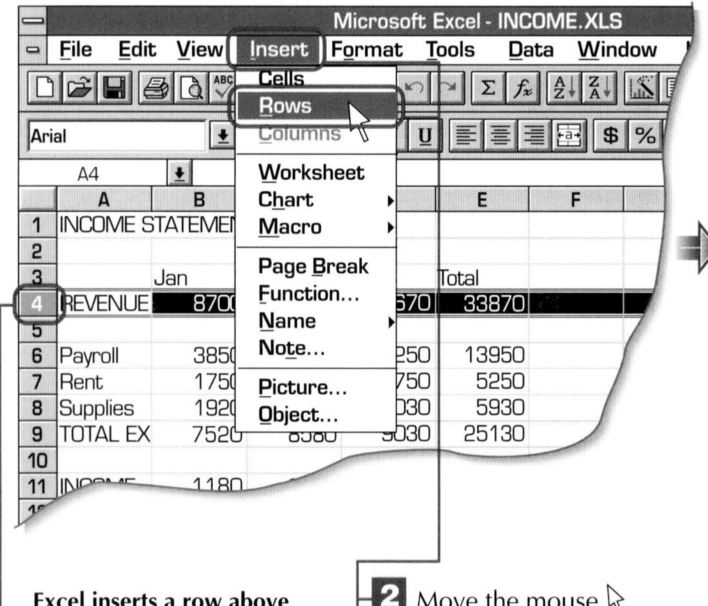

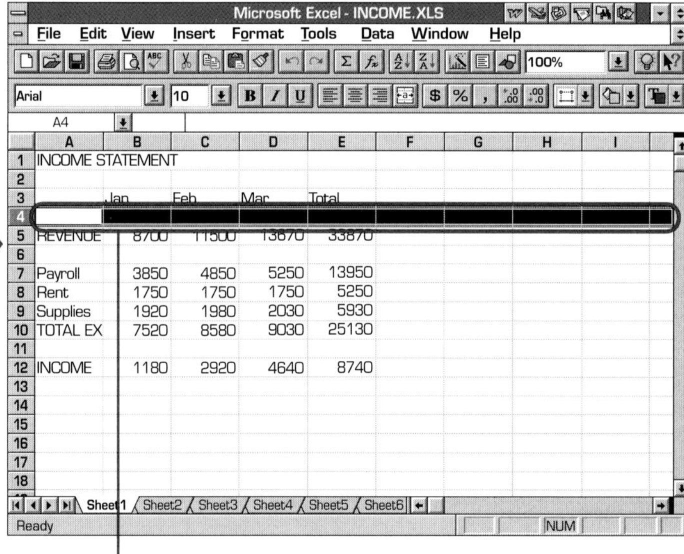

Excel inserts a row above the row you select.

1 To select a row, move the mouse over the row heading (example: **row 4**) and then press the left button.

2 Move the mouse over **Insert** and then press the left button.

3 Move the mouse over **Rows** and then press the left button.

◆ The new row appears and all the rows that follow shift downward.

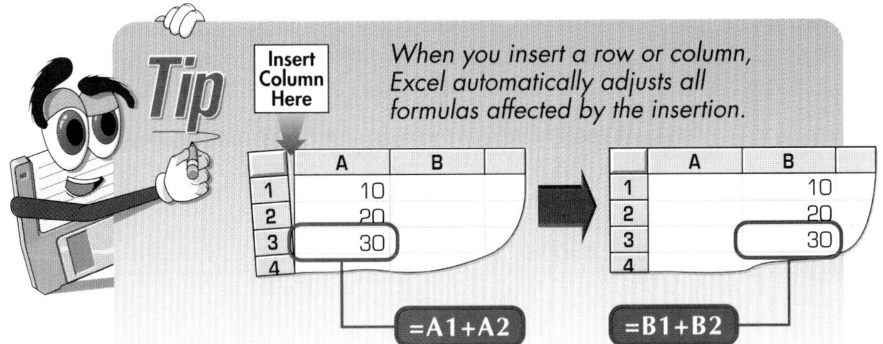

Tip
Insert Column Here
When you insert a row or column, Excel automatically adjusts all formulas affected by the insertion.
=A1+A2
=B1+B2

INSERT A COLUMN

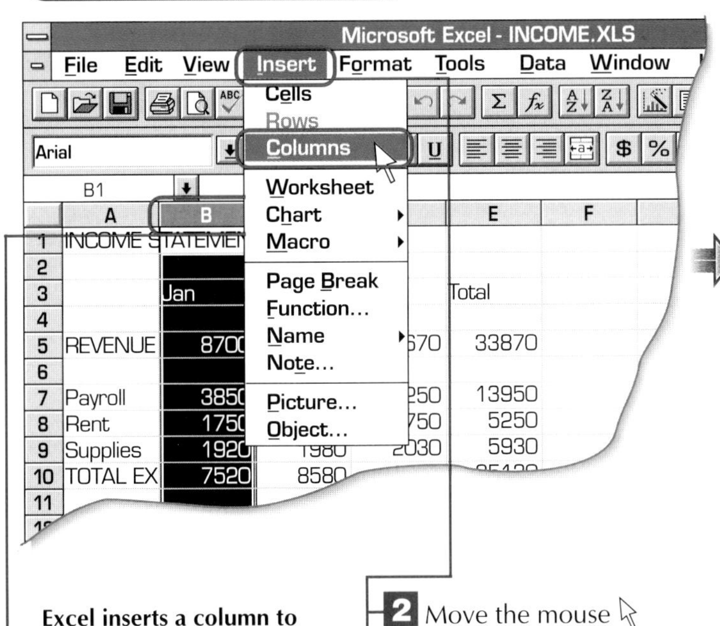

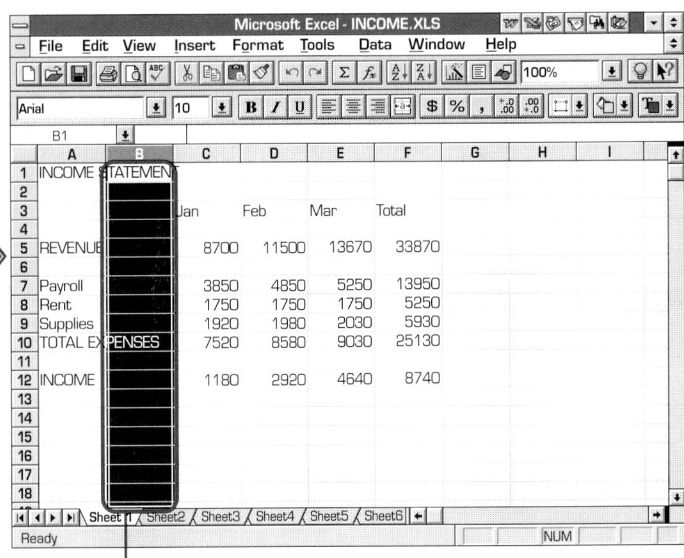

Excel inserts a column to the left of the column you select.

1 To select a column, move the mouse over the column heading (example: **column B**) and then press the left button.

2 Move the mouse over **Insert** and then press the left button.

3 Move the mouse over **Columns** and then press the left button.

◆ The new column appears and all the columns that follow shift to the right.

DELETE A ROW OR COLUMN

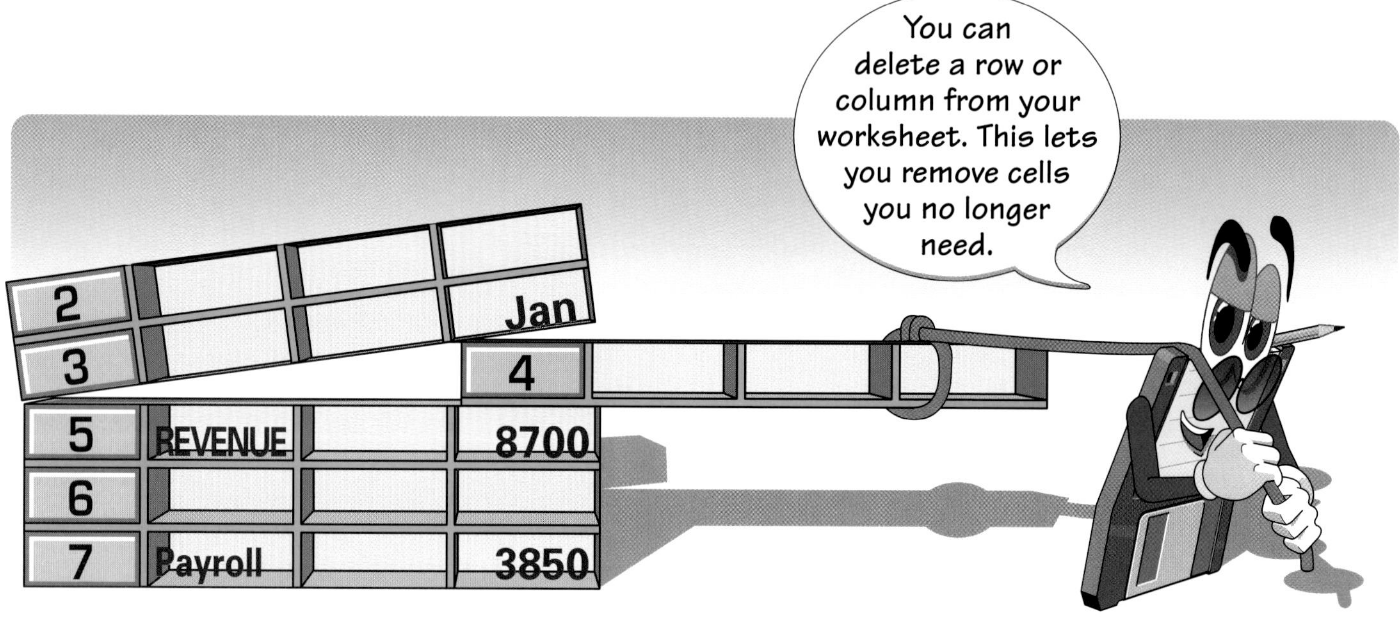

You can delete a row or column from your worksheet. This lets you remove cells you no longer need.
2
3
Jan
4
5
REVENUE
8700
6
7
Payroll
3850

DELETE A ROW

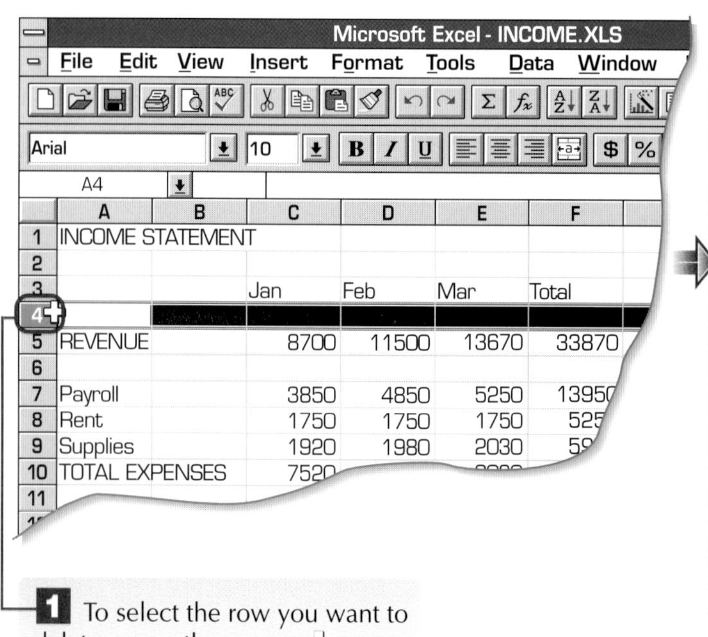

1 To select the row you want to delete, move the mouse over the row heading (example: **row 4**) and then press the left button.

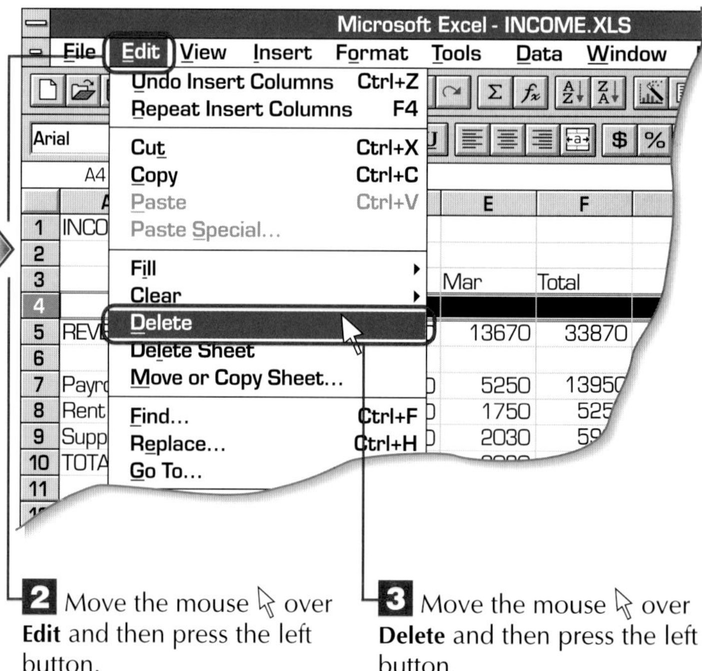

2 Move the mouse over **Edit** and then press the left button.

3 Move the mouse over **Delete** and then press the left button.

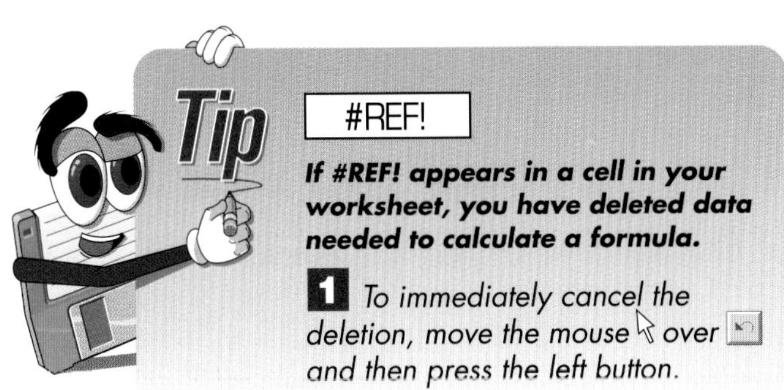

#REF!

If #REF! appears in a cell in your worksheet, you have deleted data needed to calculate a formula.

1 *To immediately cancel the deletion, move the mouse over and then press the left button.*

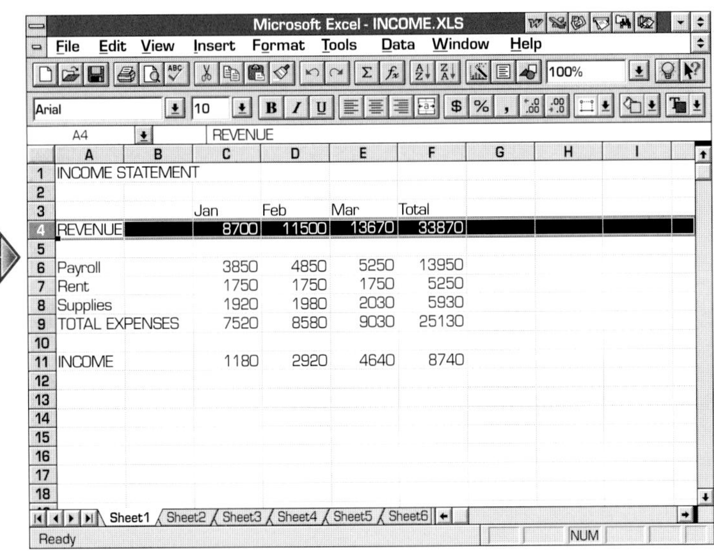

◆ The row disappears and all the rows that follow shift upward.

DELETE A COLUMN

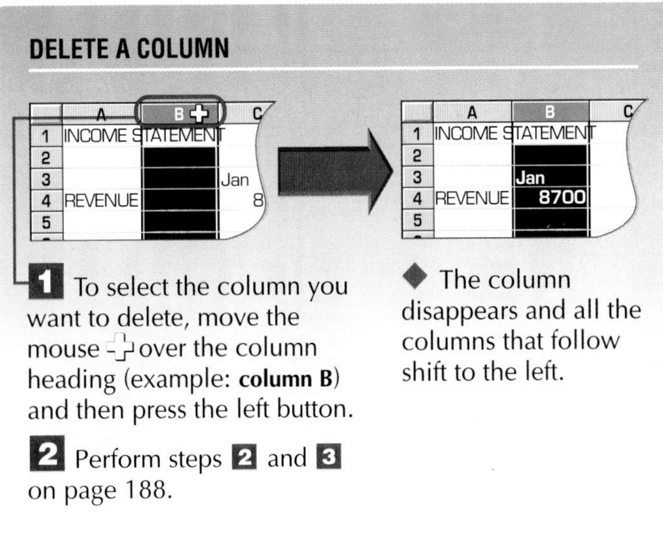

1 To select the column you want to delete, move the mouse over the column heading (example: **column B**) and then press the left button.

2 Perform steps **2** and **3** on page 188.

◆ The column disappears and all the columns that follow shift to the left.

CHANGE COLUMN WIDTH

You can improve the appearance of your worksheet and display hidden data by changing the width of columns.

CHANGE COLUMN WIDTH

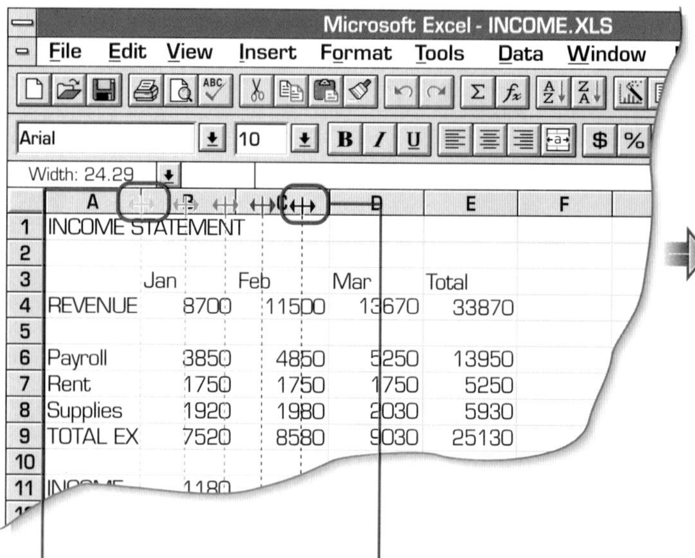

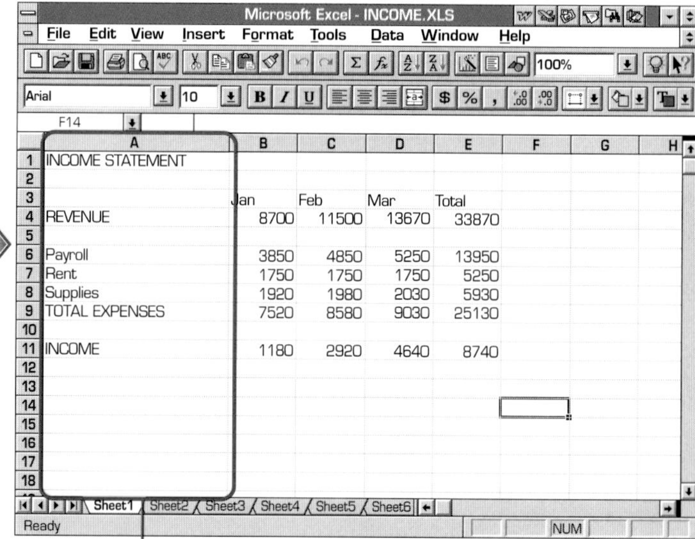

1 Move the mouse ✢ over the right edge of the column heading you want to change (example: **column A**) and ✢ changes to ↔.

2 Press and hold down the left button as you drag the edge of the column to a new position.

◆ A dotted line indicates the new column width.

3 Release the button and the new column width appears.

You can change the width of several columns at the same time.

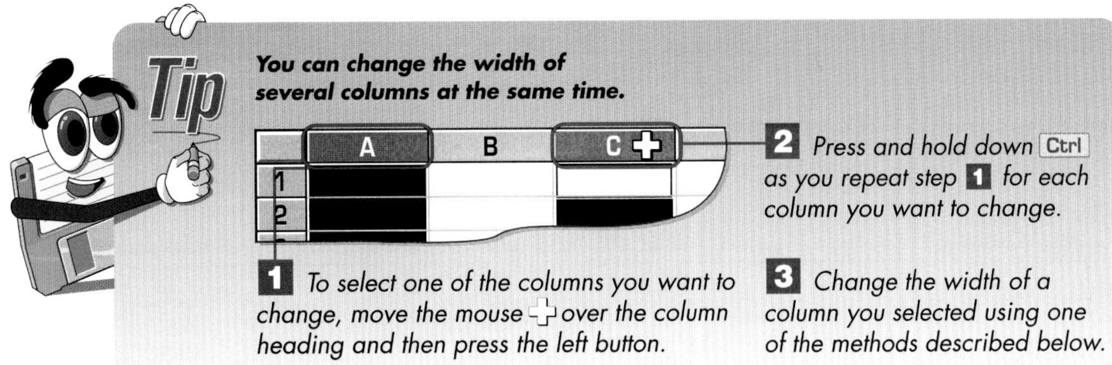

1 *To select one of the columns you want to change, move the mouse over the column heading and then press the left button.*

2 *Press and hold down Ctrl as you repeat step 1 for each column you want to change.*

3 *Change the width of a column you selected using one of the methods described below.*

CHANGE COLUMN WIDTH AUTOMATICALLY

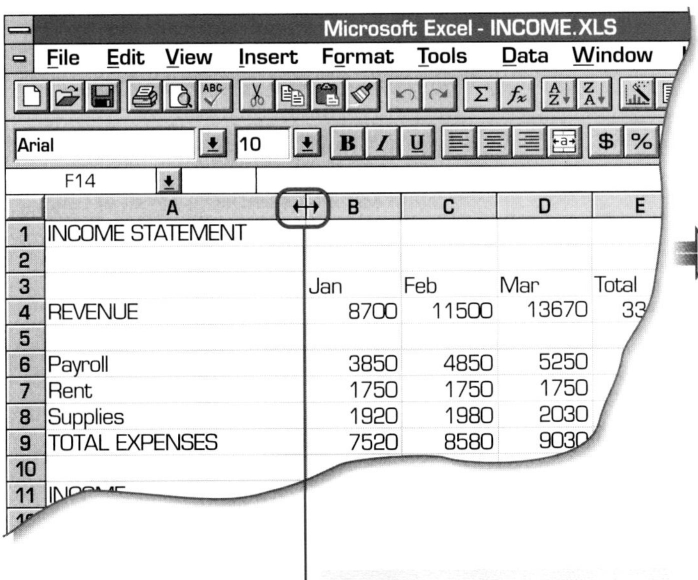

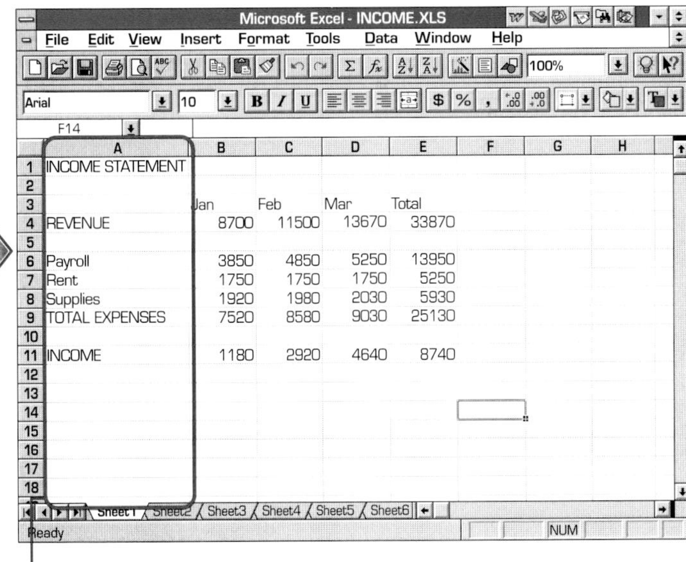

You can have Excel adjust the column width to fit the longest item in the column.

1 Move the mouse over the right edge of the column heading you want to change (example: **column A**) and changes to ↔.

2 Quickly press the left button twice.

◆ The column width changes to fit the longest item in the column.

CHANGE ROW HEIGHT

You can change the height of a row. This is useful if you want to add space between the rows of data in your worksheet.

CHANGE ROW HEIGHT

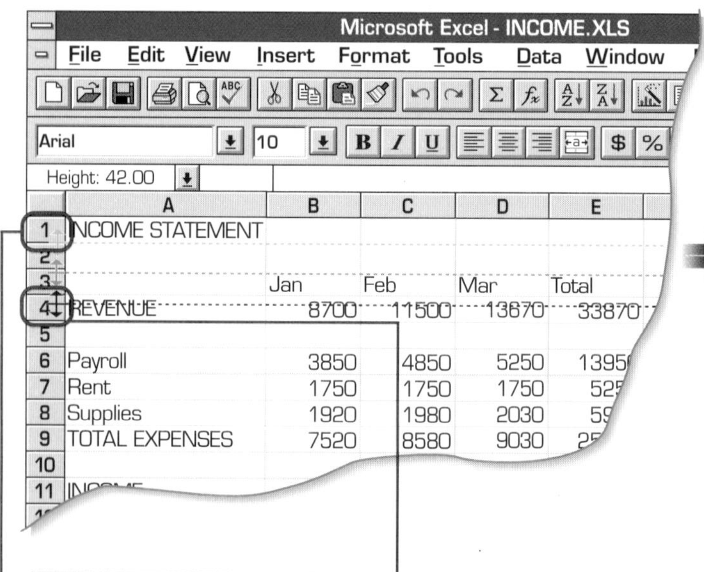

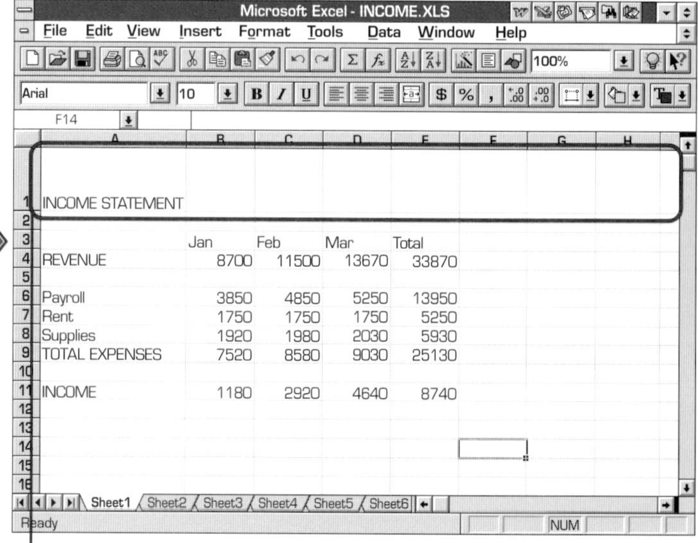

1 Move the mouse over the bottom edge of the row heading you want to change (example: **row 1**) and changes to ‡.

2 Press and hold down the left button as you drag the edge of the row to a new position.

◆ A dotted line indicates the new row height.

3 Release the button and the new row height appears.

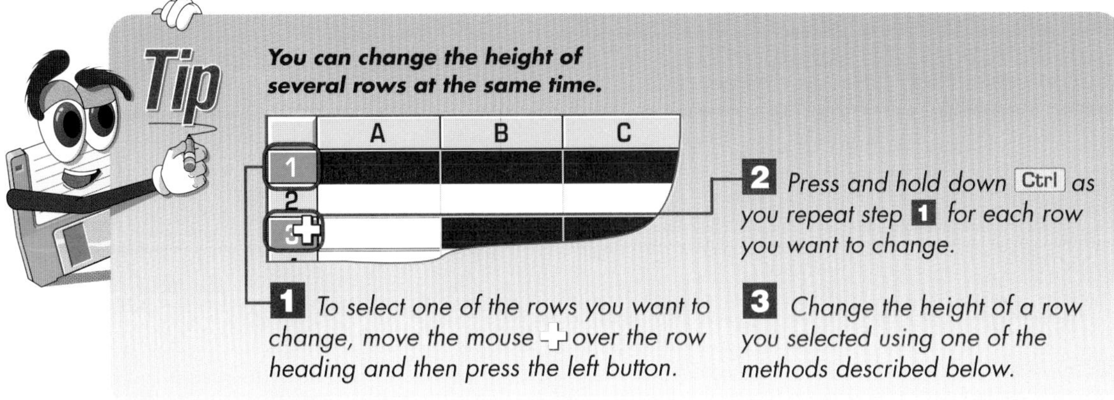

You can change the height of several rows at the same time.

1 To select one of the rows you want to change, move the mouse over the row heading and then press the left button.

2 Press and hold down Ctrl as you repeat step 1 for each row you want to change.

3 Change the height of a row you selected using one of the methods described below.

CHANGE ROW HEIGHT AUTOMATICALLY

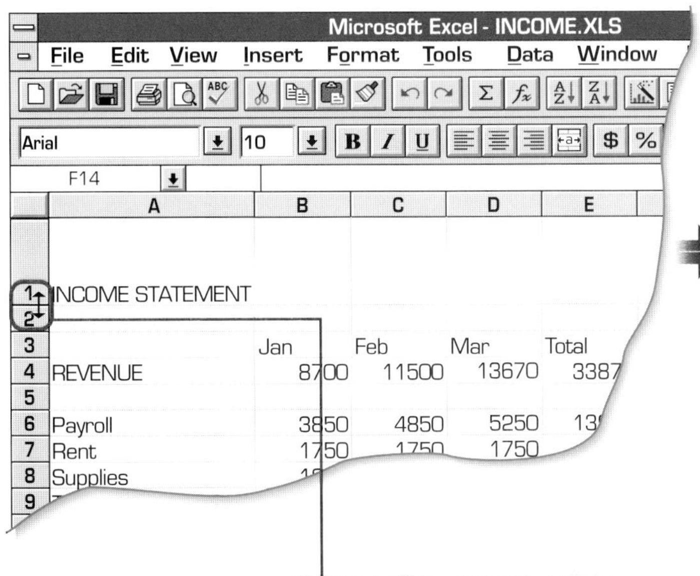

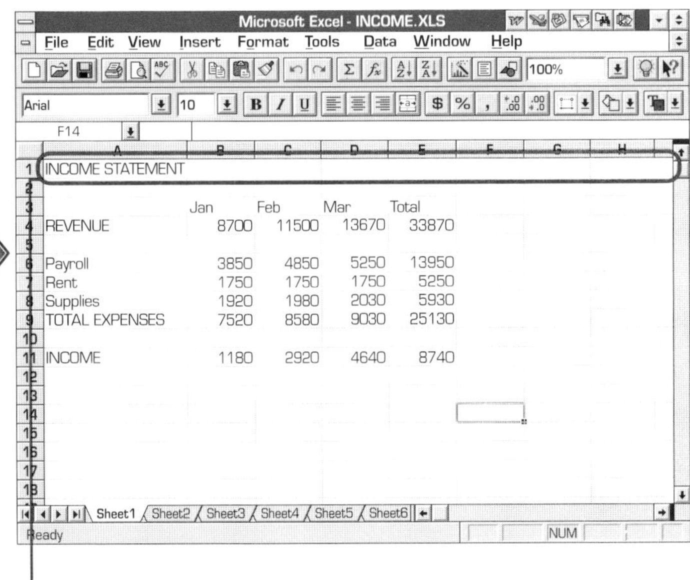

You can have Excel adjust the row height to fit the tallest item in the row.

1 Move the mouse over the bottom edge of the row heading you want to change (example: **row 1**) and changes to ‡.

2 Quickly press the left button twice.

◆ The row height changes to fit the tallest item in the row.

CHANGE APPEARANCE OF NUMBERS

You can change the appearance of numbers in your worksheet without retyping them. This can make the numbers easier to understand.

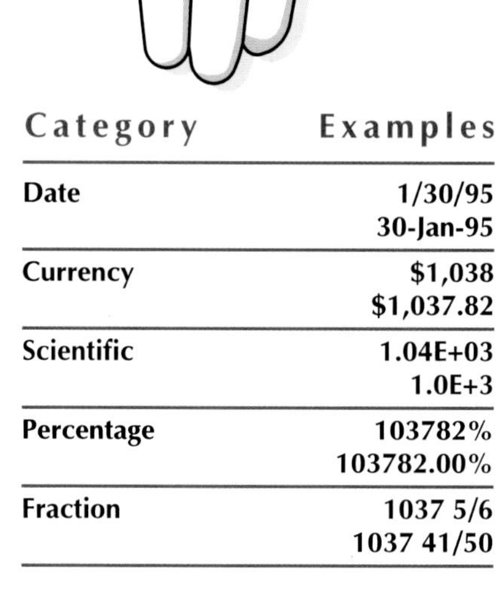

Category	Examples
Date	1/30/95 30-Jan-95
Currency	$1,038 $1,037.82
Scientific	1.04E+03 1.0E+3
Percentage	103782% 103782.00%
Fraction	1037 5/6 1037 41/50

CHANGE APPEARANCE OF NUMBERS

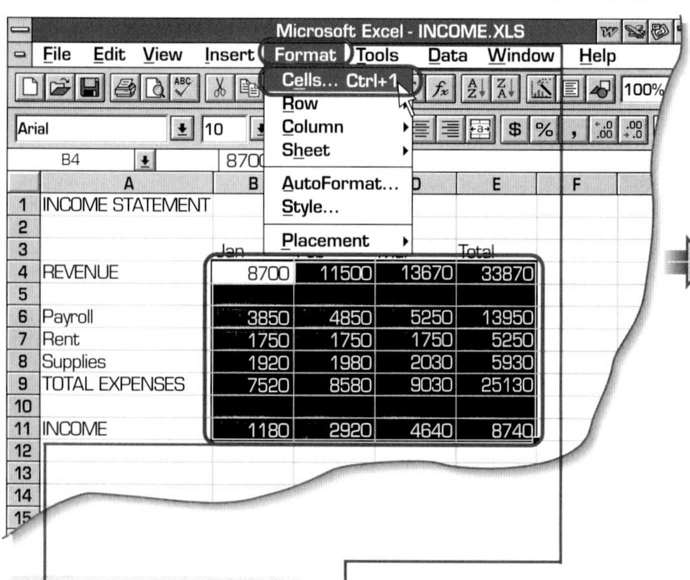

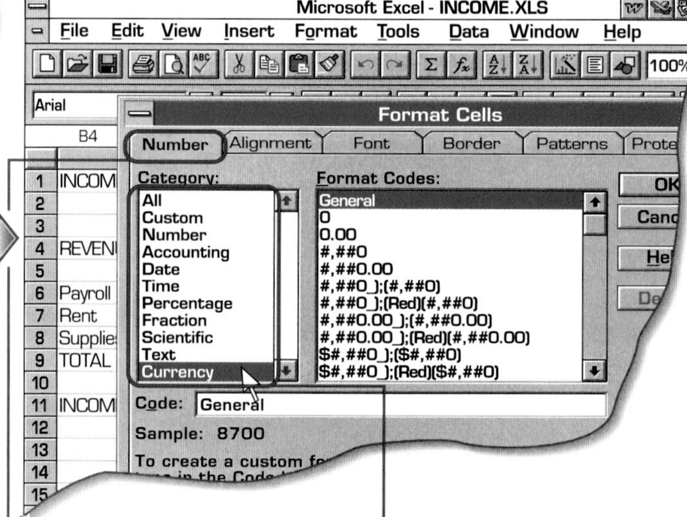

1 Select the cells containing the numbers you want to change.

Note: To select cells, refer to page 140.

2 Move the mouse over **Format** and then press the left button.

3 Move the mouse over **Cells** and then press the left button.

◆ The **Format Cells** dialog box appears.

4 Move the mouse over the **Number** tab and then press the left button.

5 Move the mouse over the category that contains the number style you want to use (example: **Currency**) and then press the left button.

Note: If you do not know which category contains the style you want to use, select ***All****. This will display a list of all the styles.*

- **Change Appearance of Numbers**
- Align Data
- Center Data Across Columns
- Bold, Italic and Underline
- Clear Formats
- Change Fonts
- Add Borders
- Format a Worksheet Automatically

To quickly change the appearance of numbers in your worksheet:

1 Select the cells containing the numbers you want to change.

2 Move the mouse over one of the following options and then press the left button.

$ Displays the number as a dollar value. Example: 7147➜ $7,147.00

% Displays the number as a percentage. Example: 0.35 ➜ 35%

, Adds a comma and two decimal places to the number. Example: 2683 ➜ 2,683.00

Adds one decimal place to the number. Example: 52.3 ➜ 52.30

Deletes one decimal place from the number. Example: 49.27 ➜ 49.3

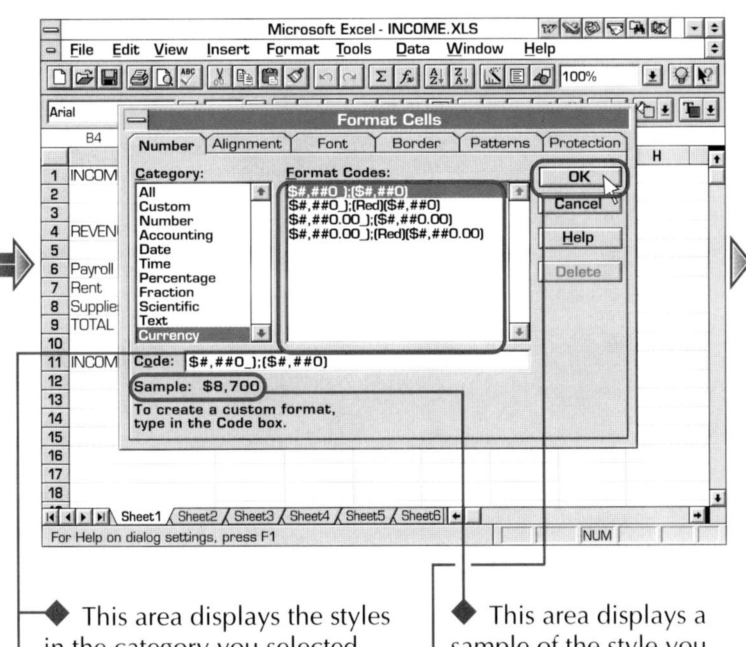

◆ This area displays the styles in the category you selected.

6 Move the mouse over the style you want to use and then press the left button.

◆ This area displays a sample of the style you selected.

7 Move the mouse over **OK** and then press the left button.

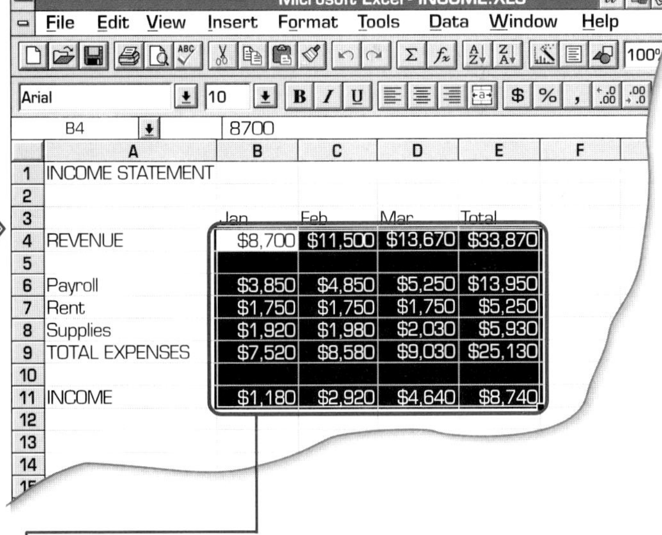

◆ The numbers in the cells you selected display the new style.

Note: If number signs (#) appear in a cell, the column is not wide enough to display the entire number. To change the column width, refer to page 190.

ALIGN DATA

CENTER DATA ACROSS COLUMNS

You can change the position of data in each cell of your worksheet. Excel offers several alignment options.
Data Left Align
Data Center
Data Right Align

ALIGN DATA

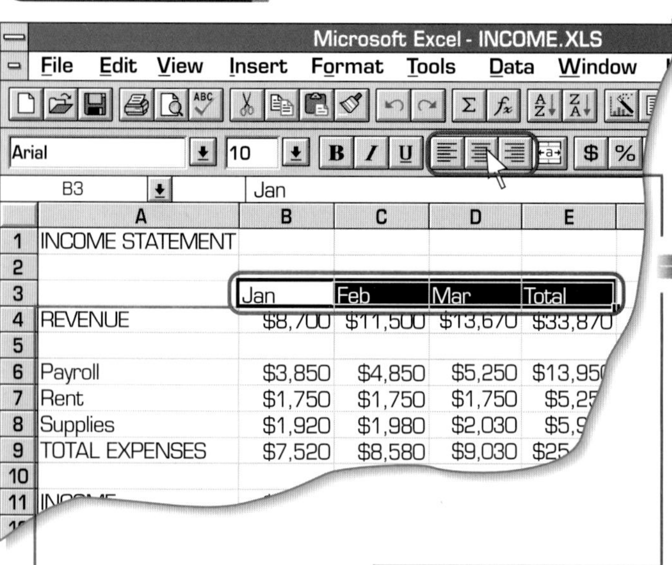

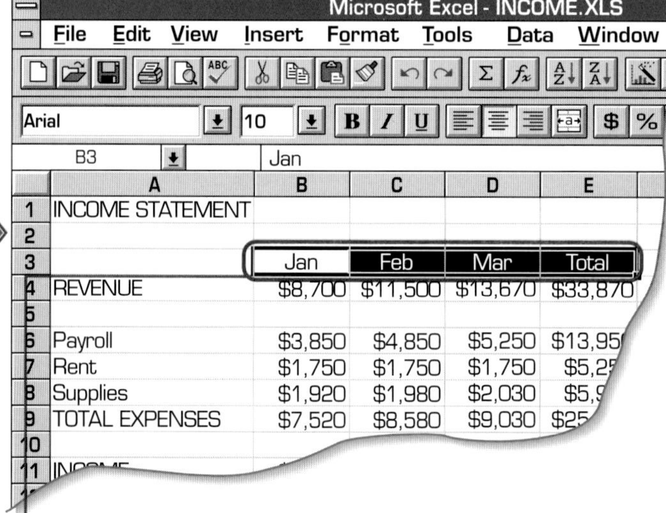

1 Select the cells containing the data you want to align.

Note: To select cells, refer to page 140.

2 Move the mouse over one of the options listed below and then press the left button.

- Left align data
- Center data
- Right align data

◆ The data in the cells you selected displays the new alignment.

Note: In this example, the data appears centered in the cells.

- Change Appearance of Numbers
- **Align Data**
- **Center Data Across Columns**
- Bold, Italic and Underline
- Clear Formats
- Change Fonts
- Add Borders
- Format a Worksheet Automatically

You can center data across columns in your worksheet. This is useful for displaying titles.

CENTER DATA ACROSS COLUMNS

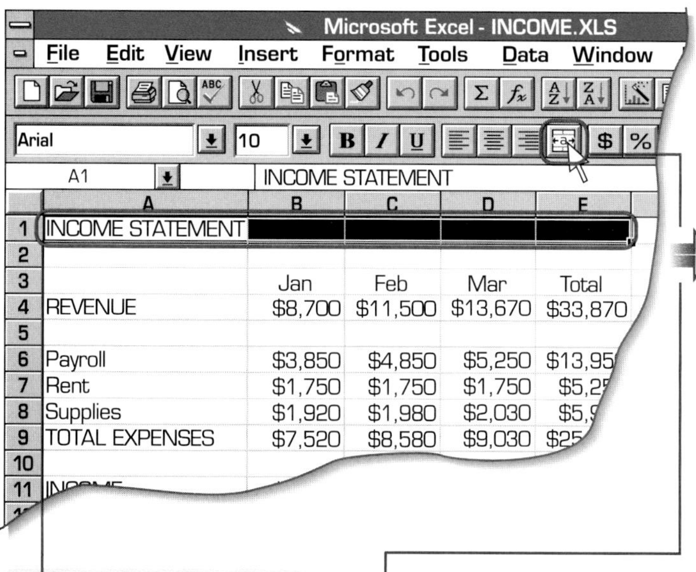

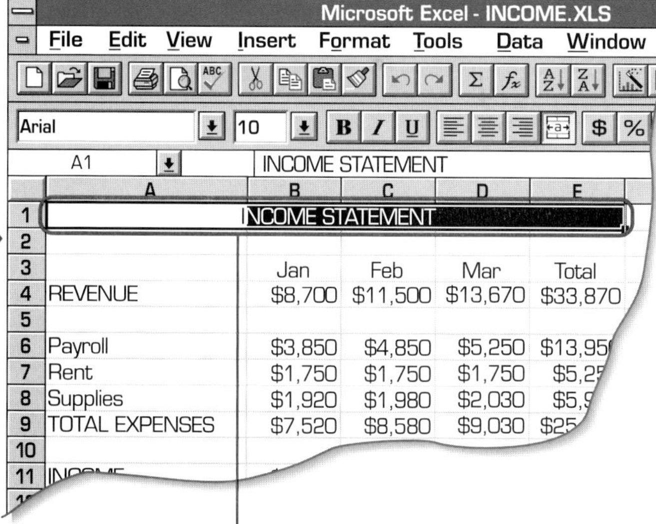

1 Select the cells you want to center the data between.

Note: For best results, the first cell you select should contain the data you want to center.

2 Move the mouse over the center across columns button and then press the left button.

◆ Excel displays the data centered between the cells you selected.

You can use the Bold, Italic and Underline features to emphasize important data.
bold italic underline

BOLD, ITALIC AND UNDERLINE

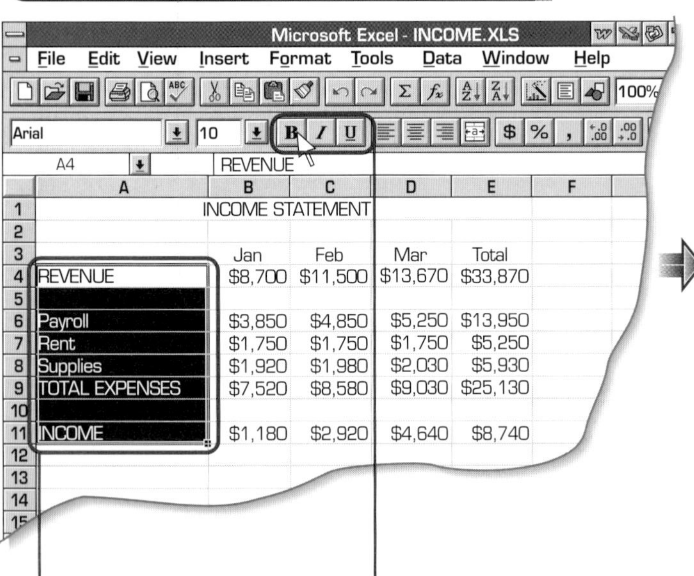

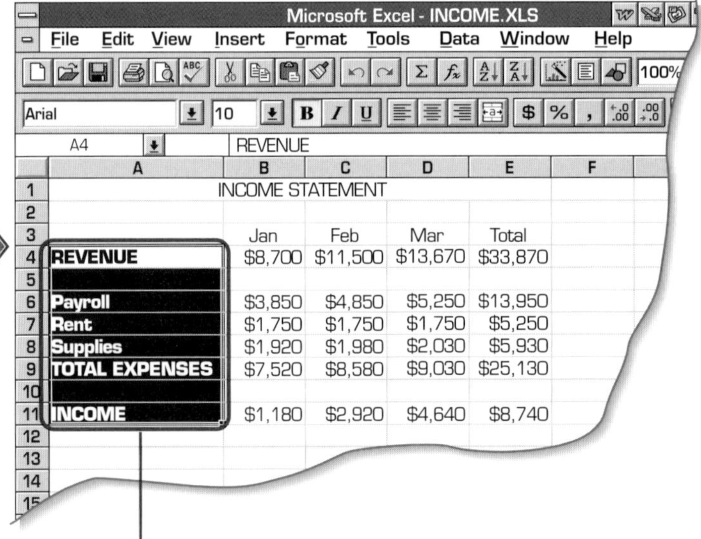

1 Select the cells containing the data you want to change.

Note: To select cells, refer to page 140.

2 Move the mouse over one of the following options and then press the left button.

- **B** Bold data
- *I* Italicize data
- U Underline data

◆ The data in the cells you selected appears in the new style.

Note: In this example, the data appears in the bold style.

Remove Bold, Italic or Underline

Repeat steps **1** and **2**.

If you have applied several formats to cells in your worksheet, you can quickly remove all the formatting at once.

CLEAR FORMATS

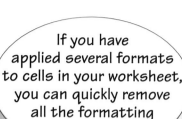

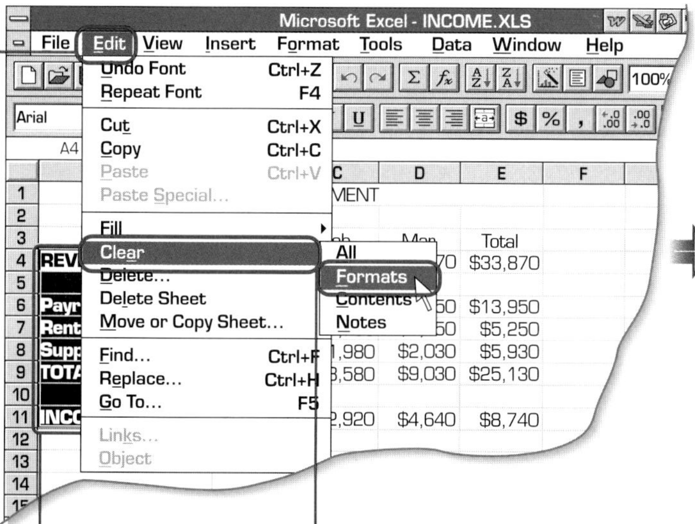

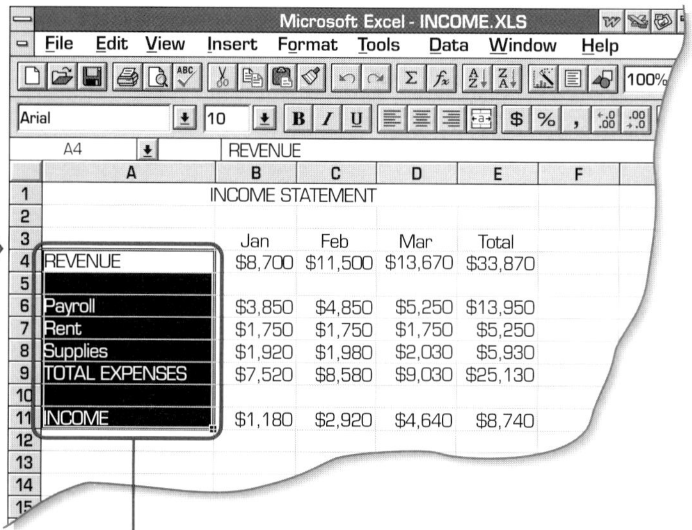

1 Select the cells displaying the formats you want to remove.

Note: To select cells, refer to page 140.

2 Move the mouse over **Edit** and then press the left button.

3 Move the mouse over **Clear** and then press the left button.

4 Move the mouse over **Formats** and then press the left button.

◆ All formats disappear from the cells you selected. The data remains unchanged.

CHANGE FONTS

You can change the design and size of data in your worksheet to emphasize headings and make data easier to read.

CHANGE FONTS

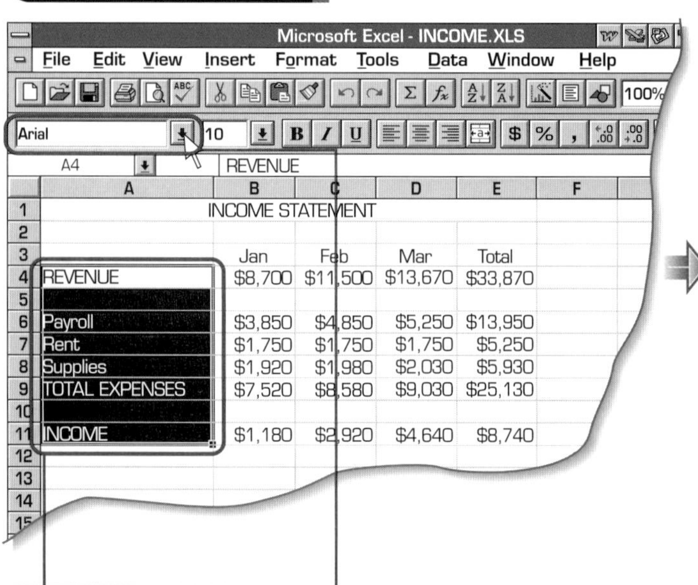

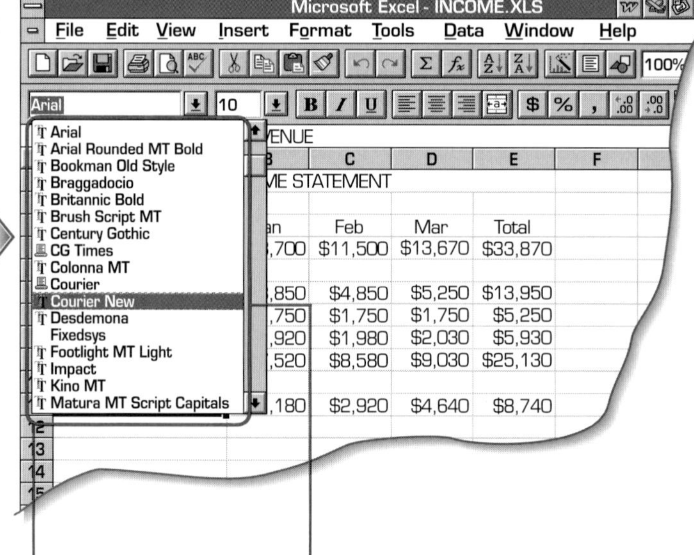

1 Select the cells containing the data you want to change to a new font.

Note: To select cells, refer to page 140.

◆ The **Font** box displays the font of the active cell (example: **Arial**).

2 To display a list of the available fonts, move the mouse over ⬇ beside the **Font** box and then press the left button.

◆ A list of the available fonts for your computer appears.

3 Press ⬇ or ⬆ on your keyboard until you highlight the font you want to use (example: **Courier New**).

4 To select the highlighted font, press Enter.

- Change Appearance of Numbers
- Align Data
- Center Data Across Columns
- Bold, Italic and Underline
- Clear Formats
- **Change Fonts**
- Add Borders
- Format a Worksheet Automatically

You can change the appearance of individual characters in a cell.

1 Move the mouse over the cell containing the characters you want to change and then quickly press the left button twice.

2 Move the mouse to the left of the first character you want to change and then press and hold down the left button.

3 Still holding down the button, drag the mouse over the characters and then release the button.

4 To change the design and size of the characters, see below.

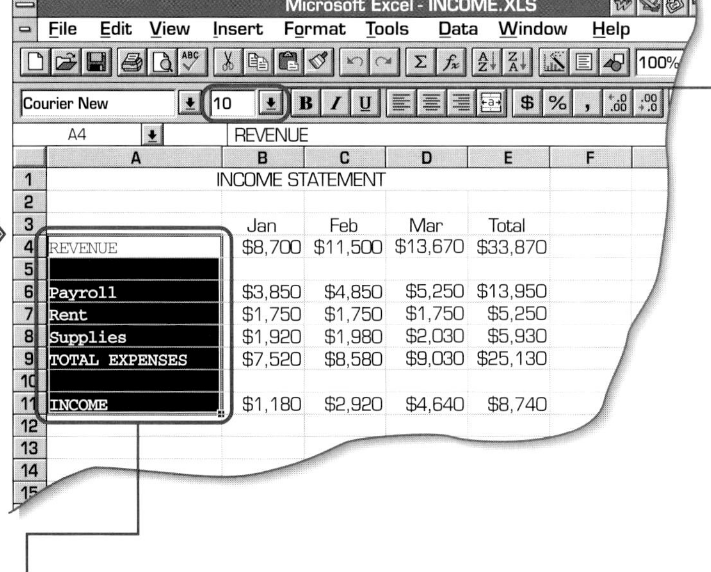

◆ The data in the cells you selected changes to the new font.

CHANGE FONT SIZE

You can increase or decrease the size of data in your worksheet.

1 Select the cells containing the data you want to change to a new font size.

Note: To select cells, refer to page 140.

2 Move the mouse over the arrow beside the **Font Size** box and then press the left button. A list of the available font sizes appears.

3 Move the mouse over the font size you want to use (example: **16**) and then press the left button.

Note: Excel measures the size of data in points. There are approximately 72 points per inch.

CHANGE FONTS

You can change the design and size of data at the same time by using the Format Cells dialog box.
INCOME STATEMENT

CHANGE FONTS

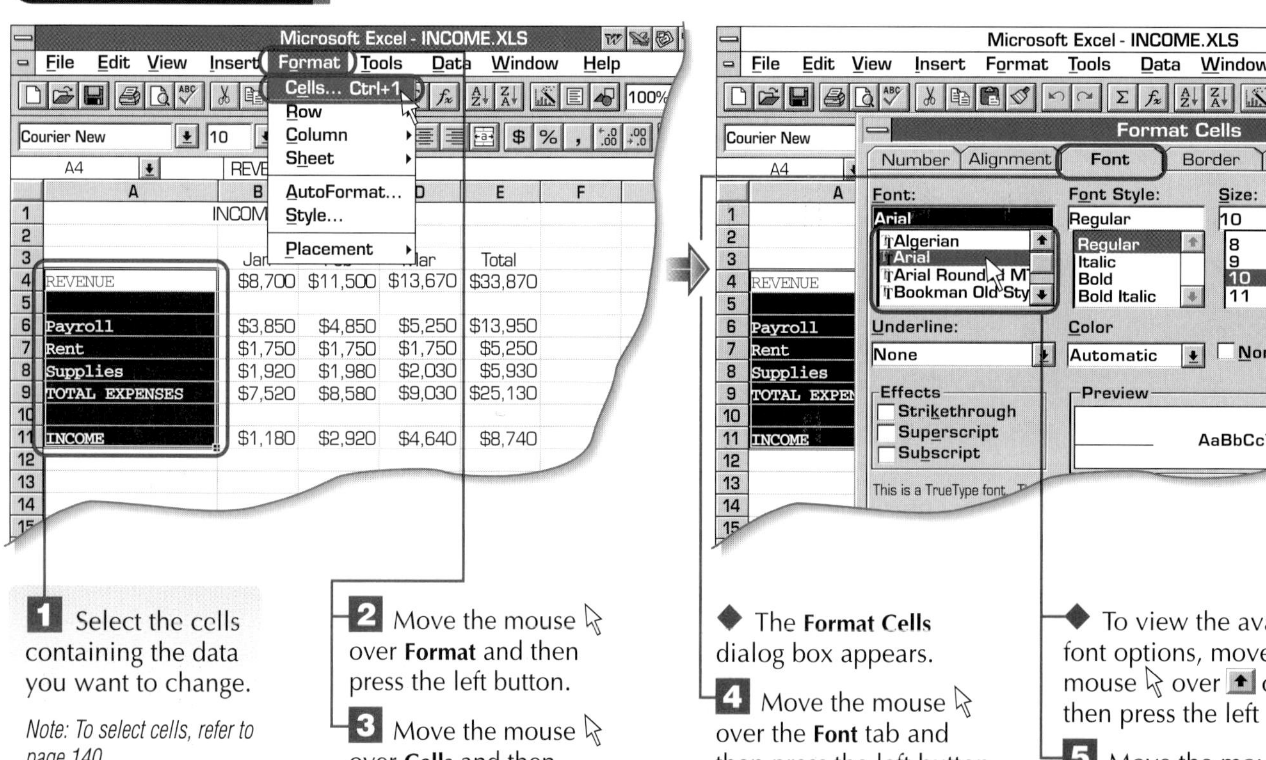

1 Select the cells containing the data you want to change.

Note: To select cells, refer to page 140.

2 Move the mouse over **Format** and then press the left button.

3 Move the mouse over **Cells** and then press the left button.

◆ The **Format Cells** dialog box appears.

4 Move the mouse over the **Font** tab and then press the left button.

◆ To view the available font options, move the mouse over ▲ or ▼ and then press the left button.

5 Move the mouse over the font you want to use (example: **Arial**) and then press the left button.

- Change Appearance of Numbers
- Align Data
- Center Data Across Columns
- Bold, Italic and Underline
- Clear Formats
- **Change Fonts**
- Add Borders
- Format a Worksheet Automatically

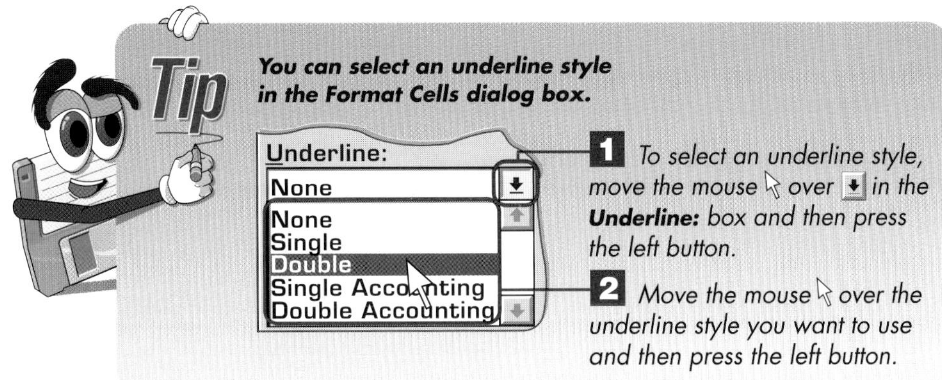

You can select an underline style in the Format Cells dialog box.

1 *To select an underline style, move the mouse over ⬇ in the* ***Underline:*** *box and then press the left button.*

2 *Move the mouse over the underline style you want to use and then press the left button.*

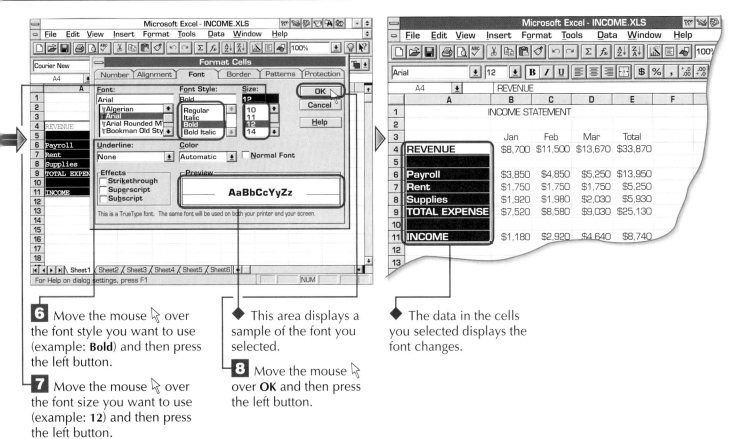

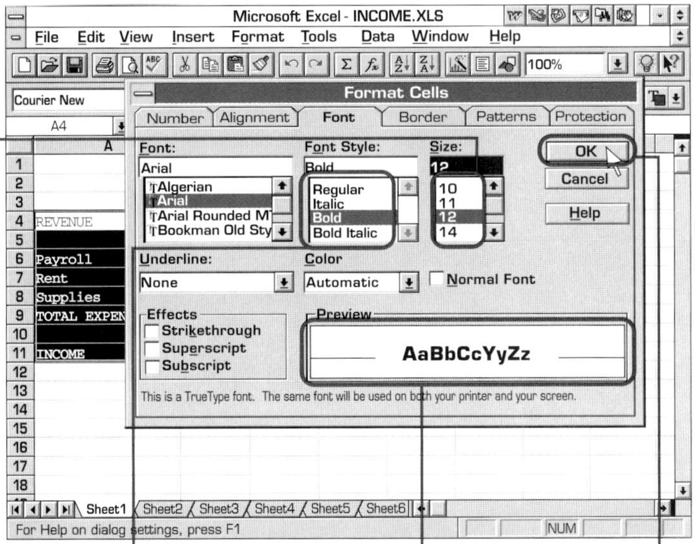

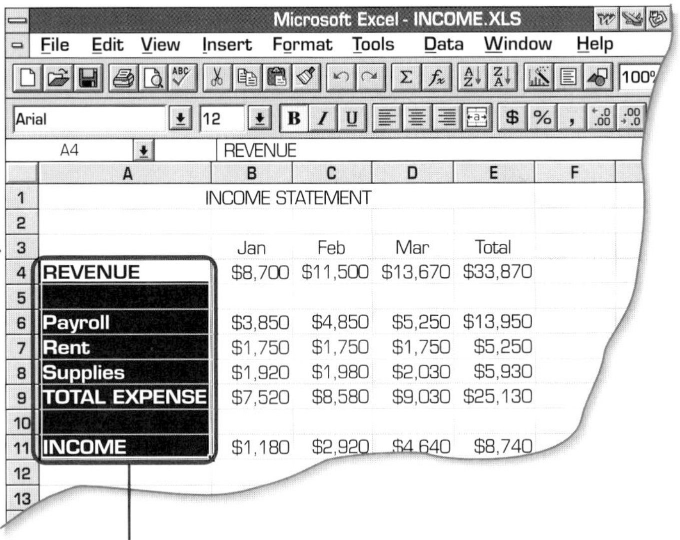

6 Move the mouse over the font style you want to use (example: **Bold**) and then press the left button.

7 Move the mouse over the font size you want to use (example: **12**) and then press the left button.

Note: To select an underline style, see the ***Tip*** *above.*

◆ This area displays a sample of the font you selected.

8 Move the mouse over **OK** and then press the left button.

◆ The data in the cells you selected displays the font changes.

ADD BORDERS

You can add borders to draw attention to important data in your worksheet.

ADD BORDERS

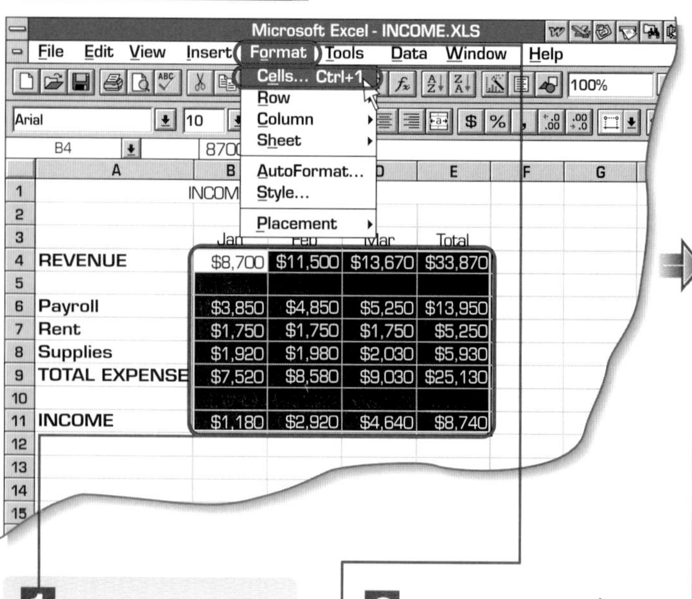

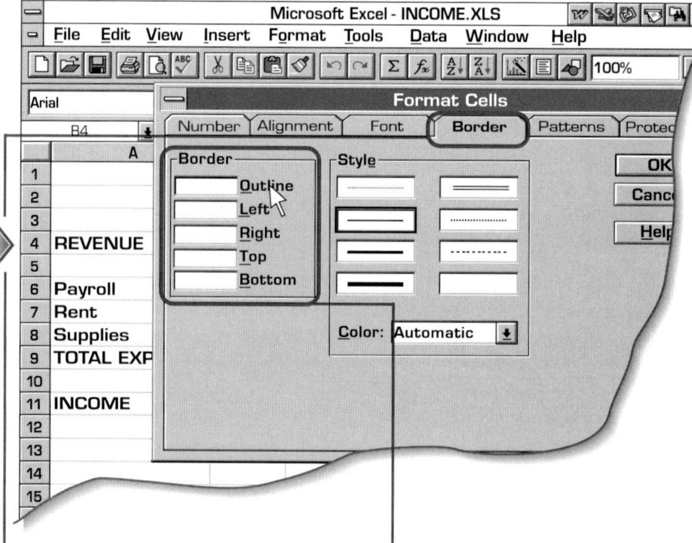

1 Select the cells you want to display borders.

Note: To select cells, refer to page 140.

2 Move the mouse over **Format** and then press the left button.

3 Move the mouse over **Cells** and then press the left button.

◆ The **Format Cells** dialog box appears.

4 Move the mouse over the **Border** tab and then press the left button.

5 Move the mouse over the border you want to add (example: **Outline**) and then press the left button.

- Change Appearance of Numbers
- Align Data
- Center Data Across Columns
- Bold, Italic and Underline
- Clear Formats
- Change Fonts
- **Add Borders**
- Format a Worksheet Automatically

SHORTCUT

To quickly add borders to cells in your worksheet:

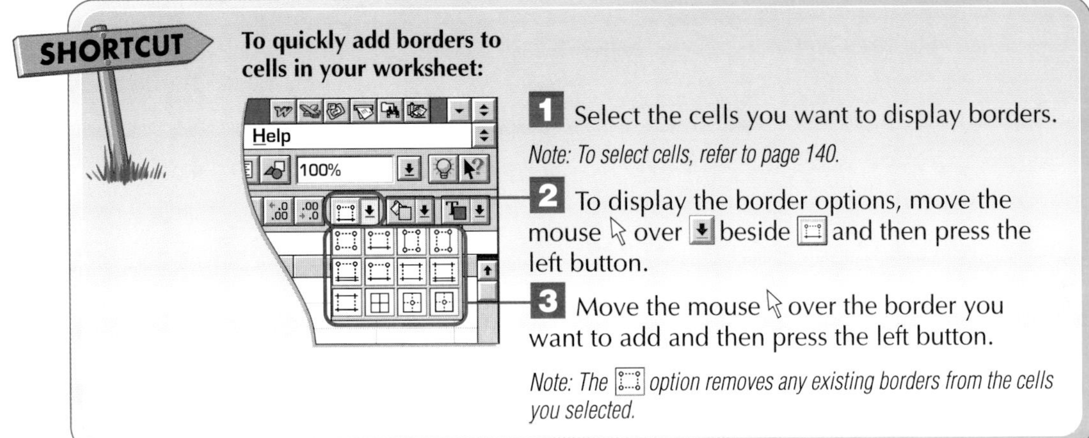

1 Select the cells you want to display borders.

Note: To select cells, refer to page 140.

2 To display the border options, move the mouse over ⬇ beside ☐ and then press the left button.

3 Move the mouse over the border you want to add and then press the left button.

Note: The ☐ option removes any existing borders from the cells you selected.

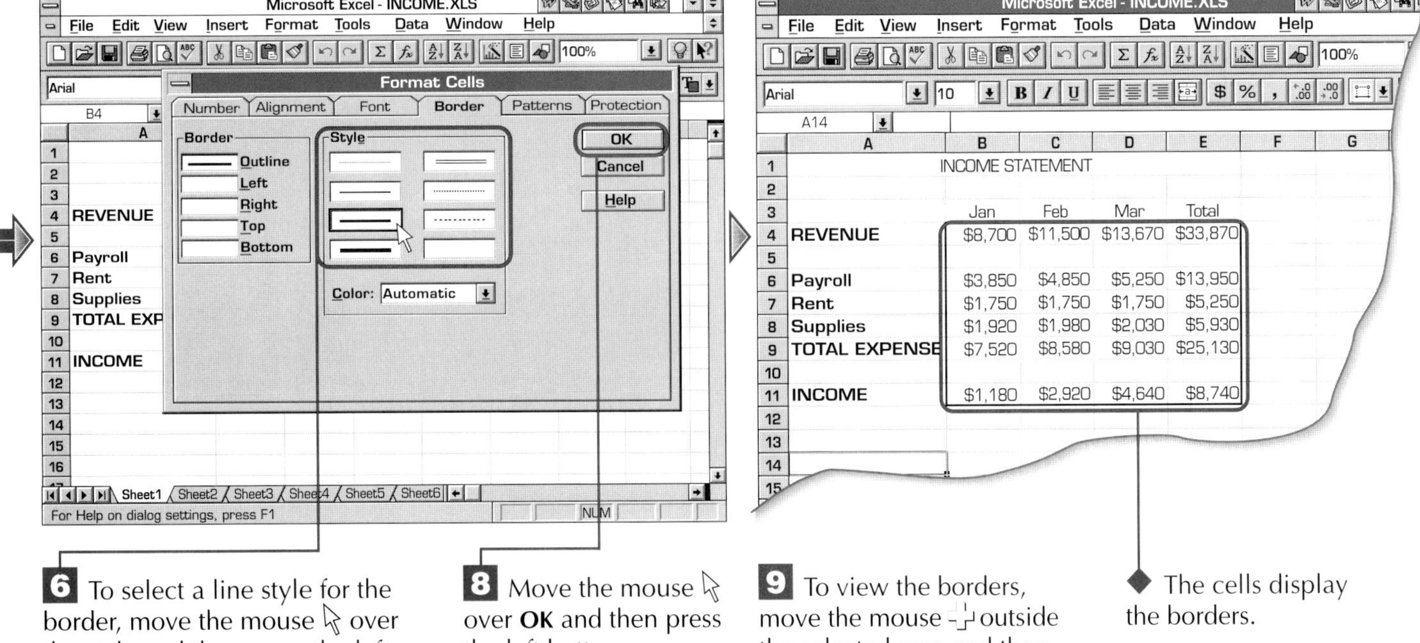

6 To select a line style for the border, move the mouse over the style and then press the left button.

7 Repeat steps 5 and 6 for each border you want to add.

8 Move the mouse over **OK** and then press the left button.

9 To view the borders, move the mouse outside the selected area and then press the left button.

◆ The cells display the borders.

FORMAT A WORKSHEET AUTOMATICALLY

Excel provides a selection of designs that you can choose from to quickly format your worksheet.

FORMAT A WORKSHEET AUTOMATICALLY

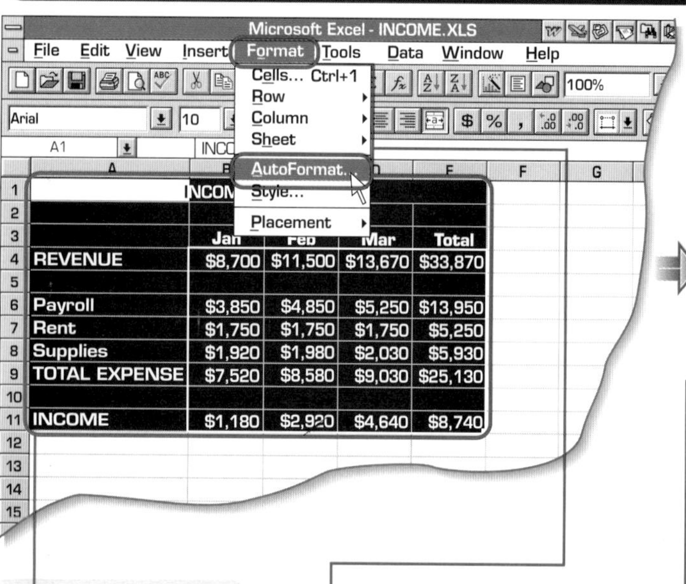

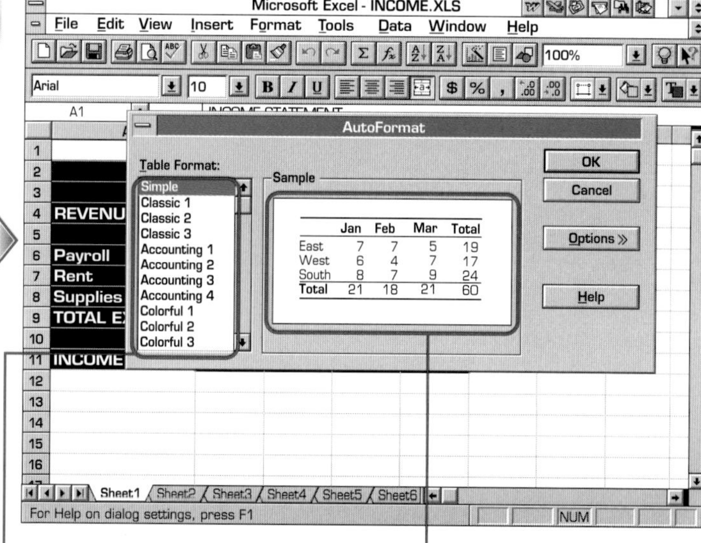

1 Select the cells you want to format.

Note: To select cells, refer to page 140.

2 Move the mouse over **Format** and then press the left button.

3 Move the mouse over **AutoFormat** and then press the left button.

◆ The **AutoFormat** dialog box appears.

◆ This area displays a list of the available designs.

◆ This area displays a sample of the highlighted design.

- Change Appearance of Numbers
- Align Data
- Center Data Across Columns
- Bold, Italic and Underline
- Clear Formats
- Change Fonts
- Add Borders
- **Format a Worksheet Automatically**

To remove an AutoFormat design from your worksheet:

1 Select the cells displaying the design you want to remove.

Note: To select cells, refer to page 140.

*2 Perform steps 2 to 5 below, selecting **None** in step 4.*

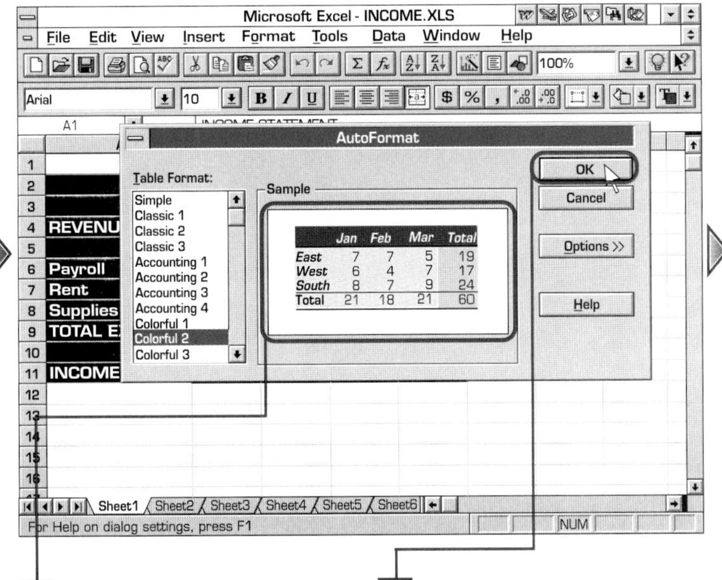

Microsoft Excel - INCOME.XLS

	A	B	C	D	E
1	INCOME STATEMENT				
3		Jan	Feb	Mar	Total
4	REVENUE	$8,700	$11,500	$13,670	$33,870
6	Payroll	$3,850	$4,850	$5,250	$13,950
7	Rent	$1,750	$1,750	$1,750	$5,250
8	Supplies	$1,920	$1,980	$2,030	$5,930
9	TOTAL EXPENSES	$7,520	$8,580	$9,030	$25,130
11	INCOME	$1,180	$2,920	$4,640	$8,740

4 Press ↓ or ↑ on your keyboard until the **Sample** box displays the design you want to use (example: **Colorful 2**).

5 To select the design, move the mouse over **OK** and then press the left button.

◆ Excel applies the design to the cells you selected.

Note: To deselect cells, move the mouse over any cell in your worksheet and then press the left button.

PREVIEW A WORKSHEET

The Print Preview feature lets you see on screen what your worksheet will look like when printed.

PREVIEW A WORKSHEET

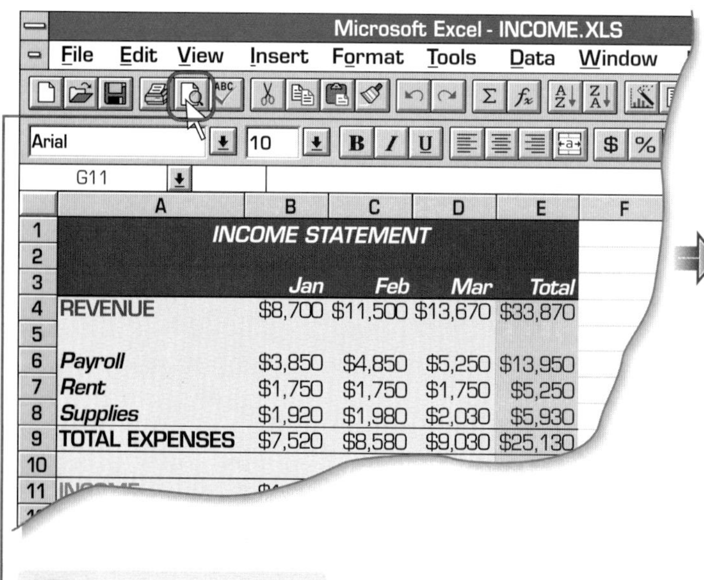

1 To display your worksheet in the Print Preview window, move the mouse over [icon] and then press the left button.

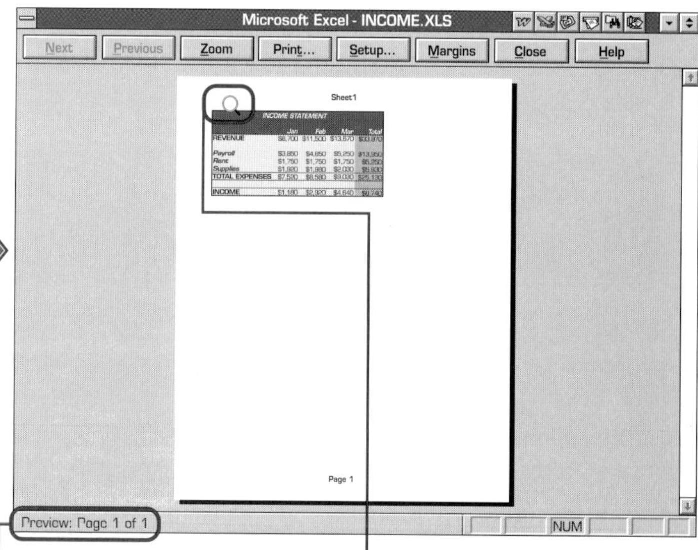

◆ The first page of your worksheet appears.

◆ The status bar at the bottom of your screen tells you which page you are viewing.

2 To magnify an area of the page, move the mouse over the area (changes to [magnifier]) and then press the left button.

If your worksheet consists of more than one page, you can use these buttons to switch between the pages in the Print Preview window.

Next

◆ *To view the next page, move the mouse over* ***Next*** *and then press the left button.*

Previous

◆ *To view the previous page, move the mouse over* ***Previous*** *and then press the left button.*

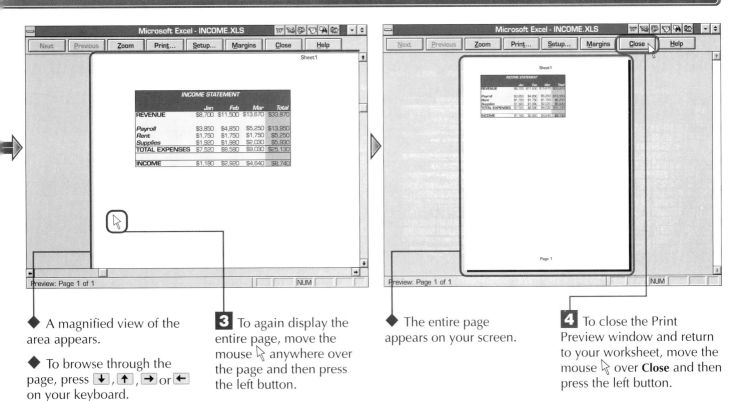

◆ A magnified view of the area appears.

◆ To browse through the page, press ↓, ↑, → or ← on your keyboard.

3 To again display the entire page, move the mouse anywhere over the page and then press the left button.

◆ The entire page appears on your screen.

4 To close the Print Preview window and return to your worksheet, move the mouse over **Close** and then press the left button.

CHANGE MARGINS

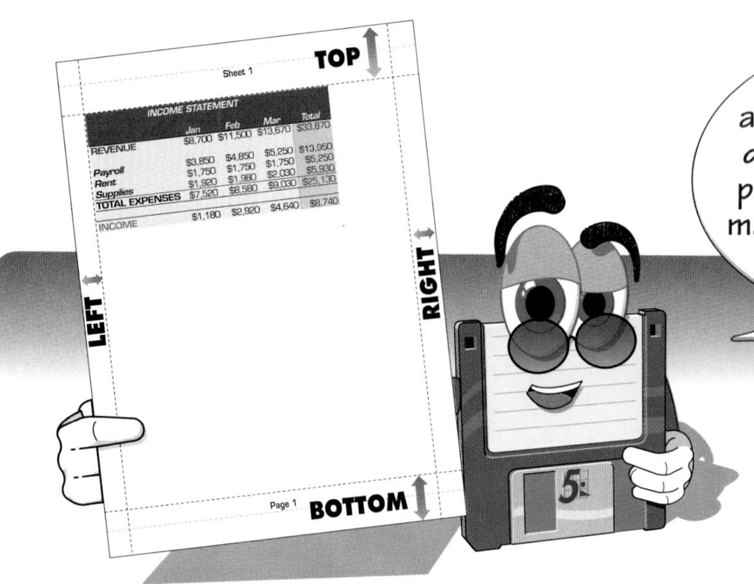

When you begin a worksheet, the top and bottom margins are set at 1 inch. The left and right margins are set at 0.75 inches.

CHANGE MARGINS

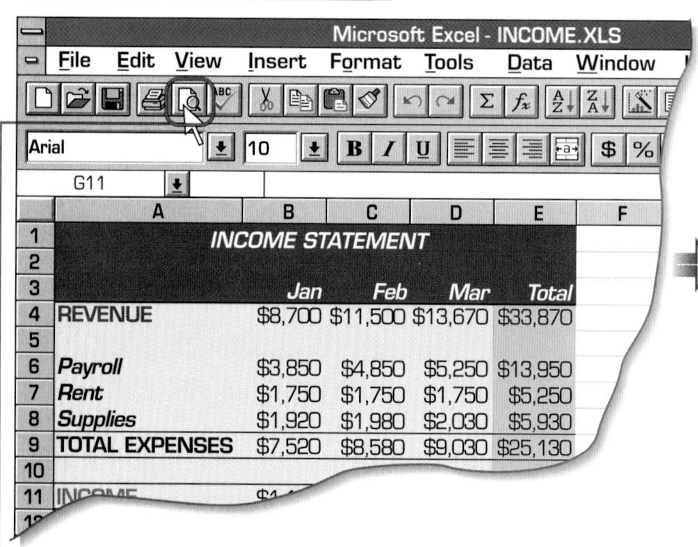

1 To display your worksheet in the Print Preview window, move the mouse over and then press the left button.

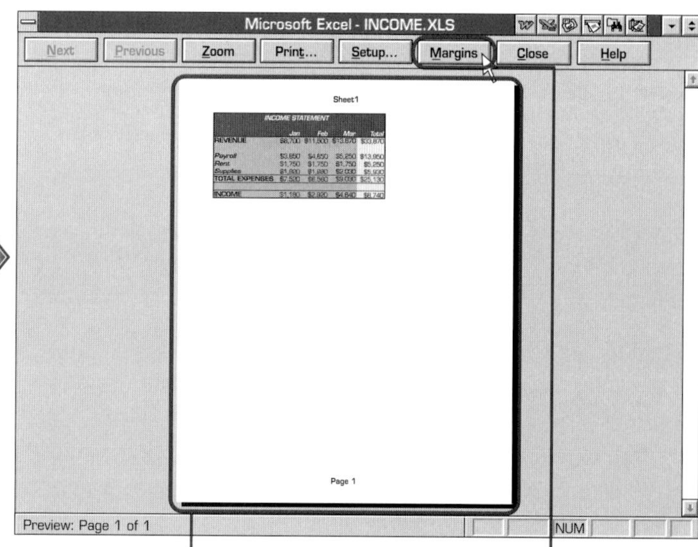

◆ The first page of your worksheet appears.

Note: For more information on using the Print Preview feature, refer to page 208.

2 To display the margins, move the mouse over **Margins** and then press the left button.

Note: To hide the margins, repeat step **2**.

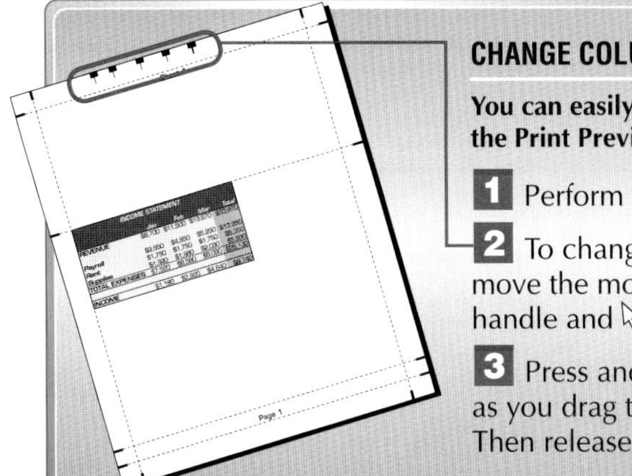

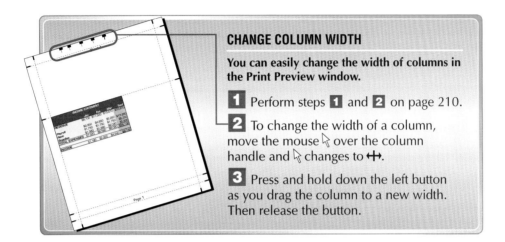

CHANGE COLUMN WIDTH

You can easily change the width of columns in the Print Preview window.

1 Perform steps **1** and **2** on page 210.

2 To change the width of a column, move the mouse over the column handle and changes to ↔.

3 Press and hold down the left button as you drag the column to a new width. Then release the button.

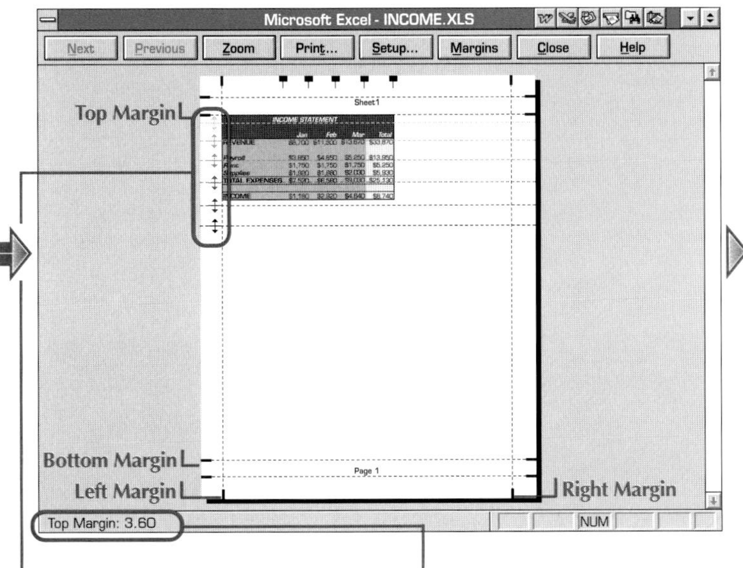

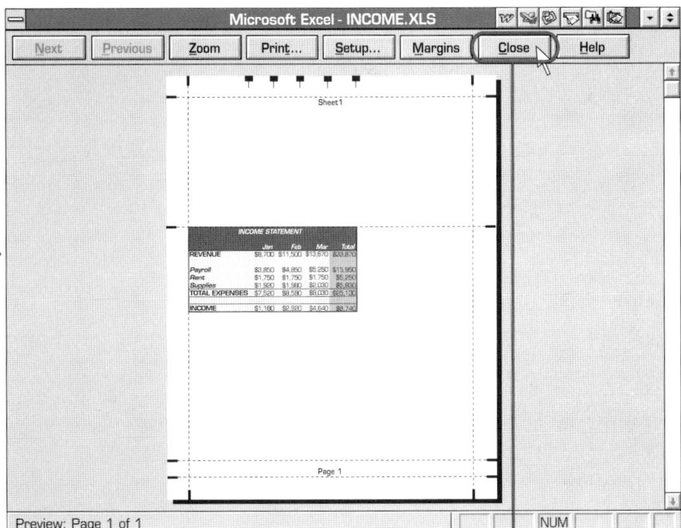

3 To change the position of a margin, move the mouse over the margin handle and changes to ↕ or ↔.

4 Press and hold down the left button as you drag the margin to a new location.

◆ A dotted line indicates the location of the new margin.

◆ The bottom of your screen displays the new measurement as you drag the margin.

5 Release the button to display the new margin.

6 To close the Print Preview window and return to your worksheet, move the mouse over **Close** and then press the left button.

Note: Margins are only visible when you display your worksheet in the Print Preview window.

PRINT A WORKSHEET

You can print a section of data or your entire worksheet. Before printing, make sure your printer is on and contains paper.

PRINT A WORKSHEET

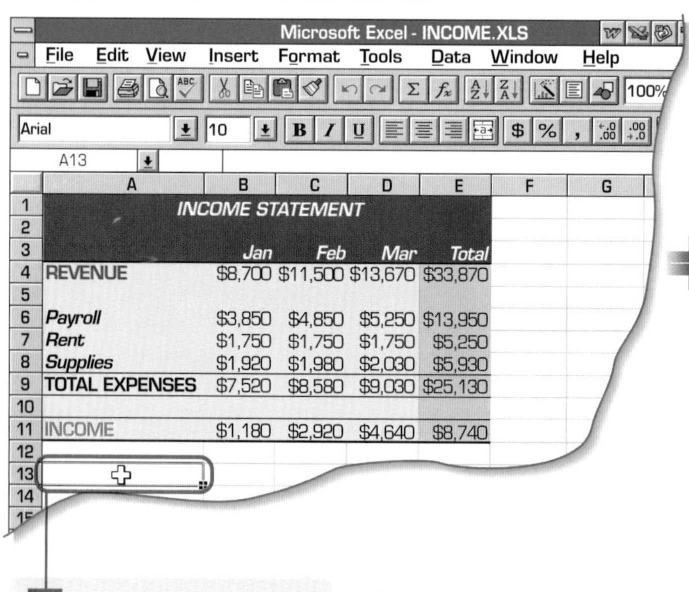

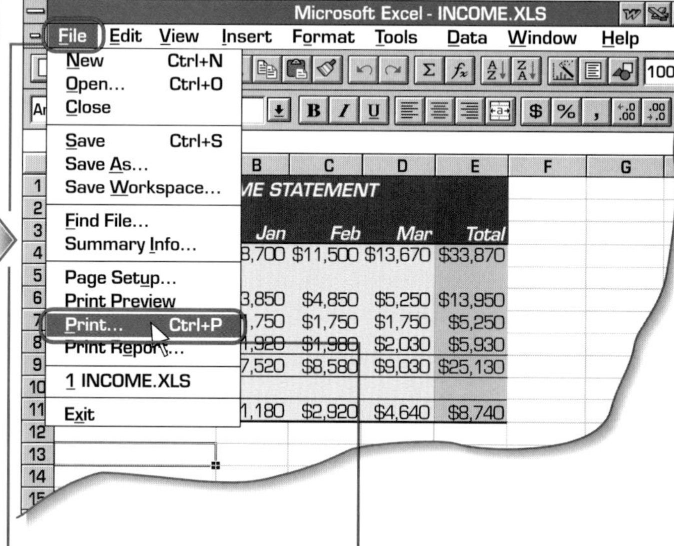

1 To print your entire worksheet, move the mouse over any cell in the worksheet and then press the left button.

◆ To print a section of your worksheet, select the cells you want to print.

Note: To select cells, refer to page 140.

2 Move the mouse over **File** and then press the left button.

3 Move the mouse over **Print** and then press the left button.

◆ The **Print** dialog box appears.

SHORTCUT
To quickly print your entire worksheet, move the mouse over and then press the left button.

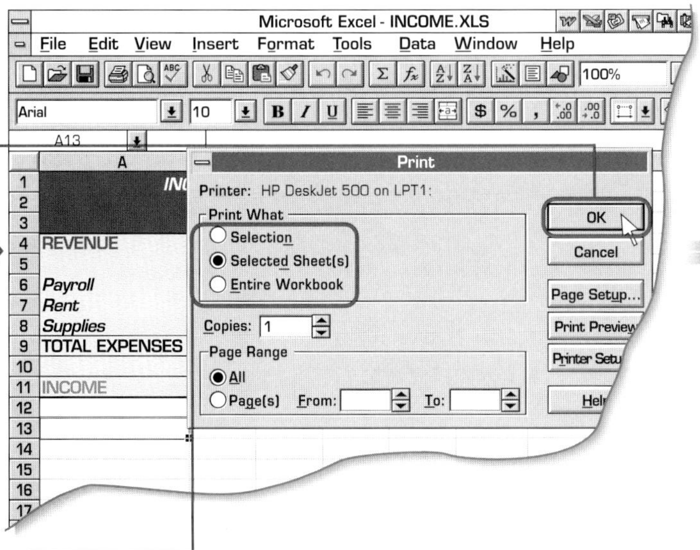

4 Move the mouse over the print option you want to use and then press the left button (○ changes to ◉).

5 Move the mouse over **OK** and then press the left button.

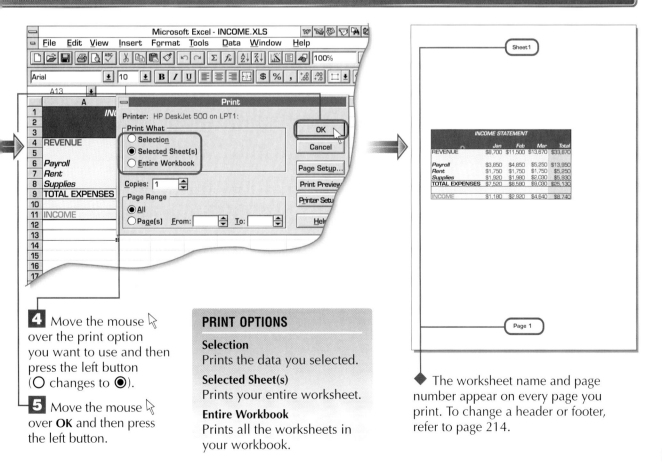

PRINT OPTIONS

Selection
Prints the data you selected.

Selected Sheet(s)
Prints your entire worksheet.

Entire Workbook
Prints all the worksheets in your workbook.

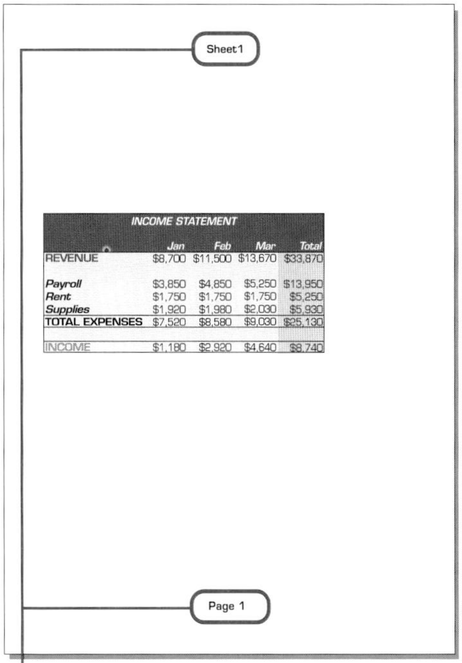

◆ The worksheet name and page number appear on every page you print. To change a header or footer, refer to page 214.

ADD A HEADER OR FOOTER

Headers and footers display information at the top and bottom of each page.
Sheet1
INCOME STATEMENT
Page 1

◆ **Header**
Excel automatically prints the name of the worksheet at the top of each page. You can change this header at any time.

◆ **Footer**
Excel automatically prints the page number at the bottom of each page. You can change this footer at any time.

ADD A HEADER OR FOOTER

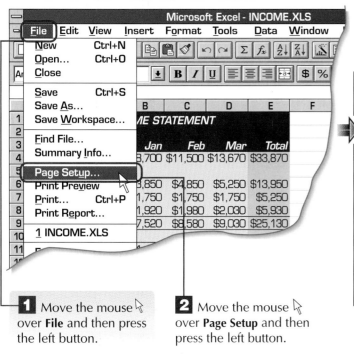

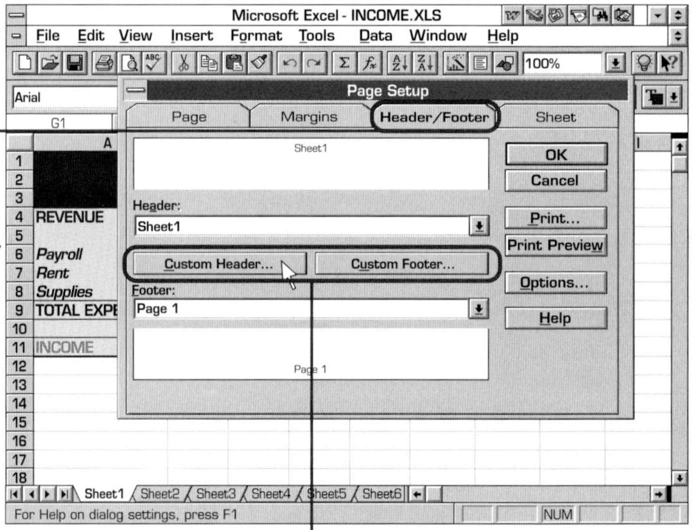

1 Move the mouse over **File** and then press the left button.

2 Move the mouse over **Page Setup** and then press the left button.

◆ The **Page Setup** dialog box appears.

3 Move the mouse over the **Header/Footer** tab and then press the left button.

4 To create a header, move the mouse over **Custom Header** and then press the left button.

◆ To create a footer, move the mouse over **Custom Footer** and then press the left button.

You can use these buttons to change the appearance of a header or footer or to add additional information. These buttons appear in both the Header and Footer dialog boxes.

 *Displays the **Font** dialog box so you can format text you have selected.*

 *Inserts the page number.*

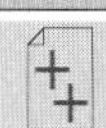 *Inserts the total number of pages in your worksheet.*

 *Inserts the current date.*

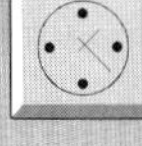 *Inserts the current time.*

 *Inserts the name of the workbook.*

 *Inserts the name of the worksheet.*

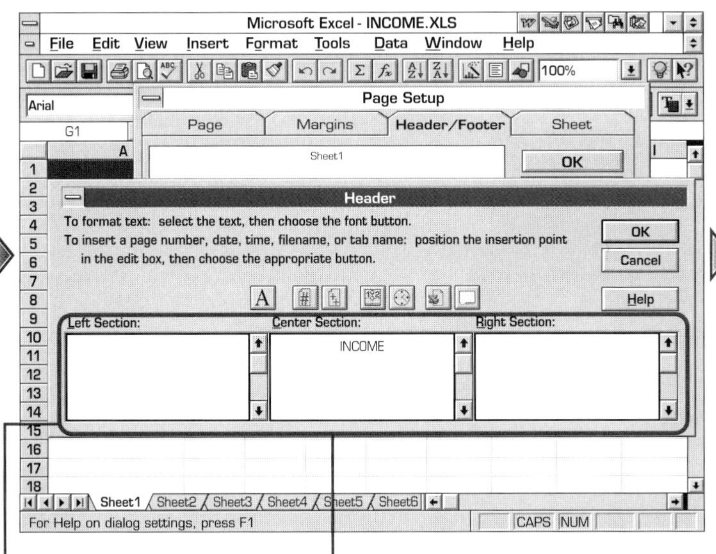

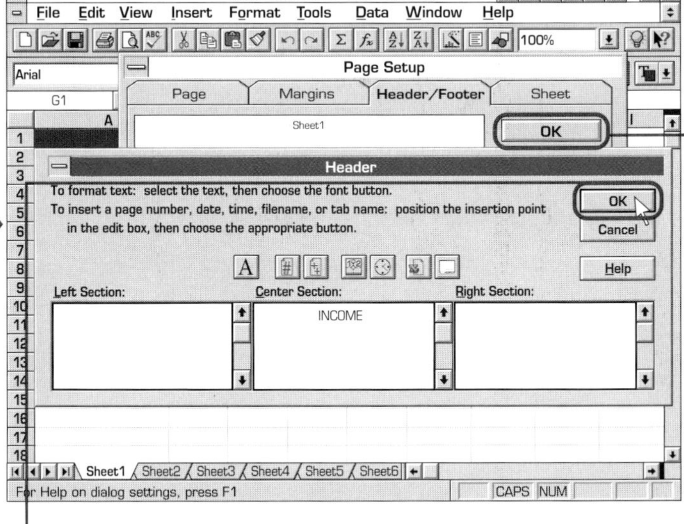

5 Move the mouse over the box under **Center Section:** and then press the left button.

6 To remove the existing text, press Delete or ←Backspace on your keyboard until the text disappears.

7 Move the mouse over the box for the area of the page where you want to display the header or footer (example: **Center Section:**) and then press the left button.

8 Type the text (example: **INCOME**).

9 Move the mouse over **OK** and then press the left button.

10 Move the mouse over **OK** in the **Page Setup** dialog box and then press the left button.

*Note: Headers and footers are only visible when you display your worksheet in the **Print Preview** window. For more information, refer to page 208.*

SWITCH BETWEEN WORKSHEETS

The worksheet displayed on your screen is part of a workbook. Like a three-ring binder, a workbook contains several sheets that you can easily flip through. This lets you view the contents of each worksheet.

SWITCH BETWEEN WORKSHEETS

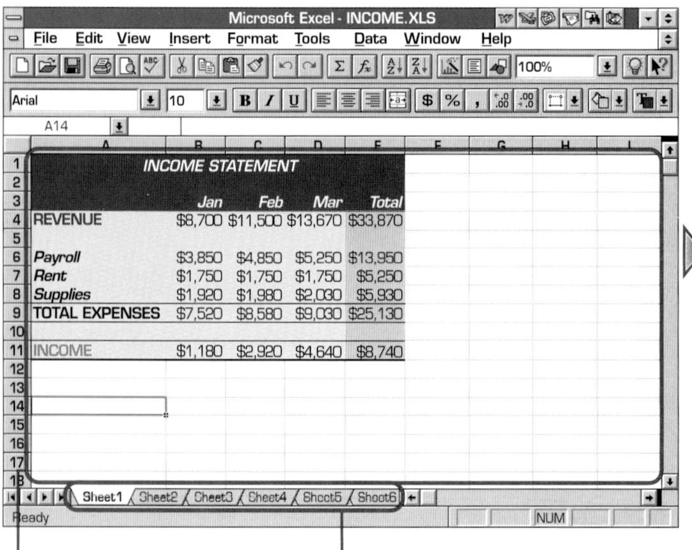

◆ The worksheet displayed on your screen is one of 16 worksheets in the current workbook.

◆ The current worksheet displays a white tab.

◆ The other worksheets display gray tabs.

◆ The contents of the current worksheet are displayed on your screen. The contents of the other worksheets are hidden behind this worksheet.

1 To display the contents of another worksheet, move the mouse over the worksheet tab (example: **Sheet2**) and then press the left button.

- **Switch Between Worksheets**
- Copy or Move Data Between Worksheets
- Enter a Formula Across Worksheets

You can use the worksheets in a workbook to store related information. For example, you can store information for each division of a company on separate worksheets.

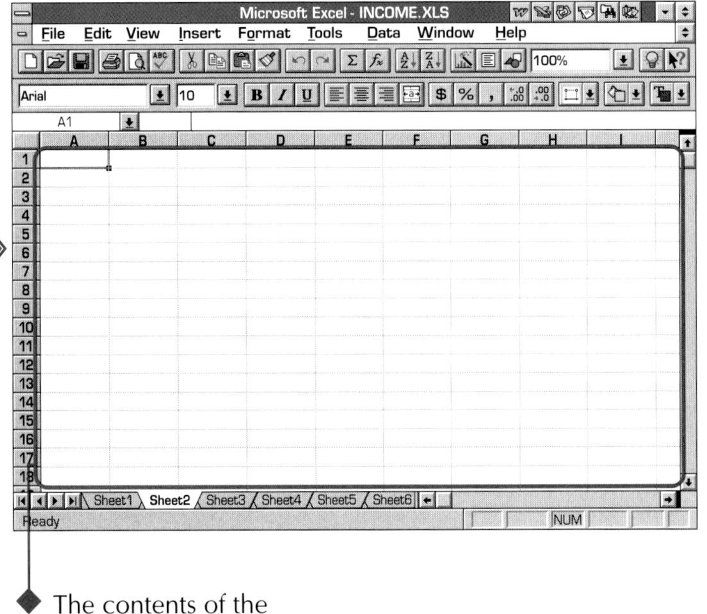

◆ The contents of the worksheet appear.

Excel cannot fit the names of all the worksheets at the bottom of your screen. You can use these buttons to display the other worksheet tabs.

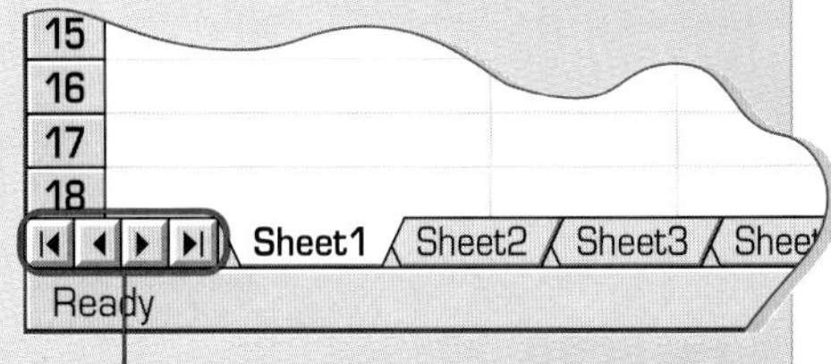

To display the first worksheet tab, move the mouse over and then press the left button.

To scroll left through the worksheet tabs, move the mouse over and then press the left button.

To scroll right through the worksheet tabs, move the mouse over and then press the left button.

To display the last worksheet tab, move the mouse over and then press the left button.

COPY OR MOVE DATA BETWEEN WORKSHEETS

Copying or moving data between worksheets saves you time when you are working in one worksheet and want to use data from another.
data
Sheet1
Sheet2

COPY OR MOVE DATA BETWEEN WORKSHEETS

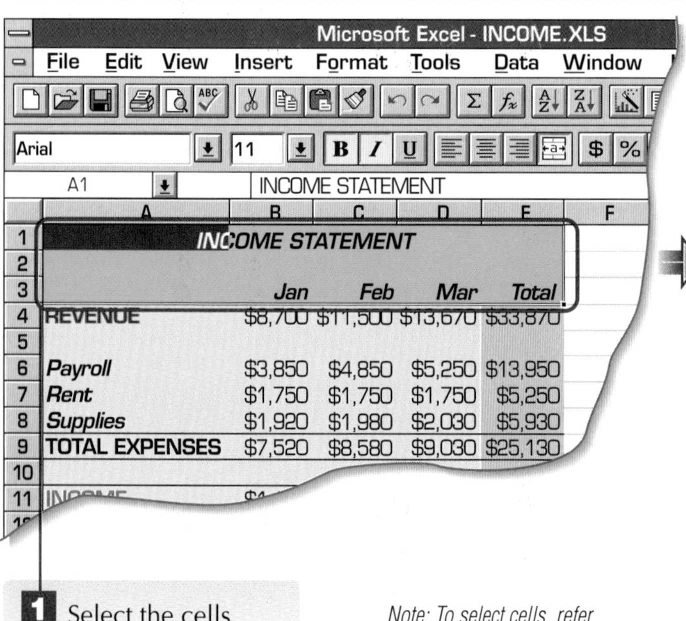

1 Select the cells containing the data you want to copy or move to another worksheet.

Note: To select cells, refer to page 140.

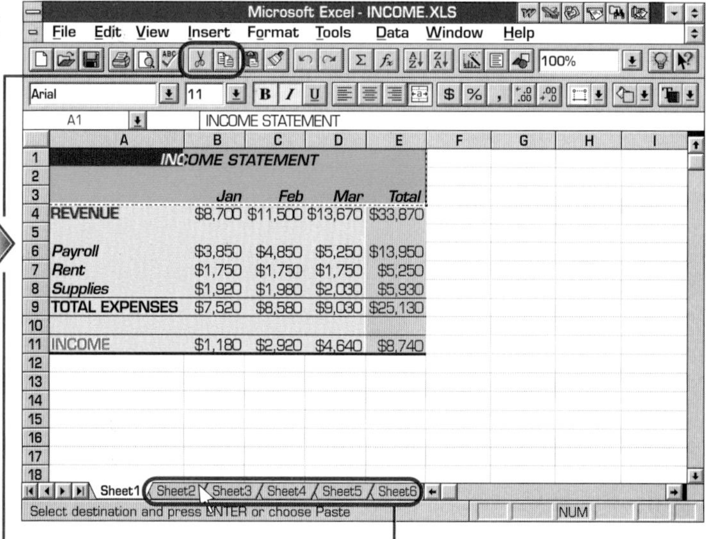

2 To copy the data, move the mouse over the copy button and then press the left button.

◆ To move the data, move the mouse over the cut button and then press the left button.

3 Move the mouse over the tab of the worksheet where you want to place the data and then press the left button.

The Copy and Move features both place data in a new location, but they have one distinct difference.

COPY DATA

When you copy data, the original data remains in its place.

MOVE DATA

When you move data, the original data disappears.

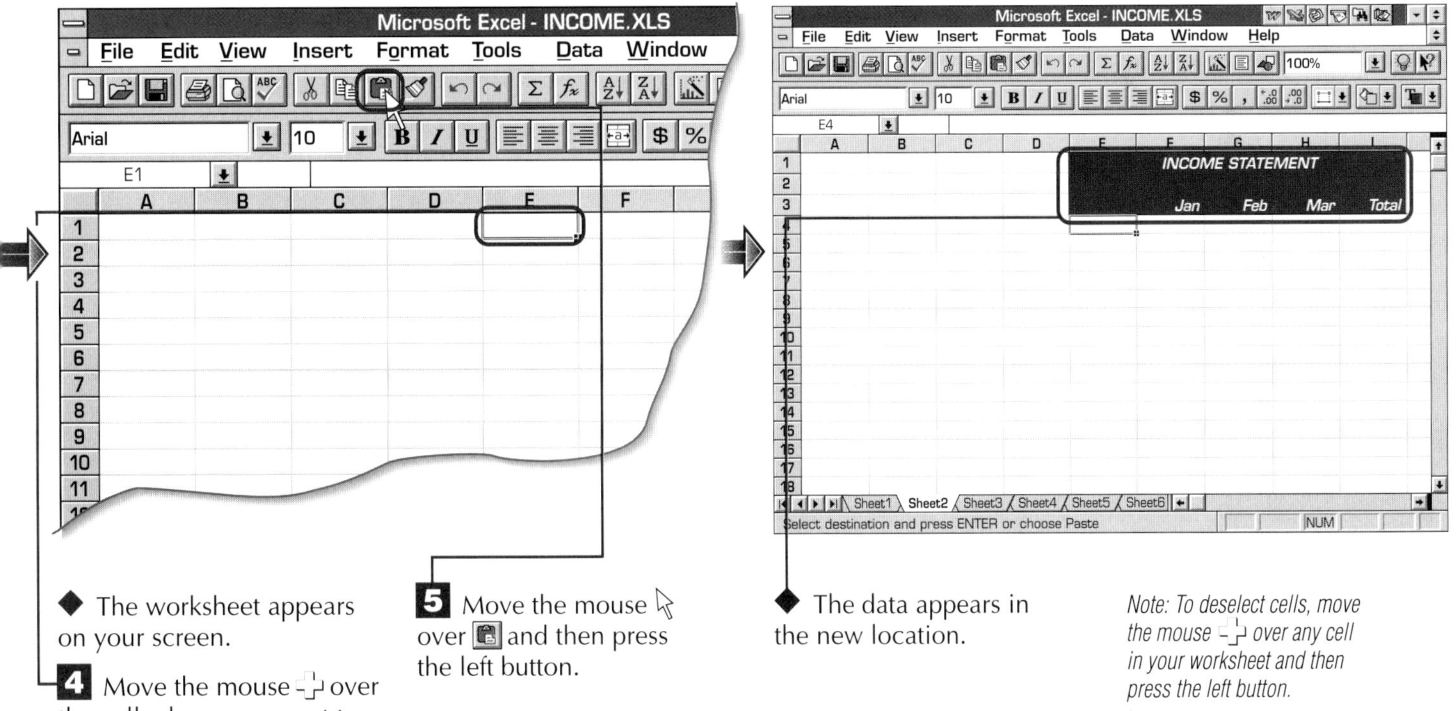

◆ The worksheet appears on your screen.

4 Move the mouse over the cell where you want to place the data and then press the left button. This cell will become the top left cell of the new location.

5 Move the mouse over and then press the left button.

◆ The data appears in the new location.

Note: To deselect cells, move the mouse over any cell in your worksheet and then press the left button.

ENTER A FORMULA ACROSS WORKSHEETS

You can enter a formula in one worksheet that uses data from other worksheets.
Sheet1
Sheet2
Sheet3

ENTER A FORMULA ACROSS WORKSHEETS

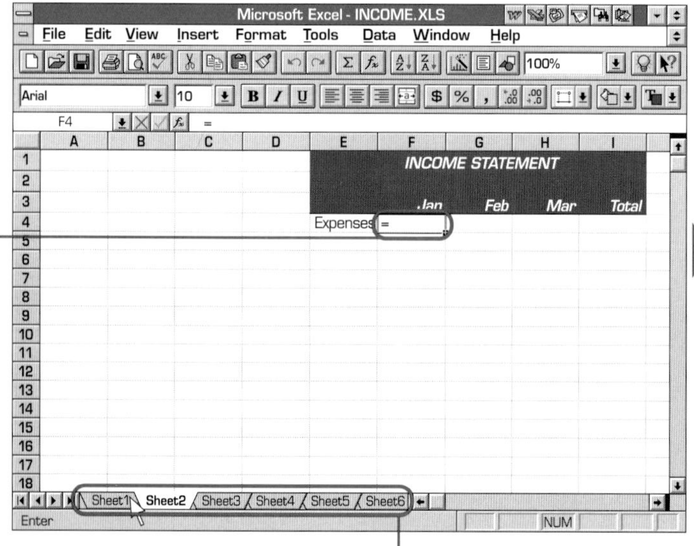

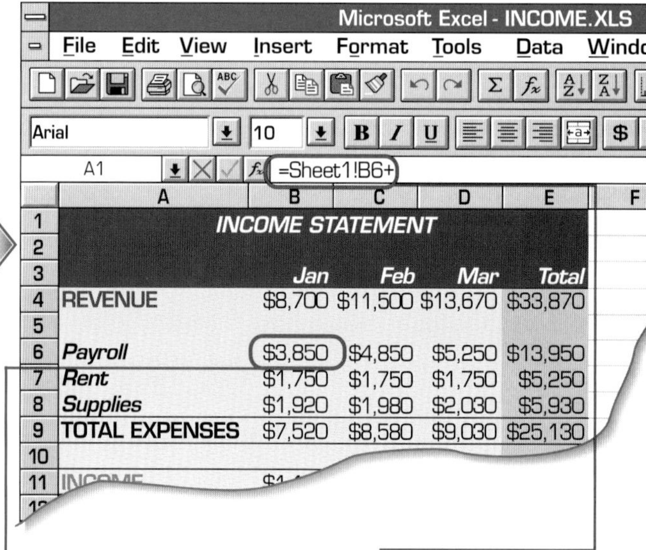

1 Move the mouse over the cell where you want to display the result of the formula and then press the left button.

2 To begin the formula, type an equal sign (=).

3 Move the mouse over the tab of the worksheet containing the data you want to use in the formula and then press the left button.

◆ The worksheet appears on your screen.

4 Move the mouse over a cell containing the data you want to use in the formula (example: **B6**) and then press the left button.

5 Type an operator for the formula (example: **+**).

Tip

The formula bar displays the worksheets and cells used to calculate a formula.

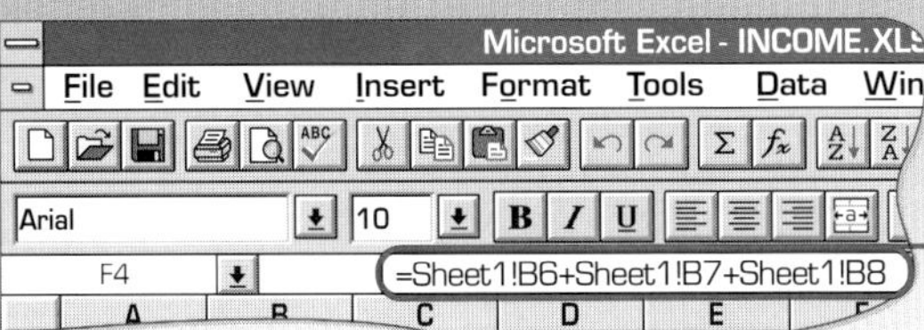

1 *Move the mouse over the cell containing the formula and then press the left button.*

◆ *The formula bar displays the worksheet name and cell reference for each cell used in the formula.*

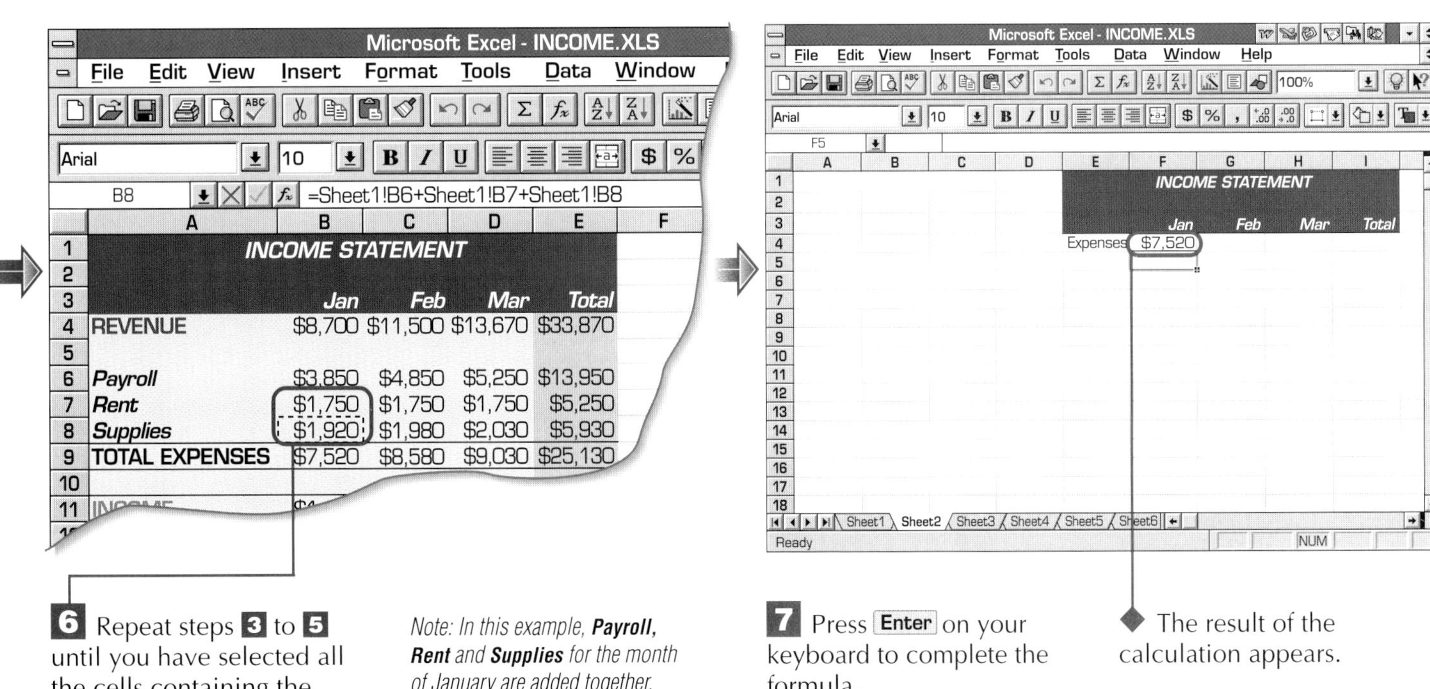

6 Repeat steps **3** to **5** until you have selected all the cells containing the data you want to use in the formula.

*Note: In this example, **Payroll**, **Rent** and **Supplies** for the month of January are added together.*

7 Press Enter on your keyboard to complete the formula.

◆ The result of the calculation appears.

CREATE A CHART

You can create a chart directly from your worksheet data. Excel provides a ChartWizard to lead you through each step.

CREATE A CHART

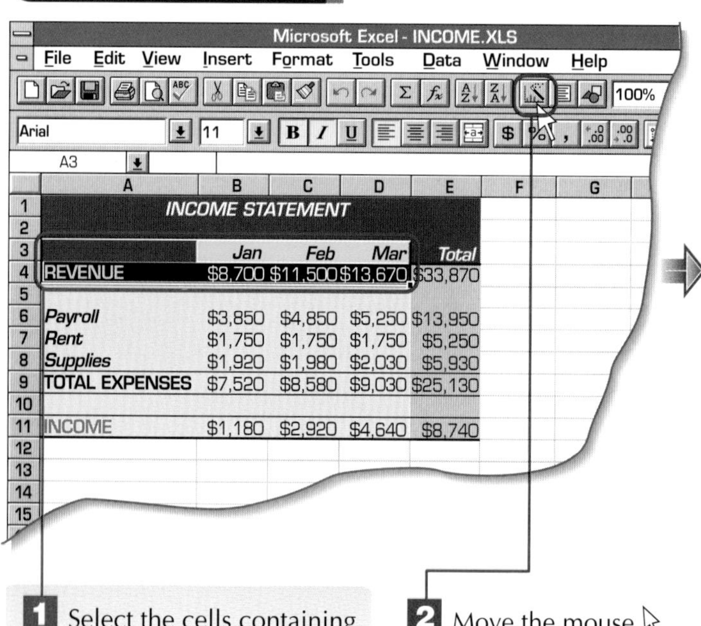

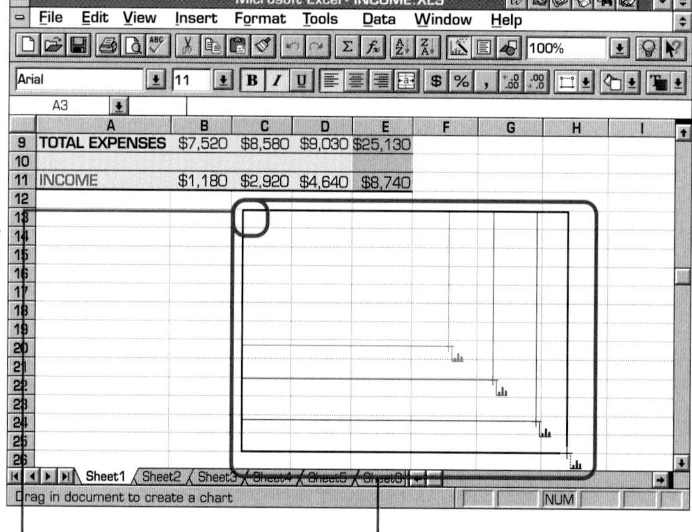

1 Select the cells containing the data you want to chart, including the row and column headings.

Note: To select cells, refer to page 140.

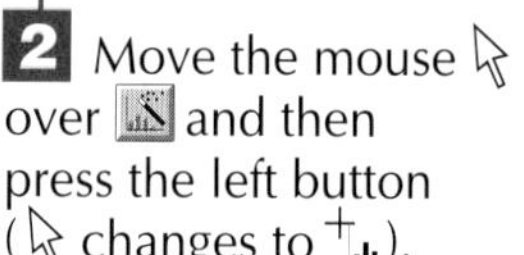

2 Move the mouse over the ChartWizard button and then press the left button (the pointer changes).

3 Move the mouse over the location where you want the top left corner of the chart to appear.

4 Press and hold down the left button as you drag the mouse until the rectangle displays the size of the chart you want. Then release the button.

- **Create a Chart**
- Move a Chart
- Size a Chart
- Add a Data Series to a Chart
- Print a Chart
- Change Chart Type
- Format a Chart Automatically

When creating a chart, you can easily return to the previous step.

◆ *To return to the previous step, move the mouse over* ***Back*** *and then press the left button.*

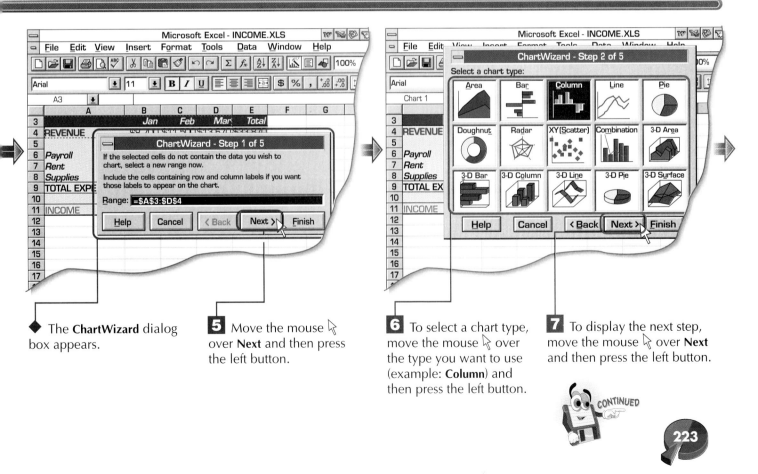

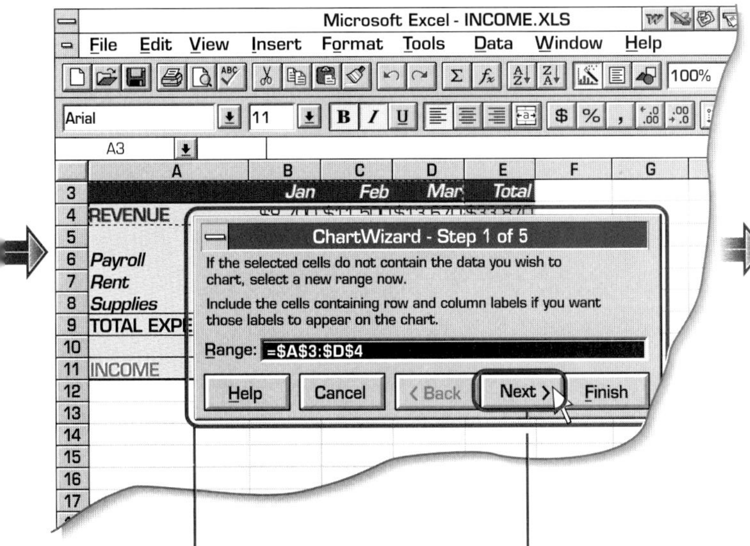

◆ The **ChartWizard** dialog box appears.

5 Move the mouse over **Next** and then press the left button.

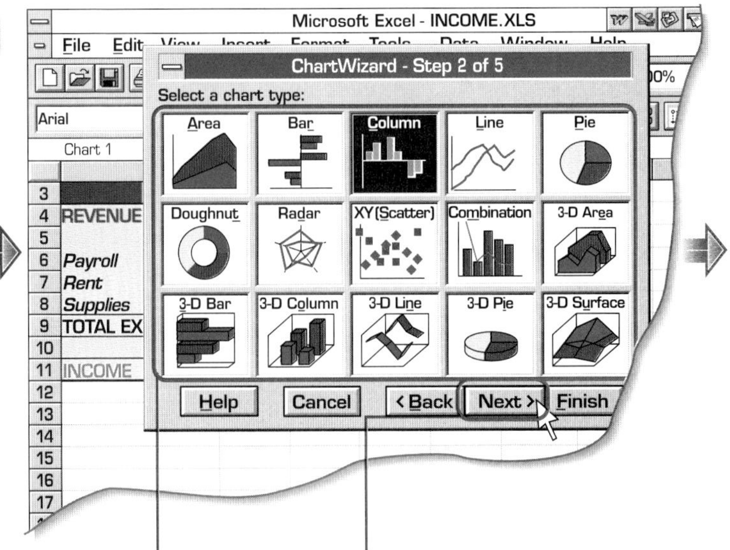

6 To select a chart type, move the mouse over the type you want to use (example: **Column**) and then press the left button.

7 To display the next step, move the mouse over **Next** and then press the left button.

CONTINUED

CREATE A CHART

A chart lets you visually display your worksheet data.

CREATE A CHART (CONTINUED)

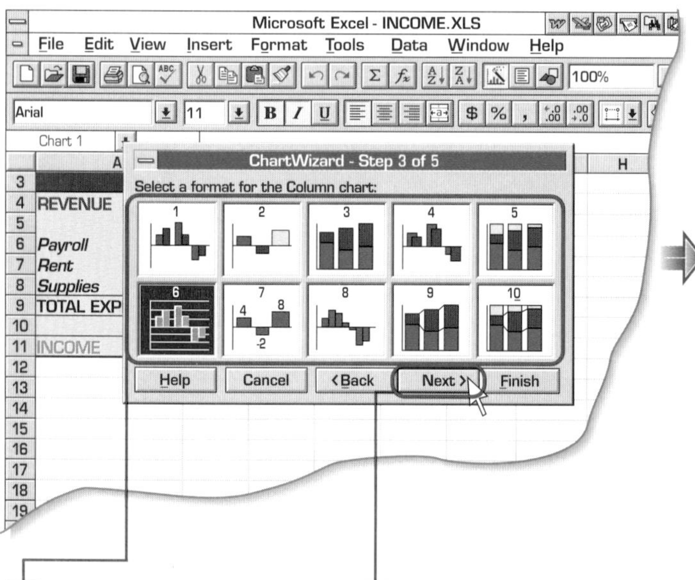

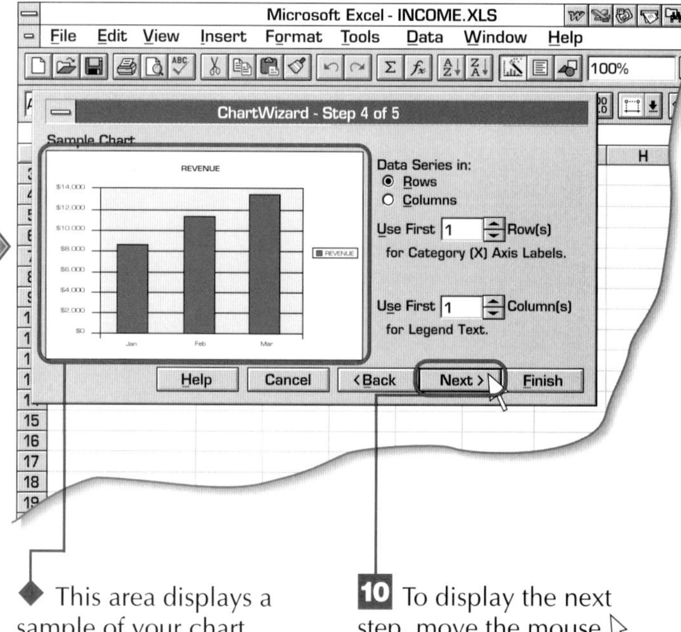

8 To select a format for the chart type you selected, move the mouse over the format you want to use (example: **6**) and then press the left button.

9 To display the next step, move the mouse over **Next** and then press the left button.

◆ This area displays a sample of your chart.

10 To display the next step, move the mouse over **Next** and then press the left button.

- **Create a Chart**
- Move a Chart
- Size a Chart
- Add a Data Series to a Chart
- Print a Chart
- Change Chart Type
- Format a Chart Automatically

If you make changes to the data in your worksheet, Excel will automatically update the chart to reflect the changes.

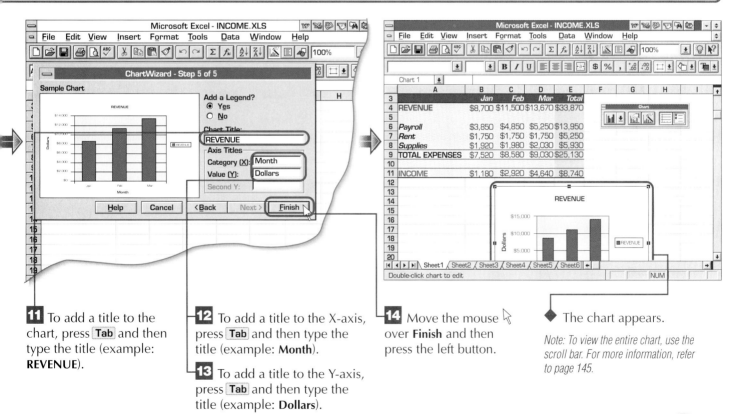

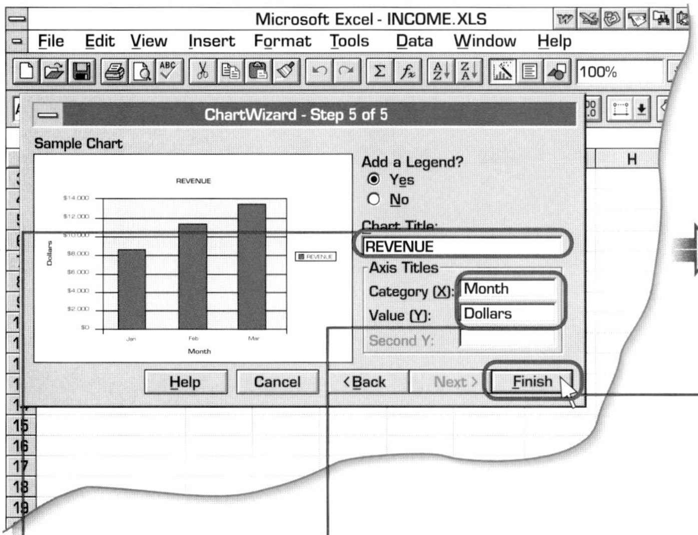

11 To add a title to the chart, press Tab and then type the title (example: **REVENUE**).

12 To add a title to the X-axis, press Tab and then type the title (example: **Month**).

13 To add a title to the Y-axis, press Tab and then type the title (example: **Dollars**).

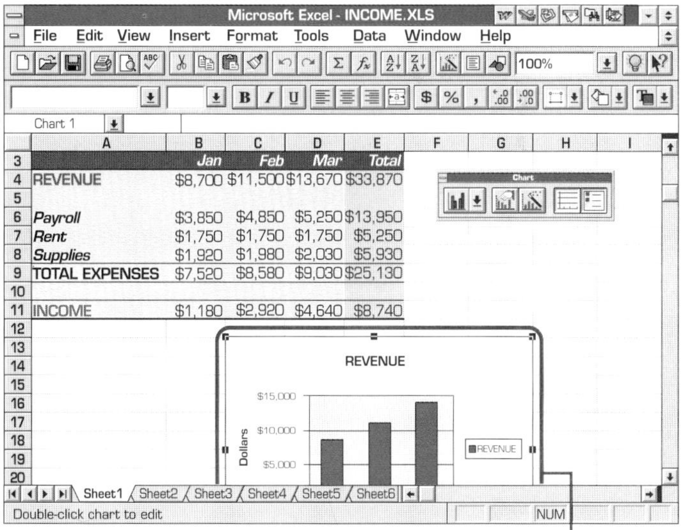

14 Move the mouse over **Finish** and then press the left button.

◆ The chart appears.

Note: To view the entire chart, use the scroll bar. For more information, refer to page 145.

MOVE A CHART

SIZE A CHART

After you create a chart, you can move it to a more suitable location in your worksheet. You can also change the overall size of the chart.

MOVE A CHART

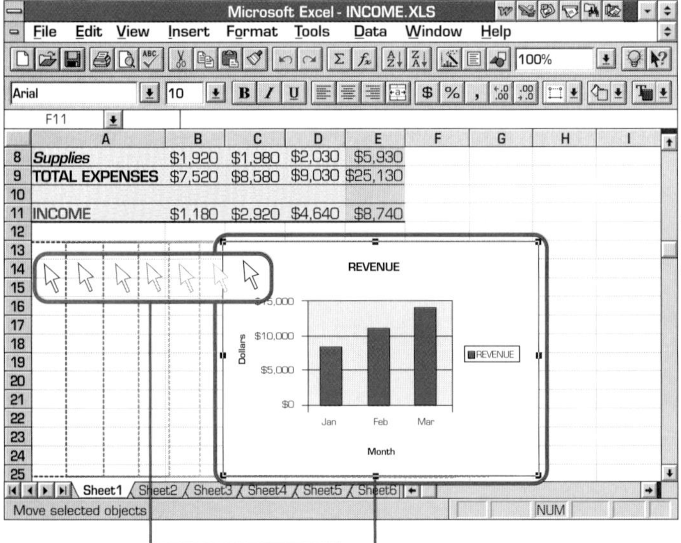

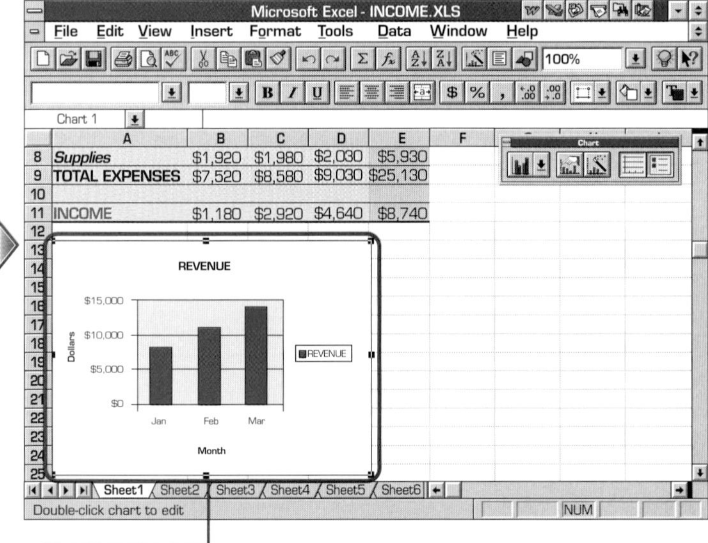

1 To deselect a chart, move the mouse ✚ over any cell outside the chart and then press the left button.

2 To move a chart, move the mouse ↖ anywhere over the chart.

3 Press and hold down the left button as you drag the chart to a new location.

◆ A dotted box shows the new location.

4 Release the button and the chart moves to the new location.

Tip

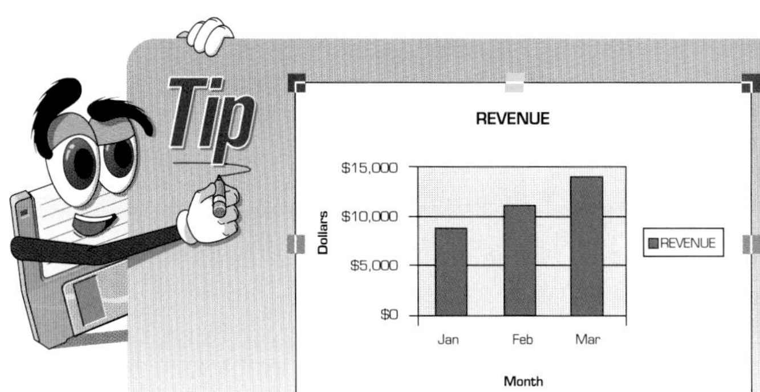

You can change the size of a chart using any handle around the chart.

You can use these handles to change the height of a chart.

You can use these handles to change the width of a chart.

You can use these handles to change the height and width of a chart at the same time.

SIZE A CHART

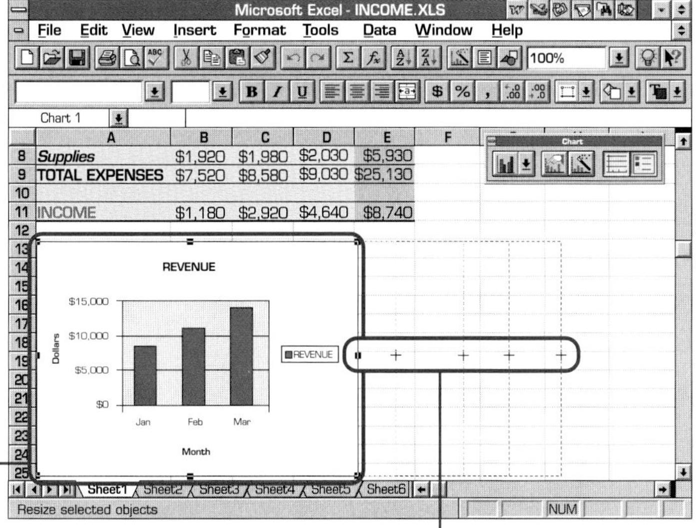

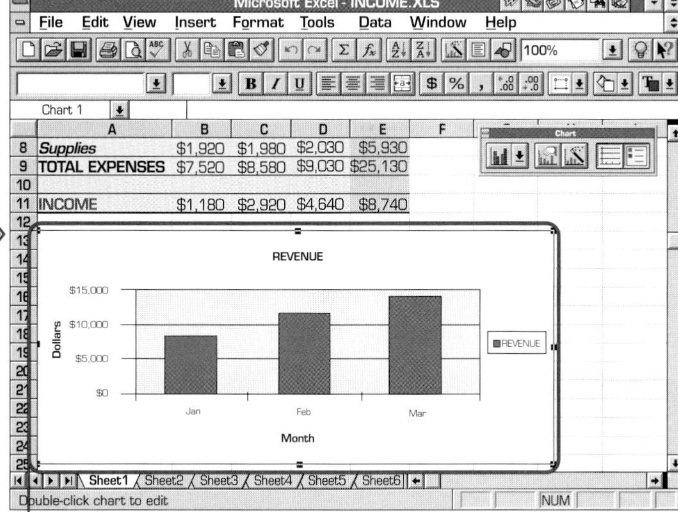

1 To deselect a chart, move the mouse over any cell outside the chart and then press the left button.

2 Move the mouse anywhere over the chart and then press the left button. Handles (■) appear around the chart.

3 Move the mouse over one of the handles (■) and changes to ↔.

4 Press and hold down the left button as you drag the chart to the new size.

◆ A dotted box shows the new size.

5 Release the button and the chart displays the new size.

ADD A DATA SERIES TO A CHART

After you create a chart, you can easily add another data series.

A data series is a group of related data representing a row or column from your worksheet.

ADD A DATA SERIES TO A CHART

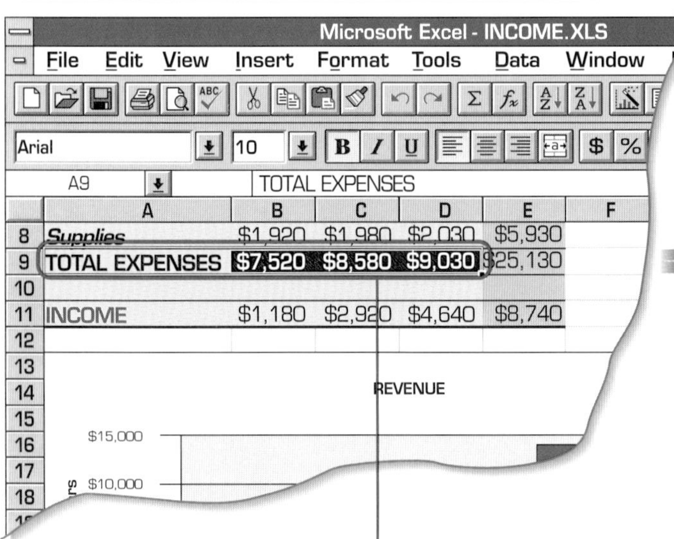

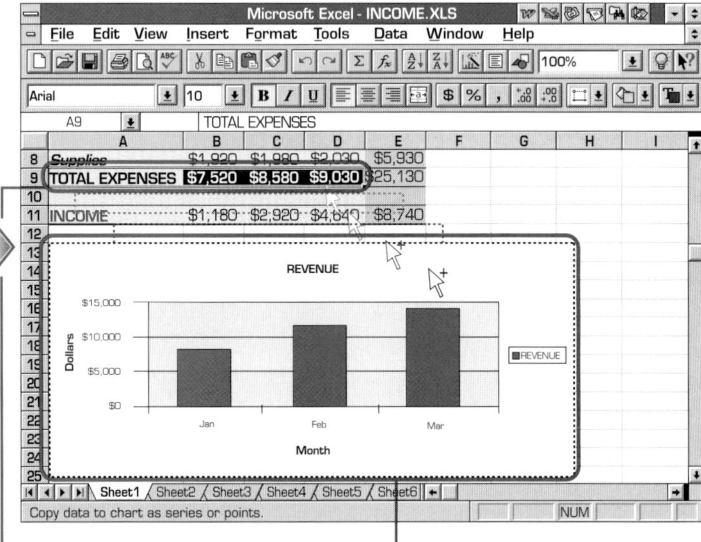

1 To deselect a chart, move the mouse over any cell outside the chart and then press the left button.

2 Select the cells containing the data you want to add to the chart.

Note: To select cells, refer to page 140.

3 Move the mouse over a border of the cells you selected (changes to) and then press and hold down the left button.

4 Still holding down the button, drag the mouse anywhere over the chart. Then release the button.

- Create a Chart
- Move a Chart
- Size a Chart
- **Add a Data Series to a Chart**
- Print a Chart
- Change Chart Type
- Format a Chart Automatically

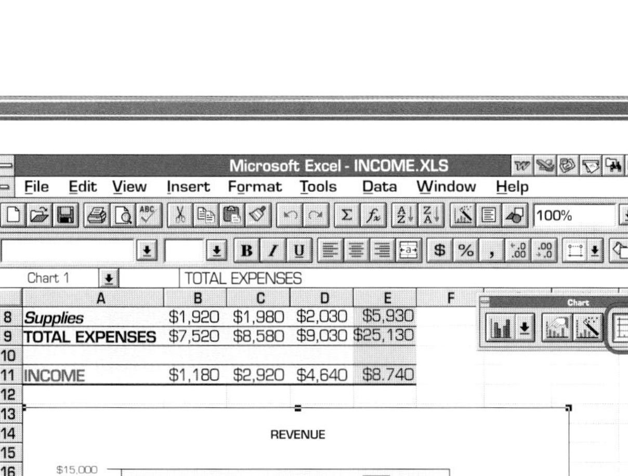

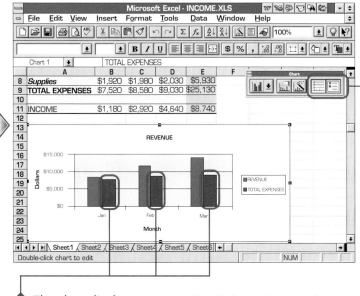

◆ The chart displays the new data series.

*Note: To display the **Chart** toolbar, refer to the **Tip** on page 233.*

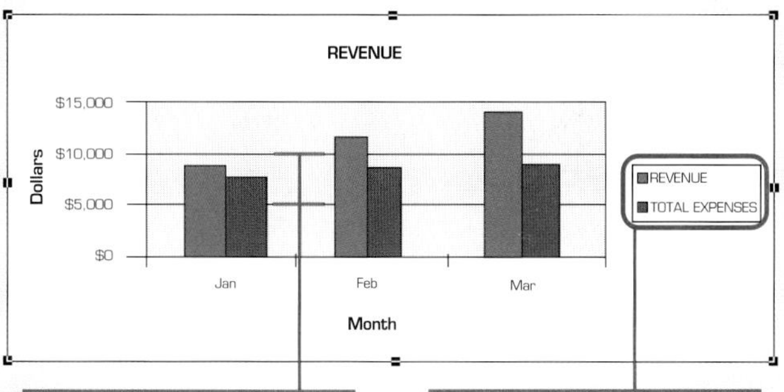

GRIDLINES

You can quickly remove or add horizontal gridlines in your chart.

1 Move the mouse anywhere over the chart and then press the left button.

2 Move the mouse over [icon] on the **Chart** toolbar and then press the left button.

LEGEND

You can quickly remove or add a legend in your chart.

1 Move the mouse anywhere over the chart and then press the left button.

2 Move the mouse over [icon] on the **Chart** toolbar and then press the left button.

PRINT A CHART

You can print your chart with the worksheet data or on its own page.

PRINT A CHART WITH WORKSHEET DATA

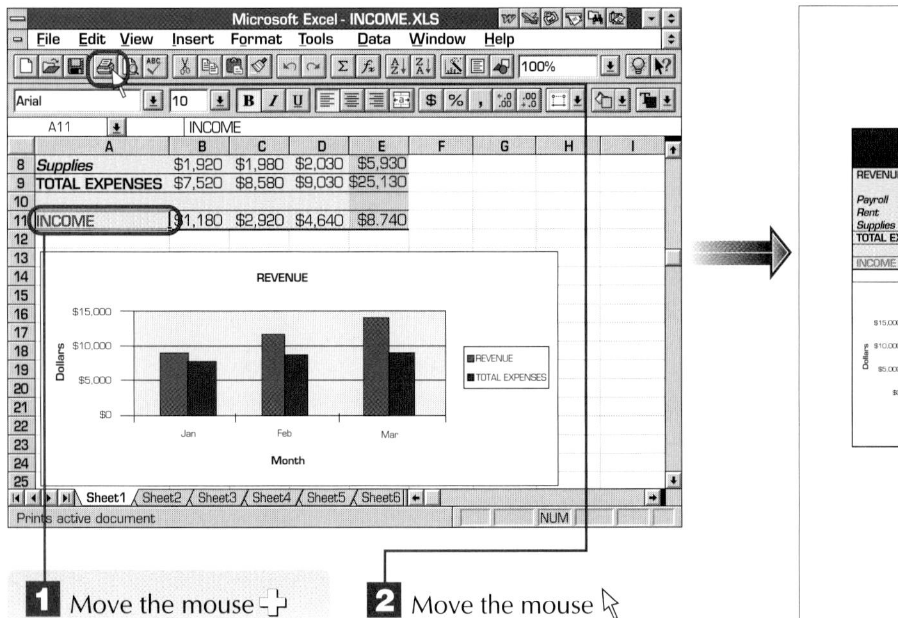

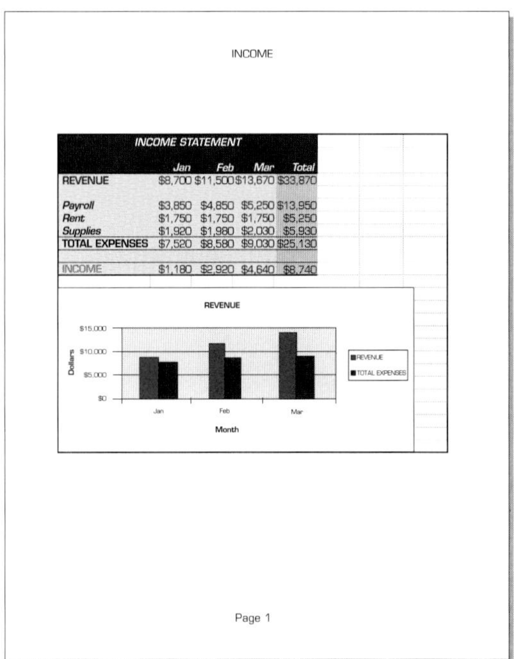

1 Move the mouse over any cell outside the chart and then press the left button.

2 Move the mouse over and then press the left button.

- Create a Chart
- Move a Chart
- Size a Chart
- Add a Data Series to a Chart
- **Print a Chart**
- Change Chart Type
- Format a Chart Automatically

For more information on printing your worksheet data, refer to page 212.

PRINT A CHART ON ITS OWN PAGE

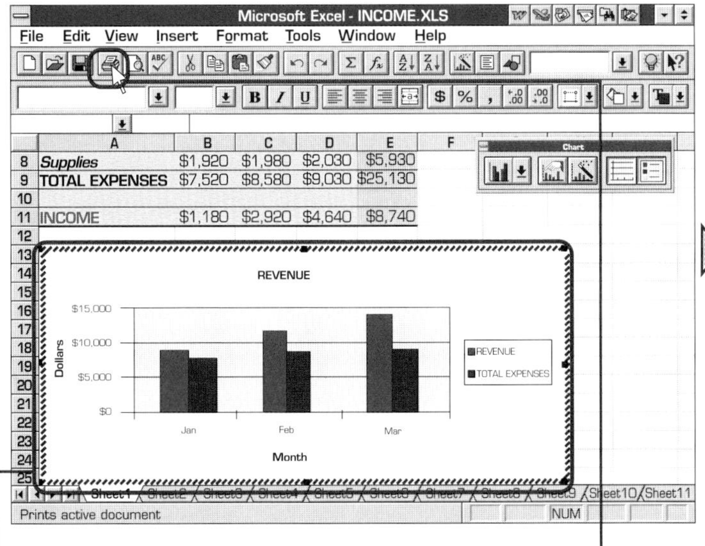

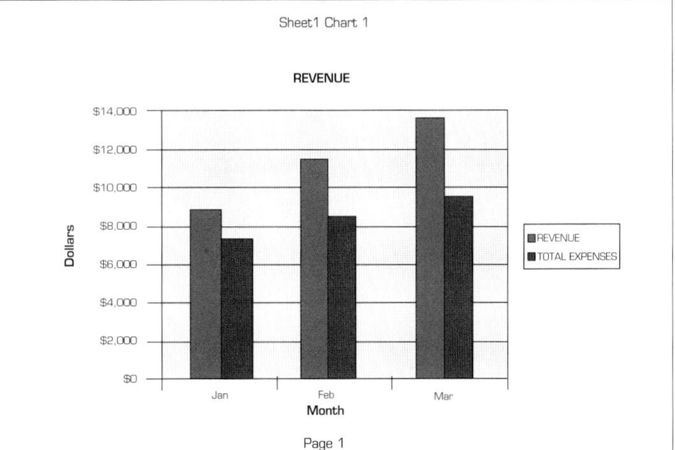

◆ To print a chart on its own page, you must first select the chart. A selected chart displays a colored border.

1 To select a chart, move the mouse anywhere over the chart and then quickly press the left button twice.

2 Move the mouse over the print button and then press the left button.

CHANGE CHART TYPE

After creating a chart, you can select a new type that will better suit your data.

CHANGE CHART TYPE

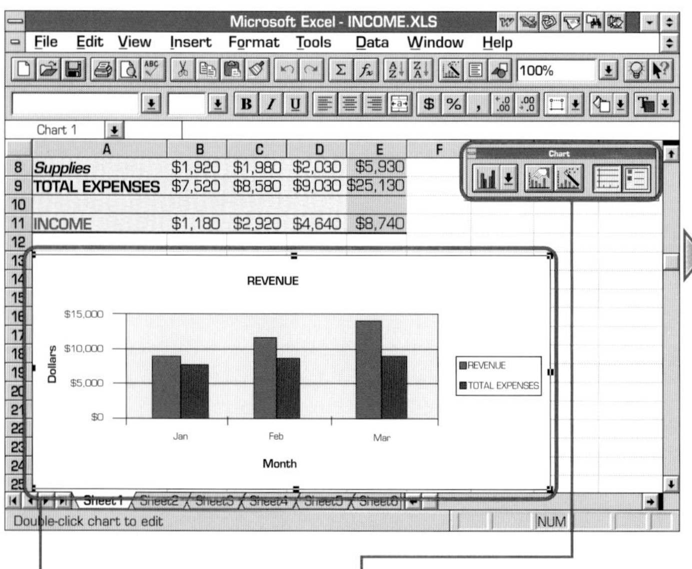

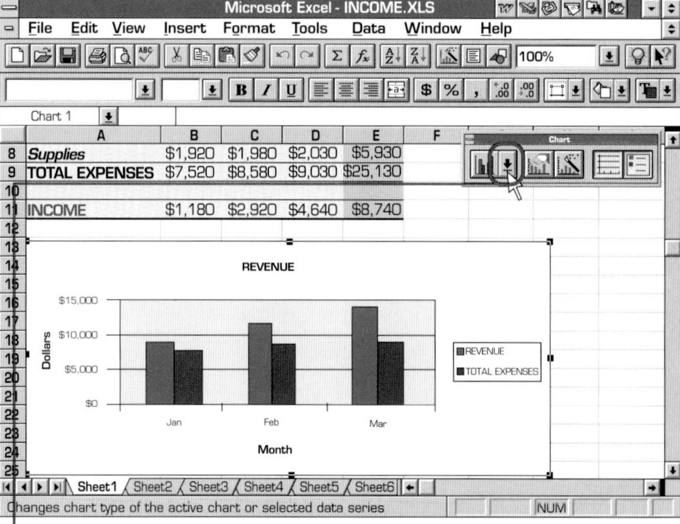

1 Move the mouse anywhere over the chart and then press the left button.

◆ The **Chart** toolbar appears.

*Note: If the **Chart** toolbar does not appear on your screen, refer to the **Tip** on page 233.*

2 Move the mouse over ⬇ on the **Chart** toolbar and then press the left button.

- Create a Chart
- Move a Chart
- Size a Chart
- Add a Data Series to a Chart
- Print a Chart
- **Change Chart Type**
- Format a Chart Automatically

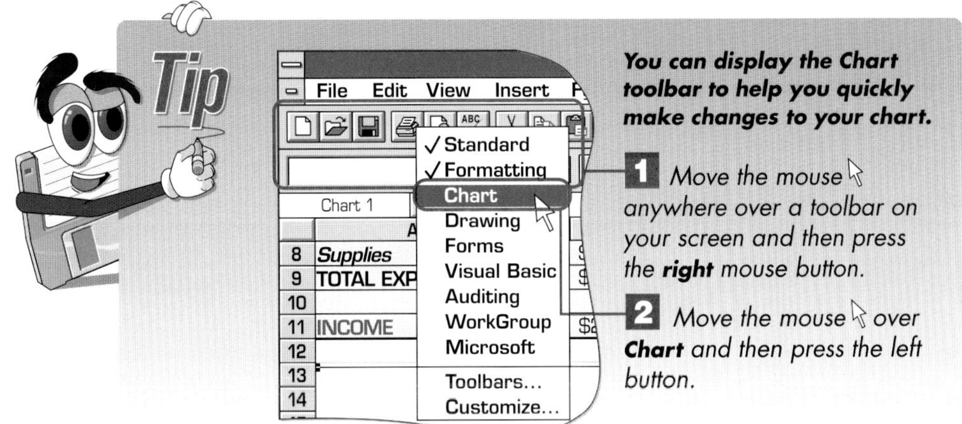

You can display the Chart toolbar to help you quickly make changes to your chart.

1 *Move the mouse anywhere over a toolbar on your screen and then press the* ***right*** *mouse button.*

2 *Move the mouse over* ***Chart*** *and then press the left button.*

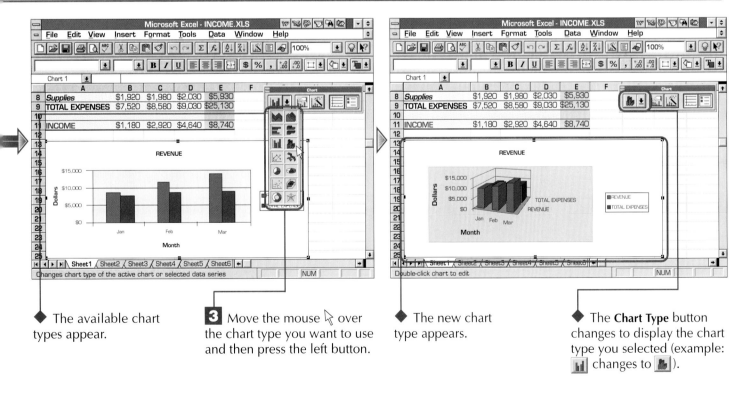

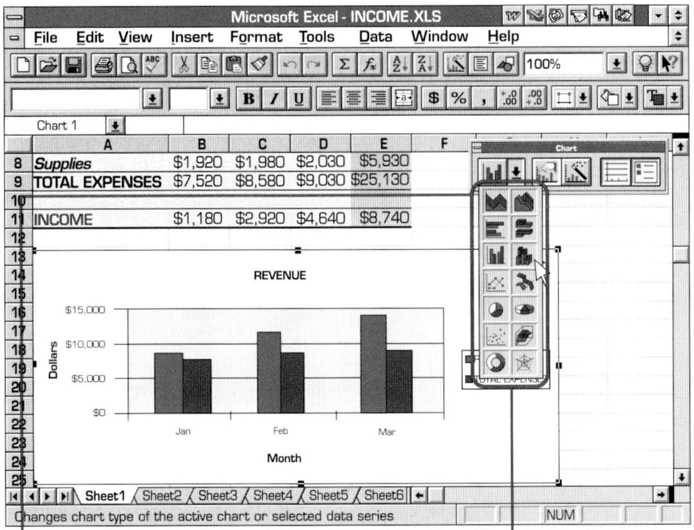

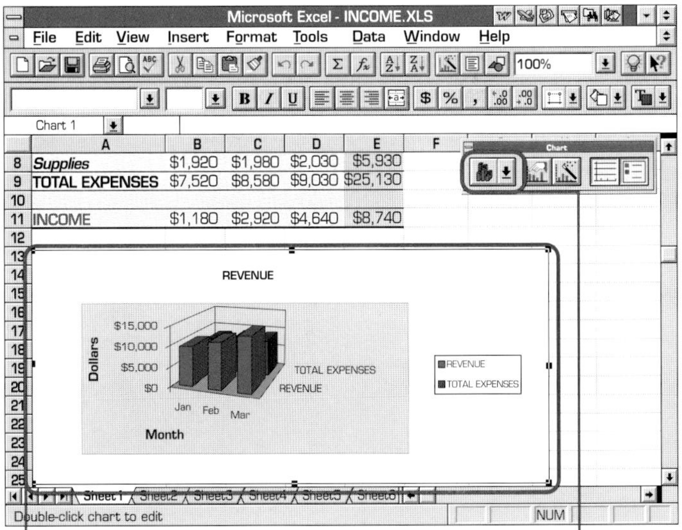

◆ The available chart types appear.

3 Move the mouse over the chart type you want to use and then press the left button.

◆ The new chart type appears.

◆ The **Chart Type** button changes to display the chart type you selected (example: changes to).

FORMAT A CHART AUTOMATICALLY

The AutoFormat feature provides a selection of formats that you can choose from to enhance the appearance of your chart.
Auto Format
REVENUE
Dollars
Jan
Feb
Month

FORMAT A CHART AUTOMATICALLY

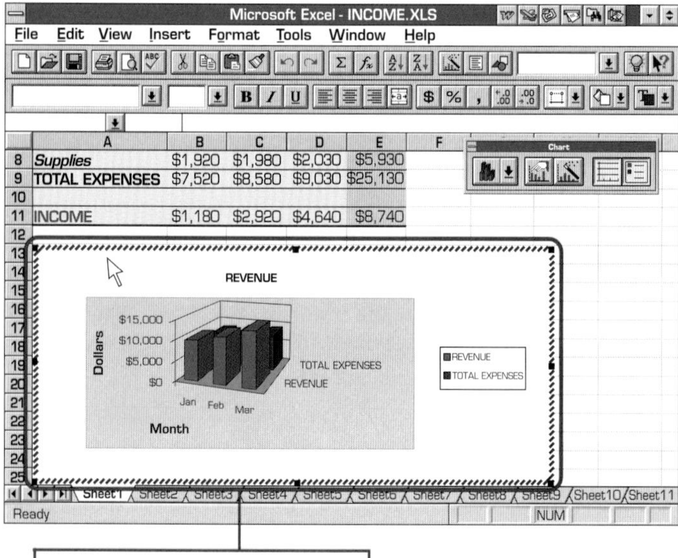

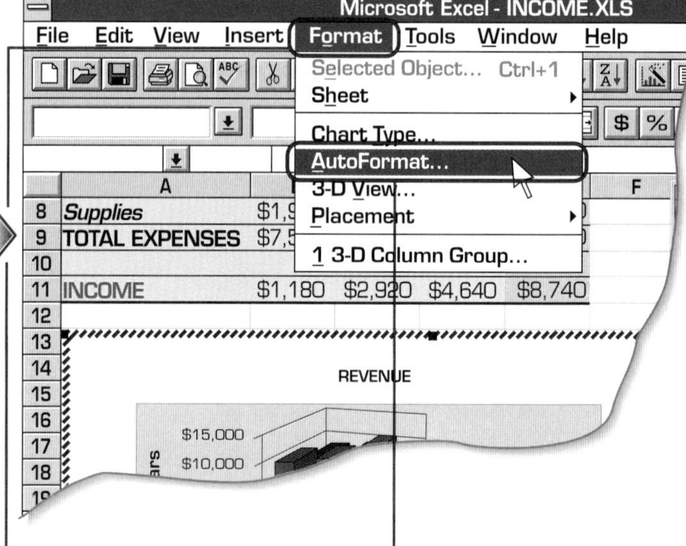

◆ You must first select the chart you want to format. A selected chart displays a colored border.

1 To select a chart, move the mouse anywhere over the chart and then quickly press the left button twice.

2 Move the mouse over **Format** and then press the left button.

3 Move the mouse over **AutoFormat** and then press the left button.

- Create a Chart
- Move a Chart
- Size a Chart
- Add a Data Series to a Chart
- Print a Chart
- Change Chart Type
- **Format a Chart Automatically**

If you are not satisfied with the results of the AutoFormat feature, you can undo the changes.

1 *To undo the AutoFormat immediately after applying the format, move the mouse over and then press the left button.*

Note: For more information on the Undo feature, refer to page 161.

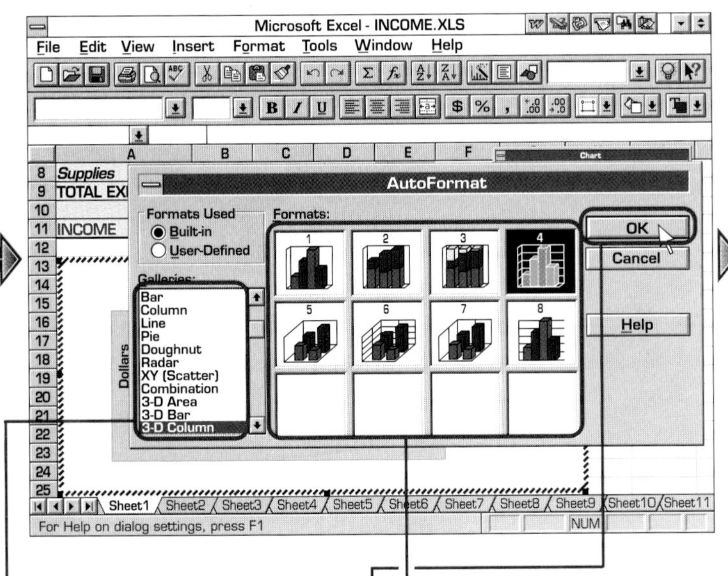

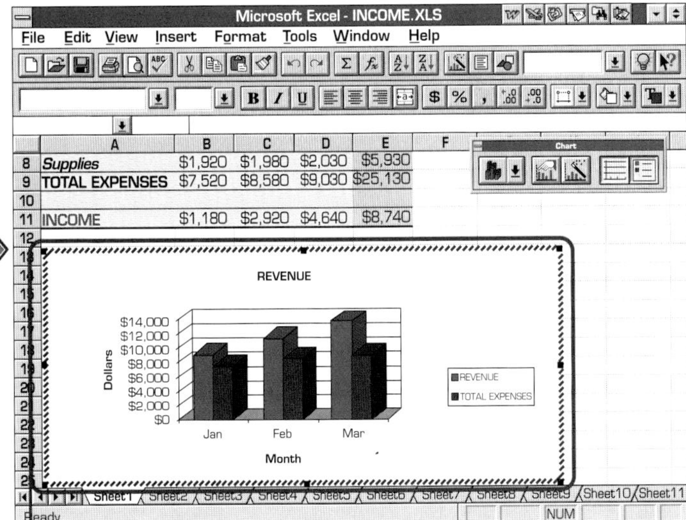

◆ The **AutoFormat** dialog box appears.

4 Move the mouse over the chart type you want to use (example: **3-D Column**) and then press the left button.

5 Move the mouse over the format you want to use (example: **4**) and then press the left button.

6 Move the mouse over **OK** and then press the left button.

◆ Your chart displays the new formats.

In this section you will learn how to create professional-looking presentations.
Lorem Ipsum
Dolot et ipsum no numi sit luxor ver
ipsum no
luxor ver batim
- no numi sit
- ver batim
t ipsum no numi
Etc cetra nobis pachem pronos no
sib non compus mentus locus.

POWERPOINT

INTRODUCTION

Microsoft® PowerPoint® helps you create, organize and design effective presentations.

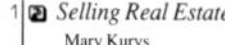

1 *Selling Real Estate*
Mary Kurys
2 *Objective*
- State the desired objective
- Use multiple points if necessary

3 *Customer Requirements*
- State the needs of the audience
- Confirm the audience's needs if you are not sure

4 *Meeting the Needs*
- List the products and features, and how each addresses a specific need or solves a specific problem
- This section may require multiple slides

5 *Cost Analysis*
- Point out financial benefits to the customer
- Compare cost-benefits between you and your competitors

6 *Our Strengths*
7 *Key Benefits*
- Summarize the key benefits provided by the product, service, or idea being promoted

8 *Next Steps*
- Specify the actions required of your audience

OUTLINE

You can print an outline that contains just the text from your presentation. This lets you view the overall content of your presentation.

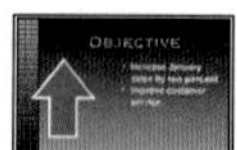

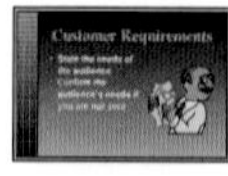

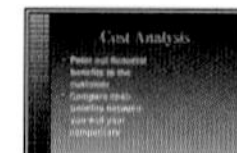

HANDOUTS

You can create handouts to help your audience follow your presentation. Handouts contain copies of your slides.

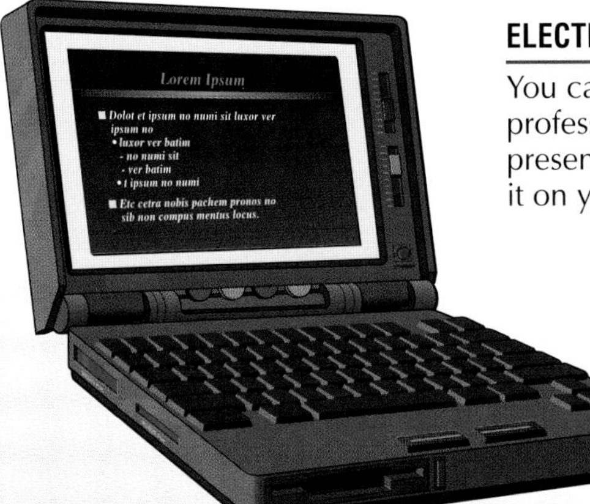

ELECTRONIC PRESENTATIONS

You can create a colorful, professional-looking presentation and then display it on your computer screen.

OVERHEADS

You can create overhead transparencies for your presentation.

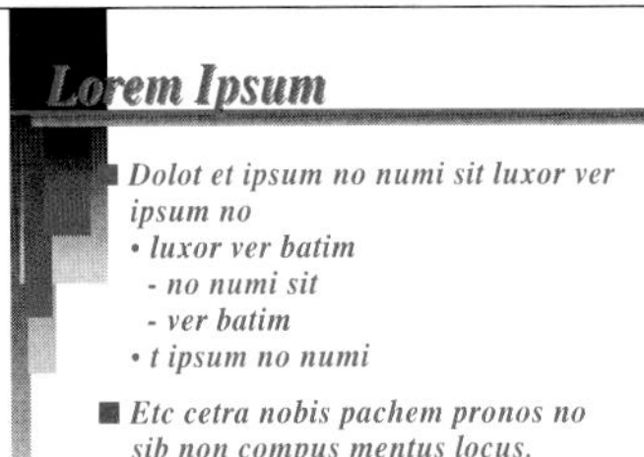

35MM SLIDES

You can create 35mm slides for your presentation.

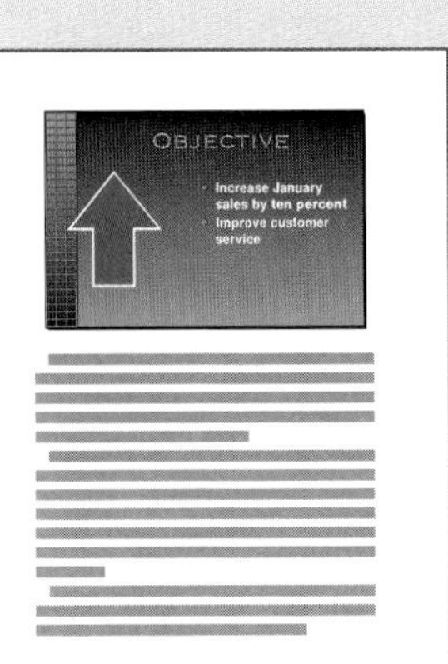

SPEAKER'S NOTES

You can create speaker's notes to help you deliver your presentation. These notes contain copies of your slides with all the ideas you want to discuss.

START POWERPOINT

START POWERPOINT

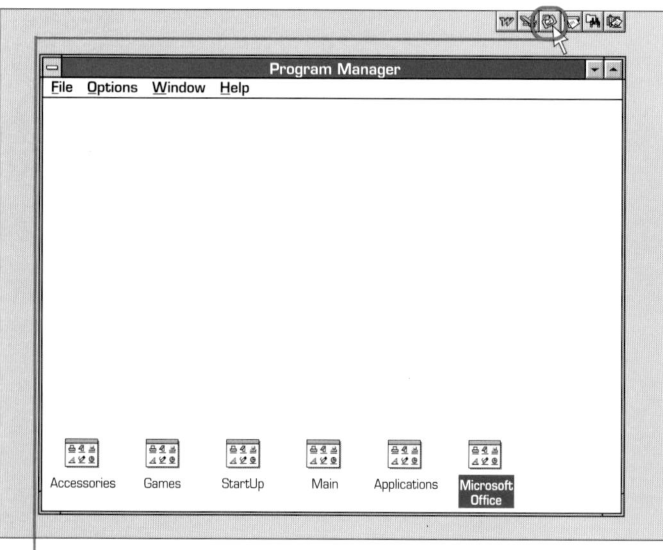

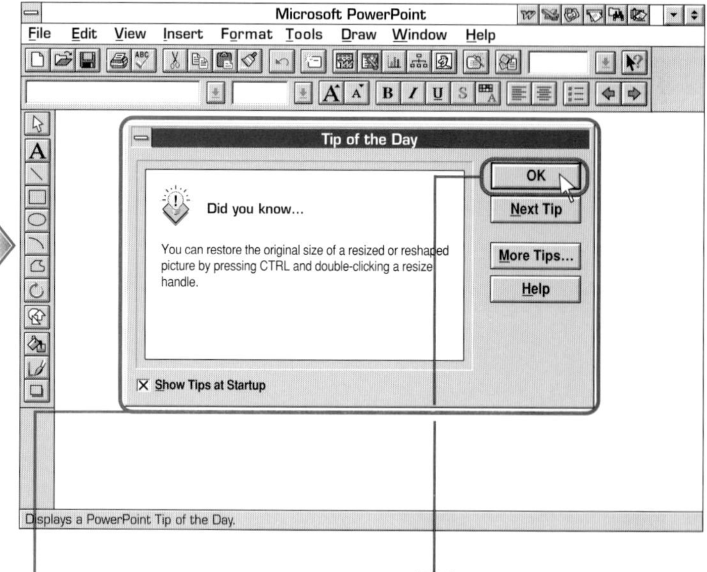

1 Move the mouse over and then press the left button.

◆ When you start PowerPoint, the **Tip of the Day** dialog box appears. It displays a tip about using PowerPoint.

2 To close this dialog box, move the mouse over **OK** and then press the left button.

*To learn how to use the mouse or select commands, refer to the first section of this book, called **Introduction to Microsoft Office**, starting on page 4.*

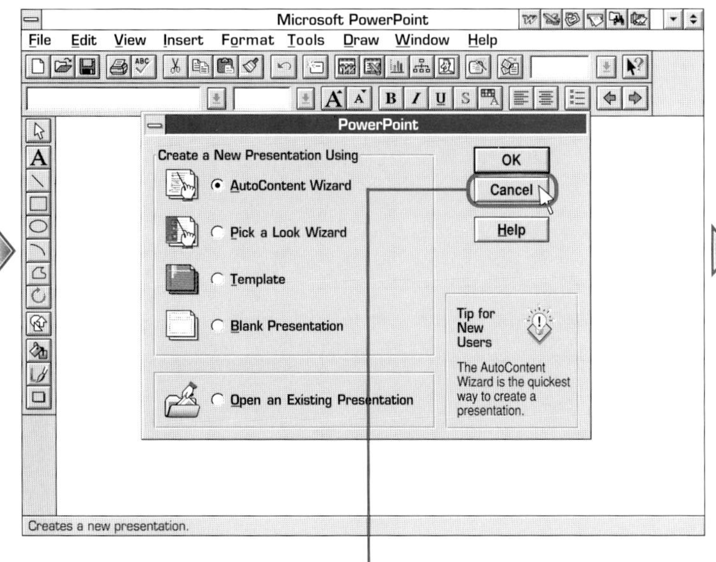

◆ The **PowerPoint** dialog box appears.

3 To close this dialog box, move the mouse over **Cancel** and then press the left button.

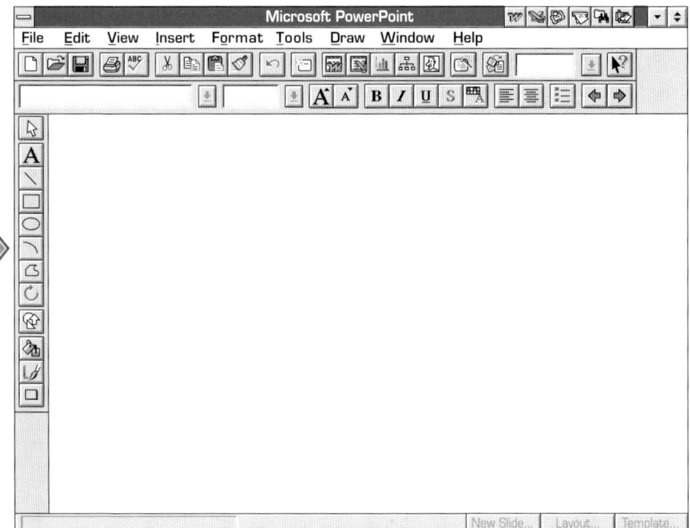

◆ You can now use PowerPoint to create a presentation.

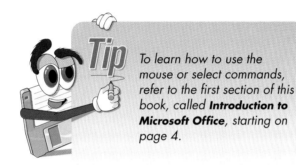

GETTING HELP

If you forget how to perform a task, you can use the Help feature to obtain information. This can save you time by eliminating the need to refer to other sources.
HELP

GETTING HELP

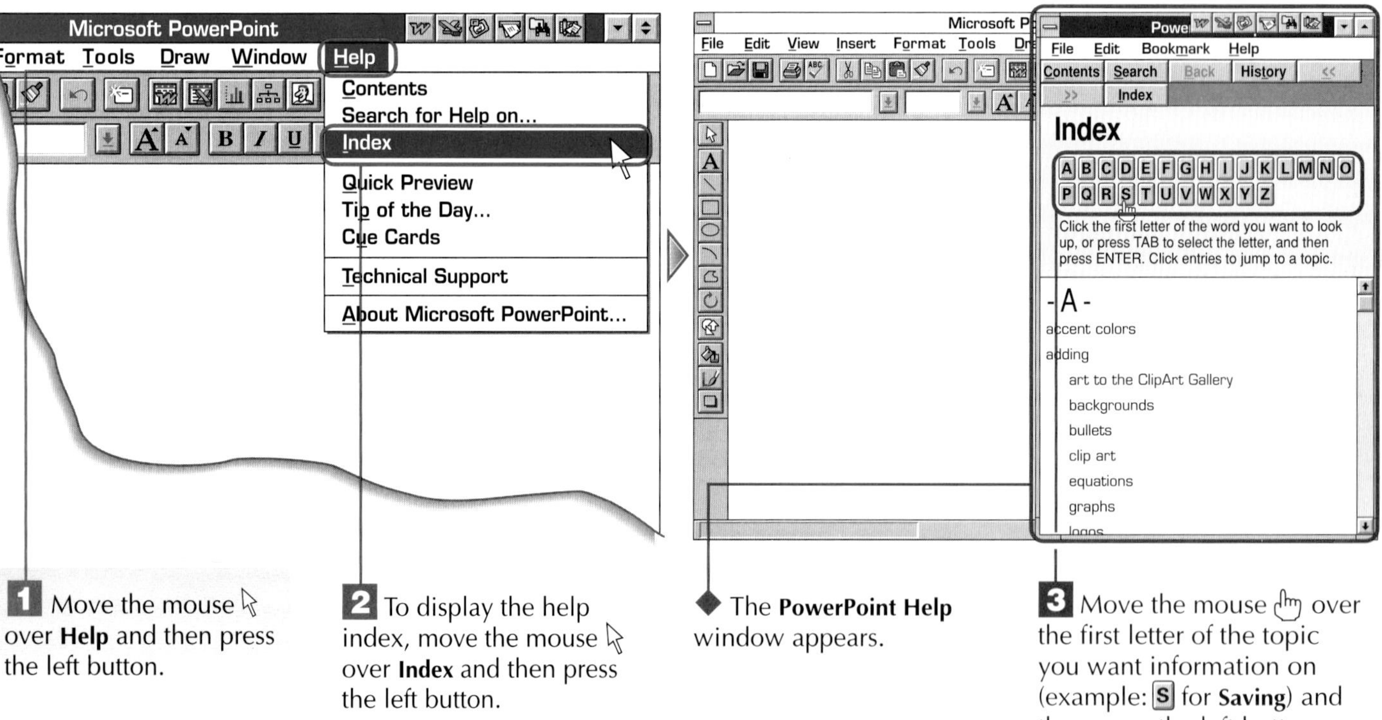

1 Move the mouse over **Help** and then press the left button.

2 To display the help index, move the mouse over **Index** and then press the left button.

◆ The **PowerPoint Help** window appears.

3 Move the mouse over the first letter of the topic you want information on (example: **S** for **Saving**) and then press the left button.

EXIT HELP

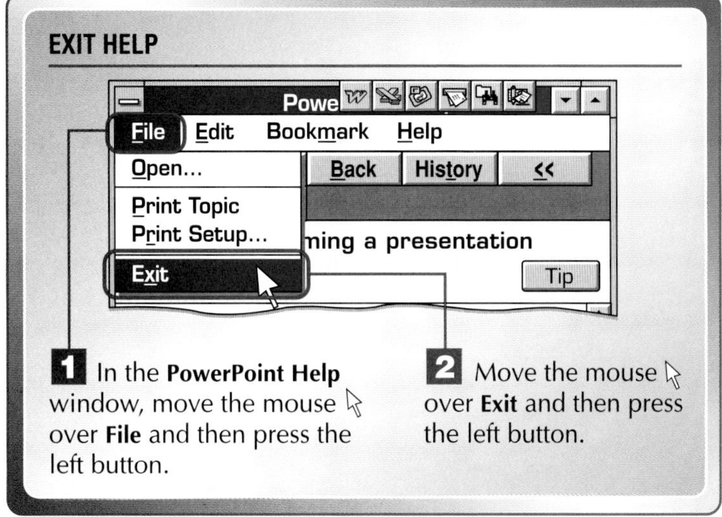

1 In the **PowerPoint Help** window, move the mouse over **File** and then press the left button.

2 Move the mouse over **Exit** and then press the left button.

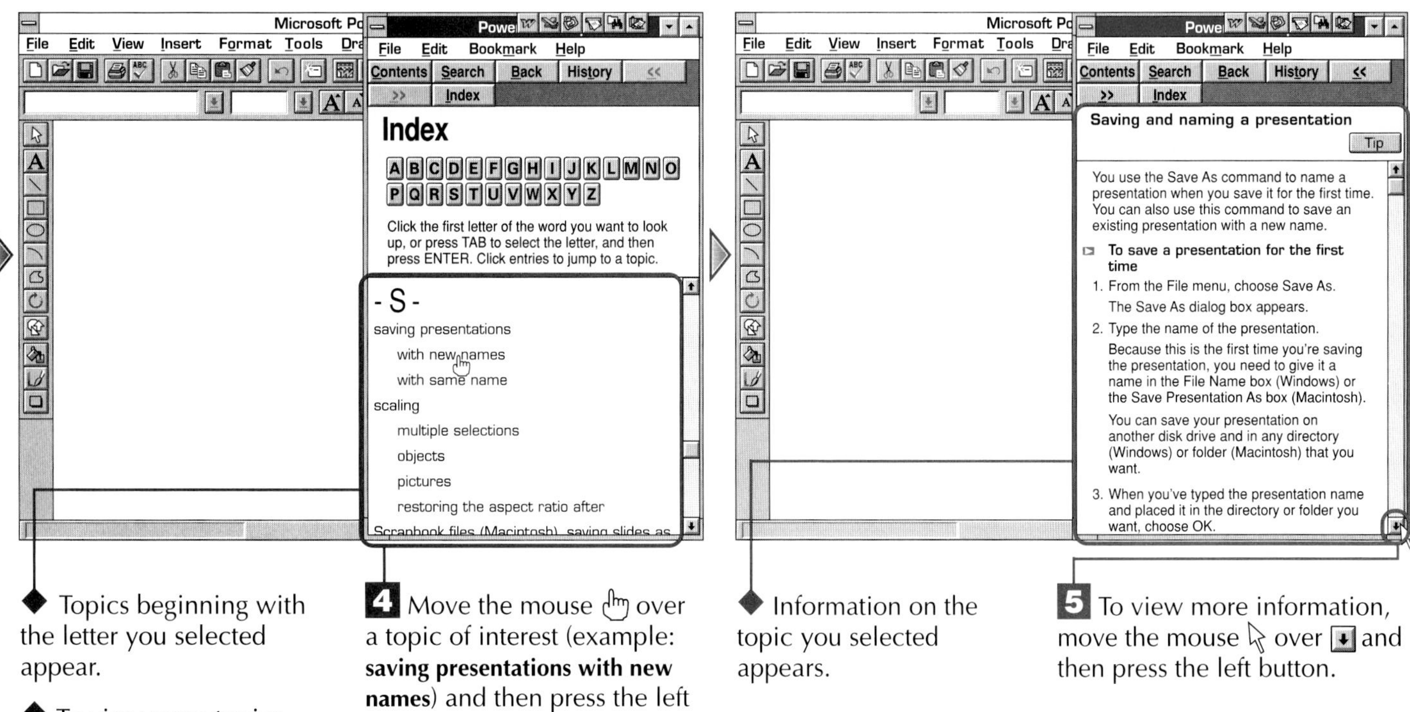

◆ Topics beginning with the letter you selected appear.

◆ To view more topics beginning with that letter, press PageDown on your keyboard.

4 Move the mouse over a topic of interest (example: **saving presentations with new names**) and then press the left button.

◆ Information on the topic you selected appears.

5 To view more information, move the mouse over ⬇ and then press the left button.

USING THE AUTOCONTENT WIZARD

The AutoContent Wizard is the quickest way to create a new presentation. This Wizard provides a basic outline that you can personalize to suit your needs.

USING THE AUTOCONTENT WIZARD

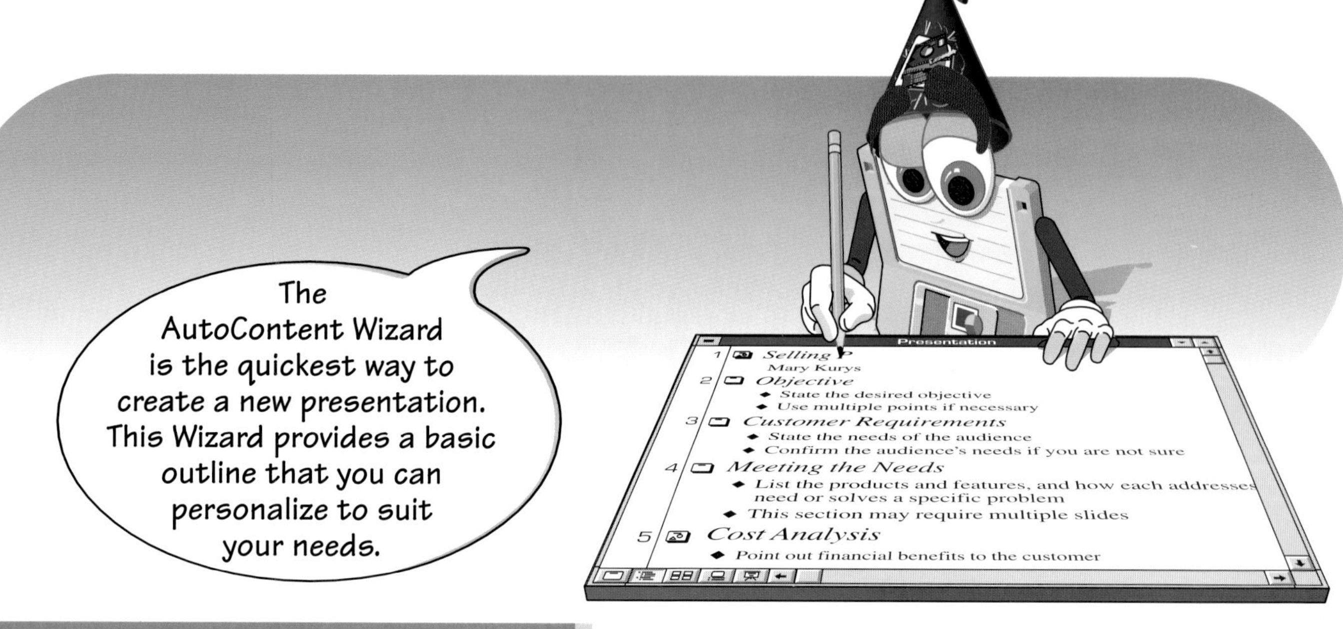

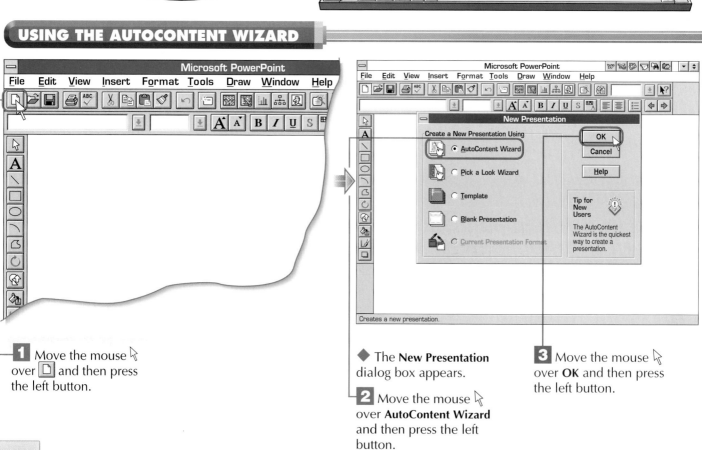

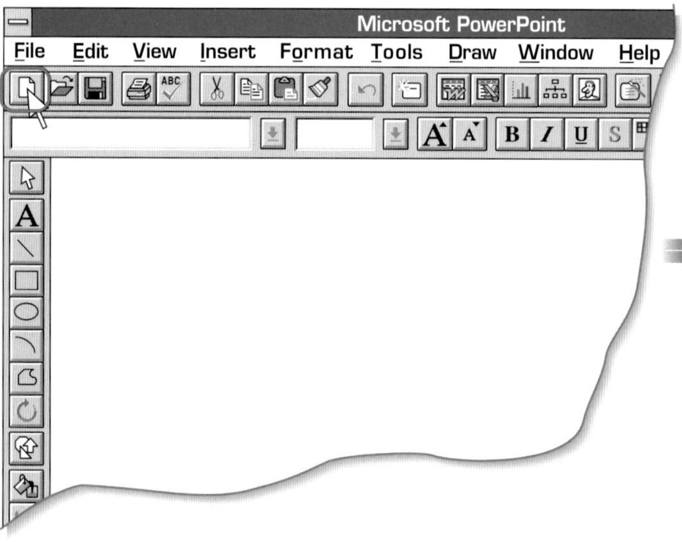

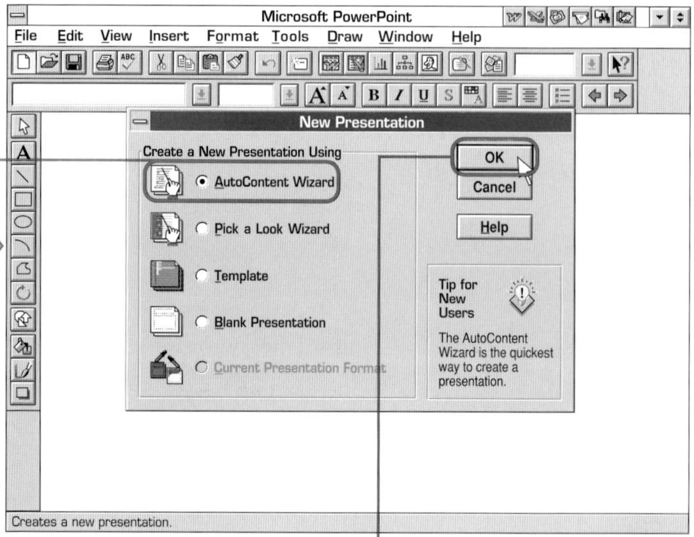

1 Move the mouse over and then press the left button.

◆ The **New Presentation** dialog box appears.

2 Move the mouse over **AutoContent Wizard** and then press the left button.

3 Move the mouse over **OK** and then press the left button.

- **Using the AutoContent Wizard**
- Change Views
- Move Between Slides

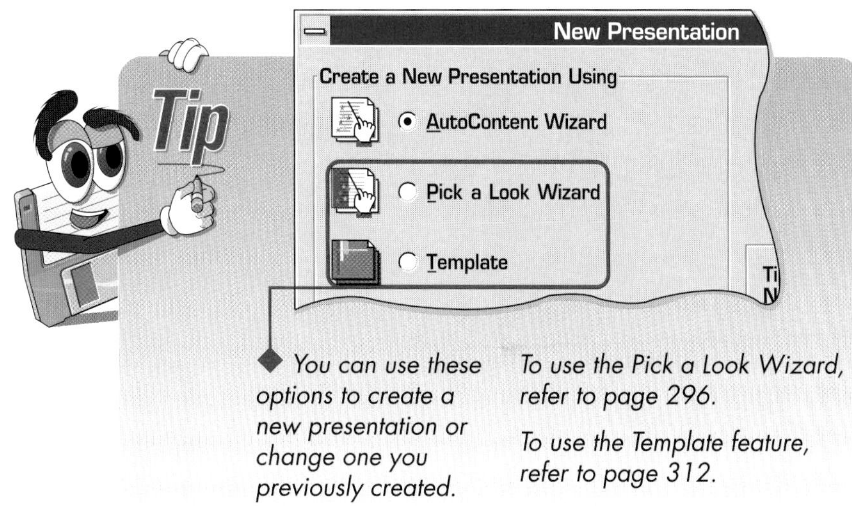

◆ *You can use these options to create a new presentation or change one you previously created.*

To use the Pick a Look Wizard, refer to page 296.

To use the Template feature, refer to page 312.

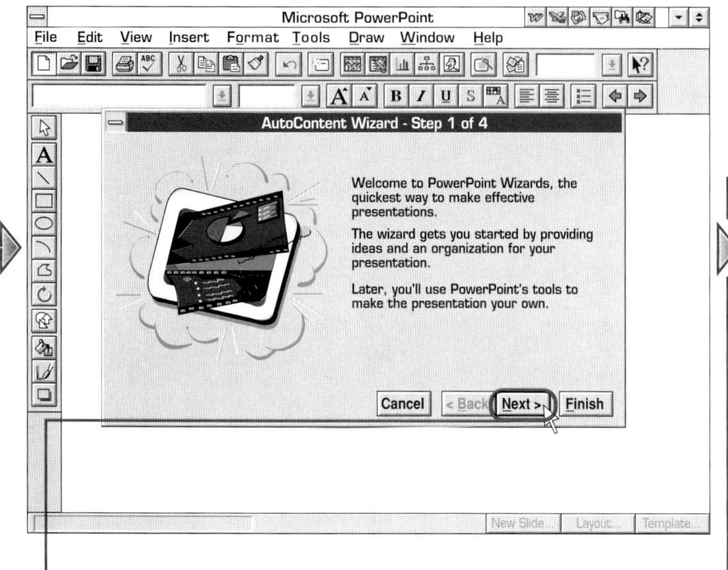

4 Move the mouse over **Next** and then press the left button.

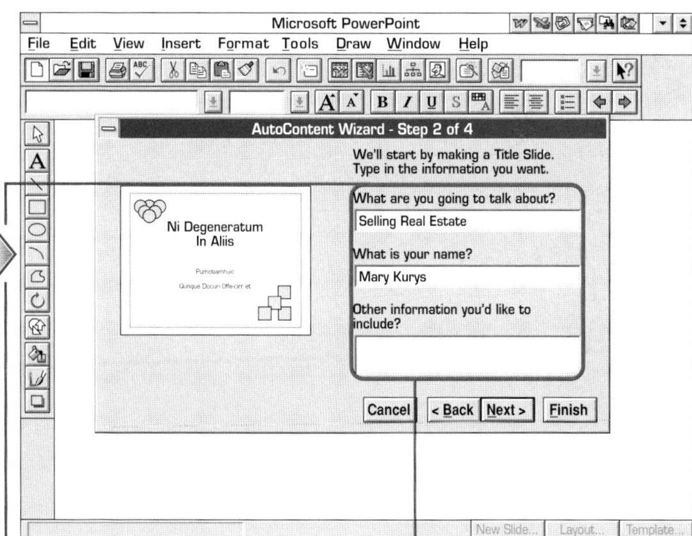

◆ The information you enter in this area will appear on the first slide in your presentation.

5 Type a title for your presentation. Then press Tab to move to the next box.

6 Type your name. Then press Tab to move to the next box.

USING THE AUTOCONTENT WIZARD

USING THE AUTOCONTENT WIZARD (CONTINUED)

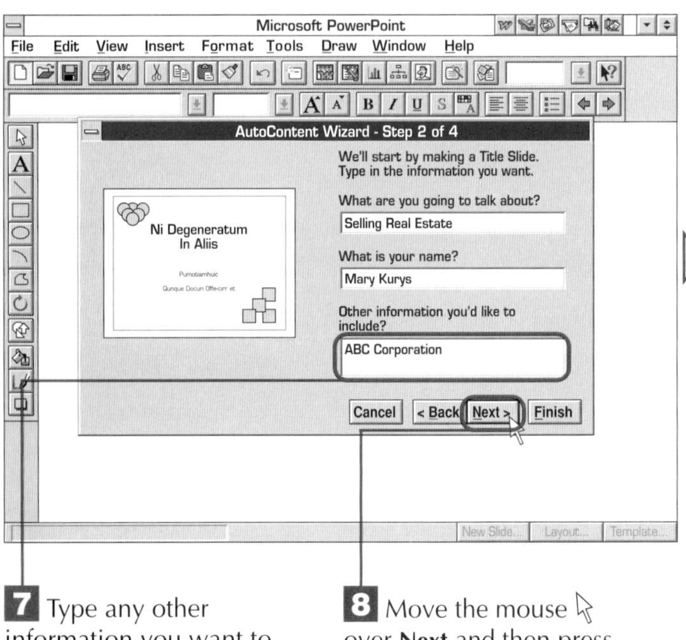

Microsoft PowerPoint

File Edit View Insert Format Tools Draw Window Help

AutoContent Wizard - Step 3 of 4

- Objective
- Customer Requirements
- Features
- Competitive Strengths
- Key Benefits
- Next Steps

Select the type of presentation you're going to give.

- Recommending a Strategy
- Selling a Product, Service or Idea
- Training
- Reporting Progress
- Communicating Bad News
- General

Cancel | < Back | Next > | Finish

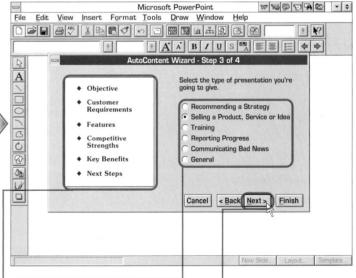

7 Type any other information you want to appear on the first slide.

8 Move the mouse over **Next** and then press the left button.

9 Move the mouse over the type of presentation you want to create and then press the left button (○ changes to ◉).

◆ This area displays the main topics for the presentation you selected.

10 Move the mouse over **Next** and then press the left button.

- **Using the AutoContent Wizard**
- Change Views
- Move Between Slides

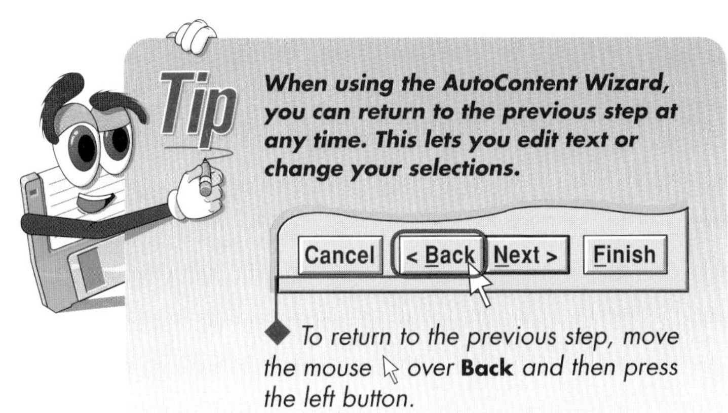

Tip
When using the AutoContent Wizard, you can return to the previous step at any time. This lets you edit text or change your selections.
Cancel
< Back
Next >
Finish

◆ *To return to the previous step, move the mouse over* ***Back*** *and then press the left button.*

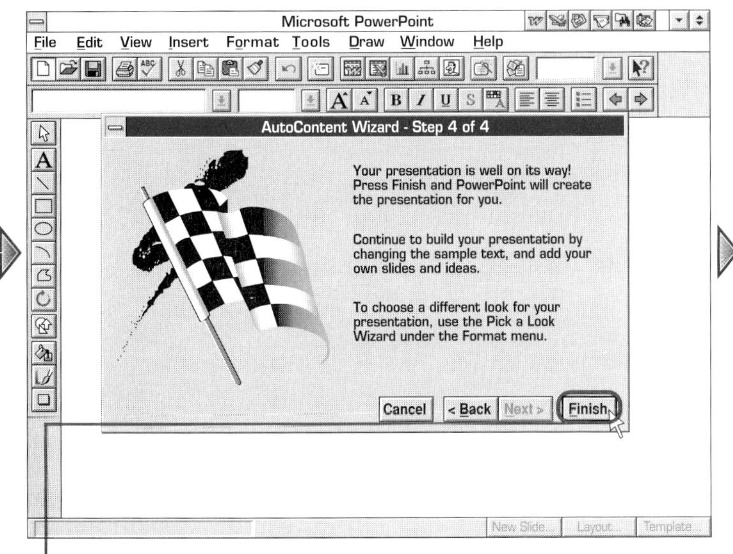

11 Move the mouse over **Finish** and then press the left button.

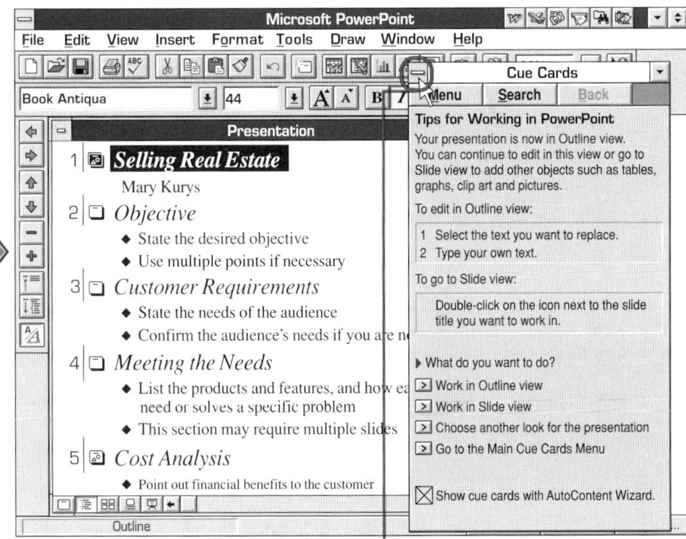

◆ A sample presentation appears.

◆ Cue Cards also appear, providing step-by-step instructions on how to perform tasks.

12 To remove the Cue Cards from your screen, move the mouse over ▭ and then quickly press the left button twice.

CHANGE VIEWS

PowerPoint offers four ways to view your presentation.

SLIDE VIEW

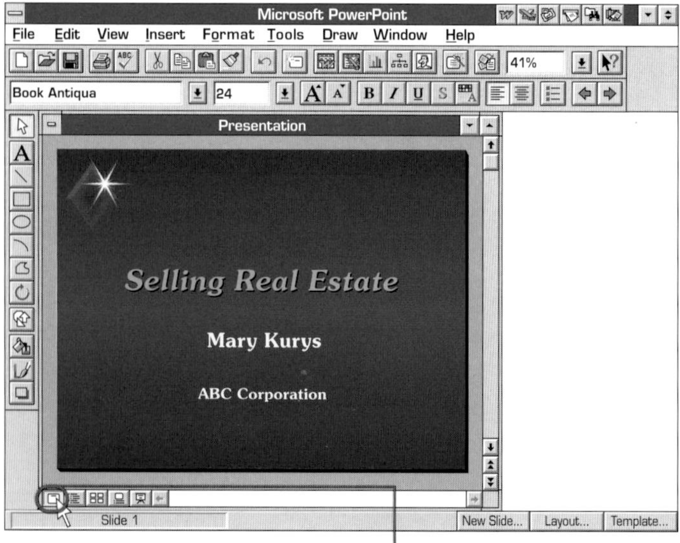

The Slide view displays one slide at a time, complete with text and graphics. You can use this view when changing the layout or design of your slides.

1 To change to the Slide view, move the mouse over and then press the left button.

OUTLINE VIEW

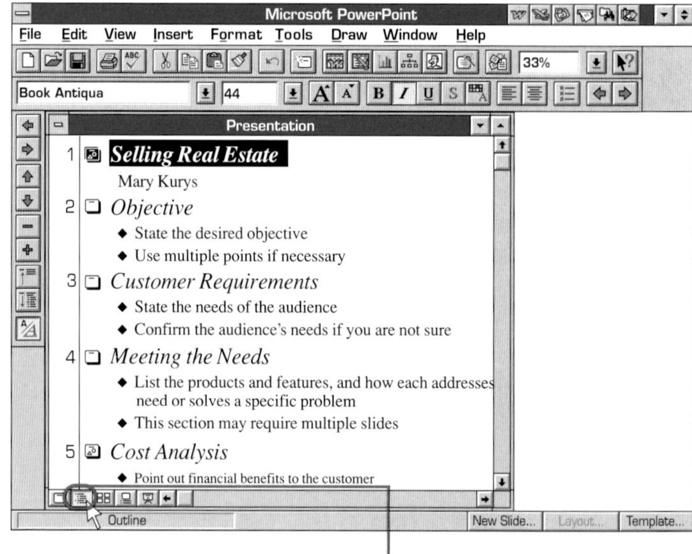

The Outline view displays the text for each slide. You can use this view to see the content of your entire presentation.

1 To change to the Outline view, move the mouse over and then press the left button.

IMPORTANT!

All views display the same slides. If you change a slide in one view, the other views will also display the change.

SLIDE SORTER VIEW

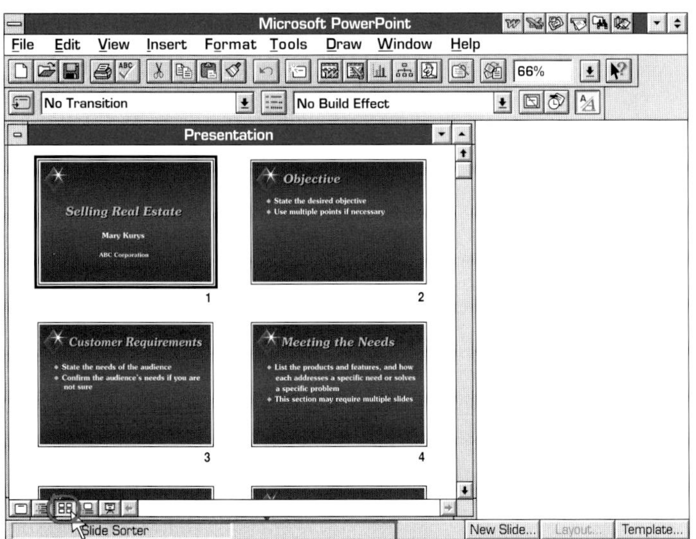

The Slide Sorter view displays a miniature version of each slide. You can use this view to see the order of your slides.

1 To change to the Slide Sorter view, move the mouse over ▦ and then press the left button.

NOTES PAGES VIEW

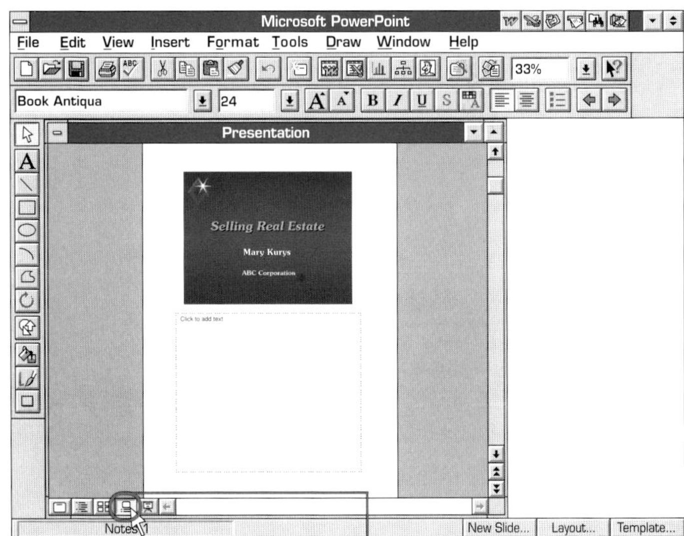

The Notes Pages view lets you add comments about each slide. You can use these comments as a guide when delivering your presentation.

1 To change to the Notes Pages view, move the mouse over ▭ and then press the left button.

MOVE BETWEEN SLIDES

The Slide view displays one slide at a time. You can easily move between the slides.

SLIDE VIEW

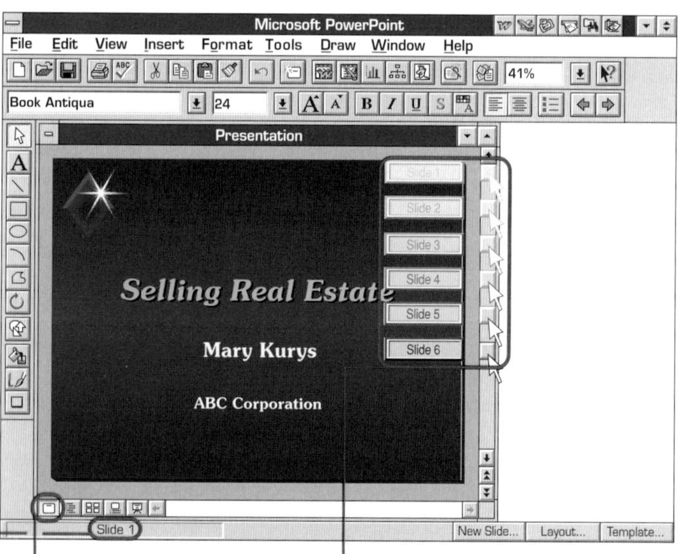

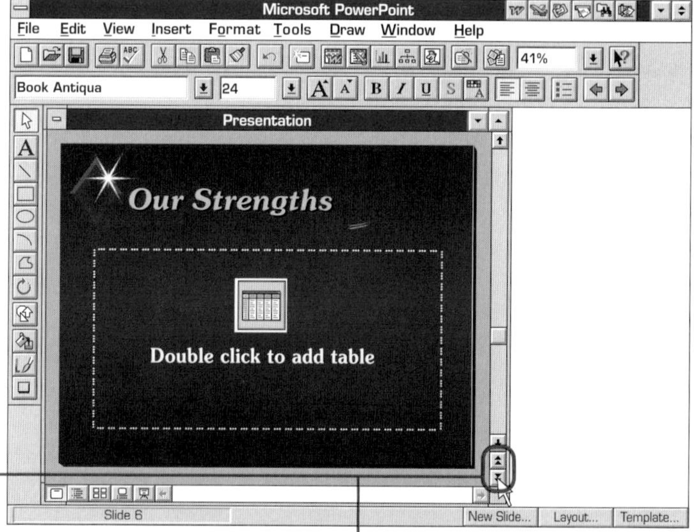

1 To change to the Slide view, move the mouse over ▭ and then press the left button.

◆ This area displays the number of the slide displayed on your screen.

QUICKLY SCROLL DOWN

1 Move the mouse over ▢ and then press and hold down the left button.

2 Still holding down the left button, drag the mouse down the scroll bar until the number of the slide you want to display appears. Then release the button.

MOVE TO PREVIOUS SLIDE

◆ Move the mouse over ⇞ and then press the left button.

MOVE TO NEXT SLIDE

◆ Move the mouse over ⇟ and then press the left button.

- Using the AutoContent Wizard
- Change Views
- **Move Between Slides**

The Outline view displays the text for all of your slides. If the text extends beyond one screen, you can scroll up or down to view the hidden text.

OUTLINE VIEW

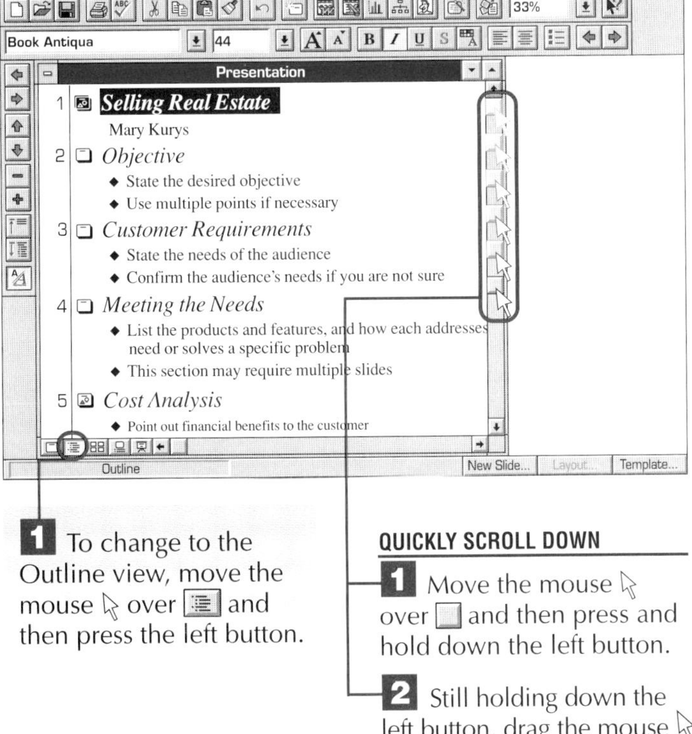

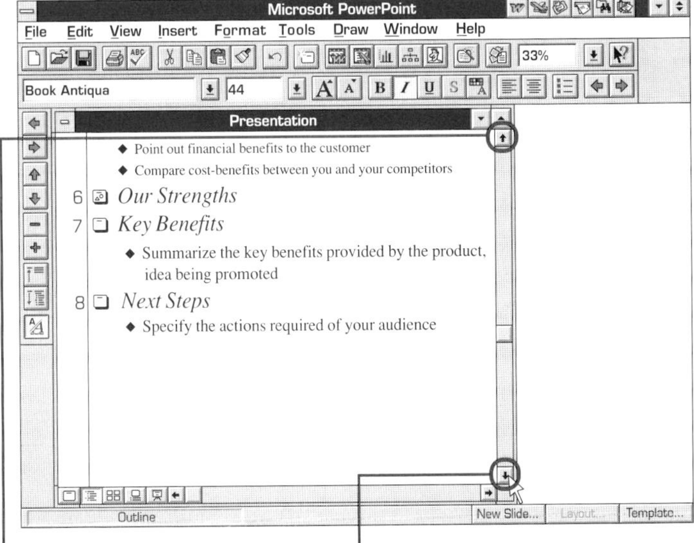

1 To change to the Outline view, move the mouse over and then press the left button.

QUICKLY SCROLL DOWN

1 Move the mouse over and then press and hold down the left button.

2 Still holding down the left button, drag the mouse down the scroll bar. Then release the button.

SCROLL UP ONE LINE

◆ Move the mouse over and then press the left button.

SCROLL DOWN ONE LINE

◆ Move the mouse over and then press the left button.

MOVE BETWEEN SLIDES

Presentation
Cost Analysis
Our Strengths
Key Benefits
Next Steps
The Slide Sorter view displays many slides on your screen. If all the slides do not fit on your screen, you can scroll up or down to view the hidden slides.

SLIDE SORTER VIEW

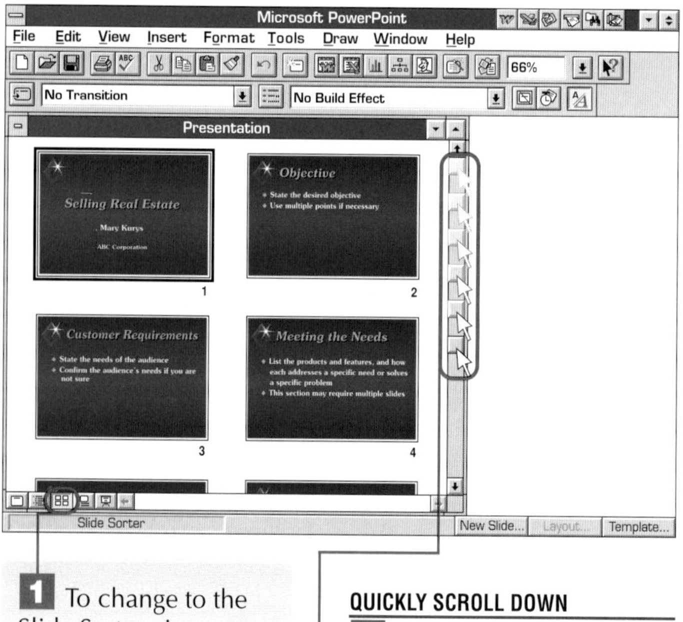

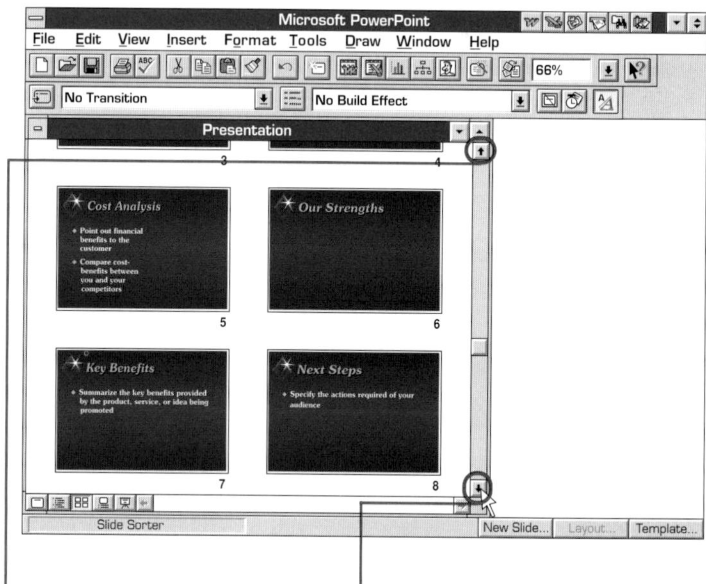

1 To change to the Slide Sorter view, move the mouse ⇖ over ⊞ and then press the left button.

QUICKLY SCROLL DOWN

1 Move the mouse ⇖ over ▭ and then press and hold down the left button.

2 Still holding down the left button, drag the mouse ⇖ down the scroll bar. Then release the button.

SCROLL UP ONE LINE

◆ Move the mouse ⇖ over ⬆ and then press the left button.

SCROLL DOWN ONE LINE

◆ Move the mouse ⇖ over ⬇ and then press the left button.

- Using the AutoContent Wizard
- Change Views
- **Move Between Slides**

The Notes Pages view displays one slide at a time. You can easily move between the slides.

NOTES PAGES VIEW

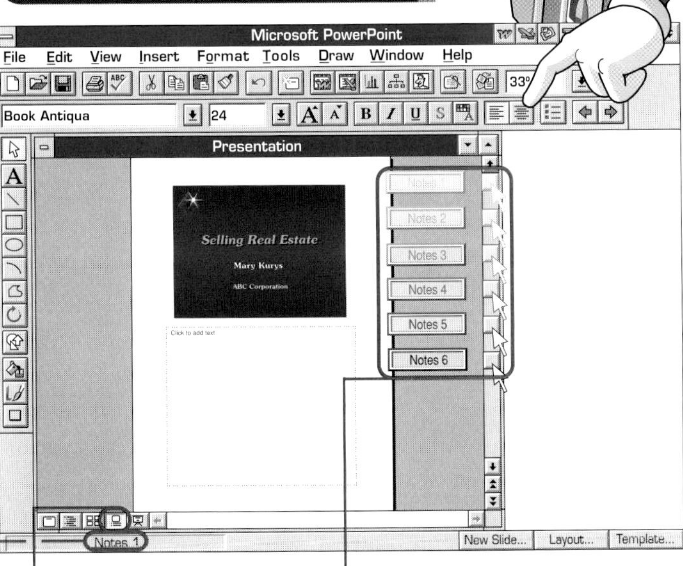

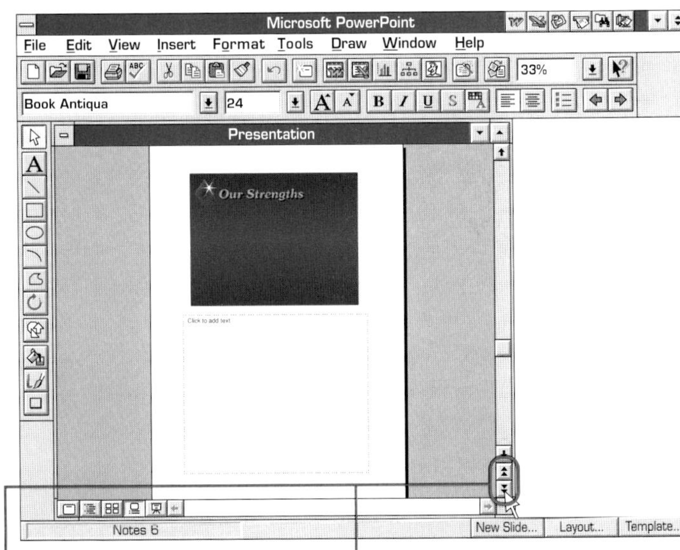

1 To change to the Notes Pages view, move the mouse over ▭ and then press the left button.

◆ This area displays the number of the slide displayed on your screen.

QUICKLY SCROLL DOWN

1 Move the mouse over ▭ and then press and hold down the left button.

2 Still holding down the left button, drag the mouse down the scroll bar until the number of the slide you want to display appears. Then release the button.

MOVE TO PREVIOUS SLIDE

◆ Move the mouse over ▭ and then press the left button.

MOVE TO NEXT SLIDE

◆ Move the mouse over ▭ and then press the left button.

SAVE A PRESENTATION

SAVE A PRESENTATION

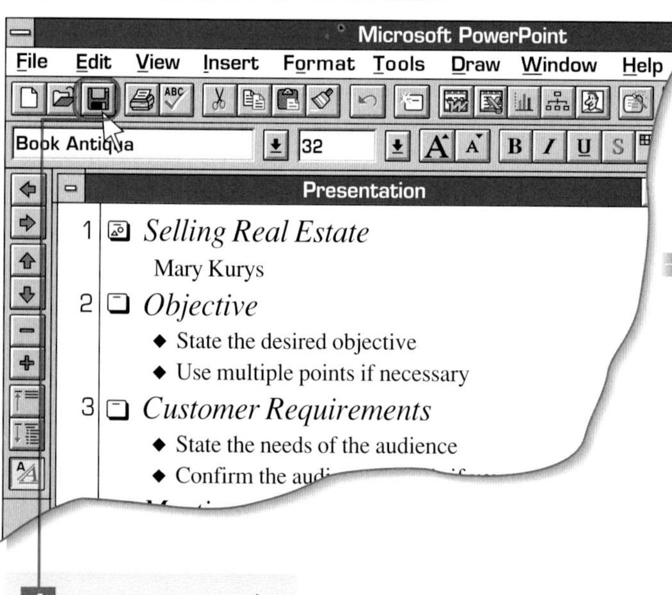

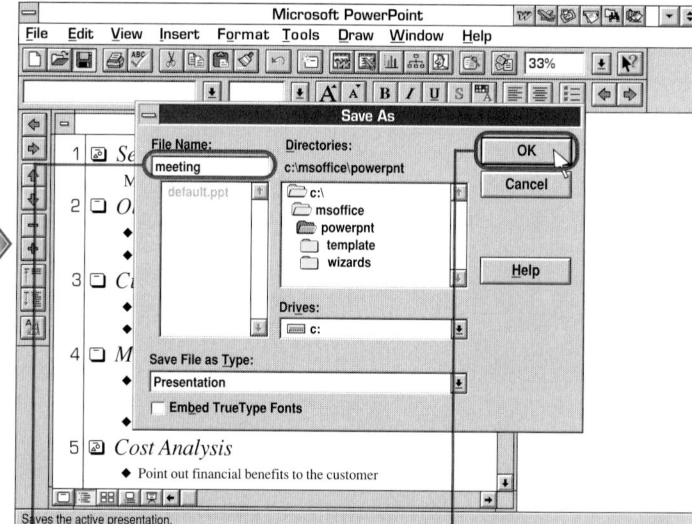

1 Move the mouse over 💾 and then press the left button.

◆ The **Save As** dialog box appears.

*Note: If you previously saved your presentation, the **Save As** dialog box will not appear since you have already named the presentation.*

2 Type a name for the presentation (example: **meeting**). The name can have up to eight characters.

*Note: To make it easier to find your presentation later on, do not type an extension. PowerPoint will automatically add the **ppt** extension to the name (example: **meeting.ppt**).*

3 Move the mouse over **OK** and then press the left button.

◆ The **Summary Info** dialog box appears.

IMPORTANT!
You should save your presentation every 5 to 10 minutes to store any changes made since the last time you saved the presentation.
File Edit View Ins
Book Antiqua
To save changes, move the mouse over and then press the left button.

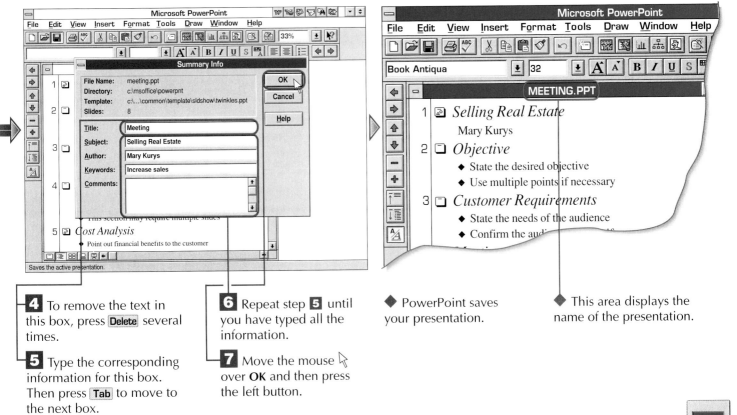

4 To remove the text in this box, press **Delete** several times.

5 Type the corresponding information for this box. Then press **Tab** to move to the next box.

6 Repeat step **5** until you have typed all the information.

7 Move the mouse over **OK** and then press the left button.

◆ PowerPoint saves your presentation.

◆ This area displays the name of the presentation.

CLOSE A PRESENTATION

EXIT POWERPOINT

When you finish working with a presentation, you can close the presentation to remove it from your screen.

CLOSE A PRESENTATION

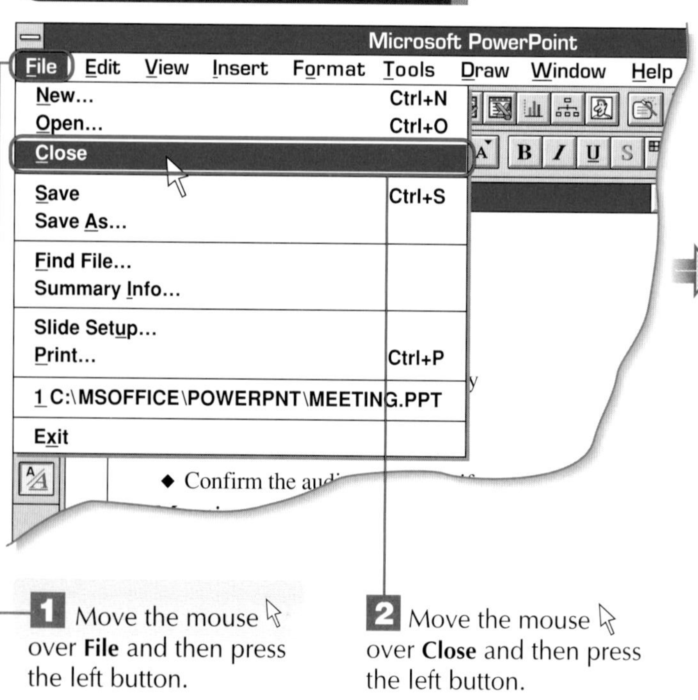

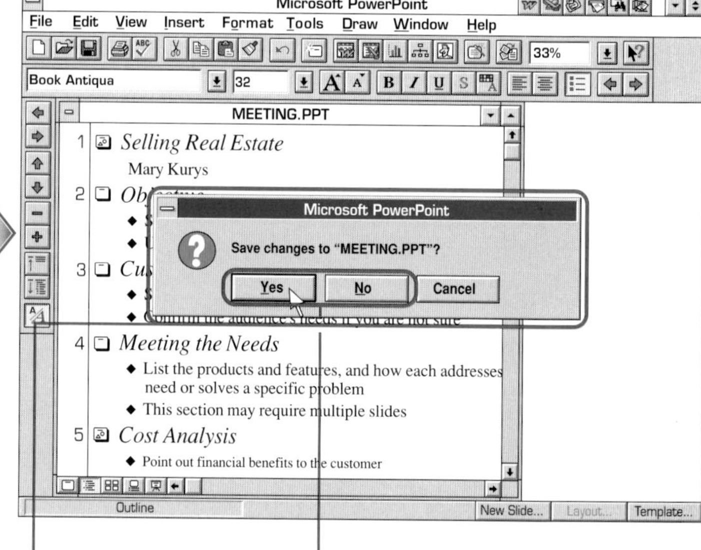

1 Move the mouse over **File** and then press the left button.

2 Move the mouse over **Close** and then press the left button.

◆ This dialog box appears if you have not saved changes made to your presentation.

3 To save the changes, move the mouse over **Yes** and then press the left button.

◆ To close the presentation without saving the changes, move the mouse over **No** and then press the left button.

When you finish using PowerPoint, you can easily exit the program.

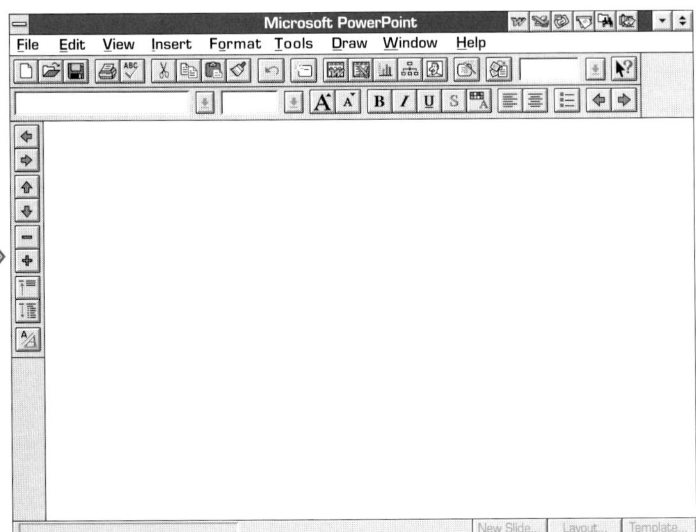

◆ The presentation disappears from your screen.

EXIT POWERPOINT

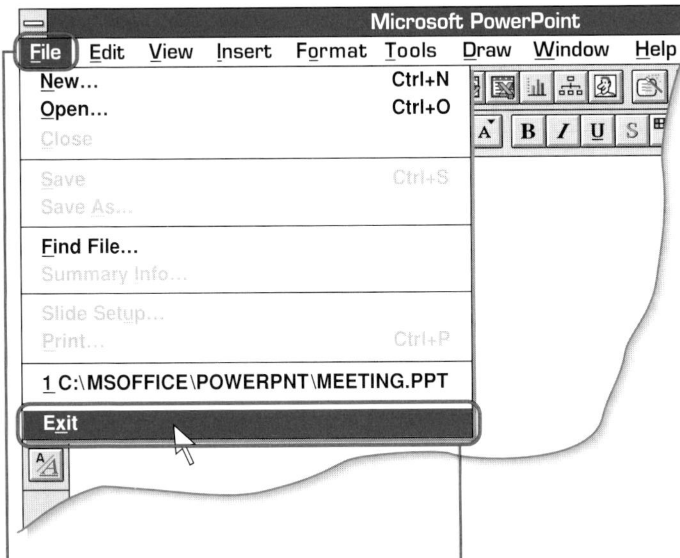

1 To save your presentation before exiting, refer to page 254.

2 Move the mouse over **File** and then press the left button.

3 Move the mouse over **Exit** and then press the left button.

Note: To restart PowerPoint, refer to page 240.

OPEN A PRESENTATION

You can open a saved presentation and display it on your screen. This lets you review and edit the presentation.

OPEN A PRESENTATION

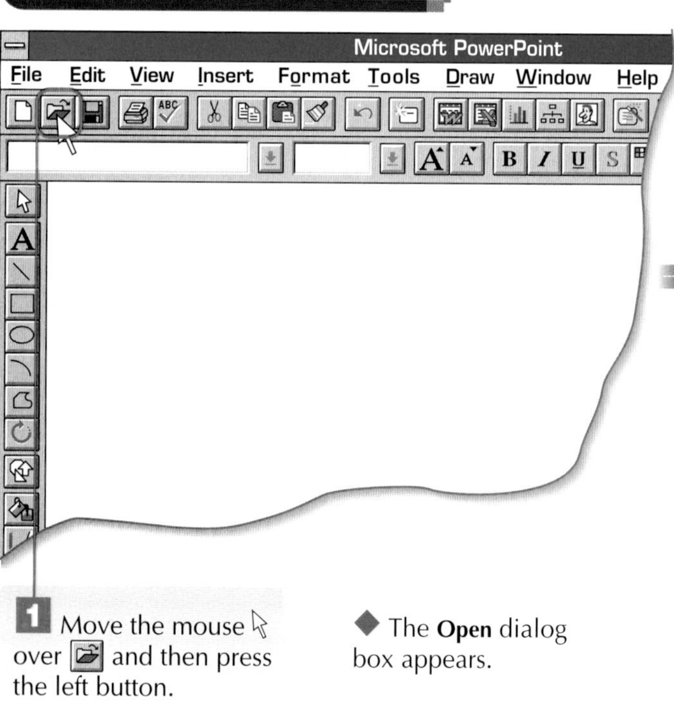

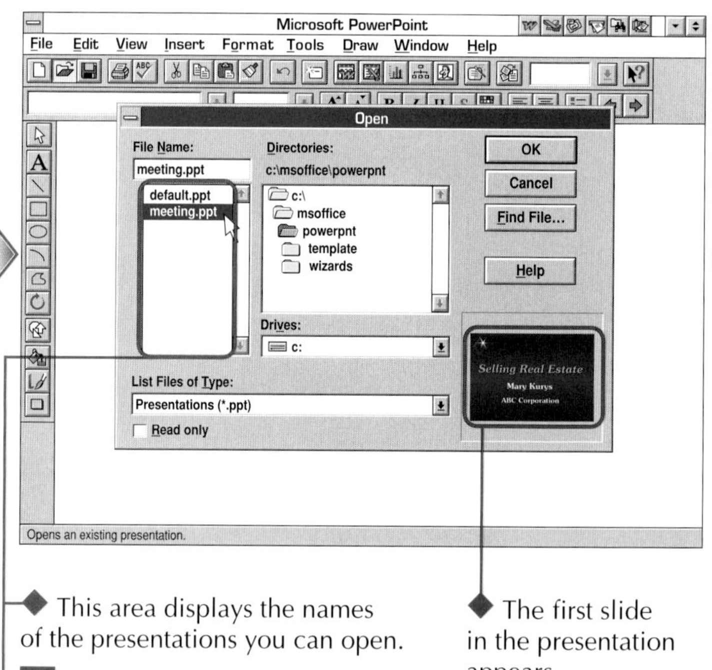

1 Move the mouse over the open button and then press the left button.

◆ The **Open** dialog box appears.

◆ This area displays the names of the presentations you can open.

2 To view the first slide of a presentation in this list, move the mouse over the name (example: **meeting.ppt**) and then press the left button.

◆ The first slide in the presentation appears.

SHORTCUT

The File menu displays the names of the last four presentations you opened.

Note: In this example, only one presentation has been opened.

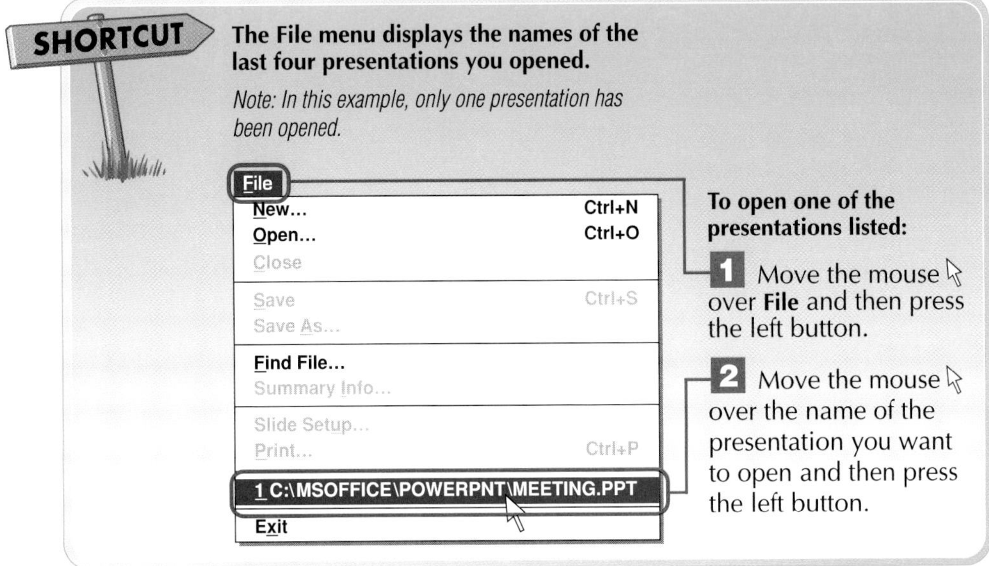

To open one of the presentations listed:

1 Move the mouse over **File** and then press the left button.

2 Move the mouse over the name of the presentation you want to open and then press the left button.

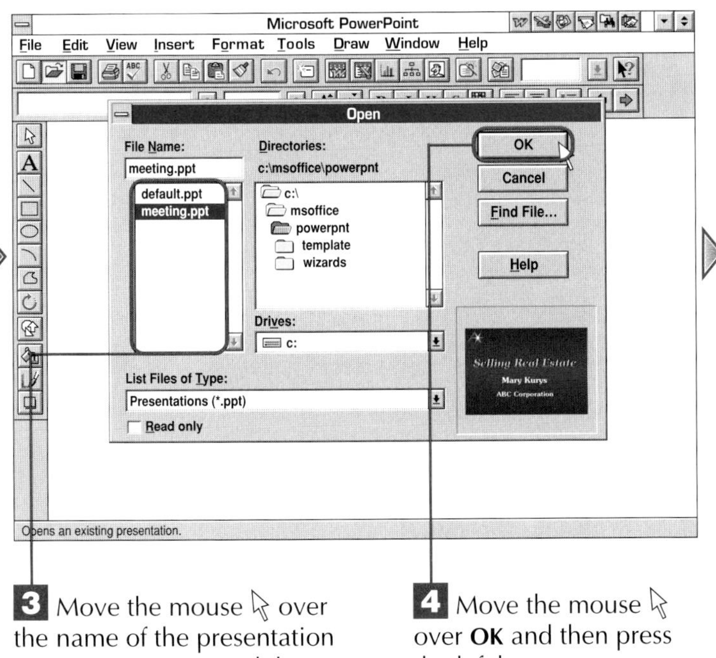

3 Move the mouse over the name of the presentation you want to open and then press the left button.

4 Move the mouse over **OK** and then press the left button.

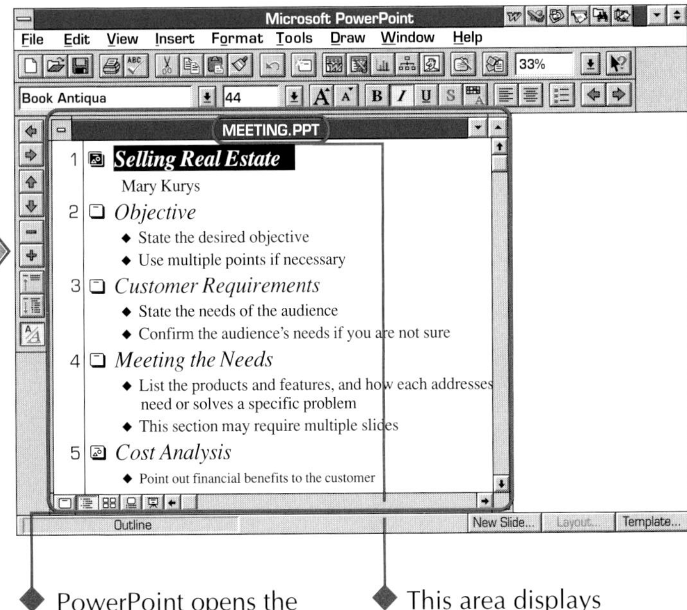

◆ PowerPoint opens the presentation and displays it on your screen. You can now make changes to the presentation.

◆ This area displays the name of the presentation.

You can enlarge the presentation window to fill your screen. This lets you view more of your presentation.

MAXIMIZE A WINDOW

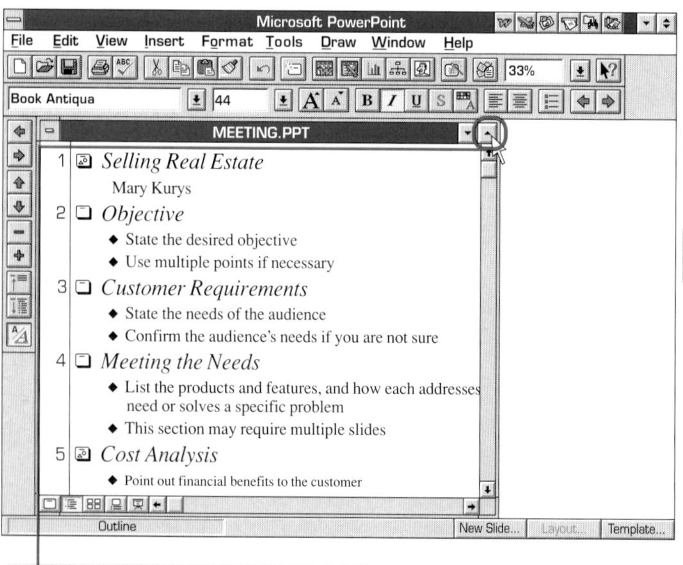

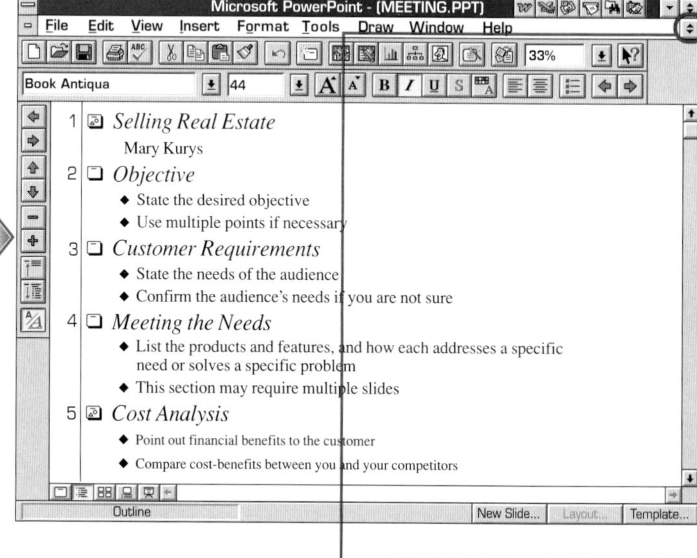

1 To enlarge the presentation window, move the mouse over ▲ and then press the left button.

◆ The window enlarges to fill your screen.

RESTORE A WINDOW

1 To restore the window to its original size, move the mouse over ⬍ and then press the left button.

- **Maximize a Window**
- **Show Titles**
- Select Text
- Delete Text
- Replace Text
- Undo Last Change
- Insert Text
- Move Text
- Check Spelling

You can display just the titles for each slide and hide the remaining text. This lets you view the overall structure of your presentation.

SHOW TITLES

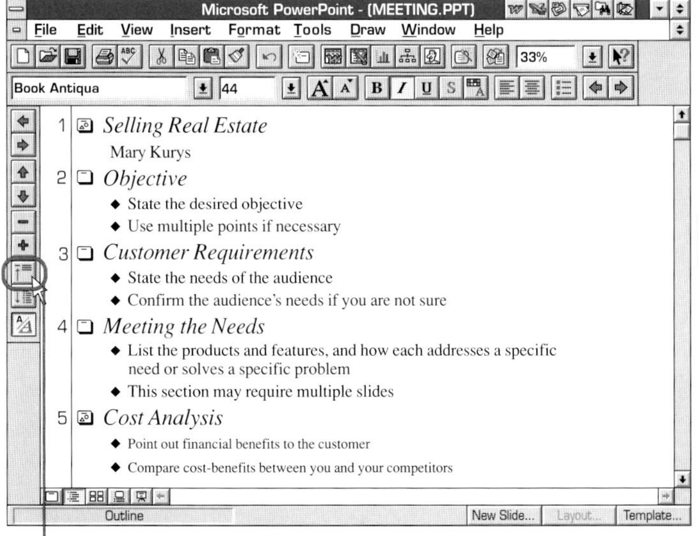

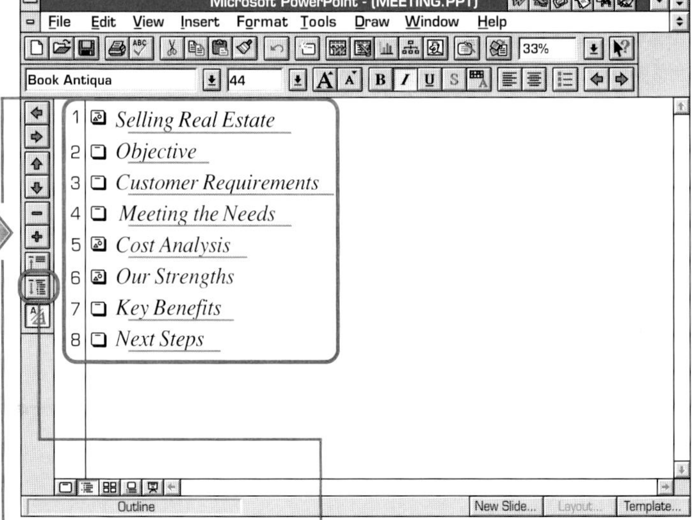

1 To show just the titles for the slides in your presentation, move the mouse over [icon] and then press the left button.

◆ PowerPoint shows only the titles for the slides.

◆ A gray line below a title indicates the text for the slide is hidden.

SHOW ALL

1 To again show the titles and the text for the slides, move the mouse over [icon] and then press the left button.

SELECT TEXT

Before editing or changing the look of text in your presentation, you must select the text you want to work with. Selected text appears highlighted on your screen.

SELECT A WORD

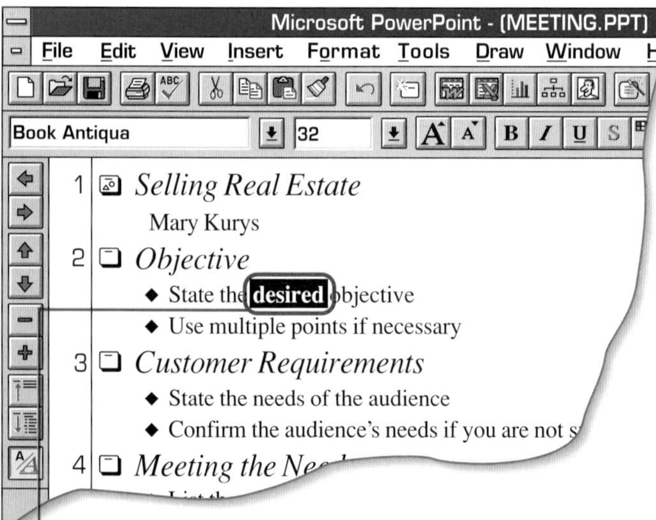

1 Move the mouse I over the word you want to select and then quickly press the left button twice.

Note: To cancel a text selection, move the mouse I outside the selected area and then press the left button.

SELECT ANY AMOUNT OF TEXT

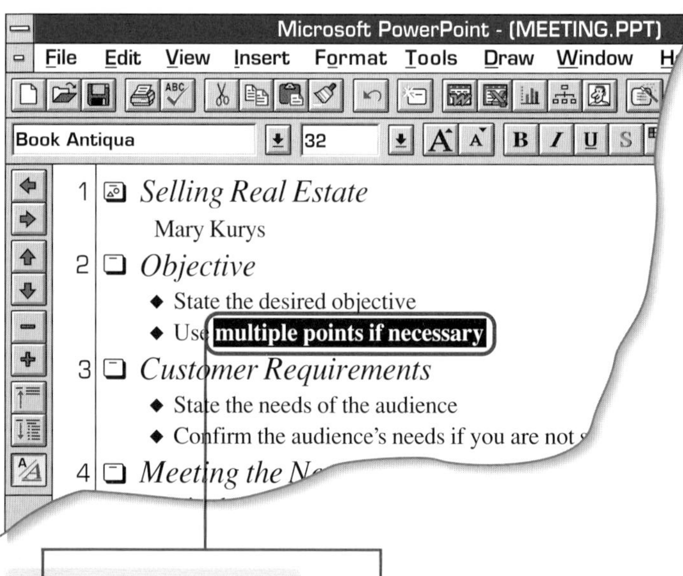

1 Move the mouse I over the first word you want to select.

2 Press and hold down the left button as you drag the mouse I over the text. Then release the button.

SELECT A POINT

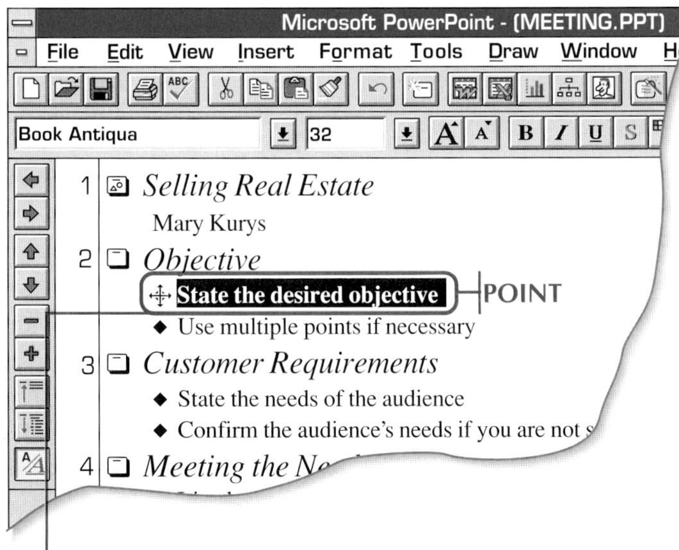

1 Move the mouse I over the symbol (◆) beside the point you want to select and I changes to ✥. Then press the left button.

SELECT AN ENTIRE SLIDE

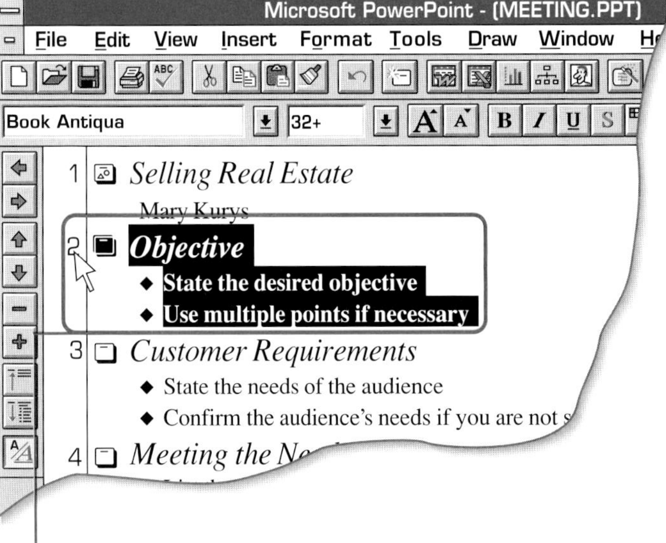

1 Move the mouse ↖ over the number of the slide you want to select (example: **2**) and then press the left button.

DELETE TEXT

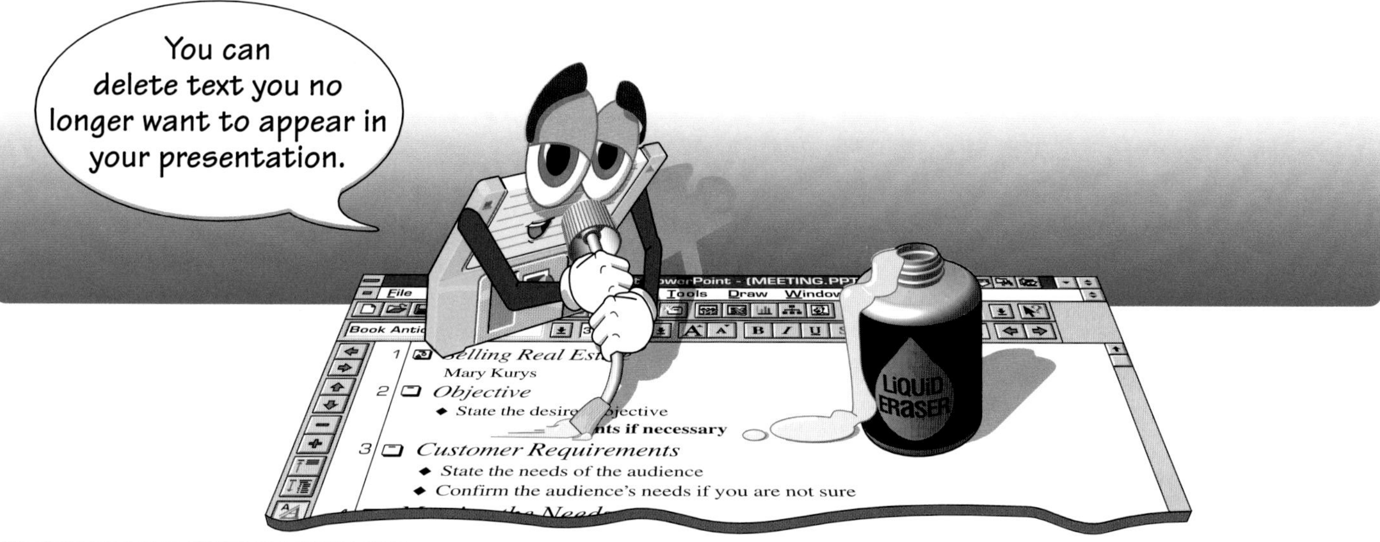

You can delete text you no longer want to appear in your presentation.
LIQUID ERASER

DELETE A CHARACTER

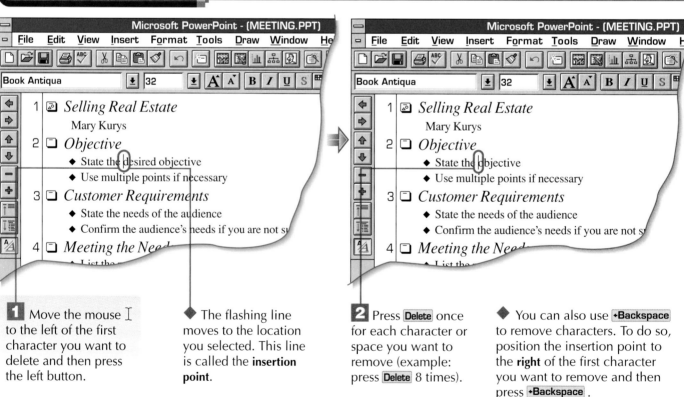

1 Move the mouse I to the left of the first character you want to delete and then press the left button.

◆ The flashing line moves to the location you selected. This line is called the **insertion point**.

2 Press Delete once for each character or space you want to remove (example: press Delete 8 times).

◆ You can also use ←Backspace to remove characters. To do so, position the insertion point to the **right** of the first character you want to remove and then press ←Backspace .

To immediately restore text you deleted:

Move the mouse over and then press the left button.

DELETE SELECTED TEXT

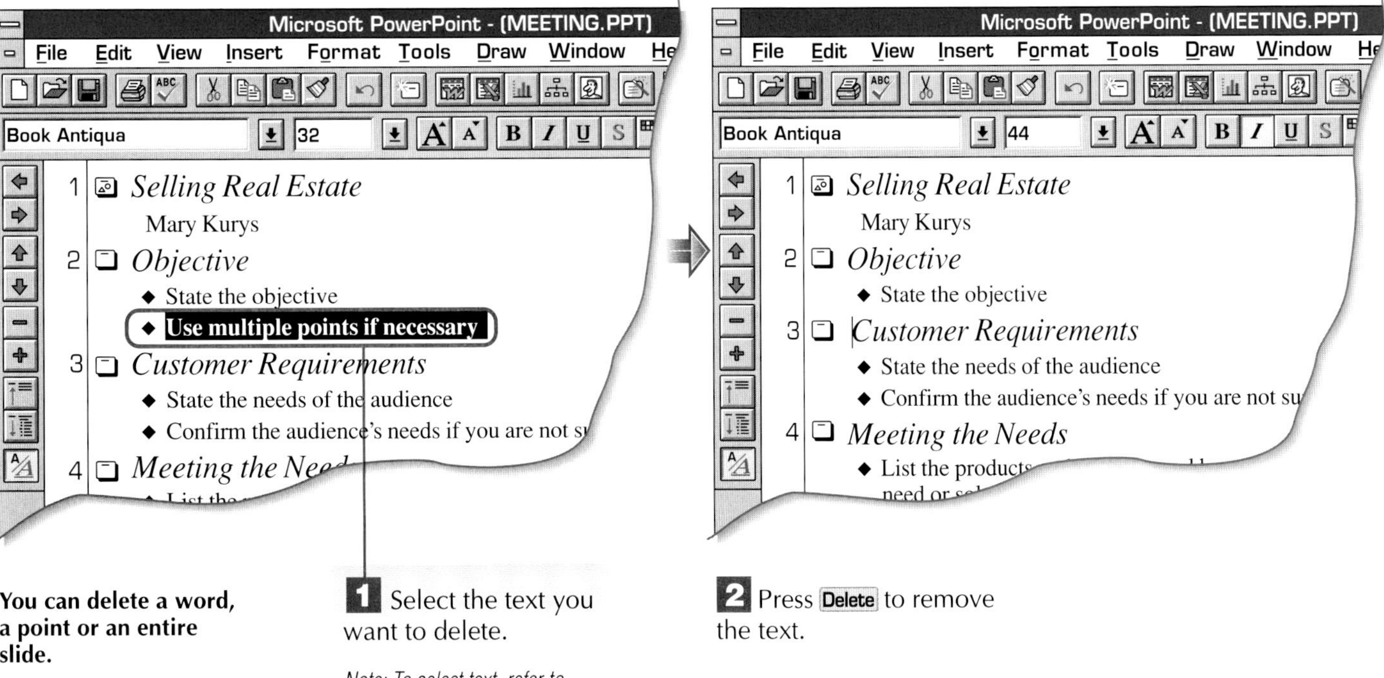

You can delete a word, a point or an entire slide.

1 Select the text you want to delete.

Note: To select text, refer to page 262.

2 Press Delete to remove the text.

REPLACE TEXT

UNDO LAST CHANGE

You can replace the text displayed on your screen with your own text.

REPLACE TEXT

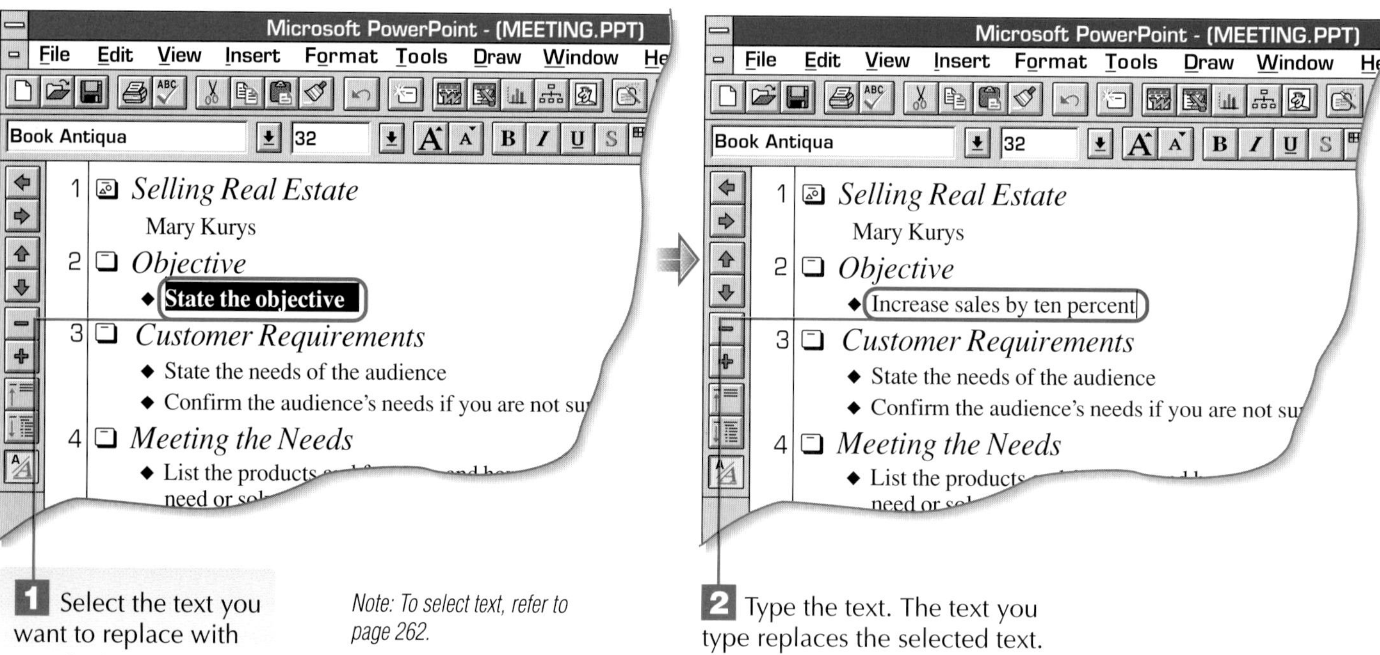

1 Select the text you want to replace with new text.

Note: To select text, refer to page 262.

2 Type the text. The text you type replaces the selected text.

- Maximize a Window
- Show Titles
- Select Text
- Delete Text
- **Replace Text**
- **Undo Last Change**
- Insert Text
- Move Text
- Check Spelling

PowerPoint remembers the last change you made to your presentation. If you regret this change, you can cancel it by using the Undo feature.

UNDO YOUR LAST CHANGE

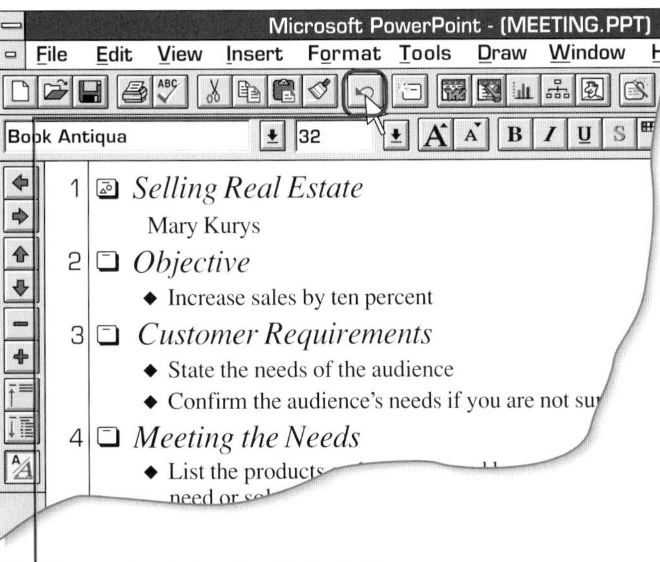

1 To cancel the last change you made to your presentation, move the mouse over and then press the left button.

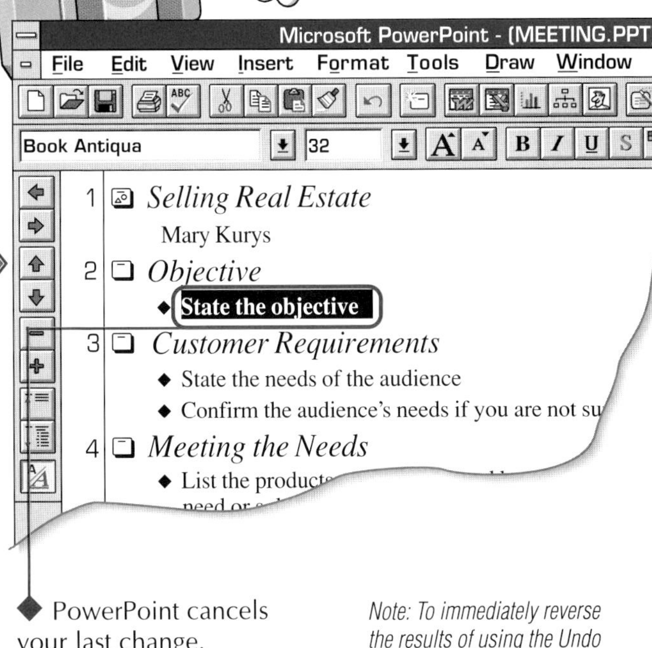

◆ PowerPoint cancels your last change.

Note: To immediately reverse the results of using the Undo feature, repeat step **1**.

INSERT TEXT

INSERT TEXT

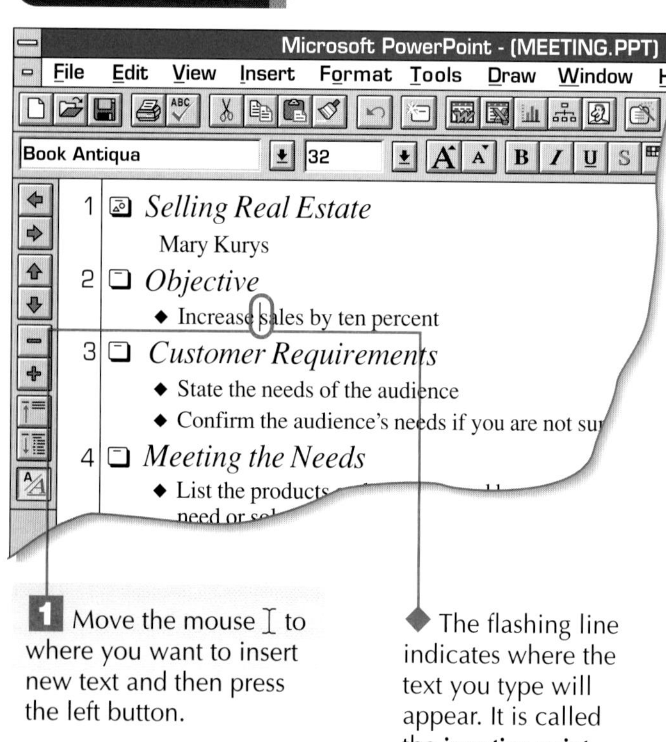

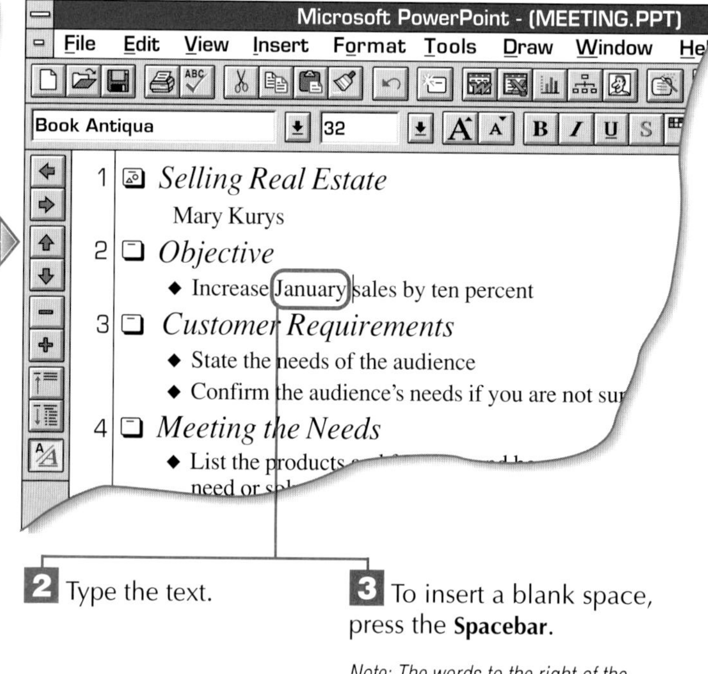

1 Move the mouse I to where you want to insert new text and then press the left button.

◆ The flashing line indicates where the text you type will appear. It is called the **insertion point**.

2 Type the text.

3 To insert a blank space, press the **Spacebar**.

Note: The words to the right of the new text are pushed forward.

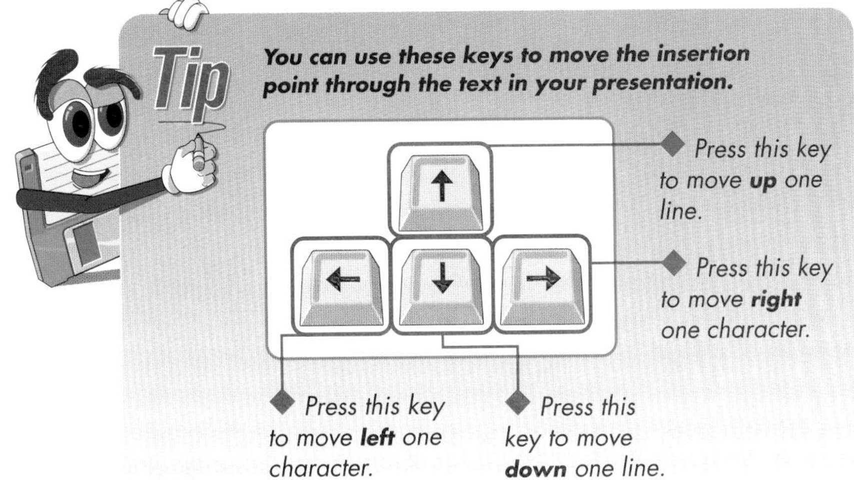

Tip
You can use these keys to move the insertion point through the text in your presentation.
Press this key to move **up** one line.
Press this key to move **right** one character.
Press this key to move **left** one character.
Press this key to move **down** one line.

INSERT A NEW POINT

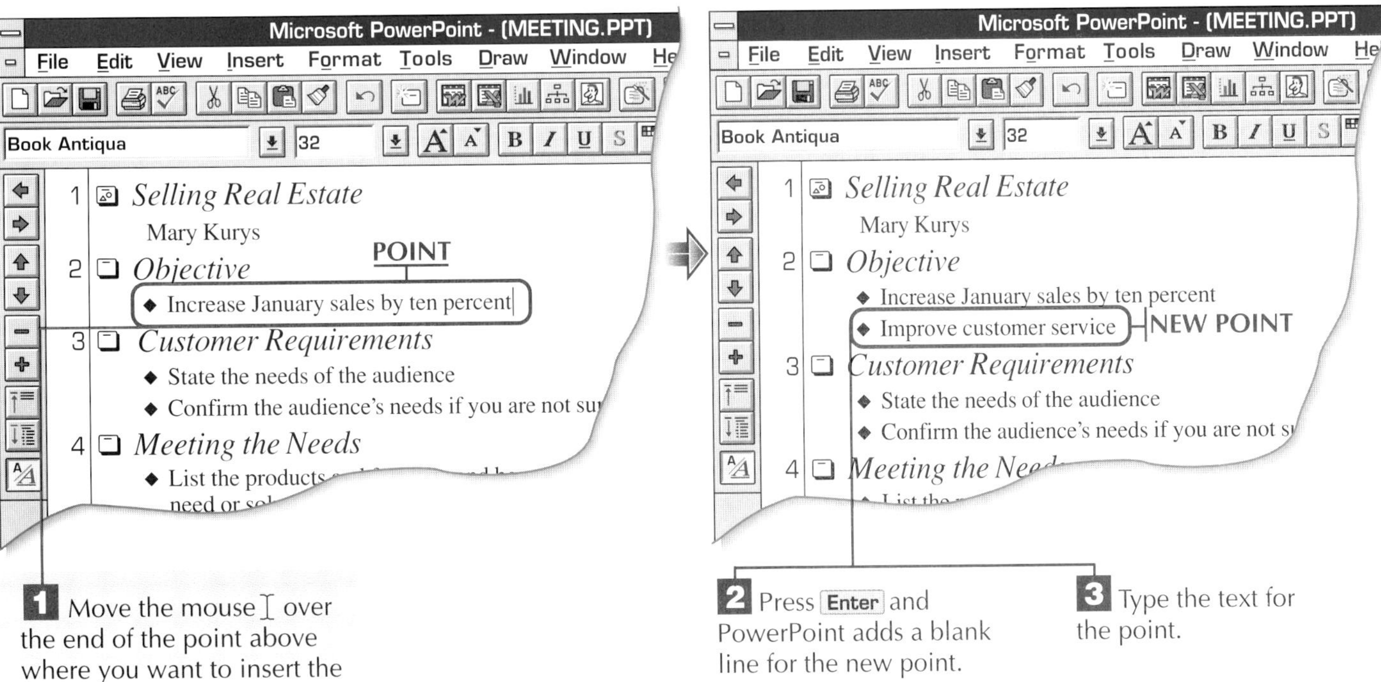

1 Move the mouse I over the end of the point above where you want to insert the new point and then press the left button.

2 Press Enter and PowerPoint adds a blank line for the new point.

3 Type the text for the point.

MOVE TEXT

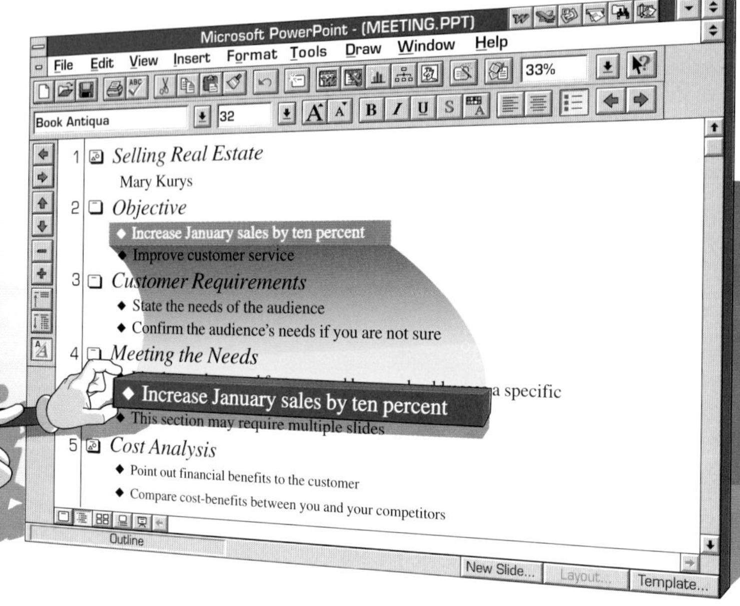

MOVE A POINT

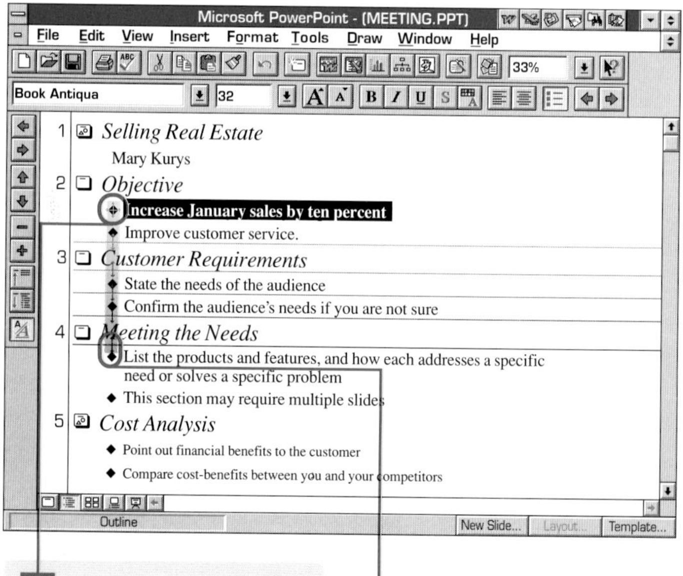

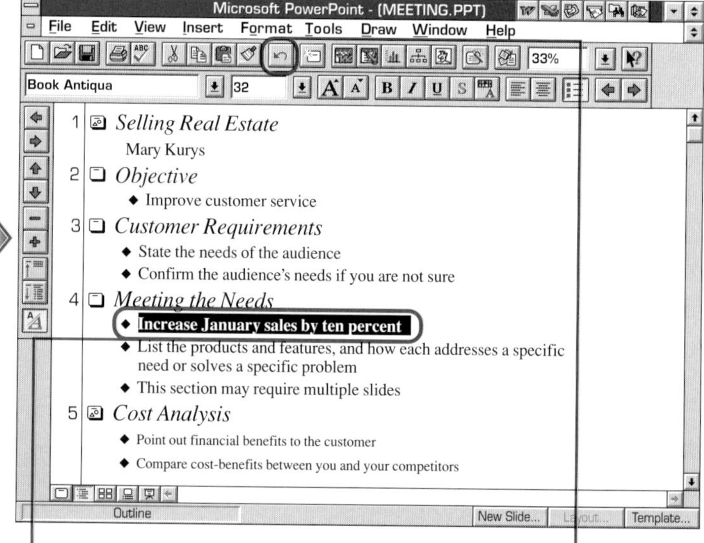

1 Move the mouse ✢ over the symbol (◆) beside the point you want to move.

2 Press and hold down the left button as you drag the mouse ↕ to where you want to place the point.

◆ A black line indicates where the point will appear.

3 Release the left button and the point appears in the new location.

◆ To immediately cancel the move, position the mouse ↖ over ↶ and then press the left button.

You can also use the Slide Sorter view to change the order of your slides.

For more information, refer to page 317.

MOVE A SLIDE

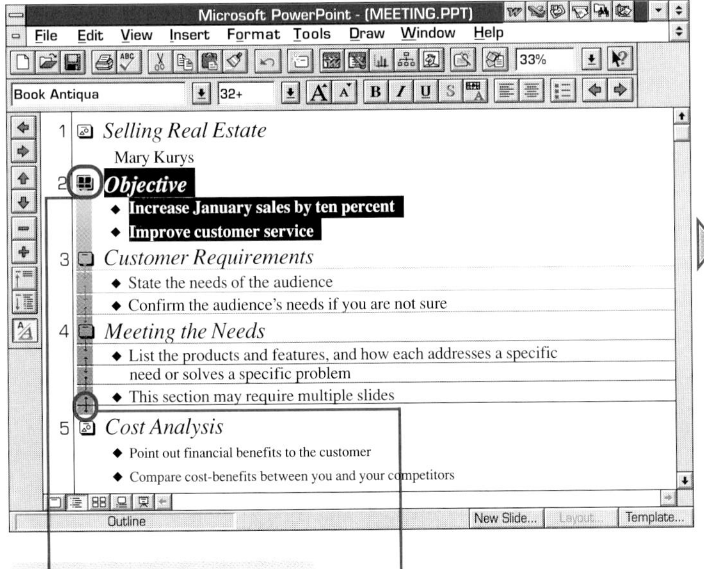

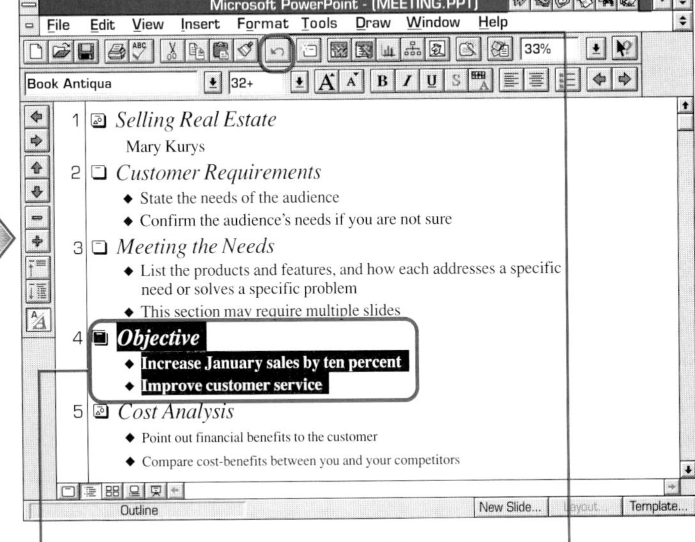

1 Move the mouse ✥ over the symbol (□) beside the number of the slide you want to move.

2 Press and hold down the left button as you drag the mouse ↕ to where you want to place the slide.

◆ A black line indicates where the slide will appear.

3 Release the left button and the slide appears in the new location.

◆ To immediately cancel the move, position the mouse ↖ over ↶ and then press the left button.

CHECK SPELLING

PowerPoint compares every word in your presentation to words in its own dictionary. If a word does not exist in the dictionary, PowerPoint considers it misspelled.

CHECK SPELLING

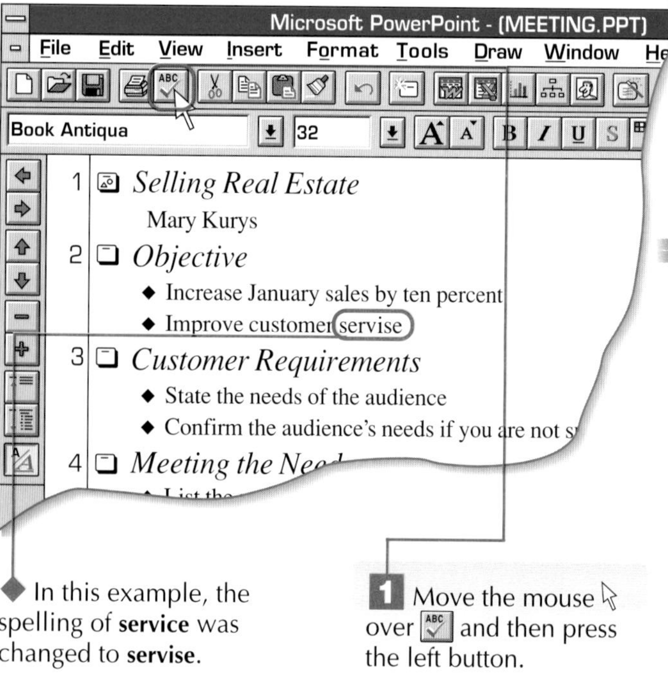

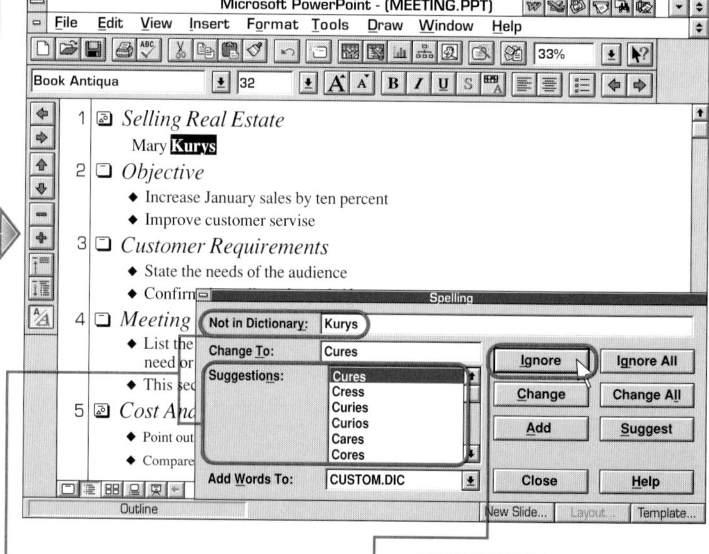

◆ In this example, the spelling of **service** was changed to **servise**.

1 Move the mouse over the spelling button and then press the left button.

◆ The **Spelling** dialog box appears if PowerPoint finds a spelling error.

◆ PowerPoint displays the first word it does not recognize and suggestions to correct the error.

IGNORE MISSPELLED WORD

2 If you do not want to change the spelling of the word, move the mouse over **Ignore** and then press the left button.

- Maximize a Window
- Show Titles
- Select Text
- Delete Text
- Replace Text
- Undo Last Change
- Insert Text
- Move Text
- **Check Spelling**

The spell check will not find a correctly spelled word used in the wrong context.

Example:

*The girl is **sit** years old.*

You must review your presentation carefully to find this type of error.

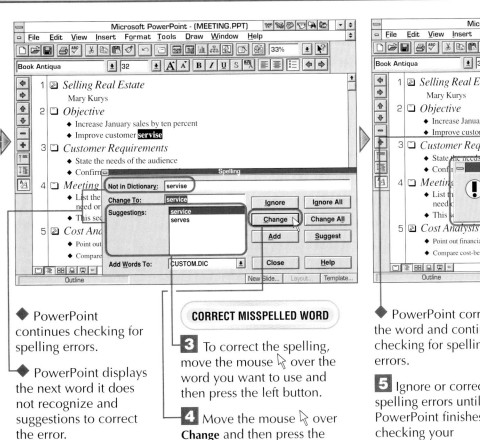

◆ PowerPoint continues checking for spelling errors.

◆ PowerPoint displays the next word it does not recognize and suggestions to correct the error.

CORRECT MISSPELLED WORD

3 To correct the spelling, move the mouse over the word you want to use and then press the left button.

4 Move the mouse over **Change** and then press the left button.

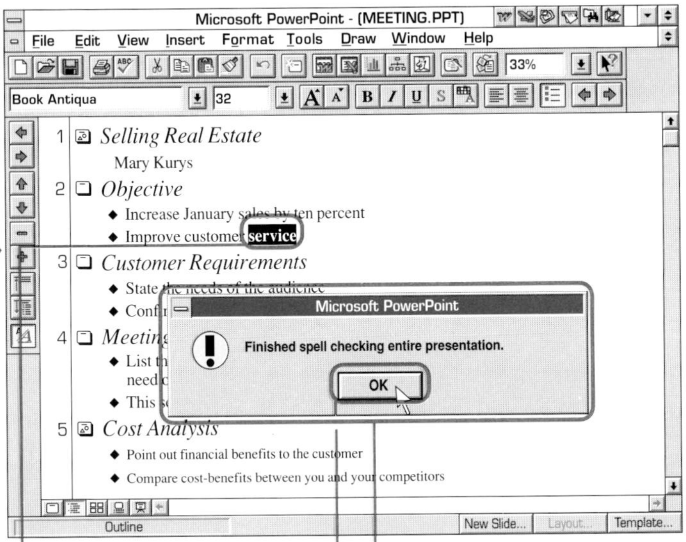

◆ PowerPoint corrects the word and continues checking for spelling errors.

5 Ignore or correct spelling errors until PowerPoint finishes checking your presentation.

◆ This dialog box appears when the spell check is complete.

6 To close the dialog box, move the mouse over **OK** and then press the left button.

CHANGE THE SLIDE LAYOUT

You can have PowerPoint arrange text and graphics on a slide for you.
Customer Requirements

CHANGE THE SLIDE LAYOUT

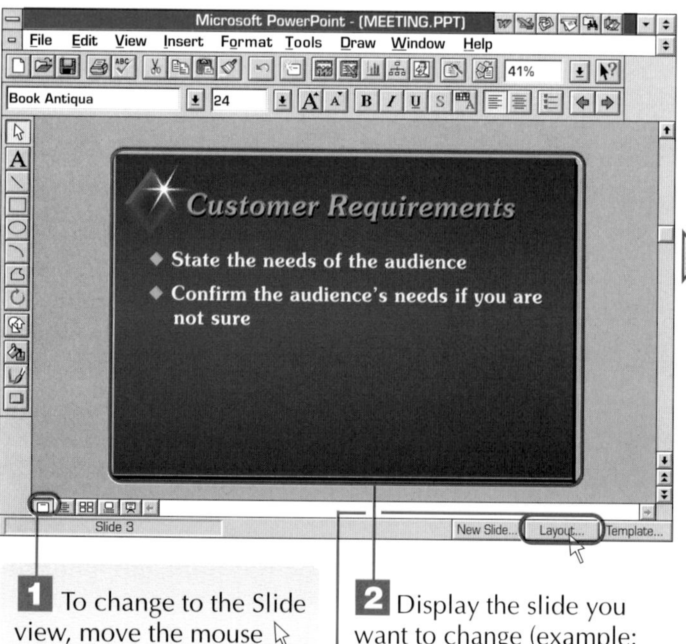

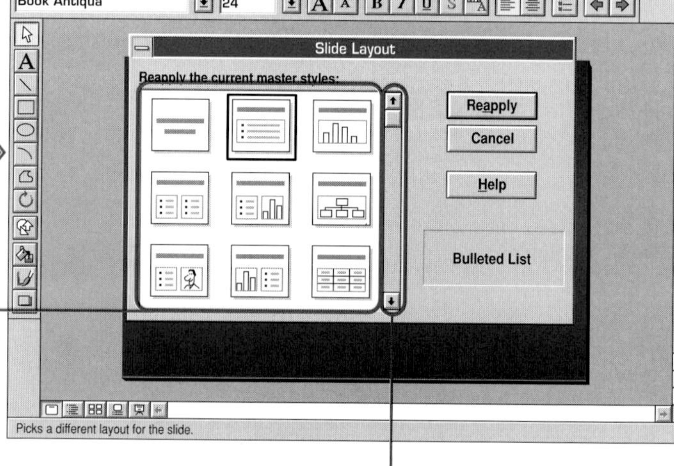

1 To change to the Slide view, move the mouse over ▭ and then press the left button.

2 Display the slide you want to change (example: slide 3).

Note: To move between slides, refer to page 250.

3 Move the mouse over **Layout** and then press the left button.

◆ The **Slide Layout** dialog box appears.

◆ This area displays the available layouts.

◆ To browse through the available layouts, move the mouse over ⬇ or ⬆ and then press the left button.

- **Change the Slide Layout**
- Add a New Slide
- Add Clip Art
- Add an Organization Chart
- Add a Graph
- Change Graph Type

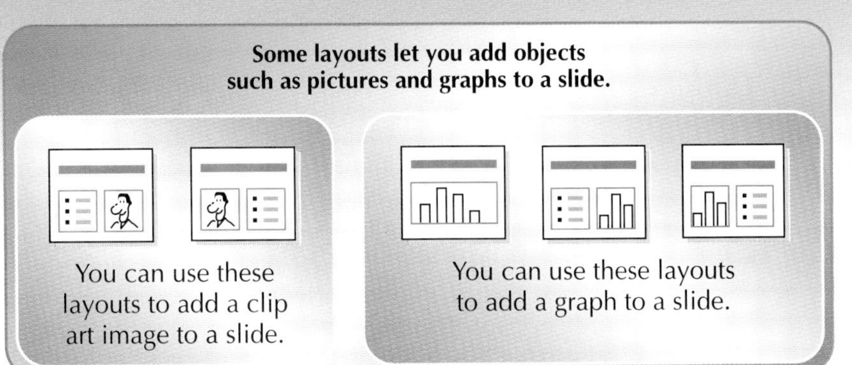

Some layouts let you add objects such as pictures and graphs to a slide.
You can use these layouts to add a clip art image to a slide.
You can use these layouts to add a graph to a slide.

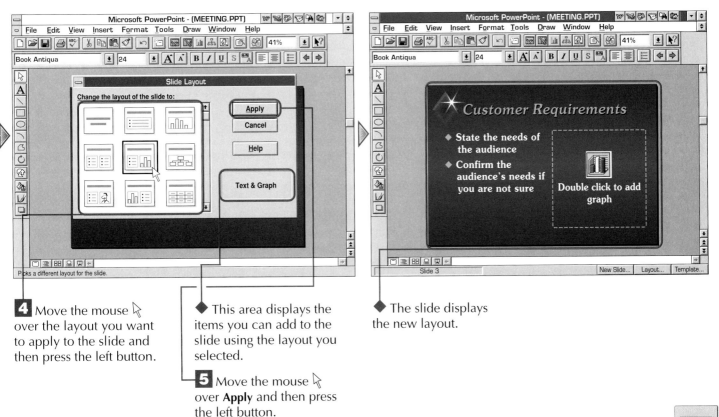

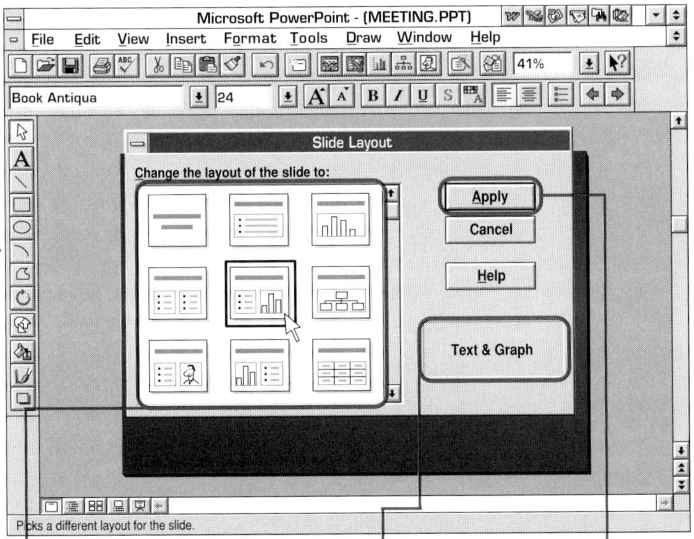

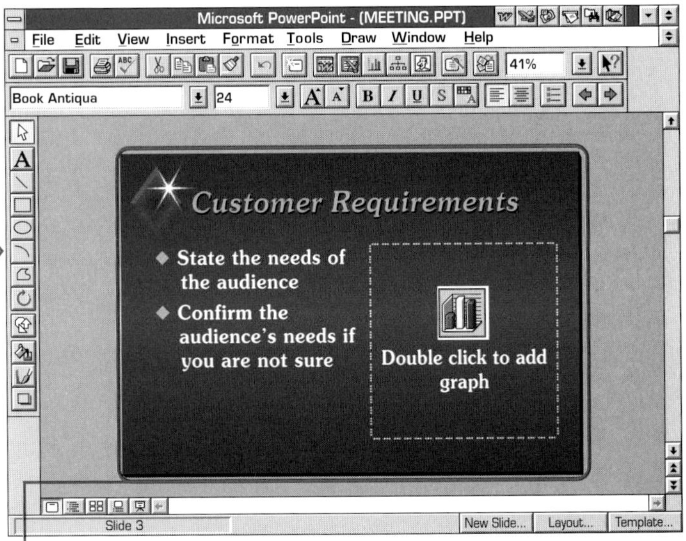

4 Move the mouse over the layout you want to apply to the slide and then press the left button.

◆ This area displays the items you can add to the slide using the layout you selected.

5 Move the mouse over **Apply** and then press the left button.

◆ The slide displays the new layout.

ADD A NEW SLIDE

You can add a new slide to your presentation at any time. This lets you add a new topic that you want to discuss.

ADD A NEW SLIDE

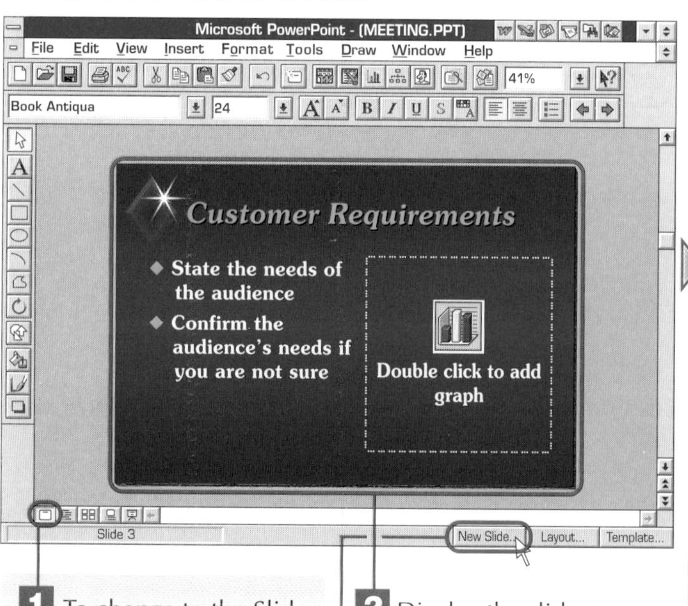

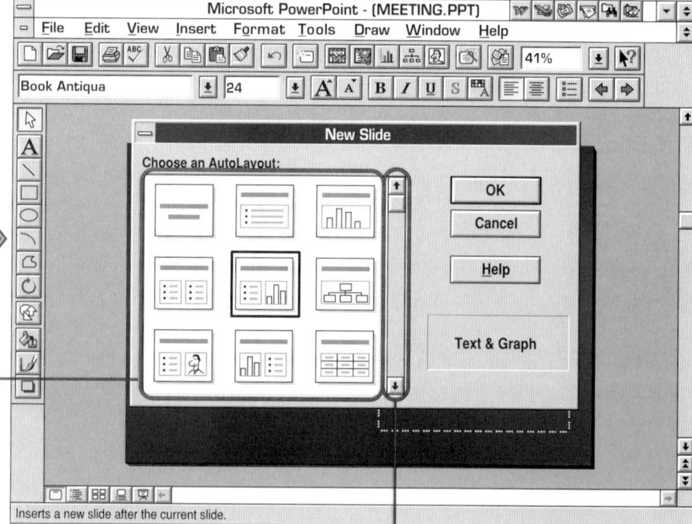

1 To change to the Slide view, move the mouse over and then press the left button.

2 Display the slide you want to appear before the new slide (example: slide 3).

Note: To move between slides, refer to page 250.

3 Move the mouse over **New Slide** and then press the left button.

◆ The **New Slide** dialog box appears.

◆ This area displays the available layouts for the new slide.

◆ To browse through the available layouts, move the mouse over or and then press the left button.

You can select a different layout for a slide at any time.

Note: For more information, refer to page 274.

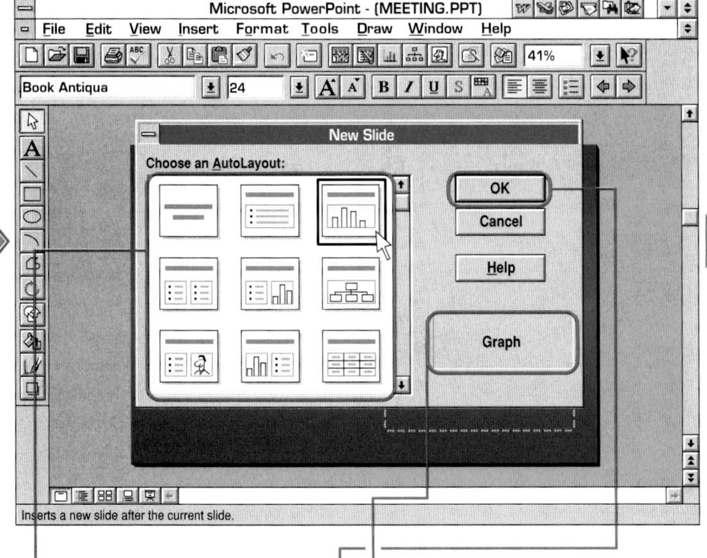

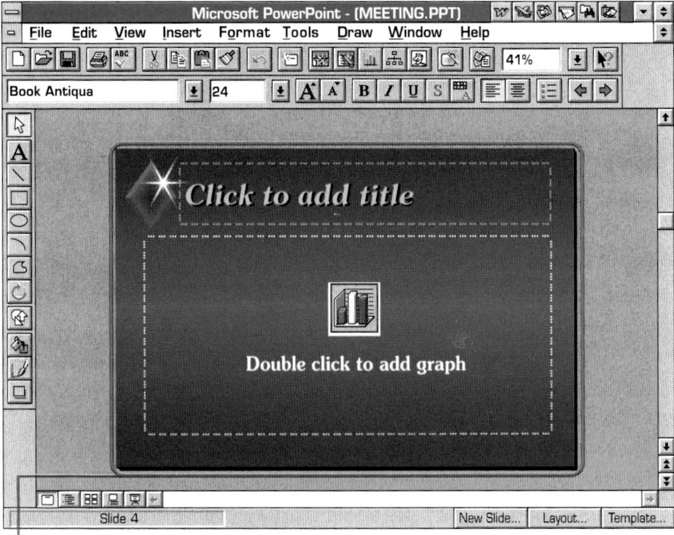

4 Move the mouse over the layout you want to apply to the new slide and then press the left button.

◆ This area displays the items you can add to the slide using the layout you selected.

5 Move the mouse over **OK** and then press the left button.

◆ The new slide appears, displaying the layout you selected.

ADD CLIP ART

PowerPoint provides hundreds of clip art images that you can add to your slides. These images will enhance your presentation.

ADD CLIP ART

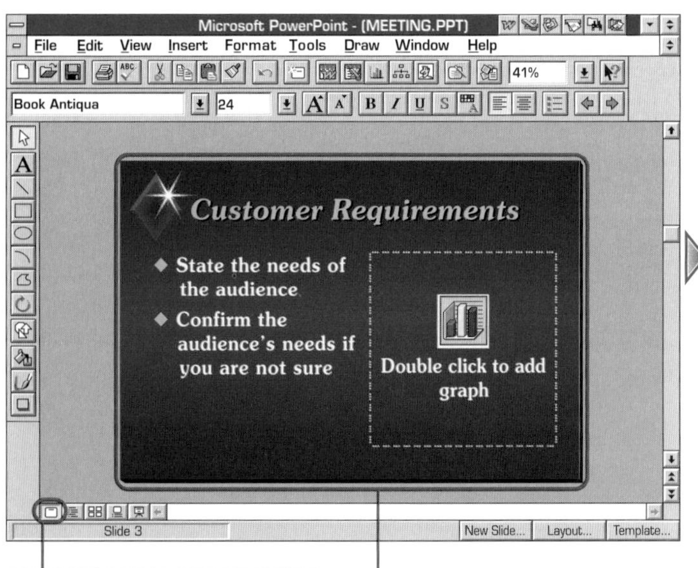

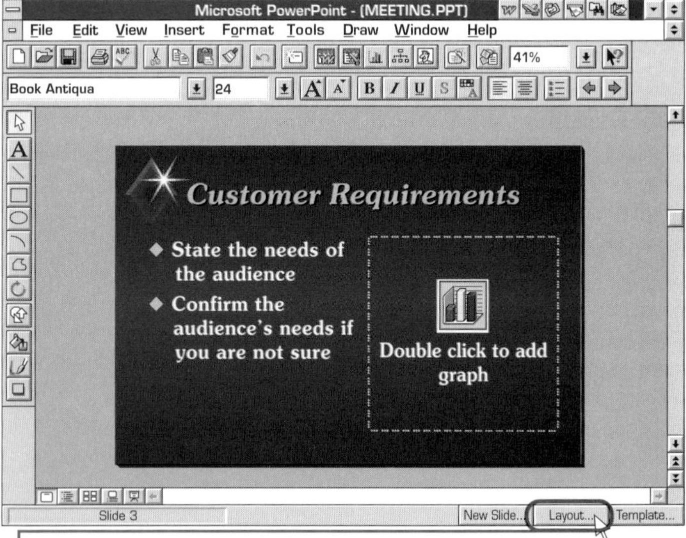

1 To change to the Slide view, move the mouse over ▭ and then press the left button.

2 Display the slide you want to add a clip art image to (example: slide 3).

Note: To move between slides, refer to page 250.

3 To change the layout of the slide, move the mouse over **Layout** and then press the left button.

- Change the Slide Layout
- Add a New Slide
- **Add Clip Art**
- Add an Organization Chart
- Add a Graph
- Change Graph Type

A clip art image is a professionally designed drawing that you can add to your slides. Clip art images can include such items as maps, cartoons or buildings.

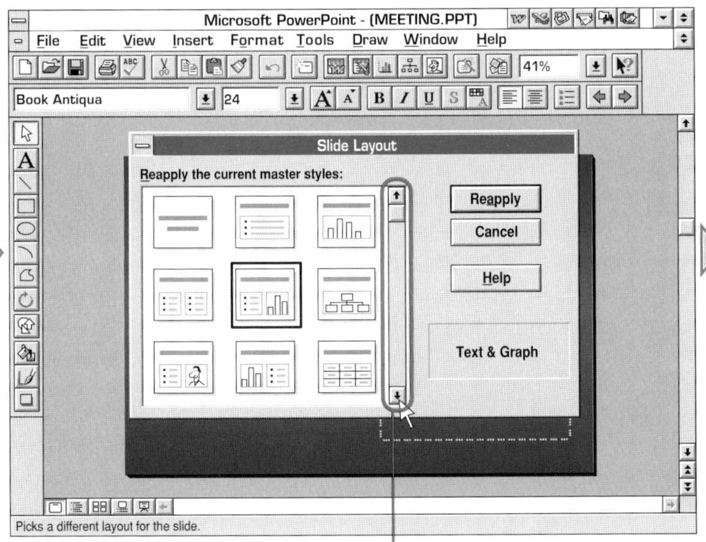

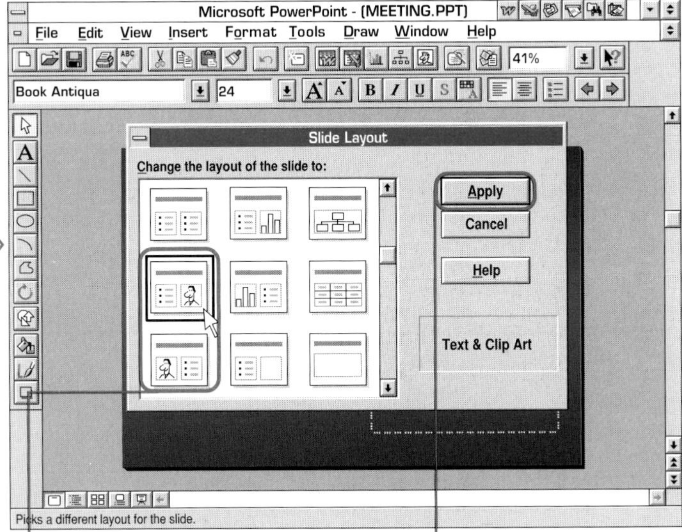

◆ The **Slide Layout** dialog box appears.

4 To browse through the available layouts, move the mouse over ⬇ or ⬆ and then press the left button.

5 To add a clip art image to the slide, move the mouse over one of these layouts and then press the left button.

6 Move the mouse over **Apply** and then press the left button.

ADD CLIP ART

ADD CLIP ART (CONTINUED)

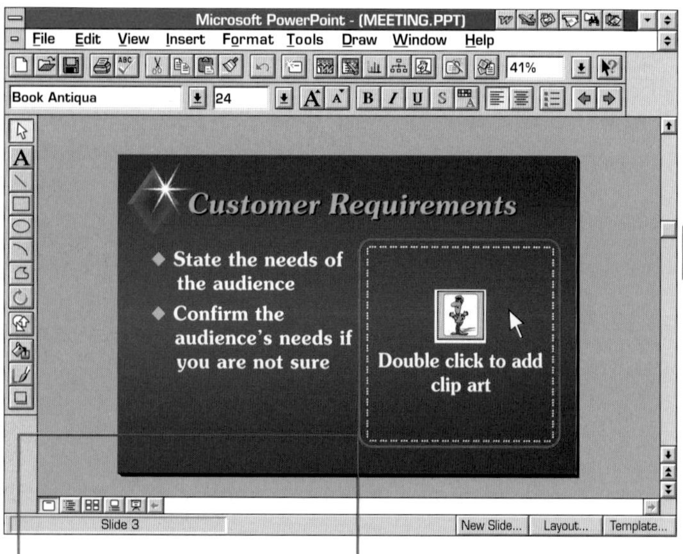

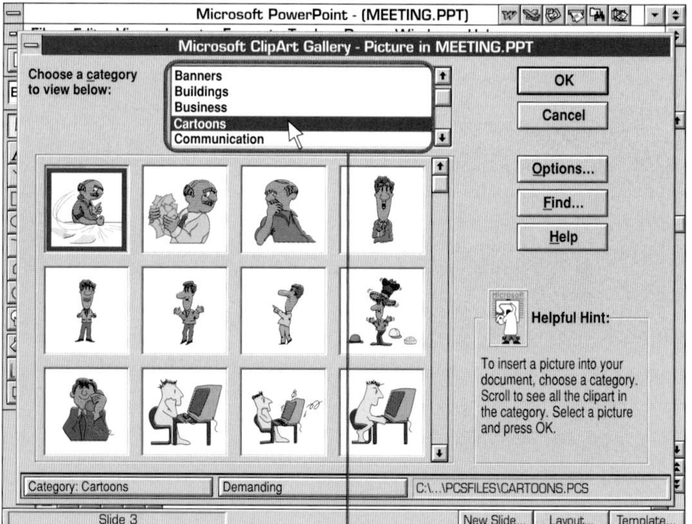

◆ The slide now displays an area for the clip art image.

7 To add a clip art image, move the mouse ↖ over this area and then quickly press the left button twice.

*Note: If this is the first time you are adding a clip art image to a presentation, refer to the **Tip** on page 281.*

◆ The **Microsoft ClipArt Gallery** dialog box appears.

8 Move the mouse ↖ over the clip art images you want to view and then press the left button.

*Note: To view all of the clip art images, select **All Categories**.*

***Tip* This dialog box appears the first time you add clip art to a presentation.**

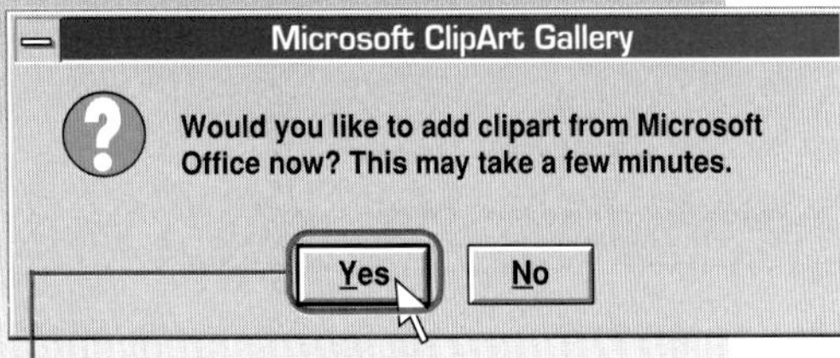

Microsoft ClipArt Gallery
Would you like to add clipart from Microsoft Office now? This may take a few minutes.
Yes
No

◆ *To add the clip art, move the mouse over **Yes** and then press the left button.*

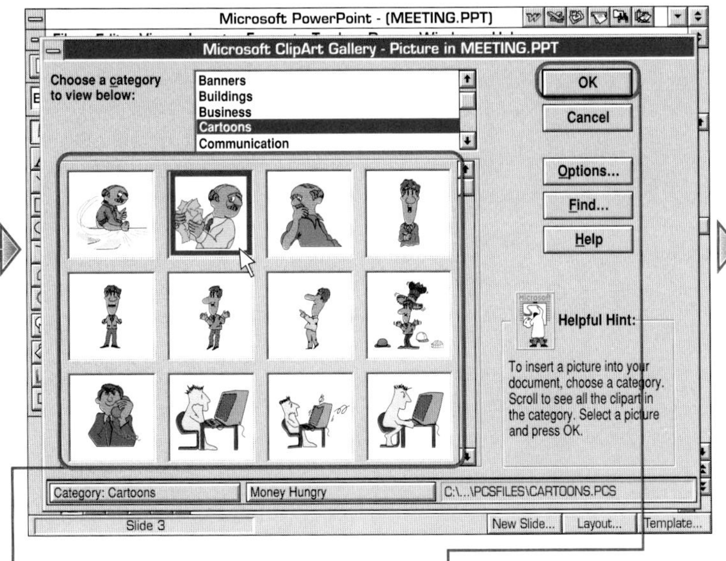

◆ The clip art images appear.

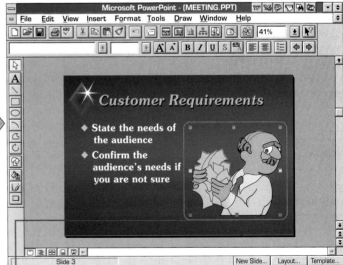

9 Move the mouse over the clip art image you want to use and then press the left button.

10 Move the mouse over **OK** and then press the left button.

◆ The clip art image you selected appears on the slide.

11 The squares around the image let you size the image. To remove these squares, move the mouse outside the image area and then press the left button.

Note: To move or size a clip art image, refer to page 306.

ADD AN ORGANIZATION CHART

You can add an organization chart to a slide. This is useful if you want to show the structure of a company.

ADD AN ORGANIZATION CHART

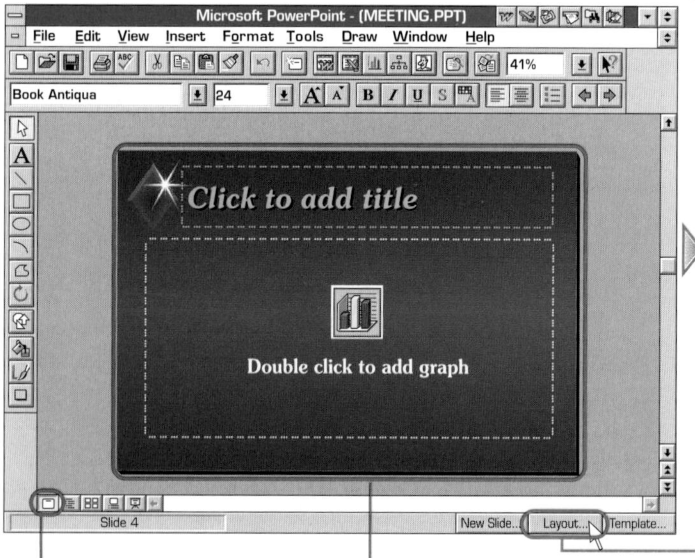

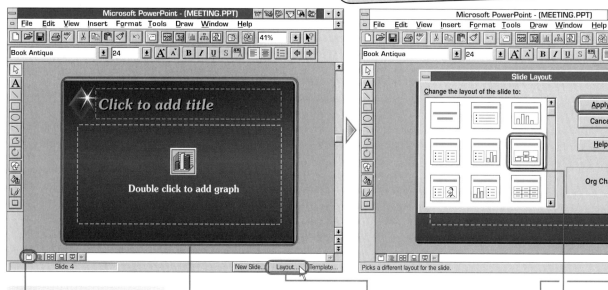

1 To change to the Slide view, move the mouse over ▢ and then press the left button.

2 Display the slide you want to add an organization chart to (example: slide 4).

Note: To move between slides, refer to page 250.

3 To change the layout of the slide, move the mouse over **Layout** and then press the left button.

◆ The **Slide Layout** dialog box appears.

4 Move the mouse over the layout displaying the organization chart and then press the left button.

5 Move the mouse over **Apply** and then press the left button.

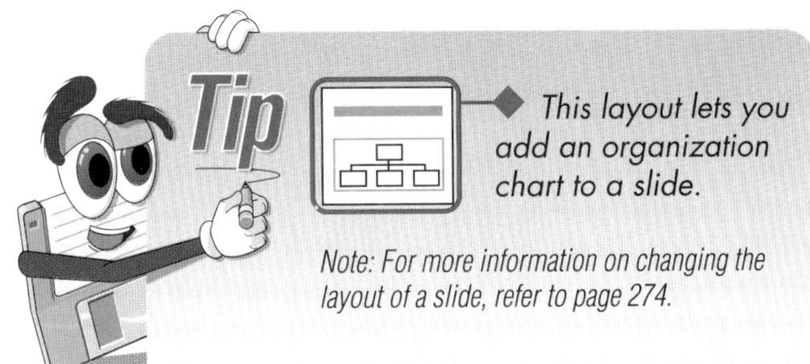

◆ *This layout lets you add an organization chart to a slide.*

Note: For more information on changing the layout of a slide, refer to page 274.

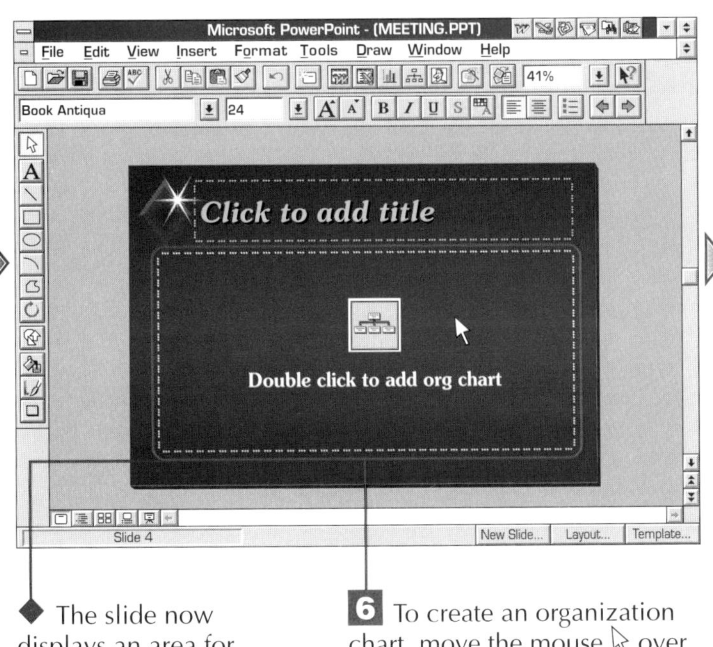

◆ The slide now displays an area for the organization chart.

6 To create an organization chart, move the mouse over this area and then quickly press the left button twice.

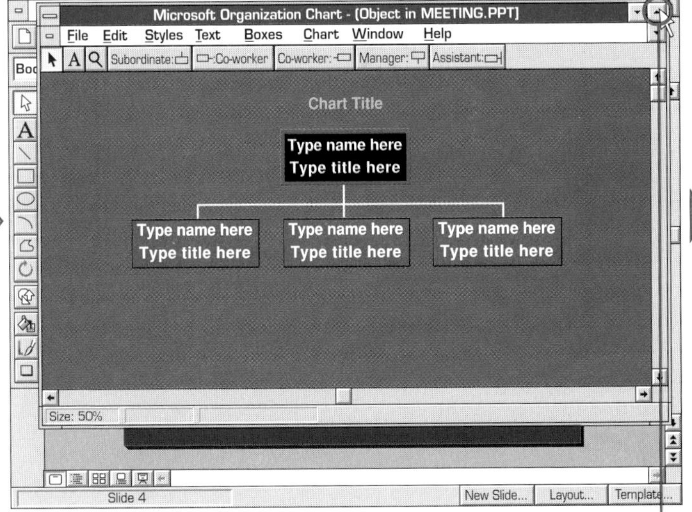

◆ **The Microsoft Organization Chart** window appears.

7 To enlarge this window to fill your screen, move the mouse over ▲ and then press the left button.

ADD AN ORGANIZATION CHART

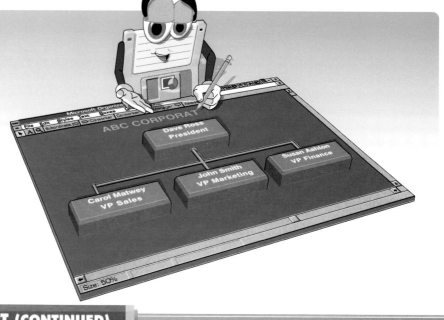

PowerPoint creates a simple organization chart that you can customize.

ADD AN ORGANIZATION CHART (CONTINUED)

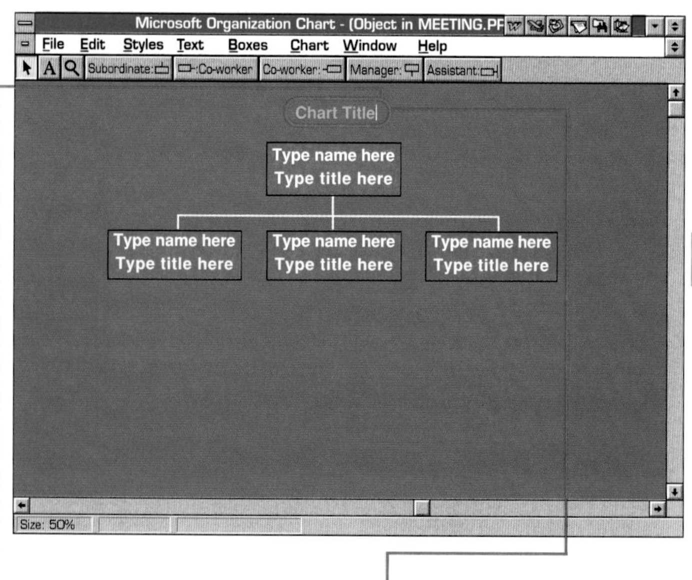

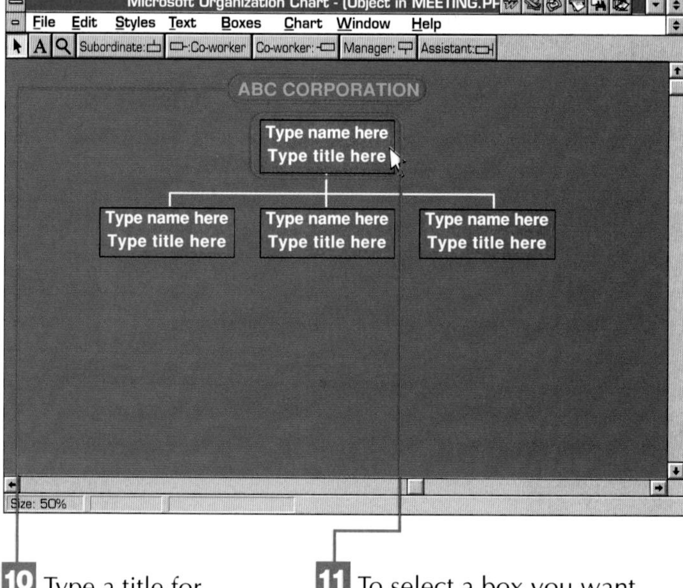

◆ The organization chart fills your screen.

8 To change the title of the chart, move the mouse I to the right of the title and then press the left button.

◆ A flashing line appears after the last character in the title.

9 Press **Backspace** until the existing title disappears.

10 Type a title for your chart.

11 To select a box you want to replace with new text, move the mouse over the box and then press the left button.

You can enter four lines of information for each person in an organization chart.

Type name here Type title here <Comment 1> <Comment 2>

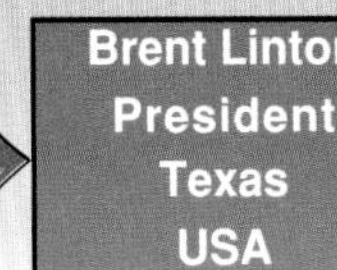

Brent Linton President Texas USA

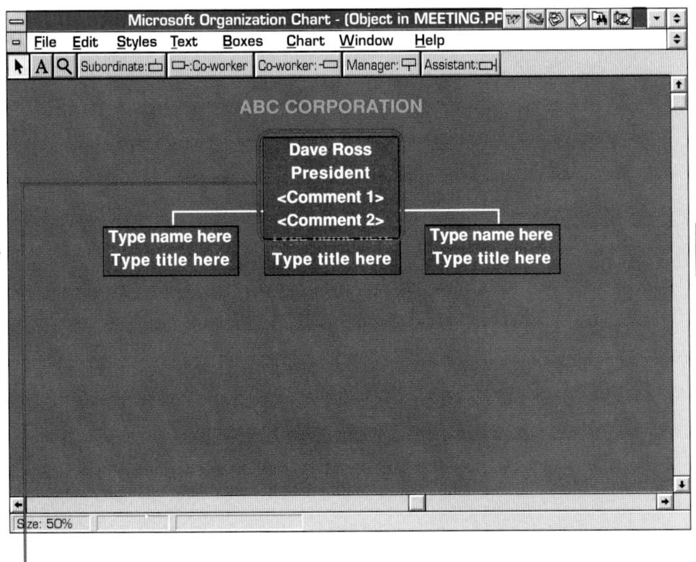

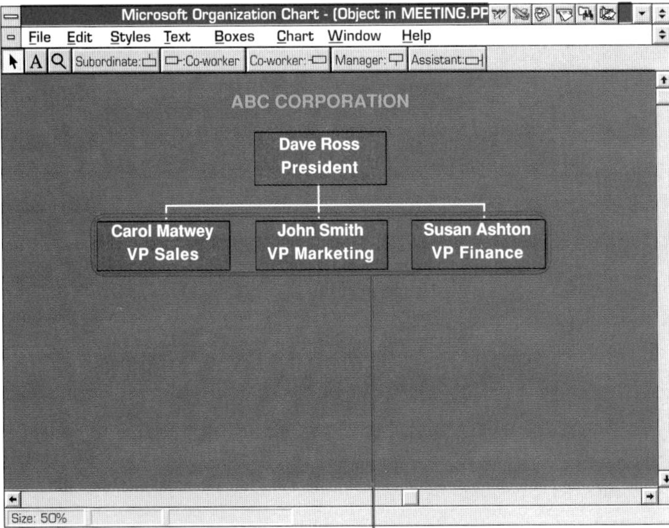

12 Type the text.

◆ To start a new line of text in a box, press **Enter**.

13 When you finish typing the information for the person, move the mouse outside the box and then press the left button.

14 Repeat steps **11** to **13** for each person you want to include in the chart.

ADD AN ORGANIZATION CHART

You can add another person to your organization chart, such as a co-worker or manager.

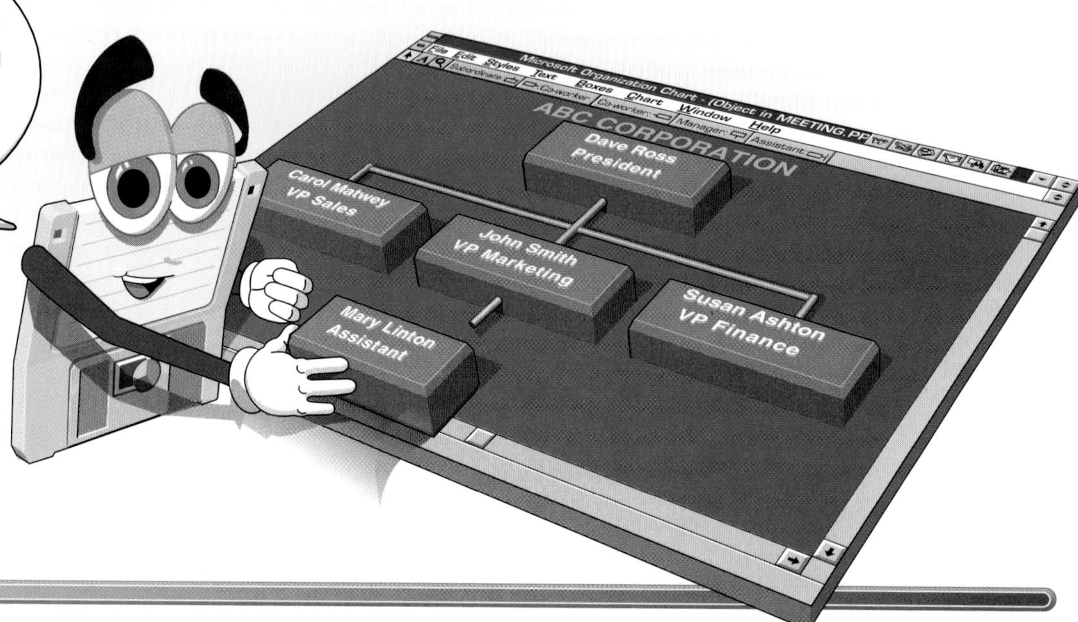

ADD A BOX

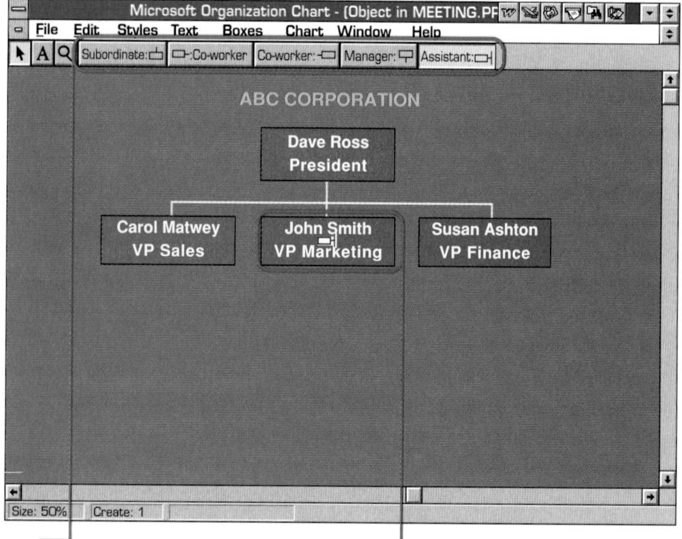

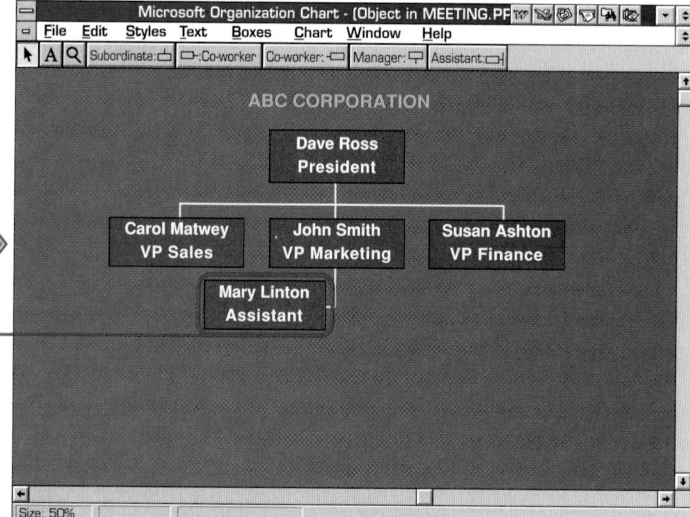

1 Move the mouse over the type of box you want to add (example: **Assistant**) and then press the left button.

2 Move the mouse over the box you want to connect the new box to and then press the left button.

◆ The new box appears.

3 Type the text you want to appear in the new box.

◆ To start a new line of text, press **Enter**.

4 When you finish typing the text, move the mouse outside the box and then press the left button.

DELETE A BOX

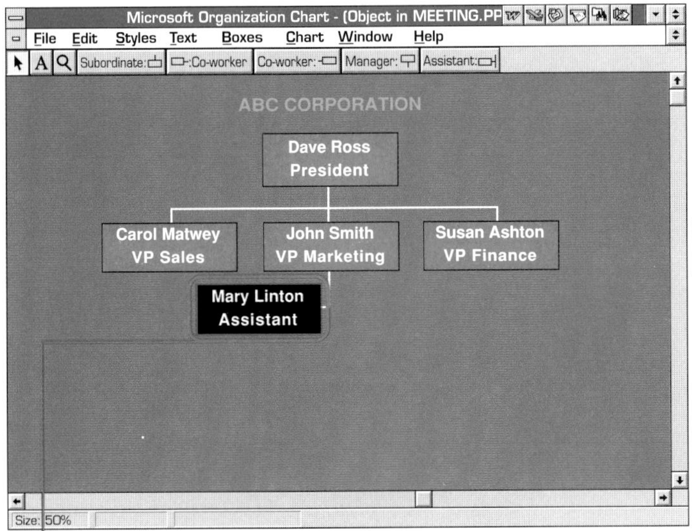

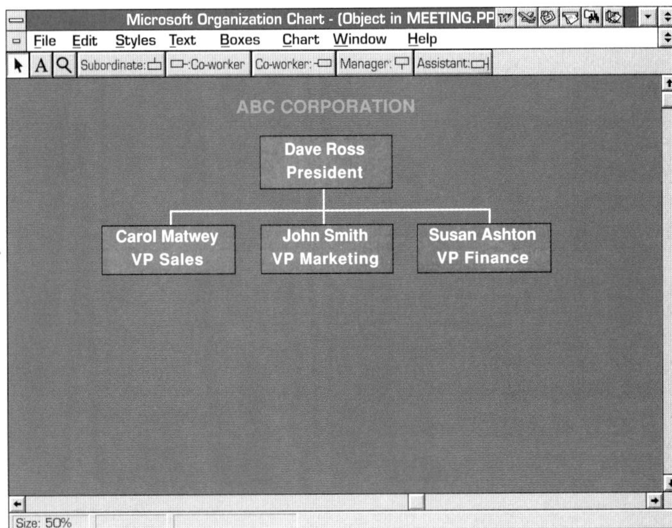

1 Move the mouse over the box you want to delete and then press the left button.

2 Press Delete on your keyboard.

◆ The box disappears.

ADD AN ORGANIZATION CHART

EXIT AND RETURN TO THE SLIDE

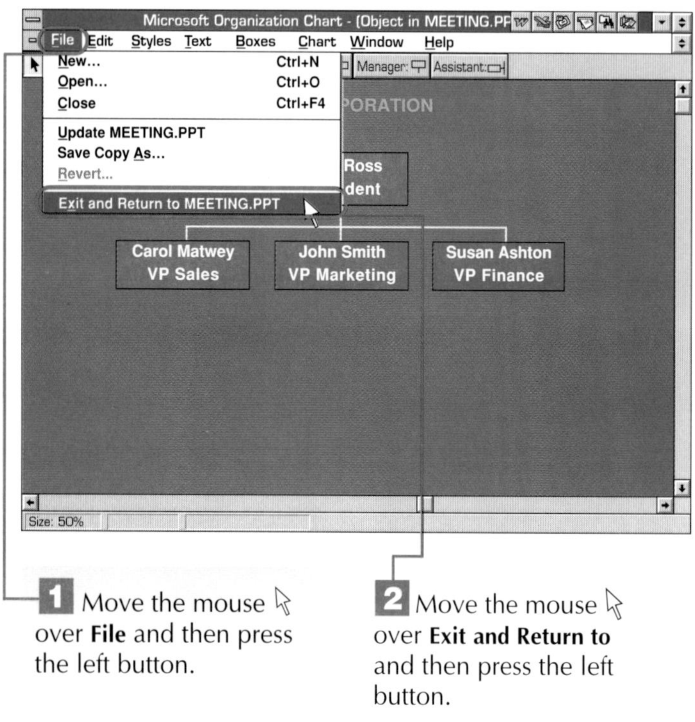

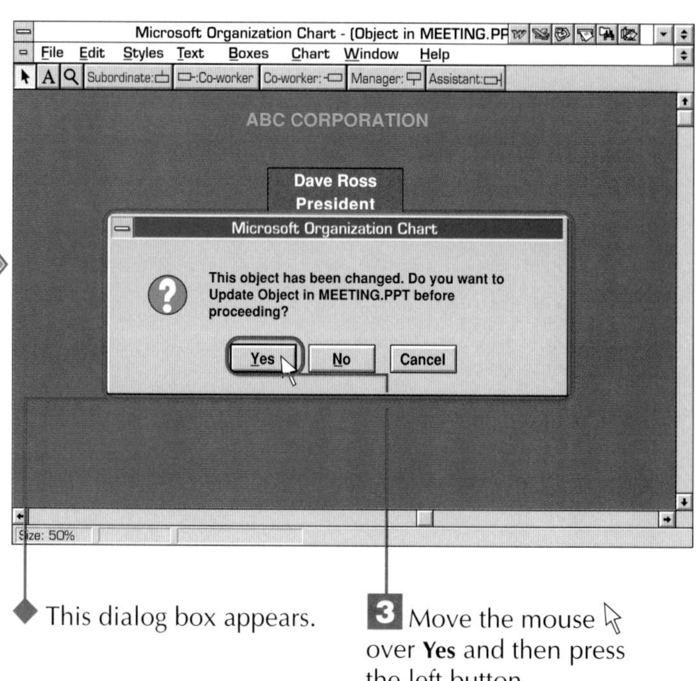

1 Move the mouse over **File** and then press the left button.

2 Move the mouse over **Exit and Return to** and then press the left button.

◆ This dialog box appears.

3 Move the mouse over **Yes** and then press the left button.

IMPORTANT!

You cannot make changes to an organization chart directly on a slide. To make changes, move the mouse over the chart and then quickly press the left button twice. This starts the **Microsoft Organization Chart** program and lets you modify the chart.

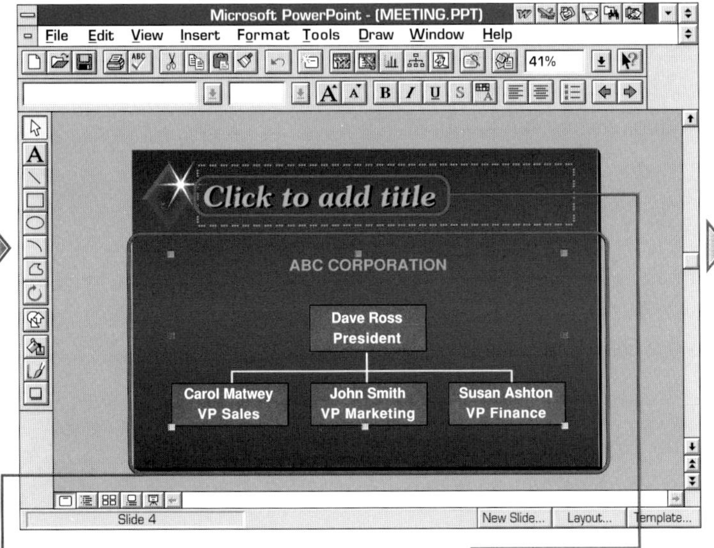

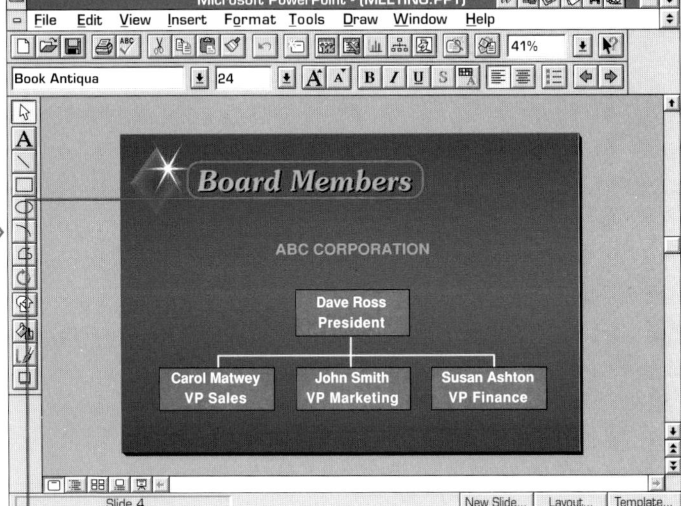

◆ The organization chart appears on the slide.

◆ The squares around the chart let you size the chart. To remove these squares, move the mouse outside the chart area and then press the left button.

4 To add a title to the slide, move the mouse over this area and then press the left button.

5 Type a title.

6 To deselect the title, move the mouse outside the title area and then press the left button.

Note: To move or size a chart, refer to page 306.

ADD A GRAPH

You can show trends and compare data by adding a graph to a slide. A graph has a greater impact than a simple list of numbers.

ADD A GRAPH

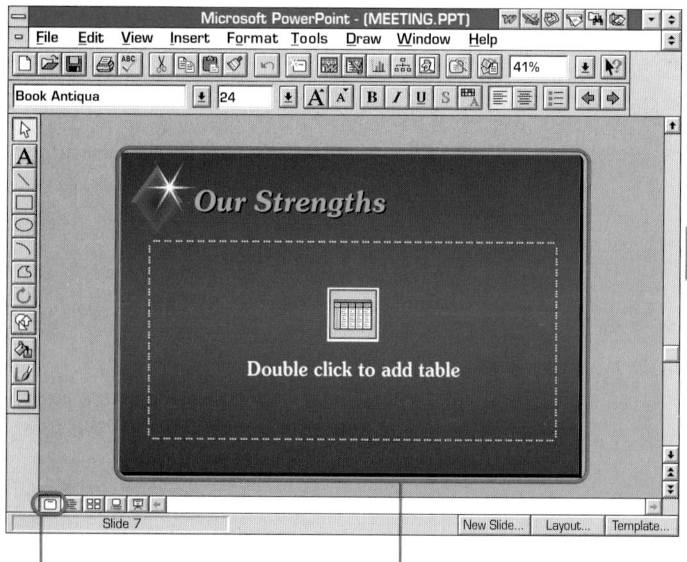

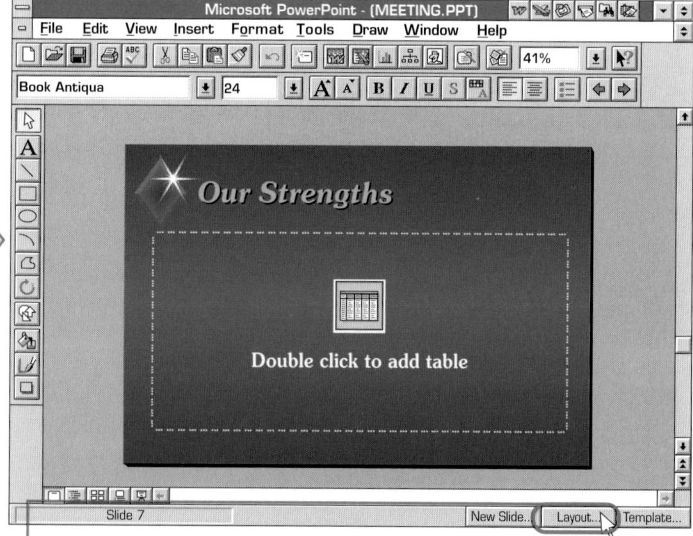

1 To change to the Slide view, move the mouse ↖ over ▭ and then press the left button.

2 Display the slide you want to add a graph to (example: slide 7).

Note: To move between slides, refer to page 250.

3 To change the layout of the slide, move the mouse ↖ over **Layout** and then press the left button.

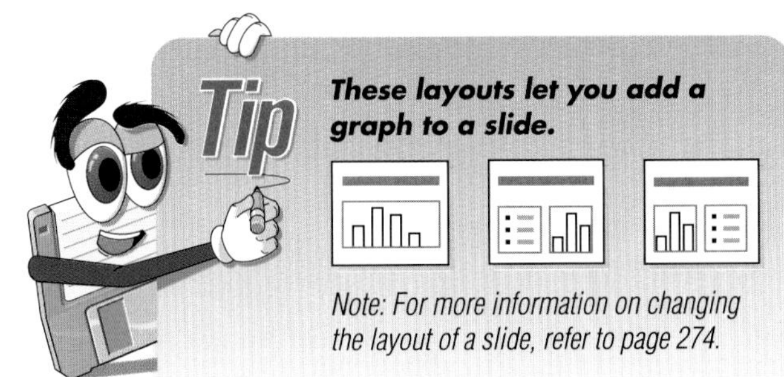

These layouts let you add a graph to a slide.

Note: For more information on changing the layout of a slide, refer to page 274.

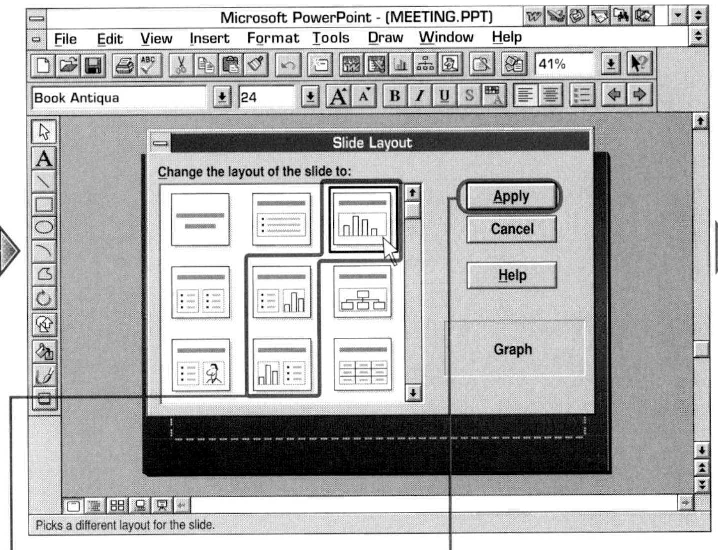

◆ The **Slide Layout** dialog box appears.

4 To add a graph to the slide, move the mouse over one of these layouts and then press the left button.

5 Move the mouse over **Apply** and then press the left button.

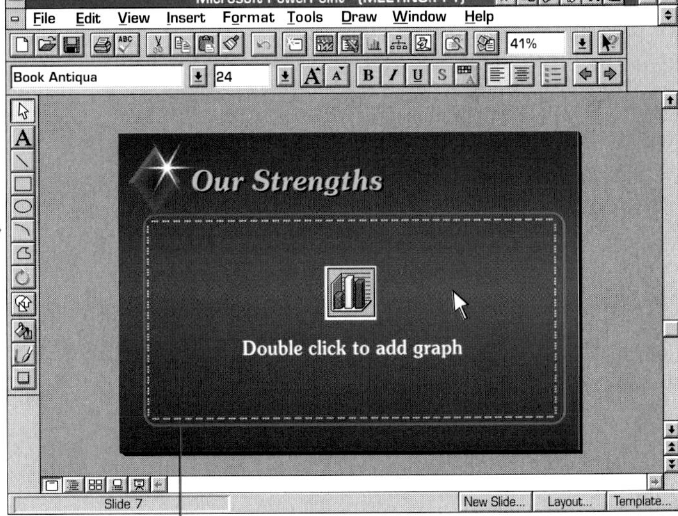

◆ The slide now displays an area for the graph.

6 To add a graph, move the mouse over this area and then quickly press the left button twice.

ADD A GRAPH

When you create a graph, PowerPoint provides a Datasheet where you enter data. PowerPoint uses this data to create the graph.

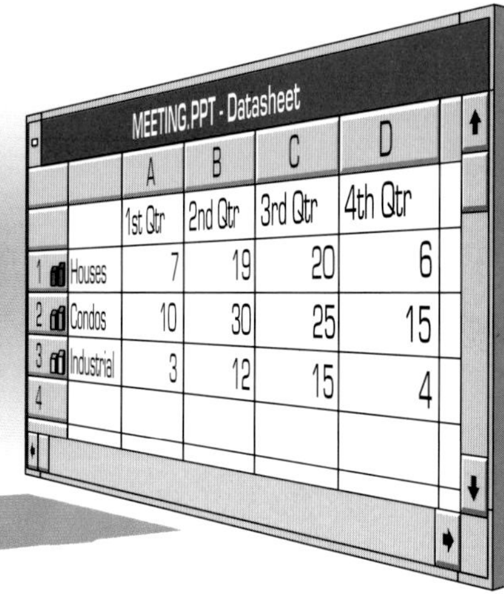

ADD A GRAPH (CONTINUED)

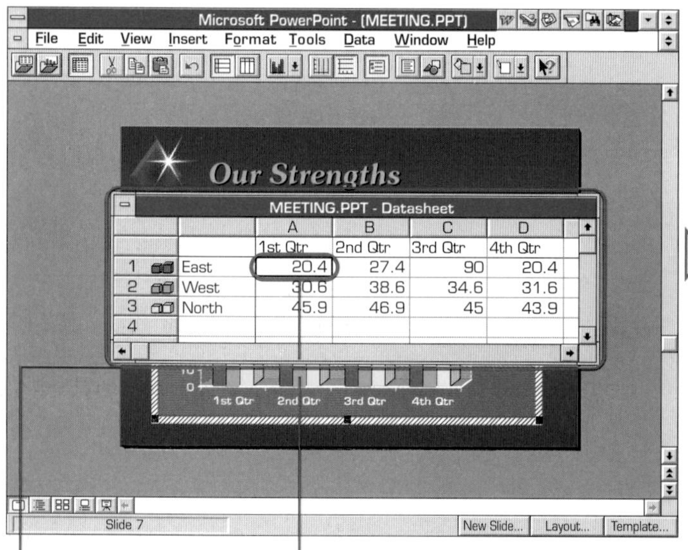

◆ A Datasheet appears, displaying sample data. This shows you where you can enter your own information.

7 To change the data in a cell, move the mouse over the cell and then press the left button.

◆ A thick border appears around the cell.

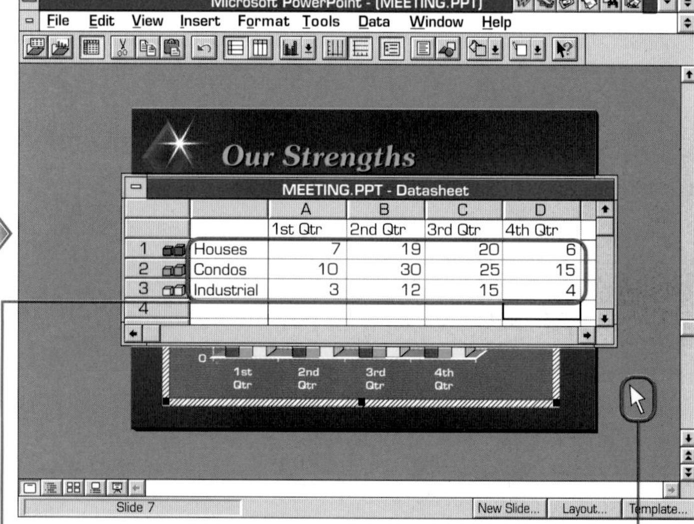

8 Type the data and then press **Enter**.

9 Repeat steps **7** and **8** until you finish entering all of your data.

Note: You can also press ↓, ↑, ← or → on your keyboard to quickly move between cells.

10 To hide the Datasheet and view the graph, move the mouse outside the Datasheet area and then press the left button.

After creating a graph, you can move or size the graph on the slide.

Note: For more information, refer to page 306.

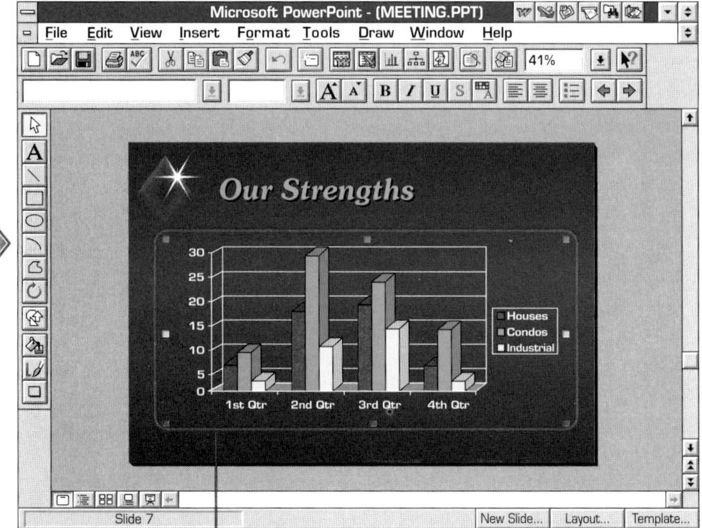

◆ The graph appears on the slide.

◆ The squares around the graph let you size the graph. To remove these squares, move the mouse outside the graph area and then press the left button.

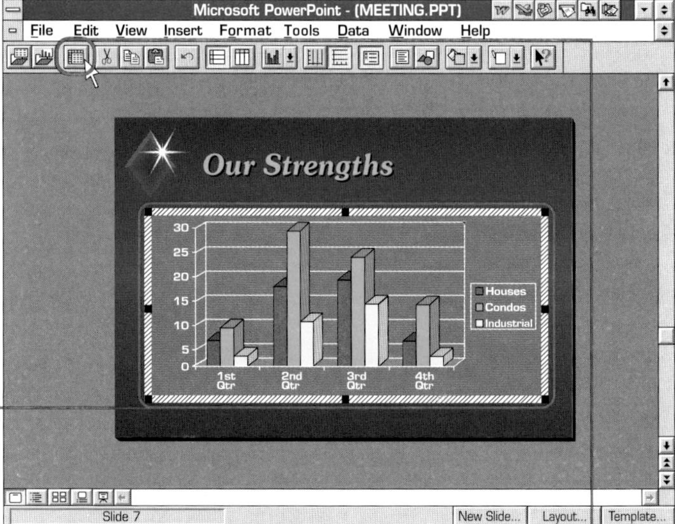

DISPLAY THE DATASHEET

1 To view or make changes to the data used in your graph, move the mouse over the graph and then quickly press the left button twice.

2 To display the Datasheet, move the mouse over and then press the left button.

◆ The graph will reflect any changes you make to the Datasheet.

CHANGE GRAPH TYPE

After creating a graph, you can select a new graph type that will better suit your data.

CHANGE GRAPH TYPE

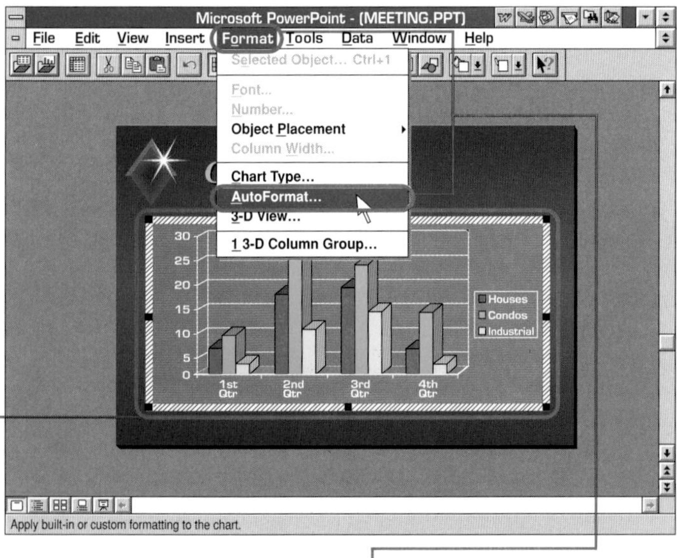

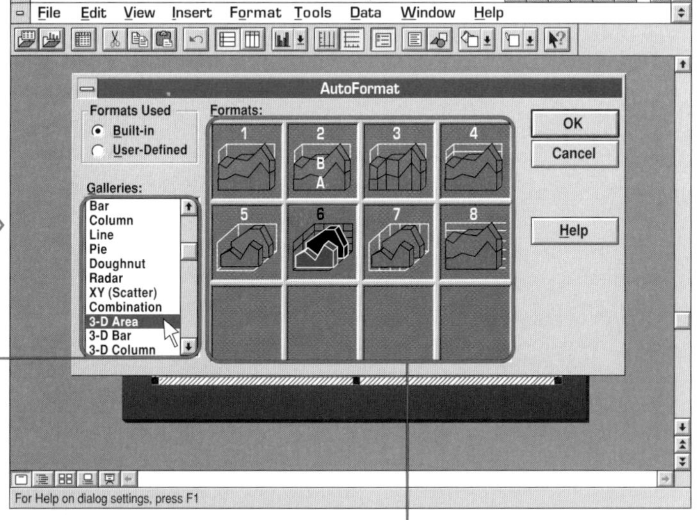

1 To select the graph, move the mouse over the graph and then quickly press the left button twice.

◆ A thick border appears around the graph.

2 Move the mouse over **Format** and then press the left button.

3 Move the mouse over **AutoFormat** and then press the left button.

◆ The **AutoFormat** dialog box appears.

4 Move the mouse over the type of graph you want to use and then press the left button.

◆ This area displays the available styles for the type of graph you selected.

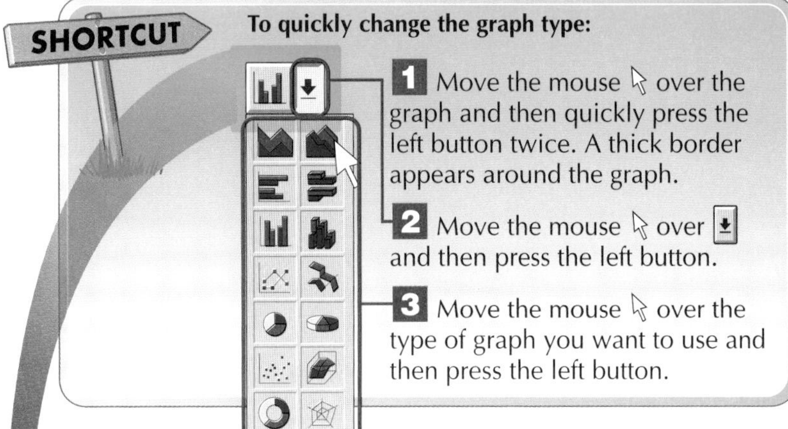

To quickly change the graph type:

1 Move the mouse over the graph and then quickly press the left button twice. A thick border appears around the graph.

2 Move the mouse over the drop-down button and then press the left button.

3 Move the mouse over the type of graph you want to use and then press the left button.

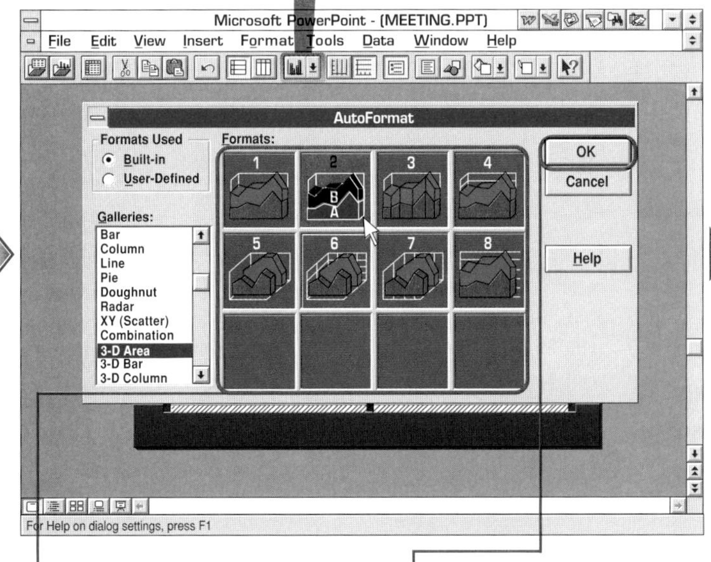

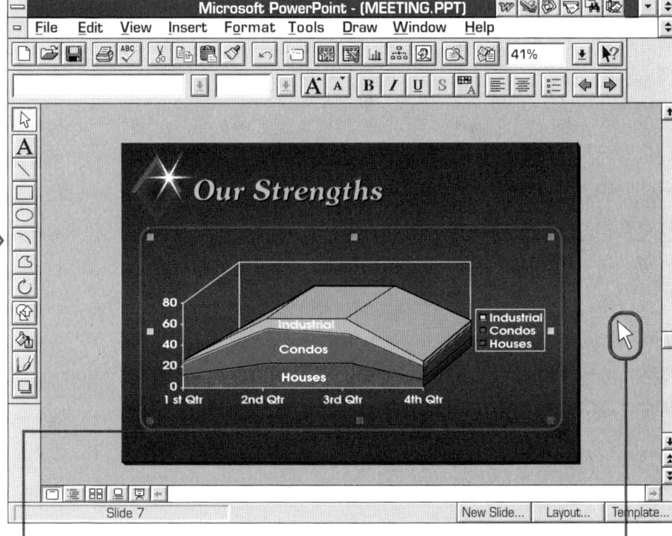

5 Move the mouse over the style you want to use (example: **2**) and then press the left button.

6 Move the mouse over **OK** and then press the left button.

◆ Your graph displays the new style.

7 To deselect the graph, move the mouse outside the graph area and then press the left button.

USING THE PICK A LOOK WIZARD

USING THE PICK A LOOK WIZARD

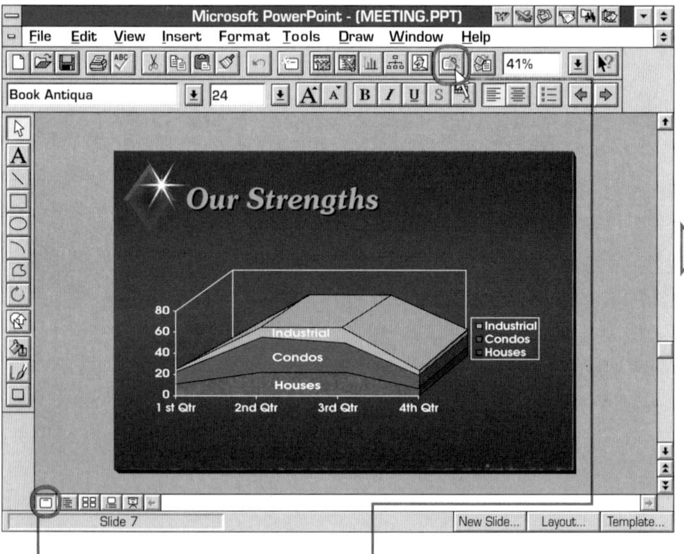

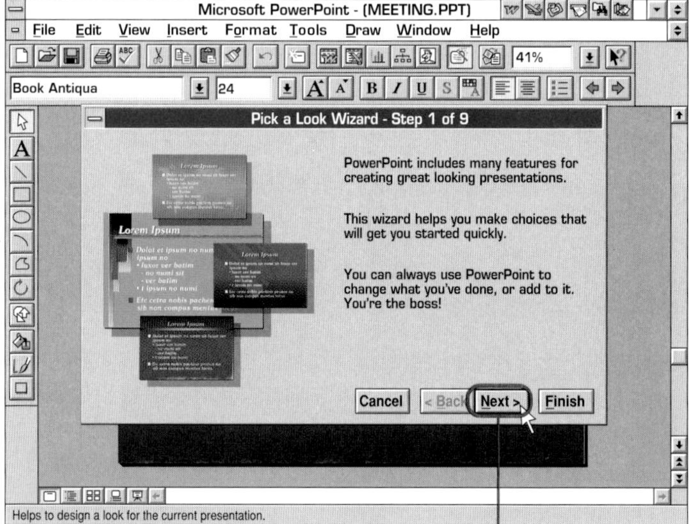

1 To change to the Slide view, move the mouse over and then press the left button.

2 Move the mouse over and then press the left button.

◆ The **Pick a Look Wizard** dialog box appears.

3 Move the mouse over **Next** and then press the left button.

- **Using the Pick a Look Wizard**
- Edit Text in Slide View
- Move and Size a Text Box
- Add an AutoShape
- Move and Size an Object
- Emphasize Text
- Change Text Size
- Change Font of Text
- Using Templates

In step 4 below, you can choose the type of output you want to use for your presentation.

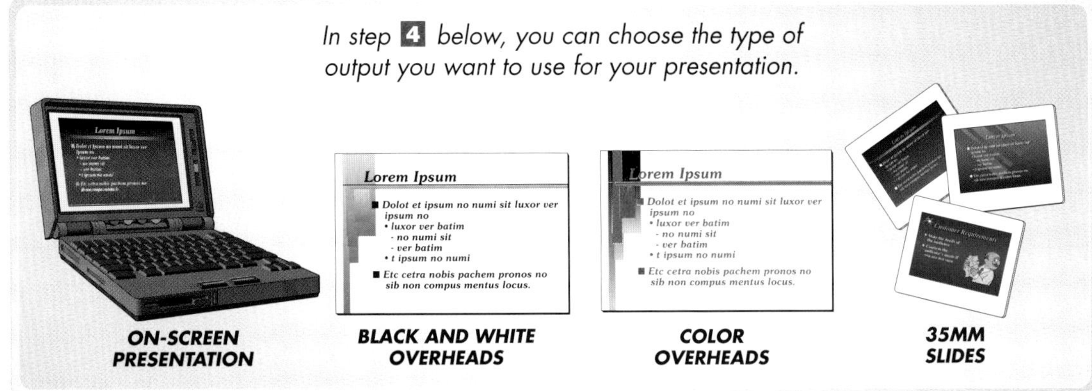

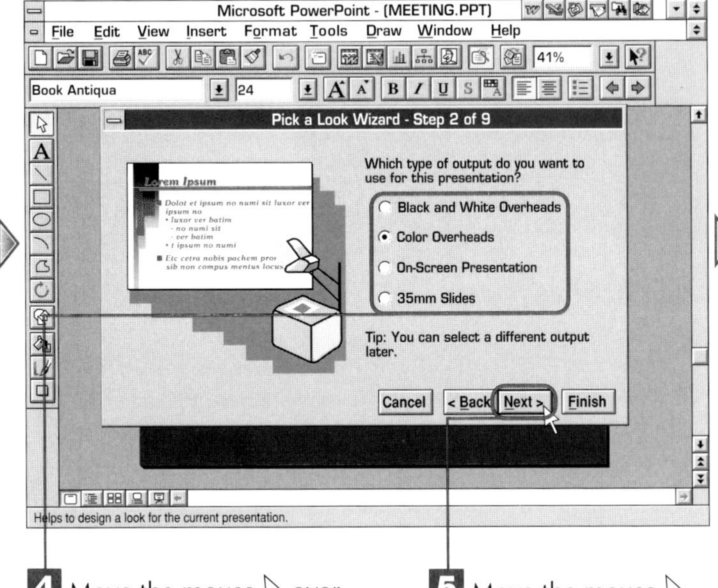

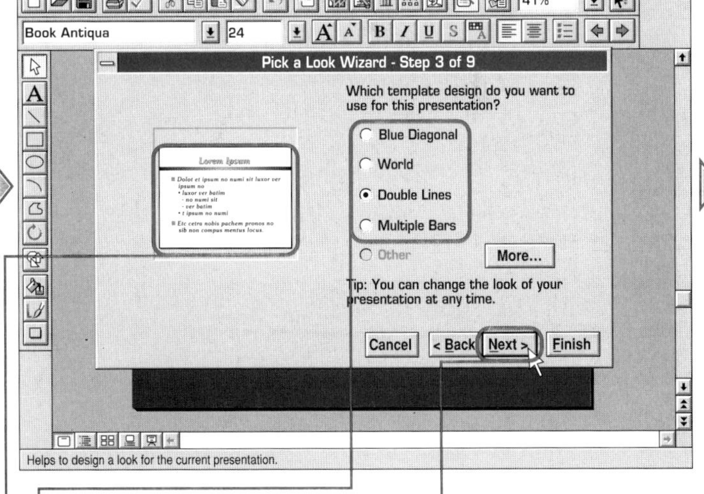

4 Move the mouse over the type of output you want to use for your presentation and then press the left button (○ changes to ◉).

5 Move the mouse over **Next** and then press the left button.

6 Move the mouse over the design you want to use and then press the left button.

Note: Only four designs are available in this dialog box. For other designs, refer to page 312.

◆ This area displays a sample of the design you selected.

7 Move the mouse over **Next** and then press the left button.

USING THE PICK A LOOK WIZARD

The Pick a Look Wizard lets you add additional information, such as the date, to your slides, notes, handouts and outline.

USING THE PICK A LOOK WIZARD (CONTINUED)

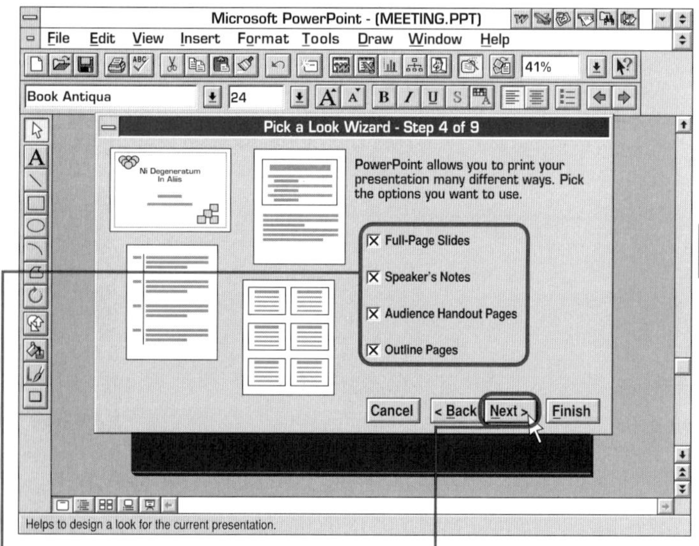

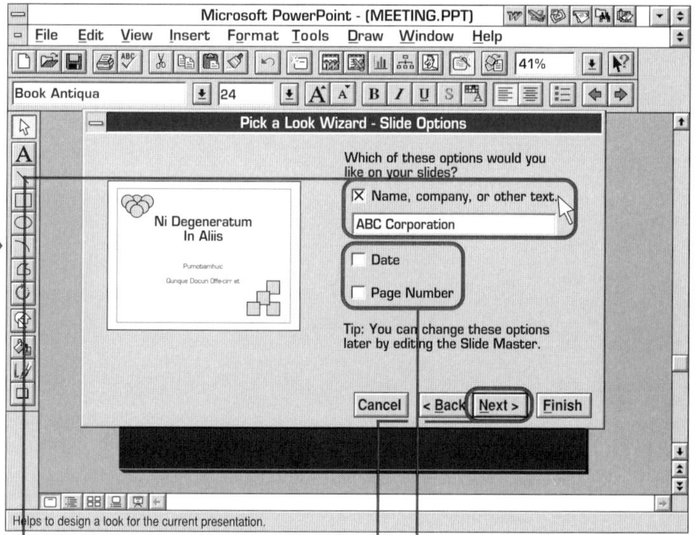

8 All of these items are part of your presentation. If you do not want to include an item, move the mouse over the item and then press the left button (☒ changes to ☐).

9 Move the mouse over **Next** and then press the left button.

Note: A dialog box will appear for each item that displays an ☒ in step 8.

10 To add text to an item in your presentation, move the mouse over this option and then press the left button (☐ changes to ☒). Press Tab and then type the text.

Note: ☒ means an option will appear on the item. ☐ means an option will not appear.

11 To add the date or page number, move the mouse over the option and then press the left button.

12 Move the mouse over **Next** and then press the left button.

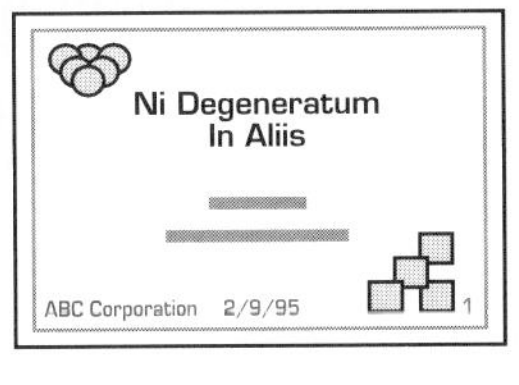

FULL-PAGE SLIDES

SPEAKER'S NOTES

AUDIENCE HANDOUT PAGES

OUTLINE PAGES

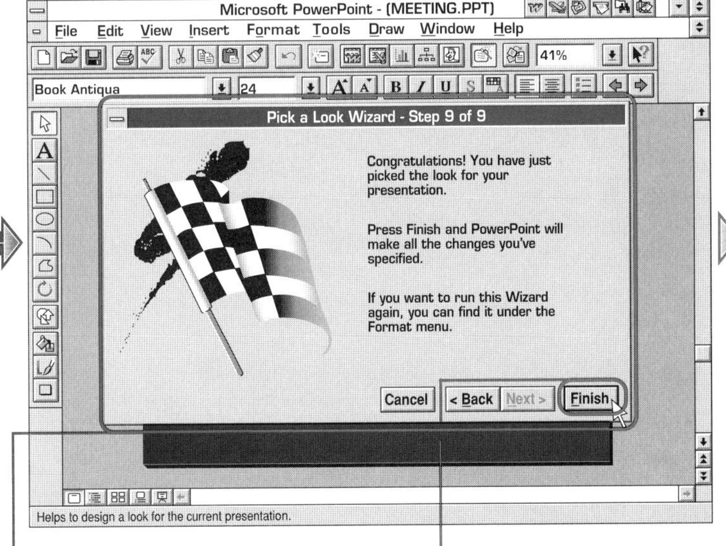

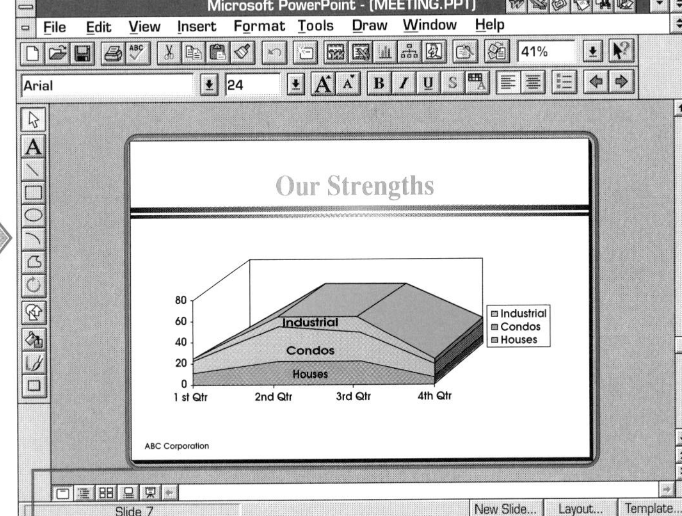

13 Repeat steps **10** to **12** for each item that displays an ☒ in step **8**.

◆ When you finish using the Pick a Look Wizard, this dialog box appears.

14 Move the mouse over **Finish** and then press the left button.

◆ PowerPoint applies the changes to your presentation.

*Note: PowerPoint displays symbols on each slide to represent the page number (**##**) and date (**II**). These symbols will be replaced with the proper information when you print your presentation.*

EDIT TEXT IN SLIDE VIEW

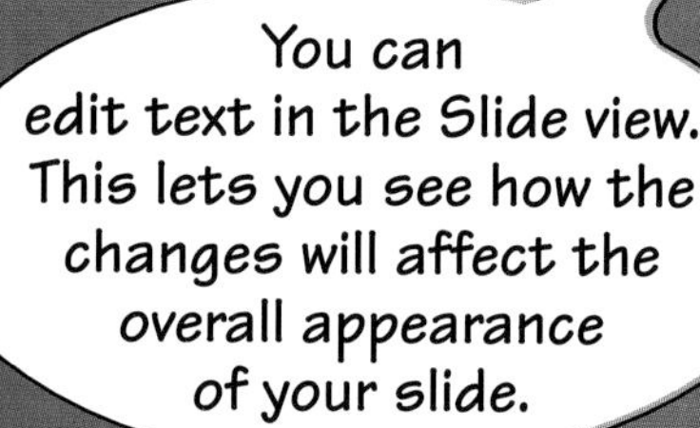

You can edit text in the Slide view. This lets you see how the changes will affect the overall appearance of your slide.

EDIT TEXT

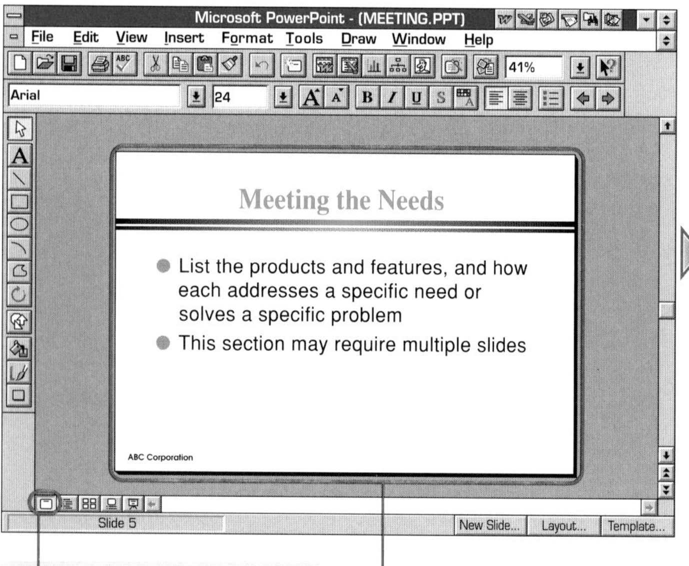

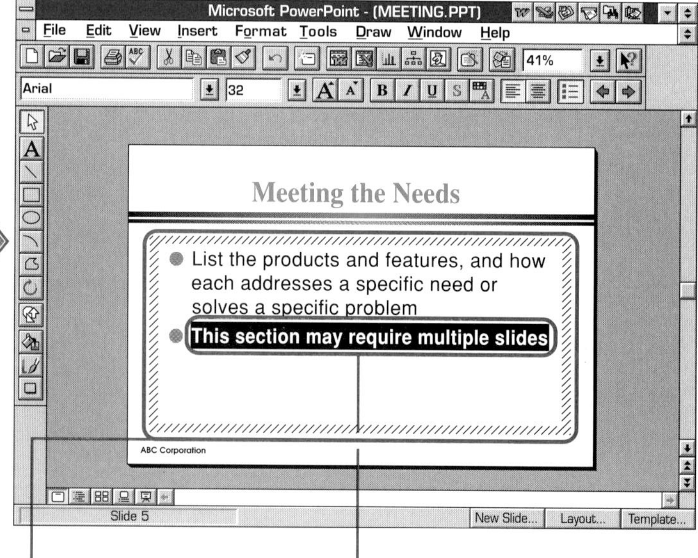

1 To change to the Slide view, move the mouse over ▭ and then press the left button.

2 Display the slide you want to edit (example: slide 5).

Note: To move between slides, refer to page 250.

3 Move the mouse I anywhere over the text you want to edit and then press the left button. A border appears around the text.

4 To delete text, select the text you want to remove. Then press **Delete**.

Note: To select text, refer to page 262.

For more information on editing text, refer to pages 264 to 270.

DELETE A LIST OF POINTS

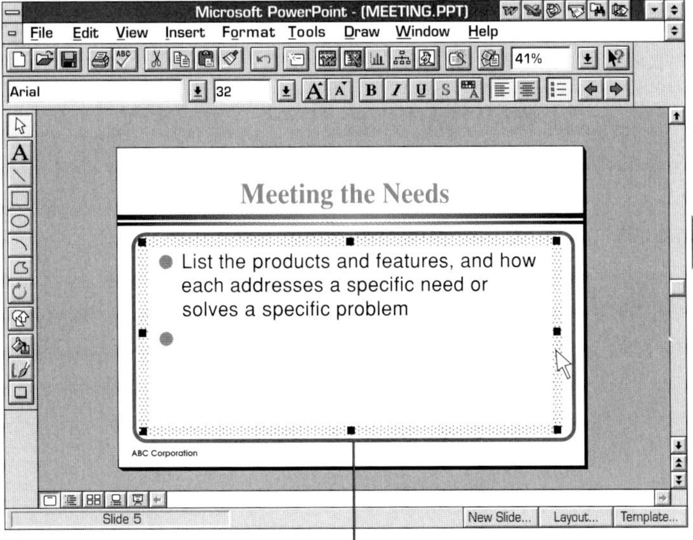

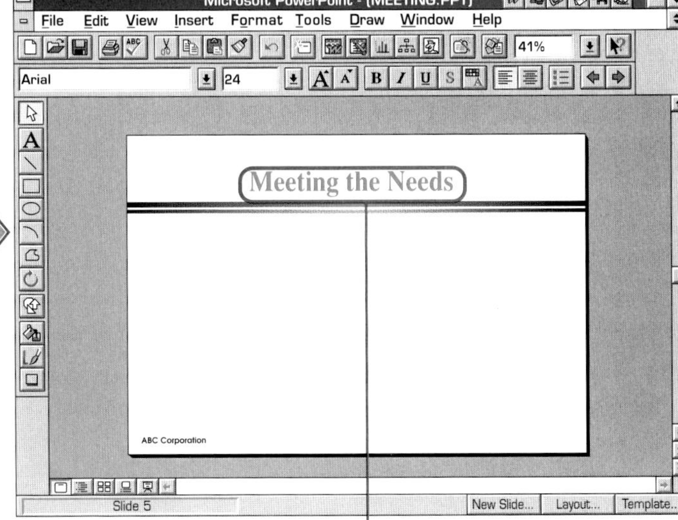

1 Move the mouse anywhere over the list of points you want to delete and then press the left button. A border appears around the list.

2 Move the mouse over the border and then press the left button. Squares appear on the border.

3 Press Delete twice and the list disappears.

◆ You can use the same method to remove a title from a slide.

MOVE AND SIZE A TEXT BOX

You can easily change the size or location of a text box on a slide. This is useful if you want to place a picture beside a list of points.

SIZE A TEXT BOX

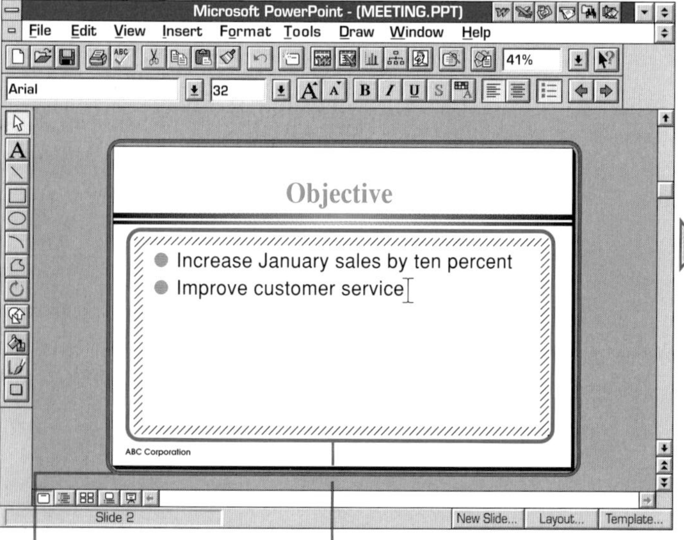

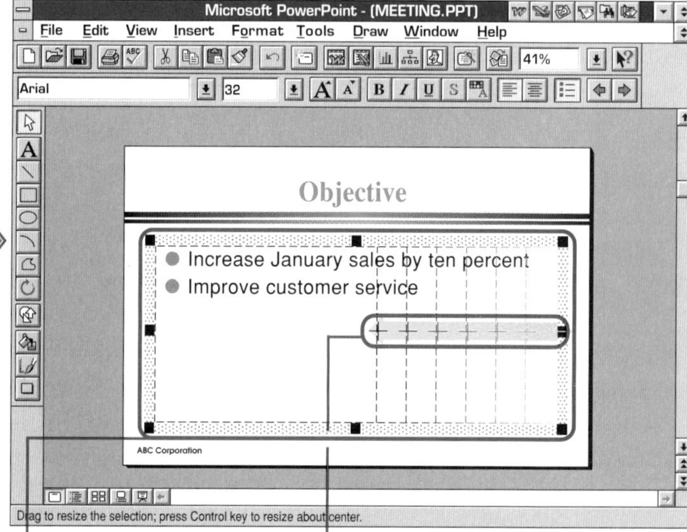

1 Display the slide you want to change (example: slide 2).

Note: To move between slides, refer to page 250.

2 Move the mouse I over the text in the text box you want to size and then press the left button. A border appears around the text.

3 Move the mouse ↖ over the border and then press the left button. Squares appear on the border.

4 Move the mouse ↖ over one of the squares and ↖ changes to ↔.

5 Press and hold down the left button as you drag the mouse + until the text box is the size you want. Then release the button.

Tip

You change the size of a text box using any square around the text.

- Increase January sales by ten percent
- Improve customer service

You can use these squares to change the height of a text box.

You can use these squares to change the width of a text box.

You can use these squares to change the height and width of a text box at the same time.

MOVE A TEXT BOX

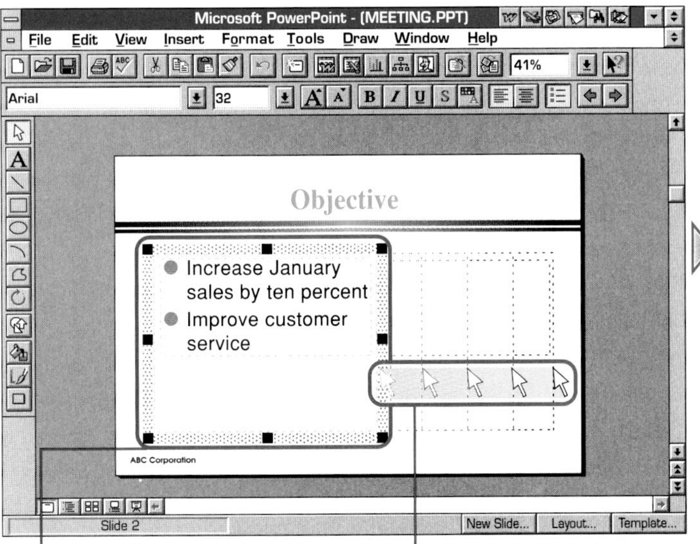

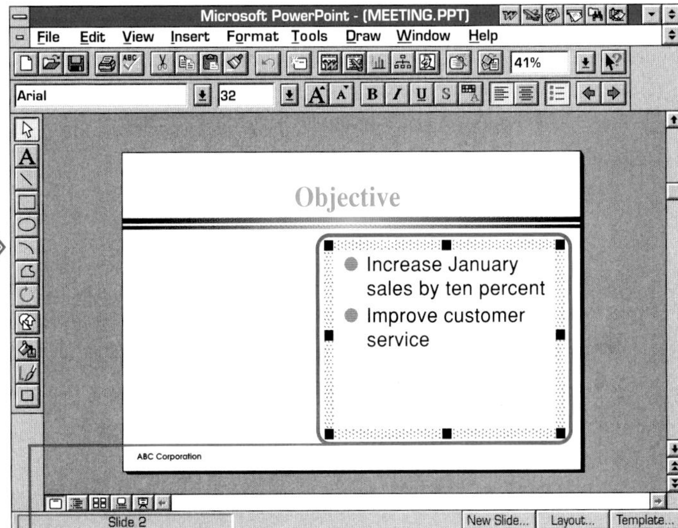

1 Move the mouse I over the text in the text box you want to move and then press the left button. A border appears around the text.

2 Move the mouse over the border and then press and hold down the left button as you drag the text box to a new location.

3 Release the button and the text box appears in the new location.

ADD AN AUTOSHAPE

You can add shapes such as arrows and stars to the slides in your presentation. A shape can help emphasize your information.

Objective

- Increase January sales by ten percent
- Improve customer service

ADD AN AUTOSHAPE

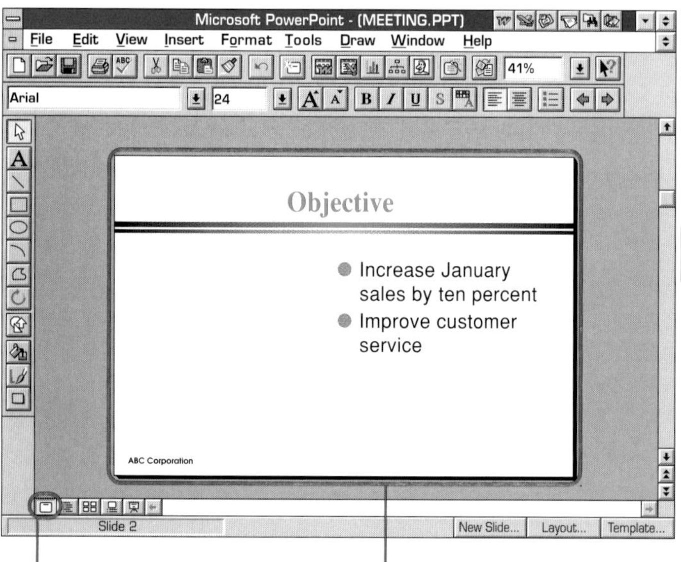

1 To change to the Slide view, move the mouse ⇖ over ▭ and then press the left button.

2 Display the slide you want to add a shape to (example: slide 2).

Note: To move between slides, refer to page 250.

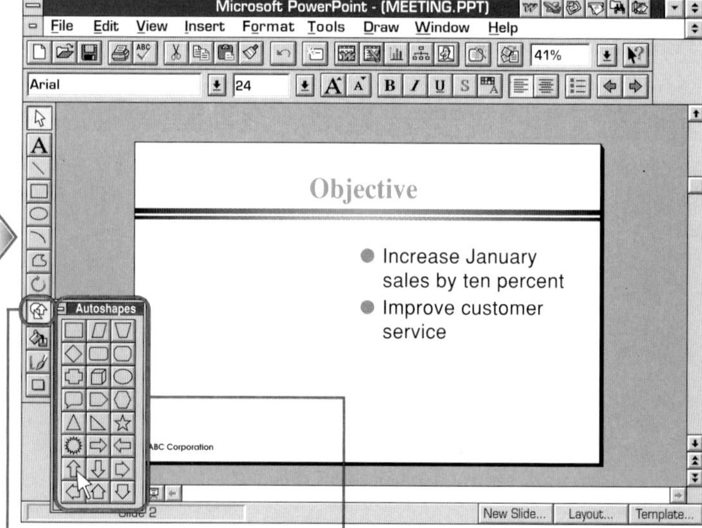

3 Move the mouse ⇖ over ▭ and then press the left button.

◆ The **Autoshapes** toolbar appears, displaying the shapes you can add to your slide.

4 Move the mouse ⇖ over the shape you want to add and then press the left button.

Tip

You can move or size a shape after you add it to a slide.

Note: For more information, refer to page 306.

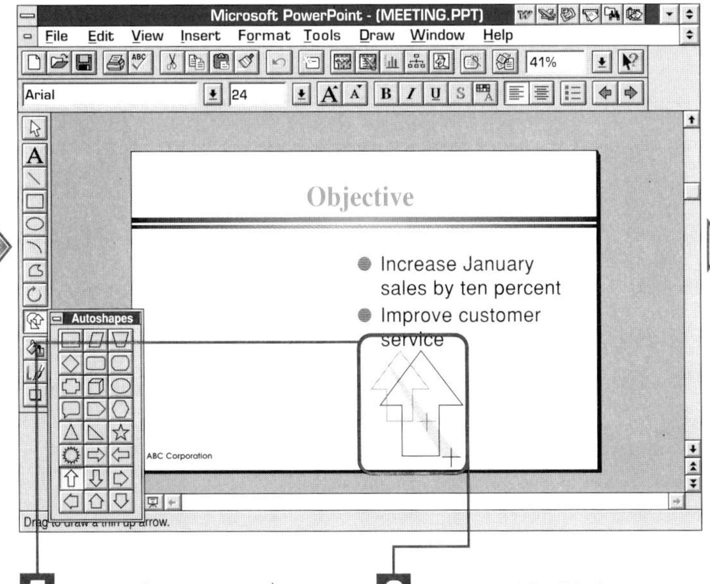

5 Move the mouse + over the location where you want the top left corner of the shape to appear.

6 Press and hold down the left button as you drag the mouse + until the shape is the size you want.

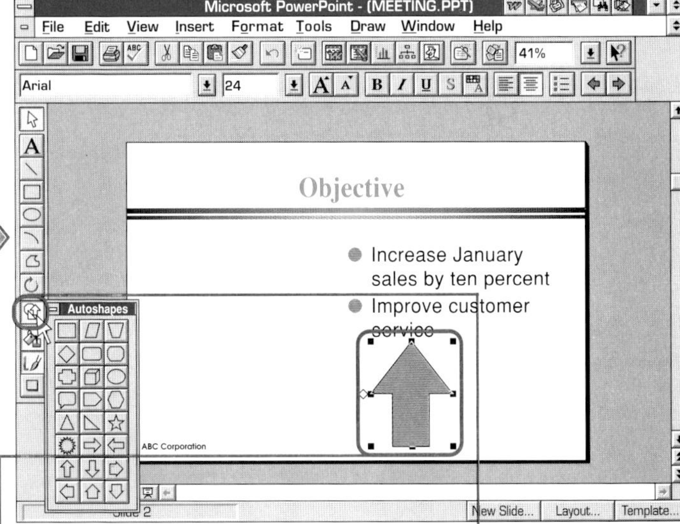

7 Release the button and the shape appears.

8 The squares around the shape let you size the shape. To remove these squares, move the mouse outside the shape area and then press the left button.

9 To hide the **Autoshapes** toolbar, move the mouse over and then press the left button.

MOVE AND SIZE AN OBJECT

MOVE AN OBJECT

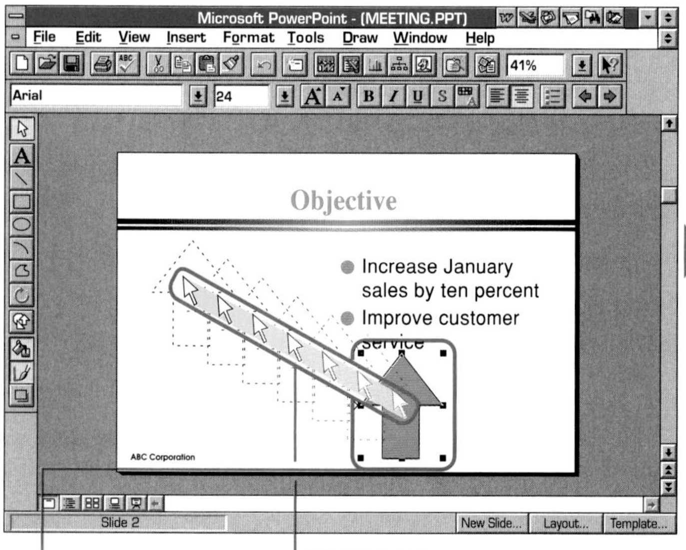

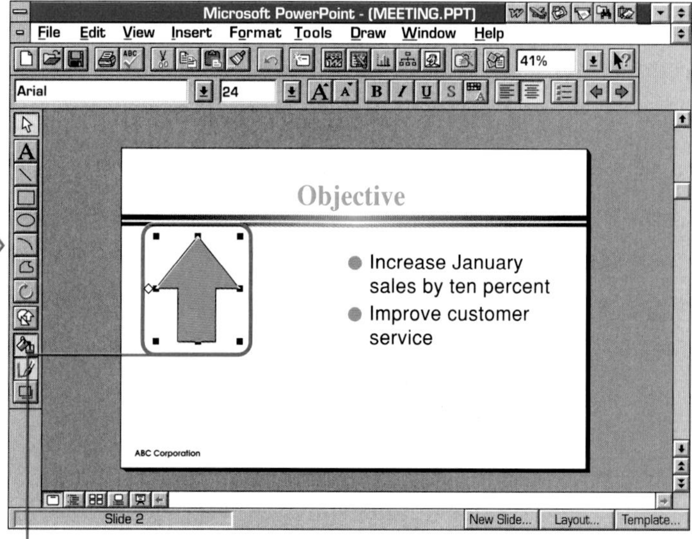

1 Move the mouse over the object you want to move and then press and hold down the left button.

2 Still holding down the left button, drag the mouse to where you want to place the object.

3 Release the button and the object appears in the new location.

DELETE AN OBJECT

1 *To select the object you want to delete, move the mouse over the object and then press the left button.*

2 *Press Delete on your keyboard.*

SIZE AN OBJECT

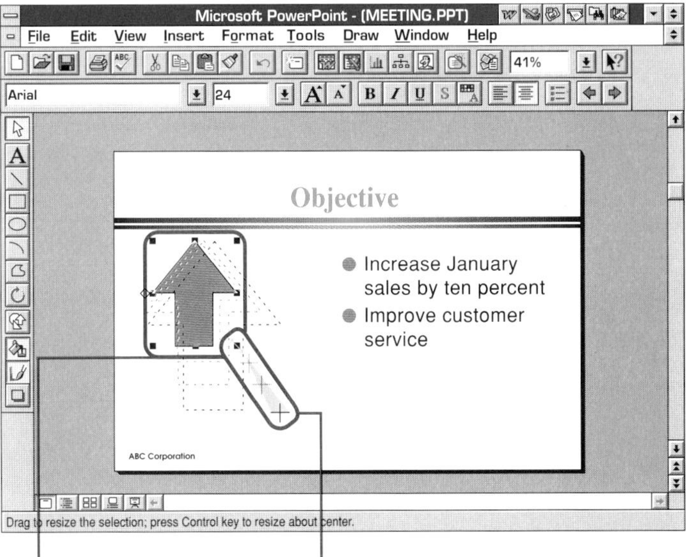

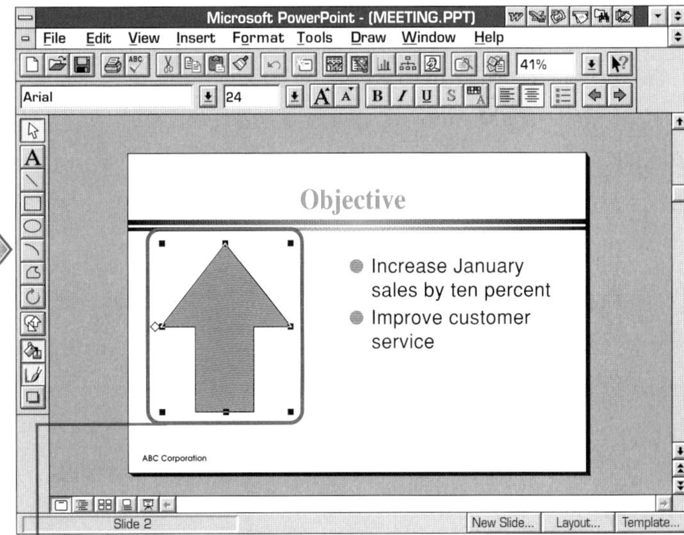

1 To select the object you want to size, move the mouse over the object and then press the left button. Squares appear around the object.

2 Move the mouse over one of the squares and changes to ↘.

3 Press and hold down the left button as you drag the mouse + until the object is the size you want.

4 Release the button and the object changes to the new size.

You can use these styles to emphasize important information in your presentation.

bold *italic* underline shadow

EMPHASIZE TEXT

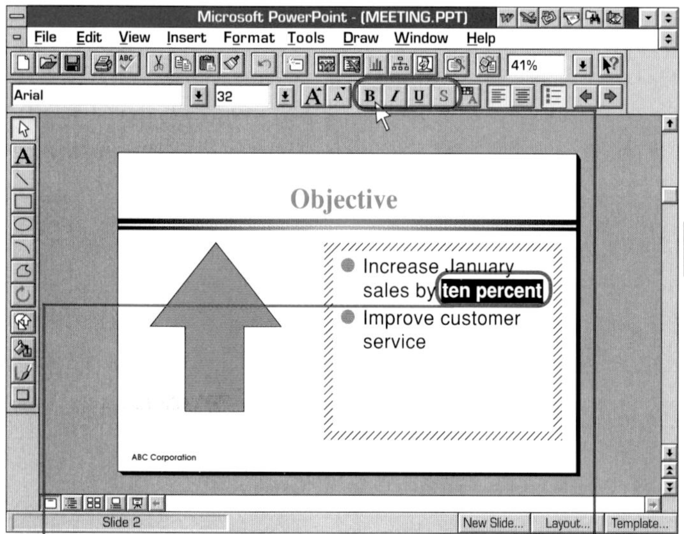

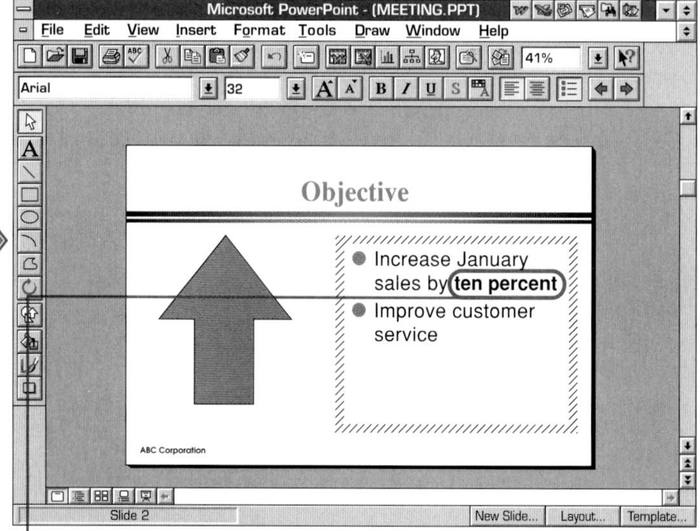

1 Select the text you want to change.

Note: To select text, refer to page 262.

2 Move the mouse over one of the following options and then press the left button.

- **B** Bold text
- *I* Italicize text
- U Underline text
- S Shadow text

◆ The text you selected appears in the new style.

Note: To deselect text, move the mouse outside the selected area and then press the left button.

◆ To remove a style, repeat steps **1** and **2**.

CHANGE TEXT SIZE

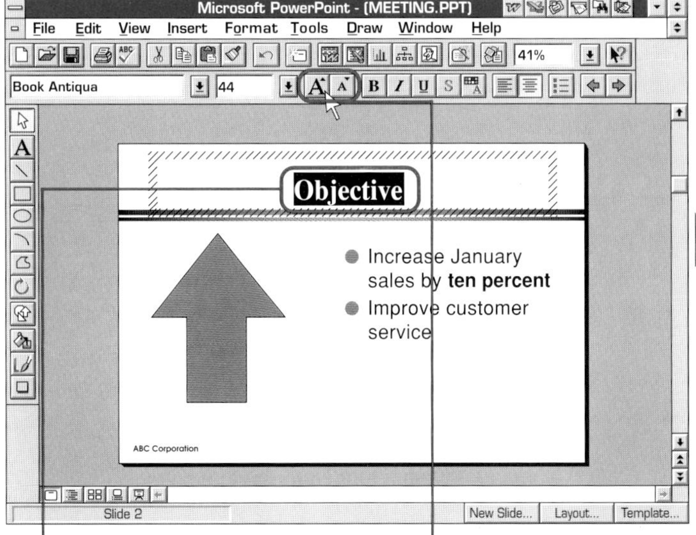

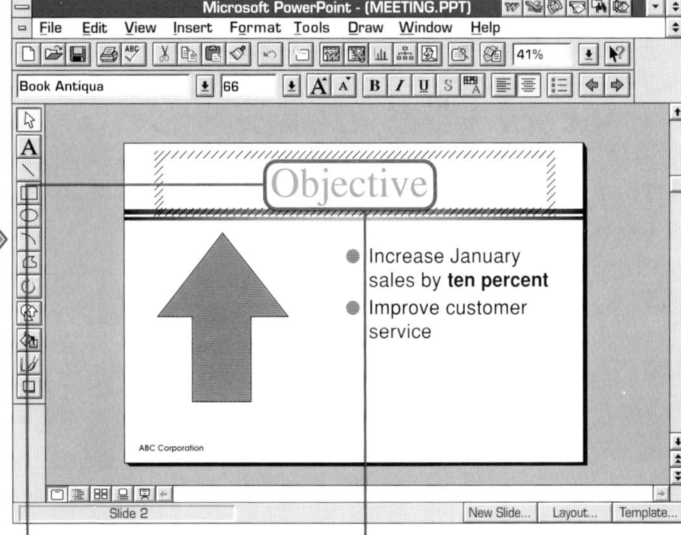

1 Select the text you want to change.

Note: To select text, refer to page 262.

2 Move the mouse over one of the following options and then press the left button.

A Increase text size

A Decrease text size

◆ The text increases or decreases in size.

3 Repeat step **2** until the text is the size you want.

Note: To deselect text, move the mouse outside the selected area and then press the left button.

CHANGE FONT OF TEXT

CHANGE FONT OF TEXT

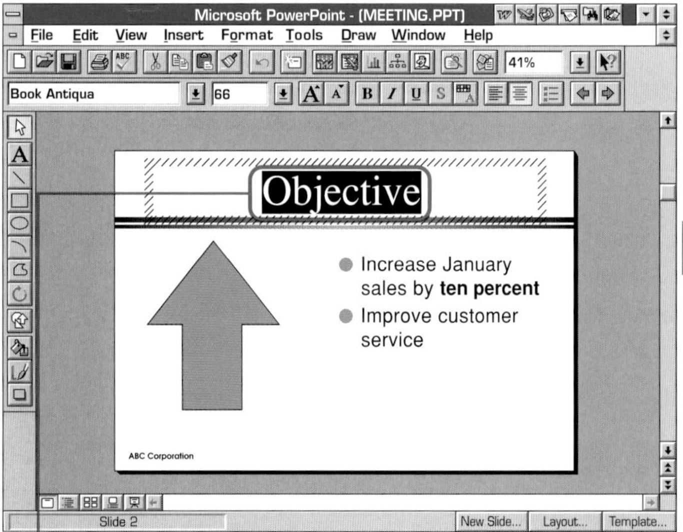

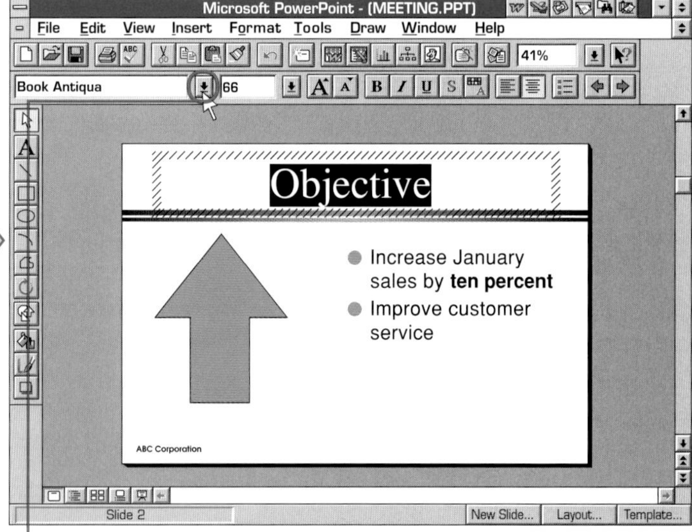

1 Select the text you want to change.

Note: To select text, refer to page 262.

2 To display a list of the available fonts, move the mouse over ⬇ beside the **Font** box and then press the left button.

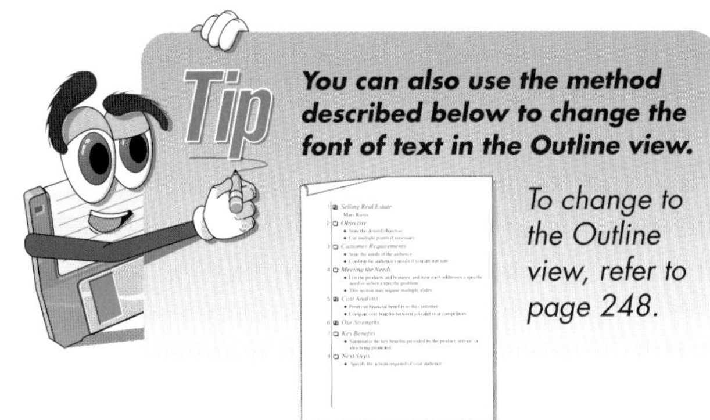

You can also use the method described below to change the font of text in the Outline view.

To change to the Outline view, refer to page 248.

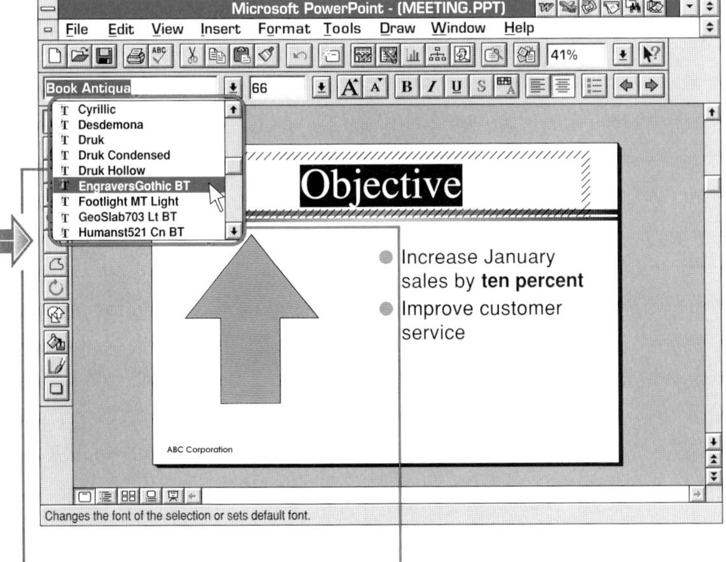

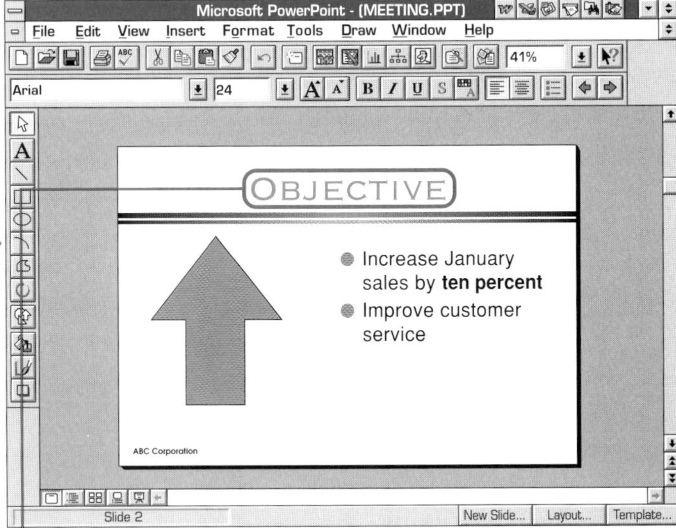

◆ A list of the available fonts for your computer appears.

3 To browse through the available fonts, move the mouse over ⬇ or ⬆ and then press the left button.

4 Move the mouse over the font you want to use and then press the left button.

◆ The text you selected changes to the new font.

Note: To deselect text, move the mouse outside the slide and then press the left button.

USING TEMPLATES

PowerPoint offers over 100 predesigned slides, called templates. You can select a different template to give your slides a new look.

USING TEMPLATES

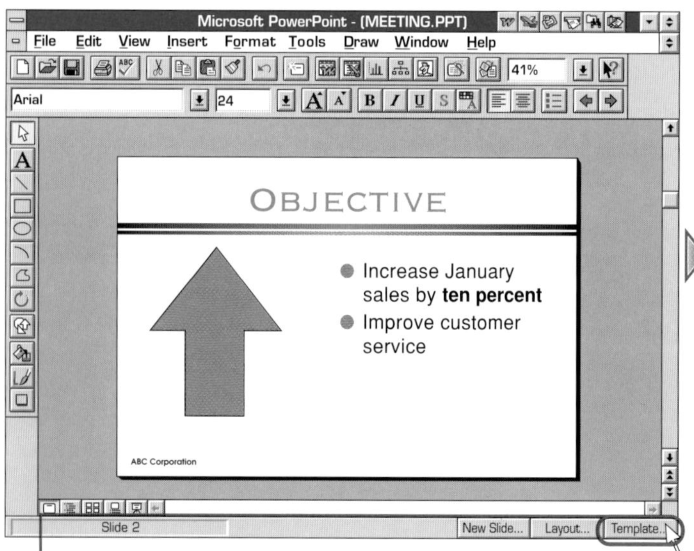

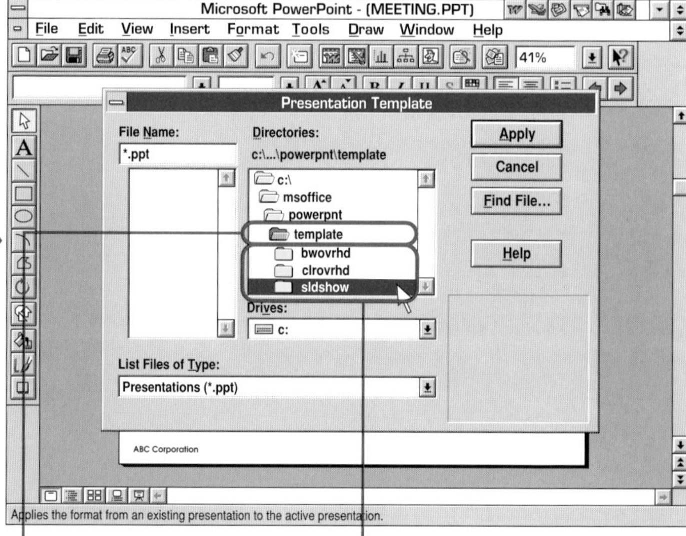

1 Move the mouse over **Template** and then press the left button.

◆ The **Presentation Template** dialog box appears.

2 Move the mouse over **template** and then quickly press the left button twice.

3 Move the mouse over the type of presentation you want to create (example: **sldshow**) and then quickly press the left button twice.

*Note: For more information, refer to the **Tip** on page 313.*

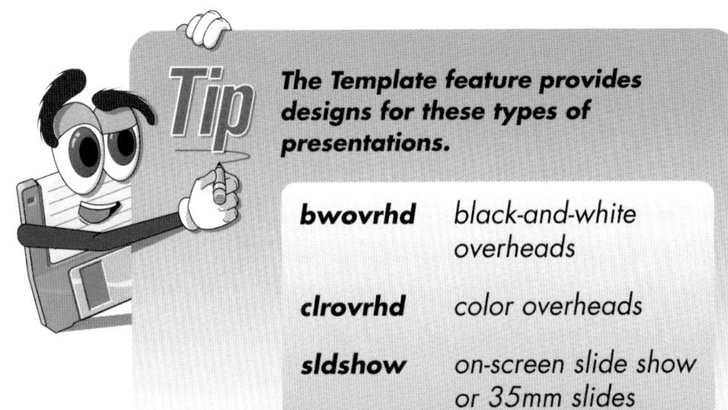

The Template feature provides designs for these types of presentations.

bwovrhd	*black-and-white overheads*
clrovrhd	*color overheads*
sldshow	*on-screen slide show or 35mm slides*

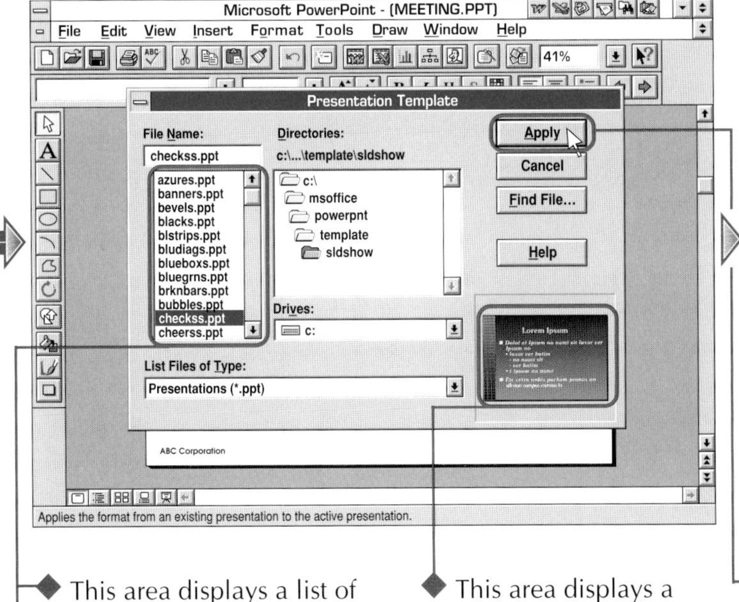

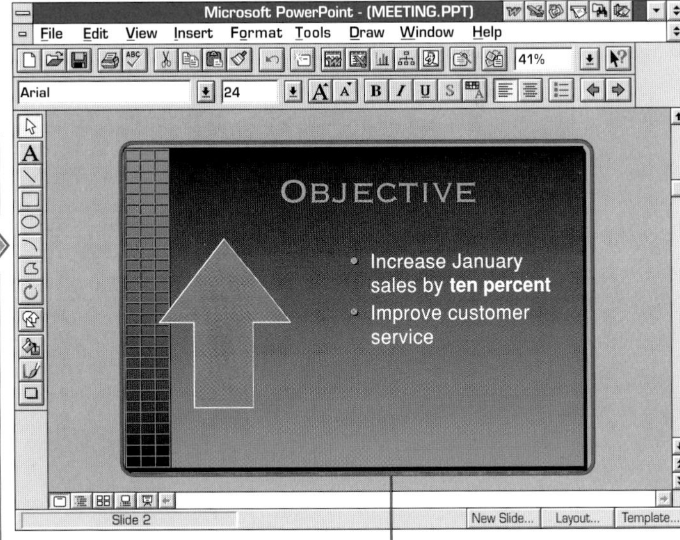

◆ This area displays a list of templates for the type of presentation you selected.

4 Move the mouse over a template you want to view (example: **checkss.ppt**) and then press the left button.

◆ This area displays a sample of the template you selected.

5 Repeat step **4** until the template you want to use appears.

6 Move the mouse over **Apply** and then press the left button.

◆ All the slides in your presentation change to the new design.

ADD SPEAKER'S NOTES

You can create speaker's notes containing copies of your slides with all the ideas you want to discuss. These notes will help guide you through your presentation.

ADD SPEAKER'S NOTES

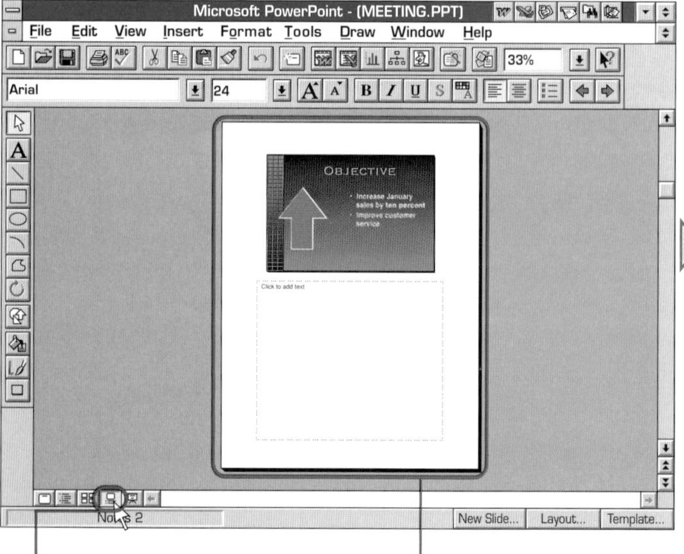

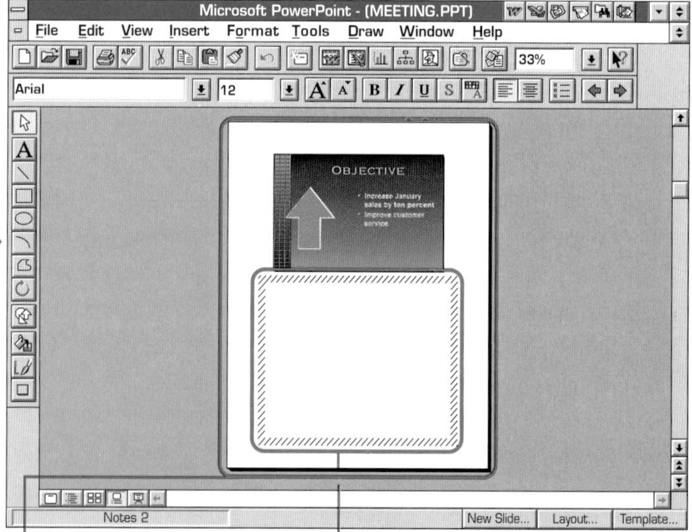

1 To change to the Notes Pages view, move the mouse over and then press the left button.

◆ A page appears, displaying a slide and an area for adding notes.

2 Display the slide you want to add notes to (example: slide 2).

Note: To move between slides, refer to page 253.

3 Move the mouse over this area and then press the left button.

◆ A border appears around the area.

Tip

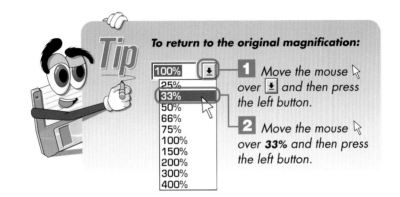

To return to the original magnification:

100%
25%
33%
50%
66%
75%
100%
150%
200%
300%
400%

1 *Move the mouse over ⬇ and then press the left button.*

2 *Move the mouse over **33%** and then press the left button.*

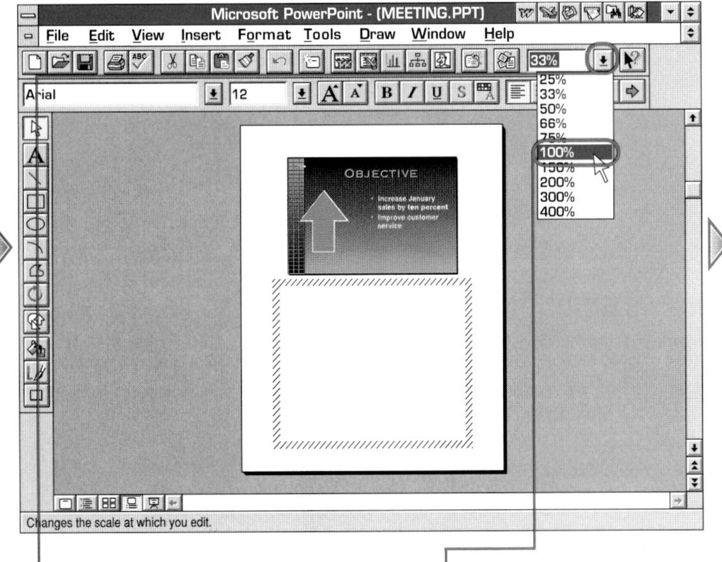

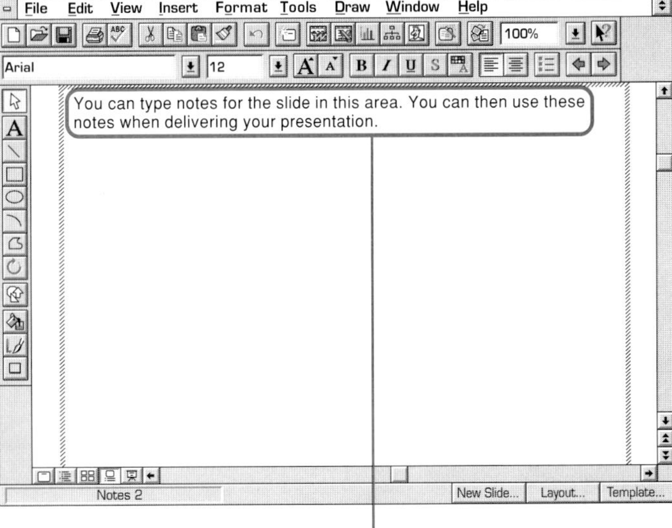

4 To magnify the text area, move the mouse over ⬇ at the top right corner of your screen and then press the left button.

5 Move the mouse over **100%** and then press the left button.

◆ The text area is magnified.

6 Type the ideas you want to discuss when you display the slide.

DELETE A SLIDE

REORDER SLIDES

You can permanently remove a slide that you no longer need.

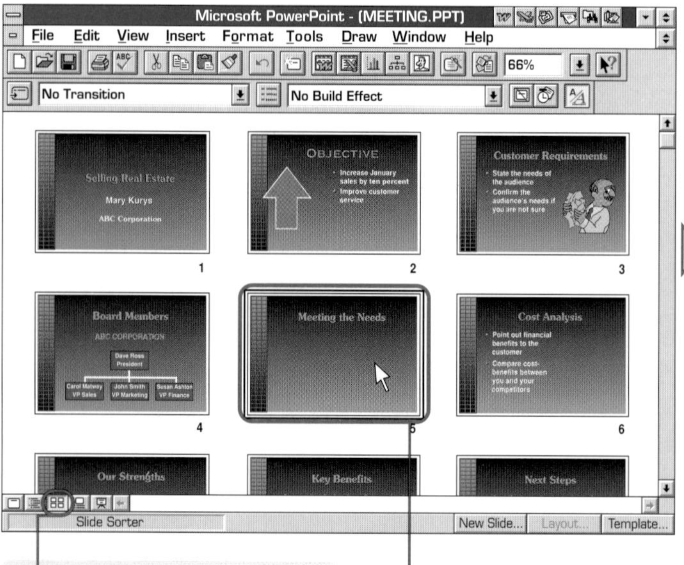

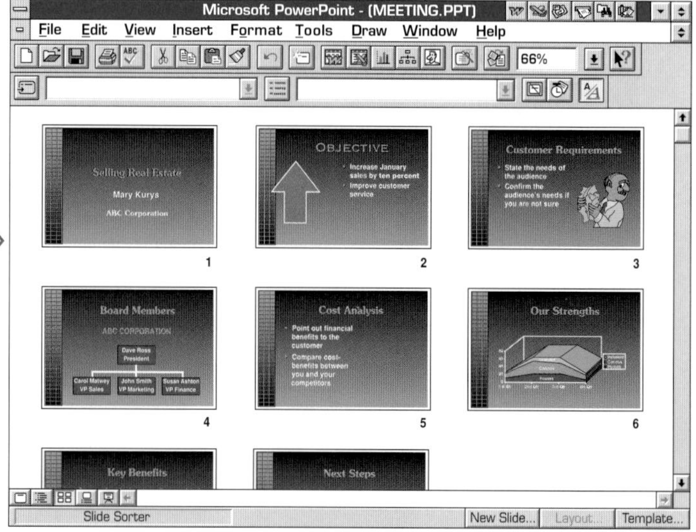

1 To change to the Slide Sorter view, move the mouse over ⊞ and then press the left button.

2 Move the mouse over the slide you want to delete and then press the left button.

3 Press **Delete** and the slide disappears.

REORDER SLIDES

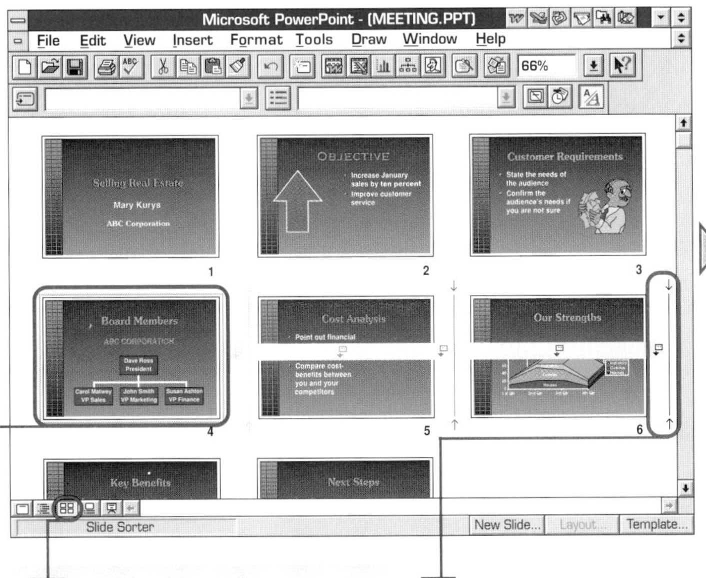

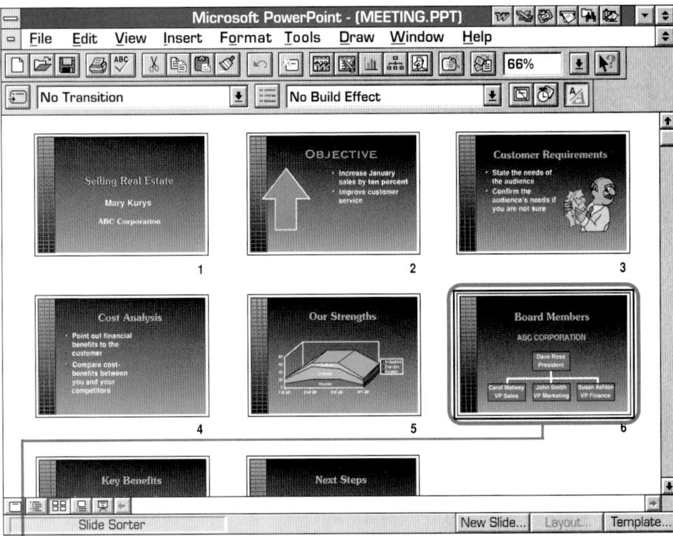

1 To change to the Slide Sorter view, move the mouse ↖ over [88] and then press the left button.

2 Move the mouse ↖ over the slide you want to move to a new location.

3 Press and hold down the left button as you drag the mouse to where you want to place the slide. A line indicates where the slide will appear.

4 Release the button and the slide appears in the new location.

SET UP SLIDES

Before printing your presentation, you must specify the size and orientation you want to use for the different parts of your presentation.

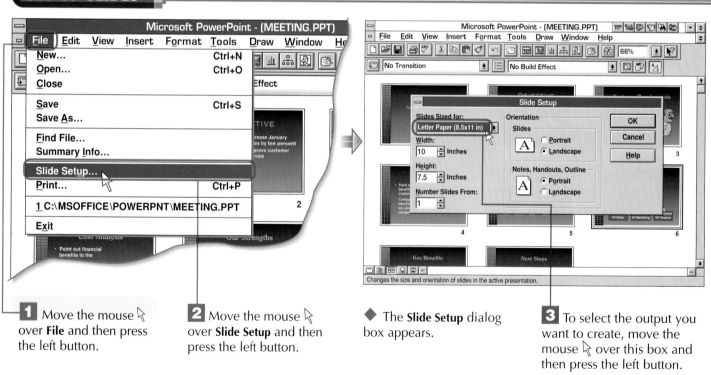

SET UP SLIDES

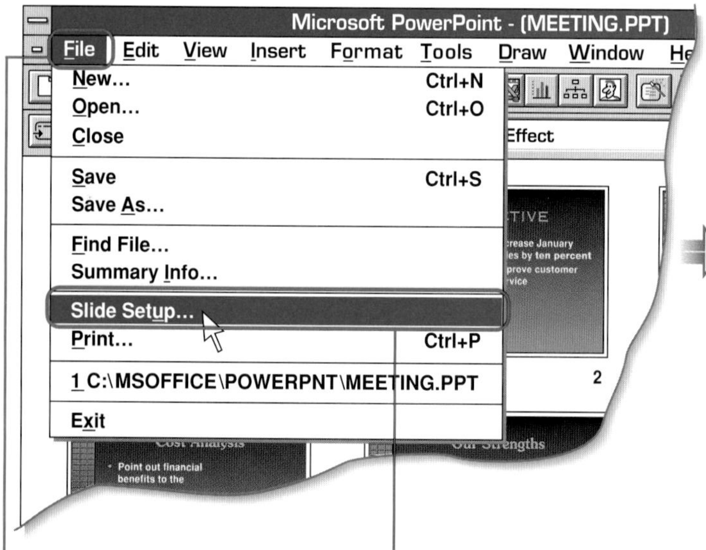

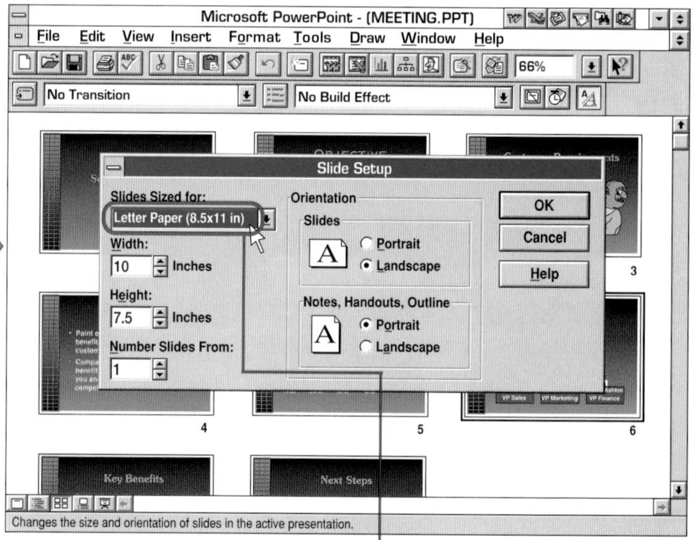

1 Move the mouse over **File** and then press the left button.

2 Move the mouse over **Slide Setup** and then press the left button.

◆ The **Slide Setup** dialog box appears.

3 To select the output you want to create, move the mouse over this box and then press the left button.

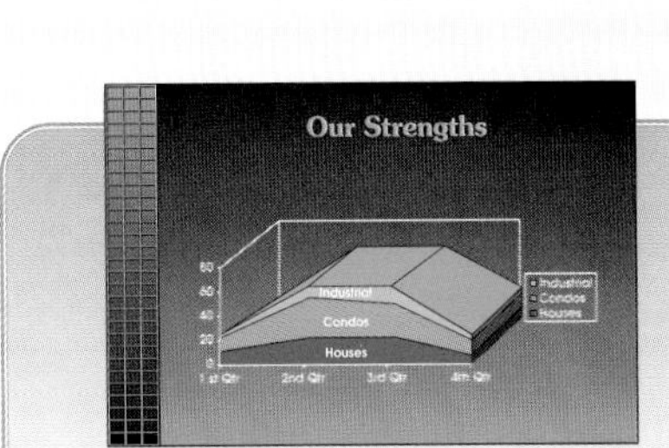

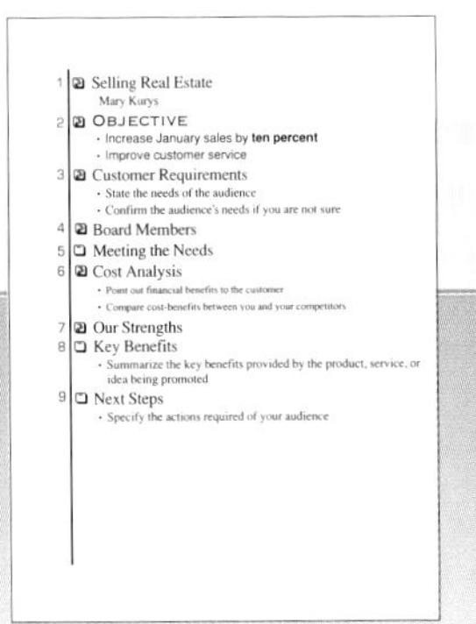

Landscape
This is the usual orientation for slides.

Portrait
This is the usual orientation for your outline, notes and handouts.

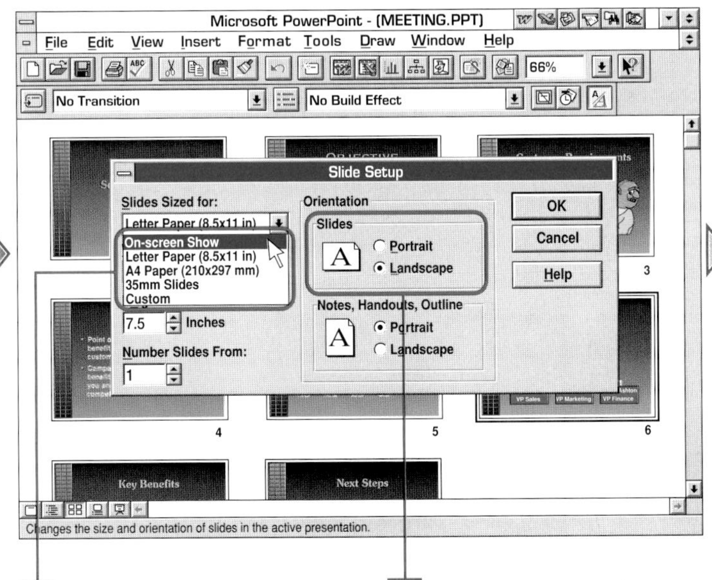

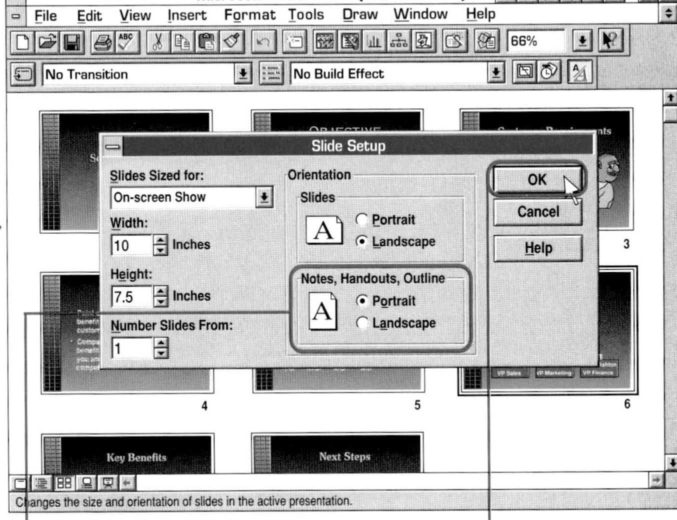

4 Move the mouse over the output you want to create and then press the left button.

*Note: To print overhead transparencies, select the **Letter Paper** option.*

5 Move the mouse over the orientation you want to use for the slides and then press the left button.

6 Move the mouse over the orientation you want to use for the notes, handouts and outline and then press the left button.

7 Move the mouse over **OK** and then press the left button.

PRINT A PRESENTATION

You can print your entire presentation, including your outline, slides, notes and handouts.

PRINT A PRESENTATION

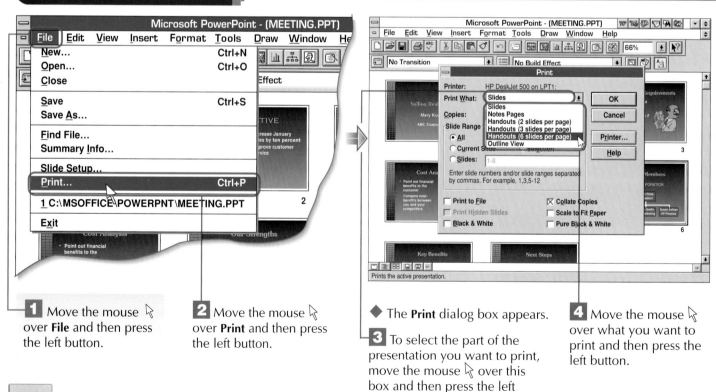

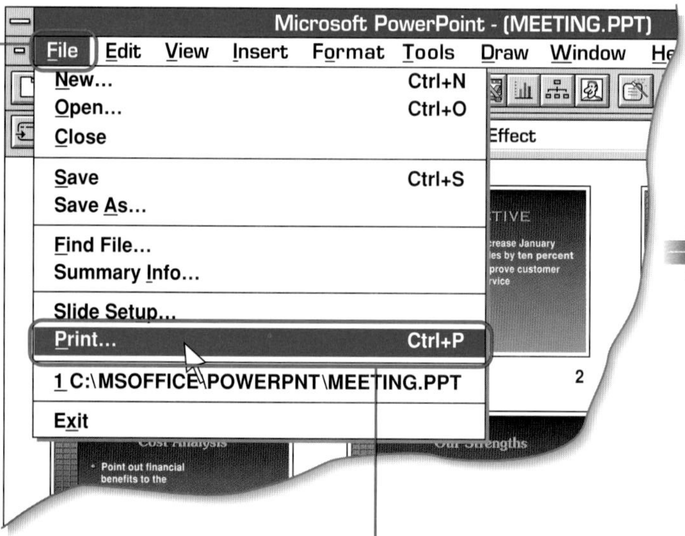

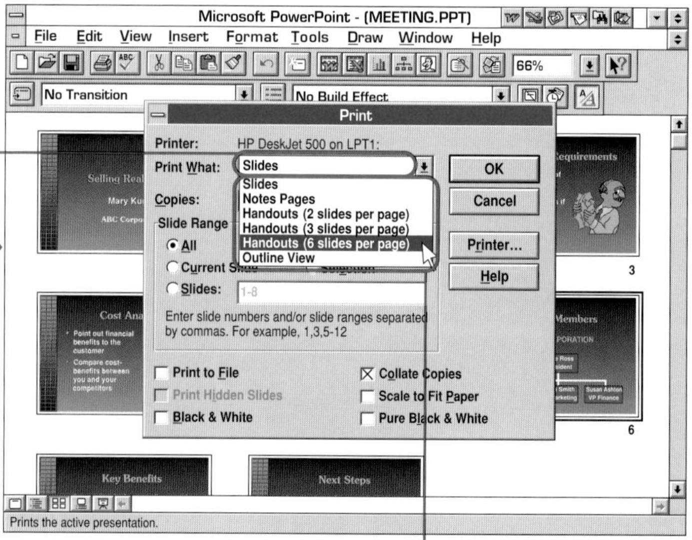

1 Move the mouse over **File** and then press the left button.

2 Move the mouse over **Print** and then press the left button.

◆ The **Print** dialog box appears.

3 To select the part of the presentation you want to print, move the mouse over this box and then press the left button.

4 Move the mouse over what you want to print and then press the left button.

Tip

You can print the following slide ranges:

All	*Prints every slide in the presentation*
Current Slide	*Prints the selected slide or the slide displayed on your screen*
Slides:	*Prints the slides you specify*

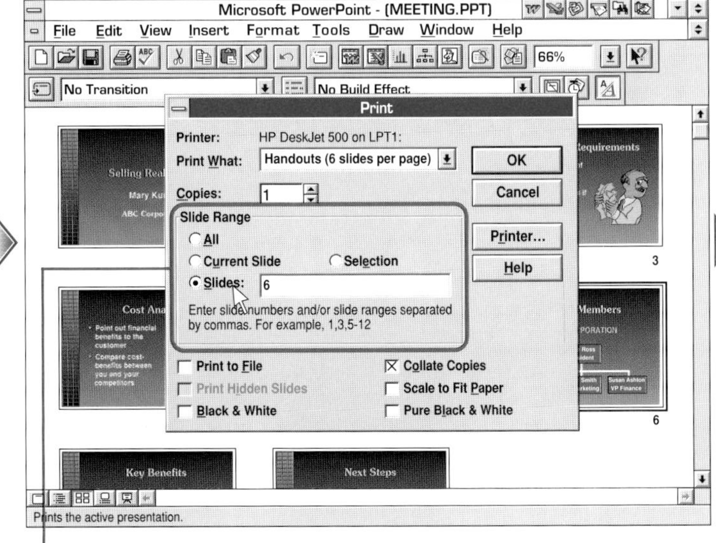

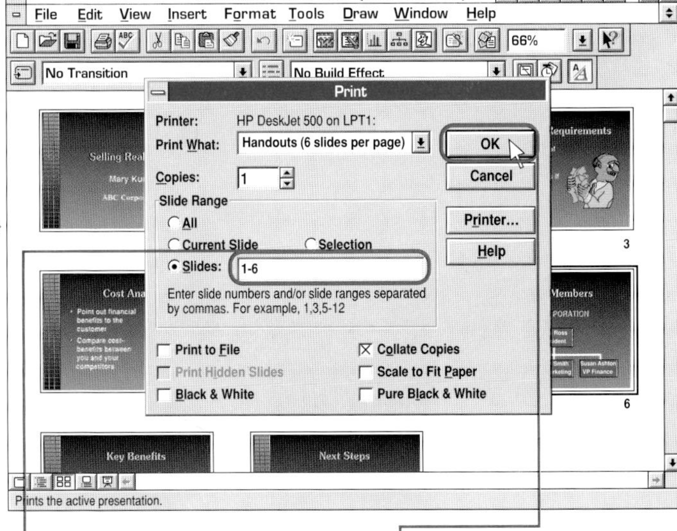

5 Move the mouse over the slide range you want to print (example: **Slides:**) and then press the left button. ○ changes to ◉.

*Note: For information on the slide range options, refer to the **Tip** above.*

6 If you selected **Slides:** in step **5**, press Delete until you remove the existing slide numbers. Then type the slides you want to print (example: **1-6**).

7 Move the mouse over **OK** and then press the left button.

VIEW A SLIDE SHOW

You can view a slide show on your computer screen. During the show, you can use your mouse to draw directly on the slides.
OBJECTIVE
Increase January sales by ten percent
Improve customer service
KRYO

VIEW A SLIDE SHOW

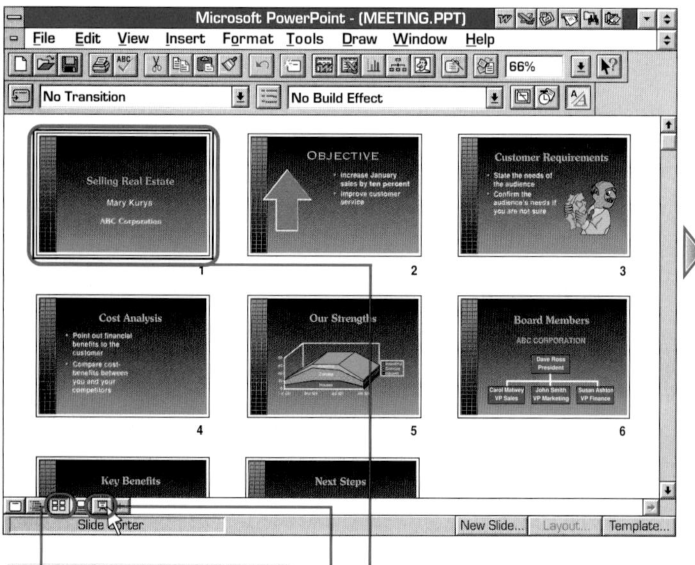

1 To change to the Slide Sorter view, move the mouse over and then press the left button.

2 To select the slide you want to begin the slide show, move the mouse over the slide and then press the left button.

3 To start the slide show, move the mouse over and then press the left button.

◆ The slide you selected appears on your screen.

*Note: You can cancel the slide show at any time by pressing **Esc** on your keyboard.*

4 To display the next slide, press the left mouse button or the **Spacebar**.

*Note: To display the previous slide, press the **right** mouse button.*

The lines you draw on a slide during a slide show are temporary. They will not appear when the slide show is over.

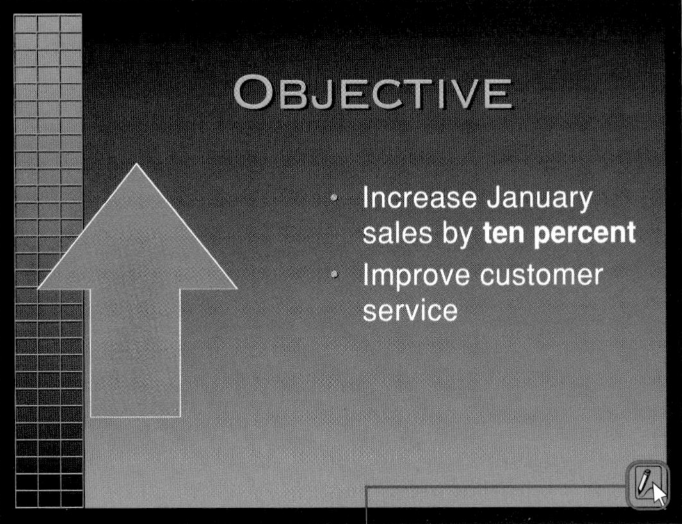

◆ The next slide appears.

5 To draw on the screen, move the mouse over and then press the left button (changes to).

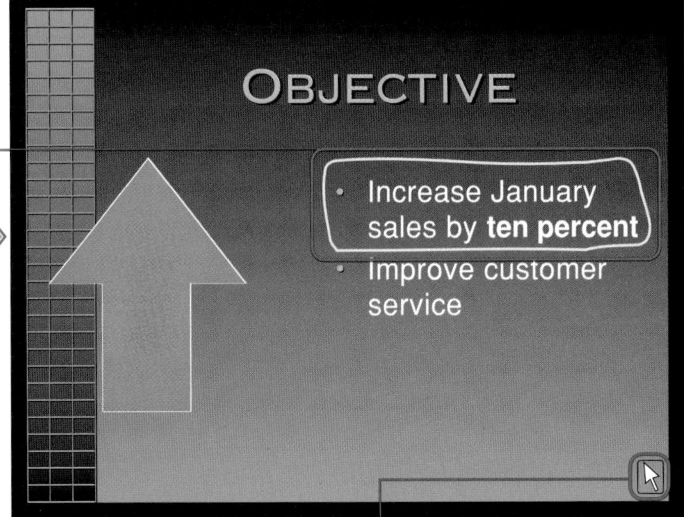

6 Move the mouse over the area where you want to begin drawing.

7 Press and hold down the left button as you drag the mouse around the area you want to emphasize. Then release the button.

8 When you finish drawing, move the mouse over and then press the left button.

9 Repeat step 4 until you finish viewing all the slides in your slide show.

REHEARSE A SLIDE SHOW

You can rehearse your slide show and have PowerPoint record the amount of time you spend on each slide.

REHEARSE A SLIDE SHOW

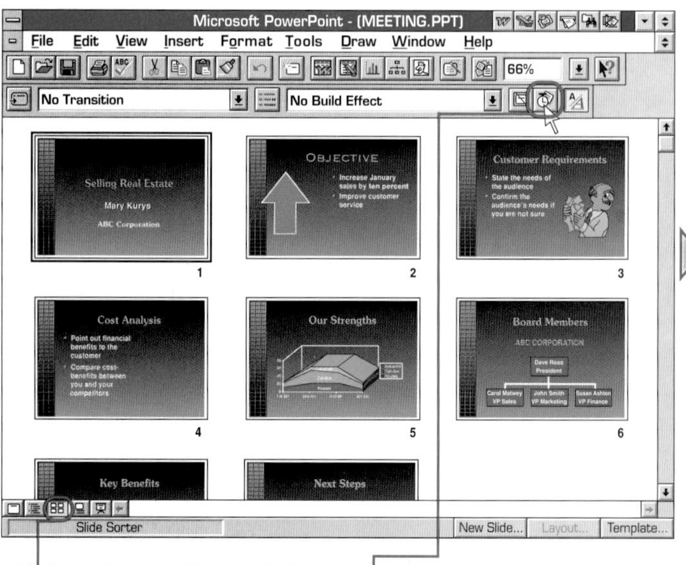

1 To change to the Slide Sorter view, move the mouse over and then press the left button.

2 To start the slide show, move the mouse over and then press the left button.

◆ The first slide in your slide show appears.

◆ A clock appears at the bottom of your screen, recording the amount of time you spend on each slide.

3 When you finish talking and want to display the next slide, press the left mouse button.

*Note: To display the previous slide, press the **right** mouse button.*

You can quit the slide show at any time by pressing Esc on your keyboard.

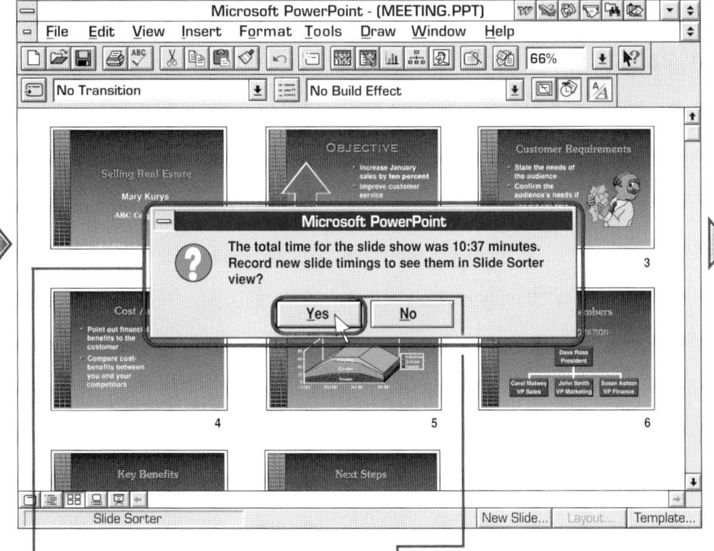

◆ This dialog box appears when you finish your slide show. It displays the total time it took to deliver your presentation.

4 To display the time you spent on each slide, move the mouse over **Yes** and then press the left button.

*Note: If you do not want to display the time, move the mouse over **No** and then press the left button.*

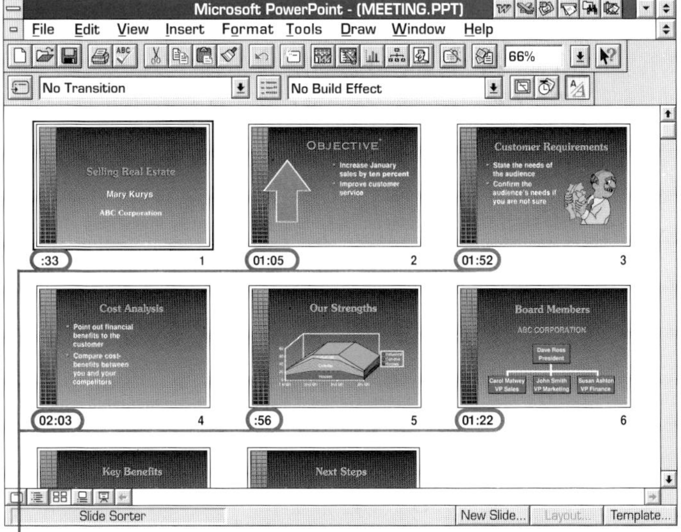

◆ PowerPoint displays the time you spent on each slide.

ADD BUILDS TO SLIDES

OBJECTIVE
Increase January sales by ten percent
During a slide show, you can increase interest by revealing the points on a slide one at a time.

ADD BUILDS TO SLIDES

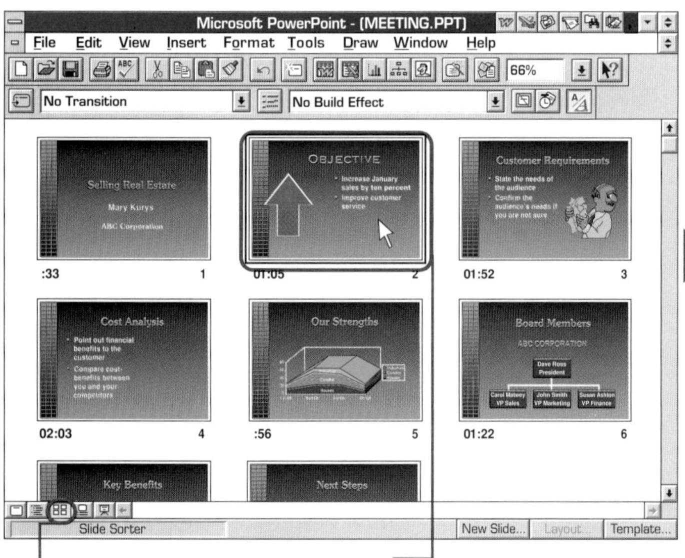

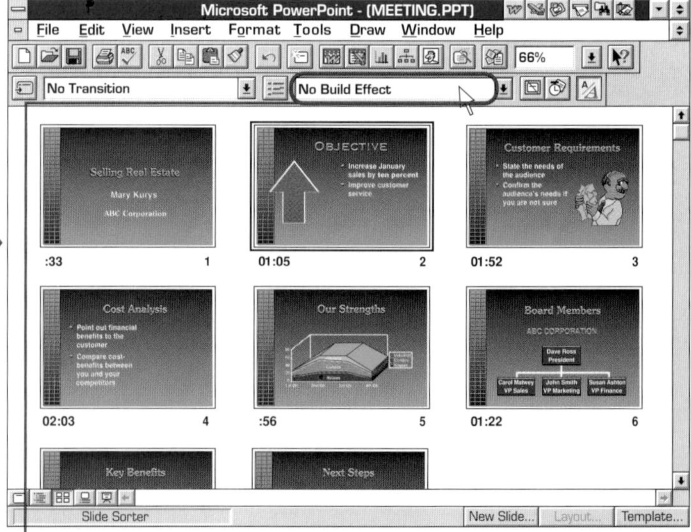

1 To change to the Slide Sorter view, move the mouse over [Slide Sorter icon] and then press the left button.

2 Move the mouse over the slide you want to reveal points one at a time and then press the left button.

3 Move the mouse over this box and then press the left button.

After you add builds to a slide, you can display the points one at a time during a slide show.

◆ *To display the next point on a slide, press the left mouse button or the* ***Spacebar****.*

Note: For information on viewing a slide show, refer to page 322.

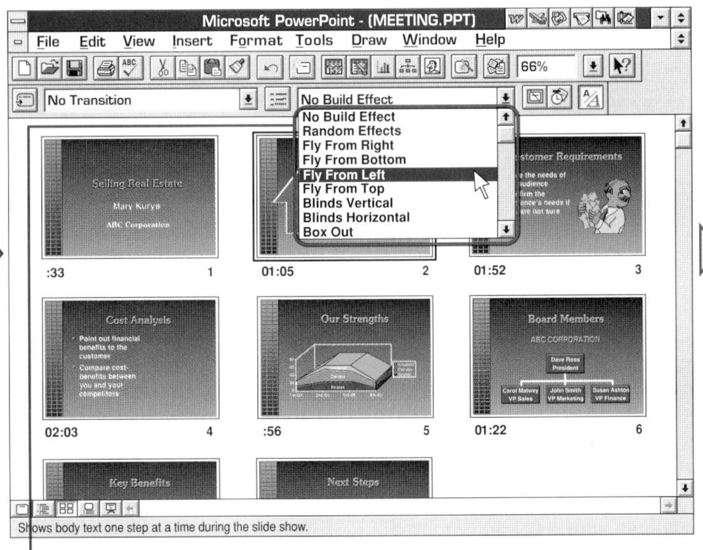

4 Move the mouse over the way you want to reveal points on the slide and then press the left button.

Note: To browse through the available options, move the mouse over ⬇ or ⬆ and then press the left button.

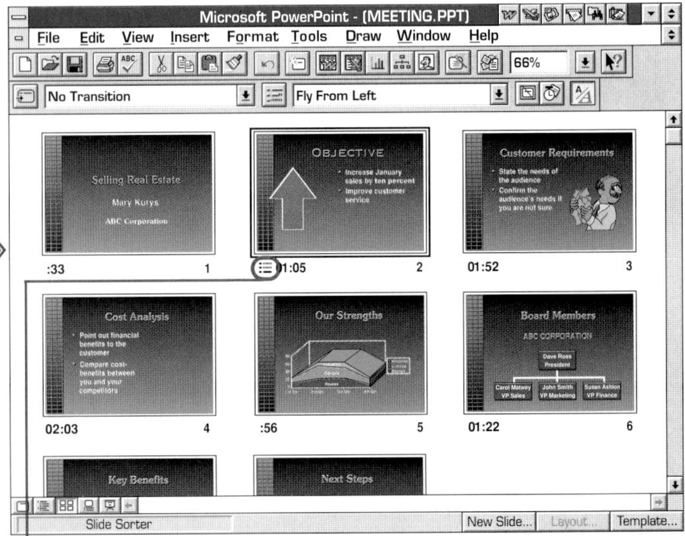

◆ The symbol appears below the slide.

ADD SLIDE TRANSITIONS

During a slide show, you can display visual effects as you move from one slide to the next. These effects are called transitions.

ADD SLIDE TRANSITIONS

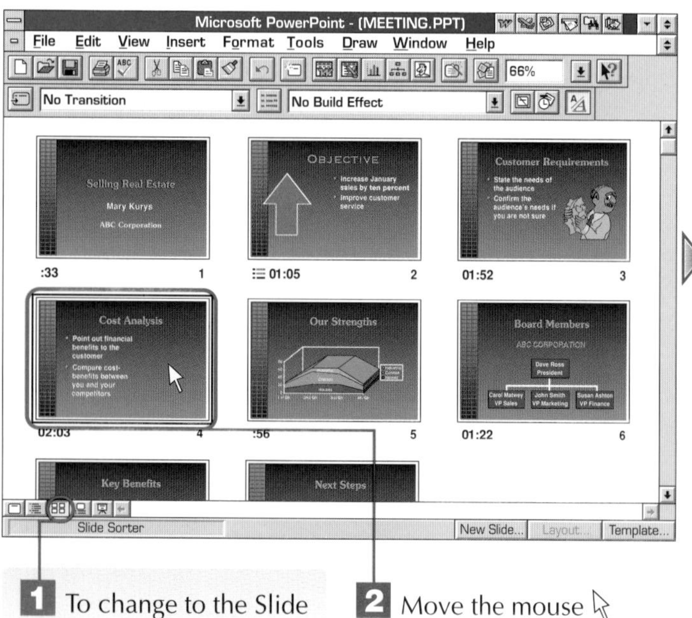

1 To change to the Slide Sorter view, move the mouse over 88 and then press the left button.

2 Move the mouse over the slide you want to display the transition and then press the left button.

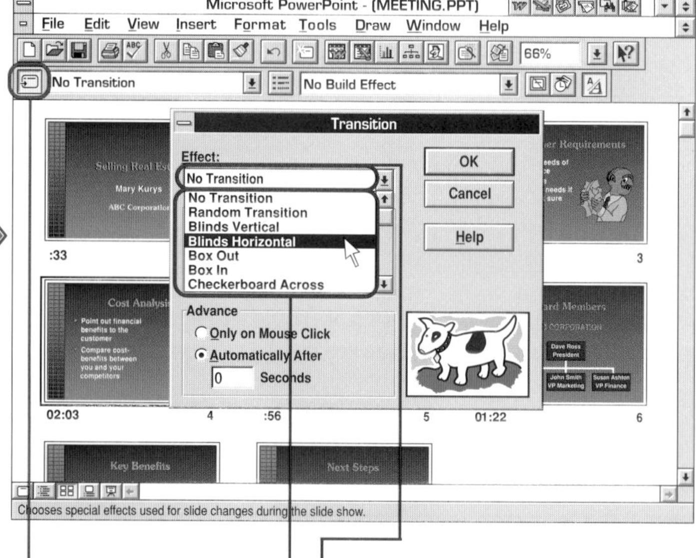

3 Move the mouse over and then press the left button.

◆ The **Transition** dialog box appears.

4 To display a list of the available transitions, move the mouse over this box and then press the left button.

5 Move the mouse over the transition you want to use and then press the left button.

- Add Speaker's Notes
- Delete a Slide
- Reorder Slides
- Set Up Slides
- Print a Presentation
- View a Slide Show
- Rehearse a Slide Show
- Add Builds to Slides
- **Add Slide Transitions**

Tip

To quickly select a transition:

1 Perform steps 1 and 2 on page 328.

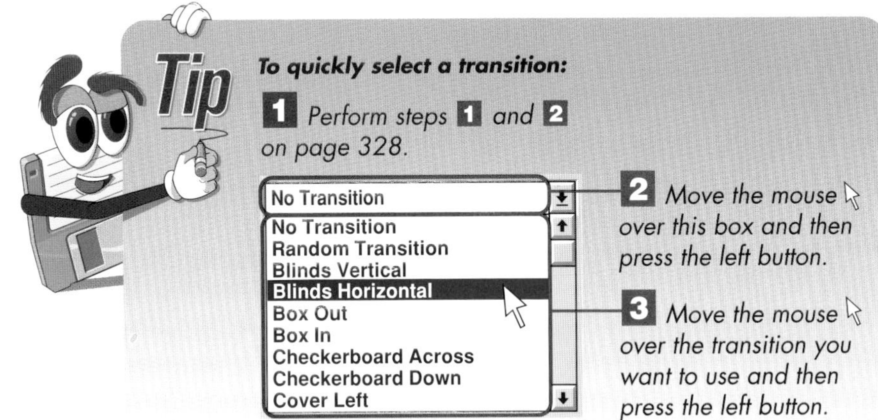

2 Move the mouse over this box and then press the left button.

3 Move the mouse over the transition you want to use and then press the left button.

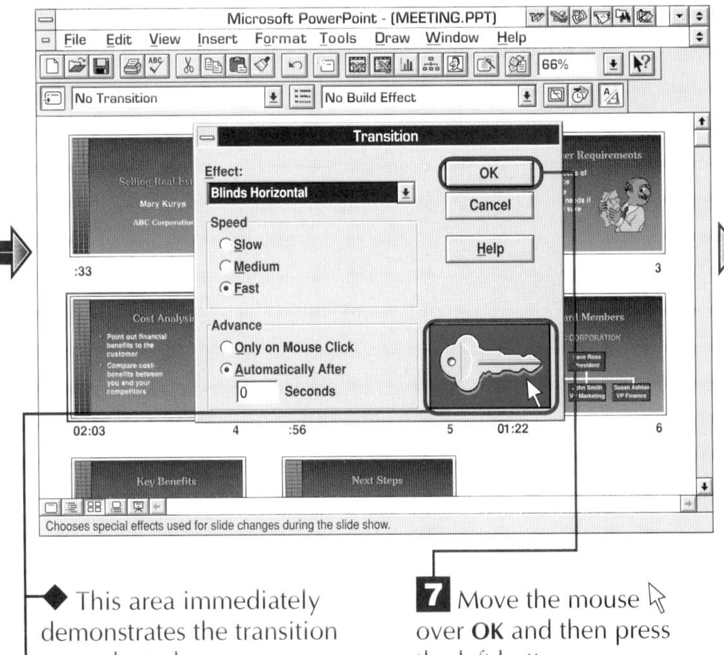

◆ This area immediately demonstrates the transition you selected.

6 To view the transition again, move the mouse over this area and then press the left button.

7 Move the mouse over **OK** and then press the left button.

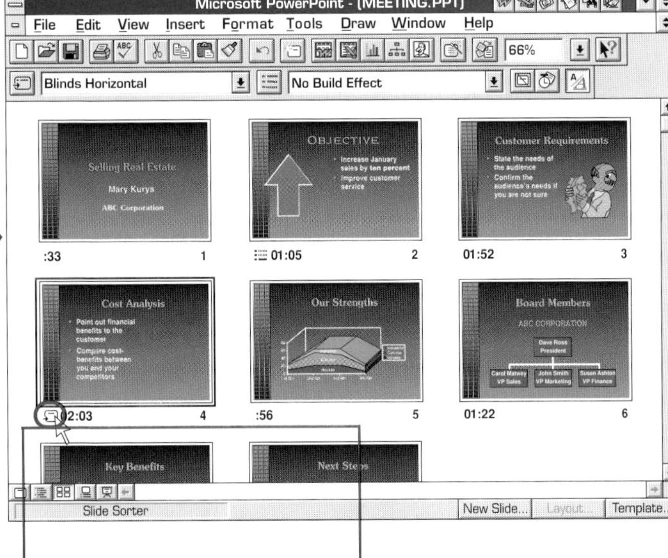

◆ The symbol appears below the slide.

8 To view the transition, move the mouse over and then press the left button.

In this section you will learn how to exchange messages with other people connected to a network.
Mary Kurys
27 Willow Avenue
Los Angeles, CA 90032
Carol Walthers
Mary Kurys
27 Willow Avenue
Los Angeles, CA 90032

MAIL

START MAIL

Microsoft Mail lets you exchange messages with other people on a network.

A network is a group of computers connected together to allow people to exchange information.

START MAIL

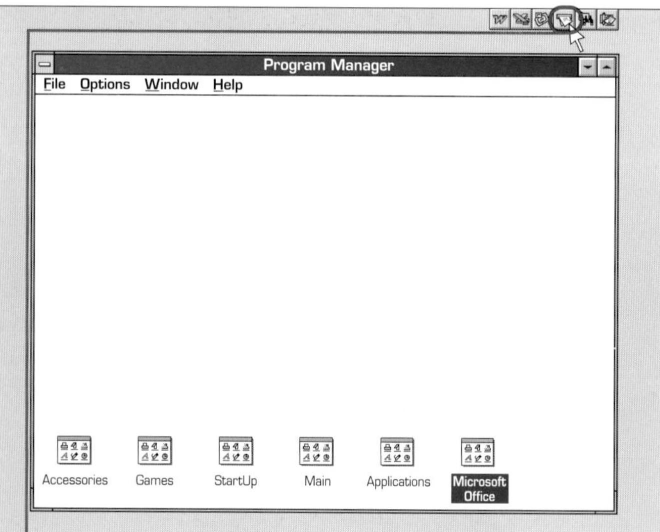

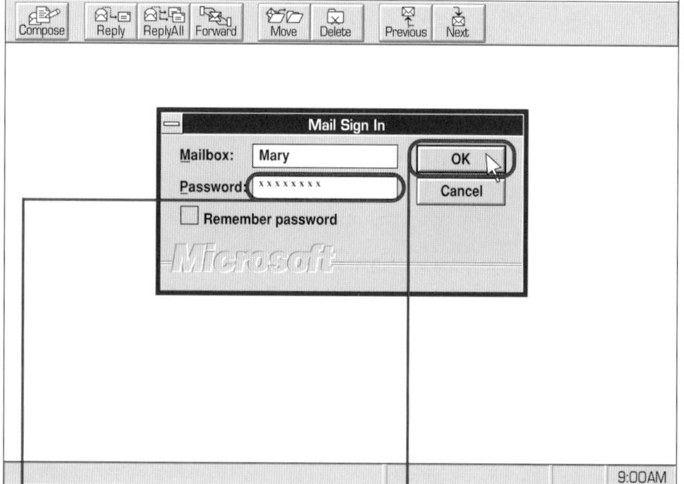

1 Move the mouse over and then press the left button.

Note: If this is the first time you are using Mail, refer to the ***Tip*** *on page 333.*

◆ The **Mail Sign In** dialog box appears.

2 Type your password. A symbol (x) appears for each character you type.

Note: A password ensures that you are the only one who can read your messages.

3 Move the mouse over **OK** and then press the left button.

This dialog box appears the first time you start Mail. Before using Mail, you must connect to a postoffice to identify where your mail will be stored.

To connect to a postoffice, ask your network or Mail administrator.

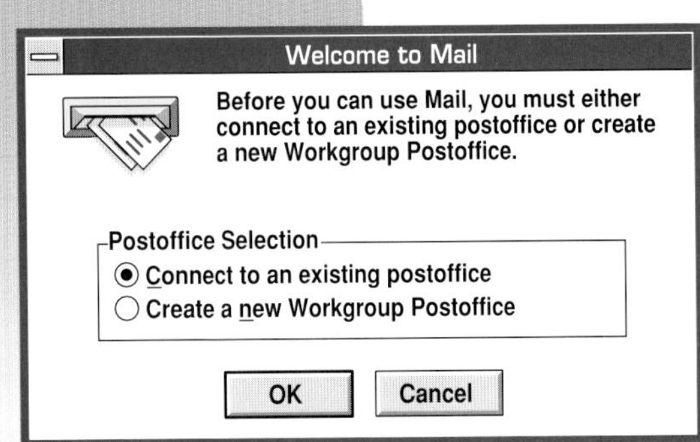

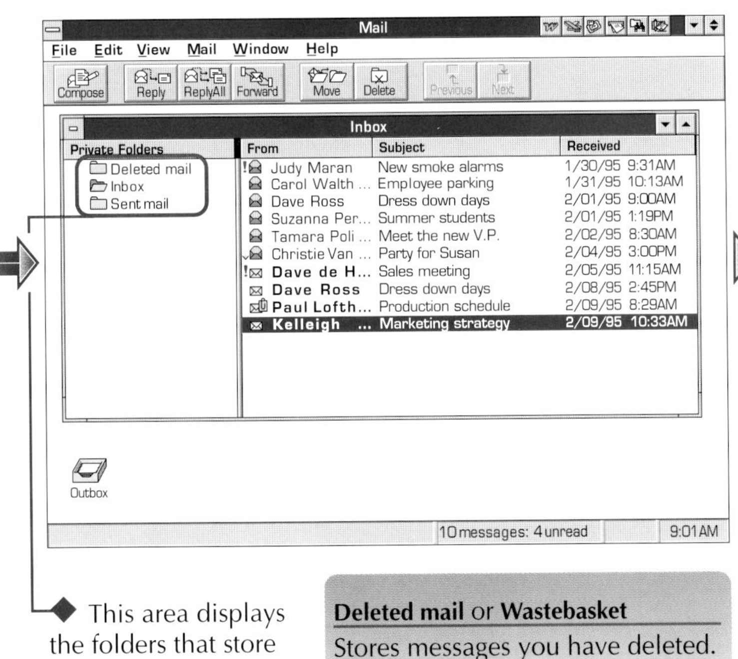

Mail
File Edit View Mail Window Help
Compose Reply ReplyAll Forward Move Delete Previous Next
Sent mail
Private Folders: Deleted mail, Inbox, Sent mail
From | Subject | Received
Outbox
0 messages
9:02AM

◆ This area displays the folders that store your messages.

Deleted mail or **Wastebasket**

Stores messages you have deleted.

Inbox

Stores messages sent to you.

Sent mail

Stores messages you have sent.

4 To display the contents of a folder, move the mouse over the folder (example: **Sent mail**) and then quickly press the left button twice.

◆ This area displays the contents of the folder you selected. You can only display the contents of one folder at a time.

Note: In this example, no messages have been sent.

SEND A MESSAGE

You can easily send a message to another person on your network.

SEND A MESSAGE

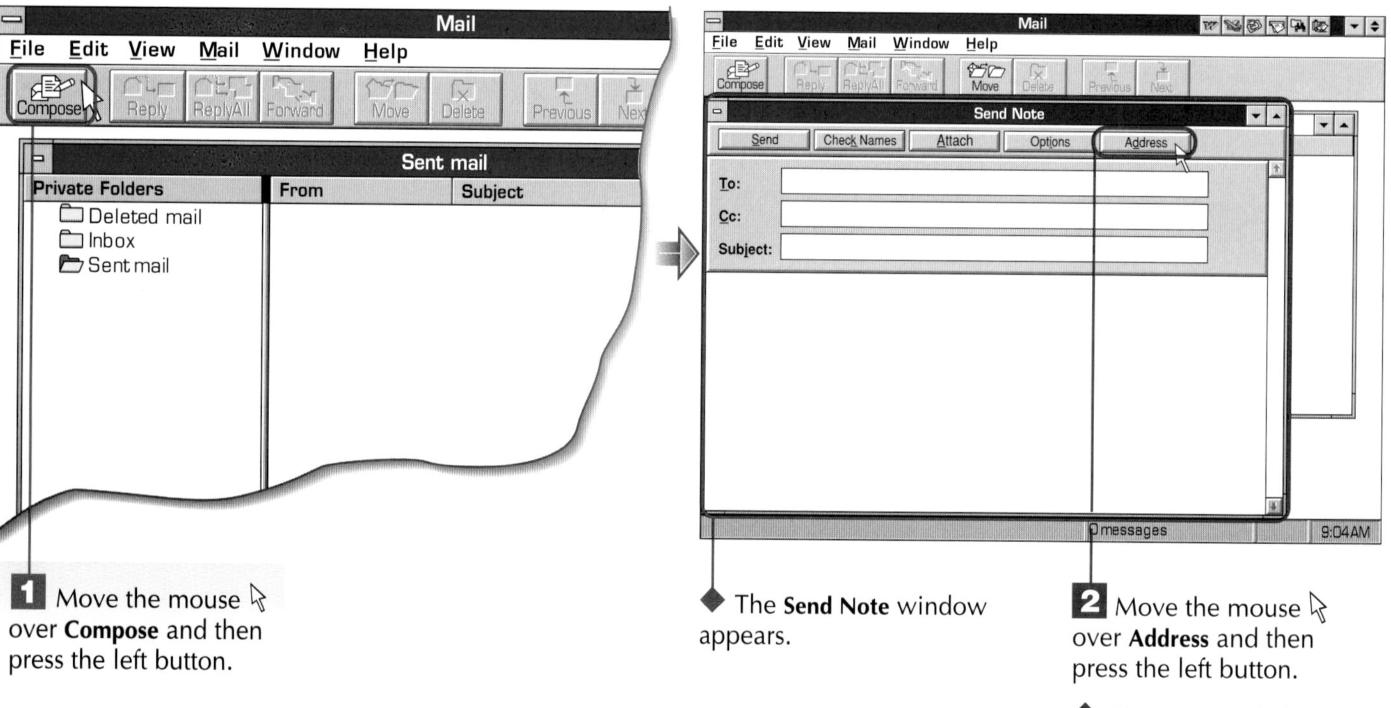

1 Move the mouse over **Compose** and then press the left button.

◆ The **Send Note** window appears.

2 Move the mouse over **Address** and then press the left button.

◆ The **Address** dialog box appears.

You can send a courtesy copy of your message to a person who is not directly involved but would be interested in your message.

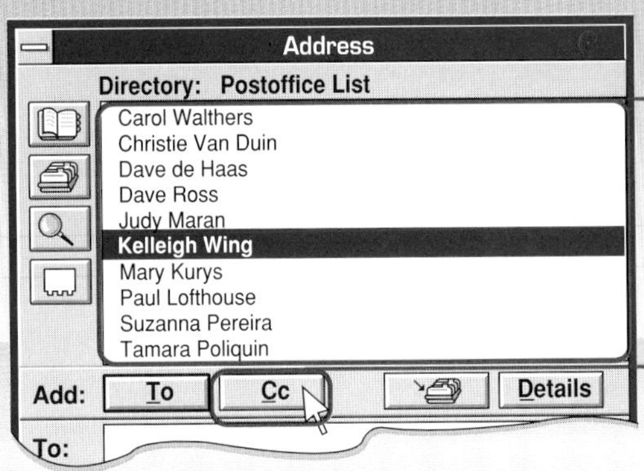

1 *In the **Address** dialog box, move the mouse over the name of the person you want to send a courtesy copy to and then press the left button.*

2 *Move the mouse over **Cc** and then press the left button.*

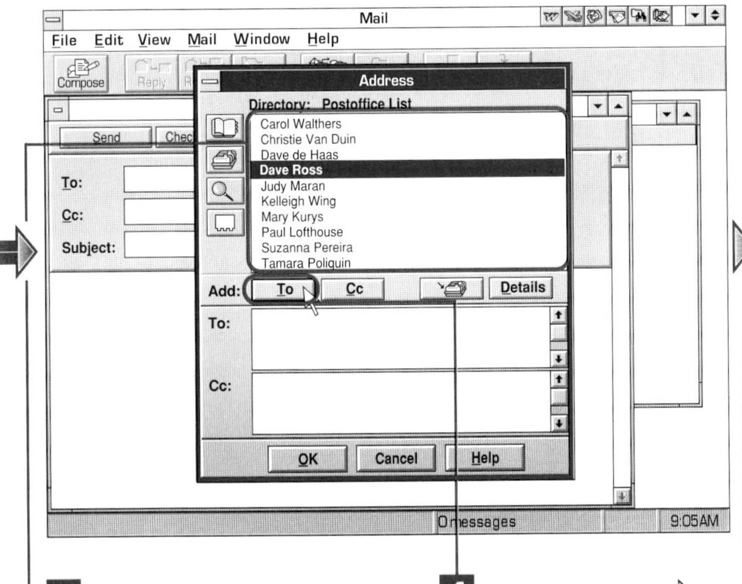

3 To select the person you want to send the message to, move the mouse over the person's name (example: **Dave Ross**) and then press the left button.

4 Move the mouse over **To** and then press the left button.

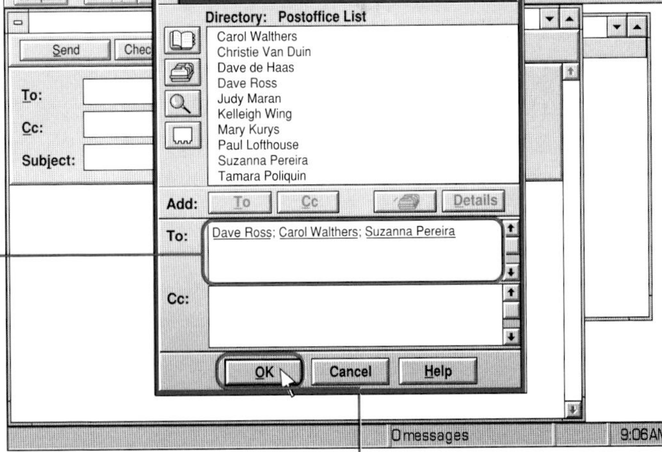

◆ This area displays the names of the people who will receive the message.

◆ To send the message to more than one person, repeat steps **3** and **4** for each person.

5 Move the mouse over **OK** and then press the left button.

SEND A MESSAGE

RECEIVED
Sending messages lets you efficiently exchange ideas, request information and organize meetings.

SEND A MESSAGE (CONTINUED)

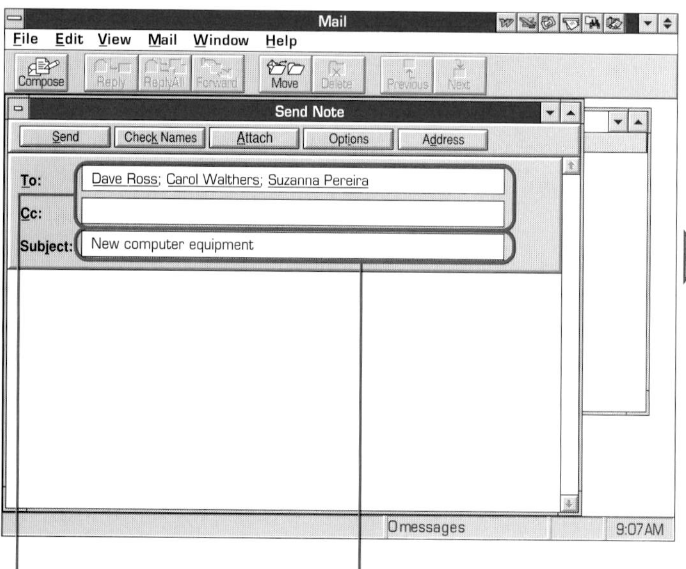

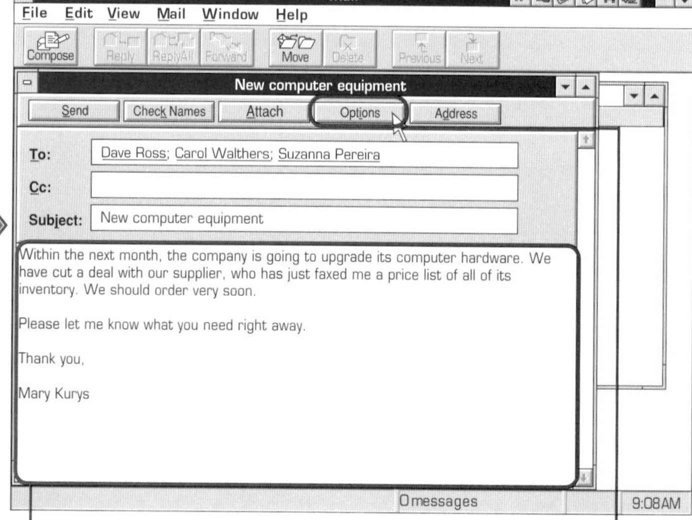

◆ This area displays the name of each person who will receive your message.

6 To enter a subject for the message, move the mouse I over the box beside **Subject:** and then press the left button. Then type the subject of your message.

7 To enter the message, move the mouse I over this area and then press the left button. Then type your message.

Note: If you make a typing error, press **←Backspace** *and then retype.*

8 To set the message options, move the mouse ↖ over **Options** and then press the left button.

◆ The **Options** dialog box appears.

You can have Mail let you know when a person has read your message by using the Return receipt option.

From	Subject	Received
! Dave Ross	Registered: Dave Ross	1/28/95 9:10AM

◆ *When a person reads your message, Mail will send you a message with the word* ***Registered:*** *displayed before the subject.*

Note: To select the ***Return receipt*** *option, perform step* **9** *below.*

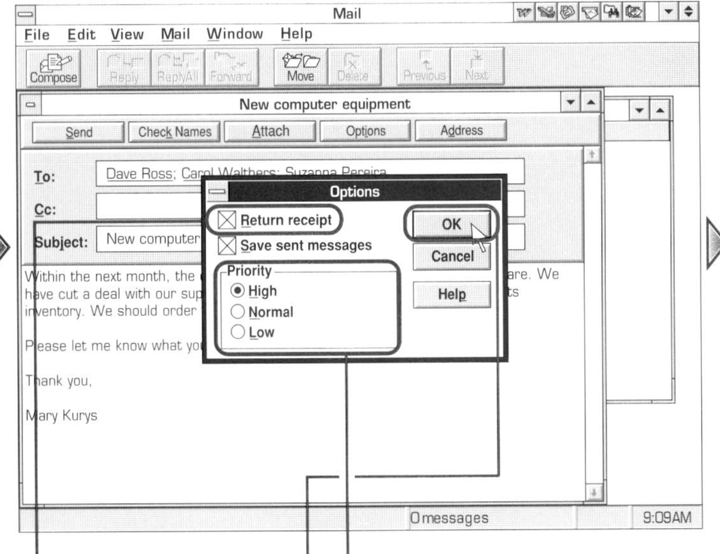

9 If you want to know when each person reads your message, move the mouse ⇖ over **Return receipt** and then press the left button (☐ changes to ☒).

10 To indicate the importance of the message, move the mouse ⇖ over a priority option and then press the left button (○ changes to ◉).

11 Move the mouse ⇖ over **OK** and then press the left button.

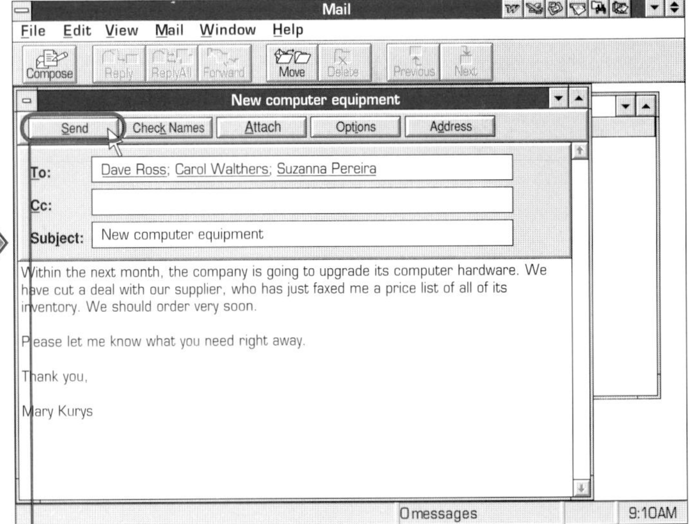

12 To send the message, move the mouse ⇖ over **Send** and then press the left button.

ATTACH A FILE TO A MESSAGE

You can attach a file to a message. This is useful when you want to include additional information with your message.
Mary Kurys
Paul Lofthouse

ATTACH A FILE TO A MESSAGE

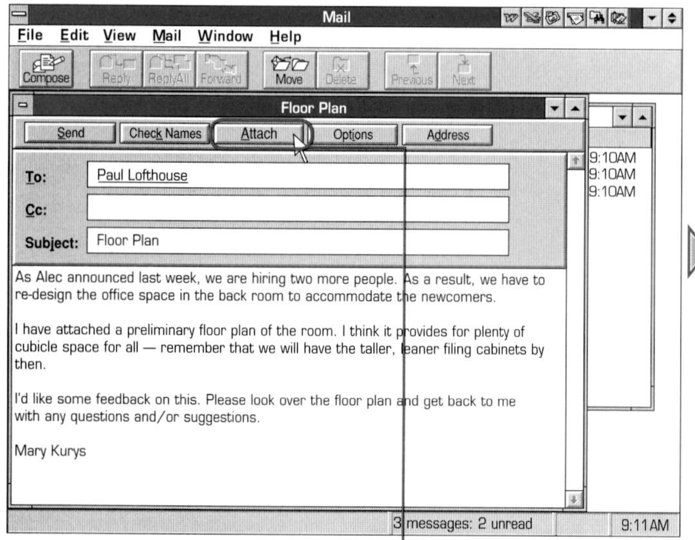

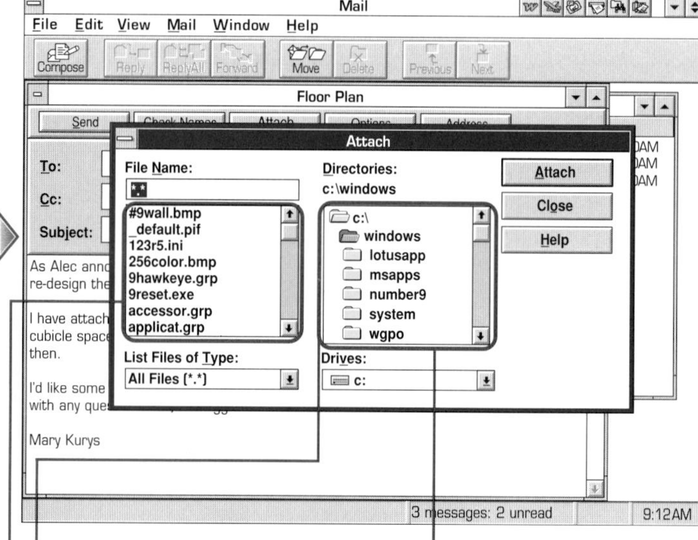

1 Create a message by performing steps **1** to **11**, starting on page 334.

2 Move the mouse over **Attach** and then press the left button.

◆ The **Attach** dialog box appears.

◆ This area displays the folders stored on your hard drive. The current folder appears darker than the other folders.

◆ This area displays the files stored in the current folder.

3 Move through the folders until you find the file you want to attach.

Note: To move through the folders, refer to your Windows manual.

Tip
To view a file attached to a message, move the mouse over the picture and then quickly press the left button twice.
FLOORPLN.BMP

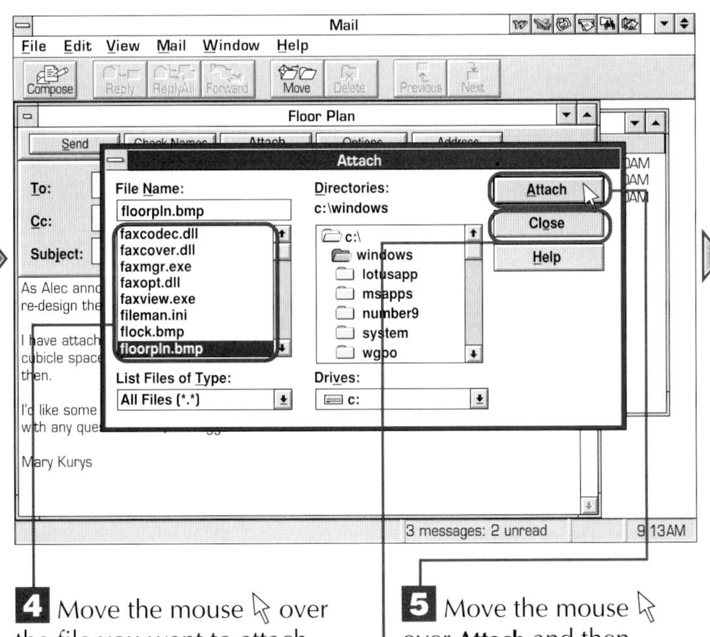

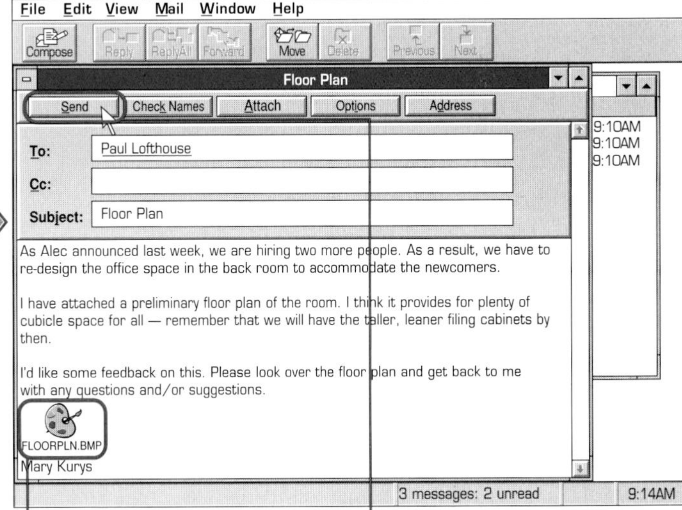

4 Move the mouse over the file you want to attach (example: **floorpln.bmp**) and then press the left button.

5 Move the mouse over **Attach** and then press the left button.

6 Move the mouse over **Close** and then press the left button.

◆ The name of the file appears with a small picture in the message.

7 To send the message, move the mouse over **Send** and then press the left button.

READ MESSAGES

READ MESSAGES

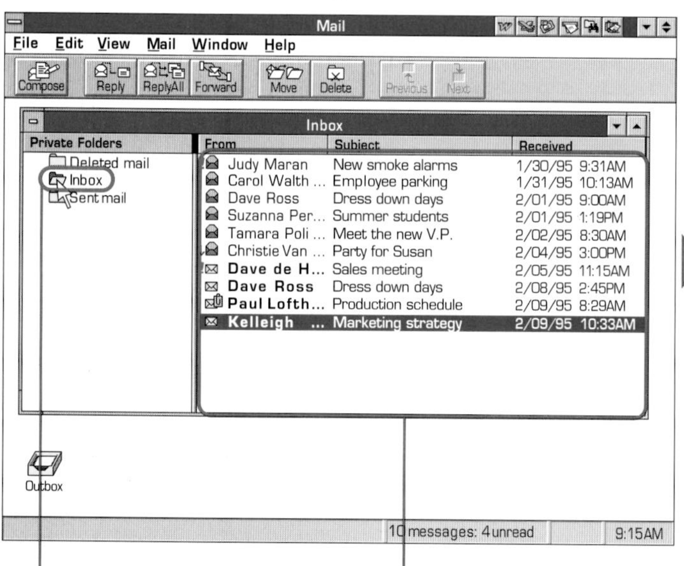

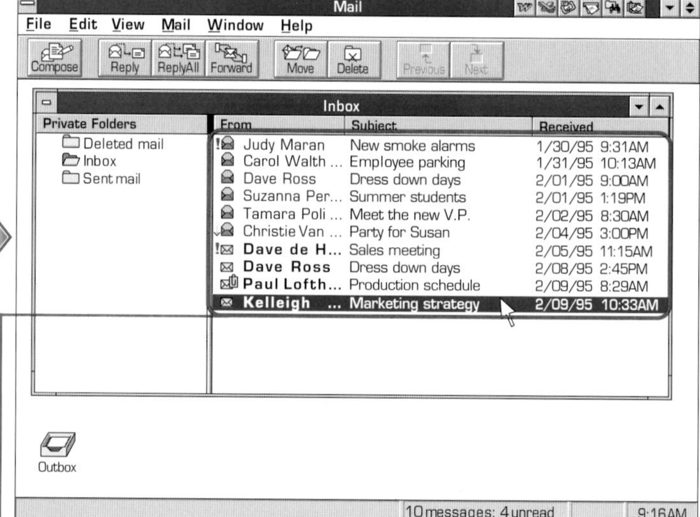

1 To display a list of all the messages sent to you, move the mouse ⇖ over the **Inbox** folder and then quickly press the left button twice.

◆ This area displays a list of all your messages. It includes the subject of each message and the date and time it was received.

2 To read a message, move the mouse ⇖ over the message and then quickly press the left button twice.

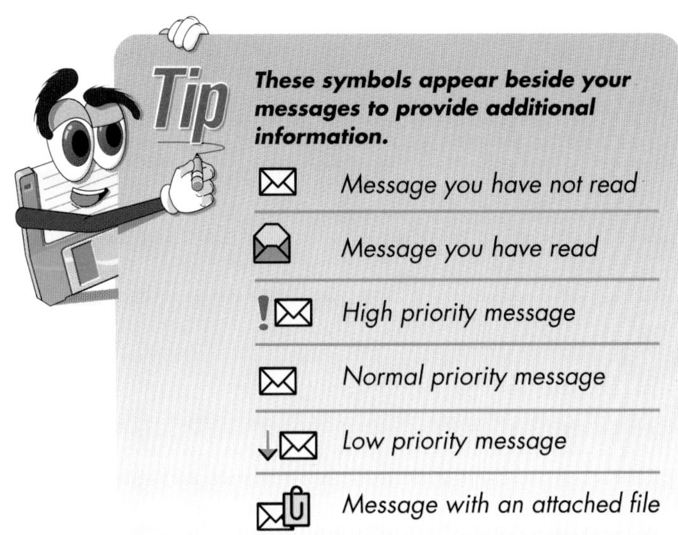

These symbols appear beside your messages to provide additional information.

Message you have not read

Message you have read

High priority message

Normal priority message

Low priority message

Message with an attached file

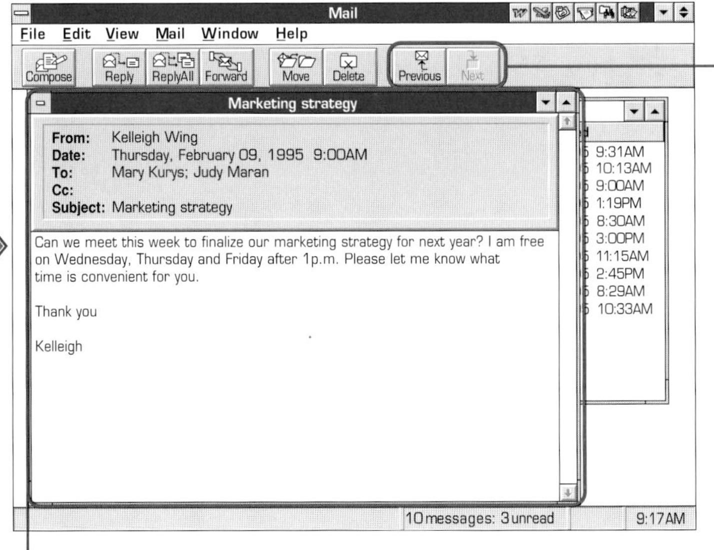

◆ The contents of the message appear.

3 When you finish reading the message, press **Esc** on your keyboard.

When you finish reading a message, you can use the Previous and Next buttons to quickly move through your messages.

◆ To read the previous message, move the mouse over **Previous** and then press the left button.

◆ To read the next message, move the mouse over **Next** and then press the left button.

REPLY TO A MESSAGE

After reading a message, you can send a reply. This lets you comment on the message or answer questions.
MESSAGES
FROM:
DATE:
SUBJECT:
MESSAGES
FROM: Kelleigh Wing
DATE: Thursday Feb. 9/95
SUBJECT: Marketing Strategy

REPLY TO A MESSAGE

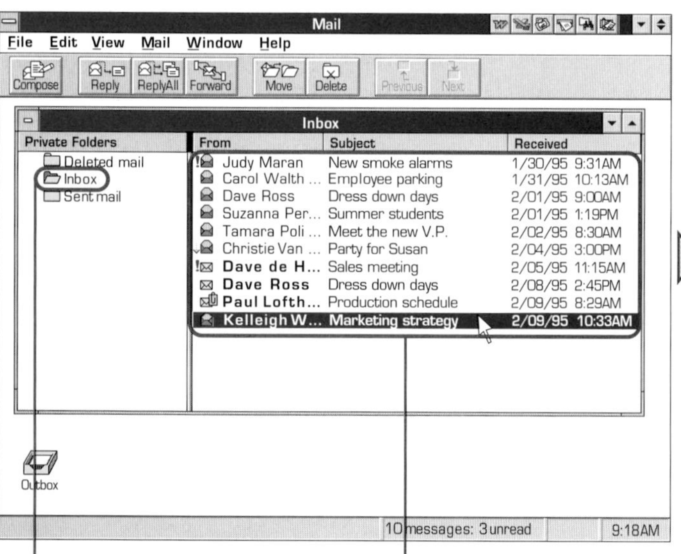

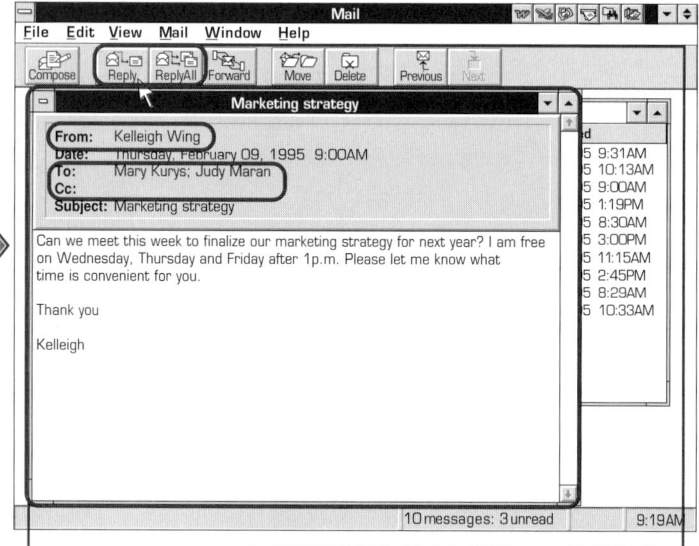

1 To display a list of all the messages sent to you, move the mouse ⇖ over the **Inbox** folder and then quickly press the left button twice.

2 To display the message you want to reply to, move the mouse ⇖ over the message and then quickly press the left button twice.

◆ The message appears.

3 To send a reply just to the person who sent the message, move the mouse ⇖ over **Reply** and then press the left button.

◆ To send a reply to the person who sent the message and to every person listed beside **To:** and **Cc:**, move the mouse ⇖ over **ReplyAll** and then press the left button.

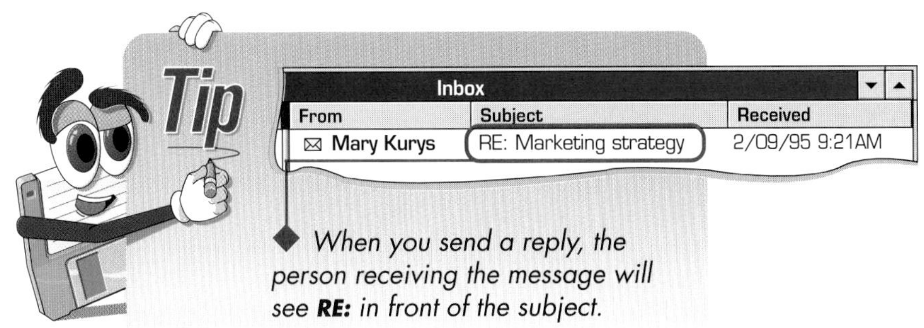

When you send a reply, the person receiving the message will see ***RE:*** *in front of the subject.*

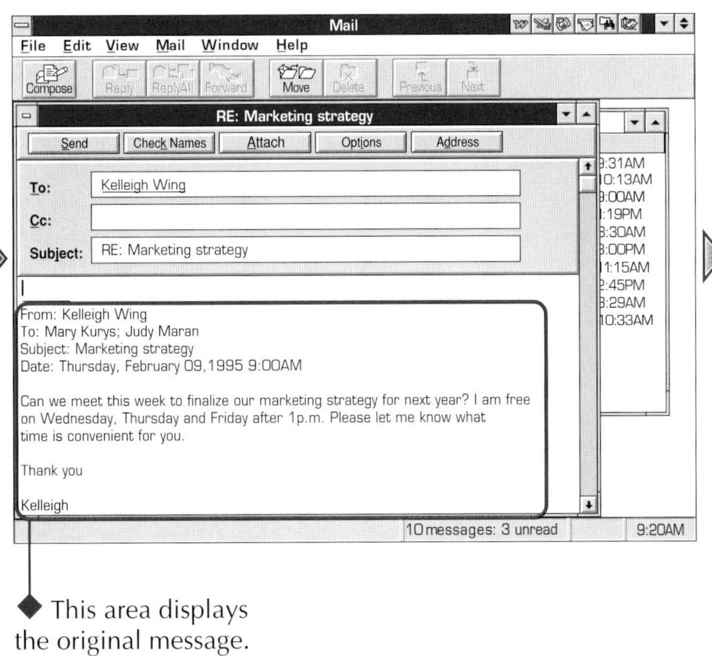

This area displays the original message.

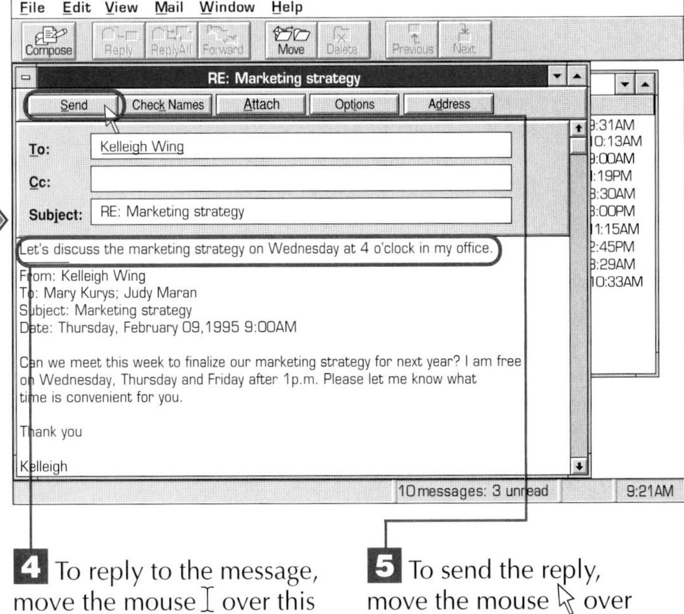

4 To reply to the message, move the mouse I over this area and then press the left button. Then type your reply.

5 To send the reply, move the mouse over **Send** and then press the left button.

FORWARD A MESSAGE

After reading a message, you can add comments and then forward the message to a colleague.

FORWARD A MESSAGE

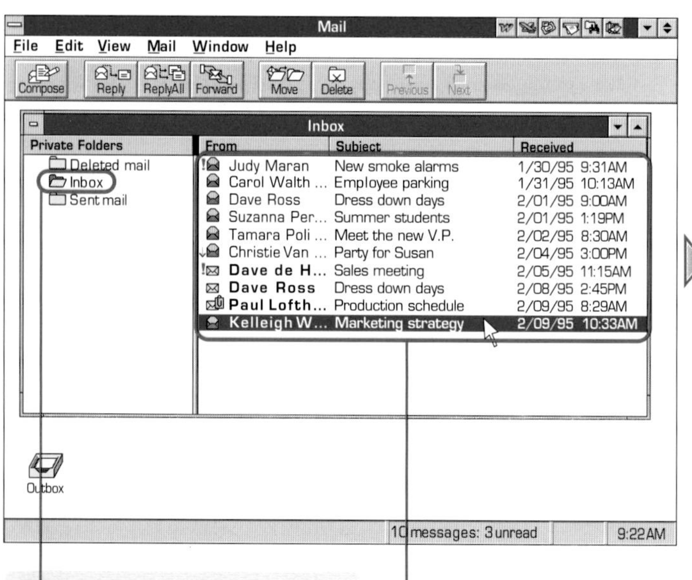

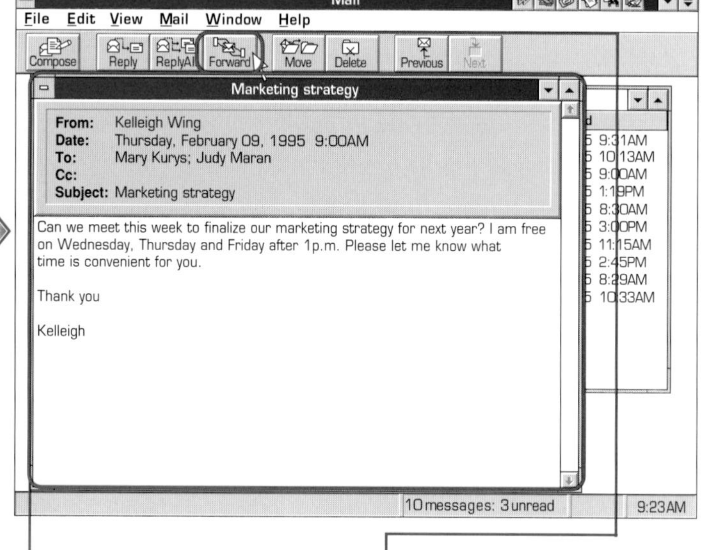

1 To display a list of all the messages sent to you, move the mouse over the **Inbox** folder and then quickly press the left button twice.

2 To display the message you want to forward, move the mouse over the message and then quickly press the left button twice.

◆ The message appears.

3 Move the mouse over **Forward** and then press the left button.

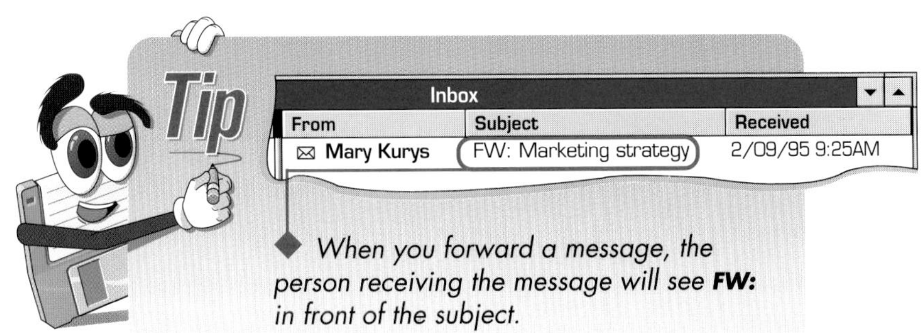

◆ *When you forward a message, the person receiving the message will see **FW:** in front of the subject.*

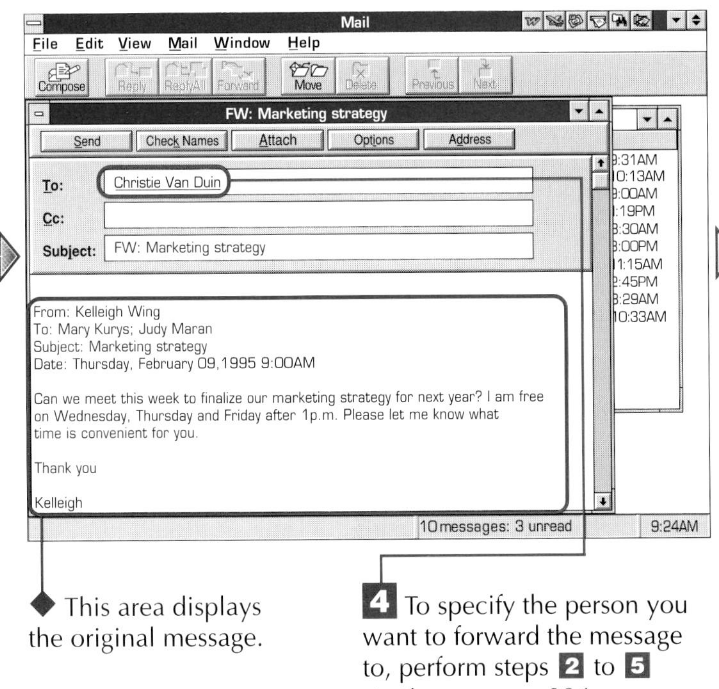

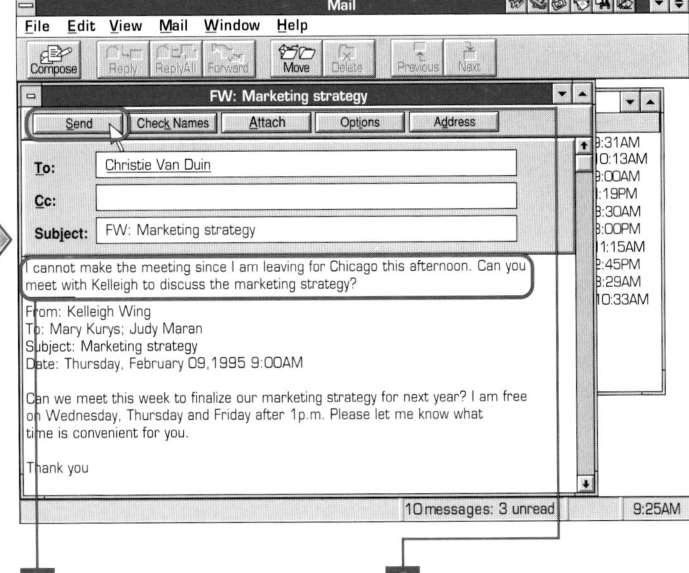

◆ This area displays the original message.

4 To specify the person you want to forward the message to, perform steps **2** to **5** starting on page 334.

5 To add your own comments to the message, move the mouse I over this area and then press the left button. Then type your comments.

6 To forward the message, move the mouse ↖ over **Send** and then press the left button.

DELETE A MESSAGE

EXIT MAIL

DELETE A MESSAGE

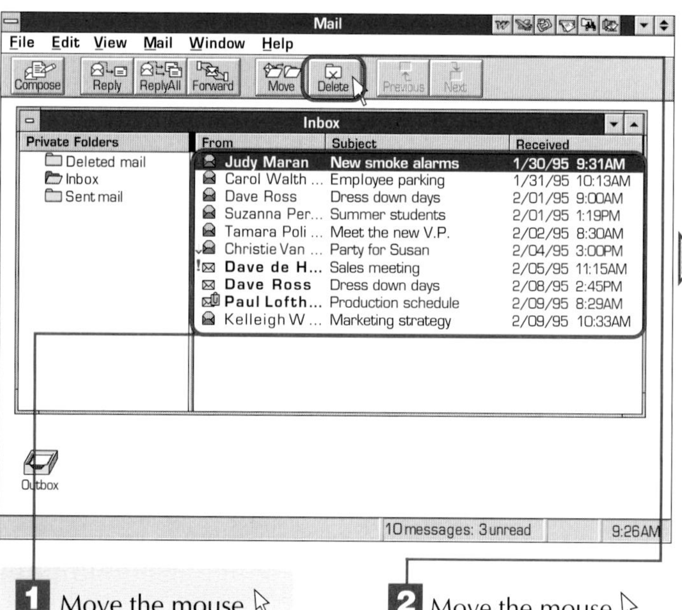

Mail
File Edit View Mail Window Help
Compose Reply ReplyAll Forward Move Delete Previous Next
Inbox
Private Folders
Deleted mail
Inbox
Sent mail
From Subject Received
Carol Walt ... Employee parking 1/31/95 10:13AM
Dave Ross Dress down days 2/01/95 9:00AM
Suzanna Per... Summer students 2/01/95 1:19PM
Tamara Poli ... Meet the new V.P. 2/02/95 8:30AM
Christie Van ... Party for Susan 2/04/95 3:00PM
Dave de H... Sales meeting 2/05/95 11:15AM
Dave Ross Dress down days 2/08/95 2:45PM
Paul Lofth... Production schedule 2/09/95 8:29AM
Kelleigh W ... Marketing strategy 2/09/95 10:33AM
Outbox
9 messages: 3 unread
9:27AM

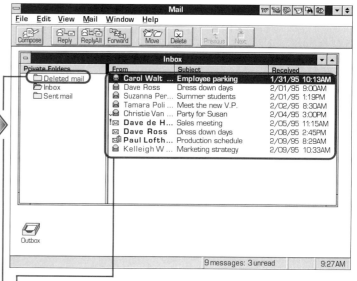

1 Move the mouse over the message you want to delete and then press the left button.

2 Move the mouse over **Delete** and then press the left button.

◆ The message disappears.

◆ Mail places deleted messages in the **Deleted mail** folder.

*Note: Your **Deleted mail** folder may be called **Wastebasket**.*

At the end of each day, you should exit Mail before turning off your computer.
EXIT

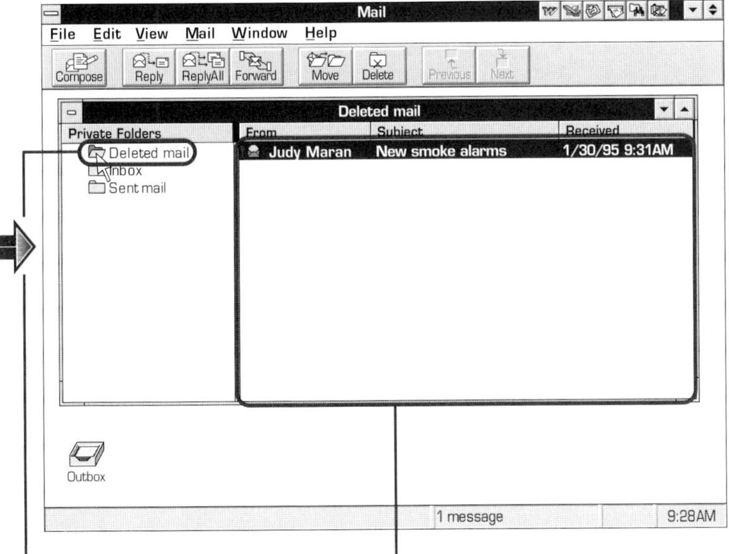

3 To view all the messages you have deleted, move the mouse over the **Deleted mail** folder and then quickly press the left button twice.

◆ This area displays all the messages you have deleted.

◆ These messages will be permanently deleted when you exit Mail.

EXIT MAIL

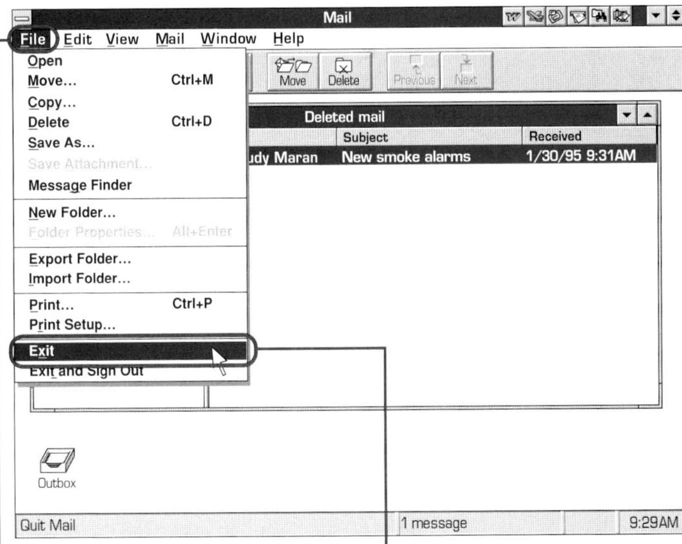

1 Move the mouse over **File** and then press the left button.

2 Move the mouse over **Exit** and then press the left button.

In this section you will learn how to place an object from one program into another. An object can include items such as a chart, text or a slide.
Customer Requirements
State the needs of the audience
Confirm the audience's needs if you are not sure
Source Document

EXCHANGE OBJECTS BETWEEN PROGRAMS

INTRODUCTION

Linking and embedding allow you to create documents containing objects from other programs. For example, you can place a chart from Excel and a slide from PowerPoint into a Word document.

The source document supplies the object.

The destination document receives the object.

EMBED AN OBJECT

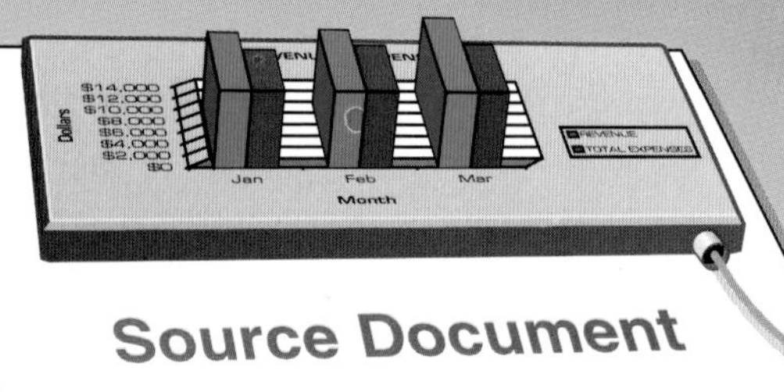

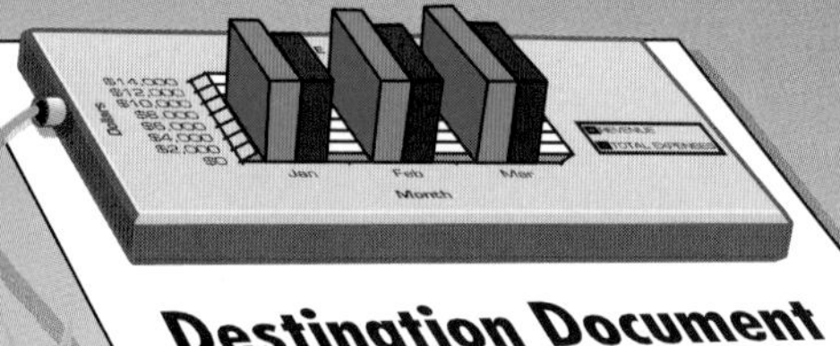

When you embed an object, it becomes part of the destination document.

When you make changes to the object in the destination document, only the destination document is affected.

The source document is no longer needed after you embed an object, since the destination document now contains the object.

OBJECT

The information you transfer between programs is called an object. An object can include items such as a picture, a chart, text, or a slide.

LINK AN OBJECT

When you link an object, the destination document receives a "screen image" of the object. The object remains in the source document.

Linking objects is useful if you want your destination documents to always contain the most up-to-date information. For example, you can link sales data to a monthly report given to all sales managers. When the sales data changes, all linked reports automatically display the change.

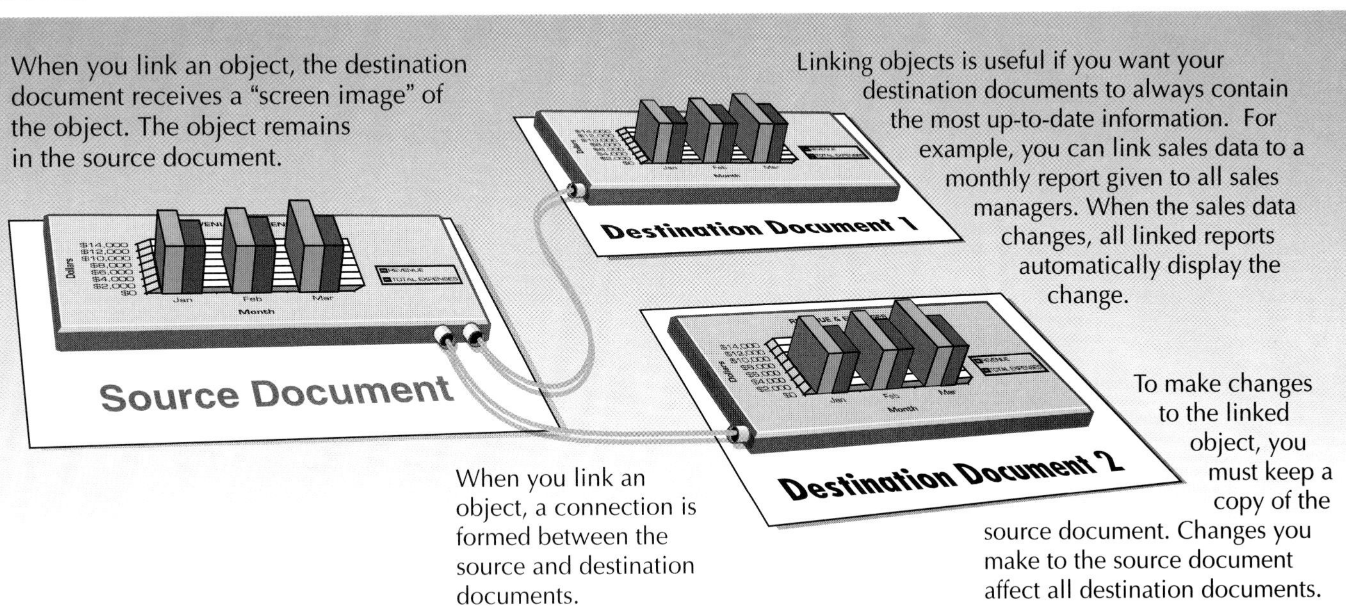

When you link an object, a connection is formed between the source and destination documents.

To make changes to the linked object, you must keep a copy of the source document. Changes you make to the source document affect all destination documents.

LINK OR EMBED AN OBJECT

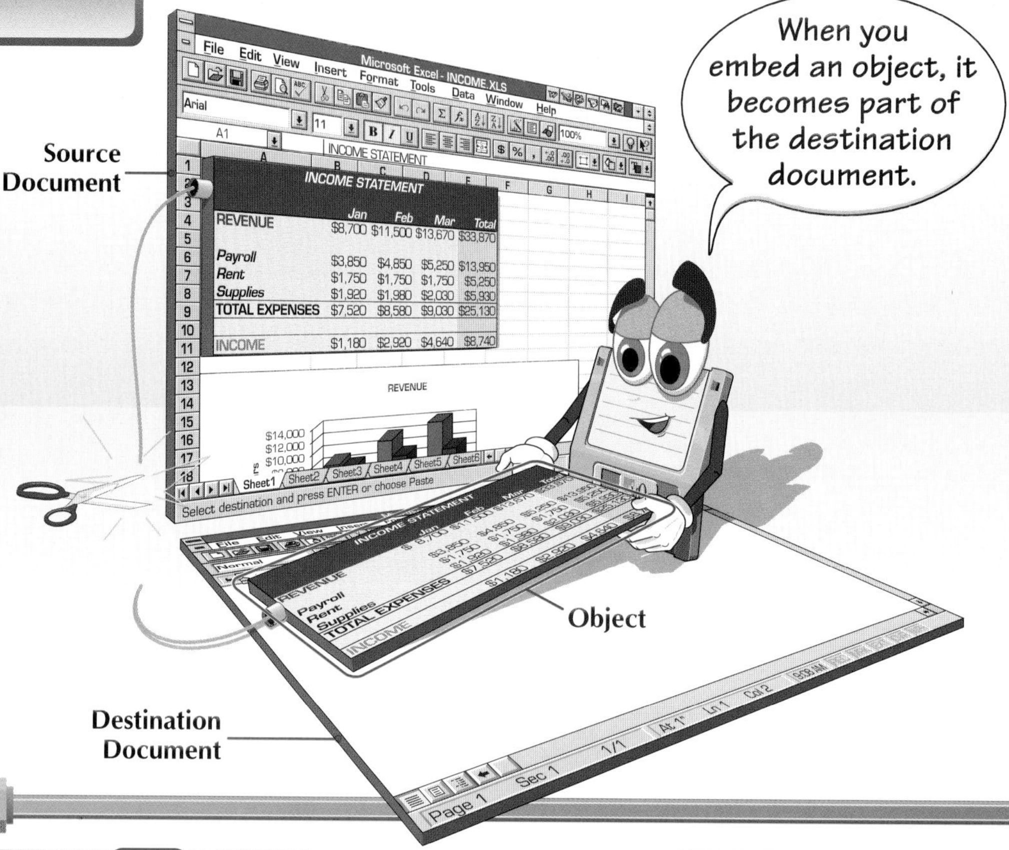

When you embed an object, it becomes part of the destination document.
Source Document
Object
Destination Document

EMBED AN OBJECT

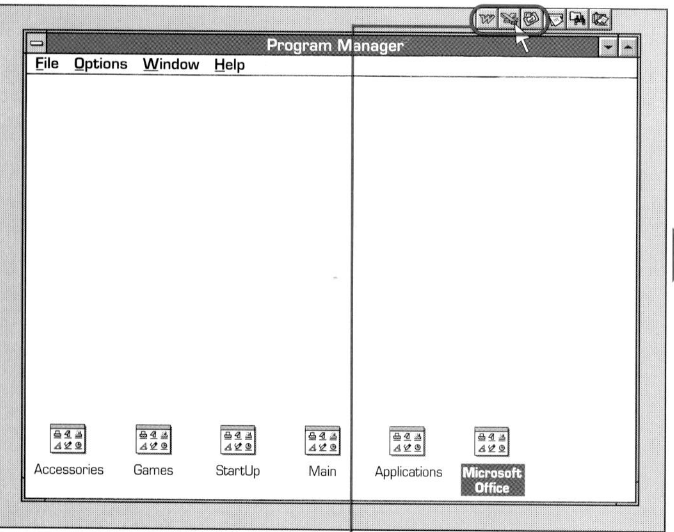

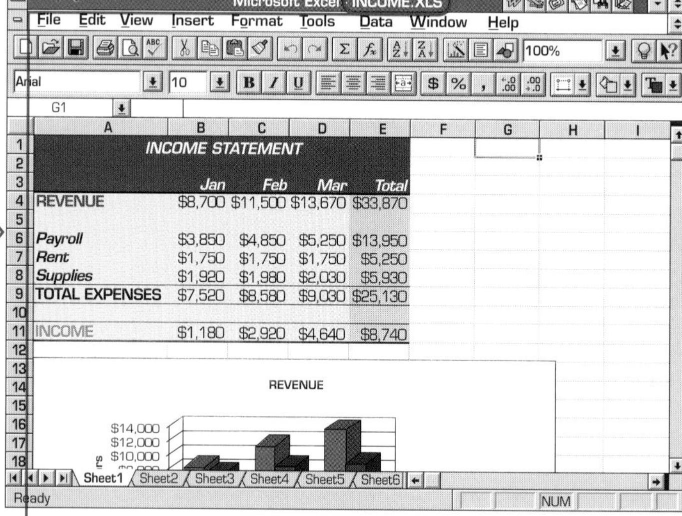

This example places an object from Excel in a Word document.

1 Start the program containing the object you want to place in another program (example: **Excel**).

Note: To start Excel, move the mouse over [icon] *and then press the left button.*

2 Open the document containing the object (example: **income.xls**).

Note: To open a document in Excel, refer to page 154.

LINK AN OBJECT

When you link an object, the destination document receives a "screen image" of the object. The object remains in the source document.

To link an object:

1 Perform steps **1** to **11** starting on page 352, selecting **Paste Link:** in step **9**.

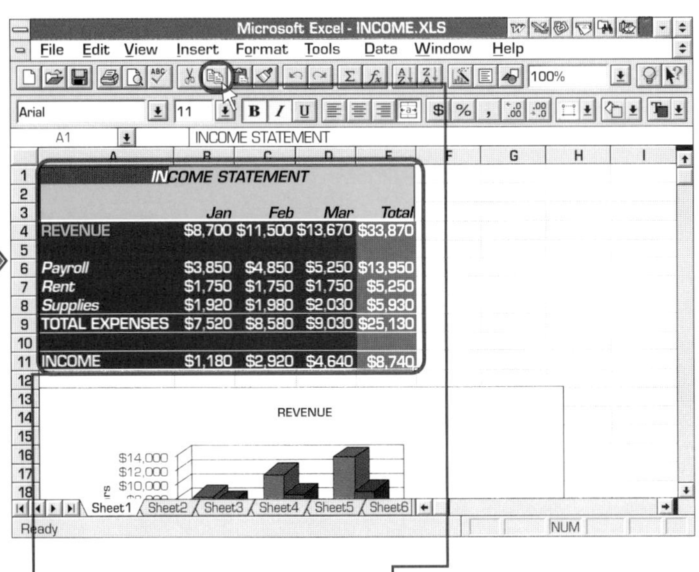

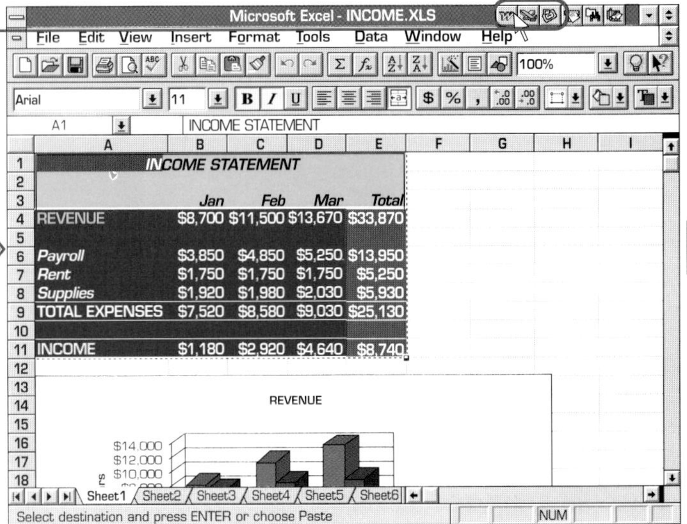

3 Select the object you want to place in another program.

Note: To select cells in Excel, refer to page 140.

4 To make a copy of the object, move the mouse over the Copy button and then press the left button.

5 Start the program you want to display a copy of the object (example: **Word**).

Note: To start Word, move the mouse over the Word button and then press the left button.

LINK OR EMBED AN OBJECT

After you embed an object, the source document is no longer needed, since the destination document now contains the object.

Source Document

Object

Destination Document

EMBED AN OBJECT (CONTINUED)

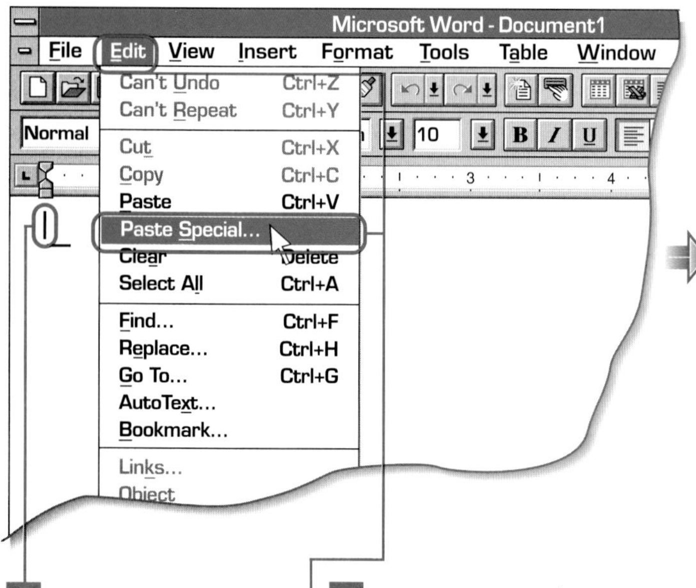

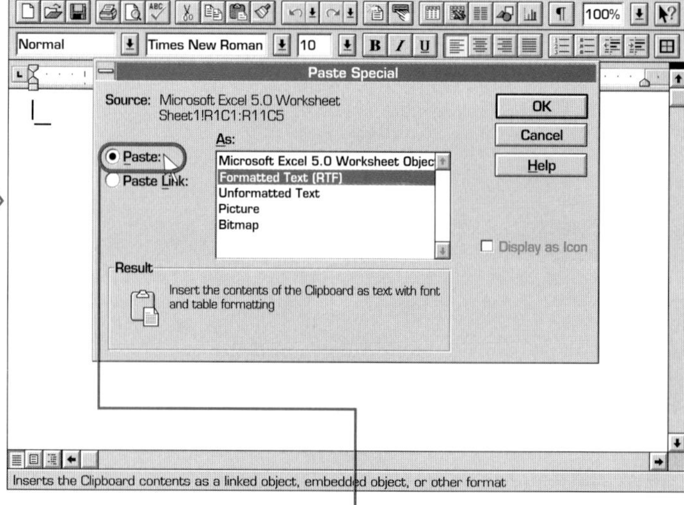

6 Position the insertion point where you want to place the object.

7 Move the mouse ↖ over **Edit** and then press the left button.

8 Move the mouse ↖ over **Paste Special** and then press the left button.

◆ The **Paste Special** dialog box appears.

9 To embed the object, move the mouse ↖ over **Paste:** and then press the left button.

Tip
A document containing an embedded object takes up more space on your computer than a document containing a linked object.

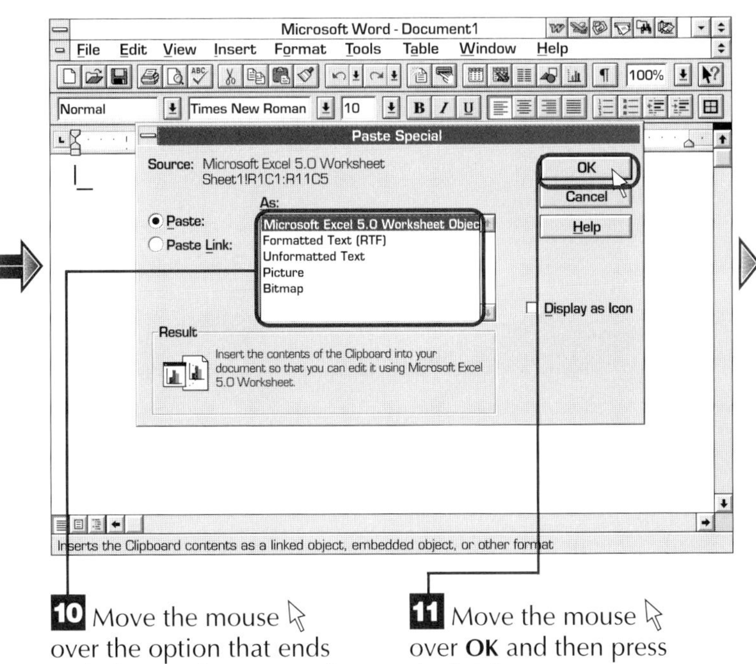

10 Move the mouse over the option that ends with the word **Object** and then press the left button.

11 Move the mouse over **OK** and then press the left button.

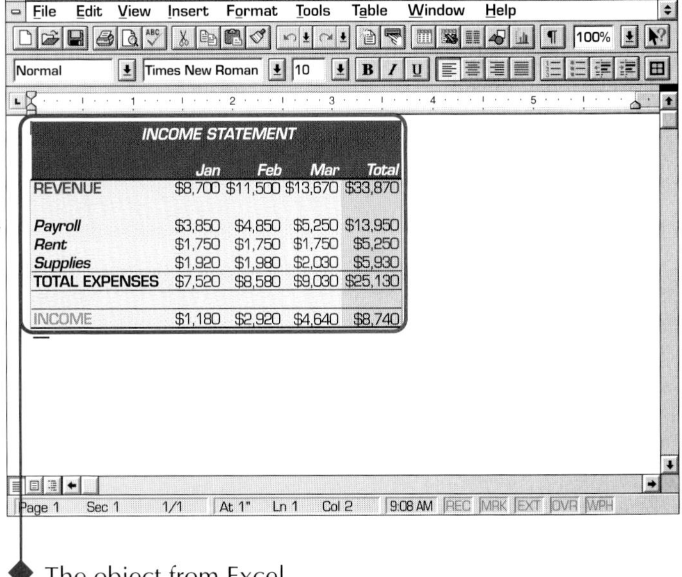

	Jan	Feb	Mar	Total
REVENUE	$8,700	$11,500	$13,670	$33,870
Payroll	$3,850	$4,850	$5,250	$13,950
Rent	$1,750	$1,750	$1,750	$5,250
Supplies	$1,920	$1,980	$2,030	$5,930
TOTAL EXPENSES	$7,520	$8,580	$9,030	$25,130
INCOME	$1,180	$2,920	$4,640	$8,740

◆ The object from Excel appears in the Word document.

EDIT AN EMBEDDED OBJECT

You can easily make changes to an embedded object in your document.
Source Document
Destination Document

When you make changes to the object in the destination document, only the destination document is affected.

EDIT AN EMBEDDED OBJECT

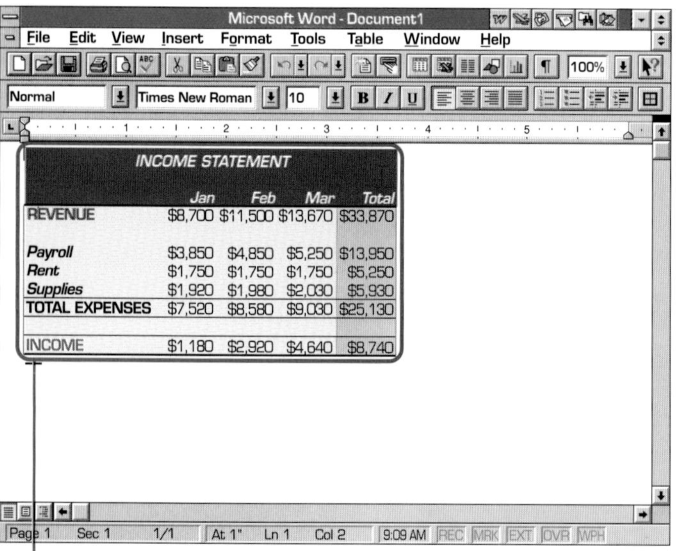

INCOME STATEMENT				
	Jan	Feb	Mar	Total
REVENUE	$8,700	$11,500	$13,670	$33,870
Payroll	$3,850	$4,850	$5,250	$13,950
Rent	$1,750	$1,750	$1,750	$5,250
Supplies	$1,920	$1,980	$2,030	$5,930
TOTAL EXPENSES	$7,520	$8,580	$9,030	$25,130
INCOME	$1,180	$2,920	$4,640	$8,740

1 To edit an object, move the mouse I over the object and then quickly press the left button twice.

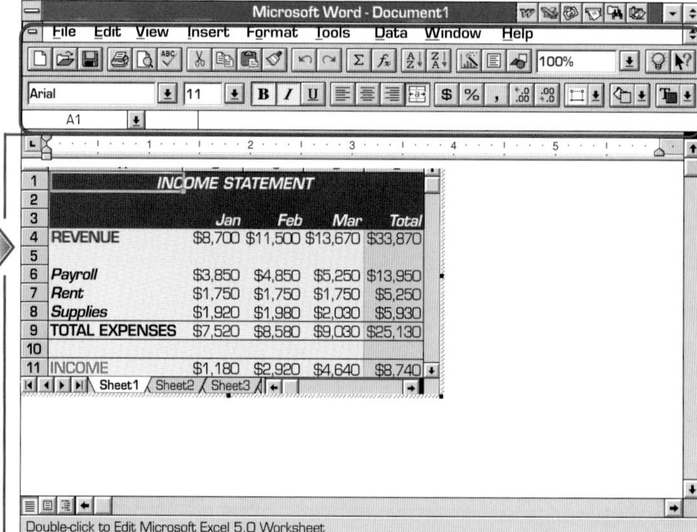

◆ In this example, the Excel menus and toolbars temporarily replace the Word menus and toolbars. This lets you access all of the Excel commands while working in the Word document.

Tip
A program that can link and embed objects supports OLE technology. OLE stands for Object Linking and Embedding.

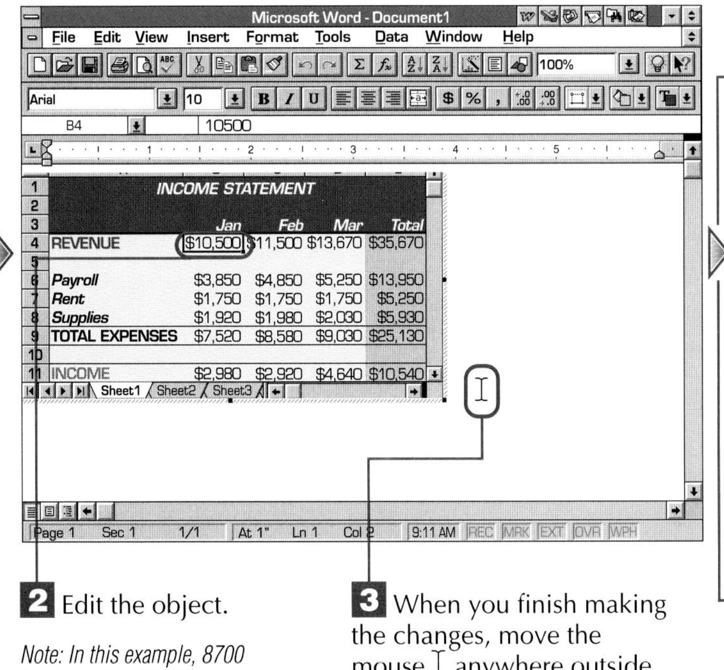

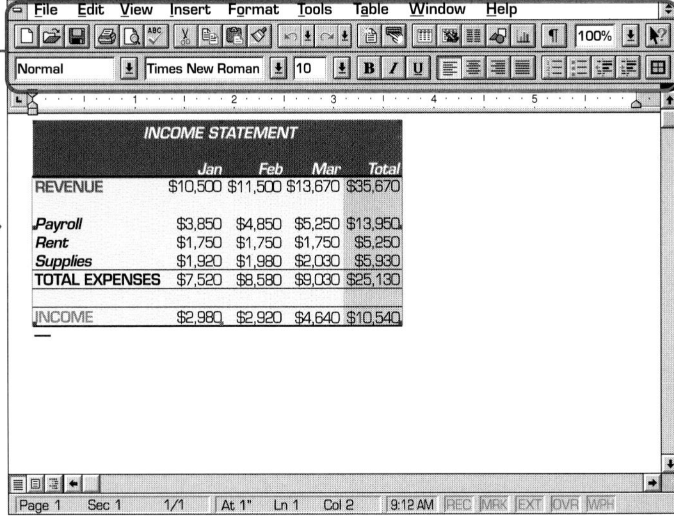

2 Edit the object.

Note: In this example, 8700 is changed to 10500.

3 When you finish making the changes, move the mouse I anywhere outside the object and then press the left button.

◆ The Word menus and toolbars reappear.

EDIT A LINKED OBJECT

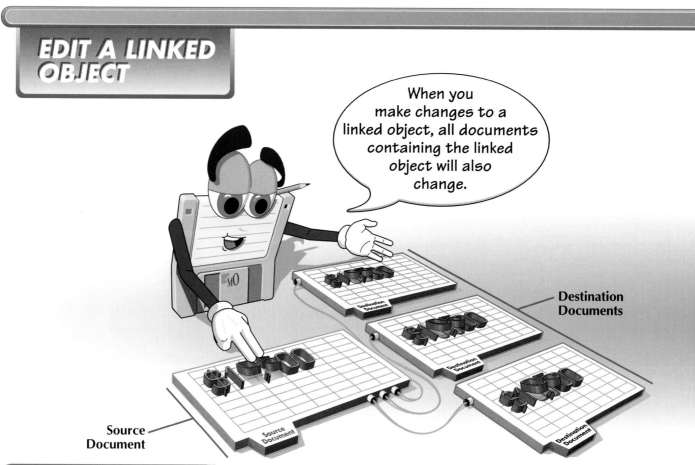

When you make changes to a linked object, all documents containing the linked object will also change.

Destination Documents

Source Document

EDIT A LINKED OBJECT

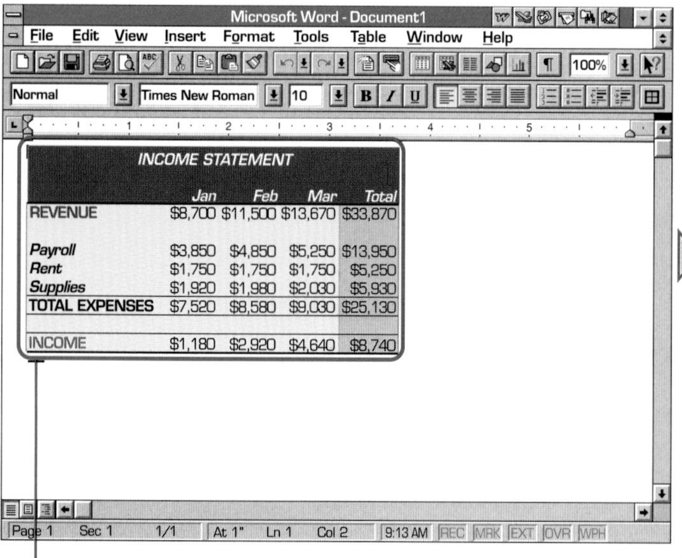

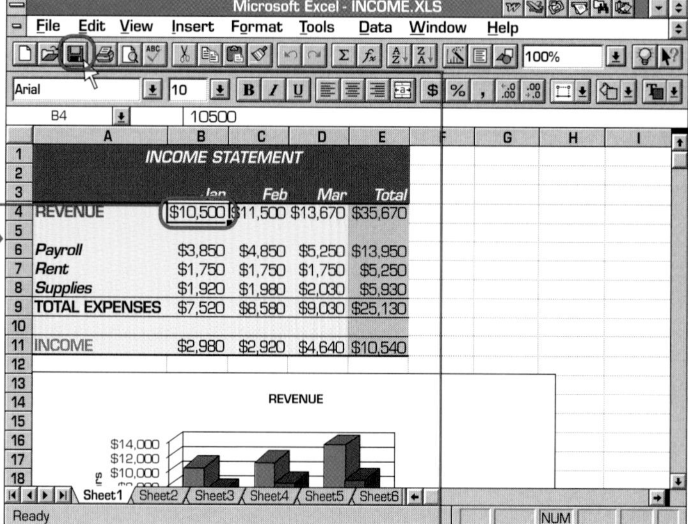

1 To edit an object, move the mouse I over the object and then quickly press the left button twice.

◆ In this example, the Excel program opens. This lets you access all of the Excel commands.

2 Edit the object.

Note: In this example, 8700 is changed to 10500.

3 To save the changes, move the mouse over 💾 and then press the left button.

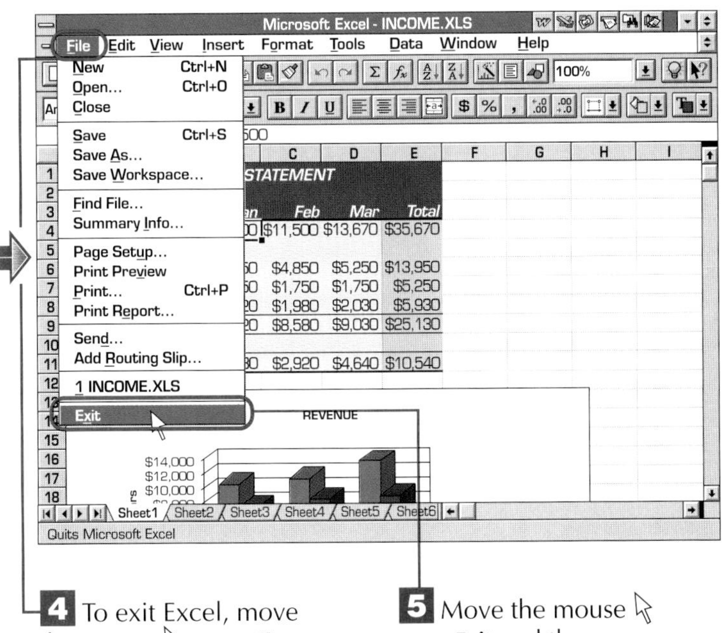

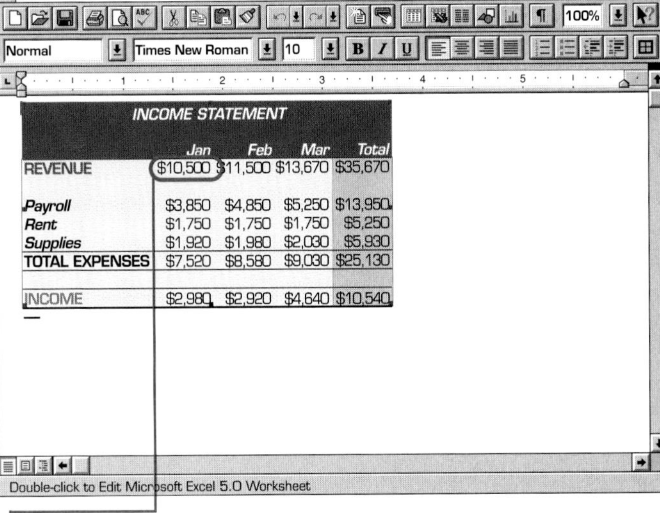

4 To exit Excel, move the mouse over **File** and then press the left button.

5 Move the mouse over **Exit** and then press the left button.

◆ The Word program reappears. The changes you made to the object in Excel appear in the Word document.

◆ All other documents containing the linked object will also change.

INDEX

D

E

P